Polishing Windows

How to Create Toolboxes, Status Bars, Excel-Style Dialogs and Other Professional User Interface Elements

Dave Jewell

 Addison-Wesley Publishing Company

Wokingham, England • Reading, Massachusetts • Menlo Park, California • New York
Don Mills, Ontario • Amsterdam • Bonn • Sydney • Singapore • Tokyo • Madrid
San Juan • Milan • Paris • Mexico City • Seoul • Taipei

Cover designed by Designers & Partners, Oxford
Typeset by Meridian Phototypesetting Ltd, Pangbourne
Printed in the United States of America by R.R. Donnelly & Sons

First printed in 1994

British Library Cataloguing in Publication Data
A catalogue record for this book is available from the British Library

Library of Congress Cataloging in Publication Data
Jewell, Dave
  Polishing Windows: how to create toolboxes, status bars, Excel style dialogs, and other professional user interface elements / Dave Jewell
    p.   cm.
  Includes index.
  ISBN 0-201-62437-0
  1. Windows (Computer programs)   2. Microsoft Windows (Computer file)   I. Title.
QA76.76.W56J49 1994
005.265-- dc20   93-49728
                                                                                 CIP

Acknowledgements
The publisher wishes to thank the following for permission to reproduce material in this book:
Screen Shot(s) © 1983–1992 Microsoft Corporation. All rights reserved. Reprinted with permission from Microsoft Corporation; Borland International Incorporated.

Dedicated to my dear wife, Janet, who single-handedly entertained
Hannah, Chris, Peter and Stephen during many hot summer days.
No words can express my thanks.

Preface

Why I wrote this book

In the course of building a number of different commercial Windows applications, I've often found myself frustrated by the lack of built-in support for the sort of easy-to-use, attractive features that users have come to expect from modern Windows software. To put it bluntly, there are a number of gaping holes in the Windows SDK (Software Development Kit) that make life more difficult than it should be for the average Windows programmer. Here are some examples of what I mean:

- Toolbox palettes. Visual Basic is one of many relatively recent programs that have a moveable palette of tool icons that can be dragged around the screen and opened and closed at will. How did the guys at Microsoft implement this sort of thing? How did they get that cute, half-height caption bar? Why aren't toolbox palettes a standard part of the Windows API?

- Spin buttons. These little double-ended arrows are used to increment or decrement a value in some associated edit control within a dialog box. If you want to see an example of a spin button, then open the Windows Control Panel, click on the Date/Time icon and you'll see a set of spin buttons next to the date and time fields. Again, spin buttons aren't a standard part of the Windows API. How do you go about building yourself reusable code that can be used to provide spin button facilities in your own programs?

- Toolbar facility. Right now, I'm using Word for Windows 2.0 to enter this text into my computer. Word has a nice toolbar displayed right across its window, just below the menu bar. The toolbar contains a number of different icons that provide shortcuts for often-used commands and procedures. Needless to say, the Windows programming interface is no help with toolbars either. (Incidentally, in this book, be careful not to get confused between a toolbar and a toolbox palette. The former are glued to the underside of a window's menu bar while the latter can be moved around the screen.)

Fancy dialog effects. Nowadays, many commercial applications have a cute three-dimensional effect to their dialog boxes. Instead of the boring, flat-looking check boxes and radio buttons that Microsoft supply as standard, you often see all sorts of attractive effects. Borland were the first to break free of the Microsoft stranglehold with their popular BWCC.DLL library. This is a custom control DLL that provides a nice 'chiseled steel' effect and allows you to easily put together attractive-looking dialog boxes. Unfortunately, the BWCC.DLL is not small: it amounts to around 100 kbytes of code and by using it, you're dependent upon a third-party DLL for your program's look and feel. In this book, I present a simple code module that you can link to your C/C++ programs and slot easily into your existing software. It's small – around 5 kbytes of code – doesn't require a separate DLL and will make your applications stand out from the crowd. (I have also provided an equivalent Turbo Pascal unit.)

This book is for those of you who, like me, find the above shortcomings irritating. If you want to add professional features to your Windows software and you don't want to spend an age doing it then read on...

The toolkit approach

Much of the software developed in this book is in the form of linkable code modules that can be incorporated into your own software with a minimum of effort. Together, the various code modules and Pascal units form an invaluable toolkit for Windows programming. I won't pretend to have covered every base, but I think you'll find that there is stuff here that you'll want to use time and time again as you create new, visually appealing Windows applications. The emphasis in this book is on creating robust, reusable code without getting bogged down in the complexities that can easily engulf and confuse the beginning Windows programmer. I've put a special emphasis on making these different code modules as easy to use as possible.

As an example, consider the dialog handling routines discussed in Chapter 5. This code has the job of providing an attractive, three-dimensional appearance for your program dialogs. Look at Figure 1 to see an example of what this code can do for your own application.

Figure 1   An example of what the Dialogs unit can do for you.

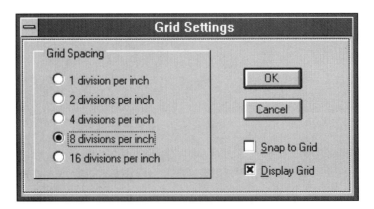

In many books on Windows programming, you'll hear about how effects like this are achieved through subclassing. When you subclass a dialog box control, such as the radio buttons shown here, it's traditional to create a new window procedure for the radio buttons. This new window procedure simply modifies the way the radio buttons are drawn, and then passes control on to the old window procedure. To make it easy to do this, Chapter 3 contains a general-purpose set of window subclassing routines. Using these routines, you can easily subclass any window you want in order to get a variety of special effects. By hiding away the details of how to subclass a window, we get a better programming interface, and we don't have to keep reinventing the wheel inside every application program we write.

The code in Chapter 5 uses these subclassing routines and the programming interface is therefore very small and simple. In fact, if you take a look at the Pascal code in Appendix 5, you'll see that there's no programming interface there at all: you can get great-looking dialog boxes and message boxes simply by including the unit into your application!

Not only that, but you don't need to fiddle around installing custom control libraries into your favorite Dialog Editor. The dialog resource used in Figure 1 was a completely standard dialog – all the magic happens at the time the dialog is invoked. That's what I mean when I talk about making my code as easy to use as possible.

Why not C++?

Although there's a perception that C++ is the 'in' language to use for Windows programming, Microsoft's own research has shown that at the present time, no more than 15–17% of professional programmers use C++ for developing commercial applications. There are probably many reasons for this, such as the steep learning curve, the run-time overheads, the difficulty of creating an object-oriented DLL that can be used with many different C++ compilers, the less than dazzling performance of some C++ development systems, and so forth.

For all these reasons, I chose to implement the code in this book using straight C. This allows me to write tight, efficient code and means that C++ programmers can also make use of the software I've developed. If I'd written the code in C++, then obviously only those 15–17% of C++ programmers would be able to benefit.

One of the much-touted advantages of C++ programming is code reusability. I think you'll find that the code in this book is just as reusable as it would be if it were developed in C++. One of the keys to writing reusable code is the reduction (and ideally, elimination) of all unnecessary global variables. You'll see this philosophy carried right through the book. It means that you can just 'drop' one of my code modules into your application with virtually no change to your existing code.

Stepwise development: a tutorial approach

Most of the chapters in this book follow a step-by-step approach to software development. If you're new to Windows programming, you can work your way through the development of a particular code module and at the end of the chapter, you'll have a good understanding of how that specific chunk of code works. More importantly, you'll understand why certain design decisions were made along the way, and you'll have a far better appreciation of the coding philosophy required to build large, complex Windows applications in a manageable way.

The importance of this tutorial approach cannot be overstated. Windows is a large and complex system which, at the time of writing, is still rapidly growing in complexity through the use of new sub-systems such as MAPI, OLE2 and so on. I wanted to present the software in this book using a tutorial approach that allows the Windows newcomer to 'get inside the head' of someone who has been programming Windows for a while. As a trainee architect, you wouldn't expect to be shown a finished apartment block and then be told to 'get on with it'. In the same way, becoming a proficient Windows developer isn't going to be easy if all you see is reams of finished code. Throughout this book, I've tried to develop certain important principles and practices that will make your software more reliable, more efficient, more understandable and more modular. To the extent to which I've succeeded, you must be the judge.

Understanding the companion disk

For each chapter, the companion disk contains source code and executables for the various code modules developed in the book. In addition, for Pascal programmers, there is a complete set of Pascal units that duplicate the functionality of the C code modules. For more up-to-the-minute information, and for details of how to install the software, please see the file README.TXT on the disk.

As an added bonus, the disk contains a copy of WiDE, an innovative British shareware program that will give your Windows system the look and feel of Windows 4 without waiting for Windows 4 to appear! This is discussed more fully in Chapter 8.

All the C code presented in this book was developed using Borland's C/C++ with Application FrameWorks, version 3.1. You may need to make very minor alterations when using other development systems, but I have steered away from using vendor-specific routines wherever possible. The Pascal code listed in the appendices was likewise developed using Borland Pascal Version 7.0. All programs and code were developed for Windows 3.1 and no guarantees are given that the code will work correctly for previous versions of Windows.

Finally, I would like to express my thanks to Geoff Chappell for encouraging me to write *Polishing Windows*, and for reviewing the manuscript and coming back with a number of helpful suggestions and bug reports. Many thanks also to Nicky Jaeger and Lesley 'Spielberg' Raper at Addison-Wesley, who demonstrated so much faith in me that I knew I just *had* to finish the book!

Dave Jewell
September 1993

email: djewell@cix.compulink.co.uk

Contents

Laying some foundations

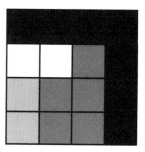

Before we look at some of the more complex code in *Polishing Windows*, please work through this introductory chapter. If you're not very familiar with Windows software development, then I'd strongly advise you to read this material. Even if you are an experienced Windows programmer, I'd still like to 'tune you in' to the coding philosophy that I use when building a Windows application. That's the real purpose behind this chapter. If you're tempted to skip on to some of the more interesting chapters, resist the temptation! Please take the time to read this introductory stuff.

In Chapter 1, we'll put together a few simple routines intended to make life easier for those programmers who use a lot of string resources in their program. The code developed here will also provide facilities for handling so-called profile strings: the special configuration strings stored in WIN.INI files and in private profile files for use by specific applications.

Why have string resources?

Many new Windows programmers are tempted to ask themselves, 'Why bother with string resources at all?' In order to understand why they ask this question, let's take a look at how we might go about implementing the error message box shown in Figure 1.1.

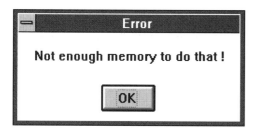

Figure 1.1 A typical use of the MessageBox API call.

If you want to have some error message come up in your program, it's very much easier just to build that error string into your code. The alternative, 'proper' way to do this is to create a string resource first, and then use the Windows LoadString routine to retrieve the string when needed. Here's an example of what I mean:

```
MessageBox (NULL, "Not enough memory to do that !", "Error", MB_OK);
```

That's the easy way of doing it. Now let's try and do it the 'right' way, like this:

```
#define    ID_ERRCAPTION      100
#define    ID_ERRMESSAGE      101

char  szCaption [40];
char  szMessage [256];

LoadString (hInstance, ID_ERRCAPTION, szCaption, sizeof (szCaption) − 1);
LoadString (hInstance, ID_ERRMESSAGE, szMessage, sizeof (szMessage) − 1);
MessageBox (NULL, szMessage, szCaption, MB_OK);
```

Given all the extra code that's necessary in order to make use of string resources, it's not surprising that a number of programmers choose to do things the easy way. Unfortunately, there are two big disadvantages to building string constants into your code and forsaking string resources.

The first and most obvious disadvantage is concerned with internationalization. If you want to sell your software around the world in non-English speaking countries, then you've got to find and modify all the strings and rebuild your software in order to come up with foreign versions of your code. On the other hand, if you use string resources, then all your string constants can be easily modified using a resource editor such as Borland's excellent Resource Workshop or the App Studio program that comes as part of Microsoft's new Visual C++ package. This string modification can be performed without access to the program source code, which can obviously be a big advantage.

There's a second and far more important reason for avoiding the use of string constants in your program code. Any Windows application, whether it's written using C, C++, or Turbo Pascal, has a special segment called the automatic data segment which cannot be greater than 64 kbytes in size. This segment contains your program's local heap and all the global variables you've defined, including any private global variables that may be used exclusively by Pascal units. If you program in C or C++, then any time you define a string constant, this string will also end up in the automatic data segment. Pascal programmers come off relatively well here: Borland's Pascal compiler takes a somewhat more intelligent approach and tries to place 'read-only' string constants into the current code segment being compiled. However, whichever way you look at it, the bottom line amounts to the same thing: your automatic data segment is a precious resource and you should try to use it wisely.

None of the relatively straightforward programs we'll be building in this book are going to push this 64 kbyte limit, but it's as well to be aware of it from the outset. More complex software often comes up against this resource limit, particularly if it contains a lot of large global variables such as arrays and look-up tables. Indeed, Windows itself has suffered from this limitation; the mysterious-sounding System Resources that you see in the Program Manager's About box is an indication of how full Windows' own automatic data segments are becoming.

There are various way around this: one approach, used by the internal Windows system code, is to allocate additional local heaps in special global memory blocks created for the purpose. Although this approach works, it does introduce additional complexity into your program. You can also tell the Microsoft C compiler to place certain variables such as string constants into the current code segment, or into some additional data segment. Again, this technique works, but it also makes your program code more complex than it needs to be.

To summarize: don't use global variables unless you have to, and avoid the use of string constants in your program code when you can get by just as well with string resources.

Treat your automatic data segment with respect and you will be able to build much bigger Windows programs before you need to resort to more specialized techniques. Even if your program is aimed specifically at the domestic market, or you just don't care about internationalizing your program, it's still important to use string resources just because of these issues.

Building a better API

OK, so we're stuck with string resources. But do we want to carry on using the cumbersome LoadString routine for the rest of our programming careers? Do we really want to keep allocating buffers, specifying buffer lengths and instance handles anytime we want a new string resource? Maybe you do, but I certainly don't!

Wouldn't it be great if we could replace all the ugly code shown above with something as concise as this:

```
MessageBox (NULL,

             GetResStr (ID_ERRMESSAGE),

             GetResStr (ID_ERRCAPTION), MB_OK);
```

We've replaced the LoadString call with a new function called GetResStr. This routine takes only one parameter, the resource ID of the string resource we're after, and returns, as a function result, a pointer to the wanted character string. Implementing a routine like this should be pretty straightforward. The code shown in Figure 1.2 is our first attempt at an implementation of the GetResStr function.

Notice that at this point our code listing has been written as a complete Windows program, complete with a WinMain function and so forth. The general rule we'll follow in this book is to develop the working code inside the main program and then move it out into a reusable module once it's tested and debugged. By doing things this way, we only have to update the one source file as we work through the process of developing the code – if we had a main program and a separate source file containing the code under development, we'd need to keep making changes to them both during the development process. If you have the disk which accompanies this book, the source code to this simple program can be found in the file STRLIB1.C.

```
// STRLIB1.C

// © 1994 Dave Jewell and Addison-Wesley, ALL RIGHTS RESERVED

#include    <windows.h>

#define     ID_ERRCAPTION      100
#define     ID_ERRMESSAGE      101

HANDLE hInstance;    // instance handle of the program

//-----------------------------------------------------------
// Name:      GetResStr
// Purpose:   This is our first try at creating a new easy-to-use replacement
//            for the Windows API LoadString routine.
//-----------------------------------------------------------

LPSTR PASCAL GetResStr (WORD id)
{
      static char szBuffer [256];

      if (LoadString (hInstance, id, szBuffer, sizeof (szBuffer) − 1) == 0)
        szBuffer [0] = '\0';

      return szBuffer;
}

#pragma argsused

int PASCAL WinMain (HANDLE hInst, HANDLE hPrevInstance,
                    LPSTR lpCmdLine, int nCmdShow)
{

      hInstance = hInst;
      MessageBox (0,
                  GetResStr (ID_ERRMESSAGE),
                  GetResStr (ID_ERRCAPTION), MB_OK);
      return (0);
}
```

You can see that the GetResStr routine simply uses the Windows API LoadString call to copy the wanted string into the szBuffer variable. This buffer has to be declared as static: if an ordinary automatic variable were used, the storage space allocated to the buffer would disappear as soon as the GetResStr routine returned control to the calling routine – this would make for an interesting debugging exercise!

Incidentally, you may be thinking that it would be better if the GetResStr routine returned a NULL value if the wanted string resource didn't exist. In other words, replace the first statement in the routine with something like this:

```
if (LoadString (hInstance, id, szBuffer, sizeof (szBuffer) −1) == 0)
    return (NULL);
```

In practice, this is a bad idea. Even though Windows 3.1 has much better parameter validation than previous versions of Windows, there are still a number of Windows API routines that will die a horrible death if you pass them invalid parameters. Coincidentally, MessageBox is just such a routine. If you make the code modification shown above and then compile the STRLIB1.C file, you'll find that the GetResStr routine will return a NULL value because we haven't yet plugged the needed string resources into our .EXE file. This NULL value will then be passed to the MessageBox routine and hey presto: a General Protection fault with very little effort. Try it if you don't believe me. It would be nicer if MessageBox was a little friendlier and interpreted NULL string parameters as empty strings, but that's life for you.

If you made the modification above, then begin by putting back the code as it was before. Now compile, link and execute the STRLIB1.C program. You should see a small message box appear on the screen with no caption and no text. That's because we still haven't provided the needed string resources. If you have the disk, copy the STRLIB.RC file from the disk and use this to create the necessary resources. How you do this will depend on the development system you're using. If you're using Borland C/C++, you can just create a new project file and add the STRLIB1.C and STRLIB.RC files to the project. The development system will then automatically take care of compiling the resource script and binding the resources into your program each time you build the project. The STRLIB.RC file is listed in Figure 1.3.

```
/* STRLIB.RC */

STRINGTABLE LOADONCALL MOVEABLE DISCARDABLE
BEGIN
        100, "Error"
        101, "Not enough memory to do that !"
END
```

Figure 1.3 STRLIB.RC: a simple resource script file for testing the GetResStr routine.

In general, because I don't know what development system you're using, I'll provide resource data in the form of .RES files or .RC files. If you have a resource editor such as Borland Resource Workshop, you can create a .RC or .RES file directly (.RES files are compiled resource scripts) by using the editor. In Figure 1.4, I'm creating STRLIB.RES using Resource Workshop's string resource editor. You should include the STRLIB.RC resource script when you compile any of the programs discussed in Chapter 1. For your convenience, pre-built versions of each .EXE file are included on the disk.

Resource Workshop - STRINGTABLE : 100		
File **Edit** **Resource** **Stringtable** **Window** **Help**		
ID Source	ID Value	String
100	100	Error
101	101	Not enough memory to do that !
Ready		

Figure 1.4 Creating the STRLIB.RES file using Borland's Resource Workshop.

Figure 1.5 The result of running the STRLIB1 program.

Once you've got the resource information compiled and linked into the STRLIB1 program, it's time to try it out. When you execute the code, you should see a message box like the one in Figure 1.5, assuming that everything has gone according to plan.

Ooops! This obviously hasn't gone according to plan. The message box we're seeing here doesn't look very much like that shown in Figure 1.1, does it? It looks as if we're getting the same string returned each time we call the GetResStr code. Actually, that's not quite true. What's really happening is that the second call to the GetResStr routine is overwriting the contents of the private string buffer that GetResStr uses to return a value. To make this a little clearer, let's have a look at the code that's actually being executed.

The code in Figure 1.6 is a disassembly of the WinMain function in our little STRLIB1 program. After making a copy of the application instance handle, the code makes the first call to the GetResStr routine at address 0035. We can see the value 65 hexadecimal (that is, 101) being pushed, which corresponds to our ID_ERRMESSAGE constant. This is what we'd expect because the MessageBox

Figure 1.6 A disassembly of part of the STRLIB1 program.

```
0028 55              WINMAIN    push   bp
0029 8b ec                      mov    bp,sp
002b 8b 46 0c                   mov    ax,+0cH[bp]
002e a3 00 01                   mov    _hInstance,ax
0031 6a 00                      push   0000H
0033 6a 65                      push   0065H
0035 e8 c8 ff                   call   _GetResStr
0038 59                         pop    cx
0039 52                         push   dx
003a 50                         push   ax
003b 6a 64                      push   0064H
003d e8 c0 ff                   call   _GetResStr
0040 59                         pop    cx
0041 52                         push   dx
0042 50                         push   ax
0043 6a 00                      push   0000H
0045 9a 00 00 00 00             call   far MESSAGEBOX
004a 33 c0                      xor    ax,ax
004c eb 00                      jmp    L3
004e 5d              L3         pop    bp
004f c2 0a 00                   ret    000aH
```

routine is a Windows API routine: it's therefore defined to use Pascal calling conventions. Pascal routines have their arguments pushed on the stack in the order in which you'd read them in the source code, that is, left to right. C routines, on the other hand, expect their arguments in reverse order. If the MessageBox routine was a C function, we'd see the MB_OK flag get pushed on the stack first.

So at this point the internal buffer inside the GetResStr routine contains the string "Not enough memory to do that !". A pointer to this buffer gets pushed onto the stack for use by the MessageBox routine and the GetResStr routine is called again, this time with the ID_ERRCAPTION value as its parameter. This is where disaster strikes: the second call to GetResStr overwrites the previous buffer contents with the string "Error" and pushes a second pointer to the *same* buffer onto the stack.

The multiple buffer problem

If you aren't familiar with machine code and you didn't follow the above discussion, then don't worry. The essential problem is that GetResStr always returns a pointer to the same buffer. Because a single buffer can only hold one string at a time, it means that any routine that needs several strings (such as MessageBox) will always get multiple copies of the same string.

There are several ways round this type of problem. One solution would be to copy each string into a temporary buffer as we receive it from GetResStr, and then pass the addresses of these buffers to MessageBox. For example, we might do something like this:

```
char buff1 [256], buff2 [256];

lstrcpy (buff1, GetResStr (ID_ERRMESSAGE));
lstrcpy (buff2, GetResStr (ID_ERRCAPTION));
MessageBox (0, buff1, buff2, MB_OK);
```

In the above code, the lstrcpy routine is used to copy the strings into temporary buffers prior to calling the MessageBox function. The problem with this approach should be pretty obvious: it's almost as much hard work as the original code which used LoadString directly! Admittedly, in this example, we could get by with only one temporary buffer, that is, use a buffer to hold the initial message text and then use GetResStr in the normal way to return a pointer to the caption string. But this solution is still clunky and inelegant.

Another technique (I've seen this one used in commercial code) is to have several hidden buffers and a corresponding version of GetResStr for each buffer. Suppose, for example, that we have four buffers. We might then have a routine called GetResStr1 that returns a pointer to the first buffer, another routine called GetResStr2 that returns a pointer to the second buffer, and so on up to GetResStr4 that points to the last buffer. Using this approach, we could rewrite WinMain to look like this:

```
#pragma argsused

int PASCAL WinMain (HANDLE hInst, HANDLE hPrevInstance,
                        LPSTR lpCmdLine, int nCmdShow)
{
    hInstance = hInst;
    MessageBox (0,
                GetResStr1 (ID_ERRMESSAGE),
                GetResStr2 (ID_ERRCAPTION), MB_OK);
    return (0);
}
```

This is clearly a lot nicer than the previous technique. It does mean, however, that we've got to have several routines all doing more or less the same job, which is very wasteful. It also means, of course, that in situations like this, we've got to remember to call GetResStr1 first followed by GetResStr2 and so on. Wouldn't it be nice if we could stick with the simplicity of a single function, and yet have the function itself return a different buffer pointer each time it's called? As it turns out, this is quite easy to achieve.

Real programmers do it statically (to start with)

The code in Figure 1.7 shows a new version of the GetResStr program. You can find this code on the accompanying disk as STRLIB2.C. You can build this program using the same resource file (STRLIB.RC) as we used earlier. When you execute the code, you'll find that this time it works as advertised, producing the message box shown in Figure 1.1.

So how does it work? The answer is that this new implementation of GetResStr uses no fewer than five 256-byte string buffers. Each time it's called, it returns a pointer to each of the string buffers in turn, and when all five buffers have been used, it starts again at the first buffer. This does mean, of course, that if we ever called a routine that needed six different string parameters, things would go wrong: the first buffer's contents would get overwritten just like the MessageBox example shown earlier. In practice, however, it's not too likely that this situation would arise. Incidentally, if you're wondering why I decided on five string buffers, the reason is that only one of the Windows API routines defined in WINDOWS.H takes this number of parameters. All the other routines defined in this header file take fewer than that number, so five seems to be a reasonable choice. (The routine that takes five string parameters is called GetPrivateProfileString.)

The new GetResStr routine works by using a two-dimensional array of string buffers. As discussed for the STRLIB1 example, any buffers have to be defined as static, allowing us to return a buffer pointer to GetResStr's caller. We've also got a new variable, called BufNum, which is used to 'remember' which of the five buffers we're going to use next. Once BufNum becomes equal to the number of buffers in the array, it's reset back to zero. For obvious reasons, BufNum also has to be defined as a static variable: if it wasn't, it would contain garbage each time the GetResStr routine was called. If you don't know how static variables are defined, just think of them as hidden global variables.

```
/* STRLIB2.C */

// © 1994 Dave Jewell and Addison-Wesley, ALL RIGHTS RESERVED

include      <windows.h>

#define      ID_ERRCAPTION      100
#define      ID_ERRMESSAGE      101

#define      MAXSTRSIZE         256
#define      NUMBUFFERS         5

HANDLE hInstance;    // instance handle of the program

//————————————————————————————————————————————
// Name:     GetResStr
// Purpose:  This is our second try at creating a new easy-to-use replacement
//           for the Windows API LoadString routine.
//————————————————————————————————————————————

LPSTR PASCAL GetResStr (WORD id)
{
       LPSTR p;
       static int BufNum = 0;
       static char szBuffer [NUMBUFFERS][MAXSTRSIZE];

       p = szBuffer [BufNum++];
       if (BufNum >= NUMBUFFERS) BufNum = 0;

       if (LoadString (hInstance, id, p, MAXSTRSIZE − 1) == 0) *p = '\0';
       return p;
}

#pragma argsused

int PASCAL WinMain (HANDLE hInst, HANDLE hPrevInstance,
                    LPSTR lpCmdLine, int nCmdShow)
{
       hInstance = hInst;
       MessageBox (0,
                   GetResStr (ID_ERRMESSAGE),
                   GetResStr (ID_ERRCAPTION), MB_OK);
       return (0);
}
```

Figure 1.7 STRLIB2.C: an updated version of the GetResStr routine.

Data segment conservation

At this point, it's tempting to sit back and feel pleased with ourselves. We've got a neat little routine that's going to save us a little future coding time whenever we need to load a resource string. Unfortunately, we've overlooked one tiny problem. Look back at the last sentence in the previous paragraph. That's right: the static variables defined inside the GetResStr routine are really hidden global variables, and global variables take up room in the automatic data segment! We began this chapter by talking about the need to treat your data segment as a precious resource and now, almost without noticing it, we've eaten up over 1 kbyte of this data segment. This is not a good thing. In small programs like STRLIB2, it doesn't matter at all, but in large Windows applications that have numerous look-up tables and other large denizens of the data segment, that small 1 kbyte could prevent the program from linking.

Ideally, we shouldn't be using the data segment in this way. We've grabbed a fair-sized chunk of a scarce resource when we've probably got a few megabytes of free memory available in the Windows global heap. The obvious answer is to allocate our string buffers in the global heap. We could easily allocate the string buffer using the Windows GlobalAlloc routine but this leaves us with the question of when we should actually perform the buffer allocation. One possibility would be to create a new routine, called InitGetResStr, which would perform the needed initialization. Unfortunately, doing things this way, we've got another routine that we must remember to call prior to using GetResStr. A better, more elegant and self-contained solution is to make use once again of the static keyword.

The code shown in Figure 1.8 represents our new approach to conservative data segment management. Once again this file, STRLIB3.C, can be found on the companion disk to *Polishing Windows*, or you can type the code in yourself. In STRLIB2.C the szBuffer variable corresponded to the actual string buffer array, but in the new code it is only a pointer to this array. By declaring szBuffer to be a static variable (remember: think of static variables as hidden global variables) and initializing it to zero, we can guarantee that this pointer will be NULL the first time the GetResStr routine is called. This initial state is detected by the code, which calls GlobalAlloc to perform the buffer allocation. It then locks the global memory handle and sets up the szBuffer pointer. If NULL is returned from the GlobalAlloc call, we're in big trouble. You should add your own application-specific error handling code here.

Note

There are a variety of different approaches that can be taken to error handling. One common approach used is to return an invalid value to the caller. For example, the C run-time library routine fopen always returns the value NULL to indicate an error, open returns −1, and so on. In our case, we could write the GetResStr routine so as to return a NULL pointer if no memory could be allocated for the string buffer. Of course, this puts the onus for error checking onto the higher-level routines, but this is no bad thing: error detection and recovery is difficult to do at a low-level because the low-level code doesn't have the 'big picture'. To illustrate this, consider what would happen if we decided to abort the program inside the GetResStr routine. We wouldn't know whether there were any files open or what other system resources should be released. For routines as simple as GetResStr, it's better just to return an 'I've screwed up' value such as NULL, and have the higher-level code take any necessary action.

Note that the code locks the global memory handle and leaves it locked. In older versions of Windows, this would have been considered bad practice. Real mode versions of Windows relied upon global memory objects being unlocked most of the time so that they could be moved around in the Windows global heap. With Windows 3.1, which only runs in protected mode, this restriction no longer applies: because of the clever protected mode addressing scheme used by your PC's processor chip, Windows can move global memory objects around without unlocking them and without altering the address of the locked object.

```
/* STRLIB3.C */

// © 1994 Dave Jewell and Addison-Wesley, ALL RIGHTS RESERVED

#include        <windows.h>

#define         ID_ERRCAPTION  100
#define         ID_ERRMESSAGE 101

#define         MAXSTRSIZE     256
#define         NUMBUFFERS     5

HANDLE hInstance;    // instance handle of the program

typedef char Buffer [MAXSTRSIZE];        // define our string buffer

//————————————————————————————————————————————————————
// Name:      GetResStr
// Purpose:   This is our third try at creating a new easy-to-use replacement
//            for the Windows API LoadString routine.
//————————————————————————————————————————————————————
LPSTR PASCAL GetResStr (WORD id)
{
     LPSTR p;
     HANDLE hBuff;
     static int BufNum = 0;
     static Buffer far * szBuffer = NULL;

     // If this is the first call, then allocate the buffer

     if (szBuffer == NULL)
     {
       hBuff = GlobalAlloc (GHND, sizeof (Buffer) * NUMBUFFERS);
       if (hBuff == NULL); // Now's the time to panic !
       szBuffer = (Buffer far *) GlobalLock (hBuff);
     }

     p = szBuffer [BufNum++];
     if (BufNum >= NUMBUFFERS) BufNum = 0;

     if (LoadString (hInstance, id, p, MAXSTRSIZE − 1) == 0) *p = '\0';
     return p;
}

#pragma argsused

int PASCAL WinMain (HANDLE hInst, HANDLE hPrevInstance,
                    LPSTR lpCmdLine, int nCmdShow)
{
     hInstance = hInst;
     MessageBox (0,
                 GetResStr (ID_ERRMESSAGE),
                 GetResStr (ID_ERRCAPTION), MB_OK);
     return (0);
}
```

Figure 1.8   STRLIB3.C:
GetResStr rewritten to allocate
its buffers in global memory.

With STRLIB2, the amount of allocated data segment space was 1914 bytes. Going over to the global memory allocation scheme brought this down to 638 bytes, a very worthwhile saving of over 1200 bytes. (These figures were obtained by running the EXEHDR program on the .EXE files to obtain the exact size of the allocated data segment. EXEHDR is a Microsoft utility that comes as part of the Windows SDK.)

To some people, considerations like this might seem over-cautious, but it isn't extreme to state that the 64 kbyte limit on the size of the automatic data segment represents something of an Achilles' heel to current implementations of Windows. Microsoft have been very concerned about this bottleneck in their own code and the Windows 3.1 version of the USER DLL (one of the major DLLs that implements a good many of the Windows API routines) has been extensively modified to get around this problem. USER.EXE actually maintains several local heaps, a specialized technique that we won't be discussing here. Naturally, all these problems go away with Windows/NT – because Windows/NT is a true 32-bit operating system, you can allocate large amounts of memory in your local heap – but if you want backward compatibility with non-32-bit versions of Windows, then you need to be aware of this restriction.

The alert reader may have noticed that there seems to be no mechanism for deallocating the global memory required by the GetResStr routine. In practice, this isn't a problem. It turns out that global memory blocks allocated by a program are automatically deallocated by Windows when that program terminates, even if the program happens to have locked the memory (as in this case). This means that we can forget about memory deallocation here: it will happen behind the scenes when any program that uses GetResStr finishes executing.

If you're even more memory-conscious than I am, you might feel that the GetResStr routine could be written to use less memory than it currently does. After all, we've assumed that a string may be up to 256 characters long (including the terminating zero character) which is quite a long string. Ordinarily, of course, you wouldn't be likely to be using such big strings. Some people might feel happier with a more sophisticated version of GetResStr that places each successive string into a single large buffer immediately after the end of the previous string. You would then return a pointer to the beginning of the new string that's just been loaded. This scheme is outlined in Figure 1.9.

Using this approach would certainly make more efficient use of memory, but it would introduce some potential complexity and problems. For example, suppose that there are only a few bytes left at the end of the buffer. When the routine was called upon to load a new string, it would have to place this string back at the beginning of the buffer. If the string were a long one, it would potentially overwrite a large number of strings that had already been stored in the buffer. A worse problem is the fact that Windows doesn't allow us to ask how long a string is before loading it. We can't say

Figure 1.9 An alternative approach to buffer management inside the GetResStr routine.

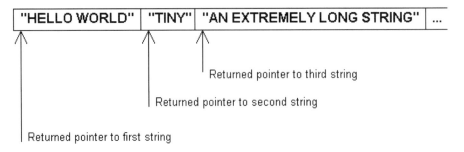

'How many bytes are used by string number 324?' Because we don't know in advance how big a string is, we have to assume that if there are less than 256 free bytes in the buffer, we might get an overflow: that is, end up writing data past the end of our globally allocated buffer. This would certainly cause a system crash. The string therefore has to be copied into a second temporary buffer and from there we can determine its size and whether it should go at the end or the beginning of the main buffer.

You can see that this is beginning to sound complicated and messy. It's no good coming up with a programming solution that saves you a few bytes of code if the added complexity needed to achieve that solution introduces more bugs into your program. Personally, I'm a great believer in the KISS concept. If you haven't come across this acronym before, KISS stands for Keep It Simple, Stupid! The basic idea is that the more 'clever' and sophisticated a piece of code becomes, the greater the opportunity for clever and sophisticated bugs to lurk in there, too!

For now, we'll stick with the GetResStr code as given in Figure 1.8, but we will revisit the code again later in this chapter. You'll understand why later.

Simpler profile string handling

So far, we've concentrated on strings held as resources, and we've developed a simple routine, GetResStr, that makes life much simpler when we come to load and use those resource strings from within a program. There is, however, another set of string-oriented Windows API routines that are even more trouble to use than the LoadString routine. These are the routines concerned with so-called profile strings. Profile strings are used by Windows programs to keep track of configuration information in the WIN.INI text file or in 'private' profile files such as PROGMAN.INI, which contains information specific to the Program Manager.

The problem with these routines is the vast number of parameters they take. Let's look at the definition for GetPrivateProfileString. As mentioned earlier in the chapter, this is the infamous routine that takes no fewer than five string pointers as parameters. Here's the definition, taken from the Borland C/C++ compiler's online help information:

```
int PASCAL GetPrivateProfileString (
    LPCSTR lpszSection,          /* address of section */
    LPCSTR lpszEntry,            /* address of entry */
    LPCSTR lpszDefault,          /* address of default string */
    LPSTR lpszReturnBuffer,      /* address of destination buffer */
    int cbReturnBuffer,          /* size of destination buffer */
    LPCSTR lpszFilename)         /* address of initialization filename */
```

For a routine that's intended to return a single resource string, this looks pretty daunting. If you find that your program needs to access a lot of profile strings, you could end up going rather cross-eyed by the time you've used this beauty a few times! Let's imagine that we've got a new routine called GetProStr which works like the GetResStr code: that is, it returns a pointer to a statically allocated string buffer rather than insisting that the calling routine supply a buffer. We might define it like this:

```
LPSTR PASCAL GetProStr (
    LPCSTR lpszSection,        /* address of section */
    LPCSTR lpszEntry,          /* address of entry */
    LPCSTR lpszDefault,        /* address of default string */
    LPCSTR lpszFilename)       /* address of initialization filename */
```

In the above definition, we've changed the function result to return a character pointer and we've also eliminated the requirement to pass a character buffer address and length. This looks a lot better, but it's still unnecessarily complex. If we dispense with the facility for providing a default string, and worry about the initialization filename later, we can simplify the function still further:

```
LPSTR PASCAL GetProStr (LPCSTR lpszSection,    /* address of section */
                        LPCSTR lpszEntry)      /* address of entry */
```

Specifying a section name and entry name every time we want to load a private profile string is no big deal. In fact, if we compare the above to the function declaration for the simpler GetProfileString routine, we can see that this too expects a section name and entry name. Ideally then, it ought to be possible to combine the two routines so that we have a common API for both our private profile strings and access to the 'public' profile strings contained within the WIN.INI file.

Note

In reality, many Windows programs tend to store their own private configuration data into the WIN.INI file even though, by rights, they should be using a private .INI file of their own. Even some Microsoft programs such as Word for Windows are guilty of this malpractice. The result is that the WIN.INI file can sometimes grow quite large and, of course, even when an offending program is removed, it will leave its 'calling card' in WIN.INI. It's a good idea to give your WIN.INI file a 'spring clean' periodically, so as to remove any unneeded rubbish. Of course, unless you really know what you're doing, you might inadvertently remove something important from WIN.INI and damage your Windows installation. The bottom line is that it's much better not to put anything into WIN.INI in the first place: make it a rule to leave WIN.INI alone in your own applications.

In the remainder of this chapter, we're going to build a simpler API for using profile strings, just as we've done for accessing resource strings. Let's begin by reviewing the list of all the routines that are concerned with manipulating entries in WIN.INI and in private profile files. If we go ahead and implement a simpler API for doing the same job, then obviously we need to ensure that we've included much of the essential functionality contained in these six routines:

```
GetProfileInt
GetProfileString
WriteProfileString
GetPrivateProfileInt
GetPrivateProfileString
WritePrivateProfileString
```

You can see that there are some holes in this programming interface. For example, there really ought to be a routine called WriteProfileInt. There should also be another routine called WritePrivateProfileInt. Both of these functions are conspicuous by their absence. In all, there should really be eight different API entry points. We'll try to plug these programming holes with our new, simpler programming interface.

Building a better mousetrap

We're dealing with three different variables here: strings versus integers, private versus public (that is, WIN.INI) files and reading versus writing. Because we're unlikely to be alternately accessing a private .INI file and the system-wide WIN.INI file, it makes sense to 'hide' the private versus public information by putting it into an API routine of its own. In other words, introduce a new function called (say) SetPublic which takes a Boolean variable as a parameter. Calling SetPublic (TRUE) would then cause all subsequent operations to refer to the WIN.INI file, while calling SetPublic (FALSE) would ensure that everything subsequent to this call would relate to our private initialization file.

We're now left with five new routines, as shown below. Things look much simpler because we're now getting two for the price of one; each routine will now access either WIN.INI or a private initialization file.

```
LPSTR PASCAL GetProStr      (LPCSTR lpszSection, LPCSTR lpszEntry);
WORD PASCAL GetProInt       (LPCSTR lpszSection, LPCSTR lpszEntry);
BOOL PASCAL WriteProStr     (LPCSTR lpszSection, LPCSTR lpszEntry, LPCSTR lpStr);
BOOL PASCAL WriteProInt     (LPCSTR lpszSection, LPCSTR lpszEntry,
                             WORD wInt, BOOL fSigned);
BOOL PASCAL SetPublic       (BOOL fPublic);
```

Here's a brief description of each of the above routines:

GetProStr   This routine retrieves a string from either WIN.INI or a private initialization file. The string is returned as the function result, just as for our earlier GetResStr routine. If the specified string does not exist, a pointer to an empty (zero-length) string is returned. Again, this is consistent with the GetResStr routine, and is done for the reasons discussed earlier.

GetProInt   This routine retrieves an integer from either WIN.INI or a private initialization file. The word is returned as the function result. If the wanted entry is not found in the initialization file, a value of -1 (0xffff) is returned. Like the GetProfileInt routine, this function can parse signed and unsigned integers from the initialization file. It's the decision of the calling routine whether or not to treat the function result as signed.

WriteProStr   This function writes a string to WIN.INI or to a private initialization file. The string is specified in the lpStr parameter. The routine behaves much like the API WriteProfileString routine: if the lpStr parameter is NULL, the designated entry is deleted. If the lpszEntry parameter is NULL, the entire designated section is deleted from the initialization file. If all three parameters are NULL, the internal Windows cache (used to optimize performance when accessing .INI files) is flushed.

WriteProInt   Writes a signed or unsigned word to WIN.INI or to a private initialization file. The parameter fSigned determines whether to treat the wInt value as a signed or an unsigned quantity. Again, the function result reports the success or failure of the routine. A non-zero value is returned if the function was successful.

SetPublic   Determines whether subsequent profile operations will apply to the WIN.INI file or to the program's private .INI file. A value of TRUE will redirect subsequent reads and writes to WIN.INI, while a value of FALSE implies use of the private file. By default, the private file is used. In other words, if you never call SetPublic, then everything will apply to the private, program-specific .INI file. The default is set that way to encourage programmers to make use of the private profile functions, rather than stuffing even more strings into the already bloated WIN.INI file.

Note carefully that the GetProInt routine returns -1 in the event of a string not being present in the initialization file. This raises the question: how do we differentiate between a missing string and one that just happens to be set to the value of -1? The short answer is, we don't. I've tried to err on the side of simplicity here and if you want to make this distinction, you'll need a more complex interface, or else more sophisticated error handling. In my own programs, I use the value -1 to indicate 'not initialized' and I don't use it for anything else (at least as far as initialization file variables are concerned). This keeps things nice and straightforward.

Where am I?

You may have noticed a rather puzzling omission from the above list of routines. There doesn't seem to be a way of specifying the name of an application's private initialization file. Provided we make the assumption that the initialization file will always have the same name (not including the file extension) as the program that owns it, this isn't a problem. For example, if we write a program called SuperShell and place it into an executable file called SUPERSHL.EXE, the routines presented here will assume that the private initialization file (if any) is going to be called SUPERSHL.INI. Although this means that we no longer have to worry about specifying the name of the private initialization file, a certain amount of flexibility is lost. We can't have an executable called SUPERSHL.EXE and an initialization file called WOMBAT.INI. In practice, it's unlikely that you'd want to do this because it would be confusing to the users of your program: they might accidentally delete the .INI file, not knowing that it relates to your application.

In those cases where you want to give your private .INI file some weird name, or you want to snoop around inside another program's .INI file (such as PROGMAN.INI), these routines won't help you. In such cases, you can always use the bare-bones API routines instead.

The code in Figure 1.10 shows how we can go about determining the name of the private initialization file. It relies on the GetModuleFileName routine to get the fully qualified name of the executable file associated with the currently running program, for example C:\MYAPPS\WIN\SUPERSHL.EXE. The 'EXE' part is then stripped off and replaced with 'INI' to yield a fully qualified name for the private .INI file. Of course, this has the side-effect of placing the .INI file into the same directory as the program that owns it. Not only is this neater, but it avoids the Windows directory becoming cluttered with .INI files, many of which can often turn out to be historical left-overs from programs long since un-installed!

There are a couple of assumptions made in the code given in Figure 1.10. Firstly, and most obviously, the code expects the calling program to have a buffer large enough to receive the full pathname of the initialization file. Secondly, it expects the filename string returned from the GetModuleFileName API call to end with a three-character suffix (usually .EXE). This assumption isn't likely to be violated, although you do need to appreciate that the returned filename string is obtained from an examination of the passed instance handle. In other words, everything will be fine so long as this routine is called from inside an application. However, if we were to put the GetPrivateProfileName routine into a DLL and call it using the instance handle of the DLL (rather than the application instance handle), then we'd get back a filename which was based on the name of the DLL file, rather than on the application file.

There may be times when the application needs to know the name of the private initialization file, such as when an error occurs and it can't be found. In these cases, the application obviously needs to display an appropriate error message. For this reason, we'll include the GetPrivateProfileName routine as part of the API we're building.

For single-user systems, the most appropriate place to put private .INI files is with the programs that own them. Unfortunately, this may not be so clear-cut when using networked systems: typically, the various users of an application that resides on a file server – let's call it a remote application – will each want their own .INI file. In this way, they can each have their own individual file of preferences and defaults. If you want to modify theses routines to make them more 'network friendly', then you can do so, although most of the code developed in this book will assume that it's running in a single-user environment. A good strategy would be to place the .INI files for local applications in the same directory as the application, and the .INI files for remote applications in the local Windows directory.

```
//----------------------------------------------------------------
// Name:      GetPrivateProfileName
// Purpose:   This routine determines the name of the private initialization
//            file, based on the executable file name.
//----------------------------------------------------------------

void PASCAL GetPrivateProfileName (LPSTR lpDest)
{
    char szBuffer [128];

    GetModuleFileName (hInstance, szBuffer, sizeof (szBuffer));
    lstrcpy (szBuffer + lstrlen (szBuffer) −3, "INI");
    lstrcpy (lpDest, szBuffer);
}
```

Figure 1.10 Determining the name of a program's private initialization file.

Figure 1.11 STRLIB4.C: a
set of routines to simplify
configuration file access.

```c
/* STRLIB4.C */

// © 1994 Dave Jewell and Addison-Wesley, ALL RIGHTS RESERVED

#include    <windows.h>
#include    <stdlib.h>

HANDLE hInstance;       // instance handle of the program
BOOL fWinIni = FALSE;   // False for private profile, True for WIN.INI

//—————————————————————————————————————————————————————
// Name:    GetPrivateProfileName
// Purpose: This routine determines the name of the private initialization
//          file, based on the executable file name.
//—————————————————————————————————————————————————————

LPSTR PASCAL GetPrivateProfileName (LPSTR lpDest)
{
    char szBuffer [128];

    if (fWinIni) lstrcpy (lpDest, "WIN.INI"),
    else
    {
        GetModuleFileName (hInstance, szBuffer, sizeof (szBuffer));
        lstrcpy (szBuffer + lstrlen (szBuffer) − 3, "INI");
        lstrcpy (lpDest, szBuffer);
    }

    return (lpDest);
}

//—————————————————————————————————————————————————————
// Name:    SetPublic
// Purpose: Specify whether to use the private initialization file or the public
//          one (WIN.INI).
//—————————————————————————————————————————————————————

BOOL PASCAL SetPublic (BOOL fPublic)
{
    BOOL temp;

    temp = fWinIni;
    fWinIni = fPublic;
    return (temp);
}

//—————————————————————————————————————————————————————
// Name:    GetProStr
// Purpose: Return the value of a designated profile string.
//—————————————————————————————————————————————————————

LPSTR PASCAL GetProStr (LPCSTR lpszSection, LPCSTR lpszEntry)
{
    static char szbuff [256];
    char szfName [128];

    GetPrivateProfileName (szfName);
    if (GetPrivateProfileString (lpszSection, lpszEntry, "", szbuff,
                          sizeof (szbuff), szfName) == 0)
                          szbuff [0] = '\0';
    return (szbuff);
}

//—————————————————————————————————————————————————————
// Name:    GetProInt
// Purpose: Return the value of a designated profile integer.
//—————————————————————————————————————————————————————
```

```
WORD PASCAL GetProInt (LPCSTR lpszSection, LPCSTR lpszEntry)
{
    LPSTR p;

    p = GetProStr (lpszSection, lpszEntry);
    return (p [0] == '\0') ? 0xffff : (WORD) atoi (p);
}

//---------------------------------------------------------------------
// Name:    WriteProStr
// Purpose: Write a profile string to an initialization file.
//---------------------------------------------------------------------

BOOL PASCAL WriteProStr (LPCSTR lpszSection, LPCSTR lpszEntry,
                         LPCSTR lpStr)
{
    char szfName [128];

    GetPrivateProfileName (szfName);
    return WritePrivateProfileString (lpszSection, lpszEntry, lpStr, szfName);
}

//---------------------------------------------------------------------
// Name:    WriteProInt
// Purpose: Write a profile integer to an initialization file.
//---------------------------------------------------------------------

BOOL PASCAL WriteProInt (LPCSTR lpszSection, LPCSTR lpszEntry, WORD
                         wInt, BOOL fSigned)
{
    char szBuff [20];

    // Special test to see if we want to remove entry

    if (wInt == 0xffff && fSigned == TRUE)
        return WriteProStr (lpszSection, lpszEntry, NULL);
    else
    {
        wsprintf (szBuff, fSigned ? "%d" : "%u", wInt);
        return WriteProStr (lpszSection, lpszEntry, szBuff);
    }
}

#pragma argsused

int PASCAL WinMain (HANDLE hInst, HANDLE hPrevInstance,
                    LPSTR lpCmdLine, int nCmdShow)
{
    char buff [128];

    // Check name of the initialization file

    hInstance = hInst;
    GetPrivateProfileName (buff);
    MessageBox (0, buff, "Initialization file name:", MB_OK);

    // Write some stuff to the file

    WriteProStr ("Gadgets", "GadgetName", "Wombat");
    WriteProInt ("Gadgets", "GadgetCount", 43, TRUE);
    WriteProInt ("Gadgets", "GadgetStyle", 0xC000, FALSE);
    return (0);
}
```

The code shown in Figure 1.11 is available on the accompanying disk as STRLIB4.C. It represents a usable implementation of the profile string routines we've been discussing. The GetPrivateProfileName routine is the same as shown in Figure 1.10 except that it will always return the string "WIN.INI" if the global variable fWinIni is set to TRUE. This is used to control whether we're accessing a program's private configuration file or the system-wide WIN.INI information. The SetPublic code sets the state of the variable fWinIni to either TRUE or FALSE and, as an added convenience to the calling program, returns the previous value of the variable.

The GetProStr code uses our old friend, the static character buffer, to return a pointer to the profile string that has just been read from the configuration file. If the wanted profile string is not found, the first character of the buffer is set to zero, thus ensuring that an empty string is returned. The corresponding GetProInt routine builds upon the functionality provided by GetProStr. It first calls the latter routine to read a profile string, and then makes use of atoi, a standard C run-time library routine that converts a character string into a number. By using atoi, we know that the GetProInt routine will correctly handle plus and minus characters ('+' and '−') before the number, and will strip any white-space characters that precede it. If the profile string corresponding to the wanted number is not present, GetProInt returns −1.

The WriteProStr routine is very straightforward and merely calls the WritePrivateProfileString Windows API call after first determining the name of the configuration file to use. The WriteProInt routine is a little more complicated, because it must be able to deal correctly with signed and unsigned integers. The wsprintf API routine is used to convert the passed 16-bit value to a string representation of a signed or unsigned number, using the format specifiers "%d" and "%u" as appropriate. Another wrinkle in this routine is concerned with the need to be able to remove existing entries in the configuration file. It's a simple matter to delete a string entry by passing a value of NULL as the final parameter to the WriteProStr routine. However, this isn't so easily accomplished with the WriteProInt routine. In the end, I decided to compromise and arranged things so that if the value passed to WriteProInt is 0xffff and the fSigned parameter is TRUE, the routine will interpret this as an attempt to delete the specified entry.

The code in WinMain is just some sample code that tests the WriteProStr and WriteProInt routines by creating a dummy initialization file. Because the executable source file is called STRLIB.EXE, we end up with a configuration file called STRLIB.INI which is located in the same directory as the executable file. As you might expect, the contents of the STRLIB.INI file will be as shown below:

```
[Gadgets]
GadgetCount=43
GadgetName=Wombat
GadgetStyle=49152
```

Unfortunately, there is one flaw in the profile string routines, and it's the same problem that we encountered when creating the GetResStr function. Because the GetProStr routine only uses a single static buffer to pass back the address of the string, things will go badly wrong when you invoke the GetProStr function more than once in the same line of code. You might consider this to be an unlikely scenario, but don't forget that the GetProStr routine is also used by GetProInt. For example, suppose that we're writing a program that makes use of a moveable, floating toolbox palette as described in Chapter 2. As an added convenience to the user of the program, we might decide to store the coordinates of the toolbox so that when the program is next restarted, the toolbox will appear in the same location, relative to the main window of the application. We might achieve the desired effect by writing a code fragment something like this:

```
GetWindowRect (hMainWnd, &WndRect);
SetWindowPos (hToolbox, HWND_TOPMOST,
              WndRect.left + GetProInt ("Toolbar", "XPos"),
              WndRect.top + GetProInt ("Toolbar", "YPos",
              0, 0, SWP_NOSIZE);
```

This code first calls GetWindowRect to obtain the screen position of the application's main window and then uses SetWindowPos in conjunction with the GetProInt routine to move the floating toolbox palette to the wanted location. Although this code looks quite elegant, it doesn't work. Since the GetProStr routine is being called twice from the same statement (via the GetProInt routine), the second call to GetProStr will overwrite the contents of the statically allocated character buffer in just the same way as happened with the GetResStr routine.

Don't do the same job twice

What's needed, of course, is a version of GetProStr that works just like our last version of the GetResStr routine. We need to allocate a global memory block and return a pointer to a different 256-byte area of that memory block each time GetProStr is called. We'll also need a static variable to remember where we got to in the buffer and… But hang on a minute: we've already written this code once, why should we need to do it again? Ideally, the best solution would be for the profile string routines (GetProStr, GetProInt) and the resource string routine (GetResStr) to use the same shared block of memory. By creating a common buffer allocation scheme that can be used by all of these routines we cut down on code. Another big advantage of doing things this way is that we can make the allocator routine available as a new call that we can add to our toolbox of useful routines. Suppose you need a temporary 256-byte buffer to perform some string manipulation: using this scheme you can access a temporary memory buffer without having to allocate memory on the heap or on the stack.

STRLIB5.C, the code shown in Figure 1.12, uses just this approach. The compiled program is available on the disk as STRLIB5.EXE, but if you want to compile the code yourself, then remember to include the STRLIB.RC file in the project or your make script. There's a new routine called GetBuff that is called from both the GetProStr and GetResStr routines. This routine 'hands out' 256-byte buffers to anyone that wants one. Notice that the NUMBUFFERS constant has now been increased to 10. That's because we're now using our statically allocated buffer pool for both resource strings and profile strings *and* we're making the GetBuff routine available for use elsewhere in an application. Ten seems a reasonable value for the number of buffers in the pool; with ten buffers, we're still only soaking up 2.5 kbytes of global memory. Bear in mind that if this constant is set too small, the buffer allocation code will 'wrap around' too quickly and use a buffer that's already in use for some other purpose. If you're of an especially nervous disposition, or you expect to make heavy use of the GetBuff routine, then you can obviously increase this value.

Figure 1.12 STRLIB5.C: the combined code for profile string and resource string handling.

```
/* STRLIB5.C */

// © 1994 Dave Jewell and Addison-Wesley, ALL RIGHTS RESERVED

#include    <windows.h>
#include    <stdlib.h>

#define     ID_ERRCAPTION       100
#define     ID_ERRMESSAGE       101

#define     MAXSTRSIZE          256
#define     NUMBUFFERS          10

HANDLE hInstance;        // instance handle of the program
BOOL fWinIni = FALSE;    // False for private profile, True for WIN.INI

//---------------------------------------------------------------
// Name:    GetBuff
// Purpose: This is the buffer allocator. Each time it's called, it returns a
//          pointer to a 256-byte temporary buffer. As a convenience to the
//          caller, the first byte of the buffer is set to zero.
//---------------------------------------------------------------

typedef char Buffer [MAXSTRSIZE];               // define our string buffer

LPSTR PASCAL GetBuff (void)
{
        LPSTR p;
        HANDLE hBuff;
        static int BufNum = 0;
        static Buffer far * szBuffer = NULL;

        // If this is the first call, then allocate the buffer

        if (szBuffer == NULL)
        {
           hBuff = GlobalAlloc (GHND, sizeof (Buffer) * NUMBUFFERS);
           if (hBuff == NULL); // Now's the time to panic !
           szBuffer = (Buffer far *) GlobalLock (hBuff);
        }

        p = szBuffer [BufNum++];
        if (BufNum >= NUMBUFFERS) BufNum = 0;
        *p = '\0';
        return p;
}

//---------------------------------------------------------------
// Name:    GetResStr
// Purpose: This new version of GetResStr uses GetBuff to get a temporary
//          buffer for holding the returned string.
//---------------------------------------------------------------

LPSTR PASCAL GetResStr (WORD id)
{
        LPSTR p;
        LoadString (hInstance, id, p = GetBuff(), MAXSTRSIZE − 1);
        return p;
}
```

```
//----------------------------------------------------------------
// Name:    GetPrivateProfileName
// Purpose: This routine determines the name of the private
//          initialization file, based on the executable file name.
//----------------------------------------------------------------

LPSTR PASCAL GetPrivateProfileName (LPSTR lpDest)
{
     char szBuffer [128];

     if (lpDest == NULL) lpDest = GetBuff();

     if (fWinIni) lstrcpy (lpDest, "WIN.INI");
     else
     {
       GetModuleFileName (hInstance, szBuffer, sizeof (szBuffer));
       lstrcpy (szBuffer + lstrlen (szBuffer) − 3, "INI");
       lstrcpy (lpDest, szBuffer);
     }

     return (lpDest);
}

//----------------------------------------------------------------
// Name:    SetPublic
// Purpose: Specify whether to use the private initialization file or the
//          public one (WIN.INI).
//----------------------------------------------------------------

BOOL PASCAL SetPublic (BOOL fPublic)
{
     BOOL temp;

     temp = fWinIni;
     fWinIni = fPublic;
     return (temp);
}

//----------------------------------------------------------------
// Name:    GetProStr
// Purpose: Return the value of a designated profile string.
//----------------------------------------------------------------

LPSTR PASCAL GetProStr (LPCSTR lpszSection, LPCSTR lpszEntry)
{
     LPSTR p;
     char szfName [128];

     GetPrivateProfileName (szfName);
     GetPrivateProfileString (lpszSection, lpszEntry, "",
                         p = GetBuff (), MAXSTRSIZE − 1, szfName);
     return p;
}

//----------------------------------------------------------------
// Name:    GetProInt
// Purpose: Return the value of a designated profile integer.
//----------------------------------------------------------------

WORD PASCAL GetProInt (LPCSTR lpszSection, LPCSTR lpszEntry)
{
     LPSTR p;

     p = GetProStr (lpszSection, lpszEntry);
     return (p [0] == '\0') ? 0xffff : (WORD) atoi (p);
}

//----------------------------------------------------------------
// Name: WriteProStr
```

```
// Purpose: Write a profile string to an initialization file.
//---------------------------------------------------------------

BOOL PASCAL WriteProStr (LPCSTR lpszSection, LPCSTR lpszEntry,
                                LPCSTR lpStr)
{
     char szfName [128];
     GetPrivateProfileName (szfName);
     return WritePrivateProfileString (lpszSection, lpszEntry, lpStr, szfName);
}

//---------------------------------------------------------------
// Name:     WriteProInt
// Purpose:  Write a profile integer to an initialization file.
//---------------------------------------------------------------

BOOL PASCAL WriteProInt (LPCSTR lpszSection, LPCSTR lpszEntry,
                                WORD wInt, BOOL fSigned)
{
     char szBuff [20];

     // Special test to see if we want to remove entry

     if (wInt = 0xffff && fSigned = TRUE)
         return WriteProStr (lpszSection, lpszEntry, NULL);
     else
     {
         wsprintf (szBuff, fSigned ? "%d" : "%u", wInt);
         return WriteProStr (lpszSection, lpszEntry, szBuff);
     }
}

#pragma argsused

int PASCAL WinMain (HANDLE hInst, HANDLE hPrevInstance,
                         LPSTR lpCmdLine, int nCmdShow)
{
     char buff [128];

     hInstance = hInst;

     MessageBox (0,
                  GetResStr (ID_ERRMESSAGE),
                  GetResStr (ID_ERRCAPTION), MB_OK);

     // Check name of the initialization file

     GetPrivateProfileName (buff);
     MessageBox (0, buff, "Initialization file name:", MB_OK);

     // Write some stuff to the file

     WriteProStr ("Gadgets", "GadgetName", "Wombat");
     WriteProInt ("Gadgets", "GadgetCount", 43, TRUE);
     WriteProInt ("Gadgets", "GadgetStyle", 0xC000, FALSE);

     return (0);
}
```

You might have noticed that as a convenience, the code inside GetBuff initializes the first byte of the returned buffer to zero. This slightly simplifies the code inside GetResStr and GetProStr (compare it with earlier versions) and it also means that if you call GetBuff directly to get a temporary buffer for string manipulation, you'll be starting off with an empty string.

That's almost the end of the road as far as these routines go. We've got a set of neat little functions that make it very easy to access string resources and .INI files. If you want, you can use this code as it is: just remove the WinMain routine and replace the declaration of the hInstance global variable with an external declaration. In other words, something like this:

```
extern HANDLE hInstance;      // instance handle of the program
```

Having done that, you've got a useful library module that you can link in to many different application programs. Obviously, you'll also need a header file that you can include into your other source files so that the compiler can see the definitions for the new routines in our string library. There are, however, just a couple more things we can do to improve the code first.

What: no global variables?

Now seems as good a place as any to confess about one of my pet hates. I loathe and detest global variables. Global variables cause a lot of headaches when making major changes to a large program. They make it difficult to understand the structure of a program and it becomes harder to write plug-in code modules which are independent of one another. Carefree use of global variables in Windows programs is particularly dangerous as we saw earlier when discussing the 64 kbyte limitation on an application's automatic data segment.

Using global variables where you don't need to use them is guaranteed to make me get very annoyed very quickly. Just the other day someone said to me, 'Gee, Windows programs have a lot of global variables, don't they?'. This guy had been looking at the example code that Microsoft supply as part of the SDK. Being fairly new to Windows programming, he'd picked up the idea that all Windows programs use a lot of global variables. Wrong. Only sloppily written Windows programs use lots of global variables. A well-written Windows program doesn't need to use any more global variables than a well-written DOS application.

Of course, there are cases where you can't get by without using global variables. A good example here is the fWinIni flag in the STRLIB code. There's really no obvious way of eliminating this global variable. The hInstance global variable is a different matter. Traditionally, Windows programs have always had a global variable called hInstance, hInst or something very similar. The reason why we have to have this global variable is because it's used to store the all-important program instance handle passed to us in a program's WinMain procedure. This handle is needed to call various API routines such as LoadString, GetModuleFileName and others. If you lose track of this handle, you've got problems.

It would have been nice if Microsoft had provided a Windows API routine that returns the instance handle of the currently executing task. That way, we could have eliminated this global variable and my arguably over-delicate sensibilities wouldn't have been offended. It's a shame they didn't. Well actually, they did... but they didn't tell anybody about it. The magic routine in question is called GetTaskDS. This routine is exported by the Windows Kernel and it returns the task handle just like we want. Unfortunately, the GetTaskDS routine is undocumented, which means that you're taking a chance if you use it. Will GetTaskDS be supported in Windows version 4.0? Will it put in an appearance under Windows/NT? Only time will tell....

I'm not going to recommend that you use GetTaskDS (or any other undocumented Windows routine), but neither am I going to recommend that you avoid doing so. My personal view of undocumented functions is that if they're good enough for Microsoft's applications, they're good enough for mine, too! For a more comprehensive discussion of undocumented Windows routines, read the excellent book *Undocumented Windows* by Andrew Schulman, David Maxey and Matt Pietrek (Addison-Wesley, 1992, ISBN: 0-201-60834-0). For those who are adventurous and like sailing close to the wind, I present one final version of our STRLIB routines in Figure 1.13.

Figure 1.13 STRLIB6.C: the final version of the STRLIB routines.

```
/* STRLIB6.C */

// © 1994 Dave Jewell and Addison-Wesley, ALL RIGHTS RESERVED

#include    <windows.h>
#include    <stdlib.h>

#define     MAXSTRSIZE          256
#define     NUMBUFFERS          10

#ifdef __cplusplus
extern "C" {
#endif
WORD FAR PASCAL GetTaskDS (void);
#ifdef __cplusplus
}
#endif

static BOOL fWinIni = FALSE; // False for private profile, True for WIN.INI

//─────────────────────────────────────────────────────────────────
// Name:    GetBuff
// Purpose: This is the buffer allocator. Each time it's called, it returns a
//          pointer to a 256-byte temporary buffer. As a convenience to the
//          caller, the first byte of the buffer is set to zero.
//─────────────────────────────────────────────────────────────────

LPSTR PASCAL GetBuff (void)
{
        typedef char Buffer [MAXSTRSIZE];   // define our string buffer

        LPSTR p;
        HANDLE hBuff;
        static int BufNum = 0;
        static Buffer far * szBuffer = NULL;

        // If this is the first call, then allocate the buffer

        if (szBuffer == NULL)
        {
            hBuff = GlobalAlloc (GHND, sizeof (Buffer) * NUMBUFFERS);
            if (hBuff == NULL); // Now's the time to panic !
            szBuffer = (Buffer far *) GlobalLock (hBuff);
        }

        p = szBuffer [BufNum++];
        if (BufNum >= NUMBUFFERS) BufNum = 0;
```

```
        *p = '\0';
        return p;
}

//------------------------------------------------------------------
// Name:     GetResStr
// Purpose:  This new version of GetResStr uses GetBuff to get a temporary
//           buffer for holding the returned string.
//------------------------------------------------------------------

LPSTR PASCAL GetResStr (WORD id)
{
        LPSTR p;

        LoadString (GetTaskDS(), id, p = GetBuff(), MAXSTRSIZE − 1);
        return p;
}

//------------------------------------------------------------------
// Name:     GetPrivateProfileName
// Purpose:  This routine determines the name of the private initialization
//           file, based on the executable file name.
//------------------------------------------------------------------

LPSTR PASCAL GetPrivateProfileName (LPSTR lpDest)
{
        char szBuffer [128];

        lp (lpDest == NULL) lpDest = GetBuff();

        if (fWinIni) lstrcpy (lpDest, "WIN.INI");
        else
        {
            GetModuleFileName (GetTaskDS(), szBuffer, sizeof (szBuffer));
            lstrcpy (szBuffer + lstrlen (szBuffer) − 3, "INI");
            lstrcpy (lpDest, szBuffer);
        }

        return (lpDest);
}

//------------------------------------------------------------------
// Name:     SetPublic
// Purpose:  Specify whether to use the private initialization file or the
//           public one (WIN.INI).
//------------------------------------------------------------------

BOOL PASCAL SetPublic (BOOL fPublic)
{
        BOOL temp;

        temp = fWinIni;
        fWinIni = fPublic;
        return (temp);
}

//------------------------------------------------------------------
// Name: GetProStr
// Purpose: Return the value of a designated profile string.
//------------------------------------------------------------------

LPSTR PASCAL GetProStr (LPCSTR lpszSection, LPCSTR lpszEntry)
{
        LPSTR p;
        char szfName [128];

        GetPrivateProfileName (szfName);
        GetPrivateProfileString (lpszSection, lpszEntry, "",
                                 p = GetBuff (), MAXSTRSIZE − 1, szfName);
```

```
            return p;
    }

    //————————————————————————————————————————————————
    // Name:    GetProInt
    // Purpose: Return the value of a designated profile integer.
    //————————————————————————————————————————————————

    WORD PASCAL GetProInt (LPCSTR lpszSection, LPCSTR lpszEntry)
    {
        LPSTR p;

        p = GetProStr (lpszSection, lpszEntry);
        return (p [0] == '\0') ? 0xffff : (WORD) atoi (p);
    }

    //————————————————————————————————————————————————
    // Name:    WriteProStr
    // Purpose: Write a profile string to an initialization file.
    //————————————————————————————————————————————————

    BOOL PASCAL WriteProStr (LPCSTR lpszSection, LPCSTR lpszEntry,
                             LPCSTR lpStr)
    {
        char szfName [128];

        GetPrivateProfileName (szfName);
        return WritePrivateProfileString (lpszSection, lpszEntry, lpStr, szfName);
    }

    //————————————————————————————————————————————————
    // Name:    WriteProInt
    // Purpose: Write a profile integer to an initialization file.
    //————————————————————————————————————————————————

    BOOL PASCAL WriteProInt (LPCSTR lpszSection, LPCSTR lpszEntry,
                             WORD wInt, BOOL fSigned)
    {
        char szBuff [20];

        // Special test to see if we want to remove entry

        if (wInt == 0xffff && fSigned == TRUE)
            return WriteProStr (lpszSection, lpszEntry, NULL);
        else
        {
            wsprintf (szBuff, fSigned ? "%d" : "%u", wInt);
            return WriteProStr (lpszSection, lpszEntry, szBuff);
        }
    }
```

You might think that eliminating the hInstance global variable is no big deal and, taken in isolation, you'd be right. What I've tried to do in this introductory chapter is teach some basic principles. One of these principles is that through the elimination of unneeded global variables, you can improve the reliability of your software by eliminating bugs such as uninitialized global variables, writing over a different module's global variables, and so forth. The hInstance global variable is but one example of many that will crop up later in the book.

The code shown in Figure 1.13 is substantially the same as that shown earlier, but it no longer relies upon a global variable called hInstance. It's also intended to be used as a general-purpose library file, linkable with your own Windows applications, so the definition of WinMain has been removed. I've also used the Pascal calling convention throughout, which improves the efficiency of the code and means that if you build these routines into a DLL, you will be able to call them easily from either C or Pascal. Incidentally, when you call the GetTaskDS routine inside a DLL, you will get the instance handle of the calling program, rather than the instance handle of the DLL. In general, this is what we want: if you put the GetResStr routine into a DLL, you would normally want the code to search the calling application for the wanted resource string. If you want to put the resource strings into the DLL, then don't use the GetTaskDS routine. Instead, use the instance handle that's passed to the DLL's LibMain routine when it's first loaded into memory.

You might be puzzled by the references to the preprocessor symbol __cplusplus around the declaration of the GetTaskDS routine. Because GetTaskDS is an undocumented routine, it has to be declared here rather than in the WINDOWS.H file. The special #ifdef statements around the function declaration ensure that if you're using C++, the name of the GetTaskDS routine won't get 'mangled'. (C++ compilers normally modify the names of declared routines so as to provide an implicit type-safe linkage mechanism even when used with simple-minded MS-DOS linkers.) If you're not using C++, then don't worry about this stuff. If you are using C++, you've probably come across it already.

Before closing the discussion of GetTaskDS, I should just mention that the code presented here was developed and tested using Borland C/C++ Version 3.1. This development system includes an import library entry for GetTaskDS in the IMPORT.LIB file, so you don't need to do anything special to link with this function. If your favourite development system doesn't include an import library entry for GetTaskDS, you'll have to create one. Details on doing this should be found in the documentation associated with your development system. If you're programming with Turbo Pascal or Borland Pascal, then just include the following function definition into your source code:

```
function GetTaskDS: Word; far; external 'KERNEL' index 155;
```

Figure 1.14 shows the header file, STRLIB.H, that would be used when using the STRLIB routines from within another source code file. Again, this has been written in such a way that it can be used when doing C++ development work.

```
/* STRLIB.H */

// © 1994 Dave Jewell and Addison-Wesley, ALL RIGHTS RESERVED

#ifndef _STRLIB
#define _STRLIB          /* #defined if strlib.h has been included */

#ifdef __cplusplus
extern "C" {
#endif

LPSTR PASCAL GetBuff (void);
```

Figure 1.14 STRLIB.H: a header file for use with the STRLIB routines.

```
LPSTR PASCAL GetResStr (WORD id);
BOOL PASCAL SetPublic (BOOL fPublic);
LPSTR PASCAL GetPrivateProfileName (LPSTR lpDest);
LPSTR PASCAL GetProStr (LPCSTR lpszSection, LPCSTR lpszEntry);
WORD PASCAL GetProInt (LPCSTR lpszSection, LPCSTR lpszEntry);
BOOL PASCAL WriteProStr (LPCSTR lpszSection, LPCSTR lpszEntry, LPCSTR
                              lpStr);
BOOL PASCAL WriteProInt (LPCSTR lpszSection, LPCSTR lpszEntry, WORD
                              wInt, BOOL fSigned);
#ifdef __cplusplus
}
#endif

#endif      /* _STRLIB */
```

Summary

In this chapter, we've worked through the development of a simple set of general-purpose library routines that can be used to simplify access to resource strings and profile strings from within any Windows application. You might be wondering what is the relevance of this material: after all, it has little to do with the development of user interface elements such as toolbars, floating tool palettes, and so on. The primary aim of Chapter 1 was to familiarize you with some of my own coding principles and practices. These can be summarized below:

- When faced with an over-complicated programming interface, build your own layer of code to insulate you from it and provide you with a simpler API.

- When writing routines that return strings, pass back a pointer to a globally allocated buffer rather than force the caller of the routine to allocate a buffer even where he or she doesn't need a buffer. This doesn't stop the caller from allocating a buffer where one really is needed. Allocating buffers is a drag.

- Be a miser when allocating storage space in your program's automatic data segment: treat it like a precious resource. Get into this habit when developing small Windows programs and when you create a large application, you'll be glad you did it. Don't use lots of string constants in your code: they have to live somewhere and they'll end up in the automatic data segment. Put them in resources where they belong.

- Don't do the same job twice. When writing code, always be on the lookout for places where you find yourself writing a bit of code that you've already written some place else. Ask yourself whether this ought to be rewritten as a subroutine. The buffer allocation code used by both GetProStr and GetResStr is an excellent example of such a situation. Bundling up common code into a subroutine saves code space but equally importantly, it localizes bugs. In other words, if you duplicate the same code in several different places and then find a bug in that code, you've got to fix that bug in several different places, too.

- Hate and detest global variables. Don't use global variables to pass stuff around between different routines. Use parameters: that's what they're there for. If you need to pass too many parameters to a particular routine, you're probably doing too much work inside that one routine. If you absolutely have to pass lots of parameters to a routine, put the parameters into a structure and pass a pointer to the structure instead. Minimizing the use of global variables is a little more work, but it's worth it, particuarly when writing large applications involving several programmers. A lot has been said about the evils of the 'goto' statement. I agree; goto statements are bad, but unnecessary global variables are equally bad. Just say no.

Note

For Pascal programmers, Appendix 1 contains the code shown in Figure 1.13 as a Pascal unit. Pascal source code is also available on the companion disk as STRLIB.PAS.

Toolboxes made easy

2

In the previous chapter, we concentrated on some of the design philosophy that goes hand in hand with efficient Windows programming. In this chapter, we're going to roll up our sleeves and dive in at the deep end. We will be developing a reusable code module that will enable us to create one or more floating tool palettes (or toolboxes) in our Windows applications. As for the introductory material in Chapter 1, we're going to work through the development of the toolbox code a step at a time, but if you're impatient and you want to begin using the code now, you can skip to the end of the chapter where you'll find the finished source code. Obviously, I recommend that you read through this chapter in order to gain an understanding of the source code and the design issues involved.

What is a floating toolbox window?

If you've ever seen or used Microsoft's popular Visual Basic for Windows development system, then you'll know all about floating toolbox windows. A toolbox window is a small moveable window that allows the user to select from one of several different tools. Each tool is represented by a small picture designed to give the user an idea about what that particular tool is intended to do. Toolbox palettes are used in many different types of program, particularly painting and drawing software where you typically select a tool and then use it to perform some operation on all or part of your document. For example, Figure 2.1 shows a typical toolbox window in action.

There are several points to note about this toolbox window. Firstly, the tools are arranged as a two-dimensional grid of controls. In this case, the grid is arranged as a 2×5 grid, although there's no reason why you couldn't organize the palette as a 5×2 grid. The software that we'll be developing will allow you to organize the palette with as many rows and columns as you like: you could even have a one-dimensional strip-shaped palette going horizontally across or vertically down the screen.

Figure 2.1 An example of a simple floating toolbox palette.

The second point to note is the way in which the selected tool is highlighted. It's important to provide the user with visual feedback so that he or she knows which tool has been selected. In this case, we do it by making the selected tool look as if it's been pressed. The bitmap image corresponding to the selected tool is drawn slightly to the right and down from its normal position so as to make it appear to be pressed in. At the same time, a different colour is used to draw the tool bitmap, with a dark red colour replacing any occurrence of black in the original bitmap. This scheme was first pioneered by Microsoft in their Visual Basic system and has now become something of an industry standard.

The third point about the toolbox window shown in Figure 2.1 is the way in which the caption bar has been drawn. Another interesting innovation in Microsoft Visual Basic was the use of toolbox palette caption bars (the topmost part of a window, which normally contains the window title) that are much smaller than usual. Microsoft reduced the height of the caption bar in their toolbox windows because this gives a much more pleasing appearance on today's high-resolution displays. When you look at a palette window that uses a normal-sized caption bar, the overall effect is clunky and amateurish. Again, this Microsoft innovation has become a standard, and has been emulated by a number of other software developers. The code presented in this chapter is designed to create toolbox windows which have this same professional look to them.

I should probably own up at this point. In case you've been admiring my artistic abilities in putting together the toolbox window shown in Figure 2.1, then please don't! The code is all mine, but the bitmaps corresponding to each tool were 'borrowed' from an early copy of one of Microsoft's Windows development tools! The essential point about creating a floating toolbox palette is that you can design your own tool icons (strictly speaking, they're not icons in the Windows programming sense of the word, but they are icons in terms of being small representative pictures) that correspond to the special painting and drawing tools you've devised for your own Windows applications. The important thing is that those icons should both look good and clearly represent the functions of the tools involved. For example, the bottom left-hand icon in Figure 2.1 is obviously a 'fill' tool, which will flood the selected area with the current pattern or colour. Try to make your icons clear and unambiguous and your users won't get any unpleasant surprises.

Creating the window class

As for the code examples in Chapter 1, we will develop the toolbox palette code as a complete program and then, once we have the final code working as we want it, we'll split the toolbox code out into a linkable code module that can be incorporated into other Windows applications.

The code in Figure 2.2 shows the beginnings of our floating toolbox palette code. This code can be found on the companion disk as PALETTE1.C and the compiled program is also on the disk as PALETTE1.EXE. In this embryonic stage, the code does very little: if you run the program, all you'll see is a window appear in the top left corner of your screen. Although the window has no title string, you can move the palette window around in the usual way and close it via the system menu or close box.

```
/* PALETTE1.C */

// © 1994 Dave Jewell and Addison-Wesley, ALL RIGHTS RESERVED

#include    <windows.h>

#define     PALETTECLASS         "Palette"

//———————————————————————————————————————————————
// Name:     PaletteWndProc
// Purpose:  Window procedure for our floating toolbox palette.
//———————————————————————————————————————————————

LONG FAR PASCAL _export PaletteWndProc (HWND Wnd, WORD Msg,
                                        WORD wParam, LONG lParam)
{
    if (Msg == WM_DESTROY)
    {
      PostQuitMessage (0);
      return (0);
    }
    return DefWindowProc (Wnd, Msg, wParam, lParam);
}


//———————————————————————————————————————————————
// Name:     InitApplication
// Purpose:  Initialization code: just registers the palette window
//           class and returns success or failure.
//———————————————————————————————————————————————

BOOL InitApplication (HANDLE hInstance)
{
    WNDCLASS cls;

    cls.style              = CS_SAVEBITS;
    cls.lpfnWndProc        = (WNDPROC) PaletteWndProc;
    cls.cbClsExtra         = 0;
    cls.cbWndExtra         = 0;
    cls.hInstance          = hInstance;
    cls.hIcon              = 0;
    cls.hCursor            = LoadCursor (0, IDC_ARROW);
    cls.hbrBackground      = GetStockObject(LTGRAY_BRUSH);
    cls.lpszMenuName       = NULL;
    cls.lpszClassName      = PALETTECLASS;
```

Figure 2.2   PALETTE1.C: the first stage in creating our floating palette window class.

```
        return RegisterClass (&cls);
}

//————————————————————————————————————————————————————————————
// Name:    WinMain
// Purpose: Program entry point.
//————————————————————————————————————————————————————————————

#pragma argsused

int PASCAL WinMain (HANDLE hInstance, HANDLE hPrevInst,
                    LPSTR lpCmdLine, int CmdShow)
{
        HWND Window;
        MSG Message;

        // If this is the first instance, then register palette window class

        if (hPrevInst == NULL)
            if (InitApplication (hInstance) == FALSE)
                return (0);

        // Create our palette window

        Window = CreateWindow (PALETTECLASS, NULL,
                    WS_VISIBLE | WS_OVERLAPPED | WS_SYSMENU,
                    0, 0, 100, 100, 0, 0, hInstance, NULL);

        ShowWindow (Window, CmdShow);
        UpdateWindow (Window);

        while (GetMessage (&Message, NULL, 0, 0))
        {
            TranslateMessage (&Message);
            DispatchMessage (&Message);
        }

        return (Message.wParam);
}
```

By and large, the code in PALETTE1.C is pretty straightforward as far as it goes, but there are a couple of points that require some explanation. Firstly, when registering the window class inside the InitApplication routine, a class style of CS_SAVEBITS has been used. You may not be familiar with this class style as it isn't often found in ordinary Windows programming. For any window that has this bit set, Windows will automatically save the contents of the screen behind the window. Thus, when the window is moved or closed, the process of repainting what was behind the window can take place without having to send a WM_PAINT message to the appropriate application.

Back in the bad old days of Windows programming, real mode Windows was forced to run in the pathetically small 640 kbytes of memory that were made available by MS-DOS. At that time, memory was *very* tight. The only window class that traditionally had the CS_SAVEBITS style set in its associated class was the menu window class. You may not realize it, but the Windows menu system is itself implemented using a special-purpose window class that's used to give drop-down menus. If you think about it, this makes a lot of sense; in a large Windows application that has many drop-down menus the system would run very slowly if a very complex drawing or picture had to be redisplayed each time the user pulled down a different menu. Microsoft solved this problem by introducing the CS_SAVEBITS class style into the system. By ensuring that Windows automatically saves the screen contents behind drop-down menus, the system runs smoothly although there's obviously an increased memory requirement: somewhere inside Windows, a buffer has to be allocated to hold the screen contents.

Nowadays, in the wonderful world of protected mode Windows, there's a lot more memory to play with. It therefore makes good sense to use the CS_SAVEBITS class style with something like a tool palette window because of the way in which you anticipate that the window is going to be used. Suppose you are creating a sophisticated CAD package that can draw very complex graphics on the screen. You really don't want every movement of the tool palette to trigger off a time-consuming redraw of the underlying screen information. This is particularly true on low-resolution screens where the user might not have much room to maneuver: on a slow machine the user would rapidly lose patience with your software.

If you look at the code for PALETTE1.C, you'll see that I've used the WS_OVERLAPPED and WS_SYSMENU window styles when creating the palette window. This is a temporary measure to allow us to close the window: with this combination of style bits, our window will have the standard system close box in the top left-hand corner. The final version of the toolbox code doesn't use the WS_SYSMENU window style because, in order to get the special narrow caption bar, we have to take responsibility for drawing the caption bar ourselves. For now, we need the WS_SYSMENU and WS_OVERLAPPED window styles, since without them we would have no way of closing the window and we'd have to shut down Windows in order to get rid of it!

Designing your toolbox bitmaps

In the code developed in this chapter, I've chosen to implement each toolbox icon as a small bitmap. Each bitmap contains a picture of the tool in its unselected state and beside it, another picture of the same tool in its selected (pushed in) state. By implementing each icon as a separate bitmap, we're free to arrange the icons as we like in the toolbox palette. An alternative arrangement would be to group all the icons together into one large bitmap. This would have the advantage that we'd only have one bitmap handle to worry about, but it could make things very messy if we wanted to rearrange the icons in the tool palette. Sticking closely to the KISS (Keep It Simple, Stupid!) principle, I've adopted a relatively straightforward but flexible approach.

One disadvantage of keeping each tool icon in a separate bitmap is clear: it increases the number of bitmap handles that we have lying around. At the same time, because of overheads in the GDI implementation of bitmaps, it means that these bitmaps will occupy somewhat more memory (in the GDI heap) than they would if they were all organized as a single large bitmap. Nevertheless, in this case flexibility and ease of implementation are more important than a slight increase in allocated memory.

One design solution that you shouldn't adopt would be to implement each tool icon as a separate window in the toolbox palette. I've seen several commercial and shareware toolbox windows that use this approach. Although it simplifies hit-testing, it needlessly uses up a lot of space in the USER module's local heap. Obviously, the more tool icons in your toolbox window, the more USER heap space will be wasted. In general, the run-time performance of Windows does suffer considerably if you create an unnecessarily large number of windows. If you don't believe me, try creating a dialog box containing a couple of hundred push-button controls (I've seen this done!) and watch performance plummet.

Figure 2.3 illustrates a 'zoomed in' view of one of the individual bitmaps that were used to construct the toolbox palette window shown in Figure 2.1. To make the toolbox, one of these bitmaps is required for each tool, making a total of ten. As pointed out earlier, you are not restricted to a 5×2 or 2×5 palette configuration, but you will obviously need to design a bitmap for each position in the window.

The bitmap shown here was loaded into Borland's Resource Workshop for display. In this illustration, note carefully that the thick black border around the bitmap is actually part of the bitmap image. The actual dimensions of the bitmap are 56 pixels horizontally and 28 pixels vertically. Effectively, the bitmap is composed of two 28×28 images placed alongside each other. Each 28×28 image has a border of black pixels. It's important to get this right if you want your toolbox window to look good. All the bitmaps you use must be of the same size, and they must all be surrounded by this black border. This is because the toolbox code doesn't explicitly draw these borders itself: it relies on them being a part of the bitmap.

Figure 2.3 An individual tool bitmap.

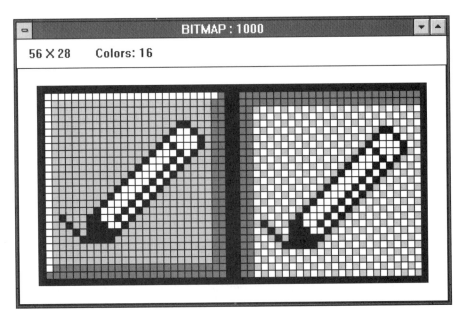

If you look very carefully at the above illustration, you'll see that in the right-hand, pressed-in image, the crayon has been drawn one pixel lower and further to the right than it appears in the left-hand image. The light gray background has been replaced by a chequered white and gray background and the raised edges in the left-hand side of the image have been replaced with a shadowed effect on the right-hand side so as to enhance the pressed-in appearance. It's important to get these details right. The worst thing you could do would be to create an ambiguous tool bitmap that didn't look as if it had been properly pressed down. This would cause all sorts of confusion to users of your program.

When designing your tool bitmaps, try to be fairly restrained in the use of color. Try to avoid using color as the sole means of identifying a tool. For example, don't create a toolbox containing nothing but a grid of plain, differently coloured squares. This would make a great color selection palette for a drawing program, but what happens if the person using the program has a high-resolution monochrome monitor? That would not be so great. It's best to use color sparingly, always bearing in mind what the tool bitmap is going to look like on a black and white monitor.

Figure 2.4 shows an enlarged view of each bitmap in the toolbox palette. If you want to replicate these particular bitmaps, there should be enough detail in this figure to allow you to create exact copies of the bitmaps involved. For the pushed-in half of each bitmap, make the changes discussed earlier. For those that have the companion disk, the resource script that contains these bitmaps is present on the disk as PALETTE.RC.

When you create your tool bitmaps, you must ensure that they have contiguous resource ID numbers in the resource file. For example, if you are creating a 3×3 toolbox palette, then you need to have nine different bitmaps in your resource script, and these bitmaps must be numbered contiguously with no intervening gaps, for example 1000 through to 1008. This is important because of the way that the code works: it takes an integer that specifies the starting ID of the first bitmap. All other bitmaps are assumed to follow sequentially. (Actually, it is possible to leave gaps in the resource ID allocation, as we shall see later.)

Incidentally, Figure 2.4 illustrates the effect of turning the toolbox palette in Figure 2.1 on to its side. The toolbox code allows you to specify the number of rows and the number of columns when creating a toolbox palette window. Figure 2.1 was created by asking for a row count of five and column count of two. By swapping these values around (two rows, five columns), the effect in Figure 2.4 was obtained. No other changes were needed to the code. The order in which each bitmap appears in the toolbox is determined solely by the resource ID numbering used.

As mentioned earlier, the bitmaps I've used are 56 pixels horizontally and 28 pixels vertically so as to give an on-screen tool bitmap which is 28 pixels square. These figures shouldn't be regarded as cast in concrete: the software that we'll be examining doesn't expect any particular bitmap size. The only real restriction is that each bitmap must be twice as wide as it is long, with the pushed-in image on the right-hand side of the bitmap. You can experiment with other bitmap sizes if you wish, although on 800×600 and 1024×768 displays I've found the 28 pixel square format to be a good compromise between compactness and readability.

Figure 2.4 An enlarged view
of all the toolbox bitmaps.

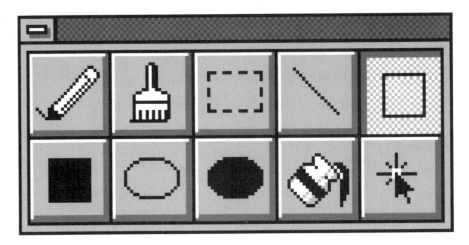

Designing a data structure

Before we can develop the main body of the code that handles the toolbox window, we need to put together a simple data structure that contains most of the information we want to keep around. The data structure that we'll be working with is shown below:

```
typedef struct ToolBoxInfo
{
    int      rows;              // number of rows of bitmaps
    int      cols;             // number of columns of bitmaps
    int      curTool;          // currently selected tool bitmap
    HWND     hWndCmd;          // window for WM_COMMAND messages
    WORD     bmBaseID;         // starting ID of bitmap resources
    int      bmWidth;          // width of each bitmap resource
    int      bmHeight;         // height of each bitmap resource
    HANDLE   bmHandles [1];    // placeholder for handle array
} ToolBoxInfo, NEAR * PToolBoxInfo;
```

This code fragment defines a data structure called ToolBoxInfo. The meanings of the various fields in the structure are as follows:

rows   The number of rows in the toolbox palette window. This is an integer value that must be greater than zero.

cols   The number of columns in the palette window. This is an integer value that must be greater than zero.

curTool   This field is used to store the index number of the currently selected tool. It can vary from 0 up to (rows * cols) − 1. When painting the palette window on the screen, this field is used to determine which tool bitmap should be drawn with a pressed-in appearance.

hWndCmd   Contains the window handle of the window to which WM_COMMAND messages are sent whenever a new tool is selected from the toolbox palette. I chose to use WM_COMMAND messages as a means of interfacing the toolbox window to a program's main application window. This is because a program will typically already have code for dealing with WM_COMMAND messages and, consequently, little extra work is involved. You must obviously ensure that there is no clash between the command IDs generated by menu commands and the WM_COMMAND messages generated by the toolbox code. This is done using the bmBaseID field as described below.

bmBaseID   This field holds the resource ID of the first toolbox bitmap. Other bitmap IDs are assumed to follow sequentially after the first. You must arrange the bmBaseID field (and the corresponding resource IDs of the bitmaps themselves) so as not to clash with the menu command IDs defined in your program.

bmWidth   This holds the width of a tool icon as displayed on the screen. Of course, this is half the width of the actual bitmap since only one half or the other of a bitmap is displayed, according to whether or not the icon is displayed in an up or down position. The value of this field is determined once only, when the bitmap resources are loaded into memory.

bmHeight   This field contains the height of a tool icon. The value of this field is determined once only, when the bitmap resources are loaded into memory.

bmHandles   This array is used to store the bitmap handles for each bitmap in the toolbox palette window. In the code fragment shown, this array only contains one element but in fact this single-element array is used as a place-holder to store the full array. When the number of expected bitmaps has been calculated (by multiplying together the rows and cols fields) an area of memory is allocated that is sufficient to store a ToolBoxInfo structure, along with a handle array of the appropriate size. This will become clearer when we examine the code in the next section.

Setting up the ToolBoxInfo data structure

The program code shown in Figure 2.5 illustrates the way in which the ToolBoxInfo data structure is initialized and used. There are many changes between this code and that previously given in Figure 2.2. The most important routine here is called CreateToolBoxWindow. The first parameter to this routine is the window handle of the toolbox palette window which is in the process of being created. CreateToolBoxWindow is called in response to a WM_CREATE message. The second parameter is the 32-bit lParam value which has been received as a part of the WM_CREATE message.

When WM_CREATE messages are generated, the lParam part of the message is used to point to a special data structure called a CREATESTRUCT record. The format of a CREATESTRUCT record is given below:

```
typedef struct tagCREATESTRUCT
{
    void FAR*    lpCreateParams;
    HINSTANCE hInstance;
    HMENU       hMenu;
    HWND        hwndParent;
    int         cy;
    int         cx;
    int         y;
    int         x;
    LONG        style;
    LPCSTR      lpszName;
    LPCSTR      lpszClass;
    DWORD       dwExStyle;
} CREATESTRUCT;
typedef CREATESTRUCT FAR* LPCREATESTRUCT;
```

For our purposes, the most important thing about the CREATESTRUCT record is the fact that it contains a field called lpCreateParams. This field is exactly the same LONG value that is passed as the final parameter to the CreateWindow routine. This mechanism was designed by Microsoft to allow an application to initialize a window in a certain way by sending some arbitrary value through to the window when it is first created, or by sending a pointer to some application-specific data structure.

If this mechanism didn't exist, things would be very much messier and it would probably be necessary to set up one or more global variables to communicate with the palette window at the time it is being created. We can make use of the CREATESTRUCT mechanism to pass the address of a ToolBoxInfo data structure through to a new toolbox window.

Figure 2.5 PALETTE2.C: creating the ToolBoxInfo data structure.

```
/* PALETTE2.C */

// © 1994 Dave Jewell and Addison-Wesley, ALL RIGHTS RESERVED

#include    <windows.h>

#define     PALETTECLASS        "Palette"

typedef struct ToolBoxInfo
{
    int     rows;            // number of rows of bitmaps
    int     cols;            // number of columns of bitmaps
    int     curTool;         // currently selected tool bitmap
    HWND    hWndCmd;         // window for WM_COMMAND messages
    WORD    bmBaseID;        // starting ID of bitmap resources
    int     bmWidth;         // width of each bitmap resource
    int     bmHeight;        // height of each bitmap resource
    HANDLE  bmHandles [1];   // placeholder for handle array

} ToolBoxInfo, NEAR * PToolBoxInfo;

HANDLE hInst;

//--------------------------------------------------------------
// Name:    FakeCaptionHeight
// Purpose: Return height of fake caption bar.
//--------------------------------------------------------------

int PASCAL FakeCaptionHeight (void)
{
        return (GetSystemMetrics (SM_CYCAPTION) / 3) + 2;
```

```
}
//————————————————————————————————————————
// Name:    CreateToolBoxWindow
// Purpose: Called in response to WM_CREATE message.
//————————————————————————————————————————

LONG PASCAL CreateToolBoxWindow (HWND hWnd, LONG lParam)
{
    BITMAP bm;
    int i, numTools;
    PToolBoxInfo NewInfo, Info;

    Info = (PToolBoxInfo) (((LPCREATESTRUCT)lParam) −>lpCreateParams);
    if (Info == NULL) return (−1);

    // Perform some sanity checks

    numTools = Info−>rows * Info−>cols;
    if (numTools == 0 || Info−>curTool >= numTools) return (−1);
    // Allocate the 'real' info structure

    NewInfo = (PToolBoxInfo) LocalAlloc (LPTR, sizeof (ToolBoxInfo) +
                                (numTools − 1) * sizeof (HANDLE));
    *NewInfo = *Info;

    // Now load the tool bitmaps

    NewInfo−>bmWidth = −1;
    for (i = 0; i < numTools; i++)
    {
       NewInfo−>bmHandles [i] = LoadBitmap (hInst,
                                MAKEINTRESOURCE
                                (NewInfo−>bmBaseID + i));

       if (NewInfo−>bmWidth == −1 && NewInfo−>bmHandles [i] != NULL)
       {
          GetObject (NewInfo−>bmHandles [i], sizeof (bm), &bm);
          NewInfo−>bmWidth = bm.bmWidth / 2;
          NewInfo−>bmHeight = bm.bmHeight;
       }
    }

    // Check we've got at least one bitmap !

    if (NewInfo−>bmWidth == −1) return (−1);

    // Calculate the required size of the window

    SetWindowPos (hWnd, 0, 0, 0,
                (NewInfo−>cols * NewInfo−>bmWidth) − (NewInfo−>cols − 1) + 6,
                (NewInfo−>rows * NewInfo−>bmHeight) − (NewInfo−>rows − 1)
                + FakeCaptionHeight() + 6,
                SWP_NOMOVE | SWP_NOACTIVATE | SWP_NOZORDER);

       // Associate the Info data structure with the window

       SetWindowWord (hWnd, 0, (WORD) NewInfo);
       return (0);
}

//————————————————————————————————————————
// Name: PaletteWndProc
// Purpose: Window procedure for our floating toolbox palette.
//————————————————————————————————————————

LONG FAR PASCAL _export PaletteWndProc (HWND Wnd, WORD Msg,
                                WORD wParam, LONG lParam)
{
```

```
        switch (Msg)
        {
          case WM_CREATE:

          return CreateToolBoxWindow (Wnd, lParam);

          case WM_DESTROY:
          PostQuitMessage (0);
          return (0);
        }

        return DefWindowProc (Wnd, Msg, wParam, lParam);
}

//————————————————————————————————————————————
// Name:    InitApplication
// Purpose: Initialization code: just registers the palette window
//          class and returns success or failure.
//————————————————————————————————————————————

BOOL InitApplication (HANDLE hInstance)
{
        WNDCLASS cls;

        cls.style              = CS_SAVEBITS;
        cls.lpfnWndProc        = (WNDPROC) PaletteWndProc;
        cls.cbClsExtra         = 0;
        cls.cbWndExtra         = 2;
        cls.hInstance          = hInstance;
        cls.hIcon              = 0;
        cls.hCursor            = LoadCursor (0, IDC_ARROW);
        cls.hbrBackground      = GetStockObject(LTGRAY_BRUSH);
        cls.lpszMenuName       = NULL;
        cls.lpszClassName      = PALETTECLASS;

        return RegisterClass (&cls);
}

//————————————————————————————————————————————
// Name:    WinMain
// Purpose: Program entry point.
//————————————————————————————————————————————

#pragma argsused

int PASCAL WinMain (HANDLE hInstance, HANDLE hPrevInst,
                    LPSTR lpCmdLine, int CmdShow)
{
        HWND Window;
        MSG Message;

        hInst = hInstance;

        // If this is the first instance, then register palette window class

        if (hPrevInst == NULL)
           if (InitApplication (hInstance) == FALSE)
              return (0);

        // Create our palette window

        Window = CreateWindow (PALETTECLASS, NULL,
                            WS_VISIBLE | WS_OVERLAPPED | WS_SYSMENU,
                            0, 0, 100, 100, 0, 0, hInstance, NULL);

        if (Window == NULL) return (0);

        ShowWindow (Window, CmdShow);
        UpdateWindow (Window);
```

```
        while (GetMessage (&Message, NULL, 0, 0))
        {
           TranslateMessage (&Message);
           DispatchMessage (&Message);
        }

        return (Message.wParam);
    }
```

The CreateToolBoxWindow uses a couple of rather messy type casts (casts are always messy!) to get a pointer to the ToolBoxInfo data structure whose address was passed through to the CreateWindow routine. If the retrieved pointer is NULL, then the routine returns a value of −1 which causes the CreateWindow operation to fail, returning a value of NULL to the caller. The CreateToolBoxWindow code then checks that the values found in the ToolBoxInfo data structure look sensible. At this point, another, more permanent ToolBoxInfo data structure is allocated using the LocalAlloc routine. This is reasonable because the data structure in question is small and isn't likely to make too much of a dent in the local heap. You could just as easily allocate the data structure in the global heap using GlobalAlloc, but there would then be a slight loss of efficiency because of the need to manipulate far rather than near pointers.

When the permanent ToolBoxInfo data structure is created, the size of the allocated memory block is adjusted according to the number of toolbox bitmaps that are expected. Recall the discussion of the bmHandles array in the ToolBoxInfo data structure: because this array already contains sufficient space to accommodate one bitmap handle, we take this into account when performing the calculation. The code given here doesn't check to ensure that the LocalAlloc routine failed: you should really insert your own error handling code here, also returning −1 as the function result.

Having allocated a permanent ToolBoxInfo data structure, the contents of the transient ToolBoxInfo record are copied across and the bmWidth field is initialized to −1. This is used as a flag to indicate that we haven't yet loaded any of the toolbox bitmaps, so we don't know what size the bitmaps are going to be.

Note
The code has been written such that it is actually possible to omit one or more bitmaps if wished: you will simply get a gap in the toolbox palette for each missing bitmap. For example, if you specify that you want a 2×3 palette and give a base resource ID of 1000, then you would normally have six bitmaps with consecutive IDs from 1000 through to 1005. If you omit bitmap 1004, for example, you will have a gray gap where that bitmap would normally be displayed. In practice, you are only ever likely to use this facility if the number of tools needed by your program doesn't quite fill the two-dimensional grid. For example, with a 2×3 grid as described above, your application might implement only five drawing tools. In such a case, you would simply omit bitmap 1005. If you omit all the bitmaps, the code will check to see if the bmWidth field is still −1 after the for loop has executed. In this case, the CreateWindow routine will again be aborted by returning −1 as the function result.

When calculating the value for bmWidth, the code calls the Windows API GetObject routine to determine the dimensions of the bitmap. The value for the width is divided by two because, as discussed earlier, the actual bitmaps are twice as long as the on-screen area used. Either the left or right half of the bitmap is painted onto the screen, depending upon whether or not that particular tool is selected.

Based on the number of rows, columns and the bitmap dimensions, the code then resizes the toolbox palette window using the SetWindowPos routine. The addition of six to the width and height is a 'fudge factor' that allows for the provision of a small border surrounding the tool icons. Look at Figure 2.4 for a closer look at this. There's also a new routine called FakeCaptionHeight which is required for the above calculations. Bear in mind that when calling the SetWindowPos routine, the specified window width and height applies to the entire window, *including* the non-client parts of the window such as the caption bar. Consequently, we need to make room for the new smaller-size caption bar that we'll be incorporating into the final version of the toolbox palette window. The FakeCaptionHeight routine returns the height (in pixels) of the new-style caption bar. The code inside this small routine might look a little odd: I discovered by trial and error that this particular formula gave a caption height size which was consistent with that used by Visual Basic's toolbox palette.

The final chunk of code in the CreateToolBoxWindow routine simply uses the SetWindowWord API call to save the permanent ToolBoxInfo pointer into a reserved location in the window data structure. If you look at the code that registers the window class in Figure 2.5, you'll see that the cbWndExtra field has now been set to two, so as to make room for this pointer value to be saved. The big advantage of this technique is that it allows us to associate a toolbox palette window with its corresponding data in a natural way that doesn't require the use of global variables. You might feel that having a global variable which points to the toolbox information is no big deal. You could even store the ToolBoxInfo structure itself as a global variable, without having to perform any explicit allocation of the data. However, aside from the data segment conservation issues we discussed in Chapter 1, consider what would happen if you wanted to implement more than one toolbox palette within the same window. You'd have to have an array of pointers to ToolBoxInfo structures... or even an array of ToolBoxInfo structures. Not a great idea. Remember: global variables – just say no.

In the PALETTE2.C code, you will also see that the PaletteWndProc routine has been modified to call the CreateToolBoxWndProc routine in response to a WM_CREATE message. Copy the PALETTE2.EXE application from the *Polishing Windows* disk and try running it. You might be surprised to see that this code seems to do nothing whatsoever. No window appears and the application terminates immediately. So what's going wrong? The answer is in the call to the CreateWindow routine: we're still passing a NULL value as the final parameter, rather than a pointer to a ToolBoxInfo data structure. Consequently, the CreateWindow routine fails in the call to CreateToolBoxWindow and no window is created.

In order to get our little palette window to reappear, we need to define a ToolBoxInfo variable inside our WinMain routine. The various fields in the structure then have to be initialized, and we then have to pass the address of the structure through to the CreateWindow routine as the final parameter. Finally, at this stage we must make sure to include our PALETTE.RC file into the project file so that the bitmap resources are linked into the final .EXE file.

With these changes, the revised version of WinMain looks as shown in Figure 2.6. You may notice that in addition to passing the address of the ToolBoxInfo structure to the CreateWindow routine, the specified initial size of the window has been changed to {0, 0, 0, 0} as passed to CreateWindow. This is because the palette window is now automatically resized according to the size of the bitmap resources and the wanted number of rows and columns as specified in the ToolBoxInfo data structure.

```
//------------------------------------------------------------
// Name:    WinMain
// Purpose: Program entry point.
//------------------------------------------------------------

#pragma argsused

int PASCAL WinMain (HANDLE hInstance, HANDLE hPrevInst,
                    LPSTR lpCmdLine, int CmdShow)
{
        HWND Window;
        MSG Message;
        ToolBoxInfo info;

        hInst = hInstance;

        // If this is the first instance, then register palette window class

        if (hPrevInst == NULL)
           if (InitApplication (hInstance) == FALSE)
              return (0);

        // Initialize our ToolBoxInfo data structure

        info.rows = 5;
        info.cols = 2;
        info.curTool = 0;
        info.hWndCmd = 0;
        info.bmBaseID = 1000;

        // Create our palette window

        Window = CreateWindow (PALETTECLASS, NULL,
                        WS_VISIBLE | WS_OVERLAPPED | WS_SYSMENU,
                        0, 0, 0, 0, 0, 0, hInstance, (LPSTR)&info);

        if (Window == NULL) return (0);

        ShowWindow (Window, CmdShow);
        UpdateWindow (Window);

        while (GetMessage (&Message, NULL, 0, 0))
        {
           TranslateMessage (&Message);
           DispatchMessage (&Message);
        }

        return (Message.wParam);
}
```

Figure 2.6 Initializing the ToolBoxInfo and passing it to the CreateWindow routine.

Painting the palette

We now have our palette window back with us again, but it still doesn't look too much like a toolbox palette: so far those pretty-looking bitmaps have been conspicuous by their absence. Now is a good time to implement the code that actually draws the bitmaps inside the palette window.

It should be apparent by now that the heart of the toolbox palette code is the small data structure we defined earlier. Given the window handle of a palette window, we need to be able to access the fields in this data structure easily. From examination of the CreateToolBoxWindow routine, you can see that we saved a near pointer to this data structure into the window itself by using the SetWindowWord API call. Let's begin by writing a simple little routine to give us back this pointer whenever we need it. Here's the code:

```
//----------------------------------------------------------------
// Name:    GetInfo
// Purpose: Return a pointer to window's associated data.
//----------------------------------------------------------------

PToolBoxInfo PASCAL GetInfo (HWND Wnd)
{
        return (PToolBoxInfo) GetWindowWord (Wnd, 0);
}
```

You can see that this routine is trivially simple. In fact, you might be strongly tempted to dispense with it altogether and explicitly call the GetWindowWord routine whenever you need to. This is a temptation that you should strongly resist: if you ever change the way that memory is allocated for the ToolBoxInfo data structure, you'd have to go all through your code, changing each of those GetWindowWord calls to something else. By localizing the details of the implementation to this one routine, future changes are very much easier to make.

One approach that you'll sometimes see used (I've used it myself in the chapter that deals with 3D dialog box effects (Chapter 5)) is the use of the GetProp and SetProp Windows API calls. These routines allow you to associate an arbitrary 'property' with a specified window. Although the Windows SDK documentation frequently refers to a property as a handle, it can actually be anything you like, with the restriction that under Windows 3.1 it can only be a 16-bit quantity. This is enormously useful when subclassing existing windows: you can't just use SetWindowWord or SetWindowLong to store data into an existing window because your code wasn't in control when the window was registered. Consequently, you weren't able to set up your own wanted values for cbWndExtra and cbClassExtra in the WNDCLASS data structure. If you try to use SetWindowWord or SetWindowLong on an unknown window type, then you're bound to run into trouble. You could easily end up corrupting the window's own private data. It's for this reason that the window property routines are extremely useful. We'll be delving deeper into the mysteries of windows' properties and the joys of subclassing in the next chapter.

Having got a pointer to the toolbox window's data, we can now write a routine that takes the number of a palette tool and fills in a bounding box rectangle for use by the drawing code. This routine, called GetBitmapRect, is shown below. The routine takes a pointer to a rectangle (in Pascal this would be a var parameter so that its contents could be changed) and an integer parameter that can vary between 0 and (cols * rows) − 1 where cols and rows are the number of columns and number of rows in the toolbox palette. Note that the code shown here doesn't actually check to see that the num parameter is within this range: that's because the checking is done elsewhere before GetBitmapRect is called.

```
//——————————————————————————————————————————————————
// Name:     GetBitmapRect
// Purpose:  Return the bounding rectangle of a specific item.
//——————————————————————————————————————————————————

void PASCAL GetBitmapRect (RECT * r, int num, PToolBoxInfo info)
{
    r−>left = (num % info−>cols) * (info−>bmWidth −1) + 3;
    r−>top = (num / info−>cols) * (info−>bmHeight −1) + FakeCaptionHeight() + 3;
    r−>right = r−>left + info−>bmWidth;
    r−>bottom = r−>top + info−>bmHeight;
}
```

The third parameter to the routine is a pointer to our old friend, the ToolBoxInfo data structure. It's important to call the FakeCaptionHeight routine again inside this code, since the height of the fake caption bar determines where the bitmaps are placed within the window and hence the position of each bitmap's bounding rectangle. At the moment, we're using a window style of WS_OVERLAPPED, but eventually, we'll be using the WS_POPUP style. When we use this window style, we will be solely responsible for drawing the fake caption bar which will actually be inside the client area of the window. We need to make room for the caption bar within the window above the bitmaps, and calling FakeCaptionHeight inside this code allows us to do just that.

I mentioned earlier that the toolbox palette code draws a small 3-pixel border around the bitmaps. This gives the palette window a more aesthetically pleasing appearance. This is the reason for the number 3 appearing in the GetBitmapRect code. Effectively, each bounding rectangle is offset vertically and horizontally by three pixels. This also fits in with the addition of six to the window height and width when the new window size is being set up via the SetWindowPos API call in the CreateToolBoxWindow routine. Rather than hard-wiring these numbers into the code, you may wish to make them into #defined constants so that they can be more easily changed.

The routine shown below takes care of the actual process of drawing the specified bitmap. Windows doesn't allow you to blit a bitmap directly onto the screen. You first have to create a memory device context using the CreateCompatibleDC function. The wanted bitmap is then selected into the memory device context and blitted from there into the wanted device context. This sounds tedious, but once you've done it a few hundred times it's not such a big deal! Those who are more experienced at Windows programming will appreciate the rationale behind Microsoft's approach: by creating a memory device context, it's possible to create a bitmap 'off-screen', which can then be blasted onto the screen in one quick operation, producing a smoother, faster response. I haven't pursued this approach in this chapter but if you want to do so, it isn't difficult to do.

One wrinkle in the code below is concerned with what happens when the currently selected tool bitmap is drawn. We want this tool to have a depressed appearance and consequently, it's important to draw the right-hand half of bitmap rather than the regular, non-depressed left-hand side. This is the function of the code that sets up the XSrc variable. Once the deed has been done, the memory device context can be deleted.

```
//————————————————————————————————————
// Name:    DrawBitmap
// Purpose: Draw a specified bitmap in its own rectangle.
//————————————————————————————————————
void PASCAL DrawBitmap (HDC dc, PToolBoxInfo info, int num)
{
        HBITMAP hbm;
        HDC hMemDC;
        RECT r;
        int XSrc;

        if (info−>bmHandles [num] != NULL)
        {
           GetBitmapRect (&r, num, info);
           hMemDC = CreateCompatibleDC (dc);
           hbm = SelectObject (hMemDC, info−>bmHandles [num]);
           XSrc = (num != info−>curTool) ? 0 : info−>bmWidth;
           BitBlt (dc, r.left, r.top, r.right − r.left, r.bottom − r.top,
                     hMemDC, XSrc, 0, SRCCOPY);
           SelectObject (hMemDC, hbm);
           DeleteDC (hMemDC);
        }
}
```

That pretty well wraps it up as far as the drawing code is concerned. All we have to do now is arrange that the DrawBitmap routine is called in response to a WM_PAINT message being received by the toolbox window procedure:

```
case WM_PAINT:
BeginPaint (Wnd, &ps);

info = GetInfo (Wnd);
for (i = 0; i < info−>rows * info−>cols; i++)
   DrawBitmap (ps.hdc, info, i);

EndPaint (Wnd, &ps);
return (0);
```

In this example, the code simply calls the GetInfo routine to retrieve a pointer to our ToolBoxInfo structure. It then loops through each of the toolbox palette positions, drawing the bitmap for each one. From the DrawBitmap code, you can see what will happen if we happen to have a missing bitmap: we'll simply get an empty gray 'gap' where the bitmap should be. This is exactly the effect that we set out to achieve.

Figure 2.7 shows the complete program when we've put it all together. This code is on the companion disk as PALETTE3.C, and the corresponding executable program is on the disk as PALETTE3.EXE.

```
/* PALETTE3.C */

// © 1994 Dave Jewell and Addison-Wesley, ALL RIGHTS RESERVED

#include    <windows.h>

#define    PALETTECLASS        "Palette"

typedef struct ToolBoxInfo
{
    int      rows;            // number of rows of bitmaps
    int      cols;            // number of columns of bitmaps
    int      curTool;         // currently selected tool bitmap
    HWND     hWndCmd;         // window for WM_COMMAND messages
    WORD     bmBaseID;        // starting ID of bitmap resources
    int      bmWidth;         // width of each bitmap resource
    int      bmHeight;        // height of each bitmap resource
    HANDLE bmHandles [1];     // placeholder for handle array

} ToolBoxInfo, NEAR * PToolBoxInfo;

HANDLE hInst;

//————————————————————————————————————————————————
// Name:    FakeCaptionHeight
// Purpose: Return height of fake caption bar.
//————————————————————————————————————————————————

int PASCAL FakeCaptionHeight (void)
{
    return (GetSystemMetrics (SM_CYCAPTION) / 3) + 2;
}

//————————————————————————————————————————————————
// Name:    GetInfo
// Purpose: Return a pointer to window's associated data.
//————————————————————————————————————————————————

PToolBoxInfo PASCAL GetInfo (HWND Wnd)
{
    return (PToolBoxInfo) GetWindowWord (Wnd, 0);
}

//————————————————————————————————————————————————
// Name:    GetBitmapRect
// Purpose: Return the bounding rectangle of a specific item.
//————————————————————————————————————————————————

void PASCAL GetBitmapRect (RECT * r, int num, PToolBoxInfo info)
{
    r->left = (num % info->cols) * (info->bmWidth − 1) + 3;
    r->top = (num / info->cols) * (info->bmHeight − 1) +
                                    FakeCaptionHeight() + 3;

    r->right = r->left + info->bmWidth;
    r->bottom = r->top + info->bmHeight;
}

//————————————————————————————————————————————————
// Name:    DrawBitmap
// Purpose: Draw a specified bitmap in its own rectangle.
//————————————————————————————————————————————————

void PASCAL DrawBitmap (HDC dc, PToolBoxInfo info, int num)
{
    HBITMAP hbm;
    HDC hMemDC;
    RECT r;
    int XSrc;
```

```
        if (info->bmHandles [num] != NULL)
        {
          GetBitmapRect (&r, num, info);
          hMemDC = CreateCompatibleDC (dc);
          hbm = SelectObject (hMemDC, info->bmHandles [num]);
          XSrc = (num != info->curTool) ? 0 : info->bmWidth;
          BitBlt (dc, r.left, r.top, r.right - r.left, r.bottom - r.top,
                hMemDC, XSrc, 0, SRCCOPY);

          SelectObject (hMemDC, hbm);
          DeleteDC (hMemDC);
        }
}

//─────────────────────────────────────────────────────────────
// Name:    CreateToolBoxWindow
// Purpose: Called in response to WM_CREATE message.
//─────────────────────────────────────────────────────────────

LONG PASCAL CreateToolBoxWindow (HWND hWnd, LONG lParam)
{
        BITMAP bm;
        int i, numTools;
        PToolBoxInfo NewInfo, Info;

        Info = (PToolBoxInfo) (((LPCREATESTRUCT)lParam)->lpCreateParams);
        if (Info == NULL) return (-1);

        // Perform some sanity checks

        numTools = Info->rows * Info->cols;
        if (numTools == 0 || Info->curTool >= numTools) return (-1);

        // Allocate the 'real' info structure

        NewInfo = (PToolBoxInfo) LocalAlloc (LPTR,
                   sizeof (ToolBoxInfo) + (numTools - 1) * sizeof (HANDLE));
        *NewInfo = *Info;

        // Now load the tool bitmaps

        NewInfo->bmWidth = -1;
        for (i = 0; i < numTools; i++)
        {
          NewInfo->bmHandles [i] = LoadBitmap (hInst,
                                       MAKEINTRESOURCE
                                       (NewInfo->bmBaseID + i));

          if (NewInfo->bmWidth == -1 &&
            NewInfo->bmHandles [i] != NULL)
          {
            GetObject (NewInfo->bmHandles [i], sizeof (bm), &bm);
            NewInfo->bmWidth = bm.bmWidth / 2;
            NewInfo->bmHeight = bm.bmHeight;
          }
        }

        // Check we've got at least one bitmap !

        if (NewInfo->bmWidth == -1) return (-1);

        // Calculate the required size of the window

        SetWindowPos (hWnd, 0, 0, 0,
                   (NewInfo->cols * NewInfo->bmWidth) - (NewInfo->cols - 1) + 6,
                   (NewInfo->rows * NewInfo->bmHeight) - (NewInfo->rows - 1)
                   + FakeCaptionHeight() + 6,
                   SWP_NOMOVE | SWP_NOACTIVATE | SWP_NOZORDER);

        // Associate the Info data structure with the window
```

```
        SetWindowWord (hWnd, 0, (WORD) NewInfo);
        return (0);
}

//————————————————————————————————————————————————
// Name:    PaletteWndProc
// Purpose: Window procedure for our floating toolbox palette.
//————————————————————————————————————————————————

LONG FAR PASCAL _export PaletteWndProc (HWND Wnd, WORD Msg,
                                        WORD wParam, LONG lParam)
{
    int i;
    PAINTSTRUCT ps;
    PToolBoxInfo info;

    switch (Msg)
    {
      case WM_PAINT:

        BeginPaint (Wnd, &ps);

        info = GetInfo (Wnd);
        for (i = 0; i < info->rows * info->cols; i++)
            DrawBitmap (ps.hdc, info, i);

        EndPaint (Wnd, &ps);
        return (0);

      case WM_CREATE:

        return CreateToolBoxWindow (Wnd, lParam);

      case WM_DESTROY:

        PostQuitMessage (0);
        return (0);
    }

    return DefWindowProc (Wnd, Msg, wParam, lParam);
}

//————————————————————————————————————————————————
// Name:    InitApplication
// Purpose: Initialization code: just registers the palette window class
//          and returns success or failure.
//————————————————————————————————————————————————

BOOL InitApplication (HANDLE hInstance)
{
    WNDCLASS cls;

    cls.style           = CS_SAVEBITS;
    cls.lpfnWndProc     = (WNDPROC) PaletteWndProc;
    cls.cbClsExtra      = 0;
    cls.cbWndExtra      = 2;
    cls.hInstance       = hInstance;
    cls.hIcon           = 0;
    cls.hCursor         = LoadCursor (0, IDC_ARROW);
    cls.hbrBackground   = GetStockObject(LTGRAY_BRUSH);
    cls.lpszMenuName    = NULL;
    cls.lpszClassName   = PALETTECLASS;

    return RegisterClass (&cls);
}

//————————————————————————————————————————————————
// Name:    WinMain
// Purpose: Program entry point.
//————————————————————————————————————————————————

#pragma argsused
```

```
int PASCAL WinMain (HANDLE hInstance, HANDLE hPrevInst,
                    LPSTR lpCmdLine, int CmdShow)
{
        HWND Window;
        MSG Message;
        ToolBoxInfo info;

        hInst = hInstance;

        // If this is the first instance, then register palette window class

        if (hPrevInst == NULL)
            if (InitApplication (hInstance) == FALSE)
                return (0);

        // Initialize our ToolBoxInfo data structure

        info.rows       = 5;
        info.cols       = 2;
        info.curTool    = 0;
        info.hWndCmd    = 0;
        info.bmBaseID   = 1000;

        // Create our palette window

        Window = CreateWindow (PALETTECLASS, NULL,
                        WS_VISIBLE | WS_OVERLAPPED | WS_SYSMENU,
                        0, 0, 0, 0, 0, 0, hInstance, (LPSTR)&info);

        if (Window == NULL) return (0);

        ShowWindow (Window, CmdShow);
        UpdateWindow (Window);

        while (GetMessage (&Message, NULL, 0, 0))
        {
            TranslateMessage (&Message);
            DispatchMessage (&Message);
        }

        return (Message.wParam);
}
```

With the foregoing in mind, you might be forgiven for expecting that when we execute the PALETTE3 code, we'll get a nice-looking palette window. In fact – this isn't the case! Figure 2.8 shows the window that results from executing the program. Something is obviously very wrong.

Clearly, the window is being given a vertical and horizontal size other than what we asked for. If you check the code that deals with sizing the window, you won't find anything obviously wrong. If you want, you can even step through the code using your favourite Windows-compatible debugger. You'll still find that the window calculations are being performed correctly.

The answer lies within Windows itself. With the code as it stands at the moment, we're using the WS_OVERLAPPED and WS_SYSMENU styles to create the window. When Windows is told to resize a window with these style bits set, it won't allow the horizontal size of the window to be reduced beyond a certain predetermined limit. This is obvious when you think about it: Windows needs to reserve sufficient horizontal space in the caption bar for the system menu close box and for a modestly

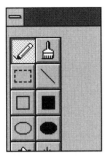

Figure 2.8 The result of executing the PALETTE3 program.

sized title string. If you try to reduce the size of the window beyond what Windows thinks is reasonable, it won't let you! Just to prove the point, you may like to try modifying the code to use the following, alternative CreateWindow call:

```
Window = CreateWindow (PALETTECLASS, NULL,
            WS_VISIBLE I WS_POPUP,
            0, 0, 0, 0, 0, 0, hInstance, (LPSTR)&info);
```

You can see that we're now using the WS_POPUP style. The resulting window no longer has a caption bar and if you compile and execute the code, you will be rewarded with a much nicer-looking palette window. One word of warning though: because there's no caption bar, there's also no system menu close box! If you want to try this out, you will have to close down Windows in order to get rid of the program.

As an alternative to the above, you might like to try swapping the values for the number of wanted rows and columns. In other words, use something like this when setting up the ToolBoxInfo data structure:

```
// Initialize our ToolBoxInfo data structure

    info.rows       = 2;
    info.cols       = 5;
    info.curTool    = 0;
    info.hWndCmd    = 0;
    info.bmBaseID   = 1000;
```

This will give us a toolbox palette that's wider than it is tall. With such a window, you'll see that the horizontal size of the window looks about right when you compile and execute the code. That's because when the SetWindowPos routine is called, the wanted window width is sufficiently large not to offend Windows' sensibilities!

OK, so we're happy with the code to calculate the window width. But what's going wrong with the window height calculation? You've probably guessed the answer already. As given, the code assumes that the window will use the WS_POPUP style and we'll be doing our own drawing of the caption bar inside what is effectively the window's client area. Because these assumptions aren't yet true, things don't look right.

The bottom line is this: there's nothing wrong with the code for calculating the width and height. But before things start looking good, we need to begin using the WS_POPUP style and we need to draw a 'fake' caption bar. Because the toolbox palette isn't going to look right until we implement these changes, it's a good idea to add this code next.

Fooling Windows with custom caption bars

If you're familiar with Visual Basic, and you've admired the neat-looking toolbox palette that forms a part of the program, you might well suspect that Microsoft are using some secret undocumented Windows API call in order to implement a window that has a reduced half-height caption bar. Although Microsoft do have a certain fondness for using secret undocumented calls in their own software, they haven't done so this time. In fact, the effect is achieved using perfectly standard, documented API routines. I'm indebted to Martin Heller (mheller@bix) for pointing me in the right direction while developing this code.

Here's how it works: an application must create a toolbox palette window using the WS_POPUP style as previously discussed. This means that the entire window is devoted to the client area – there's no caption bar at the top. The window procedure that's associated with the window has to take responsibility for drawing the fake caption bar in response to the WM_PAINT message, in just the same way as the other parts of the window are drawn. There's one extra little wrinkle, though; whenever the user clicks the mouse on our fake caption bar, we have to fool Windows into thinking that the mouse is being clicked on a real, live caption bar. This is important because it gives the user the ability to click and drag the window around the screen. In general, if a window has no caption bar, it can't be dragged around. By convincing Windows that the mouse is being clicked in the caption bar, Windows automatically 'does the right thing' as we drag the window around on the screen. If we had to implement the code to do this ourselves, it would require a lot of unnecessary work.

The routine responsible for drawing the fake caption bar, DrawFakeCaption, is given below. The routine is fairly straightforward, but in order to relate the code more easily to the actual appearance of the toolbox palette window, it's a good idea to have a look at a 'zoomed in' picture of the fake caption bar. If you look back at Figure 2.4, you'll see an enlarged view of the caption bar.

```
//————————————————————————————————————————————
// Name:     DrawFakeCaption
// Purpose:  This routine draws our fake caption bar, complete with
//           miniature system menu close box.
//————————————————————————————————————————————
void PASCAL DrawFakeCaption (HDC dc, HWND Wnd)
{
      HBRUSH hbr;
      RECT rClient;
      int width, height, brushKind;

      GetClientRect (Wnd, &rClient);
      rClient.bottom = rClient.top + FakeCaptionHeight();
      brushKind = (Wnd == GetFocus ()) ? COLOR_ACTIVECAPTION : COLOR_INACTIVECAPTION;
      hbr = CreateSolidBrush (GetSysColor (brushKind));
      FillRect (dc, &rClient, hbr);
      DeleteObject (hbr);

      MoveTo (dc, rClient.left, rClient.bottom);
      LineTo (dc, rClient.right, rClient.bottom);

      // Now draw the close box

      rClient.right = (FakeCaptionHeight() * 3) / 2;
```

```
       MoveTo (dc, rClient.right, rClient.top);
       LineTo (dc, rClient.right, rClient.bottom);
       FillRect (dc, &rClient, GetStockObject (LTGRAY_BRUSH));

       // And the close box bar

       width = rClient.right − rClient.left;
       rClient.left += (width / 4) + 1;
       rClient.right = rClient.left + (width / 2) + 1;

       height = rClient.bottom − rClient.top;
       rClient.top += height / 2;
       rClient.bottom = rClient.top + 3;

       FillRect (dc, &rClient, GetStockObject (GRAY_BRUSH));
       OffsetRect (&rClient, −1, −1);
       FillRect (dc, &rClient, GetStockObject (WHITE_BRUSH));
       FrameRect (dc, &rClient, GetStockObject (BLACK_BRUSH));
   }
```

The code begins by deciding whether or not the palette window has the input focus. Depending on the outcome of this test, it draws the caption bar using either COLOR_ACTIVECAPTION or COLOR_INACTIVECAPTION. These are system-wide color values obtained from the GetSysColor API routine. This might seem an odd thing to do but it must be remembered that because we're effectively implementing a dummy caption bar, we have got to take over some of the responsibilities of Windows. Normally, Windows will automatically take care of repainting a window's caption bar in the appropriate color when that window loses or gains the input focus. However, in this case, the window doesn't actually have a caption bar (as far as Windows is concerned) so we need to perform this job ourselves.

Having drawn the caption bar itself, the next job is to create the system menu close box. This is done in two stages: firstly, the rectangular close box area is filled in using a light gray brush and then the close box bar is drawn. The close box bar is best described as the little white horizontal 'thingumajig' that sits in the middle of the system menu close box. If you look at Microsoft's close box bar very carefully, you'll see that it has a gray shadow to give it a three-dimensional look. Accordingly, no expense spared, the DrawFakeCaption routine also draws a gray shadow one pixel below and to the right of the close box bar in our fake caption drawing code.

We can modify the toolbox palette's window procedure so as to call the DrawFakeCaption routine at the time we receive the WM_PAINT message. This is easily done like this:

```
       case WM_PAINT:

       BeginPaint (Wnd, &ps);
       DrawFakeCaption (ps.hdc, Wnd);

       info = GetInfo (Wnd);
       for (i = 0; i < info−>rows * info−>cols; i++)
           DrawBitmap (ps.hdc, info, i);

       EndPaint (Wnd, &ps);
       return (0);
```

It's also a good idea to insert code to handle the WM_ACTIVATE message at this time. The WM_ACTIVATE message is sent whenever a window is being activated or deactivated. We can use it to trigger off a WM_PAINT message so that whenever the window is activated or deactivated, the caption bar will be correctly redrawn to show the current state of the window. You might think that this is the same thing as we were discussing earlier when I talked about the two different system colors (COLOR_ACTIVECAPTION and COLOR_INACTIVECAPTION) to use when drawing the fake caption bar. It's important to be clear; the code in the DrawFakeCaption routine is responsible for telling the toolbox palette window *how* to draw itself when active and inactive. The code above, which responds to the WM_ACTIVATE message, is responsible for telling the palette window *when* to redraw the caption bar.

```
case WM_ACTIVATE:

GetClientRect (Wnd, &rClient);
rClient.bottom = rClient.top + FakeCaptionHeight();
InvalidateRect (Wnd, &rClient, FALSE);
return (0);
```

If you compile and execute the PALETTE3 program with these changes, you'll be rewarded by the bizarre sight of a window that apparently has two caption bars! Because we're still using the WS_OVERLAPPED style, the window still has a 'regular' caption bar, and our smaller fake caption bar sits immediately below it. This is illustrated in Figure 2.9.

Before we can get rid of the regular caption bar, we need to find some method of closing the application. For now, we'll do this by adding the following code to the window procedure:

```
case WM_RBUTTONDOWN:        // !! Temporary !!

PostQuitMessage (0);
return (0);
```

The effect of this code is to cause the toolbox palette window to close when the right-hand mouse button is pressed. This gives us a convenient, but strictly temporary, way of terminating the program while we develop the rest of the code. With this change, we can at last go over to using the WS_POPUP style in the CreateWindow call. This immediately makes the toolbox palette look a *lot* better. However, because of the change in window style, we now have to take responsibility for drawing our own border around the window. That's easily taken care of by adding the following two lines to the WM_PAINT drawing code:

```
GetClientRect (Wnd, &rClient);
FrameRect (ps.hdc, &rClient, GetStockObject (BLACK_BRUSH));
```

Figure 2.9 Spoilt for choice – a window with two caption bars.

At this stage, the code looks as shown in Figure 2.10. We've now got a great-looking tool palette which can easily be reconfigured by varying the number of rows and columns specified in the initial ToolBoxInfo data structure. Let's now continue by implementing the code that allows us to drag the window around just as if the fake caption bar were the genuine article.

Figure 2.10 PALETTE4.C: at this point, only the hit-testing code remains to be added.

```c
/* PALETTE4.C */

// © 1994 Dave Jewell and Addison-Wesley, ALL RIGHTS RESERVED

#include    <windows.h>

#define     PALETTECLASS        "Palette"

typedef struct ToolBoxInfo
{
    int     rows;               // number of rows of bitmaps
    int     cols;               // number of columns of bitmaps
    int     curTool;            // currently selected tool bitmap
    HWND    hWndCmd;            // window for WM_COMMAND messages
    WORD    bmBaseID;          // starting ID of bitmap resources
    int     bmWidth;           // width of each bitmap resource
    int     bmHeight;          // height of each bitmap resource
    HANDLE bmHandles [1];       // placeholder for handle array

} ToolBoxInfo, NEAR * PToolBoxInfo;

HANDLE hInst;

//————————————————————————————————————————————————————————————
// Name:     FakeCaptionHeight
// Purpose:  Return height of fake caption bar.
//————————————————————————————————————————————————————————————

int PASCAL FakeCaptionHeight (void)
{
    return (GetSystemMetrics (SM_CYCAPTION) / 3) + 2;
}

//————————————————————————————————————————————————————————————
// Name:     DrawFakeCaption
// Purpose:  This routine draws our fake caption bar, complete with miniature
//           system menu close box.
//————————————————————————————————————————————————————————————

void PASCAL DrawFakeCaption (HDC dc, HWND Wnd)
{
    HBRUSH hbr;
    RECT rClient;
    int width, height, brushKind;

    GetClientRect (Wnd, &rClient);
    rClient.bottom = rClient.top + FakeCaptionHeight();
    brushKind = (Wnd == GetFocus ()) ? COLOR_ACTIVECAPTION :
                COLOR_INACTIVECAPTION;

    hbr = CreateSolidBrush (GetSysColor (brushKind));
    FillRect (dc, &rClient, hbr);
    DeleteObject (hbr);

    MoveTo (dc, rClient.left, rClient.bottom);
    LineTo (dc, rClient.right, rClient.bottom);

    // Now draw the close box

    rClient.right = (FakeCaptionHeight() * 3) / 2;
```

```
        MoveTo (dc, rClient.right, rClient.top);
        LineTo (dc, rClient.right, rClient.bottom);
        FillRect (dc, &rClient, GetStockObject (LTGRAY_BRUSH));

        // And the close box bar

        width = rClient.right – rClient.left;
        rClient.left += (width / 4) + 1;
        rClient.right = rClient.left + (width / 2) + 1;

        height = rClient.bottom – rClient.top;
        rClient.top += height / 2;
        rClient.bottom = rClient.top + 3;

        FillRect (dc, &rClient, GetStockObject (GRAY_BRUSH));
        OffsetRect (&rClient, −1, −1);
        FillRect (dc, &rClient, GetStockObject (WHITE_BRUSH));
        FrameRect (dc, &rClient, GetStockObject (BLACK_BRUSH));
}

//————————————————————————————————————————————
// Name:    GetInfo
// Purpose: Return a pointer to window's associated data.
//————————————————————————————————————————————

PToolBoxInfo PASCAL GetInfo (HWND Wnd)
{
        return (PToolBoxInfo) GetWindowWord (Wnd, 0);
}

//————————————————————————————————————————————
// Name:    GetBitmapRect
// Purpose: Return the bounding rectangle of a specific item.
//————————————————————————————————————————————

void PASCAL GetBitmapRect (RECT * r, int num, PToolBoxInfo info)
{
        r−>left = (num % info−>cols) * (info−>bmWidth − 1) + 3;
        r−>top = (num / info−>cols) * (info−>bmHeight − 1) +
                        FakeCaptionHeight() + 3;

        r−>right = r−>left + info−>bmWidth;
        r−>bottom = r−>top + info−>bmHeight;
}

//————————————————————————————————————————————
// Name:    DrawBitmap
// Purpose: Draw a specified bitmap in its own rectangle.
//————————————————————————————————————————————

void PASCAL DrawBitmap (HDC dc, PToolBoxInfo info, int num)

{
        HBITMAP hbm;
        HDC hMemDC;
        RECT r;
        int XSrc;

        if (info−>bmHandles [num] != NULL)
        {
          GetBitmapRect (&r, num, info);
          hMemDC = CreateCompatibleDC (dc);
          hbm = SelectObject (hMemDC, info−>bmHandles [num]);
          XSrc = (num != info−>curTool) ? 0 : info−>bmWidth;
          BitBlt (dc, r.left, r.top, r.right − r.left, r.bottom − r.top,
                  hMemDC, XSrc, 0, SRCCOPY);
          SelectObject (hMemDC, hbm);
          DeleteDC (hMemDC);
        }
```

```
}

//————————————————————————————————————————————
// Name:    CreateToolBoxWindow
// Purpose: Called in response to WM_CREATE message.
//————————————————————————————————————————————

LONG PASCAL CreateToolBoxWindow (HWND hWnd, LONG lParam)
{
        BITMAP bm;
        int i, numTools;
        PToolBoxInfo NewInfo, Info;

        Info = (PToolBoxInfo)(((LPCREATESTRUCT)lParam)−>lpCreateParams);
        if (Info == NULL) return (−1);

        // Perform some sanity checks

        numTools = Info−>rows * Info−>cols;
        if (numTools == 0 || Info−>curTool >= numTools) return (−1);

        // Allocate the 'real' info structure

        NewInfo = (PToolBoxInfo) LocalAlloc (LPTR, sizeof (ToolBoxInfo) +
                                         (numTools − 1) * sizeof (HANDLE));
        *NewInfo = *Info;

        // Now load the tool bitmaps

        NewInfo−>bmWidth = −1;
        for (i = 0; i < numTools; i++)
        {
           NewInfo−>bmHandles [i] = LoadBitmap (hInst,
                                      MAKEINTRESOURCE
                                      (NewInfo−>bmBaseID + i));

           if (NewInfo−>bmWidth == −1 && NewInfo−>bmHandles [i] != NULL)

           {
              GetObject (NewInfo−>bmHandles [i], sizeof (bm), &bm);
              NewInfo−>bmWidth = bm.bmWidth / 2;
              NewInfo−>bmHeight = bm.bmHeight;
           }
        }

        // Check we've got at least one bitmap !

        if (NewInfo−>bmWidth == −1) return (−1);

        // Calculate the required size of the window

        SetWindowPos (hWnd, 0, 0, 0,
                     (NewInfo−>cols * NewInfo−>bmWidth) − (NewInfo−>cols − 1) + 6,
                     (NewInfo−>rows * NewInfo−>bmHeight) − (NewInfo−>rows − 1)
                     + FakeCaptionHeight() + 6,
                     SWP_NOMOVE | SWP  NOACTIVATE | SWP_NOZORDER);

        // Associate the Info data structure with the window

        SetWindowWord (hWnd, 0, (WORD) NewInfo);
        return (0);
}

//————————————————————————————————————————————
// Name:    PaletteWndProc
// Purpose: Window procedure for our floating toolbox palette.
//————————————————————————————————————————————

LONG FAR PASCAL _export PaletteWndProc (HWND Wnd, WORD Msg,
                                   WORD wParam, LONG lParam)
```

```
{
      int i;
      RECT rClient;
      PAINTSTRUCT ps;
      PToolBoxInfo info;

      switch (Msg)
      {
        case WM_RBUTTONDOWN:   // !! Temporary !!

        PostQuitMessage (0);
        return (0);

        case WM_ACTIVATE:

        GetClientRect (Wnd, &rClient);
        rClient.bottom = rClient.top + FakeCaptionHeight();
        InvalidateRect (Wnd, &rClient, FALSE);
        return (0);

        case WM_PAINT:

        BeginPaint (Wnd, &ps);
        DrawFakeCaption (ps.hdc, Wnd);
        info = GetInfo (Wnd);
        for (i = 0; i < info->rows * info->cols; i++)
           DrawBitmap (ps.hdc, info, i);

        GetClientRect (Wnd, &rClient);
        FrameRect (ps.hdc, &rClient, GetStockObject (BLACK_BRUSH));

        EndPaint (Wnd, &ps);
        return (0);

        case WM_CREATE:

        return CreateToolBoxWindow (Wnd, lParam);

        case WM_DESTROY:

        PostQuitMessage (0);
        return (0);
      }

      return DefWindowProc (Wnd, Msg, wParam, lParam);
}

//----------------------------------------------------------------
// Name:      InitApplication
// Purpose:   Initialization code: just registers the palette window
//            class and returns success or failure.
//----------------------------------------------------------------

BOOL InitApplication (HANDLE hInstance)
{
      WNDCLASS cls;

      cls.style            = CS_SAVEBITS;
      cls.lpfnWndProc      = (WNDPROC) PaletteWndProc;
      cls.cbClsExtra       = 0;
      cls.cbWndExtra       = 2;
      cls.hInstance        = hInstance;
      cls.hIcon            = 0;
      cls.hCursor          = LoadCursor (0, IDC_ARROW);
      cls.hbrBackground    = GetStockObject(LTGRAY_BRUSH);
      cls.lpszMenuName     = NULL;
      cls.lpszClassName    = PALETTECLASS;

      return RegisterClass (&cls);
}
```

```
//------------------------------------------------------------------
// Name:    WinMain
// Purpose: Program entry point.
//------------------------------------------------------------------

#pragma argsused

int PASCAL WinMain (HANDLE hInstance, HANDLE hPrevInst,
                    LPSTR lpCmdLine, int CmdShow)
{
    HWND Window;
    MSG Message;
    ToolBoxInfo info;

    hInst = hInstance;

    // If this is the first instance, then register palette window class

    if (hPrevInst == NULL)
        if (InitApplication (hInstance) == FALSE)
            return (0);

    // Initialize our ToolBoxInfo data structure

    info.rows      = 5;
    info.cols      = 2;
    info.curTool   = 0;
    info.hWndCmd   = 0;
    info.bmBaseID  = 1000;

    // Create our palette window

    Window = CreateWindow (PALETTECLASS, NULL,
                           WS_VISIBLE | WS_POPUP,
                           0, 0, 0, 0, 0, 0, hInstance, (LPSTR)&info);

    if (Window == NULL) return (0);

    ShowWindow (Window, CmdShow);
    UpdateWindow (Window);

    while (GetMessage (&Message, NULL, 0, 0))
    {
        TranslateMessage (&Message);
        DispatchMessage (&Message);
    }

    return (Message.wParam);
}
```

Hitting the spot

Obviously, there are two different cases where we need to respond to mouse clicks.
We want to receive mouse clicks on the caption bar so that the palette window can
be dragged around the screen, and we also want to receive clicks on the actual toolbox buttons so that the user can choose from among the available tools – without this
latter facility, our tool palette window wouldn't be of much use.

If you're new to Windows programming, you might suppose that these two cases
will be handled in pretty much the same way, that is, by intercepting and responding
to the WM_LBUTTONDOWN message. (This message is sent to the active window

whenever the left-hand mouse button is clicked.) In fact, this isn't so. Some extra code is required to convince Windows that our palette window has got a caption bar. So far, we've looked at the code for drawing the fake caption bar; now it's time to examine the code that convinces Windows that the caption bar is real.

Because of the way that Windows works, it needs to find out which parts of a window constitute the client area and which is the non-client area. In order to do this, it sends a special message, WM_NCHITTEST, whenever the mouse moves over a window. Most ordinary application windows don't handle this message, so the message 'falls through' the window procedure and gets handled by the DefWindowProc routine. The code inside DefWindowProc calls an internal routine called FindNCHit which examines the window style and decides, on this basis, where the mouse has hit. A number of different 'area codes' can be returned from the WM_NCHITTEST message, such as:

HTCAPTION	Mouse is in a title bar area
HTCLIENT	Mouse is in a client area
HTMAXBUTTON	Mouse is in a Maximize button
HTMENU	Mouse is in a menu area
HTMINBUTTON	Mouse is in a Minimize button

The problem, of course, is that because the internal FindNCHit routine doesn't understand our special palette window, it won't be able to 'see' our fake caption bar. For this reason, we need to intercept the WM_NCHITTEST routine and return the HTCAPTION area code when the mouse is pressed on the caption bar of the palette window. This will cause Windows to take responsibility automatically for dragging the window around until the mouse button is released.

The routine shown below, CaptionHitTest, is called by the palette window procedure in response to a WM_NCHITTEST. It's also called in response to another Windows message, as we shall see.

```
//--------------------------------------------------------------
// Name:    CaptionHitTest
// Purpose: Test for mouse hits in the caption bar.
//--------------------------------------------------------------

BOOL PASCAL CaptionHitTest (HWND Wnd, LONG lParam, BOOL CloseBoxOnly)
{
    POINT pt;
    RECT rClient;

    GetClientRect (Wnd, &rClient);
    rClient.bottom = rClient.top + FakeCaptionHeight();
    if (CloseBoxOnly) rClient.right = (FakeCaptionHeight() * 3) / 2;
    pt.x = LOWORD (lParam);
    pt.y = HIWORD (lParam);
    ScreenToClient (Wnd, &pt);
    return PtInRect (&rClient, pt);
}
```

The CaptionHitTest routine is passed the window handle of the toolbox window, a 32-bit parameter that specifies the mouse position, and a Boolean parameter, CloseBoxOnly, that's used to limit the extent of the test. If this parameter is FALSE, the routine tests for a mouse hit over the whole width of the caption bar. If the parameter is TRUE, the hit test is limited to the screen area that corresponds to our little system menu close box on the left-hand side of the fake caption bar.

This distinction is important because the WM_NCHITTEST routine is used to test for a hit over the whole area of the caption bar whereas the WM_NCLBUTTONDOWN message (which we'll look at in a moment) is limited to testing for a mouse click on the close box. Type in the source code to the CaptionHitTest routine and then add the following message handling case statement to the PaletteWndProc code:

```
case WM_NCHITTEST:

if (CaptionHitTest (Wnd, lParam, FALSE)) return (HTCAPTION);
return DefWindowProc (Wnd, Msg, wParam, lParam);
```

If you now compile and link the program, you should find that you can now use the caption bar to drag the toolbox palette window around the screen to your heart's content. The CaptionHitTest routine is returning HTCAPTION area codes to Windows whenever the mouse is clicked in the fake caption bar area. You have probably noticed that if you click the mouse button in the window's close box, nothing happens. Or at least, the window doesn't get closed. In fact, with the code as it stands at the moment, the close box is being treated just like the rest of the caption bar – you can use the close box to drag the window around if you wish.

Naturally, this is happening because we haven't yet done anything special to cater for the close box. Let's now add the code that will cause the window to respond properly when the close box is clicked on.

Now we've convinced Windows that the toolbox palette window has a caption bar, the system will automatically send us a WM_NCLBUTTONDOWN message whenever the mouse button is clicked in this caption bar area. In general, WM_NCLBUTTONDOWN messages are sent whenever the left mouse button is pressed on any non-client area of the window. However, since our window only has one non-client area (the caption bar) we can pretty well guarantee that if we receive this message, the user must have clicked on the caption bar.

The following code responds to WM_NCLBUTTONDOWN messages. It calls the CaptionHitTest routine to determine whether the mouse click occurred in the close box area. If it did, a WM_SYSCOMMAND message is posted back to the toolbox palette window, using a wParam value of SC_CLOSE. This is exactly the behavior that would result if the close box of an ordinary application window were pressed. If the click didn't occur in the close box area, the DefWindowProc routine is called to enable default message processing. Since Windows already knows (from looking at the response to the WM_NCHITTEST message) that it's in the caption area of the window, this has the effect of enabling the standard window-dragging behaviour.

```
case WM_NCLBUTTONDOWN:

if (CaptionHitTest (Wnd, lParam, TRUE)
{
    PostMessage (Wnd, WM_SYSCOMMAND, SC_CLOSE, 0);
    return (0);
}
return DefWindowProc (Wnd, Msg, wParam, lParam);
```

From this discussion, you may have gathered that by intercepting the WM_NCHITTEST and WM_NCLBUTTONDOWN routines, it should be possible to implement a wide variety of non-standard windows. For example, you could create a window that had its client area around the outside and a non-client area in the middle! You might want to implement a window that had a little 'handle' in the middle of the client area. By grabbing the handle with the mouse, you could drag the window around. Your users might not thank you for your decision to break with convention, but the Windows architecture is flexible enough to do these things if you really want to. By intercepting the WM_NCPAINT routine, it's even possible to create windows with non-rectangular frames.

It's also perfectly feasible to create a window that doesn't appear to have any non-client area at all but that can be moved around the screen simply by clicking and dragging. I almost decided to implement the toolbox palette this way, but I considered it important to give users a visual 'cue' via the caption bar. If a user saw no caption bar, he or she might conclude that it wasn't possible to move the window around.

With the above code in place, you should now find that clicking the mouse on the system close box will indeed shut down the toolbox palette window. Some people might argue that it would be better to display a small system menu when the close box is clicked. Again, implementing this would be very straightforward via the TrackPopupMenu API routine. I felt, however, that anyone clicking on the close box was most likely to want to simply dismiss the toolbox palette rather than choose one of the other system menu options, which are not particularly relevant to palette windows. Implementation of the extra code therefore seemed rather pointless. This is particularly true since Microsoft Excel's own sophisticated floating toolbars adopt the same approach.

Now that the toolbox palette's close box is working, the temporary code that responds to right-hand mouse button clicks can also be removed at this point.

This leaves us with only one real chunk of code left to implement – we need to add in the code that deals with mouse clicks in the actual tool slots: the buttons in our toolbox palette window. This code is shown below:

```
//————————————————————————————————————————————
// Name:    ButtonHitTest
// Purpose: This routine tests for a mouse click in a tool slot.
//————————————————————————————————————————————

VOID PASCAL ButtonHitTest (HWND Wnd, LONG lParam)
{
        RECT r;
        int num;
        POINT pt;
        PToolBoxInfo info;

        info = GetInfo (Wnd);
        pt.x = LOWORD (lParam);
        pt.y = HIWORD (lParam);

        for (num = 0; num < info->rows * info->cols; num++)
          if (info->bmHandles [num] != 0)
            {
              GetBitmapRect (&r, num, info);
              if (PtInRect (&r, pt))
                {
                  if (num != info->curTool)
                    {
                      InvalidateRect (Wnd, &r, TRUE);
                      GetBitmapRect (&r, info->curTool, info);
```

```
            InvalidateRect (Wnd, &r, TRUE);
            info->curTool = num;
            if (info->hWndCmd != NULL)
                SendMessage (info->hWndCmd, WM_COMMAND,
                                    info->bmBaseID + num, 0);
          }
       break;
     }
   }
}
```

The ButtonHitTest routine is fairly straightforward, although there are a couple of optimizations which have been made. If the routine determines that the clicked-on tool is the same as the existing tool, then it does nothing. This is a useful little trick, since it means that we've saved ourselves the bother of redrawing the toolbox palette window when, in fact, nothing was changed.

When the code determines that a tool other than the currently selected tool has been clicked, the InvalidateRect routine is used to force the changed parts of the toolbox palette window to be redrawn. Again, we ensure that only those parts of the window that really have changed are invalidated.

If a window handle is stored in the hWndCmd field of the ToolBoxInfo data structure, a WM_COMMAND is sent to this window to indicate that a tool selection has been made.

There is one final addition that we can and should make to the existing code. We ought to modify the WM_DESTROY code so that when the toolbox palette window is destroyed, the associated bitmaps are automatically deleted. The ToolBoxInfo data structure is also deallocated at this time. You might think that there's no point in deal-locating the ToolBoxInfo data structure since it forms a part of the application's local heap – consequently, it will be deleted anyway when the application terminates. However, it's very important to distinguish clearly between the termination of the toolbox palette window and the termination of the application itself. So far, we've developed the code as a single program, but the next step will entail moving the tool-box code into a linkable module that can then be incorporated into larger applica-tions. In a typical Windows application, the user should be able to dismiss an unwanted toolbox palette and then (via a menu option) make the palette appear once more when needed. You can see, therefore, that the code needs to be written such that the palette window can be created and destroyed many times. The WM_DESTROY code therefore needs to do a thorough job of cleaning up.

```
case WM_DESTROY:

   info = GetInfo (Wnd);
   for (i = 0; i < info->rows * info->cols; i++)
      if (info->bmHandles [i] != NULL)
         DeleteObject (info->bmHandles [i]);

   LocalFree ((HANDLE) info);
   PostQuitMessage(0);
   return (0);
```

On a related subject, you can see that the WM_DESTROY code still contains a call to the PostQuitMessage routine. Although this makes perfect sense here, it would be very bad news after we convert the toolbox code into a separately linked module. The PostQuitMessage routine effectively terminates message processing by the current application. Typically, the user would not want her application to terminate just because she's closed the application's toolbox palette window! This is an area that we'll need to revisit once the library version of the code is developed.

Figure 2.11 shows the complete source code as it stands at the present time. You can find this source code on the disk as PALETTE5.C and the accompanying executable code as PALETTE5.EXE. From here on, we'll split the code into two chunks: a sample application and a separate linkable module which will encapsulate the functionality of the toolbox code.

Figure 2.11 PALETTE5.C: the fully functional toolbox palette code.

```
/* PALETTE5.C */

// © 1994 Dave Jewell and Addison-Wesley, ALL RIGHTS RESERVED

#include    <windows.h>

#define     PALETTECLASS        "Palette"

typedef struct ToolBoxInfo
{
    int       rows;          // number of rows of bitmaps
    int       cols;          // number of columns of bitmaps
    int       curTool;       // currently selected tool bitmap
    HWND      hWndCmd;       // window for WM_COMMAND messages
    WORD      bmBaseID;      // starting ID of bitmap resources
    int       bmWidth;       // width of each bitmap resource
    int       bmHeight;      // height of each bitmap resource
    HANDLE bmHandles [1];    // placeholder for handle array

} ToolBoxInfo, NEAR * PToolBoxInfo;

HANDLE hInst;

//─────────────────────────────────────────────────────────
// Name:    FakeCaptionHeight
// Purpose: Return height of fake caption bar.
//─────────────────────────────────────────────────────────

int PASCAL FakeCaptionHeight (void)
{
    return (GetSystemMetrics (SM_CYCAPTION) / 3) + 2;
}

//─────────────────────────────────────────────────────────
// Name:    DrawFakeCaption
// Purpose: This routine draws our fake caption bar, complete with
//          miniature system menu close box.
//─────────────────────────────────────────────────────────

void PASCAL DrawFakeCaption (HDC dc, HWND Wnd)
{
    HBRUSH hbr;
    RECT rClient;
    int width, height, brushKind;

    GetClientRect (Wnd, &rClient);
    rClient.bottom = rClient.top + FakeCaptionHeight();
    brushKind = (Wnd == GetFocus ()) ? COLOR_ACTIVECAPTION :
        COLOR_INACTIVECAPTION;

    hbr = CreateSolidBrush (GetSysColor (brushKind));
    FillRect (dc, &rClient, hbr);
    DeleteObject (hbr);
```

```
      MoveTo (dc, rClient.left, rClient.bottom);
      LineTo (dc, rClient.right, rClient.bottom);

      // Now draw the close box

      rClient.right = (FakeCaptionHeight() * 3) / 2;
      MoveTo (dc, rClient.right, rClient.top);
      LineTo (dc, rClient.right, rClient.bottom);
      FillRect (dc, &rClient, GetStockObject (LTGRAY_BRUSH));

      // And the close box bar

      width = rClient.right − rClient.left;
      rClient.left += (width / 4) + 1;
      rClient.right = rClient.left + (width / 2) + 1;

      height = rClient.bottom − rClient.top;
      rClient.top += height / 2;
      rClient.bottom = rClient.top + 3;

      FillRect (dc, &rClient, GetStockObject (GRAY_BRUSH));
      OffsetRect (&rClient, −1, −1);
      FillRect (dc, &rClient, GetStockObject (WHITE_BRUSH));
      FrameRect (dc, &rClient, GetStockObject (BLACK_BRUSH));
}

//─────────────────────────────────────────────────────────
// Name:    GetInfo
// Purpose: Return a pointer to window's associated data.
//─────────────────────────────────────────────────────────

PToolBoxInfo PASCAL GetInfo (HWND Wnd)
{
      return (PToolBoxInfo) GetWindowWord (Wnd, 0);
}

//─────────────────────────────────────────────────────────
// Name:    GetBitmapRect
// Purpose: Return the bounding rectangle of a specific item.
//─────────────────────────────────────────────────────────

void PASCAL GetBitmapRect (RECT * r, int num, PToolBoxInfo info)
{
      r−>left = (num % info−>cols) * (info−>bmWidth − 1) + 3;
      r−>top = (num / info−>cols) * (info−>bmHeight − 1) +
               FakeCaptionHeight() + 3;

      r−>right = r−>left + info−>bmWidth;
      r−>bottom = r−>top + info−>bmHeight;
}

//─────────────────────────────────────────────────────────
// Name:    DrawBitmap
// Purpose: Draw a specified bitmap in its own rectangle.
//─────────────────────────────────────────────────────────

void PASCAL DrawBitmap (HDC dc, PToolBoxInfo info, int num)
{
      HBITMAP hbm;
      HDC hMemDC;
      RECT r;
      int XSrc;

      if (info−>bmHandles [num] != NULL)
      {
        GetBitmapRect (&r, num, info);
        hMemDC = CreateCompatibleDC (dc);
        hbm = SelectObject (hMemDC, info−>bmHandles [num]);
        XSrc = (num != info−>curTool) ? 0 : info−>bmWidth;
```

```
                    BitBlt (dc, r.left, r.top, r.right − r.left, r.bottom − r.top,
                            hMemDC, XSrc, 0, SRCCOPY);

                    SelectObject (hMemDC, hbm);
                    DeleteDC (hMemDC);
            }
    }

    //───────────────────────────────────────────────────────────────
    // Name:     CreateToolBoxWindow
    // Purpose:  Called in response to WM_CREATE message.
    //───────────────────────────────────────────────────────────────

    LONG PASCAL CreateToolBoxWindow (HWND hWnd, LONG lParam)
    {
            BITMAP bm;
            int i, numTools;
            PToolBoxInfo NewInfo, Info;

            Info = (PToolBoxInfo)(((LPCREATESTRUCT)lParam)−>lpCreateParams);
            if (Info == NULL) return (−1);

            // Perform some sanity checks

            numTools = Info−>rows * Info−>cols;
            if (numTools == 0 || Info−>curTool >= numTools) return (−1);

            // Allocate the 'real' info structure

            NewInfo = (PToolBoxInfo) LocalAlloc (LPTR, sizeof (ToolBoxInfo) +
                                                 (numTools − 1) * sizeof (HANDLE));
            *NewInfo = *Info;

            // Now load the tool bitmaps

            NewInfo−>bmWidth = −1;
            for (i = 0; i < numTools; i++)
            {
                NewInfo−>bmHandles [i] = LoadBitmap (hInst,
                                                     MAKEINTRESOURCE
                                                     (NewInfo−>bmBaseID + i));

                if (NewInfo−>bmWidth == −1 && NewInfo−>bmHandles [i] != NULL)
                {
                    GetObject (NewInfo−>bmHandles [i], sizeof (bm), &bm);
                    NewInfo−>bmWidth = bm.bmWidth / 2;
                    NewInfo−>bmHeight = bm.bmHeight;
                }
            }

            // Check we've got at least one bitmap !

            if (NewInfo−>bmWidth == −1) return (−1);

            // Calculate the required size of the window

            SetWindowPos (hWnd, 0, 0, 0,
                          (NewInfo−>cols * NewInfo−>bmWidth) − (NewInfo−>cols − 1) + 6,
                          (NewInfo−>rows * NewInfo−>bmHeight) − (NewInfo−>rows − 1)
                          + FakeCaptionHeight() + 6,
                          SWP_NOMOVE | SWP_NOACTIVATE | SWP_NOZORDER);

            // Associate the Info data structure with the window

            SetWindowWord (hWnd, 0, (WORD) NewInfo);
            return (0);
    }

    //───────────────────────────────────────────────────────────────
    // Name:     CaptionHitTest
```

```
// Purpose:  Test for mouse hits in the caption bar.
//————————————————————————————————————————————————————————————

BOOL PASCAL CaptionHitTest (HWND Wnd, LONG lParam, BOOL CloseBoxOnly)
{
      POINT pt;
      RECT rClient;

      GetClientRect (Wnd, &rClient);
      rClient.bottom = rClient.top + FakeCaptionHeight();
      if (CloseBoxOnly) rClient.right = (FakeCaptionHeight() * 3) / 2;
      pt.x = LOWORD (lParam);
      pt.y = HIWORD (lParam);
      ScreenToClient (Wnd, &pt);
      return PtInRect (&rClient, pt);
}

//————————————————————————————————————————————————————————————
// Name:     ButtonHitTest
// Purpose:  This routine tests for a mouse click in a tool slot.
//————————————————————————————————————————————————————————————

VOID PASCAL ButtonHitTest (HWND Wnd, LONG lParam)
{
      RECT r;
      int num;
      POINT pt;
      PToolBoxInfo info;

      info = GetInfo (Wnd);
      pt.x = LOWORD (lParam);
      pt.y = HIWORD (lParam);

      for (num = 0; num < info->rows * info->cols; num++)
         if (info->bmHandles [num] != 0)
         {
            GetBitmapRect (&r, num, info);
            if (PtInRect (&r, pt))
            {
               if (num != info->curTool)
               {
                  InvalidateRect (Wnd, &r, TRUE);
                  GetBitmapRect (&r, info->curTool, info);
                  InvalidateRect (Wnd, &r, TRUE);
                  info->curTool = num;
                  if (info->hWndCmd != NULL) SendMessage
                    (info->hWndCmd,
                      WM_COMMAND, info->bmBaseID + num, 0);
               }
            break;
            }
         }
}

//————————————————————————————————————————————————————————————
// Name:     PaletteWndProc
// Purpose:  Window procedure for our floating toolbox palette.
//————————————————————————————————————————————————————————————

LONG FAR PASCAL _export PaletteWndProc (HWND Wnd, WORD Msg,
                                        WORD wParam, LONG lParam)
{
      int i;
      RECT rClient;
      PAINTSTRUCT ps;
      PToolBoxInfo info;

      switch (Msg)
```

```
        {
          case WM_LBUTTONDOWN:

          ButtonHitTest (Wnd, lParam);
          return (0);

          case WM_NCLBUTTONDOWN:

          if (CaptionHitTest (Wnd, lParam, TRUE))
          {
             PostMessage (Wnd, WM_SYSCOMMAND, SC_CLOSE, 0);
             return (0);
          }
          return DefWindowProc (Wnd, Msg, wParam, lParam);

          case WM_NCHITTEST:

          if (CaptionHitTest (Wnd, lParam, FALSE)) return (HTCAPTION);
          return DefWindowProc (Wnd, Msg, wParam, lParam);

          case WM_ACTIVATE:

          GetClientRect (Wnd, &rClient);
          rClient.bottom = rClient.top + FakeCaptionHeight();
          InvalidateRect (Wnd, &rClient, FALSE);
          return (0);

          case WM_PAINT:

          BeginPaint (Wnd, &ps);

          DrawFakeCaption (ps.hdc, Wnd);

          info = GetInfo (Wnd);
          for (i = 0; i < info->rows * info->cols; i++)
             DrawBitmap (ps.hdc, info, i);

          GetClientRect (Wnd, &rClient);
          FrameRect (ps.hdc, &rClient, GetStockObject (BLACK_BRUSH));

          EndPaint (Wnd, &ps);
          return (0);

          case WM_CREATE:

          return CreateToolBoxWindow (Wnd, lParam);

          case WM_DESTROY:

          info = GetInfo (Wnd);
          for (i = 0; i < info->rows * info->cols; i++)
             if (info->bmHandles [i] != NULL)
                DeleteObject (info->bmHandles [i]);

          LocalFree ((HANDLE) info);
          PostQuitMessage(0);
          return (0);
        }

     return DefWindowProc (Wnd, Msg, wParam, lParam);
}

//—————————————————————————————————————————————————————
// Name:    InitApplication
// Purpose: Initialization code: just registers the palette window
//          class and returns success or failure.
//—————————————————————————————————————————————————————

BOOL InitApplication (HANDLE hInstance)
{
     WNDCLASS cls;
```

```
            cls.style             = CS_SAVEBITS;
            cls.lpfnWndProc       = (WNDPROC) PaletteWndProc;
            cls.cbClsExtra        = 0;
            cls.cbWndExtra        = 2;
            cls.hInstance         = hInstance;
            cls.hIcon             = 0;
            cls.hCursor           = LoadCursor (0, IDC_ARROW);
            cls.hbrBackground     = GetStockObject(LTGRAY_BRUSH);
            cls.lpszMenuName      = NULL;
            cls.lpszClassName     = PALETTECLASS;

            return RegisterClass (&cls);
}

//------------------------------------------------------------------
// Name:    WinMain
// Purpose: Program entry point.
//------------------------------------------------------------------

#pragma argsused

int PASCAL WinMain (HANDLE hInstance, HANDLE hPrevInst,
                    LPSTR lpCmdLine, int CmdShow)
{
            HWND Window;
            MSG Message;
            ToolBoxInfo info;

            hInst = hInstance;

            // If this is the first instance, then register palette window class

            if (hPrevInst == NULL)
                if (InitApplication (hInstance) == FALSE)
                    return (0);

            // Initialize our ToolBoxInfo data structure

            info.rows       = 5;
            info.cols       = 2;
            info.curTool    = 0;
            info.hWndCmd    = 0;
            info.bmBaseID   = 1000;

            // Create our palette window

            Window = CreateWindow (PALETTECLASS, NULL,
                                    WS_VISIBLE | WS_POPUP,
                                    0, 0, 0, 0, 0, 0, hInstance, (LPSTR)&info);

            if (Window == NULL) return (0);

            ShowWindow (Window, CmdShow);
            UpdateWindow (Window);

            while (GetMessage (&Message, NULL, 0, 0))
            {
                TranslateMessage (&Message);
                DispatchMessage (&Message);
            }

            return (Message.wParam);
}
```

Putting it all together: making a reusable module

I began this chapter by promising to develop a reusable code module that would allow you to incorporate toolbox palettes easily into your own applications. Unfortunately, as the palette code stands at the present time, it isn't yet structured in this way. But here's the good news: there aren't many changes we need to make to the code to get it into this state.

The first change we must make involves the use of the global variable hInst, which crops up in several of the code listings we've looked at so far. I've already spent some time trying to convince you of the evils of global variables and I don't want to labor the point! Instead, I'll give you a completely different reason for wanting to get rid of this global variable. Suppose you like the toolbox palette code so much that you want to incorporate it into several of your applications. Windows provides a very neat way of doing this through the use of DLLs. If you were to package the palette code up into a DLL, it could be used by several different applications at the same time. Now you see the problem: every Windows program has its own unique instance handle and any piece of code that forms part of a DLL must be able to work properly in this situation. That's why we need to get rid of the instance handle.

By the way, even if you're writing a chunk of code that you don't expect to place into a DLL, it's always a good idea to try to implement the code as if it might, one day, need to go into a DLL. Always ask yourself the question, 'Could this API routine work properly with several different customers?'. Learning to think in this way will encourage you to think about reentrance issues, which also have a strong impact on global variable usage.

The logical place to put our instance handle is, of course, into the ToolBoxInfo data structure. From there, it can be easily accessed by the code inside the CreateToolBoxWindow routine. The instance handle is needed here in order to load the display bitmaps required by the palette window. In fact, with the exception of the code that registers the palette window class, this is really the only place that the instance handle is needed.

One of the most important aspects of a good programming interface is concerned with the concept known as 'information hiding'. This involves building a program-ming interface that's organized on a need-to-know basis. Application programs shouldn't be complicated with details of the underlying implementation. Let's take a concrete example such as a memory handle. Under Windows, Microsoft don't tell you anything about what a memory handle is. All you know is that it's a magic cookie that can be used to access a corresponding block of memory. This means that you can't take liberties with memory handles such as 'peeking' at the data without both-ering to lock the handle first. This decision of Microsoft's was the right thing to do; by shielding application developers from the underlying details of how Windows memory management worked, it became very much easier to move Windows over to protected mode when the time was right.

Now contrast this with the Apple Macintosh approach. Right from the word go, Apple told application developers that a handle was just a pointer to another pointer called a 'master pointer'. This master pointer pointed, in turn, to the block of memory that was being referenced. This simple-minded double-indirection scheme allowed memory objects to move around in the Macintosh's memory without the need for the corresponding memory handle to change – only the master pointer was updated as memory moved. Unfortunately, because developers knew that a handle was just a pointer to a pointer to their application data, they often didn't bother to lock the handle before referencing the data. They just went ahead and doubly indirected the handle, like this:

```
(*h)->SomeField = SomeValue;
```

For this, and for many other reasons, the Macintosh still lacks a protected mode operating system which effectively isolates executing application programs from the underlying memory management implementation. This should serve as a lesson to us all: when designing effective programming interfaces, don't divulge unnecessary implementation details.

With this in mind, the code below shows a new routine called InitToolPalette. This is the first of two routines that will be used by the application program to communicate with the toolbox palette code. This routine must be called by the application before a toolbox palette window can be created. The only real job of this routine is to register the palette window class – it effectively replaces the InitApplication routine used in previous code. Indeed (just to keep you on your toes!), there's now a new InitApplication routine inside the application code that is responsible for registering the main application window.

The routine below takes two parameters: the instance handle of the application and the hPrevInst handle that's passed into the program via the WinMain function. We have to examine the hPrevInst handle in order to determine whether or not the palette window class should be registered – if it's already been registered once, an error will result if subsequent instances of the application try to register the same window class.

In theory, the InitToolPalette routine should only be called once within a single specific instance of the program. However, mistakes do happen, and for this reason the palette code is now equipped with a private static variable called fInit. This variable isn't shown below. Setting the fInit variable to TRUE at the end of the InitToolPalette code ensures that if the routine is inadvertently called more than once, no harm will result.

```
//---------------------------------------------------------------
// Name:    InitToolPalette
// Purpose: Routine to initialize palette code.
//---------------------------------------------------------------
BOOL PASCAL InitToolPalette (HANDLE hInstance, HANDLE hPrevInst)
{
       WNDCLASS cls;

       // If first instance, then register palette window class

       if (hPrevInst == NULL)
       {
          cls.style            = CS_SAVEBITS;
          cls.lpfnWndProc      = (WNDPROC) PaletteWndProc;
          cls.cbClsExtra       = 0;
          cls.cbWndExtra       = 2;
          cls.hInstance        = hInstance;
          cls.hIcon            = 0;
```

```
        cls.hCursor              = LoadCursor (0, IDC_ARROW);
        cls.hbrBackground        = GetStockObject (LTGRAY_BRUSH);
        cls.lpszMenuName         = NULL;
        cls.lpszClassName        = PALETTECLASS;

        if (RegisterClass (&cls) == FALSE) return (FALSE);
    }
    fInit = TRUE;
    return (TRUE);
}
```

The fInit variable is also used in the second of our two API routines, as shown below. This routine, CreatePaletteWindow, must be called each time that the application program wishes to create a new palette window. The routine checks the fInit variable to see if the palette window class has been registered. If it hasn't, it simply returns a NULL window handle to the calling routine, which is interpreted as failure.

One of the most important points about this routine is the fact that it 'hides' the ToolBoxInfo data structure. This structure forms a part of the internal implementation of the palette code and therefore it's of no concern to the application program. Instead, each of the fields in the ToolboxInfo structure is represented as a parameter to the routine. This is just about acceptable in this case, although if there were many more fields, it would be better to pass a pointer to a ToolBoxInfo structure as a single parameter, rather than contending with a confusingly large number of parameters.

```
//—————————————————————————————————————————————————
// Name:     CreatePaletteWindow
// Purpose:  Create a new toolbox palette and return handle.
//—————————————————————————————————————————————————
HWND PASCAL CreatePaletteWindow (HANDLE hInstance, int rows, int cols,
                        int curTool, HWND hWndCmd, WORD bmBaseID)
{
    HWND hwnd = NULL;
    ToolBoxInfo info;

    if (hWndCmd != NULL && fInit == TRUE)
    {
        // Initialize ToolBoxInfo data structure

        info.rows        = rows;
        info.cols        = cols;
        info.curTool     = curTool;
        info.hWndCmd     = hWndCmd;
        info.bmBaseID    = bmBaseID;
        info.hInst       = hInstance;

        // Create the palette window

        hwnd = CreateWindow (PALETTECLASS, NULL, WS_CHILD,
                        GetSystemMetrics (SM_CXFRAME),
                        GetSystemMetrics (SM_CXFRAME),
                        0, 0, hWndCmd, 0, hInstance,
                        (LPSTR)&info);

        // If you've got it, flaunt it...

        if (hwnd != NULL)
        {
            ShowWindow (hwnd, SW_SHOW);
            UpdateWindow (hwnd);
        }
    }

    return (hwnd);
}
```

The toolbox palette window is still created via a call to the Windows API CreateWindow routine, but in this case, we've now changed over to using a WS_CHILD window style. This means that the toolbox palette becomes a child of the main application window. This has some advantages and some disadvantages, as we shall see later. Because the palette window is now a child window, it's essential to specify the handle of a parent window when calling the CreateWindow routine. For this reason, the CreatePaletteWindow code will fail if a NULL handle is passed as the hWndCmd parameter – it is not allowable to create a child window with a NULL parent handle.

Maybe you're thinking that it would be nice if the InitToolPalette routine could be dispensed with. Wouldn't it be great if the CreatePaletteWindow routine could simply check to see if the fInit variable is TRUE and, if not, call the InitToolPalette routine internally? That way, we'd only need the one API call (CreatePaletteWindow) and we wouldn't have to worry about remembering to call the InitToolPalette routine from within the main application program. The problem with this approach is that it requires the hPrevInst variable to be available 'after the event'. The hPrevInst instance handle would have to be stashed somewhere, ready for when we wanted to make the call to hPrevInst. If we were using Borland C/C++ (my favourite development system) we could cheat by using the undocumented global variable _hPrev to obtain the hPrevInst handle at any point in the program. Unfortunately, this leads to even worse problems: suppose that hPrevInst is zero on entry to the application. In other words, this is the first instance of the code. Another instance of the program then starts up and initializes the palette window class. When it's time for us to register the palette window class, we examine our hPrevInst handle (which is still zero) and, thinking that we're still the first instance of the program, try to register the window class. The RegisterClass call fails and we have to abort the program. You see the problem? The hPrevInst handle is only valid at the time that WinMain is called. You can't preserve it for posterity and use it at some later time. For this reason, we stick with the code as it's described here.

Note

The real problem here is with the behavior of the RegisterClass routine. The Microsoft SDK documentation states: 'A task cannot register two local classes with the same name. However, two different tasks can register task-specific classes using the same name.' From this, you might conclude that two different instances of the same program can register task-specific classes with the same name. However, this isn't true. What the SDK documentation really means is that two different tasks *that are instances of different applications* can register task-specific classes with the same name. In my view, the RegisterClass routine should return success if asked to re-register a class that has already been registered by another instance of the same application. This would save a lot of fooling around with the hPrevInst instance handle.

If you look at the way in which the CreateWindow routine is called, you may notice another change. Rather than having an initial X, Y position of {0, 0}, the GetSystemMetrics routine is being used to return an initial location for the window. Again, this relates to the use of the WS_CHILD window style. Because the palette window is now a child of the main application window, the initial window position is relative to the parent window rather than relative to the entire screen as it was before. Using X, Y coordinates which are both zero would cause the palette window to appear jammed into the top left corner of the application window. While this won't do any harm, it doesn't look very nice. By moving the window slightly down and to the right, the initial appearance of your program will be more pleasing. Obviously, once the program is running, the user can move the palette window to any location that he or she wants. The SM_CXFRAME metric was used to give a suitable small off-set from the top left corner of the application window.

Because the palette window is now a child window, it's important to remove the PostQuitMessage API routine from the WM_DESTROY part of the toolbox palette's window procedure. With this call still in there, closing the palette window would terminate the entire application – probably not what the user wanted to do!

The changes to the palette code are summarized in Figure 2.12 as PALETTE6.C. Note that this code can no longer be compiled and linked as a single source file: it no longer contains a WinMain routine. PALETTE6.C has been organized as a linkable module that is to be incorporated into a larger application. Figure 2.13 contains a simple test application, PALAPP1.C, that can be used to try out the palette code. Finally, Figure 2.14 shows a small header file, PALETTE.H, that is included by the main application code. All three files can be found on the companion disk along with the resulting executable file, PALAPP1.EXE. If you want to build these files from scratch, you will need to include PALAPP1.C and PALETTE6.C into the project file so that they get linked together.

Figure 2.12 PALETTE6.C: the toolbox code in separately linkable form.

```
/* PALETTE6.C */

// © 1994 Dave Jewell and Addison-Wesley, ALL RIGHTS RESERVED

#include    <windows.h>
#include    "palette.h"

#define    PALETTECLASS        "Palette"

typedef struct ToolBoxInfo
{
        int        rows;          // number of rows of bitmaps
        int        cols;          // number of columns of bitmaps
        int        curTool;       // currently selected tool bitmap
        HWND       hWndCmd;       // window for WM_COMMAND messages
        HANDLE     hInst;         // instance handle for resource loads
        WORD       bmBaseID;      // starting ID of bitmap resources
        int        bmWidth;       // width of each bitmap resource
        int        bmHeight;      // height of each bitmap resource
        HANDLE     bmHandles [1]; // placeholder for handle array

} ToolBoxInfo, NEAR * PToolBoxInfo;

static BOOL fInit = FALSE;       // TRUE if module initialized

//--------------------------------------------------------------
// Name:    FakeCaptionHeight
// Purpose: Return height of fake caption bar.
//--------------------------------------------------------------

static int PASCAL FakeCaptionHeight (void)
{
```

```
        return (GetSystemMetrics (SM_CYCAPTION) / 3) + 2;
}

//——————————————————————————————————————————————————————
// Name:      DrawFakeCaption
// Purpose:   This routine draws our fake caption bar, complete with
//            miniature system menu close box.
//——————————————————————————————————————————————————————
static void PASCAL DrawFakeCaption (HDC dc, HWND Wnd)
{
        HBRUSH hbr;
        RECT rClient;
        int width, height, brushKind;

        GetClientRect (Wnd, &rClient);
        rClient.bottom = rClient.top + FakeCaptionHeight();
        brushKind = (Wnd == GetFocus ()) ? COLOR_ACTIVECAPTION :
            COLOR_INACTIVECAPTION;

        hbr = CreateSolidBrush (GetSysColor (brushKind));
        FillRect (dc, &rClient, hbr);
        DeleteObject (hbr);

        MoveTo (dc, rClient.left, rClient.bottom);
        LineTo (dc, rClient.right, rClient.bottom);

        // Now draw the close box

        rClient.right = (FakeCaptionHeight() * 3) / 2;
        MoveTo (dc, rClient.right, rClient.top);
        LineTo (dc, rClient.right, rClient.bottom);
        FillRect (dc, &rClient, GetStockObject (LTGRAY_BRUSH));

        // And the close box bar

        width = rClient.right − rClient.left;
        rClient.left += (width / 4) + 1;
        rClient.right = rClient.left + (width / 2) + 1;

        height = rClient.bottom − rClient.top;
        rClient.top += height / 2;
        rClient.bottom = rClient.top + 3;

        FillRect (dc, &rClient, GetStockObject (GRAY_BRUSH));
        OffsetRect (&rClient, −1, −1);
        FillRect (dc, &rClient, GetStockObject (WHITE_BRUSH));
        FrameRect (dc, &rClient, GetStockObject (BLACK_BRUSH));
}

//——————————————————————————————————————————————————————
// Name:      GetInfo
// Purpose:   Return a pointer to window's associated data.
//——————————————————————————————————————————————————————
static PToolBoxInfo PASCAL GetInfo (HWND Wnd)
{
        return (PToolBoxInfo) GetWindowWord (Wnd, 0);
}

//——————————————————————————————————————————————————————
// Name:      GetBitmapRect
// Purpose:   Return the bounding rectangle of a specific item.
//——————————————————————————————————————————————————————
static void PASCAL GetBitmapRect (RECT * r, int num, PToolBoxInfo info)
{
        r−>left = (num % info−>cols) * (info−>bmWidth − 1) + 3;
        r−>top = (num / info−>cols) * (info−>bmHeight − 1) +
                    FakeCaptionHeight() + 3;
```

```
            r->right = r->left + info->bmWidth;
            r->bottom = r->top + info->bmHeight;
    }

    //—————————————————————————————————————————————————————
    // Name:    DrawBitmap
    // Purpose: Draw a specified bitmap in its own rectangle.
    //—————————————————————————————————————————————————————

    static void PASCAL DrawBitmap (HDC dc, PToolBoxInfo info, int num)
    {
            HBITMAP hbm;
            HDC hMemDC;
            RECT r;
            int XSrc;

            if (info->bmHandles [num] != NULL)
            {
                GetBitmapRect (&r, num, info);
                hMemDC = CreateCompatibleDC (dc);

                hbm = SelectObject (hMemDC, info->bmHandles [num]);
                XSrc = (num != info->curTool) ? 0 : info->bmWidth;
                BitBlt (dc, r.left, r.top, r.right – r.left, r.bottom – r.top,
                        hMemDC, XSrc, 0, SRCCOPY);

                SelectObject (hMemDC, hbm);
                DeleteDC (hMemDC);
            }
    }

    //—————————————————————————————————————————————————————
    // Name:    CreateToolBoxWindow
    // Purpose: Called in response to WM_CREATE message.
    //—————————————————————————————————————————————————————

    static LONG PASCAL CreateToolBoxWindow (HWND hWnd, LONG lParam)
    {
            BITMAP bm;
            int i, numTools;
            PToolBoxInfo NewInfo, Info;

            Info = (PToolBoxInfo)(((LPCREATESTRUCT)lParam)->lpCreateParams);
            if (Info == NULL) return (–1);

            // Perform some sanity checks

            numTools = Info->rows * Info->cols;
            if (numTools == 0 || Info->curTool >= numTools) return (–1);

            // Allocate the 'real' info structure

            NewInfo = (PToolBoxInfo) LocalAlloc (LPTR, sizeof (ToolBoxInfo) +
                        (numTools – 1) * sizeof (HANDLE));

            *NewInfo = *Info;

            // Now load the tool bitmaps

            NewInfo->bmWidth = –1;
            for (i = 0; i < numTools; i++)
            {
                NewInfo->bmHandles [i] = LoadBitmap (NewInfo->hInst,
                                            MAKEINTRESOURCE
                                            (NewInfo->bmBaseID + i));

                if (NewInfo->bmWidth == –1 && NewInfo->bmHandles [i] != NULL)
                {
                    GetObject (NewInfo->bmHandles [i], sizeof (bm), &bm);
```

```
                NewInfo->bmWidth = bm.bmWidth / 2;
                NewInfo->bmHeight = bm.bmHeight;
            }
        }

        // Check we've got at least one bitmap !

        if (NewInfo->bmWidth == -1) return (-1);

        // Calculate the required size of the window

        SetWindowPos (hWnd, 0, 0, 0,
                        (NewInfo->cols * NewInfo->bmWidth) - (NewInfo->cols - 1) + 6,
                        (NewInfo->rows * NewInfo->bmHeight) - (NewInfo->rows - 1)
                        + FakeCaptionHeight() + 6,
                        SWP_NOMOVE | SWP_NOACTIVATE | SWP_NOZORDER);

        // Associate the Info data structure with the window

        SetWindowWord (hWnd, 0, (WORD) NewInfo);
        return (0);
}

//----------------------------------------------------------------
// Name:     CaptionHitTest
// Purpose:  Test for mouse hits in the caption bar.
//----------------------------------------------------------------

static BOOL PASCAL CaptionHitTest (HWND Wnd, LONG lParam, BOOL CloseBoxOnly)
{
        POINT pt;
        RECT rClient;

        GetClientRect (Wnd, &rClient);
        rClient.bottom = rClient.top + FakeCaptionHeight();
        if (CloseBoxOnly) rClient.right = (FakeCaptionHeight() * 3) / 2;
        pt.x = LOWORD (lParam);
        pt.y = HIWORD (lParam);
        ScreenToClient (Wnd, &pt);
        return PtInRect (&rClient, pt);
}

//----------------------------------------------------------------
// Name:     ButtonHitTest
// Purpose:  This routine tests for a mouse click in a tool slot.
//----------------------------------------------------------------

static VOID PASCAL ButtonHitTest (HWND Wnd, LONG lParam)
{
        RECT r;
        int num;
        POINT pt;
        PToolBoxInfo info;

        info = GetInfo (Wnd);
        pt.x = LOWORD (lParam);
        pt.y = HIWORD (lParam);

        for (num = 0; num < info->rows * info->cols; num++)
            if (info->bmHandles [num] != 0)
            {
                GetBitmapRect (&r, num, info);
                if (PtInRect (&r, pt))
                {
                    if (num != info->curTool)
                    {
                        InvalidateRect (Wnd, &r, TRUE);
                        GetBitmapRect (&r, info->curTool, info);
                        InvalidateRect (Wnd, &r, TRUE);
```

```
                    info−>curTool = num;
                    if (info−>hWndCmd != NULL) SendMessage
                      (info−>hWndCmd,
                        WM_COMMAND, info−>bmBaseID + num, 0);
                }
              break;
          }
        }
}

//────────────────────────────────────────────────────────────
// Name:    PaletteWndProc
// Purpose: Window procedure for our floating toolbox palette.
//────────────────────────────────────────────────────────────

LONG FAR PASCAL _export PaletteWndProc (HWND Wnd, WORD Msg,
                                        WORD wParam, LONG lParam)
{
      int i;
      RECT r;
      LONG ret;
      PAINTSTRUCT ps;
      PToolBoxInfo info;

      switch (Msg)
      {
        case WM_LBUTTONDOWN:
        ButtonHitTest (Wnd, lParam);
        return (0);

        case WM_NCLBUTTONDOWN:

        if (CaptionHitTest (Wnd, lParam, TRUE))
        {
          PostMessage (Wnd, WM_SYSCOMMAND, SC_CLOSE, 0);
          return (0);
        }
        return DefWindowProc (Wnd, Msg, wParam, lParam);

        case WM_NCHITTEST:

        if (CaptionHitTest (Wnd, lParam, FALSE)) return (HTCAPTION);
        return DefWindowProc (Wnd, Msg, wParam, lParam);

        case WM_ACTIVATE:

        GetClientRect (Wnd, &r);
        r.bottom = r.top + FakeCaptionHeight();
        InvalidateRect (Wnd, &r, FALSE);
        return (0);

        case WM_PAINT:

        BeginPaint (Wnd, &ps);
        DrawFakeCaption (ps.hdc, Wnd);
        info = GetInfo (Wnd);
        for (i = 0; i < info−>rows * info−>cols; i++)
          DrawBitmap (ps.hdc, info, i);

        GetClientRect (Wnd, &r);
        FrameRect (ps.hdc, &r, GetStockObject (BLACK_BRUSH));

        EndPaint (Wnd, &ps);
        return (0);

      case WM_CREATE:

        if ((ret = CreateToolBoxWindow (Wnd, lParam)) == 0)
        {
```

```
            info = GetInfo (Wnd);
            if (info−>hWndCmd != NULL) SendMessage
              (info−>hWndCmd,
              WM_COMMAND, info−>bmBaseID + info−>curTool, 0);
          }
          return (ret);

        case WM_DESTROY:

          info = GetInfo (Wnd);
          for (i = 0; i < info−>rows * info−>cols; i++)
            if (info−>bmHandles [i] != NULL)
                DeleteObject (info−>bmHandles [i]);

          // Send good-bye kiss…

          if (info−>hWndCmd != NULL) SendMessage
            (info−>hWndCmd,
            WM_COMMAND, 0xFFFF, 0);

          LocalFree ((HANDLE) info);
          return (0);

        case PM_GETTOOL:

          info = GetInfo (Wnd);
          return (info−>curTool + info−>bmBaseID);

        case PM_SETTOOL:

          info = GetInfo (Wnd);
          wParam −= info−>bmBaseID;
          if ((int)wParam >= 0 && (int)wParam < info−>rows * info−>cols)
            if (info−>bmHandles [wParam] != NULL && wParam != info−>curTool)
              {
                GetBitmapRect (&r, wParam, info);
                InvalidateRect (Wnd, &r, TRUE);
                GetBitmapRect (&r, info−>curTool, info);
                InvalidateRect (Wnd, &r, TRUE);
                info−>curTool = wParam;
                if (info−>hWndCmd != NULL) SendMessage
                  (info−>hWndCmd,
                  WM_COMMAND, info−>bmBaseID + wParam, 0);
                return (1);
              }
          return (0);
      }

    return DefWindowProc (Wnd, Msg, wParam, lParam);
}

//────────────────────────────────────────────────────
// Name:    InitToolPalette
// Purpose: Routine to initialize palette code.
//────────────────────────────────────────────────────

BOOL PASCAL InitToolPalette (HANDLE hInstance, HANDLE hPrevInst)
{
    WNDCLASS cls;

    // If first instance, then register palette window class

    if (hPrevInst == NULL)
    {
      cls.style           = CS_SAVEBITS;
      cls.lpfnWndProc     = (WNDPROC) PaletteWndProc;
      cls.cbClsExtra      = 0;
      cls.cbWndExtra      = 2;
      cls.hInstance       = hInstance;
```

```
            cls.hIcon          = 0;
            cls.hCursor        = LoadCursor (0, IDC_ARROW);
            cls.hbrBackground  = GetStockObject (LTGRAY_BRUSH);
            cls.lpszMenuName   = NULL;
            cls.lpszClassName  = PALETTECLASS;

            if (RegisterClass (&cls) == FALSE) return (FALSE);
        }

        fInit = TRUE;
        return (TRUE);
}

//─────────────────────────────────────────────────────────
// Name:    CreatePaletteWindow
// Purpose: Create a new toolbox palette and return handle.
//─────────────────────────────────────────────────────────

HWND PASCAL CreatePaletteWindow (HANDLE hInstance, int rows, int cols,
                                 int curTool, HWND hWndCmd,
                                 WORD bmBaseID)
{
        HWND hwnd = NULL;
        ToolBoxInfo info;

        if (hWndCmd != NULL && fInit == TRUE)
        {
            // Initialize ToolBoxInfo data structure

            info.rows      = rows;
            info.cols      = cols;
            info.curTool   = curTool;
            info.hWndCmd   = hWndCmd;
            info.bmBaseID  = bmBaseID;
            info.hInst     = hInstance;

            // Create the palette window

            hwnd = CreateWindow (PALETTECLASS, NULL, WS_CHILD,
                                 GetSystemMetrics (SM_CXFRAME),
                                 GetSystemMetrics (SM_CXFRAME),
                                 0, 0, hWndCmd, 0, hInstance,
                                 (LPSTR)&info);

            // If you've got it, flaunt it...

            if (hwnd != NULL)
            {
                ShowWindow (hwnd, SW_SHOW);
                UpdateWindow (hwnd);
            }
        }

        return (hwnd);
}
```

Figure 2.13 PALAPP1.C: a sample application used to test the palette code.

```
/* PALAPP1.C */

// © 1994 Dave Jewell and Addison-Wesley, ALL RIGHTS RESERVED

#include    <windows.h>
#include    "palette.h"
```

```
#define    APPCLASS    "MyApp"
#define    TOOLBASEID  1000

HWND hPalWnd;        // Handle to palette window

LONG FAR PASCAL _export AppWndProc (HWND Wnd, WORD Msg,
                                    WORD wParam, LONG lParam)
{
    int curTool;
    char szBuffer [128];
    PAINTSTRUCT ps;

    switch (Msg)
    {
      case WM_CHAR:

        wParam -= '0';
        if ((int)wParam >= 0 && (int)wParam <= 9)
        {
            if (hPalWnd == NULL) MessageBeep (0);
            else SendMessage (hPalWnd, PM_SETTOOL, wParam + TOOLBASEID, 0);
        }
        return (0);

      case WM_COMMAND:

        if (wParam >= TOOLBASEID && wParam <= TOOLBASEID + 9)
            InvalidateRect (Wnd, NULL, TRUE);
        if (wParam == 0xFFFF) // Good-bye kiss ?
        {
            InvalidateRect (Wnd, NULL, TRUE);
            hPalWnd = NULL;
        }

        return (0);

      case WM_PAINT:

        BeginPaint (Wnd, &ps);
        if (hPalWnd == NULL) lstrcpy (szBuffer,
                                    "Palette window is out to lunch");
        else
        {
            curTool = SendMessage (hPalWnd, PM_GETTOOL, 0, 0);
            wsprintf (szBuffer, "Currently selected tool is %d !", curTool);
        }

        TextOut (ps.hdc, 10, 10, szBuffer, lstrlen (szBuffer));
        EndPaint (Wnd, &ps);
        return (0);

      case WM_DESTROY:

        PostQuitMessage (0);
        return (0);
    }

    return DefWindowProc (Wnd, Msg, wParam, lParam);

}
//————————————————————————————————————————————————
// Name:    InitApplication
// Purpose: Register application window class.
//————————————————————————————————————————————————

BOOL PASCAL InitApplication (HANDLE hInstance)
{
    WNDCLASS cls;
```

```
        // If first instance, then register application window class

        cls.style              = CS_HREDRAW | CS_VREDRAW;
        cls.lpfnWndProc        = (WNDPROC) AppWndProc;
        cls.cbClsExtra         = 0;
        cls.cbWndExtra         = 0;
        cls.hInstance          = hInstance;
        cls.hIcon              = LoadIcon (0, IDI_APPLICATION);
        cls.hCursor            = LoadCursor (0, IDC_ARROW);
        cls.hbrBackground      = GetStockObject (WHITE_BRUSH);
        cls.lpszMenuName       = NULL;
        cls.lpszClassName      = APPCLASS;

        return RegisterClass (&cls);
}

//───────────────────────────────────────────────────────────────
// Name:    WinMain
// Purpose: Program entry point.
//───────────────────────────────────────────────────────────────

#pragma argsused

int PASCAL WinMain (HANDLE hInstance, HANDLE hPrevInst,
                    LPSTR lpCmdLine, int CmdShow)
{
        HWND Window;
        MSG Message;

        // Register the toolbox palette code

        if (InitToolPalette (hInstance, hPrevInst) == FALSE)
            return (0);

        if (hPrevInst == NULL)
            if (InitApplication (hInstance) == FALSE)
                return (0);

        // Create main application window

        Window = CreateWindow (APPCLASS, "Sample Application",
                            WS_OVERLAPPEDWINDOW,
                            CW_USEDEFAULT, 0,
                            CW_USEDEFAULT, 0, 0, 0, hInstance, NULL);

        if (Window == NULL) return (0);

        ShowWindow (Window, CmdShow);
        UpdateWindow (Window);

        // Create palette window

        hPalWnd = CreatePaletteWindow (hInstance, 5, 2, 0, Window, TOOLBASEID);
        if (hPalWnd == NULL) return (0);

        while (GetMessage (&Message, NULL, 0, 0))
        {
            TranslateMessage (&Message);
            DispatchMessage (&Message);
        }

        return (Message.wParam);
}
```

```
/* PALETTE.H */

// © 1994 Dave Jewell and Addison-Wesley, ALL RIGHTS RESERVED

#ifndef _PALETTE
#define _PALETTE        /* #defined if palette.h has been included */

#ifdef __cplusplus
extern "C" {
#endif

// Custom Windows messages

#define    PM_GETTOOL          WM_USER
#define    PM_SETTOOL          WM_USER + 1

// Palette code API routines

BOOL PASCAL InitToolPalette (HANDLE hInstance, HANDLE hPrevInst);
HWND PASCAL CreatePaletteWindow (HANDLE hInstance, int rows, int cols, int
                        curTool, HWND hWndCmd, WORD
                        bmBaseID);

#ifdef __cplusplus
}
#endif

#endif      /* _PALETTE */
```

Figure 2.14 PALETTE.H: the header file used by the palette code.

If you examine the header file, you'll see that in addition to the two API routines, we've also defined a couple of private messages. These are called PM_GETTOOL and PM_SETTOOL. You can use these messages to ask a palette window for the number of the currently selected tool, or to select a new tool under program control. It's always nice to provide more than one way of doing the same job, for those users who don't like using mice. You might, for example, decide to implement a drawing package where a toolbox palette might contain a 'fill' tool. You could use the Control-F key combination as an alternative means of selecting the fill tool.

The code to implement the PM_GETTOOL and PM_SETTOOL code is implemented inside the PaletteWndProc routine. It should be fairly obvious how this code works, but you do need to bear in mind that the value returned from issuing a PM_GETTOOL message includes the base resource offset. In other words, if you have ten bitmaps in your toolbox palette and a starting bitmap resource ID of 500, then you'll get returned values in the range 500–509, rather than 0–9. This is important because it simplifies the code in the application program itself. The whole idea is that you use the base resource offset to allocate a unique range of numbers that don't conflict with those generated from using the menu in your application. Similarly, you would use numbers in the range 500–509 in order to set the currently selected tool via the PM_SETTOOL message.

It's very important to have a rigidly defined interface between different chunks of code. In our case, we have the two API routines and these two special messages that can be sent to palette windows. That's all. There are no shared global variables, and the main application code doesn't even know the class name used by the palette window. If you really do want to write code that's simple to reuse from one application to the next, then it's crucially important to bolt down programming interfaces in this way.

Figure 2.15   Running the
sample application.

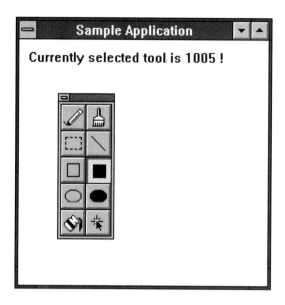

Figure 2.15 shows the sample application in use. The toolbox palette window
can be dragged around within the main application window, but because it's a child
of the application window, it cannot appear outside it. As you move the palette
window to the edge of the application window, it is progressively 'clipped'. If you
iconize the application window and then restore it to its previous size, you'll see that
the palette window will maintain the same position with respect to the application
window. This behavior comes 'for free' with child windows.

Each time that a new tool is selected from the palette window, the corresponding WM_COMMAND message is sent to the main application window. This causes it
to invalidate its client area, causing a WM_PAINT message to be generated. This in
turn causes the application to query the palette window for the currently selected tool
via the PM_GETTOOL message. An appropriate text string is then displayed in the
main window. In a real-life application, you'd probably set up different cursors
depending upon the currently selected tool.

It might seem odd to query the palette window for the currently selected tool.
After all, we've just received a WM_COMMAND that gave us the number of the
selected tool. This is good programming practice: it saves us having to maintain a
global variable that contains the currently selected tool number. Keep in mind what
would happen if we wished to have two or three different palette windows within the
same application: we'd need a global variable for each, with further resulting
complications.

There are a couple of other points that need explaining. The palette code
has been modified such that when a palette window is closed, it sends a special
WM_COMMAND to its parent window. This special message can be recognized
by the fact that the wParam field is set to 0xFFFF. You can think of this message
as a 'good-bye kiss'. This facility is useful since, in the present case, it enables the

main application code to keep track of whether or not a toolbox palette window is active. As soon as a WM_COMMAND message is received that has wParam set to 0xFFFF, the application code knows to set the palette window handle to NULL. From then on, the message Palette window is out to lunch will be displayed in the main window. Again, in a real-world application, you would provide a menu item to make the toolbox palette window available again, simply by making a new call to the CreatePaletteWindow window routine. You can use the good-bye kiss facility in your own programs, but as discussed earlier, keep in mind what you're going to do if you find that you need more than one palette window for some specialized program.

In addition to good-bye kisses, the palette code also makes use of a 'hello kiss' feature! When you start the sample program, you may notice that for a split second the Palette window is out to lunch message appears. This is because the main application window is created first, and a WM_PAINT message is generated before the palette window comes into existence. The palette code automatically sends an initial WM_COMMAND to the parent window as part of its own WM_CREATE message processing. This ensures that the parent gets the current tool status as soon as possible, but when initializing your program, you do need to be sure that the parent window is in a fit state to receive WM_COMMAND messages before calling the CreatePaletteWindow routine.

If you look at the application source code, you'll see that you can use the keys '0' through to '9' to select the current tool. This is just to illustrate that the PM_SET-TOOL message works – you'd more likely use some control key combination as described earlier with reference to the Fill tool. If you press these keys after closing the palette window, the MessageBeep API routine is called to warn you that you're doing something wrong.

Children versus popups

You might find it a little irritating that the entire client area of the main application window is redrawn each time a new tool is selected – if you watch carefully, you'll see the palette window flicker whenever a new tool is selected. This is the inevitable result of using the InvalidateRect routine in the way that we're doing. Whenever a window gets repainted, it's taken as read that any exposed child window gets repainted too. Since the toolbox is a child of the main application window, it also receives a WM_PAINT message and has to redraw itself. Because we're calling the InvalidateRect routine with a NULL pointer, the entire client area of the application window gets redrawn each time a new tool is selected.

This is obviously a very false situation and it's easy to fix. In a real program, we'd typically only invalidate the part of the client area that had changed. In something like a drawing or painting application, changing from one tool to another might not even affect the client area at all; it would simply involve the selection of a different cursor appropriate to the new drawing mode. When the client area does change, it's a simple matter to exclude the palette window from the update region of the application window. This will prevent unnecessary redrawing taking place. We'll look at this shortly.

If you want to experiment, try using the SetWindowText routine to draw the tool selection message into the caption bar of the application window. Having done that, you can dispense with the calls to InvalidateRect, and you'll find that there's no flicker when you change from one tool to another.

So far, we've been using a toolbox palette window that's a child of the main application window. This technique works well but, as we've seen, it has a couple of disadvantages. For one thing, the palette window is constrained to the dimensions of its parent and cannot be placed anywhere on the screen (unless, of course, the parent window is maximized). At the same time, some care needs to be taken when it comes to performing updates of the application window. Ideally, when some change is made to the application window's client area, the size of the invalidated area should be minimized so that the palette window does not have to redrawn unnecessarily.

An alternative approach is to use the WS_POPUP style rather than WS_CHILD. You can do this by changing just one line of code in the PALETTE6.C file. Here's how the call to CreateWindow looks now:

```
// Create the palette window
hwnd = CreateWindow (PALETTECLASS, NULL, WS_POPUP,
                GetSystemMetrics (SM_CXFRAME),
                GetSystemMetrics (SM_CXFRAME),
                0, 0, hWndCmd, 0, hInstance,
                (LPSTR)&info);
```

Using the WS_POPUP style, the palette window is no longer a child of the application window, but is still 'owned' by the application window. This means that when the application window is closed, the palette window will automatically be destroyed as well, just as if it were a child window. Additionally, the position of the palette window is preserved each time the application window is iconized and restored whenever the application window is restored.

One of the nicest things about the WS_POPUP style is the fact that the palette window can now be placed anywhere on the screen. Additionally, because it's no longer a child window, it isn't included in updates to the client area of the application window. If you try changing tools now, you'll see that there's no flickering in the palette. Whichever style you use (child or popup) is up to you. It's a matter of taste and how you want your application to look.

As with everything else in life, there's no such thing as a free lunch, and the WS_POPUP style is not without its problems. You may have noticed that the characters '0' through to '9' can no longer be used to select a palette tool. If you have the palette window sitting on top of the application window, you'll see that these characters seem to be ignored. The problem is that the palette window (because it's no longer a child window) will receive the input focus when it's active. When you type something on the keyboard, the WM_CHAR messages are sent to the palette window, rather than the application window. This is obviously not what we want. For this reason (and a few others), I've stuck with the WS_CHILD window style in my code. At the end of the day, it represents the simplest solution to the problem.

I mentioned earlier that it was fairly easy to remove the palette window from the update region of the application window. Doing so leads to smoother performance, and eliminates flicker when changing from one tool to another. The code to do this is shown below – it can be added to the end of the application code that processes WM_COMMAND messages received from the client. In an actual application, you'd normally only do this when you knew that the client area needed to be updated.

```
if (hPalWnd != NULL)
{
        GetWindowRect (hPalWnd, &ToolRect);
        ScreenToClient (Wnd, (POINT FAR *) &ToolRect.left);
        ScreenToClient (Wnd, (POINT FAR *) &ToolRect.right);
        ValidateRect (Wnd, &ToolRect);
}
```

At the same time, it's necessary to add a couple of calls to the UpdateWindow routine inside the palette code. This forces the palette window to be redrawn before the WM_COMMAND message is passed to the application. In the code that you'll see later, I've take the opportunity to common up some existing code by introducing a new routine, ChangeTool. This is called in response to mouse clicks on the palette window, and whenever a PM_SETTOOL message is received.

There are a couple more things we should do to the palette code in order to get a really professional effect. For one thing, we need to take a look at the way the caption bar is highlighted. If you remember, a caption bar can be displayed in either a highlighted or a non-highlighted state, depending on whether or not the application is active. Because we've settled on the idea of using a child window, we really want the palette window to mimic the highlighted state of its parent. This means that when we 'switch away' from the main application window to another Windows program, the fake caption bar in the palette needs to become inactive. Similarly, when we 'switch back' to our test application, the palette window's caption bar should become active, along with the caption bar of the main application window. This is fairly easy to do: we need to change one line of code in the DrawFakeCaption routine so as to look like this:

```
brushKind = (GetParent (Wnd) == GetFocus ())
        ? COLOR_ACTIVECAPTION : COLOR_INACTIVECAPTION;
```

In other words, the palette window is now looking at its parent (the main application window) to decide how to draw the caption bar. Bear in mind that with this code change, we're now committed to the palette window being a child window.

This is reflected in the code shown in PALETTE7.C at the end of this chapter. At the expense of some loss of generality, the code has been simplified and now assumes that the hWndCmd handle in the ToolBoxInfo structure is non-NULL: child windows *have* to have a parent. In fact, the hWndCmd field has been eliminated altogether from the ToolBoxInfo data structure: we simply use the GetParent API routine to find the parent window handle.

In order to get the palette window's caption bar redrawn, we also have to respond to a special message that's received by the application window. This message, WM_ACTIVATEAPP, is received whenever the current application is about to be activated or deactivated in favor of another Windows program. The code to handle the WM_ACTIVATEAPP message looks like this:

```
case WM_ACTIVATEAPP:
if (hPalWnd != NULL)
{
        GetWindowRect (hPalWnd, &ToolRect);
        ScreenToClient (Wnd, (POINT FAR *) &ToolRect.left);
        ScreenToClient (Wnd, (POINT FAR *) &ToolRect.right);
        InvalidateRect (Wnd, &ToolRect, TRUE);
}
return (0);
```

These changes pretty well wrap things up as far as the toolbox palette code is concerned. The final code listings are shown in Figures 2.16 and 2.17.

Figure 2.16 PALETTE7.C: the finished palette window code module.

```
/* PALETTE7.C */

// © 1994 Dave Jewell and Addison-Wesley, ALL RIGHTS RESERVED

#include    <windows.h>
#include    "palette.h"

#define    PALETTECLASS        "Palette"

typedef struct ToolBoxInfo
{
        int        rows;           // number of rows of bitmaps
        int        cols;           // number of columns of bitmaps
        int        curTool;        // currently selected tool bitmap
        HANDLE hInst;              // instance handle for resource loads
        WORD    bmBaseID;          // starting ID of bitmap resources
        int        bmWidth;        // width of each bitmap resource
        int        bmHeight;       // height of each bitmap resource
        HANDLE bmHandles [1];      // placeholder for handle array

} ToolBoxInfo, NEAR * PToolBoxInfo;

static BOOL fInit = FALSE;         // TRUE if module initialized

//────────────────────────────────────────────────────────────
// Name:    FakeCaptionHeight
// Purpose: Return height of fake caption bar.
//────────────────────────────────────────────────────────────

static int PASCAL FakeCaptionHeight (void)
{
        return (GetSystemMetrics (SM_CYCAPTION) / 3) + 2;
}

//────────────────────────────────────────────────────────────
// Name:    DrawFakeCaption
// Purpose: This routine draws our fake caption bar, complete with
//          miniature system menu close box.
//────────────────────────────────────────────────────────────

static void PASCAL DrawFakeCaption (HDC dc, HWND Wnd)
{
        HBRUSH hbr;
        RECT rClient;
        int width, height, brushKind;

        GetClientRect (Wnd, &rClient);
        rClient.bottom = rClient.top + FakeCaptionHeight();
        brushKind = (GetParent (Wnd) == GetFocus ())
            ? COLOR_ACTIVECAPTION : COLOR_INACTIVECAPTION;

        hbr = CreateSolidBrush (GetSysColor (brushKind));
```

```
        FillRect (dc, &rClient, hbr);
        DeleteObject (hbr);

        MoveTo (dc, rClient.left, rClient.bottom);
        LineTo (dc, rClient.right, rClient.bottom);

        // Now draw the close box

        rClient.right = (FakeCaptionHeight() * 3) / 2;
        MoveTo (dc, rClient.right, rClient.top);
        LineTo (dc, rClient.right, rClient.bottom);
        FillRect (dc, &rClient, GetStockObject (LTGRAY_BRUSH));

        // And the close box bar

        width = rClient.right - rClient.left;
        rClient.left += (width / 4) + 1;
        rClient.right = rClient.left + (width / 2) + 1;

        height = rClient.bottom - rClient.top;
        rClient.top += height / 2;
        rClient.bottom = rClient.top + 3;

        FillRect (dc, &rClient, GetStockObject (GRAY_BRUSH));
        OffsetRect (&rClient,-1, -1);
        FillRect (dc, &rClient, GetStockObject (WHITE_BRUSH));
        FrameRect (dc, &rClient, GetStockObject (BLACK_BRUSH));
}

//————————————————————————————————————————————————————
// Name:    GetInfo
// Purpose: Return a pointer to window's associated data.
//————————————————————————————————————————————————————

static PToolBoxInfo PASCAL GetInfo (HWND Wnd)
{
        return (PToolBoxInfo) GetWindowWord (Wnd, 0);
}

//————————————————————————————————————————————————————
// Name:    GetBitmapRect
// Purpose: Return the bounding rectangle of a specific item.
//————————————————————————————————————————————————————

static void PASCAL GetBitmapRect (RECT * r, int num, PToolBoxInfo info)
{
        r->left = (num % info->cols) * (info->bmWidth - 1) + 3;
        r->top = (num / info->cols) * (info->bmHeight - 1) +
                    FakeCaptionHeight() + 3;

        r->right = r->left + info->bmWidth;
        r->bottom = r->top + info->bmHeight;
}

//————————————————————————————————————————————————————
// Name:    DrawBitmap
// Purpose: Draw a specified bitmap in its own rectangle.
//————————————————————————————————————————————————————

static void PASCAL DrawBitmap (HDC dc, PToolBoxInfo info, int num)
{
        HBITMAP hbm;
        HDC hMemDC;
        RECT r;
        int XSrc;

        if (info->bmHandles [num] != NULL)
        {
            GetBitmapRect (&r, num, info);
            hMemDC = CreateCompatibleDC (dc);
```

```
        hbm = SelectObject (hMemDC, info->bmHandles [num]);
        XSrc = (num != info->curTool) ? 0 : info->bmWidth;
        BitBlt (dc, r.left, r.top, r.right - r.left, r.bottom - r.top,
                hMemDC, XSrc, 0, SRCCOPY);

        SelectObject (hMemDC, hbm);
        DeleteDC (hMemDC);
    }
}

//-------------------------------------------------------------------
// Name:    CreateToolBoxWindow
// Purpose: Called in response to WM_CREATE message.
//-------------------------------------------------------------------

static LONG PASCAL CreateToolBoxWindow (HWND hWnd, LONG lParam)
{
    BITMAP bm;
    int i, numTools;
    PToolBoxInfo NewInfo, Info;

    Info = (PToolBoxInfo) (((LPCREATESTRUCT)lParam)->lpCreateParams);
    if (Info == NULL) return (-1);

    // Perform some sanity checks

    numTools = Info->rows * Info->cols;
    if (numTools == 0 || Info->curTool >= numTools) return (-1);

    // Allocate the 'real' info structure

    NewInfo = (PToolBoxInfo) LocalAlloc (LPTR, sizeof (ToolBoxInfo) +
                                (numTools - 1) * sizeof (HANDLE));

    *NewInfo = *Info;

    // Now load the tool bitmaps

    NewInfo->bmWidth = -1;
    for (i = 0; i < numTools; i++)
    {
        NewInfo->bmHandles [i] = LoadBitmap
            (NewInfo->hInst,
             MAKEINTRESOURCE (NewInfo->bmBaseID + i));

        if (NewInfo->bmWidth == -1 && NewInfo->bmHandles [i] != NULL)
        {
            GetObject (NewInfo->bmHandles [i], sizeof (bm), &bm);
            NewInfo->bmWidth = bm.bmWidth / 2;
            NewInfo->bmHeight = bm.bmHeight;
        }
    }

    // Check we've got at least one bitmap !

    if (NewInfo->bmWidth == -1) return (-1);

    // Calculate the required size of the window

    SetWindowPos (hWnd, 0, 0, 0,
                    (NewInfo->cols * NewInfo->bmWidth) - (NewInfo->cols - 1) + 6,
                    (NewInfo->rows * NewInfo->bmHeight) - (NewInfo->rows - 1)
                    + FakeCaptionHeight() + 6,
                    SWP_NOMOVE | SWP_NOACTIVATE | SWP_NOZORDER);

    // Associate the Info data structure with the window

    SetWindowWord (hWnd, 0, (WORD) NewInfo);
    return (0);
}
```

```
//————————————————————————————————————————————————
// Name:    CaptionHitTest
// Purpose:  Test for mouse hits in the caption bar.
//————————————————————————————————————————————————

static BOOL PASCAL CaptionHitTest (HWND Wnd, LONG lParam, BOOL
                                   CloseBoxOnly)
{
      POINT pt;
      RECT rClient;

      GetClientRect (Wnd, &rClient);
      rClient.bottom = rClient.top + FakeCaptionHeight();
      if (CloseBoxOnly) rClient.right = (FakeCaptionHeight() * 3) / 2;
      pt.x = LOWORD (lParam);
      pt.y = HIWORD (lParam);
      ScreenToClient (Wnd, &pt);
      return PtInRect (&rClient, pt);
}

//————————————————————————————————————————————————
// Name:    ChangeTool
// Purpose:  Change to a new tool in the palette window.
//————————————————————————————————————————————————

static BOOL PASCAL ChangeTool (HWND Wnd, int newTool)
{
      RECT r;
      PToolBoxInfo info;

      info = GetInfo (Wnd);
      if (newTool != info->curTool && info->bmHandles [newTool] != NULL)
      {
          GetBitmapRect (&r, newTool, info);
          InvalidateRect (Wnd, &r, TRUE);
          GetBitmapRect (&r, info->curTool, info);
          InvalidateRect (Wnd, &r, TRUE);
          info->curTool = newTool;
          UpdateWindow (Wnd);
          SendMessage (GetParent (Wnd), WM_COMMAND, info->bmBaseID
                       + newTool, 0);
          return (TRUE);
      }

      return (FALSE);
}

//————————————————————————————————————————————————
// Name:    ButtonHitTest
// Purpose:  This routine tests for a mouse click in a tool slot.
//————————————————————————————————————————————————

static int PASCAL ButtonHitTest (HWND Wnd, LONG lParam)
{
      RECT r;
      int num;
      POINT pt;
      PToolBoxInfo info;

      info = GetInfo (Wnd);
      pt.x = LOWORD (lParam);
      pt.y = HIWORD (lParam);

      for (num = 0; num < info->rows * info->cols; num++)
      {
          GetBitmapRect (&r, num, info);
          if (PtInRect (&r, pt)) return (num);
      }
```

```
            return (−1);
    }

    //————————————————————————————————————————————————————
    // Name:    PaletteWndProc
    // Purpose: Window procedure for our floating toolbox palette.
    //————————————————————————————————————————————————————

    LONG FAR PASCAL _export PaletteWndProc (HWND Wnd, WORD Msg,
                                            WORD wParam, LONG lParam)
    {
        int i;
        RECT r;
        LONG ret;
        PAINTSTRUCT ps;
        PToolBoxInfo info;

        info = GetInfo (Wnd);

        switch (Msg)
        {
          case WM_LBUTTONDOWN:

            i = ButtonHitTest (Wnd, lParam);
            if (i != −1) ChangeTool (Wnd, i);
            return (0);

          case WM_NCLBUTTONDOWN:

            if (CaptionHitTest (Wnd, lParam, TRUE))
            {
                PostMessage (Wnd, WM_SYSCOMMAND, SC_CLOSE, 0);
                return (0);
            }
            return DefWindowProc (Wnd, Msg, wParam, lParam);

          case WM_NCHITTEST:

            if (CaptionHitTest (Wnd, lParam, FALSE))
                return (HTCAPTION);

            return DefWindowProc (Wnd, Msg, wParam, lParam);

          case WM_ACTIVATE:

            GetClientRect (Wnd, &r);
            r.bottom = r.top + FakeCaptionHeight();
            InvalidateRect (Wnd, &r, FALSE);
            return (0);

          case WM_PAINT:

            BeginPaint (Wnd, &ps);
            DrawFakeCaption (ps.hdc, Wnd);

            for (i = 0; i < info−>rows * info−>cols; i++)
                DrawBitmap (ps.hdc, info, i);

            GetClientRect (Wnd, &r);
            FrameRect (ps.hdc, &r, GetStockObject (BLACK_BRUSH));

            EndPaint (Wnd, &ps);
            return (0);

          case WM_CREATE:

            if ((ret = CreateToolBoxWindow (Wnd, lParam)) == 0)
            {
                info = GetInfo (Wnd);
                SendMessage (GetParent (Wnd), WM_COMMAND,
                            info−>bmBaseID + info−>curTool, 0);
```

```
        }
        return (ret);

    case WM_DESTROY:

        for (i = 0; i < info−>rows * info−>cols; i++)
            if (info−>bmHandles [i] != NULL)
                DeleteObject (info−>bmHandles [i]);

        // Send good-bye kiss...

        SendMessage (GetParent (Wnd), WM_COMMAND, 0xFFFF, 0);
        LocalFree ((HANDLE) info);
        return (0);

    case PM_GETTOOL:

        return (info−>curTool + info−>bmBaseID);

    case PM_SETTOOL:

        wParam −= info−>bmBaseID;
        if ((int)wParam >= 0 && (int)wParam < info−>rows * info−>cols)
            return ChangeTool (Wnd, wParam);

        return (0);
        }

        return DefWindowProc (Wnd, Msg, wParam, lParam);
}

//——————————————————————————————————————————
// Name:    InitToolPalette
// Purpose: Routine to initialize palette code.
//——————————————————————————————————————————

BOOL PASCAL InitToolPalette (HANDLE hInstance, HANDLE hPrevInst)
{
    WNDCLASS cls;

    // If first instance, then register palette window class

    if (hPrevInst == NULL)
    {
        cls.style          = CS_SAVEBITS;
        cls.lpfnWndProc    = (WNDPROC) PaletteWndProc;
        cls.cbClsExtra     = 0;
        cls.cbWndExtra     = sizeof (VOID NEAR *);
        cls.hInstance      = hInstance;
        cls.hIcon          = 0;
        cls.hCursor        = LoadCursor (0, IDC_ARROW);
        cls.hbrBackground  = GetStockObject (LTGRAY_BRUSH);
        cls.lpszMenuName   = NULL;
        cls.lpszClassName  = PALETTECLASS;

        if (RegisterClass (&cls) == FALSE) return (FALSE);
    }

    fInit = TRUE;
    return (TRUE);
}

//——————————————————————————————————————————
// Name:    CreatePaletteWindow
// Purpose: Create a new toolbox palette and———— return handle.
//——————————————————————————————————————————

HWND PASCAL CreatePaletteWindow (HANDLE hInstance, int rows, int cols,
                                 int curTool, HWND hWndCmd, WORD bmBaseID)
{
```

```
        HWND hwnd = NULL;
        ToolBoxInfo info;

        if (hWndCmd != NULL && fInit == TRUE)
        {
            // Initialize ToolBoxInfo data structure

            info.rows     = rows;
            info.cols     = cols;
            info.curTool  = curTool;
            info.bmBaseID = bmBaseID;
            info.hInst    = hInstance;

            // Create the palette window

            hwnd = CreateWindow (PALETTECLASS, NULL, WS_CHILD,
                            GetSystemMetrics (SM_CXFRAME),
                            GetSystemMetrics (SM_CXFRAME),
                            0, 0, hWndCmd, 0, hInstance,
                            (LPSTR)&info);

            // If you've got it, flaunt it...

            if (hwnd != NULL)
            {
                ShowWindow (hwnd, SW_SHOW);
                UpdateWindow (hwnd);
            }
        }

        return (hwnd);
}
```

Figure 2.17 PALAPP2.C: the
test application program.

```
/* PALAPP2.C */

// © 1994 Dave Jewell and Addison-Wesley, ALL RIGHTS RESERVED

#include    <windows.h>
#include    "palette.h"

#define     APPCLASS        "MyApp"
#define     TOOLBASEID      1000

HWND hPalWnd;        // Handle to palette window

LONG FAR PASCAL _export AppWndProc (HWND Wnd, WORD Msg,
                                WORD wParam, LONG lParam)
{
    int curTool;
    RECT ToolRect;
    char szBuffer [128];
    PAINTSTRUCT ps;

    switch (Msg)
    {
      case WM_ACTIVATEAPP:

        if (hPalWnd != NULL)
        {
            GetWindowRect (hPalWnd, &ToolRect);
            ScreenToClient (Wnd, (POINT FAR *) &ToolRect.left);
```

```
                  ScreenToClient (Wnd, (POINT FAR *) &ToolRect.right);
                  InvalidateRect (Wnd, &ToolRect, TRUE);
              }
          return (0);

          case WM_CHAR:

          wParam −= '0';
          if ((int)wParam >= 0 && (int)wParam <= 9)
          {
              if (hPalWnd == NULL) MessageBeep (0);
              else SendMessage (hPalWnd, PM_SETTOOL, wParam + TOOLBASEID, 0);
          }
          return (0);

          case WM_COMMAND:

          if (wParam >= TOOLBASEID && wParam <= TOOLBASEID + 9)
          InvalidateRect (Wnd, NULL, TRUE);

          if (wParam == 0xFFFF) // Good-bye kiss ?
          {
              InvalidateRect (Wnd, NULL, TRUE);
              hPalWnd = NULL;
          }

          if (hPalWnd != NULL)
          {
              GetWindowRect (hPalWnd, &ToolRect);
              ScreenToClient (Wnd, (POINT FAR *) &ToolRect.left);
              ScreenToClient (Wnd, (POINT FAR *) &ToolRect.right);
              ValidateRect (Wnd, &ToolRect);
          }

          return (0);

          case WM_PAINT:

          BeginPaint (Wnd, &ps);
          if (hPalWnd == NULL) lstrcpy (szBuffer,
                                          "Palette window is out to lunch");
          else
          {
              curTool = SendMessage (hPalWnd, PM_GETTOOL, 0, 0);
              wsprintf (szBuffer, "Currently selected tool is %d !", curTool);
          }

          TextOut (ps.hdc, 10, 10, szBuffer, lstrlen (szBuffer));

          EndPaint (Wnd, &ps);
          return (0);

          case WM_DESTROY:

          PostQuitMessage (0);
          return (0);
      }

      return DefWindowProc (Wnd, Msg, wParam, lParam);
}

//————————————————————————————————————————————————————————————————
// Name:    InitApplication
// Purpose: Register application window class.
//————————————————————————————————————————————————————————————————

BOOL PASCAL InitApplication (HANDLE hInstance)
{
      WNDCLASS cls;
```

```
         // If first instance, then register application window class

         cls.style              = CS_HREDRAW I CS_VREDRAW;
         cls.lpfnWndProc        = (WNDPROC) AppWndProc;
         cls.cbClsExtra         = 0;
         cls.cbWndExtra         = 0;
         cls.hInstance          = hInstance;
         cls.hIcon              = LoadIcon (0, IDI_APPLICATION);
         cls.hCursor            = LoadCursor (0, IDC_ARROW);
         cls.hbrBackground      = GetStockObject (WHITE_BRUSH);
         cls.lpszMenuName       = NULL;
         cls.lpszClassName      = APPCLASS;

         return RegisterClass (&cls);
}

//─────────────────────────────────────────────────────────────────────
// Name:    WinMain
// Purpose: Program entry point.
//─────────────────────────────────────────────────────────────────────

#pragma argsused

int PASCAL WinMain (HANDLE hInstance, HANDLE hPrevInst,
                    LPSTR lpCmdLine, int CmdShow)
{
         HWND Window;
         MSG Message;

         // Register the toolbox palette code

         if (InitToolPalette (hInstance, hPrevInst) == FALSE)
            return (0);

         if (hPrevInst == NULL)
            if (InitApplication (hInstance) == FALSE)
               return (0);

         // Create main application window

         Window = CreateWindow (APPCLASS, "Sample Application",
                           WS_OVERLAPPEDWINDOW,
                           CW_USEDEFAULT, 0,
                           CW_USEDEFAULT, 0, 0, 0, hInstance, NULL);

         if (Window == NULL) return (0);

         ShowWindow (Window, CmdShow);
         UpdateWindow (Window);

         // Create palette window

         hPalWnd = CreatePaletteWindow (hInstance, 5, 2, 0, Window, TOOLBASEID);
         if (hPalWnd == NULL) return (0);
         while (GetMessage (&Message, NULL, 0, 0))
         {
            TranslateMessage (&Message);
            DispatchMessage (&Message);
         }

         return (Message.wParam);
}
```

A word about color schemes

As you probably appreciate, it's possible for a user to change the color scheme using the Windows Control Panel application. These color changes include the color of push buttons, the color used to paint the button 'shadow' along the bottom and right edges of a button, and the color used to paint the button 'highlight' along the top and left edges of the button. This raises an obvious question: should we change the colors used by the floating toolbox palette to match the current color scheme? The short answer to this is yes, we should.

Fortunately, there's a simple technique for modifying the colors used by a bitmap 'on the fly' at the time the bitmap is loaded by your application. This technique is covered in greater detail in a later chapter. Suffice it to say that the job's very simple: it merely involves replacing the LoadBitmap routine with a new routine called LoadButtonBitmap. The code for this new routine is given in Chapter 5. If you make these changes, you will also need to alter the background color used by the palette window. This is obviously very straightforward. Finally, don't worry about altering the appearance of the close box in the fake caption bar – normal Windows close boxes are not affected by color scheme changes, so there's no reason why our fake close box should be affected either!

Note

For Pascal programmers, Appendix 2 contains the code from Figures 2.16 and 2.17 in the form of a Pascal unit and accompanying application program. Pascal source code is also available on the companion disk as PALETTE.PAS and PALTEST.PAS.

Classy subclassing

3

This chapter introduces subclassing, a popular Windows technique that allows us to add custom features easily to existing Window classes. We will examine subclassing and superclassing, and look at the relative merits of each technique. In addition, I'll develop a simple set of generic subclassing routines that will be used later when we look at how to add decorative 3D effects to the dialog boxes in your application.

What's in a class?

Before we take a look at subclassing, it's important to be very clear on what a class is, and how it works. Let's take some time out to examine how the class mechanism works under Windows. As a Windows programmer, you will no doubt be familiar with the RegisterClass routine and the associated WNDCLASS data structure. The various fields within the WNDCLASS data structure are what define a class as far as Windows is concerned. Of these fields, the lpfnWndProc field is arguably the most important since it points to the class's window procedure. This window procedure in turn defines the appearance and behaviour of every window that belongs to this particular class.

You'd be right in suspecting that Windows keeps an internal copy of most of the WNDCLASS information. After all, you can use the API routines such as GetClassInfo and GetClassWord to retrieve information about window classes that have already been registered. In fact, these routines will provide you with data about classes that haven't even been registered by your own program: you can get information on window classes registered by other applications, or by the Windows system itself.

So where does Windows store all this stuff? The answer is fairly simple. Each time the RegisterClass routine is called, Windows allocates a special internal data structure within the local heap of the USER dynamic link library. This data structure contains much the same information as the WNDCLASS structure, and in fact most of the fields are copied across in one go. However, there are also a few extra fields in the internal class record, and one of these is a pointer; it's used to link the various class records together into a linked list. Whenever you issue a Windows API routine that requires access to class information, Windows has to walk this linked list looking for the specified class. When the class record is created within the USER module's local heap, Windows examines the cbClsExtra field within the WNDCLASS record and increases the size of the class record by this amount. That's why it's crucially important to initialize the cbClsExtra field to a sensible value before calling the RegisterClass routine. I have a Windows image processing application (which had better remain nameless!) that doesn't properly initialize the cbClsExtra field. The result is that it eats up most of the USER local heap while it's running!

There's another field in the WNDCLASS record that also needs to be initialized. This is the cbWndExtra field. Each time Windows creates a window of a given class, an internal window data structure is allocated inside the USER module's local heap, just as for the class record. (Note: this approach will almost certainly change for future 16-bit versions of Windows. For 32-versions of the system, the 64-kbyte limit on the size of a local heap no longer exists). When the window record is created, it's size is boosted by the value of the cbWndExtra field in the associated class record. The cbWndExtra field is very important for the purposes of subclassing, as we shall see.

Figure 3.1 shows the relationship between window records, class records, and the associated window procedure. In this diagram, we can see three window records, all of which are allocated in USER's local heap, as explained earlier. An internal window record contains a pointer to that window's class record, and this is illustrated by the lines linking the window records to the class record. In this case, the class record corresponds to the EDIT class, which is used to implement edit boxes through-out the Windows system. The EDIT class, in turn, contains a pointer to the window procedure. This is the very same pointer that was passed as the lpfnWndProc field when the RegisterClass routine was called.

Incidentally, there is nothing 'magic' about the built-in Windows classes. They are implemented and initialized in just the same way as you would implement custom window classes inside your own program code. When you start Windows running, the initialization code inside the USER DLL will eventually be called. Amongst other things, this code is responsible for initializing all the built-in Windows classes through calls to the RegisterClass routine. Most of the built-in classes are implemented inside the USER DLL. In fact, the code for the EDIT class, which is actually quite complex, actually accounts for several of the code segments inside the USER.EXE file.

In Figure 3.1, the hatched area of each window record indicates the extra storage that's allocated in the USER local heap via the cbWndExtra field. It so happens that under Windows 3.1, the cbWndExtra field is set to six for windows of the EDIT class. Put another way, the code that implemented Windows 3.1 edit boxes needs six bytes of private storage for each window of that class. The cbWndExtra field presents a problem when subclassing, as we shall see.

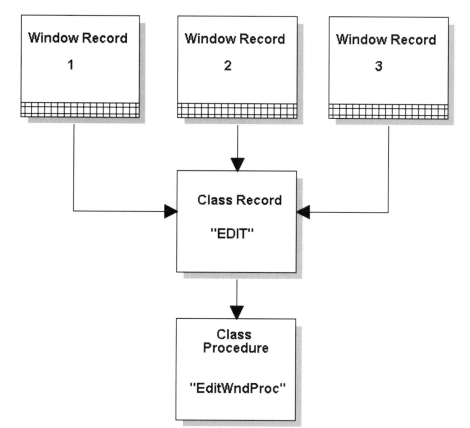

Figure 3.1   The relationship between window records, class records and window procedures.

From looking at Figure 3.1, you might suppose that all windows of the same class *have* to share the same class and window procedure. Since they're all pointing at the same class, how is it possible for different windows to be directed to different window procedures? The answer lies inside the window record itself. When a window is created, the class procedure address is copied from the class record into a field within the window record. This field is used to point to the current window procedure for that particular window. Thus, returning to Figure 3.1, when a number of windows are created, all of which belong to the same class, they all start off by pointing at the same procedure as was referenced in the class record. It's perfectly possible, however, to come along after the window has been created and point the window at some new window procedure.

So what exactly is subclassing?

In order to be able to talk about window subclassing, we need to be very clear in our terminology. Amongst Windows programmers, the phrase 'window procedure' is generally used to refer to the special exported routine that's used to field all messages for a given window class. This is the same procedure whose address you pass as the lpfnWndProc field in the WNDCLASS data structure when calling the RegisterClass routine. It needs to be said that 'window procedure' is a bad choice of term: it implies a procedure which is specific to a given window, whereas we're really talking about a procedure that's specific to a whole class; a procedure that's shared by all windows of the same class. Things get more confusing when we start subclassing windows. When we say 'window procedure', are we talking about the original procedure that was specified in the RegisterClass routine, or are we talking about the new procedure that's been bolted on to a specific window of the class?

In order to make things as clear as possible, from now on we'll try to adhere to a certain convention throughout this chapter. When I talk about the class procedure, I'm talking about the original routine whose address was passed in via the RegisterClass call. When I talk about the window procedure, I'm referring to the routine that first handles any messages for a given window. In the case of a non-subclassed window, these two routines will be one and the same. For windows that have been subclassed, the window procedure will typically process one or more messages to add some custom functionality and, for other messages which it's not concerned with, it will pass control on to the original class procedure.

In fact, with the amount of window subclassing that goes on these days, you often find that a particular window is subclassed more than once! In principle, a window can be subclassed any number of times with a 'chain' of linked window procedures, each of which passes control down the chain until the original class procedure is reached. If you're at all familiar with interrupt handling under DOS, this concept should be quite familiar to you: just think of interrupt handlers that add to or modify the functionality of some software interrupt such as INT $21.

Subclassing an existing window is very straightforward: you begin by using the GetWindowLong routine to get a pointer to the original class procedure (of course, it may not actually be the class procedure if the window has already been subclassed). You can then install a new window routine by calling SetWindowLong with the address of the new code. As soon as a new window procedure has been installed, it will immediately begin receiving any messages that are directed to that window.

The situation after a window (window number 3 in this example) has been subclassed is illustrated in Figure 3.2. Although this diagram may look a little complicated, there's no new information there, other than what we've already discussed. As you can see, each window record is shown with two pointers: a pointer to the class to which that window belongs, and a 'Proc Pointer' which points to the window procedure for that particular window. The additional memory allocation that corresponds to the cbWndExtra information (the hatched area in Figure 3.1) has been omitted from this diagram for the sake of clarity.

In the illustration, any messages received by the first two edit boxes are sent immediately to the EditWndProc class procedure which is contained in the USER library. Windows knows where to send messages by internally examining the Proc Pointer field of the window record. In the case of the third window, however, it has been subclassed so that its Proc Pointer points to a new routine called MyEditWndProc. This routine receives messages ahead of the original class procedure and can decide whether or not messages should be sent to the original code.

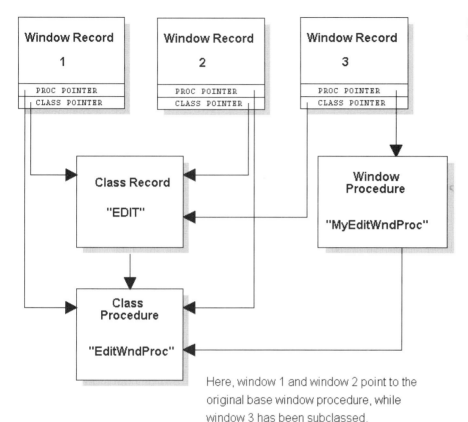

Figure 3.2 Window subclassing: the inside story.

Here, window 1 and window 2 point to the original base window procedure, while window 3 has been subclassed.

Notice that in all three cases, the class pointer of each window record still points to the EDIT class record. Subclassing an existing window does not change its class.

Let's put this into practice by attempting to subclass an application window. We'll create a very simple, skeletal Windows application and then use this as a basis for window subclassing. This simple application is shown in Figure 3.3 – it can be found on the companion disk as SCLASS1.C, and in compiled form as SCLASS1.EXE. All the program does is display a regular, overlapped application window on the screen.

```
/* SCLASS1.C */

// © 1994 Dave Jewell and Addison-Wesley, ALL RIGHTS RESERVED

#include    <windows.h>

HWND hMainWnd;      // main application window

//—————————————————————————————————————
// Name:     AppWndProc
// Purpose:  Window procedure for our application window.
//—————————————————————————————————————
```

Figure 3.3 SCLASS1.C: our skeletal Windows application.

```
LRESULT FAR PASCAL _export AppWndProc (HWND hwnd, UINT Msg, WPARAM
                                       wParam, LPARAM lParam)
{
    if (Msg == WM_DESTROY) PostQuitMessage (0);
    return DefWindowProc (hwnd, Msg, wParam, lParam);
}

//────────────────────────────────────────────────────────────
// Name:    InitApplication
// Purpose: Register application window class.
//────────────────────────────────────────────────────────────

BOOL NEAR PASCAL InitApplication (HANDLE hInstance)
{
    WNDCLASS cls;

    cls.style         = CS_VREDRAW | CS_HREDRAW;
    cls.lpfnWndProc   = AppWndProc;
    cls.cbClsExtra    = 0;
    cls.cbWndExtra    = 0;
    cls.hInstance     = hInstance;
    cls.hIcon         = LoadIcon (NULL, IDI_APPLICATION);
    cls.hCursor       = LoadCursor (0, IDC_ARROW);
    cls.hbrBackground = GetStockObject (WHITE_BRUSH);
    cls.lpszMenuName  = NULL;
    cls.lpszClassName = "SUBCLASS";

    return RegisterClass (&cls);
}

//────────────────────────────────────────────────────────────
// Name:    WinMain
// Purpose: Program entry point.
//────────────────────────────────────────────────────────────

int PASCAL WinMain (HANDLE hInstance, HANDLE hPrevInstance,
                    LPSTR lpCmdLine, int nCmdShow)
{
    MSG Message;

    // Do the usual initialization stuff....

    if (hPrevInstance == NULL)
      if (InitApplication (hInstance) == FALSE)
        return (0);

    hMainWnd = CreateWindow ("SUBCLASS", "My Application Window",
                             WS_OVERLAPPEDWINDOW,
                             CW_USEDEFAULT, 0, CW_USEDEFAULT, 0,
                             NULL, NULL, hInstance, NULL);

    if (hMainWnd == NULL) return (0);

    ShowWindow (hMainWnd, nCmdShow);
    UpdateWindow (hMainWnd);

    while (GetMessage (&Message, 0, 0, 0))
    {
      TranslateMessage (&Message);
      DispatchMessage (&Message);
    }

    return (Message.wParam);
}
```

Suppose that we wish to modify the behavior of the application window in some way – let's face it, it's somewhat boring right now! Maybe we want to arrange things so that moving the cursor across the window causes the MessageBeep routine to be called, or maybe we want to display an icon in the top left corner of the window.

The conventional way of making these changes would be to modify the AppWndProc routine to get the behavior we want. However, the essential point about subclassing a window is that we're modifying the behavior of some window whose window procedure isn't defined inside our own program. Programmers typically subclass dialog boxes to get attractive 3D effects. They might subclass edit boxes to create a new, custom edit box that will only allow numeric data to be entered. The list goes on: the possibilities are endless, but the important point is that typically we don't have any control over the window procedure of a window that we're subclassing.

Let's get some experience of subclassing techniques by subclassing the main application window in this simple program. The code to do it looks like this:

```
// Now subclass the window

lpfnOldWndProc = (FARPROC) GetWindowLong (hMainWnd, GWL_WNDPROC);
SetWindowLong (hMainWnd, GWL_WNDPROC, (LONG) NewWindowProc);
```

The GetWindowLong routine fetches a 32-bit value from a specified position in the internal window record that we discussed earlier. By specifying GWL_WNDPROC as the second parameter, we're telling Windows that we want to obtain the current value of what I called the Proc Pointer in Figure 3.2. As discussed earlier, this is a pointer to the window's current window procedure. The obtained value is saved in a global variable, lpfnOldWndProc. The SetWindowLong routine can then be called to set up a new Proc Pointer. From this point onwards, any messages directed at our application window will be directed to the NewWindowProc routine.

Here's what the NewWindowProc routine looks like:

```
//-----------------------------------------------------
// Name:    NewWindowProc
// Purpose: The subclassing routine.
//-----------------------------------------------------

LRESULT FAR PASCAL _export NewWindowProc (HWND Wnd, UINT Msg,
                                          WPARAM wParam, LPARAM lParam)
{
    int x, y;
    HICON hIcon;
    RECT rClient;
    PAINTSTRUCT ps;

    switch (Msg)
    {
      case WM_MOUSEMOVE:

        MessageBeep (0);
        break;

      case WM_PAINT:

        BeginPaint (Wnd, &ps);
        GetClientRect (Wnd, &rClient);
        hIcon = LoadIcon (0, IDI_HAND);
        for (x = 0; x < rClient.right; x += GetSystemMetrics (SM_CXICON))
          for (y = 0; y < rClient.right; y += GetSystemMetrics (SM_CYICON))
            DrawIcon (ps.hdc, x, y, hIcon);
```

```
        EndPaint (Wnd, &ps);

        return (0);
    }

    return CallWindowProc (lpfnOldWndProc, Wnd, Msg, wParam, lParam);
}
```

This routine makes two changes to the window's behavior. Firstly, every time the mouse moves over the window, it calls the Windows API MessageBeep routine to beep the speaker or play a sound file. If you have a sound board installed in your machine, and you have arranged for a .WAV file to be played each time that the MessageBeep routine is called, then I just hope it's not a long duration .WAV. You will rapidly get tired of listening to the Hallelujah Chorus each time the mouse changes position!

The second thing this little routine does is to take over the WM_PAINT message. Each time the paint message is received, the window is filled with the standard system 'Stop' icons. This might be a good window to display in a Windows-based disk formatting program when the user has inadvertently chosen to format the hard disk. The effect is shown in Figure 3.4.

The code corresponding to these changes can be found on the disk as SCLASS2.C, and the executable file as SCLASS2.EXE. Figure 3.5 shows the listing of SCLASS2.C.

Figure 3.4:   The dramatic effect of adding a little window subclassing code....

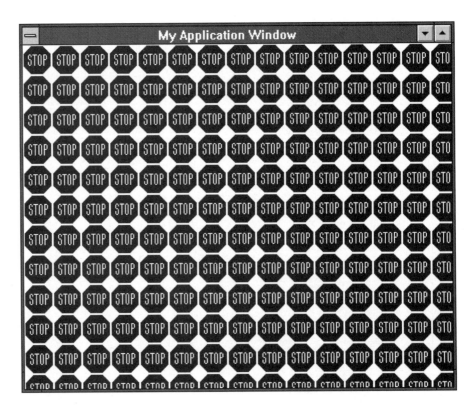

Figure 3.5   SCLASS2.C: this program demonstrates the essentials of window subclassing.

```
/* SCLASS2.C */

// © 1994 Dave Jewell and Addison-Wesley, ALL RIGHTS RESERVED

#include    <windows.h>

HWND hMainWnd;              // main application window
FARPROC lpfnOldWndProc;     // Pointer to old window procedure

//——————————————————————————————————————————————————————————
// Name:    AppWndProc
// Purpose: Window procedure for our application window.
//——————————————————————————————————————————————————————————

LRESULT FAR PASCAL _export AppWndProc (HWND Wnd, UINT Msg,
                                    WPARAM wParam, LPARAM lParam)
{
     if (Msg == WM_DESTROY) PostQuitMessage (0);
     return DefWindowProc (Wnd, Msg, wParam, lParam);
}

//——————————————————————————————————————————————————————————
// Name:    NewWindowProc
// Purpose: The subclassing routine.
//——————————————————————————————————————————————————————————

LRESULT FAR PASCAL _export NewWindowProc (HWND Wnd, UINT Msg,
                                    WPARAM wParam, LPARAM lParam)
{
     int x, y;
     HICON hIcon;
     RECT rClient;
     PAINTSTRUCT ps;

     switch (Msg)
     {
       case WM_MOUSEMOVE:

       MessageBeep (0);
       break;

       case WM_PAINT:

       BeginPaint (Wnd, &ps);
       GetClientRect (Wnd, &rClient);
       hIcon = LoadIcon (0, IDI_HAND);
       for (x = 0; x < rClient.right; x += GetSystemMetrics (SM_CXICON))
          for (y = 0; y < rClient.right; y += GetSystemMetrics (SM_CYICON))
             DrawIcon (ps.hdc, x, y, hIcon);
       EndPaint (Wnd, &ps);

       return (0);
     }

     return CallWindowProc (lpfnOldWndProc, Wnd, Msg, wParam, lParam);
}

//——————————————————————————————————————————————————————————
// Name:    InitApplication
// Purpose: Register application window class.
//——————————————————————————————————————————————————————————

BOOL NEAR PASCAL InitApplication (HANDLE hInstance)
{
     WNDCLASS cls;

     cls.style            = CS_VREDRAW | CS_HREDRAW;
     cls.lpfnWndProc      = AppWndProc;
     cls.cbClsExtra       = 0;
     cls.cbWndExtra       = 0;
```

```
        cls.hInstance          = hInstance;
        cls.hIcon              = LoadIcon (NULL, IDI_APPLICATION);
        cls.hCursor            = LoadCursor (0, IDC_ARROW);
        cls.hbrBackground      = GetStockObject (WHITE_BRUSH);
        cls.lpszMenuName       = NULL;
        cls.lpszClassName      = "SUBCLASS";

        return RegisterClass (&cls);
}

//----------------------------------------------------------------------
// Name:    WinMain
// Purpose: Program entry point.
//----------------------------------------------------------------------

#pragma argsused

int PASCAL WinMain (HANDLE hInstance, HANDLE hPrevInstance,
                    LPSTR lpCmdLine, int nCmdShow)
{
        MSG Message;

        // Do the usual initialization stuff...

        if (hPrevInstance == NULL)
           if (InitApplication (hInstance) == FALSE)
              return (0);

        hMainWnd = CreateWindow ("SUBCLASS", "My Application Window",
                         WS_OVERLAPPEDWINDOW,
                         CW_USEDEFAULT, 0, CW_USEDEFAULT, 0,
                         NULL, NULL, hInstance, NULL);

        if (hMainWnd == NULL) return (0);

        // Now subclass the window

        lpfnOldWndProc = (FARPROC) GetWindowLong (hMainWnd, GWL_WNDPROC);
        SetWindowLong (hMainWnd, GWL_WNDPROC, (LONG) NewWindowProc);

        ShowWindow (hMainWnd, nCmdShow);
        UpdateWindow (hMainWnd);

        while (GetMessage (&Message, 0, 0, 0))
        {
           TranslateMessage (&Message);
           DispatchMessage (&Message);
        }

        return (Message.wParam);
}
```

There are a few important points to note about the NewWindowProc code. It's crucially important that a subclassing routine for an existing window should use the _export keyword, just like the original class procedure with which the class was first registered. If you neglect to use the _export keyword or (depending on your development system) you omit the name of the subclassing routine from your .DEF file, then all sorts of obscure bugs will result. In particular, you'll find that the DS (Data Segment) register probably won't be set up properly on entry to the routine.

Note that the code that handles the WM_MOUSEMOVE message ends up calling the class procedure (or, to be more general, the previously installed window procedure) via CallWindowProc once the MessageBeep routine has been invoked. In other words, the WM_MOUSEMOVE message is passed on to the original window procedure so that it can perform any necessary processing that's required in response to this message. On the other hand, the code which handles the WM_PAINT message doesn't let the original code see any WM_PAINT messages at all: it returns zero as a function result. By convention, this means 'I've dealt with the WM_PAINT message' – end of story. In effect, the WM_PAINT code in the previous window procedure has been completely replaced, whereas the WM_MOUSEMOVE code has been supplemented.

This distinction is important. When you subclass an existing window, you'll want to pass the majority of messages right through to the existing window procedure, but for those messages that you intercept, you need to be quite clear what you're doing. Roughly speaking, here are the alternatives:

- Process the message and then pass control to the old code.
- Process the message and return immediately.
- Call the old code and then process the message.

The first and second alternatives correspond to the WM_MOUSEMOVE and WM_PAINT messages in our example code. The third alternative might be a bit of a surprise, but if you think about it, it's quite easy to do, like this:

```
case WM_ERASEBKGND:

result = CallWindowProc (lpfnOldWndProc, Wnd, Msg, wParam, IParam);
———— our own special processing code here ————
return (result);
```

This sort of situation is useful in cases like this, where you want, for example, to preserve an existing window's background, but you want to 'write' something else onto that background, just as if it were part of the original window background. If you're feeling adventurous, you can use exactly this technique to subclass the desktop window and draw some sort of informational display onto the desktop itself.

When handling a message inside a subclassing routine, it's important to know exactly what effect you want to achieve and which of the above three cases is the appropriate one to use.

By now, you should be getting the idea that subclassing is a very powerful tool to use. Before you get carried away, it's time to take a look at one or two pitfalls for the unwary. In particular, let's look at the problems presented by the dreaded cbWndExtra field.

Finding a home of your own

A frequent requirement in Windows programming is the need to associate some arbitrary data with a window handle. For example, the palette code developed in Chapter 2 needed to associate a small data structure with the palette window. As another example, you might want to subclass a window of the BUTTON class (the standard Windows push-button control) so as to create bitmapped push buttons like those used by Borland in their Windows programming tools. To do this, you'd naturally want to associate some bitmap handle with a particular window.

In the case of the palette window, this was done by setting up the cbWndExtra field so that a handle to the data structure could be stored into the window record. This is a simple and elegant solution: if you are in control of the window class, you can allocate the number of bytes you need by using this technique. (But please don't abuse the system; 16-bit Windows will not take kindly to you trying to tag 10 kbytes of data onto the end of your window record. This may well cause no problems under 32-bit versions of the system, but with 16-bit Windows, 10 bytes is a far more realistic limit.)

The situation isn't quite so simple when it comes to subclassing windows. The window class has already been registered, which means that we don't get an opportunity to add our own storage requirements to those that the designers of the window class have already allocated. Worse, the window we're interested in is already in existence, which means that we haven't even got the opportunity to 'tweak' the class record before the window is created. Taking the case of our bitmapped push-button control, we can certainly find out how many bytes of extra window storage are in use by the BUTTON window class by just calling the GetClassInfo routine. (If you're curious, the Windows 3.1 implementation of the BUTTON class uses three bytes of extra storage.) What the GetClassInfo routine doesn't tell us is whether any of these extra three bytes are up for grabs. The answer, in any case, is almost certain to be no: if the designer of the window class allocated three bytes of storage, then that's almost certainly the amount of memory that he or she needed.

Window superclassing

Fortunately, there are some ways around this sort of problem. One of them is to use a technique called superclassing. Superclassing is most appropriate where you do not need to change the behavior of an existing window. Let's suppose, for example, that you want to use bitmapped buttons within your application. To superclass the BUTTON window class, you'd proceed as follows.

Firstly, you would call the GetClassInfo API routine to obtain all the information about the BUTTON class. You would then use the information in the returned WNDCLASS data structure to create a new 'superclass', which you might call BITMAPBUTTON. To do this, you'd need to set up the lpszClassName field in the WNDCLASS data structure, and you'd need to set the lpszMenuName field to NULL – these two fields are not returned by the GetClassInfo call. You would also need to write a new window procedure called (say) BitMapButtonWndProc and you'd need to initialize the lpfnWndProc field in the WNDCLASS data structure to point to this new routine. Before setting up this field, store the value of the lpfnWndProc field which was returned from the call to GetClassInfo. This value will be needed later inside the BitMapButtonWndProc routine.

Now comes the sneaky bit. Suppose you've worked out that you need four bytes of storage for your bitmap button class. You might need a couple of bytes to store a handle to the bitmap, and a couple more bytes for control information. You should then add this value to the cbWndExtra value that was returned from the GetClassInfo routine. This is the biggest advantage of the superclassing technique – it allows us to link our own storage requirements to a window record without messing up the storage already in use by the BUTTON class.

Let's stick with our BUTTON class example, and say for the sake of argument that the BUTTON class requires three bytes of data. It's probably a good idea to round this up to an even number of bytes, so when we add your data requirements on to those of the BUTTON class, we get a figure of eight bytes, which is the value that must be plugged into the cbWndExtra field when the BITMAPBUTTON class is registered.

Note

In superclassing terminology, the BUTTON class is referred to as the 'base class' while the BITMAPBUTTON class is referred to as the superclass. If you're familiar with object-oriented techniques, this approach should hold few surprises for you – we've effectively derived a new class from an existing base class. The new super-class has inherited all the functionality of the base class and is free to add any new functionality of its own.

Within the new BitMapButtonWndProc, you can access your own window data in the usual way by using the GetWindowWord routine. If you want to access the first word of your own private window data, you would add the value four on to the index value. Thus the first word would be accessed with an index of four, and the second word with an index of six. This means, of course, that the BitMapButtonWndProc routine needs to know how many bytes to add to the index in order to 'skip past' the data that belongs to the base class. In other words, when you first call the GetClassInfo routine, you will need to store the returned cbWndExtra value into a global variable along with the original lpfnWndProc address. The BitmapButtonWndProc 'chains onto' the existing base class window procedure by using the CallWindowProc routine as discussed previously.

Superclassing is a powerful technique, but alas, it's not terribly useful to us. This is because we are primarily concerned with adding functionality to windows that have already been created. In this case, superclassing can't really do anything for us. Precisely why I should be so concerned with adding functionality to existing windows will become clear later when we get to the chapter on adding 3D effects to dialog boxes (Chapter 5).

Acquiring some property

Fortunately, Windows offers another solution to us. A couple of API routines called GetProp and SetProp can be used to associate a 'property' value with a specified window. The Windows SDK documentation is rather vague about what a property actually is. It refers to a 16-bit property value (32 bits under 32-bit versions of Windows) as being simply a 'data handle'. You can certainly allocate an arbitrarily large data structure on the local or global heap and store the returned handle as a window property. However, you can equally store any arbitrary value as a window property. It isn't at all necessary that a property should be a handle.

Properties are stored by reference to a string. This string identifies the property and allows us to distinguish between several different properties, all of which may be associated with the same window. Here's the SDK interface to the SetProp routine:

```
BOOL SetProp (HWND hWnd, LPSTR lpString, HANDLE hData);
```

As an example, if you wanted to associate some bitmap handle with a window, you could do so like this:

```
SetProp (hWnd, "Bitmap", hbm);
```

In this case, hWnd refers to the window to associate with the property, "Bitmap" is an identifying string that can be used to retrieve the property and hbm is, of course, the handle to the bitmap. To retrieve this bitmap handle at any time, you can do it like this:

```
hbm = GetProp (hWnd, "Bitmap");
```

Using properties is very simple, but there a couple of points to bear in mind. Firstly, when a window is destroyed, the properties that have been added to that window will not (according to the SDK documentation) be automatically deleted. The documentation states that properties must be explicitly removed using the RemoveProp routine before the window itself is deleted. Although I have some strong doubts about the truth of this (the Windows 3.0 version of the USER library certainly deleted properties before destroying a window and I see no reason why this should not be the same in Windows 3.1), the code developed in this book does explicitly delete properties before the window is destroyed.

The second point concerns the speed of the GetProp routine. In the past, this routine has received something of a bad press and has been described as far too slow to use as the basis for any subclassing technique. This is simply not the case, as we shall see later in the chapter on dialog boxes (Chapter 5). Inevitably, the GetProp routine will be slower than GetWindowWord, since the latter requires only the index retrieval of a word, while the GetProp routine requires string manipulation and calls to the internal Windows Atom manager. Nevertheless, performance is more than acceptable in the vast majority of cases.

Note

It turns out that there's a simple trick you can employ with the GetProp routine that makes it almost as fast to use as GetWindowWord. This trick exploits the internal operation of the GetProp routine. Basically, whenever GetProp receives a character string, it converts this string into an atom value and then searches the window's property list looking for a match on this value. What takes up most of the processing time is the conversion of the character string into a property value. We can exploit this behaviour by passing an atom value directly to the GetProp routine as described later in the chapter. In these circumstances, GetProp is very rapid.

You might be wondering why Microsoft implemented such an odd thing as property lists in the first place. The fact is that most of these API 'oddities' such as the

Atom Manager, properties, and so forth are reflections of the internal Windows implementation. These routines were developed to implement Windows itself and then made a part of the API when they were considered to be more generally useful. For example, when you register a window class, Windows uses the Atom Manager to convert the class name into an atom value. It's the atom value that gets stored in the class record, not the string itself. Another example is the implementation of iconized windows. If you've ever used something like the SDK Spy utility or Borland's WinSight program, you'll know that an iconized window has a separate 'title window' which sits immediately below the displayed icon. This title window is used to display the name of the window when iconized. Microsoft made use of the property list facility to link the title window to the main iconized window.

Subclassing dialog boxes

At this point, you should be feeling fairly comfortable with the essentials of window subclassing. However, the code we've looked at so far isn't too representative of what we want to achieve. As pointed out earlier, you can't really get a feel for this kind of thing if you're only subclassing a window whose window procedure you have access to anyway.

Accordingly, we'll round out this chapter by looking in more detail at some of the issues relating to dialog box subclassing. Along the way, we'll develop the promised generic window subclasser. This will lay a foundation for the later chapter on dialog box effects (Chapter 5).

The small program shown in Figure 3.6 is almost the simplest possible implementation of a program that displays a dialog box. It simply displays a dialog box on the screen and then terminates when the dialog box is closed by the user. There's no need to register a window class or implement a message loop because Windows takes care of all these things internally when you're using a dialog box.

The only out-of-the-ordinary task performed by the dialog procedure is the setting of the input focus to the dialog box edit control when the WM_INITDIALOG message is received. By convention, if you're implementing a dialog box that contains only a single 'user editable' control, then you should set the input focus to that dialog item before the dialog box is displayed.

```
/* SCLASS3.C */

// © 1994 Dave Jewell and Addison-Wesley, ALL RIGHTS RESERVED

#include    <windows.h>

#define    UNAMEBOX         100

//———————————————————————————————
// Name:     UserNameWndProc
// Purpose:  Dialog procedure for user name dialog.
//———————————————————————————————

#pragma argsused
```

Figure 3.6 SCLASS3.C: implementing a simple dialog box.

```
BOOL FAR PASCAL _export UserNameWndProc (HWND hDlg, UINT Msg,
                                         WPARAM wParam, LPARAM lParam)
{
    switch (Msg)
    {
      case WM_INITDIALOG:

      SetFocus (GetDlgItem (hDlg, UNAMEBOX));

      return (FALSE);

      case WM_COMMAND:

      if (wParam == IDOK || wParam == IDCANCEL)
         EndDialog (hDlg, wParam);
      break;

      default:

      return (FALSE);
    }

    return (TRUE);
}

//────────────────────────────────────────────────────────────────────
// Name:    WinMain
// Purpose: Program entry point.
//────────────────────────────────────────────────────────────────────

#pragma argsused

int PASCAL WinMain (HANDLE hInstance, HANDLE hPrevInstance,
                    LPSTR lpCmdLine, int nCmdShow)
{
    FARPROC lpfnDialogProc;

    lpfnDialogProc = MakeProcInstance (UserNameWndProc, hInstance);
    DialogBox (hInstance, "USERNAME", NULL, lpfnDialogProc);
    FreeProcInstance (lpfnDialogProc);
    return (0);
}
```

The program implements a simple dialog box to ask the user for his or her name. You might use a dialog like this as part of the registration procedure of a larger program. The .RC file corresponding to the dialog template I've used is shown in Figure 3.7.

Figure 3.7 SCLASS3.RC: the dialog box template required by the SCLASS3 program.

```
USERNAME DIALOG 37, 30, 165, 72
STYLE DS_MODALFRAME | WS_POPUP | WS_CAPTION | WS_SYSMENU
CAPTION "User Details"
BEGIN
      DEFPUSHBUTTON "&OK", 1, 33, 49, 35, 14, WS_CHILD | WS_VISIBLE |
            WS_TABSTOP
      PUSHBUTTON "&Cancel", 2, 87, 49, 35, 14, WS_CHILD | WS_VISIBLE |
            WS_TABSTOP
      LTEXT "Please enter your name in the box below:", -1, 10, 12, 143, 11,
            WS_CHILD | WS_VISIBLE | WS_GROUP
      EDITTEXT 100, 11, 26, 137, 12, ES_LEFT | WS_CHILD | WS_VISIBLE |
            WS_BORDER | WS_TABSTOP
END
```

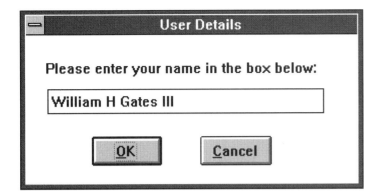

Figure 3.8   Running the SCLASS3 program.

The *Polishing Windows* disk contains the source code and executable file in the form of SCLASS3.C and SCLASS3.EXE. The resource script, SCLASS.RC, is also included. We'll be using this same resource script for the rest of the chapter. Figure 3.8 shows the effect of running the program.

I haven't bothered to add the code that would normally copy the text from the edit box and store it in a global variable somewhere. The absence of this code doesn't affect this discussion of dialog subclassing code.

Any color so long as it's gray

When a customer asked what color schemes were available for the famous Model T motor car, Henry Ford is oft-quoted as giving his anecdotal reply, 'You can have any color so long as it's black.' A little more recently, Windows users might have noticed that dialog boxes in many commercial programs have taken on a uniform gray shade. At the same time, dialog box controls have suddenly developed a fancy 3D appearance. One of the more tasteful examples of such a dialog box is shown in Figure 3.9.

Dialog boxes that look like this are generally perceived as being far more pleasing to the eye than the plain-vanilla dialog boxes that the Windows API gives you.

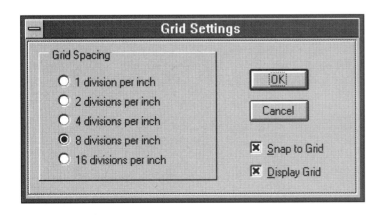

Figure 3.9   Any color so long as it's gray....

In my opinion, this is certainly the case. Borland were very quick to notice that this was an area in which the look and feel of Windows could be improved, and all the Borland development tools and application programs now sport dialog boxes with 3D effects, bitmapped buttons and (naturally) gray backgrounds.

Microsoft were a little slower on the uptake, but they introduced fancy dialog effects into Excel 4.0 in 1992, and more recent offerings such as the Access database program, Windows for Workgroups and so on, all now use dialog boxes very similar to that shown in Figure 3.9.

Incidentally, it's also widely believed that Microsoft will be building a more decorative 3D look into all the dialog box controls that come with Windows 4. This means that you'll be able to get dialog boxes like the one shown above just through using the Windows API dialog routines in the normal way. You might think that this renders my dialog subclassing code redundant, but bear in mind that I give you the source code and Microsoft almost certainly won't! This means that you can create dialog boxes with the look and feel that *you* want without relying on some external DLL. Naturally, you can take the code presented here and package it up as a DLL too, if that's what you want to do.

In addition to the gray background, the dialog box in Figure 3.9 has a decorative border around the edge, and special 3D bitmaps are used to implement the radio buttons and check boxes. The text inside the dialog box is drawn using a relatively fine Sans Serif font that looks much nicer than the standard system font used by Windows 3.1. I'll be providing the code needed to achieve all of these effects in the chapter on dialog boxes (Chapter 5).

For now though, let's continue by considering how to give a gray background effect to your dialog boxes. It turns out that this is quite straightforward. The secret to changing the background color of a dialog box is the WM_ERASEBKGND message. This message is sent to any window whenever Windows wants to erase the background of the window, prior to drawing the window contents. It's important to appreciate that there's nothing magic about dialog boxes; although there's no obvious message loop and window class, they are just like any other window in the sense that they receive a wide range of window messages through the dialog procedure. Most of these messages are ignored in a typical dialog procedure, but by handling some of these messages, such as WM_ERASEBKGND, we can create some interesting effects.

The code below shows how simple it is to give your dialog box window a gray background. This code fragment (which needs to go into the dialog procedure) intercepts the WM_ERASEBKGND message and uses the PatBlt routine to fill the entire window with a uniform gray color. When this message is received, the wParam parameter contains a device context which can be used for drawing into the window. Be sure to restore the device context to whatever state it was in before you made use of it.

```
HDC dc;
RECT r;
HBRUSH hbr;

case WM_ERASEBKGND:

dc = (HDC) wParam;
GetClientRect (hDlg, &r);
hbr = SelectObject (dc, GetStockObject (LTGRAY_BRUSH));
```

```
PatBlt (dc, r.left, r.top, r.right − r.left, r.bottom − r.top, PATCOPY);
SelectObject (dc, hbr);
return (TRUE);
```

If you add this code to the UserNameWndProc routine, you should get the effect shown in Figure 3.10. It's surprising how so little code can make such a dramatic difference to the appearance of the dialog box. One problem you can see immediately is that the static text in the dialog box (the string that begins with the words 'Please enter your name') isn't appearing on a gray background. We'll look into this problem in a little while.

You may have noticed that the above code is 'hard-wired' for light gray dialog boxes. If the user of your application ever wanted to have a green or a mauve dialog box, he wouldn't be able to. OK, I hear you say, that doesn't sound like any great loss, but believe me – you'd be surprised what wacky color schemes some people love!

The solution to this problem is to use the Windows API GetSysColor routine. This function takes an integer parameter and returns one of the built-in 'system colors'. When the Control Panel is used to change the color scheme, the system colors change also. By using the GetSysColor function, we can be sure that our dialog box subclassing code is always in line with whatever color scheme the user has selected.

The table in Figure 3.11 shows the possible arguments to the GetSysColor routine and, in each case, the color information that's returned. Unfortunately, since Windows 3.1 doesn't directly support the idea of variable dialog box colors, there's no entry for dialog box color backgrounds. Under bare-bones Windows 3.1, you can have any dialog box background so long as it's white! You might think that the best candidate to use would be COLOR_WINDOW (color of the window background), but unfortunately it isn't. The majority of people tend to prefer white as their window background color, so we'd be right back where we started with a plain, boring dialog box with a white background.

In fact, the best color to use is COLOR_BTNFACE. This corresponds to the color that Windows uses to draw the face shading on a button. Using this as the dialog box background color produces a good-looking color scheme that won't go to pieces no matter what bizarre color combinations the user wants to use!

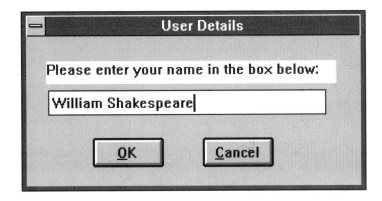

Figure 3.10 Intercepting the WM_ERASEBKGND message.

Figure 3.11 Possible
arguments to the GetSysColor
API routine.

COLOR_ACTIVEBORDER	Color of active window's border.
COLOR_ACTIVECAPTION	Color of active window's title.
COLOR_APPWORKSPACE	Background color of multiple document interface (MDI) application 'main' window.
COLOR_BACKGROUND	Color of desktop.
COLOR_BTNFACE	Color of face shading on push buttons.
COLOR_BTNHIGHLIGHT	Color of selected button in a control.
COLOR_BTNSHADOW	Color of edge shading on push buttons.
COLOR_BTNTEXT	Color of text on push buttons.
COLOR_CAPTIONTEXT	Color of text in title bar, size button, scroll-bar or arrow button.
COLOR_GRAYTEXT	Color of grayed (dimmed) text. This color is zero if the current display driver does not support a solid gray color.
COLOR_HIGHLIGHT	Color of background of selected item in a control.
COLOR_HIGHLIGHTTEXT	Color of text of selected item in a control.
COLOR_INACTIVEBORDER	Color of inactive window border.
COLOR_INACTIVECAPTION	Color of inactive window title.
COLOR_INACTIVECAPTIONTEXT	Color of text in an inactive title.
COLOR_MENU	Color of menu background.
COLOR_MENUTEXT	Color of text in menus.
COLOR_SCROLLBAR	Color of scroll-bar area.
COLOR_WINDOW	Color of window background.
COLOR_WINDOWFRAME	Color of window frame.
COLOR_WINDOWTEXT	Color of text in windows.

Using the GetSysColor routine, we can rewrite our little code fragment to look like this:

```
case WM_ERASEBKGND:

dc = (HDC) wParam;
GetClientRect (hDlg, &r);
hbr = SelectObject (dc, GetControlBrush (COLOR_BTNFACE));
PatBlt (dc, r.left, r.top, r.right − r.left, r.bottom − r.top, PATCOPY);
DeleteObject (SelectObject (dc, hbr));
return (TRUE);
```

This introduces a new routine called GetControlBrush. The code for this routine is trivially simple and is given below. The reason that I've made this into a routine is because we'll be needing it again in several other places, as we shall see. Also notice that because we're now using a custom brush (rather than one of the stock, built-in brushes), it's necessary to delete it after use.

```
//————————————————————————————————————————
// Name:    GetControlBrush
// Purpose: Create a control brush for a given system color.
//————————————————————————————————————————
HBRUSH GetControlBrush (int sysColor)
{
    COLORREF color;

    color = GetSysColor (sysColor);
    return (CreateSolidBrush (color));
}
```

Let's now turn our attention to the fancy border around the dialog. (Remember Figure 3.9.) Once again, adding an attractive border around the dialog box is easy if we put the actual drawing code into the WM_ERASEBKGND handler. Effectively, the border becomes part of the dialog background. Here's what the code looks like:

```
// Now draw the fancy border

InflateRect (&r, −3, −3);
FrameRect (dc, &r, hbr = GetControlBrush (COLOR_BTNHIGHLIGHT));
DeleteObject (hbr);
—r.left;
—r.right;
—r.top;
—r.bottom;
FrameRect (dc, &r, hbr = GetControlBrush (COLOR_BTNSHADOW));
DeleteObject (hbr);
return (TRUE);
```

This code needs to be inserted immediately before the return statement that terminates the WM_ERASEBKGND message processing. You can see that the 3D border effect is achieved simply by drawing two rectangles, one of which is one pixel to the right and down from the other one. The first rectangle is drawn using a highlight color (corresponding to COLOR_BTNHIGHLIGHT) and the second rectangle is drawn with a (normally) dark gray brush that's obtained from the GetControlBrush routine using the COLOR_BTNSHADOW index. This corresponds to the color that Windows normally uses to draw the 3D 'shadow' along the bottom and right edges of a button. This color will almost always be darker than the COLOR_BTNFACE color, unless the user has a very weird color scheme indeed!

By the way, you might have expected me to use a call to the OffsetRect routine to shift the rectangle one pixel in each direction. This is a purely arbitrary choice – I just thought it might be a little faster than calling the OffsetRect routine in the USER library. Speed isn't really an issue here, so by all means use OffsetRect if it helps you sleep easier….

With the changes described so far, the complete program now looks as shown in Figure 3.12. Source and executable can be found on the disk as SCLASS4.C and SCLASS4.EXE respectively.

```
/* SCLASS4.C */

// © 1994 Dave Jewell and Addison-Wesley, ALL RIGHTS RESERVED

#include    <windows.h>

#define    UNAMEBOX    100

//——————————————————————————————————————
// Name:     GetControlBrush
// Purpose:  Create a control brush for a given system color.
//——————————————————————————————————————

HBRUSH GetControlBrush (int sysColor)
{
        COLORREF color;
```

Figure 3.12 SCLASS4.C : Adding the gray background and fancy dialog box border.

```
            color = GetSysColor (sysColor);
            return (CreateSolidBrush (color));
}

//————————————————————————————————————————————————————————————————
// Name:    UserNameWndProc
// Purpose: Dialog procedure for user name dialog.
//————————————————————————————————————————————————————————————————

#pragma argsused

BOOL FAR PASCAL _export UserNameWndProc (HWND hDlg, UINT Msg,
                                    WPARAM wParam, LPARAM lParam)
{
     HDC dc;
     RECT r;
     HBRUSH hbr;

     switch (Msg)
     {

        case WM_ERASEBKGND:

        dc = (HDC) wParam;
        GetClientRect (hDlg, &r);
        hbr = SelectObject (dc, GetControlBrush (COLOR_BTNFACE));
        PatBlt (dc, r.left, r.top, r.right − r.left, r.bottom − r.top, PATCOPY);
        DeleteObject (SelectObject (dc, hbr));

        // Now draw the fancy border

        InflateRect (&r, −3, −3);
        FrameRect (dc, &r, hbr = GetControlBrush (COLOR_BTNHIGHLIGHT));
        DeleteObject (hbr);
        −−r.left;
        −−r.right;
        −−r.top;
        −−r.bottom;
        FrameRect (dc, &r, hbr = GetControlBrush (COLOR_BTNSHADOW));
        DeleteObject (hbr);
        return (TRUE);

        case WM_INITDIALOG:

        SetFocus (GetDlgItem (hDlg, UNAMEBOX));
        return (FALSE);

        case WM_COMMAND:

        if (wParam == IDOK || wParam == IDCANCEL)
            EndDialog (hDlg, wParam);
        break;

        default:

        return (FALSE);
     }

     return (TRUE);
}

//————————————————————————————————————————————————————————————————
// Name:    WinMain
// Purpose: Program entry point.
//————————————————————————————————————————————————————————————————

#pragma argsused
```

```
int PASCAL WinMain (HANDLE hInstance, HANDLE hPrevInstance,
                    LPSTR lpCmdLine, int nCmdShow)
{
    FARPROC lpfnDialogProc;

    lpfnDialogProc = MakeProcInstance (UserNameWndProc, hInstance);
    DialogBox (hInstance, "USERNAME", NULL, lpfnDialogProc);
    FreeProcInstance (lpfnDialogProc);
    return (0);
}
```

Figure 3.13 shows what the dialog looks like now. As you can see, the new border looks good. The dialog is now almost good enough to eat, but we still have a problem with the white background color used by the static text item.

You can fix this last problem by adding code to intercept the WM_CTLCOLOR message. This is a special message that's sent by Windows to request the background brush that should be used to draw controls. Here's how it works:

```
static HBRUSH hbrBack = NULL;

    switch (Msg)
    {
      case WM_CTLCOLOR:

        SetBkColor ((HDC) wParam, GetSysColor (COLOR_BTNFACE));
        if (hbrBack == NULL) hbrBack = GetControlBrush (COLOR_BTNFACE);
        return (hbrBack);

      case WM_DESTROY:

        if (hbrBack != NULL)
        {
          DeleteObject (hbrBack);
          hbrBack = NULL;
        }
        return (FALSE);
```

Figure 3.13   The dialog box with its new-look border.

This code fragment introduces a new static variable into the window procedure. This variable, hbrBack, is a handle to a brush that is used to draw the background color of the various controls. When the WM_CTLCOLOR message is processed for the first time, this brush is created, and it's destroyed when the WM_DESTROY message is processed when the dialog box is closed down. Of course, you could simplify this code by using a stock brush. For example, the following code fragment would simplify things and eliminate the need for any special processing of the WM_DESTROY message.

```
case WM_CTLCOLOR:

    SetBkColor ((HDC) wParam, GetSysColor (COLOR_BTNFACE));
    return GetStockObject (LTGRAY_BRUSH);
```

Because we're using a stock brush, there's now no need to maintain a static variable or destroy the brush when the dialog box is closed. The disadvantage of this technique, however, should be pretty obvious. By limiting ourselves to stock brushes, we're unable to make use of the GetSysColor API routine which allows us to fit in with the user-selected color scheme. For this reason, we'll stick with the former technique.

If you make these changes to the code and then rerun the program, you'll see that the static text item now has a background color that blends in with the rest of the dialog. Not only that, but the edit text item has now also got a matching background color. This may or may not be what you want, and it's a matter of personal taste. A lot of people prefer their edit boxes to retain a white background because this provides better contrast. It also helps distinguish edit boxes from static text items.

Fortunately, it's easy to assign different background colors to different control types. When the WM_CTLCOLOR message is called, the high word of the lParam field contains an identifier that specifies the type of control that's requesting information. In the case of edit boxes, the high word of lParam is set to the value CTLCOLOR_EDIT. By explicitly checking for this value, we can ensure that the edit box controls in the dialog get a white background. This is shown below:

```
case WM_CTLCOLOR:

    if (HIWORD (lParam) == CTLCOLOR_EDIT)
    {
      SetBkColor ((HDC) wParam, 0xFFFFFF);
      return GetStockObject (WHITE_BRUSH);
    }
    else
    {
      SetBkColor ((HDC) wParam, GetSysColor (COLOR_BTNFACE));
      if (hbrBack == NULL) hbrBack = GetControlBrush (COLOR_BTNFACE);
      return (hbrBack);
    }
```

Using this approach, it's perfectly possible to assign a different background color to each different control type. However, I wouldn't recommend that you pursue this line of thought – you don't really want to give your users eyestrain each time they use one of your multi-colored dialog boxes!

You may notice that the edit box is still lacking a good 3D effect and all the controls in the dialog box are still using the standard system font. We'll be addressing these issues in more detail in the chapter devoted to dialog box effects (Chapter 5).

Generic subclassing

OK, so where does the subclassing come in? So far, we've just been adding code to the UserNameWndProc routine, but we haven't been subclassing the dialog box. By automatically subclassing a dialog procedure, we ought to be able to take all the code discussed above, and effectively add it to every dialog procedure in our Windows application, just as if that code were already there.

This is a great advantage; imagine that you've written a large, complex application with a couple of dozen different dialog boxes that are required for the program's operation. Now that you know how to create dialog boxes with fancy borders, gray backgrounds and so forth, do you really want to go through your entire application, adding all this code to each of your dialog procedures? Of course not. The good news is that you don't have to. At the end of the day, you'll only need to add one routine call to the WM_INITDIALOG handler of each of your dialog boxes. Simple.

Let's call this new routine SubClassDialog. It takes only one parameter, the handle of the dialog window. Suppose, for example, that you've got an existing dialog procedure that contains a WM_INITDIALOG entry something like this:

```
case WM_INITDIALOG:

CheckDlgButton (hDlg, IDButton1, bRegistered);
CheckDlgButton (hDlg, IDButton2, bSaveOnly);
...
```

This is a very typical state of affairs; the WM_INITDIALOG message is generally used to initialize the state of the various controls in a dialog, based upon the values of one or more global variables. All we need do in order to get our fancy dialog effects is to call the SubClassDialog routine like this:

```
case WM_INITDIALOG:

SubClassDialog (hDlg);
CheckDlgButton (hDlg, IDButton1, bRegistered);
CheckDlgButton (hDlg, IDButton2, bSaveOnly);
...
```

So how exactly does this new SubClassDialog routine work? The answer is that it internally subclasses the existing dialog procedure by using the SetWindowLong routine. Once done, everything happens as before. Let's look first at HookWindow, one of the functions called by the SubClassDialog routine.

```
//------------------------------------------------------------
// Name:     HookWindow
// Purpose:  Hook the window with our new window procedure.
//------------------------------------------------------------
void PASCAL HookWindow (HWND Wnd, FARPROC proc)
{
      LONG oldProc;

      // Check if we're already hooked...

      if (GetProp (Wnd, PROPLO) == 0 && GetProp (Wnd, PROPHI) == 0)
      {
        // Stash the old proc
```

```
oldProc = GetWindowLong (Wnd, GWL_WNDPROC);
SetProp (Wnd, PROPLO, LOWORD (oldProc));
SetProp (Wnd, PROPHI, HIWORD (oldProc));

// And set the new one...

SetWindowLong (Wnd, GWL_WNDPROC, (LONG) proc);
   }
}
```

This is the first routine in our generic window subclasser. It can be used to sub-class any window and isn't specific to dialog boxes. To subclass a window, you pass it the handle of the window and the address of the intended new window procedure.

A big issue when subclassing windows is where do you store the address of the old window or class procedure? The obvious answer is to use a global variable, but what happens if you're subclassing multiple windows at the same time? This situation can arise very easily when working with dialogs. You might have a situation where one dialog box leads to another dialog box, and so forth. There's also the issue of what to do if you want to put code like this into a DLL. The simplest thing is to associate the old window procedure address with the window procedure itself. Earlier on in this chapter we discussed property lists, and this is where they really begin to come into their own. Unfortunately, a property entry can only hold a single 16-bit word. Therefore, in order to store the full 32-bit procedure address, we need to use two property entries. That's why the HookWindow routine makes use of two different properties. These properties are referenced via the constants PROPLO and PROPHI. In my code, I've set up these strings constants as follows:

```
#define        PROPLO    "SCLO"
#define        PROPHI    "SCHI"
```

However, you could equally well use any other convenient pair of string constants, such as "LO" and "HI". Please don't be tempted to use property names such as "LAUREL" and "HARDY" – you'll soon forget which is the low word and which is the high word. Well, maybe not in this case...!

Notice that the HookWindow also checks to see whether or not the specified window has already been subclassed. This is an example of 'defensive programming'. Under normal circumstances, you wouldn't call this routine twice for the same window: by checking for the existence of the PROPLO and PROPHI entries, any attempt to subclass the same routine more than once is ignored.

```
//─────────────────────────────────────────────────────────────
// Name:    UnHookWindow
// Purpose: Unhook a hooked window.
//─────────────────────────────────────────────────────────────

void PASCAL UnHookWindow (HWND Wnd)
{
    WORD lo, hi;

    lo = GetProp (Wnd, PROPLO);
    hi = GetProp (Wnd, PROPHI);

    // Check that this is a hooked window

    if (lo || hi)
    {
        RemoveProp (Wnd, PROPLO);
```

```
            RemoveProp (Wnd, PROPHI);
            SetWindowLong (Wnd, GWL_WNDPROC, MAKELONG (lo, hi));
        }
}
```

Now let's examine the counterpart of the HookWindow code. Unsurprisingly, this is called UnHookWindow. Its job is to reverse the effect of the call to HookWindow. Again, this routine adopts a fairly cautious approach to life by checking that the address returned from the property entries is not NULL. (Perhaps a more complete check would be to use the IsBadCodePtr routine that was introduced with Windows 3.1.) Having validated the old window procedure address and removed the property entries, the UnHookWindow routine then calls SetWindowLong to restore the *status quo*.

The final routine that completes the generic subclassing code is called CallOldProc. This routine is called from the subclassing window procedure and is responsible for calling the previous window procedure where appropriate. The code for the CallOldProc routine is shown below:

```
//————————————————————————————————————————————————
// Name:    CallOldProc
// Purpose: Call the old window procedure and return result.
//          For convenience, this routine takes care of unhooking
//          a window in response to a WM_DESTROY message.
//————————————————————————————————————————————————

LONG PASCAL CallOldProc (HWND Wnd, UINT Msg, WPARAM wParam, LPARAM lParam)
{
    WORD lo, hi;

    lo = GetProp (Wnd, PROPLO);
    hi = GetProp (Wnd, PROPHI);

    // Check that this is a hooked window

    if (lo || hi)
    {
        // If it's a WM_DESTROY message, then unhook now...

        if (Msg == WM_DESTROY) UnHookWindow (Wnd);

        return CallWindowProc ((FARPROC) MAKELONG (lo, hi),
                        Wnd, Msg, wParam, lParam);
    }

    return DefWindowProc (Wnd, Msg, wParam, lParam);
}
```

Based on what we've discussed, the code for this routine is actually very straightforward. CallOldProc checks to determine whether or not the window is subclassed. If it isn't, the standard DefWindowProc routine is called in the usual way. On the other hand, if the window is subclassed, the MAKELONG macro is used to build up the address of the old window procedure. This is then passed to the CallWindowProc routine. Just to make things a little easier for the higher-level routines, the CallOldProc code explicitly checks for the WM_DESTROY message. If it's seen, the UnHookWindow procedure is automatically called to restore the old window procedure.

There is one fairly subtle point here: after we receive the WM_DESTROY message and unhook the window, it's still very important to exit via a call to the CallWindowProc routine. This ensures that the original window procedure gets to see the WM_DESTROY message. Upon seeing this message, an application might call the PostQuitMessage routine. If this didn't happen, then the window would certainly be destroyed, but the application would go into a 'zombie' state whereby it continued to execute its message loop, but without any messages to process! This is why it's so important that the WM_DESTROY message is passed on.

So what does the new subclassing routine look like? This is shown below in its entirety. You can see that the new subclassing routine takes full responsibility for the WM_CTLCOLOR and WM_ERASEBKGND messages. These messages are no longer handled by the 'regular' dialog procedure, which shouldn't really change whether the dialog box is subclassed or not.

If you look closely at the DlgSubClass code, you'll see that the WM_ERASE-BKGND and WM_CTLCOLOR messages completely replace any default processing. In other words, they return from the DlgSubClass routine. On the other hand, the WM_DESTROY message (which is only intercepted in order for us to destroy the static background brush) drops through into the CallOldProc routine. This is important. The CallOldProc routine must get to see the WM_DESTROY message in order for it to be able to unhook the window as described earlier.

```
//—————————————————————————————————————————————
// Name:    DlgSubClass
// Purpose: This is the subclasser for the dialog box itself.
//          Main embellishments are "gray" background for dialog and
//          any controls. Also draws a fancy border around the box.
//—————————————————————————————————————————————
LONG FAR PASCAL _export DlgSubClass (HWND hDlg, UINT Msg,
                                     WPARAM wParam, LPARAM lParam)
{
    HDC dc;
    RECT r;
    HBRUSH hbr;
    static HBRUSH hbrBack = NULL;

    switch (Msg)
    {
      case WM_CTLCOLOR:

        if (HIWORD (lParam) == CTLCOLOR_EDIT)
        {
        SetBkColor ((HDC) wParam, 0xFFFFFF);
        return GetStockObject (WHITE_BRUSH);
        }
        else
        {
          SetBkColor ((HDC) wParam, GetSysColor (COLOR_BTNFACE));
          if (hbrBack == NULL) hbrBack = GetControlBrush (COLOR_BTNFACE);
          return (hbrBack);
        }

      case WM_ERASEBKGND:

        dc = (HDC) wParam;
        GetClientRect (hDlg, &r);
        hbr = SelectObject (dc, GetControlBrush (COLOR_BTNFACE));
        PatBlt (dc, r.left, r.top, r.right − r.left, r.bottom − r.top, PATCOPY);
        DeleteObject (SelectObject (dc, hbr));

        // Now draw the fancy border

        InflateRect (&r, −3, −3);
        FrameRect (dc, &r, hbr = GetControlBrush (COLOR_BTNHIGHLIGHT));
        DeleteObject (hbr);
```

```
            —r.left;
            —r.right;
            —r.top;
            —r.bottom;
            FrameRect (dc, &r, hbr = GetControlBrush (COLOR_BTNSHADOW));
            DeleteObject (hbr);
            return (TRUE);

        case WM_DESTROY:

            if (hbrBack != NULL)
            {
                DeleteObject (hbrBack);
                hbrBack = NULL;
            }
    }

    return CallOldProc (hDlg, Msg, wParam, lParam);
}
```

The final piece in the jigsaw is the SubClassDialog code. This must be called from the initial dialog box procedure. The SubClassDialog routine doesn't really have to do much more than call the HookWindow routine, passing it the dialog window handle and the address of the DlgSubClass routine. There is, however, one little wrinkle. At the time of writing, Windows 4.0 is an unannounced product, but it is widely expected that it will contain some (but hopefully not all!) of the visual enhancements that are presented in this book. In order to guard against the possibility of a clash between Windows 4 and my dialog subclassing code, I've written the SubClassDialog routine to bow out gracefully if Windows 4 (or later) is detected.

Here's what the code looks like:

```
//————————————————————————————————————————
// Name:      SubClassDialog
// Purpose:   This routine does the actual job of subclassing a
//            dialog. It should be called from WM_INITDIALOG.
//————————————————————————————————————————

void PASCAL SubClassDialog (HWND hDlg)
{
        if (LOBYTE (LOWORD (GetVersion())) < 4)
        HookWindow (hDlg, (FARPROC) DlgSubClass);
}
```

As you can see, if this routine is executed on a version of Windows greater than or equal to 4, it will have no effect whatsoever. Whether or not this check is desirable remains to be seen – it's impossible to say until the new version of Windows is available.

Whoops!

There is one serious limitation with the generic subclassing routines as they stand at the moment. The HookWindow code has been written in such a way as to prevent the same window from being subclassed more than once. In practice, there will often be times where it's essential to subclass the same window more than once. From where you're sitting, this might seem an odd thing to say. However, in later chapters of this book, I'll be using the generic subclassing routines to perform a certain amount of behind-the-scenes work. For example, the status bar code in Chapter 4 actually sub-classes its parent window. By doing so, any WM_SIZE messages that are received by the main application window are automatically handled by the status bar, causing its size to change in step with the parent window. This technique allows unnecessary implementation detail to be hidden away and presents a simpler, more reusable interface to the main application code.

Problems arise with this technique, however. What if we want our application to have both a status bar and a toolbar – hardly an unlikely proposition! This means that the application window must be subclassed twice, which we can't do with the existing HookWindows code. Clearly, this calls for some serious thought.

In addition to this problem, we'd also like to be able to use global atom names whenever a property is accessed. As discussed earlier in the chapter, this can drasti-cally speed up property access as it means that string manipulation does not have to take place each time a property list is accessed. Combining these two approaches allows us to come up with a different strategy as shown below:

```
//——————————————————————————————————————————————
// Name:      RegisterHookClient
// Purpose:  Register a client name and get back the atom-pair.
//——————————————————————————————————————————————

static LONG PASCAL RegisterHookClient (LPCSTR ClientName)
{
        int len;
        LPCSTR p;
        ATOM lo, hi;
        char szBuff [41];

        // Make a reversed copy of the ClientName string
        len = lstrlen (ClientName);
        if (len <= 0 || len >= sizeof (szBuff)) return (0);
        p = ClientName;
        szBuff [len] = '\0';
        while (len—) szBuff [len] = *p++;

        // Now get the atom values

        hi = GlobalAddAtom (ClientName);
        lo = GlobalAddAtom (szBuff);
        return MAKELONG (lo, hi);
}
```

In the previous version of the code, we used two hard-wired strings called PROPLO and PROPHI to identify the properties attached to the subclassed window. Because we want to be able to subclass the same window more than once, we can't use just these two hard-wired strings. It's the job of the RegisterHookClient routine to generate two unique atom values that will be used in place of the old PROPLO and PROPHI strings. It does this by deriving the atoms from a supplied client name. A client name uniquely identifies a set of routines that require the services of the generic subclassing code. In this way, different client modules can all subclass the same window, provided that they each have a unique client name.

The code calls the GlobalAddAtom routine with the supplied client name to obtain one of the needed atom values. The other atom value is obtained by reversing the string and calling GlobalAddAtom again on the reversed string. This guarantees that the two atom values we end up with will be both unique and different, provided, of course, that the client names are unique. In the example dialog subclassing code developed here, we'll use the string "DIALOGSHOOK" as the client name. The RegisterHookClient routine returns a long integer made up of the two global atom numbers. This long integer will be returned as a 'hook key'. It's effectively a magic cookie that is passed back to the generic subclassing code, allowing the needed property words to be accessed.

Note
OK, I admit that this approach is not 100% foolproof. My daughter's name is Hannah, which happens to be a palindrome. In other words, it reads the same backwards as it does forwards! If you happened to pass a palindromic ClientName to the RegisterHookClient name, you'd get two identical atom values and things would go badly wrong. If this bothers you, then I'd suggest that you concatenate something (say, a couple of underscore characters) onto one of the strings to ensure uniqueness.

```
#define      PROPLO        (MAKEINTATOM(LOWORD(hookkey)))
#define      PROPHI        (MAKEINTATOM(HIWORD(hookkey)))
```

Replacing PROPLO and PROPHI with a couple of macros allows us to 'crack open' a hook key into its component parts. Using these macros, PROPLO and PROPHI can still be used with the GetProp and SetProp API routines as before. With these changes, the HookWindow routine now looks as below. It's actually the HookWindow code that is responsible for calling the RegisterHookClient routine, and it passes back the hook key as a function result. If the window in question has already been subclassed by the specified module, a hook key of zero is returned, indicating an error. The client name is passed to the HookWindow procedure as an additional parameter.

```
//─────────────────────────────────────────────────────────────
// Name:     HookWindow
// Purpose:  Hook the window with our new window procedure.
//─────────────────────────────────────────────────────────────
LONG PASCAL HookWindow (HWND Wnd, FARPROC proc, LPCSTR ClientName)
{
      LONG oldProc;
      LONG hookkey;

      hookkey = RegisterHookClient (ClientName);

      // Check if we're already hooked...

      if (GetProp (Wnd, PROPLO) == 0 && GetProp (Wnd, PROPHI) == 0)
      {
        // Stash the old proc

        oldProc = GetWindowLong (Wnd, GWL_WNDPROC);
        SetProp (Wnd, PROPLO, LOWORD (oldProc));
        SetProp (Wnd, PROPHI, HIWORD (oldProc));

        // And set the new one...

        SetWindowLong (Wnd, GWL_WNDPROC, (LONG) proc);
        return hookkey;
      }

      UnRegisterHookClient (hookkey);
      return (0);
}
```

If the HookWindow routine determines that the window in question has already been subclassed by the specified client, it calls the UnRegisterHookClient code to destroy the hook key that's just been created. The code for this is trivial, and simply involves a couple of calls to the GlobalDeleteAtom routine:

```
//————————————————————————————————————————
// Name:    UnRegisterHookClient
// Purpose: Unregister a client hook atom-pair.
//————————————————————————————————————————
static void PASCAL UnRegisterHookClient (LONG hookKey)
{
    GlobalDeleteAtom (LOWORD (hookKey));
    GlobalDeleteAtom (HIWORD (hookKey));
}
```

With all of this in mind, the new UnHookWindow code is quite straightforward. It takes a hook key as a parameter and uses this to determine if the window is subclassed. As a convenience, the new UnHookWindow routine calls the UnRegisterHookClient code to delete the global atoms associated with the hook key. In this way, neither the RegisterHookClient nor the UnRegisterHookClient routine needs to be made part of the interface, and the fact that a hook key is comprised of two global atoms is completely transparent to the application code – it's simply a magic cookie.

```
//————————————————————————————————————————
// Name:    UnHookWindow
// Purpose: Unhook a hooked window....
//————————————————————————————————————————
void PASCAL UnHookWindow (HWND Wnd, LONG hookkey)
{
    WORD lo, hi;

    lo = GetProp (Wnd, PROPLO);
    hi = GetProp (Wnd, PROPHI);

    // Check that this is a hooked window

    if (lo || hi)
    {
      RemoveProp (Wnd, PROPLO);
      RemoveProp (Wnd, PROPHI);
      UnRegisterHookClient (hookkey);
      SetWindowLong (Wnd, GWL_WNDPROC, MAKELONG (lo, hi));
    }
}
```

The CallOldProc routine looks almost identical to the previous version, except that it also takes a hook key parameter and must pass this on to the UnHookWindow code when a WM_DESTROY message is received. The PROPLO and PROPHI macros take care of any other changes.

```
//————————————————————————————————————————
// Name:    CallOldProc
// Purpose: Call the old window procedure and return result.
//          For convenience, this routine takes care of unhooking
//          a window in response to a WM_DESTROY message.
//————————————————————————————————————————
LONG PASCAL CallOldProc (HWND Wnd, UINT Msg, WPARAM wParam,
                 LPARAM lParam, LONG hookkey)
{
```

```
        WORD lo, hi;

        lo = GetProp (Wnd, PROPLO);
        hi = GetProp (Wnd, PROPHI);

        // Check that this is a hooked window

        if (lo || hi)
        {
            // If it's a WM_DESTROY message, then unhook now…

            if (Msg == WM_DESTROY) UnHookWindow (Wnd, hookkey);

            return CallWindowProc ((FARPROC) MAKELONG (lo, hi),
                                Wnd, Msg, wParam, lParam);

        }

        return DefWindowProc (Wnd, Msg, wParam, lParam);
}
```

Putting it all together

The full source code of our new, linkable dialog subclassing module is shown in
Figure 3.14. This file can be found on the disk as SCLASLIB.C. To incorporate 3D
effects into your application program, all you need do is link this module into your
code and call the SubClassDialog routine at the start of your WM_INITDIALOG
processing code. This being the case, you could optionally make the other routines
in the code module static. This means that only the SubClassDialog routine would
be accessible to clients of the code module.

I chose not to do this because of course the generic subclassing mechanism is
very useful in its own right. It needs to be stressed that the HookWindow,
UnHookWindow and CallOldProc routines really do constitute a generic window subclassing mechanism. It just so happens that we've used them here to subclass dialog
windows, but you can use them just as easily to subclass any other type of window.
For this reason, these routines have been placed in the module's interface so that they
can be used for other purposes. The same argument applies to the GetControlBrush
routine.

Note
With regard to the code under discussion, you might be tempted to apply the static
specifier to the DlgSubClass routine because this function is only ever referenced
from inside the dialog subclasser code module. Don't do it! If you're using Borland
C/C++ (I used version 3.1 of the development system to create all the code in this
book), be very careful NEVER to use the static keyword in conjunction with the
_export specifier. I inadvertently did this while developing the code for Chapter 2 of
Polishing Windows. This resulted in serious problems. If you combine the static and
_export specifiers, the static specifier takes precedence: I eventually tracked down
my problems to the fact that the DS register was not being properly set up on entry
to the exported routine – it was still pointing at the data segment of some other
Windows program! Ideally, the Borland compiler should complain if you combine
these two incompatible function specifiers but it doesn't, so be warned and be careful!

Figure 3.14 SCLASLIB.C: the completed dialog subclassing code.

```
/* SCLASLIB.C */

// © 1994 Dave Jewell and Addison-Wesley, ALL RIGHTS RESERVED

#include    <windows.h>
#include    "sclaslib.h"

#define    PROPLO    (MAKEINTATOM(LOWORD(hookkey)))
#define    PROPHI    (MAKEINTATOM(HIWORD(hookkey)))

static LONG MyHookKey = 0;

//──────────────────────────────────────────────
// Name:     RegisterHookClient
// Purpose:  Register a client name and get back the atom-pair.
//──────────────────────────────────────────────

static LONG PASCAL RegisterHookClient (LPCSTR ClientName)
{
      int len;
      LPCSTR p;
      ATOM lo, hi;
      char szBuff [41];

      // Make a reversed copy of the ClientName string

      len = lstrlen (ClientName);
      if (len <= 0 || len >= sizeof (szBuff)) return (0);
      p = ClientName;
      szBuff [len] = '\0';
      while (len—) szBuff [len] = *p++;

      // Now get the atom values

      hi = GlobalAddAtom (ClientName);
      lo = GlobalAddAtom (szBuff);
      return MAKELONG (lo, hi);
}

//──────────────────────────────────────────────
// Name:     UnRegisterHookClient
// Purpose:  Unregister a client hook atom-pair.
//──────────────────────────────────────────────

static void PASCAL UnRegisterHookClient (LONG hookKey)
{
      GlobalDeleteAtom (LOWORD (hookKey));
      GlobalDeleteAtom (HIWORD (hookKey));
}

//──────────────────────────────────────────────
// Name:     HookWindow
// Purpose:  Hook the window with our new window procedure.
//──────────────────────────────────────────────

LONG PASCAL HookWindow (HWND Wnd, FARPROC proc, LPCSTR ClientName)
{
      LONG oldProc;
      LONG hookkey;

      hookkey = RegisterHookClient (ClientName);

      // Check if we're already hooked...

      if (GetProp (Wnd, PROPLO) == 0 && GetProp (Wnd, PROPHI) == 0)
      {
            // Stash the old proc
            oldProc = GetWindowLong (Wnd, GWL_WNDPROC);
            SetProp (Wnd, PROPLO, LOWORD (oldProc));
            SetProp (Wnd, PROPHI, HIWORD (oldProc));
```

```
            // And set the new one...

            SetWindowLong (Wnd, GWL_WNDPROC, (LONG) proc);
            return hookkey;
        }

        UnRegisterHookClient (hookkey);
        return (0);
    }

//───────────────────────────────────────────────
// Name:    UnHookWindow
// Purpose: Unhook a hooked window.
//───────────────────────────────────────────────

void PASCAL UnHookWindow (HWND Wnd, LONG hookkey)
{
        WORD lo, hi;

        lo = GetProp (Wnd, PROPLO);
        hi = GetProp (Wnd, PROPHI);

        // Check that this is a hooked window

        if (lo || hi)
        {
            RemoveProp (Wnd, PROPLO);
            RemoveProp (Wnd, PROPHI);
            UnRegisterHookClient (hookkey);
            SetWindowLong (Wnd, GWL_WNDPROC, MAKELONG (lo, hi));
        }
}

//───────────────────────────────────────────────
// Name:    CallOldProc
// Purpose: Call the old window procedure and return result.
//          For convenience, this routine takes care of unhooking
//          a window in response to a WM_DESTROY message.
//───────────────────────────────────────────────

LONG PASCAL CallOldProc (HWND Wnd, UINT Msg, WPARAM wParam,
                            LPARAM lParam, LONG hookkey)
{
        WORD lo, hi;

        lo = GetProp (Wnd, PROPLO);
        hi = GetProp (Wnd, PROPHI);

        // Check that this is a hooked window

        if (lo || hi)
        {
            // If it's a WM_DESTROY message, then unhook now...

            if (Msg == WM_DESTROY) UnHookWindow (Wnd, hookkey);

            return CallWindowProc ((FARPROC) MAKELONG (lo, hi),
                            Wnd, Msg, wParam, lParam);

        }

        return DefWindowProc (Wnd, Msg, wParam, lParam);
}

//───────────────────────────────────────────────
// Name:    GetControlBrush
// Purpose: Create a control brush for a given system color.
//───────────────────────────────────────────────

HBRUSH PASCAL GetControlBrush (int sysColor)
```

```
{
     COLORREF color;

     color = GetSysColor (sysColor);
     return (CreateSolidBrush (color));
}
//─────────────────────────────────────────────────────
// Name:    DlgSubClass
// Purpose: This is the subclasser for the dialog box itself.
//          Main embellishments are "gray" background for dialog and
//          any controls. Also draws a fancy border around the box.
//─────────────────────────────────────────────────────

LONG FAR PASCAL _export DlgSubClass (HWND hDlg, UINT Msg,
                                     WPARAM wParam, LPARAM lParam)
{
     HDC dc;
     RECT r;
     HBRUSH hbr;
     static HBRUSH hbrBack = NULL;

     switch (Msg)
     {
       case WM_CTLCOLOR:

         if (HIWORD (lParam) == CTLCOLOR_EDIT)
         {
            SetBkColor ((HDC) wParam, 0xFFFFFF);
            return GetStockObject (WHITE_BRUSH);
         }
         else
         {
            SetBkColor ((HDC) wParam, GetSysColor (COLOR_BTNFACE));
            if (hbrBack == NULL) hbrBack = GetControlBrush (COLOR_BTNFACE);
            return (hbrBack);
         }

       case WM_ERASEBKGND:

         dc = (HDC) wParam;
         GetClientRect (hDlg, &r);
         hbr = SelectObject (dc, GetControlBrush (COLOR_BTNFACE));
         PatBlt (dc, r.left, r.top, r.right − r.left, r.bottom − r.top, PATCOPY);
         DeleteObject (SelectObject (dc, hbr));

         // Now draw the fancy border

         InflateRect (&r, −3, −3);
         FrameRect (dc, &r, hbr = GetControlBrush (COLOR_BTNHIGHLIGHT));
         DeleteObject (hbr);
         —r.left;
         —r.right;
         —r.top;
         —r.bottom;
         FrameRect (dc, &r, hbr = GetControlBrush (COLOR_BTNSHADOW));
         DeleteObject (hbr);
         return (TRUE);

       case WM_DESTROY:

         if (hbrBack != NULL)
         {
            DeleteObject (hbrBack);
            hbrBack = NULL;
         }
     }

     return CallOldProc (hDlg, Msg, wParam, lParam, MyHookKey);
```

```
        }
        //─────────────────────────────────────────────
        // Name:    SubClassDialog
        // Purpose: This routine does the actual job of subclassing a
        //          dialog. It should be called from WM_INITDIALOG.
        //─────────────────────────────────────────────

        void PASCAL SubClassDialog (HWND hDlg)
        {
            if (LOBYTE (LOWORD (GetVersion()))) < 4)
                MyHookKey = HookWindow (hDlg, (FARPROC) DlgSubClass, "DIALOGSHOOK");
        }
```

Figure 3.15 shows the accompanying header file, SCLASLIB.H. This file is included by both the library code and the application itself. As before, the header file has been constructed for compatibility with C++ applications.

```
        /* SCLASLIB.H */

        // © 1994 Dave Jewell and Addison-Wesley, ALL RIGHTS RESERVED

        #ifndef _INC_SCLASS

        #define _INC_SCLASS /* #defined if sclaslib.h has been included */

        #ifdef __cplusplus
        extern "C" {
        #endif

        void PASCAL      SubClassDialog (HWND hDlg);
        LONG PASCAL      HookWindow (HWND Wnd, FARPROC proc, LPCSTR ClientName);
        void PASCAL      UnHookWindow (HWND Wnd, LONG hookkey);
        LONG PASCAL      CallOldProc (HWND Wnd, UINT Msg, WPARAM wParam,
                                      LPARAM lParam, LONG hookkey);
        HBRUSH PASCAL GetControlBrush (int sysColor);

        #ifdef __cplusplus
        }
        #endif

        #endif
```

Figure 3.15 SCLASLIB.H: the header file for dialog and window subclassing.

Finally, Figure 3.16 shows the application program, SCLASS5.C. Again, this can be found on the disk, together with the compiled .EXE file, SCLASS5.EXE. You'll notice that the program has now shrunk back down to almost the same size that it had in Figure 3.6. In fact, the application code is now exactly the same as it was before, with the exception of the call to SubClassDialog and the #include statement for the header file. That's the power of window subclassing for you.

```
/* SCLASS5.C */

// © 1994 Dave Jewell and Addison-Wesley, ALL RIGHTS RESERVED

#include    <windows.h>
#include    "sclaslib.h"

#define      UNAMEBOX            100

//------------------------------------------------------------------------
// Name:      UserNameWndProc
// Purpose:  Dialog procedure for user name dialog.
//------------------------------------------------------------------------

#pragma argsused

BOOL FAR PASCAL _export UserNameWndProc (HWND hDlg, UINT Msg,
                                      WPARAM wParam, LPARAM lParam)
{
     switch (Msg)
     {
       case WM_INITDIALOG:

       SubClassDialog (hDlg);
       SetFocus (GetDlgItem (hDlg, UNAMEBOX));
       return (FALSE);

         case WM_COMMAND:

         if (wParam == IDOK || wParam == IDCANCEL)
            EndDialog (hDlg, wParam);
         break;

         default:

         return (FALSE);
       }

       return (TRUE);
}

//------------------------------------------------------------------------
// Name:     WinMain
// Purpose:  Program entry point.
//------------------------------------------------------------------------

#pragma argsused

int PASCAL WinMain (HANDLE hInstance, HANDLE hPrevInstance,
                        LPSTR lpCmdLine, int nCmdShow)
{
       FARPROC lpfnDialogProc;

       lpfnDialogProc = MakeProcInstance (UserNameWndProc, hInstance);
       DialogBox (hInstance, "USERNAME", NULL, lpfnDialogProc);
       FreeProcInstance (lpfnDialogProc);
       return (0);
}
```

Figure 3.17 shows the dialog box as it now appears. The edit box sports a white background, while everything else is matched to the current Windows color scheme. Henry Ford would have been proud....

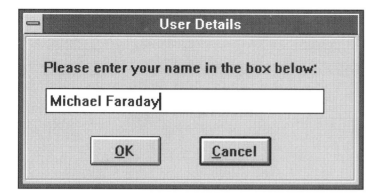

Figure 3.17   The final state
of the user name dialog box.

Conclusions

In this chapter, I've tried to demonstrate some of the power of window subclassing. In particular, we've looked at a very simple set of routines that can be used to subclass any window easily, including dialog windows. Finally, we built a linkable code module that can be used to add 3D dialog effects to your application through the inclusion of only one routine call.

In Chapter 5 on dialog boxes, we'll use the code developed here as a basis for making dialogs look even better. We'll use the same subclassing routines to subclass push buttons, check boxes, edit boxes and so forth, so as to get dialog boxes that look just as good as the one shown in Figure 3.9. What might surprise you is the fact that all this can be accomplished through just a single routine call. We won't need to add anything else to the programming interface – everything happens behind the scenes in the call to DialogSubClass.

There are other big advantages to using these techniques. Some third-party programming tools will give you pretty-looking dialogs, but at a price. You have to use a dialog box that has a certain special class name, and if you want a gray background, you have to create a special 'canvas-style' custom control which fills the whole of the dialog. Similarly, you have to use non-standard push buttons and check boxes to get all the effects you want, and so on. My response to all this is, why bother? By subclassing *standard* dialog boxes on the fly, you can end up with a dialog box that looks just as good as the others, but hasn't required any special contortions with resource editors, third-party DLLs or any of that stuff.

Of course, subclassing is good for far more than just fancy dialog boxes. In the next chapter, we'll develop a professional-looking status bar, and in Chapter 6 we'll build a toolbar for your applications. Both of these code modules will make use of the generic subclasser developed here, and you'll see just why being able to subclass the same window more than once is so useful.

Note
Pascal programmers can find a Pascal listing of the generic subclassing code presented here in Appendix 3. Pascal source code can also be found on the companion disk as SUBCLASS.PAS.

Getting some status

4

In this chapter, we focus on how to build status bars into your own programs. Status bars are an important new aspect of the Windows graphical interface and many commercial applications implement status bars to great effect. A number of the standard Microsoft applications bundled with Windows 3.1 implement a status bar: you will find them in the File Manager, Control Panel and the PIF Editor. More 'heavyweight' programs such as Microsoft's Word for Windows (which I'm using now) also provide a status bar, and so do non-Microsoft applications such as Serif's PagePlus desktop publishing package. Status bars are here to stay and, like most of the other techniques described in this book, they allow you to give your application a more professional 'look' without having to write enormous amounts of code.

So what's a status bar?

A status bar is generally implemented as a small window that sits at the bottom of the application's main window. As the name suggests, a status bar is primarily concerned with status: it's used to show the current status of the application. In Word for Windows, it's used to show the current line number and column position. These figures change as text is entered into the current document. The Word for Windows status bar also shows the current page number, the current section number and the zoom factor: the percentage by which the current page view is scaled up or down. Other parts (or 'cells') of the status bar indicate whether the CapsLock and NumLock keys are pressed, whether the word processor is in insert mode or overwrite mode, and so forth.

All this information is just that – informational data that should be presented to the user but shouldn't be used to clutter up the client area of the application. Putting this sort of stuff into the status bar is a neat way of presenting data without having it mess up the main part of the application window. Status bars are generally not interactive – you can see the information in a status bar, but you can't directly edit it. This is an area where PagePlus rather flies in the face of convention. Many of the items in the PagePlus status bar are actually buttons you can press to affect the operation of the program. Strictly speaking, the status bar in PagePlus is as much of a toolbar as a status bar since it includes elements of both. As a general rule, though, status bars go at the bottom of the main application window and are informational only, while toolbars go at the top of the application window and contain buttons and other control elements that can be used to affect the operation of the program.

There's another important use for status bars, called 'menu hinting'. Menu hinting is used in complex applications such as Word for Windows. The basic idea works like this: as the user drags the mouse around the various parts of the application's menu structure, the status bar displays a hint string that's intended to provide information on what that menu selection actually does. As the mouse moves up and down through a pull-down menu, and causes other pull-down menus to be displayed, the hint string displayed in the status bar keeps track, always providing information that corresponds to the menu item currently under the cursor. In addition to developing a general-purpose status bar in this chapter, we'll also be looking at how to add menu hinting capabilities to your application.

Status bars are often divided into one or more cells. For example, the Word for Windows status bar shown in Figure 4.1 has no fewer than nine individual cells in which different categories of information can be displayed. In this screen shot, the CapsLock, NumLock and Overwrite indicators are all turned on.

Before we begin work on the actual code for the status bar, there are a few other points that need to be made. Firstly, notice that the text in the status bar is shown using the same font that's used to display titles under minimized application icons. We'll be using the same font in our own status bar code and, in fact, this is the same font effect that we'll be using for the enhanced dialog effects in Chapter 5.

Secondly, when the main window of an application is changed in size, the status bar window has to be changed in size and position to reflect the new size of its parent. (The status bar is implemented as a child of the main application window.) The status bar must always be at the bottom of the application window client area and must always fill the entire width available.

This raises the question of what happens when the width of the main application window is reduced. The approach taken by almost all applications is simply to clip the status bar display to the available width. In other words, if the user reduces the width of the main window to such an extent that he can't see some cells of the status bar display, then that's his problem. I think that this is a reasonable approach, and

Figure 4.1   The Word for
Windows status bar.

certainly preferable to trying to 'shrink' the status bar so that the whole thing remains visible. This would introduce all sorts of unpleasant effects. Accordingly, in the code described here, we will take the same approach.

Figure 4.2 shows the source code for STATUS1.C. This is a simple generic application that's intended to do nothing more than display a main application window. We'll take this skeletal application framework as a starting point, and hang on it the extra code needed to implement a status bar.

```
/* STATUS1.C */

// © 1994 Dave Jewell and Addison-Wesley, ALL RIGHTS RESERVED

#include   <windows.h>

char szAppName[] = "StatusTest";

//——————————————————————————————————————————————
// Name:    WindowProc
// Purpose:  Window procedure for main application window.
//——————————————————————————————————————————————

LONG FAR PASCAL _export WindowProc (HWND Wnd, WORD Msg,
                                    WPARAM wParam, LPARAM lParam)
{
    switch (Msg)
    {
      case WM_DESTROY:

      PostQuitMessage (0);
      return (0);
    }

    return DefWindowProc (Wnd, Msg, wParam, lParam);
}

//——————————————————————————————————————————————
// Name:    InitAppClass
// Purpose:  Register the main application window class.
//——————————————————————————————————————————————

BOOL PASCAL InitAppClass (HANDLE hInstance)
{
    WNDCLASS cls;

    cls.style           = CS_VREDRAW | CS_HREDRAW;
    cls.lpfnWndProc     = (WNDPROC) WindowProc;
    cls.cbClsExtra      = 0;
    cls.cbWndExtra      = 0;
    cls.hInstance       = hInstance;
    cls.hIcon           = LoadIcon (NULL, IDI_APPLICATION);
    cls.hCursor         = LoadCursor (NULL, IDC_ARROW);
    cls.hbrBackground   = GetStockObject (WHITE_BRUSH);
    cls.lpszMenuName    = NULL;
    cls.lpszClassName   = szAppName;
    return RegisterClass (&cls);
}

//——————————————————————————————————————————————
// Name:    WinMain
// Purpose: Main application entry point.
//——————————————————————————————————————————————

int PASCAL WinMain (HANDLE hInstance, HANDLE hPrevInstance,
                    LPSTR lpCmdLine, int nCmdShow)
```

Figure 4.2   STATUS1.C: the starting point for the status bar application.

```
{
    HWND Wnd;
    MSG Msg;

    // Register application class if needed

    if (hPrevInstance == NULL)
        if (InitAppClass (hInstance) == FALSE)
            return (0);

    // Create the main application window

    Wnd = CreateWindow (szAppName, szAppName, WS_OVERLAPPEDWINDOW,
                        CW_USEDEFAULT, CW_USEDEFAULT,
                        CW_USEDEFAULT, CW_USEDEFAULT,
                        0, 0, hInstance, NULL);

    if (Wnd != NULL)
    {
        ShowWindow (Wnd, nCmdShow);
        UpdateWindow (Wnd);
    }

    while (GetMessage (&Msg, 0, 0, 0))
    {
        TranslateMessage (&Msg);
        DispatchMessage (&Msg);
    }

    return (Msg.wParam);
}
```

The death of hPrevInst

Let's begin by examining the code needed to initialize the status bar. If you look back
at Chapter 2, you'll see that two API routines were needed to get the toolbox code
working. The first of these was the InitToolPalette routine which took the instance
handle and the hPrevInst handle as parameters. The hPrevInst handle was used to
determine whether or not it was necessary to register the window class for the floating toolbox palette window. Ideally, it would be nice to eliminate the InitToolPalette
routine and have the window class registration happen transparently inside the call
to the CreatePaletteWindow routine. The simpler an interface is, the less room there
is for making a programming error.

Fortunately, it's possible to eliminate the hPrevInst variable from the equation.
From Windows 3.0 onwards, the API has contained a useful routine called
GetClassInfo. This routine takes an instance handle and class name as parameters. It
returns information on the specified class. If the class hasn't been registered, the
GetClassInfo routine returns zero. This is a simple, non-invasive and portable
technique for determining whether or not a window class has been registered. It's
used by Microsoft in much of their own software.

Note
You might think I'm making a big deal out of hPrevInst, but the fact is that this
parameter is a historical anachronism. Support for it is going to be dropped in a

future version of Windows, so it's best to remove it from your code now. There are three situations where programs tend to make use of the hPrevInst handle.

Firstly, for applications that only allow one instance of themselves to execute, it's used to determine whether another instance is running. If it is, then such a program typically switches over to the previous instance. Try running the Windows 3.1 File Manager for an example of this behavior. When writing new code, you should use the FindWindow API routine to determine whether a previous instance of your code is already executing.

Secondly, some applications pass the hPrevInst handle to the GetInstanceData routine in order to 'peek' at global variables in previous instances of the code. This is strictly historical, and goes all the way back to real mode Windows. The idea was that the GetInstanceData mechanism allowed programs to reuse resources such as icons, cursors, and so forth that had already been loaded by a previous instance. The saving on memory was small, and in these days of protected mode Windows, it's definitely not worth bothering about. In any event, the GetInstanceData routine will no longer exist in Windows NT. Make sure that you're not using it in your code.

Thirdly, and most typically, programs use the hPrevInst handle to determine whether or not a window class needs to be registered. This is where the GetClassInfo technique is useful.

Using the GetClassInfo routine, we can rewrite the InitAppClass routine to look like this:

```
//------------------------------------------------------------
// Name:     InitAppClass
// Purpose:  Register the main application window class.
//------------------------------------------------------------

BOOL PASCAL InitAppClass (HANDLE hInstance)
{
    WNDCLASS cls;

    if (GetClassInfo (hInstance, szAppName, &cls) == 0)
    {
        cls.style           = CS_VREDRAW | CS_HREDRAW;
        cls.lpfnWndProc     = (WNDPROC) WindowProc;
        cls.cbClsExtra      = 0;
        cls.cbWndExtra      = 0;
        cls.hInstance       = hInstance;
        cls.hIcon           = LoadIcon (NULL, IDI_APPLICATION);
        cls.hCursor         = LoadCursor (NULL, IDC_ARROW);
        cls.hbrBackground   = GetStockObject (WHITE_BRUSH);
        cls.lpszMenuName    = NULL;
        cls.lpszClassName   = szAppName;
        return RegisterClass (&cls);
    }
    return (TRUE);
}
```

This code can now be called unreservedly from the WinMain routine without having to look at the value of the hPrevInst parameter. Similar improvements can also be made to the floating toolbox palette code: it's obviously very easy to arrange for the CreatePaletteWindow routine to call internally a class registration procedure very similar to the one above.

Let's now look at some of the requirements for our new status bar window class. I mentioned in Chapter 3 that the color gray is enjoying unprecedented popularity amongst Windows programmers. Consequently, we want our new status bar to have a gray background color. More generally, we want it to have the same color that Windows itself uses to paint the surface of push controls. This will allow us to fit in (reasonably harmoniously!) with any color scheme changes that the user makes. Accordingly, the background color is derived from the COLOR_BTNFACE system constant.

We also want to associate an arbitrary amount of data with each window of this class. I mentioned earlier that a status bar can contain one or more cells, each of which can be used to display a different text message. In order to do this, we need to be able to define some sort of data structure that can describe each of these cells. As for the toolbox palette code, we'll allocate this data structure using the LocalAlloc API routine. This means that we'll be using 16-bit near pointers, which in turn means that we only need to allocate room for a single word using the cbWndExtra field at the time the status bar window class is registered.

Let's break with tradition and develop the code for the main application side by side with the linkable module containing the status bar code. A little later, you'll see that now we have a generic subclassing mechanism from the previous chapter, we can use this to put a lot more functionality into the library module without affecting the main application code.

Figure 4.3 shows the source code for STATBAR1.C, which is also included on the companion disk. The code is very self-contained and makes no references to global variables in the main application module. At this stage of the development process, there's just a single API routine called CreateStatusWindow. This routine is called from the parent application. It takes two parameters: the program instance handle and the window handle of the parent window.

The CreateStatusWindow routine first calls the RegisterStatusBar routine to ensure that the status bar window class is registered. Note that the szClassName variable corresponding to our chosen window class is declared as static so that it does not conflict with a like-named variable elsewhere in the application. If the window class registration process should fail (an unlikely event which under 16-bit versions of Windows will be almost certainly due to lack of space in the USER heap), the CreateStatusWindow routine returns a NULL window handle.

The CreateStatusWindow code then creates a child window of the main application and returns a handle to this window. I've temporarily set the size of this child window to 100 units high and 100 units wide. This is just to make the window 'big enough to be noticed'. As we develop the code further, we'll see that the status bar code will itself be responsible for sizing the window at the time the window is created. This is just like the floating toolbox palette window, which resized itself according to the number of rows and columns required and the size of the bitmaps involved.

Figure 4.3 STATBAR1.C: the beginnings of the status bar linkable module.

```
/* STATBAR1.C */
// © 1994 Dave Jewell and Addison-Wesley, ALL RIGHTS RESERVED
#include    <windows.h>
#include    "statbar.h"
static char szClassName[] = "StatusBar";       // name of our window class
```

```
//————————————————————————————————————————————————————————————
// Name:    StatusBarWndProc
// Purpose: Window procedure for status bar windows.
//————————————————————————————————————————————————————————————

LONG FAR PASCAL _export StatusBarWndProc (HWND Wnd, WORD Msg,
                                  WPARAM wParam, LPARAM lParam)
{
    return DefWindowProc (Wnd, Msg, wParam, lParam);
}

//————————————————————————————————————————————————————————————
// Name:    RegisterStatusBar
// Purpose: Register the status bar window procedure.
//————————————————————————————————————————————————————————————

BOOL PASCAL RegisterStatusBar (HANDLE hInstance)
{
    WNDCLASS cls;

    if (GetClassInfo (hInstance, szClassName, &cls) == 0)
    {
        cls.style          = 0;
        cls.lpfnWndProc    = (WNDPROC) StatusBarWndProc;
        cls.cbClsExtra     = 0;
        cls.cbWndExtra     = sizeof (void NEAR *);
        cls.hInstance      = hInstance;
        cls.hIcon          = 0;
        cls.hCursor        = LoadCursor (NULL, IDC_ARROW);
        cls.hbrBackground  = COLOR_BTNFACE + 1;
        cls.lpszMenuName   = NULL;
        cls.lpszClassName  = szClassName;

        return RegisterClass (&cls);
    }

    return TRUE;
}

//————————————————————————————————————————————————————————————
// Name:    CreateStatusWindow
// Purpose: Create a status window and attach it to the designated parent.
//————————————————————————————————————————————————————————————

HWND PASCAL CreateStatusWindow (HANDLE hInstance, HWND hWndParent)
{
    HWND Wnd = NULL;

    // Check that we've got a valid parent window

    if (hWndParent != NULL && IsWindow (hWndParent))
        if (RegisterStatusBar (hInstance))
        Wnd = CreateWindow (szClassName, "",
                        WS_CHILD | WS_BORDER | WS_VISIBLE,
                        0, 0, 100, 100, hWndParent, NULL, hInstance, NULL);

    return (Wnd);
}
```

Figure 4.4 shows the corresponding application code, STATUS2.C. This hasn't changed much from Figure 4.2 and we won't need to make any more changes to it for some time. The header file is shown in Figure 4.5 and the result of running this code in Figure 4.6. The executable file can be found on the companion disk as STATUS2.EXE, and the header file as STATBAR1.H.

```
/* STATUS2.C */

// © 1994 Dave Jewell and Addison-Wesley, ALL RIGHTS RESERVED

#include    <windows.h>

#include    "statbar.h"

char szAppName[] = "StatusTest";

//----------------------------------------------------------------------
// Name:     WindowProc
// Purpose:  Window procedure for main application window.
//----------------------------------------------------------------------

LONG FAR PASCAL _export WindowProc (HWND Wnd, WORD Msg,
                                        WPARAM wParam, LPARAM lParam)
{
    switch (Msg)
    {
      case WM_DESTROY:

      PostQuitMessage (0);
      return (0);
    }

    return DefWindowProc (Wnd, Msg, wParam, lParam);
}

//----------------------------------------------------------------------
// Name:     InitAppClass
// Purpose:  Register the main application window class.
//----------------------------------------------------------------------

BOOL PASCAL InitAppClass (HANDLE hInstance)
{
    WNDCLASS cls;

    if (GetClassInfo (hInstance, szAppName, &cls) == 0)
    {
        cls.style            = CS_VREDRAW | CS_HREDRAW;
        cls.lpfnWndProc      = (WNDPROC) WindowProc;
        cls.cbClsExtra       = 0;
        cls.cbWndExtra       = 0;
        cls.hInstance        = hInstance;
        cls.hIcon            = LoadIcon (NULL, IDI_APPLICATION);
        cls.hCursor          = LoadCursor (NULL, IDC_ARROW);
        cls.hbrBackground    = GetStockObject (WHITE_BRUSH);
        cls.lpszMenuName     = NULL;
        cls.lpszClassName    = szAppName;
        return RegisterClass (&cls);
    }

    return (TRUE);
}

//----------------------------------------------------------------------
// Name:     WinMain
// Purpose:  Main application entry point.
//----------------------------------------------------------------------

#pragma argsused

int PASCAL WinMain (HANDLE hInstance, HANDLE hPrevInstance,
                    LPSTR lpCmdLine, int nCmdShow)
{
    HWND Wnd;
```

```
     MSG Msg;
     HWND statusWnd;

     // Register application class if needed

     if (InitAppClass (hInstance) == FALSE)
         return (0);

     // Create the main application window

     Wnd = CreateWindow
         (szAppName, szAppName, WS_OVERLAPPEDWINDOW,
          CW_USEDEFAULT, CW_USEDEFAULT,
          CW_USEDEFAULT, CW_USEDEFAULT,
          0, 0, hInstance, NULL);    /

     if (Wnd != NULL)
     {
         ShowWindow (Wnd, nCmdShow);
         UpdateWindow (Wnd);
         statusWnd = CreateStatusWindow (hInstance, Wnd);
     }

     while (GetMessage (&Msg, 0, 0, 0))
     {
         TranslateMessage (&Msg);
         DispatchMessage (&Msg);
     }

     return (Msg.wParam);
}
```

```
/* STATBAR1.H */

// © 1994 Dave Jewell and Addison-Wesley, ALL RIGHTS RESERVED

#ifndef _INC_STATBAR
#define    _INC_STATBAR    /* #defined if statlib.h has been included */

#ifdef        __cplusplus
extern        "C" {
#endif

HWND PASCAL CreateStatusWindow (HANDLE hInstance, HWND hWndParent);

#ifdef        __cplusplus
}
#endif

#endif
```

Figure 4.5   STATBAR1.H: the header file for the status bar code module.

Figure 4.6 The effect of
running the STATUS2 program.

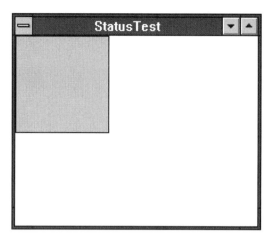

Figure 4.6 The effect of
running the STATUS2 program.

Cutting the status bar down to size

As might be expected, the child window shown in Figure 4.6 doesn't look very much like a status bar. It needs to be moved down to the bottom of the main application window and should occupy the whole width of the parent window. It also needs to have an appropriate height so that text strings can be easily accommodated in the status bar without it taking up too much unnecessary space. Let's make these changes our first priority.

Figure 4.7 shows a close-up of the left-hand corner of a typical status bar. There are a few points to notice here. Firstly, I've followed convention by drawing the text inside a 'sunken rectangle'. In other words, a rectangle which is drawn in such a way as to appear recessed into the screen. Secondly, the text is centered vertically within this rectangle. Clearly, the wanted height for the status bar will depend on the height of the font used and on the size of the borders that are required around the status bar. In Figure 4.7, you may feel that the text doesn't appear to be exactly centered vertically, that it's a little higher than it should be. This is because the status bar code we're developing leaves room for descenders (that is, characters such as g, y, and so on, which have a tail below the base line). If any descenders were present in the string shown, you would see that the centering is correct.

Figure 4.7 Anatomy of a
status bar.

The routine shown below, GetStatusFont, is intended to return a handle to the font we'll be using for drawing text inside the status bar. The font used is really the same font that's employed when drawing the titles of minimized window icons. When the USER DLL is initialized, it stores a handle to this font as a private global variable and uses it subsequently for all drawing of icon titles. Unfortunately, this font handle is not made available to application programs via a Windows API call. Consequently, we have to get a handle to the font ourselves by calling the CreateFont routine.

```
//————————————————————————————————————————————————
// Name:    GetStatusFont
// Purpose: Return a handle to our special font.
//————————————————————————————————————————————————
HFONT PASCAL GetStatusFont (int * height)
{
    HDC dc;
    int nHeight;
    HFONT font;
    TEXTMETRIC tm;

    dc = GetDC (NULL);
    nHeight = (GetDeviceCaps (dc, LOGPIXELSY) * 8) / −72;

    font = CreateFont (nHeight, 0, 0, 0, FW_NORMAL,
                    FALSE, FALSE, FALSE,
                    ANSI_CHARSET,
                    OUT_DEFAULT_PRECIS,
                    CLIP_DEFAULT_PRECIS,
                    DEFAULT_QUALITY,
                    FF_SWISS | VARIABLE_PITCH,
                    "MS Sans Serif");

    font = SelectObject (dc, font);
    GetTextMetrics (dc, &tm);
    font = SelectObject (dc, font);
    ReleaseDC (NULL, dc);
    if (height != NULL) *height = tm.tmHeight;
    return (font);
}
```

The call to CreateFont looks a bit fearsome for those unfamiliar with the Windows font manager, but it's actually reasonably straightforward. The important bit is really the line above the call, which calculates the value of the nHeight variable. Although not documented until relatively recently, passing a negative number as the first parameter to the CreateFont routine allows us to specify a font size in points, rather than in logical units. That's the purpose of this line of code, which calls GetDeviceCaps to determine the number of logical units in an inch and divides by 72 (the number of points in an inch). In this case, we're asking Windows for an eight-point font. You may wish to fool around with this – try replacing the 8 with 100, and you'll get a real monster of a status bar! When you've finished fooling around, set it back to 8, because this is the *de facto* size of fonts in a status bar.

If the height parameter is non-zero, the routine passes back the value of the tmHeight field, obtained by calling the GetTextMetrics routine. We need to know the height of the font so that we can figure out how tall to make the status bar. A status bar normally only contains a single row of characters, and ours isn't going to be any different, so I haven't bothered to add in the tmExternalLeading field to the value for the font height. This would normally only be necessary if we were displaying multiple character rows above each other.

Having obtained a handle to the font, we should store this handle in an easily accessible location so that we don't need to call the font manager again. Therefore, we'll put it into the data record that's associated with the status bar window. At the same time, we need to have an integer field that specifies the number of cells currently in the status bar. We end up with a data structure something like this:

```
typedef struct StatusRec
{
        HFONT     statusFont;   // handle to our special font
        int       border;       // width of border
        int       height;       // height of status bar
        int       numParts;     // number of defined parts
} StatusRec, NEAR * PStatusRec;
```

The distance between the edges of the status bar window and the edges of the framing rectangle (see Figure 4.7) is defined by the border field in the above data structure. Between the framing rectangle and the text, there exists another border of the same width. Effectively, therefore, the total height of the status bar is equal to the height of the font, plus four times the border size defined in the above data structure.

The logical place to have this initialization code executed is in response to the WM_CREATE message in the status bar window procedure. In other words, we need to add the following lines of code to the StatusBarWndProc routine.

```
case WM_CREATE:

return InitStatusWindow (Wnd);
```

If the InitStatusWindow call returns −1, this indicates an error condition and the window is destroyed internally within Windows, causing a NULL handle to be returned as the result of the CreateWindow call. If the InitStatusWindow routine returns a function result of zero, this is interpreted as success. Here's the code for the initialization routine itself:

```
//————————————————————————————————————————————
// Name:    InitStatusWindow
// Purpose: Initialization code for setting up the status window.
//————————————————————————————————————————————

static LONG PASCAL InitStatusWindow (HWND Wnd)
{
     PStatusRec p;
     LONG res = −1L;

     p = (PStatusRec) LocalAlloc (LPTR, sizeof (StatusRec));
     if (p != NULL)
     {
        // Initialize the StatusRec data structure

        p−>numParts = 1;
        p−>statusFont = GetStatusFont (&p−>height);
        p−>border = (GetSystemMetrics (SM_CXFRAME) + 1) / 2;
        p−>height += (p−>border * 4);
        SetWindowWord (Wnd, 0, (WORD) p);
        res = 0;
     }

     return (res);
}
```

Because the value returned from GetSystemMetrics (SM_CXFRAME) is typically quite small, one is added to it in order to ensure that rounding errors are not too significant when dividing by two. The height of the status bar is then calculated by multiplying the border width by four and adding to the height of the font.

This is all very well, but we still haven't adjusted the size and position of the status window. A good place to do that would be inside InitStatusWindow, but the resizing code must be written as a procedure so that it can be called from elsewhere. This is important because we need to resize the status bar window whenever the user changes the size of the parent window, not merely at the time the window is created.

```
//————————————————————————————————————————————————————
// Name:     ResizeWindow
// Purpose:  Routine to force status bar to proper size and position.
//————————————————————————————————————————————————————

static void PASCAL ResizeWindow (HWND Wnd)
{
    RECT r;
    PStatusRec p;

    p = (PStatusRec) GetWindowWord (Wnd, 0);
    GetClientRect (GetParent (Wnd), &r);
    SetWindowPos (Wnd, 0, 0, r.bottom − p−>height, r.right, p−>height, SWP_NOZORDER);
}
```

The routine above, ResizeWindow, is used to adjust the size and position of the status window so that it remains at the bottom of the main application window. Change the InitStatusWindow code so that the ResizeWindow routine is called immediately after the call to SetWindowWord.

With these changes in place, we have the STATBAR2.C file shown in Figure 4.8. There are no changes to the main application module, so I haven't shown it again. Note that the WS_BORDER style has been removed from the status bar window: this is because a bordered child window causes a two-pixel-wide border to be drawn between the junction of a child window and the parent window's frame. Having no border gives us better control over the visual appearance of the status bar. The GetStatusRec routine has also been added to compartmentalize the mechanism whereby a StatusRec pointer is obtained from the status bar window handle. This obviously minimizes future changes to the code in the event that you decide (for example) to use GlobalAlloc instead.

Figure 4.8 STATBAR2.C: the status bar code, with initialization code added.

```
/* STATBAR2.C */

// © 1994 Dave Jewell and Addison-Wesley, ALL RIGHTS RESERVED

#include    <windows.h>
#include    "statbar.h"

static char szClassName[] = "StatusBar";       // name of our window class

typedef struct StatusRec
{
    HFONT   statusFont;    // handle to our special font
    int     border;        // width of border
    int     height;        // height of status bar
```

```
        int      numParts;    // number of defined parts
    }    StatusRec, NEAR * PStatusRec;

//——————————————————————————————————————————————————————————
// Name:    GetStatusFont
// Purpose: Return a handle to our special font.
//——————————————————————————————————————————————————————————

static HFONT PASCAL GetStatusFont (int * height)
{
    HDC dc;
    int nHeight;
    HFONT font;
    TEXTMETRIC tm;

    dc = GetDC (NULL);
    nHeight = (GetDeviceCaps (dc, LOGPIXELSY) * 8) / −72;

    font = CreateFont (nHeight, 0, 0, 0, FW_NORMAL, 0, 0, 0,
                    ANSI_CHARSET,
                    OUT_DEFAULT_PRECIS,
                    CLIP_DEFAULT_PRECIS,
                    DEFAULT_QUALITY,
                    FF_SWISS | VARIABLE_PITCH,
                    "MS Sans Serif");

    font = SelectObject (dc, font);
    GetTextMetrics (dc, &tm);
    font = SelectObject (dc, font);
    ReleaseDC (NULL, dc);
    if (height != NULL) *height = tm.tmHeight;
    return (font);
}

//——————————————————————————————————————————————————————————
// Name:    GetStatusRec
// Purpose: Given a window handle, return a pointer to the corresponding
//          status record.
//——————————————————————————————————————————————————————————

static PStatusRec PASCAL GetStatusRec (HWND Wnd)
{
    return (PStatusRec) GetWindowWord (Wnd, 0);
}

//——————————————————————————————————————————————————————————
// Name:    ResizeWindow
// Purpose: Routine to force status bar to proper size and position.
//——————————————————————————————————————————————————————————

static void PASCAL ResizeWindow (HWND Wnd)
{
    RECT r;
    PStatusRec p;

    p = GetStatusRec (Wnd);
    GetClientRect (GetParent (Wnd), &r);
    SetWindowPos (Wnd, 0, 0, r.bottom − p−>height, r.right, p−>height,
                SWP_NOZORDER);
}

//——————————————————————————————————————————————————————————
// Name:    InitStatusWindow
// Purpose: Initialization code for setting up the status window.
//——————————————————————————————————————————————————————————

static LONG PASCAL InitStatusWindow (HWND Wnd)
{
        PStatusRec p;
```

```
        LONG res = −1L;

        p = (PStatusRec) LocalAlloc (LPTR, sizeof (StatusRec));
        if (p != NULL)
        {
            // Initialize the StatusRec data structure

            p−>numParts = 1;
            p−>statusFont = GetStatusFont (&p−>height);
            p−>border = (GetSystemMetrics (SM_CXFRAME) + 1) / 2;
            p−>height += (p−>border * 4);
            SetWindowWord (Wnd, 0, (WORD) p);
            ResizeWindow (Wnd);
            res = 0;
        }

        return (res);
}

//──────────────────────────────────────────────────────────────────
// Name:    StatusBarWndProc
// Purpose: Window procedure for status bar windows.
//──────────────────────────────────────────────────────────────────

LONG FAR PASCAL _export StatusBarWndProc (HWND Wnd, WORD Msg,
                                          WPARAM wParam, LPARAM lParam)
{
        switch (Msg)
        {
            case WM_CREATE:

            return InitStatusWindow (Wnd);
        }

        return DefWindowProc (Wnd, Msg, wParam, lParam);
}

//──────────────────────────────────────────────────────────────────
// Name:    RegisterStatusBar
// Purpose: Register the status bar window procedure.
//──────────────────────────────────────────────────────────────────

static BOOL PASCAL RegisterStatusBar (HANDLE hInstance)
{
        WNDCLASS cls;

        if (GetClassInfo (hInstance, szClassName, &cls) == 0)
        {
            cls.style           = 0;
            cls.lpfnWndProc     = (WNDPROC) StatusBarWndProc;
            cls.cbClsExtra      = 0;
            cls.cbWndExtra      = sizeof (void NEAR *);
            cls.hInstance       = hInstance;
            cls.hIcon           = 0;
            cls.hCursor         − LoadCursor (NULL, IDC_ARROW);
            cls.hbrBackground   = COLOR_BTNFACE + 1;
            cls.lpszMenuName    = NULL;
            cls.lpszClassName   = szClassName;

            return RegisterClass (&cls);
        }

        return TRUE;
}

//──────────────────────────────────────────────────────────────────
// Name:    CreateStatusWindow
// Purpose: Create a status window and attach it to the designated parent.
//──────────────────────────────────────────────────────────────────
```

```
HWND PASCAL CreateStatusWindow (HANDLE hInstance, HWND hWndParent)
{
        HWND Wnd = NULL;
        PStatusRec p;
        int fontHeight;

        // Check that we've got a valid parent window

        if (hWndParent != NULL && IsWindow (hWndParent))
          if (RegisterStatusBar (hInstance))
            Wnd = CreateWindow (szClassName, "", WS_CHILD | WS_VISIBLE, 0, 0,
                                100, 100, hWndParent, NULL, hInstance, NULL);

        return (Wnd);
}
```

The compiled program is included on the disk as STATUS3.EXE. If you execute it, you'll see that the initial position of the status bar looks good, but if you increase the size of the parent window, the status bar will stay right where it is. Obviously, there's more work to do here.

Fixing things up is relatively straightforward: we merely have to ensure that the ResizeWindow routine is called each time the main application window receives a WM_SIZE message. This message is sent to a window each time its size is changed. The obvious place to modify the code is in WindowProc, the main window's window procedure. However, if we were to call the ResizeWindow from this place, we would have to make ResizeWindow available as an API routine. Currently it's defined as being static and it isn't mentioned in the header file. Not only that, but why should the main application window have to care about resizing the status bar? Once we've created the status bar we want to be able to forget about it, except when we want to do something with it, like setting the text in one of the cells. It seems a pity to have to mess up the interface in this way. Surely there's a better way….

Subclassing to the rescue

If you read Chapter 2, which was concerned with implementing floating toolbox palettes, you'll know that we did end up muddying the waters a little. The main application window and the toolbox palette were quite tightly coupled together. For example, when the WM_ACTIVATEAPP message was received by the main window, it knew that it had to invalidate the rectangle corresponding to the position of the toolbox. This sort of interaction can't be eliminated, of course, but using subclassing we can effectively hide it away so that the person responsible for writing the main application doesn't have to concern herself with these irrelevant details. This concept is often called 'information hiding' and it's one of the cornerstones of good programming interface design. If it's not relevant to you, then you shouldn't need to know about it.

With the previous chapter under your belt, you should begin to see what I'm getting at. We can subclass the main application window internally (that is, within the STATBAR code module) and use the subclassing routine to take care of any modifications we might need to make to the window procedure of the application window. That way, the main application doesn't get cluttered up with unnecessary detail. Let's examine this approach now.

First off, we need to include the header file for the subclassing routines into the STATBAR source code. We just need to add the line:

```
#include        "sclaslib.h"
```

You'll also need to add the SCLASLIB.C source file to your project. How you do this depends on which Windows development environment you're using. See your compiler's documentation for more information on creating and managing projects. You should end up with three source files in the project. These are the main application, the status bar code, and the subclassing routines.

```
//————————————————————————————————————————————————
// Name:     SubclassParentWndProc
// Purpose:  Subclassing routine for the main application window.
//————————————————————————————————————————————————

#pragma argsused

LONG FAR PASCAL _export SubclassParentWndProc (HWND Wnd, WORD Msg,
                                 WPARAM wParam, LPARAM lParam)
{
    if (Msg == WM_SIZE) ResizeWindow (GetProp (Wnd, szClassName));
    return CallOldProc (Wnd, Msg, wParam, lParam, hookKey);
}
```

Now we need to add the above routine to the status bar source code. This is the subclassing procedure for the main application window. All it does here is call the ResizeWindow routine every time a WM_SIZE message is received, that is, every time the main window size is changed. This allows the status bar to keep track of the parent window's size. Notice that we don't exit after processing the WM_SIZE message. It's important to 'fall through' into the CallOldProc routine, thereby passing the WM_SIZE message on to the old application window procedure. This particular message is typically used by an application to do things like setting scroll bar ranges and so forth. If we didn't pass it on to the existing window procedure, the results could be disastrous.

In general, when subclassing the main application window like this, it's important to allow the old window procedure to 'see' all the messages it receives. We can't predict which messages are important to the application code and which aren't. Therefore, we try to pass them all through. The only exceptions to this are special messages that might be specifically defined for private communication between the application window and the status bar window. See the floating toolbox palette code in Chapter 2 for an example of such messages.

OK, so how do we hook into the main application window? We can do this using our old friend, HookWindow, from the subclassing module. We can modify the InitStatusWindow routine defined earlier by adding the following two lines of code after the call to ResizeWindow:

```
SetProp (GetParent (Wnd), szClassName, Wnd);
hookKey = HookWindow (GetParent (Wnd), (FARPROC) SubclassParentWndProc,
            szHookName);
```

Here, HookWindow is called using the GetParent routine to specify that it's the parent window of the status bar window that should be hooked. You'll also notice that I've used the SetProp routine to set up a property for the parent window. This property entry contains the window handle of the status bar. The idea is that given the handle of the main application window, we can determine the window handle of the status bar using the GetProp call. Similarly, given the window handle of the status window, we can determine the handle of the application window using the GetParent routine. This sort of 'either-way' identification is important, and makes the code a lot simpler. I've used the status bar class name as the name of the property. This is fine, provided, of course, that the application window isn't also using properties of the same name.

Note

Be careful not to use the status bar class name as the service or client name when calling the HookWindow code. This might at first sight seem like a sensible idea, but since the statement above has already attached a property of that name to the window, if we then used the same string as the client name, the subclassing code would be fooled into thinking that the window had already been subclassed. This would mean that the window wouldn't actually get subclassed. Of course, you could move the SetProp statement immediately *after* the HookWindow call, but I wouldn't advise this either. It's better to use different property names for different functions.

Of course, if we felt like being lazy, we could dispense with this property business and just use a static global variable inside the status bar module. This would contain the window handle of the status bar. By now, you should realize that this isn't a good idea. What happens if our application has several windows open, each of which has a status bar? What happens if we want to package this code up as a DLL, with multiple clients? No – do it properly with properties!

Having hooked the main application window, we need to arrange for it to get unhooked at the appropriate time. The subclassing routine contains code that will automatically unhook the main application window if it receives a WM_DESTROY message. However, this is not sufficiently flexible for our purposes: it implies that the status bar will only be destroyed at the time the parent window is closed. Ideally, we'd like to write the code such that the status bar can be destroyed at other times, too. A hypothetical application might only display a status bar when in some specific state; at other times the status bar would be removed.

With this in mind, the code below shows our revised status bar window procedure:

```
//----------------------------------------------------------------
// Name:    StatusBarWndProc
// Purpose: Window procedure for status bar windows.
//----------------------------------------------------------------

LONG FAR PASCAL _export StatusBarWndProc (HWND Wnd, WORD Msg,
                                          WPARAM wParam, LPARAM lParam)
{
    PStatusRec p;

    switch (Msg)
    {
      case WM_CREATE:
```

```
        return InitStatusWindow (Wnd);

    case WM_DESTROY:

        p = GetStatusRec (Wnd);
        DeleteObject (p->statusFont);
        RemoveProp (GetParent (Wnd), szClassName);
        UnHookWindow (GetParent (Wnd), hookKey);
        LocalFree ((HLOCAL) p);
        return (0);
    }

    return DefWindowProc (Wnd, Msg, wParam, IParam);
}
```

When the status bar receives a WM_DESTROY message, it first removes the special associating property that we discussed earlier and then calls the UnHookWindow routine to restore the parent's original window procedure. Notice that we also destroy the special status font and deallocate the status record at this time.

This leaves us with one residual problem: how do we ensure that the status bar window is destroyed when the main application window is closed? This might seem like a very odd thing to say – after all, the status bar window is a child of the application window and so it will inevitably be destroyed when the application window is closed. The real question is precisely *when* it will be destroyed. Ideally, when a parent window is destroyed, all child windows should be destroyed first. This would mean that when we receive the WM_DESTROY message in the code above, the parent window handle would still be valid. Unfortunately, however, the Microsoft SDK information specifically states that the WM_DESTROY message is sent first to the parent window and *then* to all the child windows. The question therefore is: how valid is the parent window handle at the time the status bar receives its WM_DESTROY message?

My own observations suggest that the parent window is actually perfectly valid. You might be tempted to modify the SubclassParentWndProc routine so as to explicitly destroy the status bar window. Here's how the code might look:

```
//─────────────────────────────────────────────────────────────
// Name:    SubclassParentWndProc
// Purpose: Subclassing routine for the main application window.
//─────────────────────────────────────────────────────────────

#pragma argsused

LONG FAR PASCAL _export SubclassParentWndProc (HWND Wnd, WORD Msg,
                                WPARAM wParam, LPARAM IParam)
{
    HWND hWndStatus;
    hWndStatus = GetProp (Wnd, szClassName);
    if (Msg == WM_SIZE) ResizeWindow (hWndStatus);
    if (Msg == WM_DESTROY && IsWindow (hWndStatus)) DestroyWindow (hWndStatus);
    return CallOldProc (Wnd, Msg, wParam, IParam, hookKey);
}
```

Unfortunately, doing this would be a big mistake, although the reason is perhaps a little subtle. When the DestroyWindow API routine is called to terminate the status bar window, the WM_DESTROY handling code in the StatusBarWndProc routine is called. This in turn calls the UnHookWindow routine. In other words, by the time the CallOldProc routine in the above code is called, the application window will no longer be subclassed and the WM_DESTROY message will be passed directly to the DefWindowProc routine, avoiding the original application window procedure. As pointed out in the previous chapter, it's important that the application window procedure 'sees' this message. Without it, the PostQuitMessage routine is never called, and the application goes into a limbo state where it's still loaded in memory, but has no active windows or messages.

Because of considerations like this, you need to take care when subclassing windows. Although the generic subclassing routines we developed in Chapter 3 are a help, they can't do all the work for you. When subclassing a window, always think carefully about the exact sequence of events as a particular message is processed.

```
//-----------------------------------------------------------------
// Name:     CreateStatusWindow
// Purpose:  Create a status window and attach it to the designated parent.
//-----------------------------------------------------------------

HWND PASCAL CreateStatusWindow (HANDLE hInstance, HWND hWndParent)
{
     HWND Wnd = NULL;
     PStatusRec p;
     int fontHeight;

     // Check that we've got a valid parent window

     if (hWndParent != NULL && IsWindow (hWndParent))
     {
        // Ok so far, but has window already got a status bar ?

        Wnd = GetProp (hWndParent, szClassName);
        if (Wnd == NULL)
          if (RegisterStatusBar (hInstance))
            Wnd = CreateWindow (szClassName, "", WS_CHILD | WS_VISIBLE,
                            0, 0, 100, 100, hWndParent, NULL, hInstance, NULL);
     }

     return (Wnd);
}
```

One final change is indicated, and that's shown above. If the CreateStatusWindow is inadvertently called twice for the same parent window, we want to ensure that the code does something sensible. Internally, the HookWindow routine will ensure that a window that has already been subclassed will not be subclassed again. However, we do want to ensure that an application window doesn't end up with two status bars! The code above uses the GetProp routine to see if a status bar window is already associated with the parent window. If it is, the window handle of the existing status bar is returned to the caller and no new window is created.

The changes made so far are summarized in Figure 4.9 and the corresponding code can be found on the disk as STATBAR3.C. The compiled program is STATUS4.EXE. When you run it this time, you'll see that the status bar faithfully tracks the size of the parent window, and the subclassing mechanism we now have can be used as the basis of any needed interaction between the status bar and its parent window.

Figure 4.9 STATBAR3.C: subclassing the main application window can simplify the API.

```
/* STATBAR3.C */

// © 1994 Dave Jewell and Addison-Wesley, ALL RIGHTS RESERVED

#include   <windows.h>
#include   "statbar.h"
#include   "sclaslib.h"

static char szClassName[] = "StatusBar";        // name of our window class
static char szHookName[] = "StatusBarHook";  // name of our hook

typedef struct StatusRec
{
     HFONT      statusFont;                   // handle to our special font
     int        border;                       // width of border
     int        height;                       // height of status bar
     int        numParts;                     // number of defined parts
} StatusRec, NEAR * PStatusRec;
static LONG hookKey;

//-------------------------------------------------------------------------
// Name:     GetStatusFont
// Purpose:  Return a handle to our special font.
//-------------------------------------------------------------------------

static HFONT PASCAL GetStatusFont (int * height)
{
     HDC dc;
     int nHeight;
     HFONT font;
     TEXTMETRIC tm;

     dc = GetDC (NULL);
     nHeight = (GetDeviceCaps (dc, LOGPIXELSY) * 8) / -72;

     font = CreateFont (nHeight, 0, 0, 0, FW_NORMAL, 0, 0, 0,
                        ANSI_CHARSET,
                        OUT_DEFAULT_PRECIS,
                        CLIP_DEFAULT_PRECIS,
                        DEFAULT_QUALITY,
                        FF_SWISS | VARIABLE_PITCH,
                        "MS Sans Serif");

     font = SelectObject (dc, font);
     GetTextMetrics (dc, &tm);
     font = SelectObject (dc, font);
     ReleaseDC (NULL, dc);
     if (height != NULL) *height = tm.tmHeight;
     return (font);
}

//-------------------------------------------------------------------------
// Name:     GetStatusRec
// Purpose:  Given a window handle, return a pointer to the corresponding
//           status record.
//-------------------------------------------------------------------------

static PStatusRec PASCAL GetStatusRec (HWND Wnd)
{
     return (PStatusRec) GetWindowWord (Wnd, 0);
}

//-------------------------------------------------------------------------
// Name:     ResizeWindow
// Purpose:  Routine to force status bar to proper size and position.
//-------------------------------------------------------------------------

static void PASCAL ResizeWindow (HWND Wnd)
{
```

```
        RECT r;
        PStatusRec p;

        p = GetStatusRec (Wnd);
        GetClientRect (GetParent (Wnd), &r);
        SetWindowPos (Wnd, 0, 0, r.bottom − p−>height, r.right, p−>height,
                        SWP_NOZORDER);
}

//─────────────────────────────────────────────────────────────
// Name:    SubclassParentWndProc
// Purpose: Subclassing routine for the main application window.
//─────────────────────────────────────────────────────────────

#pragma argsused

LONG FAR PASCAL _export SubclassParentWndProc
    (HWND Wnd, WORD Msg, WPARAM wParam, LPARAM lParam)
{
        if (Msg = WM_SIZE) ResizeWindow (GetProp (Wnd, szClassName));
        return CallOldProc (Wnd, Msg, wParam, lParam, hookKey);
}

//─────────────────────────────────────────────────────────────
// Name:    InitStatusWindow
// Purpose: Initialization code for setting up the status window.
//─────────────────────────────────────────────────────────────

static LONG PASCAL InitStatusWindow (HWND Wnd)
{
        PStatusRec p;
        LONG res = −1L;

        p = (PStatusRec) LocalAlloc (LPTR, sizeof (StatusRec));
        if (p != NULL)
        {
          // Initialize the StatusRec data structure

          p−>numParts = 1;
          p−>statusFont = GetStatusFont (&p−>height);
          p−>border = (GetSystemMetrics (SM_CXFRAME) + 1) / 2;
          p−>height += (p−>border * 4);
          SetWindowWord (Wnd, 0, (WORD) p);
          ResizeWindow (Wnd);
          SetProp (GetParent (Wnd), szClassName, Wnd);
          hookKey = HookWindow (GetParent (Wnd), (FARPROC)
                                    SubclassParentWndProc, szHookName);

          res = 0;
        }

        return (res);
}

//─────────────────────────────────────────────────────────────
// Name:    StatusBarWndProc
// Purpose: Window procedure for status bar windows.
//─────────────────────────────────────────────────────────────

LONG FAR PASCAL _export StatusBarWndProc (HWND Wnd, WORD Msg,
                                    WPARAM wParam, LPARAM lParam)
{
        PStatusRec p;

        switch (Msg)
        {
          case WM_CREATE:

          return InitStatusWindow (Wnd);
```

```
        case WM_DESTROY:

            p = GetStatusRec (Wnd);
            DeleteObject (p->statusFont);
            RemoveProp (GetParent (Wnd), szClassName);
            UnHookWindow (GetParent (Wnd), hookKey);
            LocalFree ((HLOCAL) p);
            return (0);
        }

        return DefWindowProc (Wnd, Msg, wParam, lParam);
}

//------------------------------------------------------------
// Name:    RegisterStatusBar
// Purpose: Register the status bar window procedure.
//------------------------------------------------------------

static BOOL PASCAL RegisterStatusBar (HANDLE hInstance)
{
        WNDCLASS cls;

        if (GetClassInfo (hInstance, szClassName, &cls) == 0)
        {
            cls.style           = 0;
            cls.lpfnWndProc     = (WNDPROC) StatusBarWndProc;
            cls.cbClsExtra      = 0;
            cls.cbWndExtra      = sizeof (void NEAR *);
            cls.hInstance       = hInstance;
            cls.hIcon           = 0;
            cls.hCursor         = LoadCursor (NULL, IDC_ARROW);
            cls.hbrBackground   = COLOR_BTNFACE + 1;
            cls.lpszMenuName    = NULL;
            cls.lpszClassName   = szClassName;

            return RegisterClass (&cls);
        }

        return TRUE;
}

//------------------------------------------------------------
// Name:    CreateStatusWindow
// Purpose: Create a status window and attach it to the designated parent.
//------------------------------------------------------------

HWND PASCAL CreateStatusWindow (HANDLE hInstance, HWND hWndParent)

{
        HWND Wnd = NULL;
        PStatusRec p;
        int fontHeight;

        // Check that we've got a valid parent window

        if (hWndParent != NULL && IsWindow (hWndParent))
        {
            // Ok so far, but has window already got a status bar ?

            Wnd = GetProp (hWndParent, szClassName);
            if (Wnd == NULL)
              if (RegisterStatusBar (hInstance))
                  Wnd = CreateWindow (szClassName, "", WS_CHILD | WS_VISIBLE,
                                      0, 0, 100, 100, hWndParent, NULL,
                                      hInstance, NULL);
        }

        return (Wnd);
```

A bar of many parts

That was a fairly lengthy introduction, but we now have a good foundation on which to write the rest of the status bar code.

When we created the StatusRect data structure earlier, we didn't incorporate any place to save the text information. Nor did we define any storage space for holding the size of each cell of the status rectangle. Let's do that now.

For each cell of the status bar (by 'cell', I mean a separate rectangular area in which text can be displayed), we need to store a handle to the associated text. Additionally, we need some way of storing the size of each cell. The most obvious way of doing this would be to use an array of rectangles, one for each cell of the status box. However, this would not be particularly efficient. For one thing, all the cells are guaranteed to have the same height, so the top and bottom fields of each rectangle are essentially superfluous. Further, if we assume a fixed distance between each cell and the next cell in the status bar, we can store just a single integer for each cell. This integer represents the position of the right-hand edge of that particular cell in client coordinates. The first cell is assumed to start a certain predefined distance from the left-hand edge of the status bar, and the remaining cells follow on in order.

```
#define          MAXCELLS          10

typedef struct StatusRec
{
      HFONT    statusFont;              // handle to our special font
      int      border;                 // width of border
      int      height;                 // height of status bar
      int      numParts;               // number of defined cells
      HLOCAL   hText [MAXCELLS];       // handle to text data
      int      frames [MAXCELLS];      // right edge of each cell
      int      flags [MAXCELLS];       // flag information
} StatusRec, NEAR * PStatusRec;
```

This gives us the data structure shown above. The #define is used to specify the maximum number of cells that can be contained within the status bar; ten seems like a reasonable number, but you can increase it at the expense of a slight increase in the size of the allocated data structure. In principle, you could remove this limitation by using the LocalReAlloc API routine to dynamically reallocate the size of the StatusRec as more cells are added to the status bar. You could even build up the status bar data structure as a linked list of structures, each of which describes an individual cell. However, the additional code complexity isn't really worth it in this particular case.

The hText array is used to hold a LocalAlloc'd handle for the text which is associated with a particular cell. When the code encounters a NULL handle, it knows that this particular cell does not currently have any text associated with it. The cell is drawn, but it's left blank. As mentioned earlier, the frames array is used to specify the right-edge boundary of each cell in client coordinates. The flags field is used to alter the appearance of text within a particular cell. It can be used, for example, to specify that text in the cell be left-aligned, right-aligned, or centered.

With this in mind, when creating the status bar window we should really set the numParts field to zero, indicating that no cells have so far been defined. A better approach (similar to what we did in Chapter 2 with the floating palette toolbox window) would be to pass a pointer to an initial text string as a third parameter to the CreateStatusWindow routine, like this:

```
HWND PASCAL CreateStatusWindow (HANDLE hInstance, HWND hWndParent, LPCSTR lpText);
```

This is a pretty reasonable thing to do, since we're not likely to create a status bar window unless we want to add at least one cell to it. By allowing the application window to specify the text to appear in the first cell at the same time as it creates the status bar, we've provided a more flexible interface. Of course, if the application doesn't want to create an initial cell at this time, it can pass either NULL or a pointer to an empty string as the third parameter.

```
//------------------------------------------------------------
// Name:     InitStatusWindow
// Purpose:  Initialization code for setting up the status window.
//------------------------------------------------------------

static LONG PASCAL InitStatusWindow (HWND Wnd, LONG lParam)
{
    LPCSTR text;
    PStatusRec p;
    LONG res = -1L;

    p = (PStatusRec) LocalAlloc (LPTR, sizeof (StatusRec));
    if (p != NULL)
    {
        // Initialize the StatusRec data structure

        p->numParts = 0;
        p->statusFont = GetStatusFont (&p->height);
        p->border = (GetSystemMetrics (SM_CXFRAME) + 1) / 2;
        p->height += (p->border * 4);
        SetWindowWord (Wnd, 0, (WORD) p);
        ResizeWindow (Wnd);
        SetProp (GetParent (Wnd), szClassName, Wnd);
        hookKey = HookWindow (GetParent (Wnd), (FARPROC) SubclassParentWndProc,
                              szHookName);

        // Now check for any initial text

        text = ((LPCREATESTRUCT) lParam)->lpCreateParams;
        if (text != NULL && *text != '\0') AddCell (Wnd, text, -1);
        res = 0;
    }

    return (res);
}
```

This results in the modifications to the InitStatusWindow routine shown above. The CreateStatusWindow routine passes the lpText window on to the CreateWindow routine. The lParam field of the WM_CREATE message is then passed to the InitStatusWindow for interpretation as above. This is the standard way of passing initialization information to a window that is being created, so we may as well make use of the mechanism here. The numParts field of the StatusRec data structure is initialized to zero and, if a text string has been supplied to the CreateStatusWindow routine, the AddCell code is called to create a new cell in the status window. It's assumed that this routine will be responsible for incrementing the numParts field.

So far, so good. Now we need to develop the code for the AddCell routine. This routine always adds a single cell to the status bar.

```
//——————————————————————————————————————————————
// Name:    AddCell
// Purpose: Add a cell to the status bar.
// Returns: TRUE on success, FALSE on failure.
//——————————————————————————————————————————————

BOOL PASCAL AddCell (HWND Wnd, LPCSTR text, int nWidth)
{
    HDC dc;
    int left;
    HFONT hFont;
    PStatusRec p;

    p = GetStatusRec (Wnd);
    if (p−>numParts < MAXCELLS)
    {
        p−>hText [p−>numParts] = AllocText (text);
        p−>flags [p−>numParts] = DT_LEFT;

        // Calculate left edge of cell

        if (p−>numParts) left = p−>frames [p−>numParts − 1] + (p−>border * 2);
        else left = p−>border;

        // Calculate width of string if necessary

        if (nWidth == −1 && p−>hText [p−>numParts] != NULL)
        {
            dc = GetDC (NULL);
            hFont = SelectObject (dc, p−>statusFont);
            nWidth = LOWORD(GetTextExtent (dc, text, lstrlen (text))) + p−>border * 3;
            SelectObject (dc, hFont);
            ReleaseDC (NULL, dc);
        }

        // And calculate position of right edge

        if (nWidth != −1)
        {
            p−>frames [p−>numParts] = left + nWidth;
            ++p−>numParts;
            return (TRUE);
        }
    }

    return (FALSE);
}
```

The AddCell routine takes three parameters: the window handle of the status bar, a pointer to the text that's to appear in the new cell, and a width specifier. This third parameter is used to specify the width of the new cell. If a value of −1 is used, the cell width is set to match the dimensions of the passed text string. Any other value is taken to be the wanted cell width in client coordinates.

The routine starts off by checking to see whether the numParts field is already up to the maximum. If not, the AllocText routine is called to allocate a handle, copy the text into the newly created local memory block, and return the handle. If the text string pointer is NULL or points to an empty string, a NULL handle is returned. The initial value of the flags entry is set to DT_LEFT, which left-aligns the text within the cell.

The right-hand edge of the cell is then calculated and stored in the frames array. This is done by first calculating the position of the left-hand side of the cell, determining the cell width, and then adding the two together to find the position of the right edge. Note that there are two alternatives here:

- You can pass −1 as the nWidth parameter. In this case, you must supply a valid non-empty string.
- You can set up a specific width for the cell. In this case, it doesn't matter whether or not the text string is empty.

What you can't do is pass an empty or NULL string and set the nWidth parameter to −1. This is invalid and will cause the routine to return FALSE as the function result.

```
//————————————————————————————————————————————
// Name:    AllocText
// Purpose: Allocate a chunk of text, and return a handle to it.
//————————————————————————————————————————————
static HLOCAL PASCAL AllocText (LPCSTR text)
{
    HLOCAL hText;

    if (text == NULL || *text == '\0') return (NULL);
    hText = LocalAlloc (LHND, lstrlen (text) + 1);
    lstrcpy (LocalLock (hText), text);
    LocalUnlock (hText);
    return (hText);
}
```

The code for the AllocText routine is very straightforward. It merely calls the LocalAlloc routine to allocate space for the supplied text, copies the text to its new location and returns the handle. If you prefer, you could use the C run-time strdup routine here.

Now let's look at the code required to draw the status bar. We'll use the following routine to draw sunken rectangles at various places in the status bar window.

```
//————————————————————————————————————————————
// Name:    DrawSunkenRect
// Purpose: Draw a sunken rectangle at specified location.
//————————————————————————————————————————————
static void PASCAL DrawSunkenRect (HDC dc, LPRECT lpr)
{
    HBRUSH hbr;
    int width, height;

    width = lpr−>right − lpr−>left;
    height = lpr−>bottom − lpr−>top;
    hbr = SelectObject (dc, CreateSolidBrush (GetSysColor (COLOR_BTNHIGHLIGHT)));
    PatBlt (dc, lpr−>right, lpr−>top, 1, height, PATCOPY);
    PatBlt (dc, lpr−>left, lpr−>bottom, width, 1, PATCOPY);
    DeleteObject (SelectObject (dc,CreateSolidBrush(GetSysColor(COLOR_BTNSHADOW))));
    PatBlt (dc, lpr−>left, lpr−>top, 1, height, PATCOPY);
    PatBlt (dc, lpr−>left, lpr−>top, width, 1, PATCOPY);
    DeleteObject (SelectObject (dc, hbr));
}
```

This code takes a device context and a pointer to a rectangle. The sunken rectangle is drawn using a highlighted one-pixel line for the bottom and right side and a shadowed line for the top and left side. The color of this second line corresponds to the COLOR_BTNSHADOW system color because we're using it to give a shadowed effect. Figure 4.7 shows the sort of effect you will get from using this code.

The code described here, and the code built into the internal Windows classes such as the BUTTON class, assumes that the COLOR_BTNSHADOW color is darker than the COLOR_BTNFACE color. After all, shadows are supposed to be darker than the object casting the shadow, aren't they? Realistically, there's nothing we can do to enforce this; as stated earlier, if the user wants to come up with some wacky color scheme, then that's up to him. You can content yourself with the knowledge that if the status bar ends up looking weird, so will all the other Windows elements such as push buttons, scroll bars and so forth. Fortunately, many Windows users are happy to stick with the built-in color schemes provided by the Control Panel.

```
//——————————————————————————————————————————
// Name:    StatusBarPaint
// Purpose: This routine is responsible for painting the status bar.
//——————————————————————————————————————————
static int PASCAL StatusBarPaint (HWND Wnd)
{
        int i;
        RECT r;
        PStatusRec p;
        PAINTSTRUCT ps;

        BeginPaint (Wnd, &ps);
        p = GetStatusRec (Wnd);

        // First, draw the top edge of the status bar

        GetClientRect (Wnd, &r);
        MoveTo (ps.hdc, 0, 0);
        LineTo (ps.hdc, r.right, 0);
        PatBlt (ps.hdc, 0, 1, r.right − r.left, 1, WHITENESS);

        // Now draw each cell in turn

        for (i = 0; i < p−>numParts; i++)
           PaintCell (ps.hdc, p, i);

        EndPaint (Wnd, &ps);
        return (0);
}
```

The StatusBarPaint routine is responsible for drawing the status bar whenever a WM_PAINT message is received. The routine first draws a double line along the top edge of the status bar (recall that the status bar does not have the WS_BORDER style bit set, so it's up to us to draw the border ourselves). The topmost line is drawn in black and the line below in white. This gives a nice, trendy 3D edge to our status bar although, strictly speaking, the second line should probably also be drawn using the button highlight color. You can make this change if you want to.

You might find it a little odd that I've used the PatBlt routine to draw the white line here. The reason is that it's quick and simple. If you're not too familiar with using the PatBlt routine, then I recommend that you get some practice with it. If I'd used the LineTo routine to draw a white line, I would have had to select a white pen into the device context, reposition the drawing position and so forth. PatBlt lets us eliminate all that, and it's also considerably faster in execution.

The PaintCell routine is used to draw a specified cell. Firstly, the dimensions of the rectangle are calculated and the DrawSunkenRect routine is called to draw the cell frame. If there is any text associated with the cell, the text is retrieved using the

LocalLock function and displayed in the cell frame using the DrawText routine. Note that the appropriate member of the flags array is OR'ed with the DT_VCENTER specifier to obtain the wanted text alignment for the cell. This ensures that the text is always centered vertically within the cell rectangle.

```
//——————————————————————————————————————————————————————————
// Name:    PaintCell
// Purpose: Paint a specified cell in the status bar.
//——————————————————————————————————————————————————————————
static VOID PASCAL PaintCell (HDC dc, PStatusRec p, int cellNum)
{
        RECT r;
        int mode;
        LPSTR theText;

        r.left      = (cellNum) ? p—>frames [cellNum — 1] + (p—>border * 2) : p—>border;
        r.top       = p—>border + 1;
        r.right     = p—>frames [cellNum];
        r.bottom    = p—>height — p—>border;
        DrawSunkenRect (dc, &r);

        if (p—>hText [cellNum] != NULL)
        {
          mode = SetBkMode (dc, TRANSPARENT);
          p—>statusFont = SelectObject (dc, p—>statusFont);
          InflateRect (&r, —p—>border, —p—>border);
          theText = LocalLock (p—>hText [cellNum]);
          DrawText (dc, theText, —1, &r, p—>flags [cellNum] | DT_VCENTER);
          LocalUnlock (p—>hText [cellNum]);
          p->statusFont = SelectObject (dc, p—>statusFont);
          SetBkMode (dc, mode);
        }
}
```

There's one more job to be done before building the code to see if it works. Now that we're allocating text strings as part of the StatusRec, we need to ensure that these strings are deallocated when the status bar window is destroyed. This is a convenient place at which to introduce a new routine, DestroyStatusWindow. This routine is called from StatusBarWndProc in response to a WM_DESTROY message.

```
//——————————————————————————————————————————————————————————
// Name:    DestroyStatusWindow
// Purpose: Clean-up code for the status window.
//——————————————————————————————————————————————————————————
static int PASCAL DestroyStatusWindow (HWND Wnd)
{
        int i;
        PStatusRec p;

        p = GetStatusRec (Wnd);
        DeleteObject (p—>statusFont);
        RemoveProp (GetParent (Wnd), szClassName);
        UnHookWindow (GetParent (Wnd), hookKey);

        // Deallocate text buffers

        for (i = 0; i < p—>numParts; i++)
          if (p—>hText [i] != NULL)
            LocalFree (p—>hText [i]);

        LocalFree ((HLOCAL) p);
        return (0);
}
```

I've also added the AddCell routine to the STATBAR.H include file, so as to make it part of the programming interface that can be called from the main program. Figure 4.10 shows the complete picture; this code can be found on the disk as STATBAR4.C and the modified header file as STATBAR2.H.

Figure 4.10 STATBAR4.C: the status bar code with painting and cell manipulation in place.

```
/* STATBAR4.C */

// © 1994 Dave Jewell and Addison-Wesley, ALL RIGHTS RESERVED

#include    <windows.h>
#include    "statbar.h"
#include    "sclaslib.h"

static char szClassName[] = "StatusBar";      // name of our window class
static char szHookName[] = "StatusBarHook";// name of our hook

#define     MAXCELLS            10

typedef struct StatusRec
{
       HFONT    statusFont;              // handle to our special font
       int      border;                  // width of border
       int      height;                  // height of status bar
       int      numParts;                // number of defined cells
       HLOCAL hText [MAXCELLS];          // handle to text data
       int      frames [MAXCELLS];       // right edge of each cell
       int      flags [MAXCELLS];        // flag information

} StatusRec, NEAR * PStatusRec;

static LONG hookKey;

//-----------------------------------------------------------------
// Name:    DrawSunkenRect
// Purpose: Draw a sunken rectangle at specified location.
//-----------------------------------------------------------------

static void PASCAL DrawSunkenRect (HDC dc, LPRECT lpr)
{
       HBRUSH hbr;
       int width, height;

       width = lpr−>right − lpr−>left;
       height = lpr−>bottom − lpr−>top;

       hbr = SelectObject (dc, CreateSolidBrush (GetSysColor
                   (COLOR_BTNHIGHLIGHT)));
       PatBlt (dc, lpr−>right, lpr−>top, 1, height, PATCOPY);
       PatBlt (dc, lpr−>left, lpr−>bottom, width, 1, PATCOPY);
       DeleteObject (SelectObject (dc,CreateSolidBrush
                         (GetSysColor(COLOR_BTNSHADOW))));
       PatBlt (dc, lpr−>left, lpr−>top, 1, height, PATCOPY);
       PatBlt (dc, lpr−>left, lpr−>top, width, 1, PATCOPY);
       DeleteObject (SelectObject (dc, hbr));
}

//-----------------------------------------------------------------
// Name:    GetStatusFont
// Purpose: Return a handle to our special font.
//-----------------------------------------------------------------

static HFONT PASCAL GetStatusFont (int * height)
{
       HDC dc;
```

```
        int nHeight;
        HFONT font;
        TEXTMETRIC tm;

        dc = GetDC (NULL);
        nHeight = (GetDeviceCaps (dc, LOGPIXELSY) * 8) / −72;

        font = CreateFont (nHeight, 0, 0, 0, FW_NORMAL, 0, 0, 0,
                        ANSI_CHARSET,
                        OUT_DEFAULT_PRECIS,
                        CLIP_DEFAULT_PRECIS,
                        DEFAULT_QUALITY,
                        FF_SWISS | VARIABLE_PITCH,
                        "MS Sans Serif");

        font = SelectObject (dc, font);
        GetTextMetrics (dc, &tm);
        font = SelectObject (dc, font);
        ReleaseDC (NULL, dc);
        if (height != NULL) *height = tm.tmHeight;
        return (font);
}

//————————————————————————————————————————————————————————
// Name:    GetStatusRec
// Purpose: Given a window handle, return a pointer to the corresponding
//          status record.
//————————————————————————————————————————————————————————

static PStatusRec PASCAL GetStatusRec (HWND Wnd)
{
        return (PStatusRec) GetWindowWord (Wnd, 0);
}

//————————————————————————————————————————————————————————
// Name:    AllocText
// Purpose: Allocate a chunk of text, and return a handle to it.
//————————————————————————————————————————————————————————

static HLOCAL PASCAL AllocText (LPCSTR text)
{
        HLOCAL hText;

        if (text == NULL || *text == '\0') return (NULL);
        hText = LocalAlloc (LHND, lstrlen (text) + 1);
        lstrcpy (LocalLock (hText), text);
        LocalUnlock (hText);
        return (hText);
}

//————————————————————————————————————————————————————————
// Name:    AddCell
// Purpose: Add a cell to the status bar.
// Returns: TRUE on success, FALSE on failure.
//————————————————————————————————————————————————————————

BOOL PASCAL AddCell (HWND Wnd, LPCSTR text, int nWidth)
{
        HDC dc;
        int left;
        HFONT hFont;
        PStatusRec p;

        p = GetStatusRec (Wnd);
        if (p−>numParts < MAXCELLS)
        {
            p−>hText [p−>numParts] = AllocText (text);
            p−>flags [p−>numParts] = DT_LEFT;
```

```
            // Calculate left edge of cell

            if (p->numParts) left = p->frames [p->numParts - 1] + (p->border * 2);
            else left = p->border;

            // Calculate width of string if necessary

            if (nWidth == -1 && p->hText [p->numParts] != NULL)
            {
                dc = GetDC (NULL);
                hFont = SelectObject (dc, p->statusFont);
                nWidth = LOWORD (GetTextExtent (dc, text, lstrlen (text)))
                    + p->border * 3;
                SelectObject (dc, hFont);
                ReleaseDC (NULL, dc);
            }

            // And calculate position of right edge

            if (nWidth != -1)
            {
                p->frames [p->numParts] = left + nWidth;
                ++p->numParts;
                return (TRUE);
            }
        }

    return (FALSE);
}

//------------------------------------------------------------------
// Name:    ResizeWindow
// Purpose: Routine to force status bar to proper size and position.
//------------------------------------------------------------------

static void PASCAL ResizeWindow (HWND Wnd)
{
    RECT r;
    PStatusRec p;

    p = GetStatusRec (Wnd);
    GetClientRect (GetParent (Wnd), &r);
    SetWindowPos (Wnd, 0, 0, r.bottom - p->height, r.right,
                p->height, SWP_NOZORDER);
}

//------------------------------------------------------------------
// Name:    SubclassParentWndProc
// Purpose: Subclassing routine for the main application window.
//------------------------------------------------------------------

#pragma argsused

LONG FAR PASCAL _export SubclassParentWndProc
    (HWND Wnd, WORD Msg, WPARAM wParam, LPARAM lParam)
{
    if (Msg == WM_SIZE) ResizeWindow (GetProp (Wnd, szClassName));
    return CallOldProc (Wnd, Msg, wParam, lParam, hookKey);
}

//------------------------------------------------------------------
// Name:    InitStatusWindow
// Purpose: Initialization code for setting up the status window.
//------------------------------------------------------------------

static LONG PASCAL InitStatusWindow (HWND Wnd, LONG lParam)
{
    LPCSTR text;
    PStatusRec p;
    LONG res = -1L;
```

```
        p = (PStatusRec) LocalAlloc (LPTR, sizeof (StatusRec));
        if (p != NULL)
        {
            // Initialize the StatusRec data structure

            p->numParts = 0;
            p->statusFont = GetStatusFont (&p->height);
            p->border = (GetSystemMetrics (SM_CXFRAME) + 1) / 2;
            p->height += (p->border * 4) + 1;
            SetWindowWord (Wnd, 0, (WORD) p);
            ResizeWindow (Wnd);
            SetProp (GetParent (Wnd), szClassName, Wnd);
            hookKey = HookWindow (GetParent (Wnd), (FARPROC)
                                SubclassParentWndProc, szHookName);
            // Now check for any initial text

            text = ((LPCREATESTRUCT) lParam)->lpCreateParams;
            if (text != NULL && *text != '\0') AddCell (Wnd, text, -1);

            res = 0;
        }

        return (res);
}

//------------------------------------------------------------------------
// Name:    PaintCell
// Purpose: Paint a specified cell in the status bar.
//------------------------------------------------------------------------

static VOID PASCAL PaintCell (HDC dc, PStatusRec p, int cellNum)
{
        RECT r;
        int mode;
        LPSTR theText;

        r.left    = (cellNum) ? p->frames [cellNum - 1] +
                    (p->border * 2) : p->border;
        r.top     = p->border + 1;
        r.right   = p->frames [cellNum];
        r.bottom  = p->height - p->border;
        DrawSunkenRect (dc, &r);

        if (p->hText [cellNum] != NULL)
        {
            mode = SetBkMode (dc, TRANSPARENT);
            p->statusFont = SelectObject (dc, p->statusFont);
            InflateRect (&r, -p->border, -p->border);
            theText = LocalLock (p->hText [cellNum]);
            DrawText (dc, theText, -1, &r, p->flags [cellNum] | DT_VCENTER);
            LocalUnlock (p->hText [cellNum]);
            p->statusFont = SelectObject (dc, p->statusFont);
            SetBkMode (dc, mode);
        }
}

//------------------------------------------------------------------------
// Name:    StatusBarPaint
// Purpose: This routine is responsible for painting the status bar.
//------------------------------------------------------------------------

static int PASCAL StatusBarPaint (HWND Wnd)
{
        int i;
        RECT r;
        PStatusRec p;
        PAINTSTRUCT ps;
```

```
        BeginPaint (Wnd, &ps);
        p = GetStatusRec (Wnd);

        // First, draw the top edge of the status bar

        GetClientRect (Wnd, &r);
        MoveTo (ps.hdc, 0, 0);
        LineTo (ps.hdc, r.right, 0);
        PatBlt (ps.hdc, 0, 1, r.right − r.left, 1, WHITENESS);

        // Now draw each cell in turn

        for (i = 0; i < p−>numParts; i++)
            PaintCell (ps.hdc, p, i);

        EndPaint (Wnd, &ps);
        return (0);
}

//─────────────────────────────────────────────────────────────
// Name:    DestroyStatusWindow
// Purpose: Clean-up code for the status window.
//─────────────────────────────────────────────────────────────

static int PASCAL DestroyStatusWindow (HWND Wnd)
{
        int i;
        PStatusRec p;

        p = GetStatusRec (Wnd);
        DeleteObject (p−>statusFont);
        RemoveProp (GetParent (Wnd), szClassName);
        UnHookWindow (GetParent (Wnd), hookKey);

        // Deallocate text buffers

        for (i = 0; i < p−>numParts; i++)
        if (p−>hText [i] != NULL)
        LocalFree (p−>hText [i]);
        LocalFree ((HLOCAL) p);
        return (0);
}

//─────────────────────────────────────────────────────────────
// Name:    StatusBarWndProc
// Purpose: Window procedure for status bar windows.
//─────────────────────────────────────────────────────────────

LONG FAR PASCAL _export StatusBarWndProc
    (HWND Wnd, WORD Msg, WPARAM wParam, LPARAM lParam)
{
        switch (Msg)

        {

            case WM_PAINT:

            return StatusBarPaint (Wnd);

            case WM_CREATE:

            return InitStatusWindow (Wnd, lParam);

            case WM_DESTROY:

            return DestroyStatusWindow (Wnd);
        }

        return DefWindowProc (Wnd, Msg, wParam, lParam);
}
```

```
//------------------------------------------------------------------
// Name:    RegisterStatusBar
// Purpose: Register the status bar window procedure.
//------------------------------------------------------------------

static BOOL PASCAL RegisterStatusBar (HANDLE hInstance)
{
    WNDCLASS cls;

    if (GetClassInfo (hInstance, szClassName, &cls) == 0)
    {
        cls.style            = 0;
        cls.lpfnWndProc      = (WNDPROC) StatusBarWndProc;
        cls.cbClsExtra       = 0;
        cls.cbWndExtra       = sizeof (void NEAR *);
        cls.hInstance        = hInstance;
        cls.hIcon            = 0;
        cls.hCursor          = LoadCursor (NULL, IDC_ARROW);
        cls.hbrBackground    = COLOR_BTNFACE + 1;
        cls.lpszMenuName     = NULL;
        cls.lpszClassName    = szClassName;

      return RegisterClass (&cls);
    }

    return TRUE;
}

//------------------------------------------------------------------
// Name:    CreateStatusWindow
// Purpose: Create a status window and attach it to the designated parent.
//------------------------------------------------------------------

HWND PASCAL CreateStatusWindow (HANDLE hInstance,
                                HWND hWndParent, LPCSTR lpText)
{
    HWND Wnd = NULL;
    PStatusRec p;
    int fontHeight;

    // Check that we've got a valid parent window

    if (hWndParent != NULL && IsWindow (hWndParent))
    {
        // Ok so far, but has window already got a status bar ?

      Wnd = GetProp (hWndParent, szClassName);
      if (Wnd == NULL)
        if (RegisterStatusBar (hInstance))
            Wnd = CreateWindow (szClassName, "", WS_CHILD | WS_VISIBLE,
                                0, 0, 100, 100, hWndParent, NULL,
                                hInstance, lpText);
    }

    return (Wnd);
}
```

In order to test the new code, I modified the WinMain routine in the main application program to look as below. As you can see, the call to the CreateStatusWindow routine has been supplemented with two further calls to AddCell. The first of these specifies a default cell width, while the second specifies a cell width equivalent to 200 in client coordinates.

```
// Create the main application window
Wnd = CreateWindow (szAppName, szAppName, WS_OVERLAPPEDWINDOW,
                    CW_USEDEFAULT, CW_USEDEFAULT,
                    CW_USEDEFAULT, CW_USEDEFAULT,
                    0, 0, hInstance, NULL);

if (Wnd != NULL)
{
    ShowWindow (Wnd, nCmdShow);
    UpdateWindow (Wnd);
    statusWnd = CreateStatusWindow (hInstance, Wnd, "Getting some status");
    if (statusWnd != NULL)
    {
        AddCell (statusWnd, "Coming soon in Part 2....", −1);
        AddCell (statusWnd, "Developing the API", 200);
    }
}
```

The complete source code for the main application is on the disk as STATUS3.C, and the compiled application as STATUS5.EXE. Running this program produces the status bar display shown in Figure 4.11. As we would expect, the first and second cells are sized appropriately for the text, while the third cell has some extra space. The left alignment of text is particularly apparent in the third cell.

From my totally unbiased perspective, the status bar shown in Figure 4.11 is a vision of loveliness. However, I do appreciate that not everyone has such a developed sense of aesthetics as I do! More seriously, some users of your application will be using large high-definition monitors with 1024×768 (or higher) resolution while other users may be using a plain-vanilla VGA system with 640×480 resolution.

With this in mind, it's a good idea to give your users some control over the point size of the text used in the status bar display. Word for Windows uses the same font as I do, in an eight-point, plain style. Microsoft's Control Panel application and File Manager again use the same font, but at what appears to be a slightly larger point size (it looks like ten point to me). Different again, Borland's development tools use an eight-point (I think!) font with the bold attribute turned on. The bottom line is that Windows developers (even within Microsoft) can't seem to agree on what makes the most attractive readable font. If developers can't agree, you can be sure that end users will have different opinions, too. A good solution to this problem is to provide a mechanism to allow users to change the point size and perhaps display the font in bold if preferred. These alterations are quite easy to implement and only involve

Figure 4.11 Creating three cells in the status bar.

changes to the GetStatusFont routine. Here's how you might allow selection of point size and font face name via entries in the WIN.INI initialization file:

```
//─────────────────────────────────────────────────────────────
// Name:     GetStatusFont
// Purpose:  Return a handle to our special font.
//─────────────────────────────────────────────────────────────
static HFONT PASCAL GetStatusFont (int * height)
{
    HDC dc;
    HFONT font;
    TEXTMETRIC tm;
    char faceName [50];
    int nHeight, pointSize;

    // Pickup point size and face name from WIN.INI

    pointSize = GetProfileInt ("Desktop", "StatusBarFaceHeight", 8);
    GetProfileString ("Desktop", "StatusBarFaceName", "MS Sans Serif", faceName, 50);

    // Now create the font

    dc = GetDC (NULL);
    nHeight = (GetDeviceCaps (dc, LOGPIXELSY) * pointSize) / −72;

    font = CreateFont (nHeight, 0, 0, 0, FW_NORMAL, 0, 0, 0,
                    ANSI_CHARSET,
                    OUT_DEFAULT_PRECIS,
                    CLIP_DEFAULT_PRECIS,
                    DEFAULT_QUALITY,
                    FF_SWISS | VARIABLE_PITCH,
                    faceName);

    font = SelectObject (dc, font);
    GetTextMetrics (dc, &tm);
    font = SelectObject (dc, font);
    ReleaseDC (NULL, dc);
    if (height != NULL) *height = tm.tmHeight;
    return (font);
}
```

In the same way, you could add another profile string to WIN.INI to cope with bold versus normal text, and so forth. The names that I've used here, StatusBarFaceHeight and StatusBarFaceName, are chosen for compatibility with Microsoft Windows for Workgroups. This variant of the Windows operating system contains a dynamic library called COMMCTRL.DLL. Amongst other things, this DLL implements a status bar and uses these WIN.INI entries to control the point size and face name of the font used in the status bar. By using the same names as Microsoft have chosen, we maintain compatibility with their code.

Developing the API

At this point, we've got a linkable code module that allows us to create a status bar, add cells and set up the text of each cell. Unfortunately, there's more to status bars than this. We need to be able to change the text in a cell once it's been created. Ideally, we should also be able to interrogate a cell to determine the currently selected text. It would also be nice if we could delete cells when not appropriate to the current mode of the program. Another problem concerns the operation of the AddCell routine.

Currently, it can only add cells to the end of the status bar. It would be nice if we could insert cells at an arbitrary position in the status bar. We also need a mechanism that allows us to modify the flags for each cell, so as to set text justification attributes, and so forth.

Let's write out the names of the wanted routines below:

```
SetCellText
GetCellText
DeleteCell
InsertCell
SetCellFlags
GetCellFlags
GetNumCells
GetStatusBarWindow
```

These routines seem to cover the bases described above. We'll remove the AddCell routine and replace it by the InsertCell routine, which is a more general mechanism for adding a cell at any point in the status bar. Additionally, I've added the GetNumCells routine, which returns the number of cells currently defined in the status bar.

I've also added another routine called GetStatusBarWindow, which, given the name of the parent window, returns the handle of the status bar window. This might seem like an oddity, but it's always a good idea to write a programming interface that's as easy to use as possible from the viewpoint of the application programmer. Why should he or she have to store the window handle of the status bar window that's returned from the call to CreateStatusWindow? There's no good reason why the application programmer should have to do this. If we further stipulate that the various routines above take as a parameter the window handle of the application window (rather than the window handle of the status bar), then our status bar effectively becomes an extension to the main window. In these circumstances, the GetStatusBarWindow routine is useful for explicitly destroying the status bar, as in:

```
DestroyWindow (GetStatusBarWindow (hMinWnd));
```

Let's begin by looking at the code for the new GetStatusBarWindow routine. This routine is almost trivially simple; it just checks that the passed parent window is valid and then calls GetProp to return the handle of the status bar window. If no status bar has been attached to the window, or if the parent window handle is invalid, then NULL is returned.

```
//----------------------------------------------------------------
// Name:    GetStatusBarWindow
// Purpose: Return the handle of this window's status bar.
//----------------------------------------------------------------
HWND PASCAL GetStatusBarWindow (HWND hWndParent)
{
    if (hWndParent != NULL && IsWindow (hWndParent))
        return GetProp (hWndParent, szClassName);
    else
        return NULL;
}
```

The GetNumCells routine is equally simple. It obtains a handle to the status bar window via GetStatusBarWindow and then obtains a pointer to the status bar record. If an error occurred, a value of −1 is returned, otherwise the routine returns the number of cells currently defined in the status bar. The value −1 is used to signal an error condition because this is obviously an impossible figure for the number of cells in a status bar, whereas zero would be a perfectly acceptable answer. When returning error indications, always try to use error codes that are outside the domain of what would normally be expected.

```
//─────────────────────────────────────────────────────────
// Name:     GetNumCells
// Purpose:  Return number of cells in status bar.
// Returns:  −1 on failure.
//─────────────────────────────────────────────────────────

int PASCAL GetNumCells (HWND hWndParent)
{
    PStatusRec p;
    HWND hWndStatus;

    hWndStatus = GetStatusBarWindow (hWndParent);
    p = GetStatusRec (hWndStatus);
    return (hWndStatus != NULL && p != NULL) ? p−>numParts : −1;
}
```

The GetCellFlags routine performs all the validation code mentioned above, but in addition, it checks the passed cell number to ensure that it's within the range of the cells currently defined for the status bar. In the event of an error, an error code of −1 is returned.

```
//─────────────────────────────────────────────────────────
// Name:     GetCellFlags
// Purpose:  Return the flag word for a specified cell.
// Returns:  −1 on failure.
//─────────────────────────────────────────────────────────

int PASCAL GetCellFlags (HWND hWndParent, int cellNum)
{
    PStatusRec p;
    HWND hWndStatus;

    hWndStatus = GetStatusBarWindow (hWndParent);
    p = GetStatusRec (hWndStatus);
    if (hWndStatus != NULL && p != NULL && cellNum >= 0 && cellNum < p−>numParts)
      return p−>flags [cellNum];
    else
      return −1;
}
```

The SetCellFlags routine is a little more interesting. Again, it checks the passed cell number to ensure that it's within the currently defined range for the status bar. The passed flag value is AND'ed with the combination of the DT_CENTER and DT_RIGHT. This makes sense if you look at the values for these DrawText flag values in the WINDOWS.H header file:

```
#define DT_LEFT        0x0000
#define DT_CENTER      0x0001
#define DT_RIGHT       0x0002
```

The previous value of the flag is returned as the function result from the routine. This routine also introduces another new internal routine, called GetCellRect. Given a cell number, the GetCellRect routine fills in a rectangle with the frame rectangle for that particular cell. This functionality was needed at several places in the new code, so it was made into a separate routine. By calling InvalidateRect only for the cell whose flags have been changed, we avoid having to redraw the entire status bar, which obviously reduces screen flicker and improves efficiency. As a general rule, if you can easily determine the extent of some change to a window's contents, then it's more efficient to call InvalidateRect for just that part of the window.

```
//——————————————————————————————————————————————
// Name:    SetCellFlags
// Purpose: Set the flag word for a specified cell.
// Returns: Previous flag value or −1 on failure.
//——————————————————————————————————————————————

int PASCAL SetCellFlags (HWND hWndParent, int cellNum, int flags)
{
    RECT r;
    int old;
    PStatusRec p;
    HWND hWndStatus;

    hWndStatus = GetStatusBarWindow (hWndParent);
    p = GetStatusRec (hWndStatus);
    if (hWndStatus != NULL && p != NULL && cellNum >= 0 && cellNum < p−>numParts)
    {
        old = p−>flags [cellNum];
        p−>flags [cellNum] = flags & (DT_CENTER | DT_RIGHT);
        GetCellRect (p, cellNum, &r);
        InvalidateRect (hWndStatus, &r, TRUE);
        return (old);
    }

    return −1;
}
```

The code for GetCellRect is shown below. This code should be no stranger to us, since it was previously a part of the PaintCell routine. By making it into a separate procedure, it can be called from several other places in the source module. Note that this is a static routine; it is not part of the programming interface.

```
//——————————————————————————————————————————————
// Name:    GetCellRect
// Purpose: Return the frame rectangle for a given cell.
//——————————————————————————————————————————————
static VOID PASCAL GetCellRect (PStatusRec p, int cellNum, LPRECT r)
{
    r−>left = (cellNum) ? p−>frames [cellNum − 1] + (p−>border * 2) : p−>border;
    r−>top = p−>border + 1;
    r−>right = p−>frames [cellNum];
    r−>bottom = p−>height − p−>border;
}
```

The SetCellText routine is very similar to the SetCellFlags code. It likewise calls GetCellRect to establish an invalidation rectangle. In point of fact, the rectangle returned from GetCellRect encompasses the sunken rectangle area and could therefore be shrunk further; look at the line:

```
InflateRect (&r, −p−>border, −p−>border);
```

in the PaintCell code. However, if you're worried about carrying drawing optimizations down to this sort of level, you should probably be running Windows on a faster machine! The SetCellText routine also takes care to deallocate any previously existing text before allocating room for the new text. Note that you can call the SetCellText routine with the lpText parameter set to NULL or pointing at an empty string. In this case, the old text will be removed but will not be replaced; the cell will appear as an empty box in the status bar.

```
//––––––––––––––––––––––––––––––––––––––––––––––––––––––––––––––––––
// Name:     SetCellText
// Purpose:  Set the text of a specified cell to 'lpText'.
// Returns:  TRUE on success, FALSE on failure.
//––––––––––––––––––––––––––––––––––––––––––––––––––––––––––––––––––

BOOL PASCAL SetCellText (HWND hWndParent, LPCSTR lpText, int cellNum)
{
    RECT r;
    PStatusRec p;
    HWND hWndStatus;

    hWndStatus = GetStatusBarWindow (hWndParent);
    p = GetStatusRec (hWndStatus);
    if (hWndStatus != NULL && p != NULL && cellNum >= 0 && cellNum < p–>numParts)
    {
        if (p–>hText [cellNum] != NULL) LocalFree (p–>hText [cellNum]);
        p–>hText [cellNum] = AllocText (lpText);
        GetCellRect (p, cellNum, &r);
        InvalidateRect (hWndStatus, &r, TRUE);
        return (TRUE);
    }

    return (FALSE);
}
```

The GetCellText routine is relatively complicated, mainly as a result of all the parameter validation that it needs to perform. The retrieved text is copied into the user-supplied buffer, up to the number of bytes specified by the buffSize parameter. This figure does not include the trailing null byte appended to the end of the string. If the string associated with the wanted status bar cell is longer than the available buffer length, it is truncated. I haven't used the C run-time library routine strncpy here since it will only cater for 'near' strings; you could probably use something like _fstrncpy which can cope with far pointers, but my technique saves pulling another library module into the link.

```
//––––––––––––––––––––––––––––––––––––––––––––––––––––––––––––––––––
// Name:     GetCellText
// Purpose:  Retrieve the text of a specified cell.
// Returns:  Number of bytes copied to destination (not including null byte).
//––––––––––––––––––––––––––––––––––––––––––––––––––––––––––––––––––

int PASCAL GetCellText (HWND hWndParent, int cellNum, LPSTR buffer, int buffSize)
{
    int bytes;
    LPSTR text;
    HLOCAL th;
    PStatusRec p;
    char ch = '\0';
    HWND hWndStatus;

    hWndStatus = GetStatusBarWindow (hWndParent);
    p = GetStatusRec (hWndStatus);
```

```
if (hWndStatus != NULL && p != NULL && cellNum >= 0 && cellNum < p->numParts)
    if (buffer != NULL)
    {
        *buffer = '\0';
        if ((th = p->hText [cellNum]) != NULL)
        {
            text = LocalLock (th);
            if ((bytes = lstrlen (text)) > buffSize)
            {
                ch = text [buffSize];
                text [buffSize] = '\0';
                bytes = buffSize;
            }

            lstrcpy (buffer, text);
            if (ch != '\0') text [buffSize] = ch;
            LocalUnlock (th);
            return (bytes);
        }
    }
return (0);
}
```

The InsertCell and DeleteCell routines are the most complex of the new API routines. The InsertCell routine is similar to the AddCell code that it replaces, but it's designed to be more flexible. A fourth parameter, pos, specifies the position in the status bar at which the new cell should be inserted. If the pos parameter is set to −1, the new cell is inserted at the end of any existing cells. If pos is set to 0, the new cell becomes the first cell in the status bar; setting pos to 1 makes the new cell appear as the second cell in the status bar, and so on.

Obviously, from a programming point of view, the simplest case occurs when the new cell is being inserted at the end of the status bar. In all other cases, it's necessary to 'shuffle' existing cells to the right to make room for the new cell. In the case of the InsertCell code, shown below, this shuffling is primarily accomplished through the three memmove calls which move the contents of the hText, frames and flags arrays to make room for the new cell. Whenever you use the memcpy or memmove routines to move memory around like this, always ask yourself whether the source and destination buffers overlap. In this case they do, which means that you can't use the memcpy routine. The memmove routine has to be used whenever buffer overlap takes place.

There's another point concerning the use of the memmove routine: by using it, we've effectively locked ourselves into the use of near pointers for this code. If the status bar record was allocated 'far' using GlobalAlloc, then we wouldn't be able to use memmove. This isn't likely to be a problem for you unless your application makes heavy use of the local heap. Even then, there's a lot to be said for leaving the StatusRec allocated locally for the sake of efficiency, and just moving the text string handles out to global memory. Because the StatusRec data is allocated at many points in the code, this would seem to be a reasonable trade-off between memory usage and run-time performance.

Having shuffled the other cells to the right, the code also needs to adjust the right-edge boundaries (the frames array) for all following cells in the status bar. Because all following cells will effectively change in position, the InvalidateRect routine is called with a NULL rectangle pointer so as to invalidate the entire status bar at the end of the insert operation. However, if you're really paranoid about efficiency, you could adjust the left edge of the invalidation rectangle to coincide with the left edge of the newly inserted cell. That way, nothing before the new cell would need to be redrawn.

```
//————————————————————————————————————————————————
// Name:    InsertCell
// Purpose: Insert a cell into the status bar.
// Returns: TRUE on success, FALSE on failure.
//————————————————————————————————————————————————

BOOL PASCAL InsertCell (HWND hWndParent, LPCSTR text, int nWidth, int pos)
{
    HDC dc;
    int i, left;
    HFONT hFont;
    PStatusRec p;
    HWND hWndStatus;

    hWndStatus = GetStatusBarWindow (hWndParent);
    p = GetStatusRec (hWndStatus);
    if (hWndStatus != NULL && p != NULL && p->numParts < MAXCELLS)
    {
        // Get pos parameter in range

        if (pos == -1 || pos > p->numParts) pos = p->numParts;

        // Do we need to shuffle ?

        if (pos < p->numParts)
        {
            // Yes, we do !

            memmove (&p->hText [pos + 1], &p->hText [pos],
                        (p->numParts - pos) * sizeof (p->hText [0]));
            memmove (&p->frames [pos + 1], &p->frames [pos],
                        (p->numParts - pos) * sizeof (p->frames [0]));
            memmove (&p->flags [pos + 1], &p->flags [pos],
                        (p->numParts - pos) * sizeof (p->flags [0]));
        }

        p->hText [pos] = AllocText (text);
        p->flags [pos] = DT_LEFT;

        // Calculate left edge of cell

        if (pos) left = p->frames [pos - 1] + (p->border * 2);
        else left = p->border;

        // Calculate width of string if necessary

        if (nWidth == -1 && p->hText [pos] != NULL)
        {
            dc = GetDC (NULL);
            hFont = SelectObject (dc, p->statusFont);
            nWidth = LOWORD (GetTextExtent (dc, text, lstrlen (text))) +
                            p->border * 3;

            SelectObject (dc, hFont);
            ReleaseDC (NULL, dc);
        }

        // And calculate position of right edge

        if (nWidth != -1)
        {
            p->frames [pos] = left + nWidth;

            // Do we need to shuffle position of following cells ?

            if (pos < p->numParts)
                for (i = pos + 1; i <= p->numParts; i++)
```

```
                              p–>frames [i] += nWidth + (p–>border * 2);

                    ++p–>numParts;
                    InvalidateRect (hWndStatus, NULL, TRUE);
                    return (TRUE);
                }
            }

        return (FALSE);
    }

    //————————————————————————————————————————————————
    // Name:    DeleteCell
    // Purpose: Delete a cell from the status bar.
    // Returns: TRUE on success, FALSE on failure.
    //————————————————————————————————————————————————
    BOOL PASCAL DeleteCell (HWND hWndParent, int pos)
    {
        int i;
        RECT r;
        PStatusRec p;
        HWND hWndStatus;

        hWndStatus = GetStatusBarWindow (hWndParent);
        p = GetStatusRec (hWndStatus);
        if (hWndStatus != NULL && p != NULL && pos >= 0 && pos < p–>numParts)
        {
            if (p–>hText [pos] != NULL) LocalFree (p–>hText [pos]);

            // Do we need to shuffle ?

            if (pos < p–>numParts –1)
            {
                GetCellRect (p, pos, &r);

                // Adjust any following right borders

                for (i = pos + 1; i < p–>numParts; i++)
                    p–>frames [i] –= (r.right – r.left) + (p–>border * 2);

                // And shuffle everything up one slot

                memmove (&p–>hText [pos], &p–>hText [pos + 1],
                        (p–>numParts – pos –1) * sizeof (p–>hText [0]));
                memmove (&p–>frames [pos], &p–>frames [pos + 1],
                        (p–>numParts – pos –1) * sizeof (p–>frames [0]));
                memmove (&p–>flags [pos], &p–>flags [pos + 1],
                        (p–>numParts – pos –1) * sizeof (p–>flags [0]));
            }

            ––p–>numParts;
            InvalidateRect (hWndStatus, NULL, TRUE);
            return (TRUE);
        }

        return (FALSE);
    }
```

The DeleteCell routine also needs to perform a certain amount of shuffling, but of course it's in the opposite direction; when a cell is deleted, all the cells to the right have to move one place to the left. The memmove routine calls in this routine and in the InsertCell routine both use the sizeof operator to determine the number of bytes to move. This is a useful technique; if you ever change one of these arrays to be an array of 32-bit integers or an array of bytes (or even an array of structures), the code will still work properly. Whenever you write similar code, try to make use of the sizeof operator to improve portability and make the code more future-proof.

Figure 4.12 brings this all together by showing the complete source code for STATBAR5.C. This file is on the companion disk under that name. The revised header file, including all the new API routines, is shown in Figure 4.13.

```
/* STATBAR5.C */

// © 1994 Dave Jewell and Addison-Wesley, ALL RIGHTS RESERVED

#include    <mem.h>
#include    <windows.h>
#include    "statbar.h"
#include    "sclaslib.h"

static char szClassName[ ] = "StatusBar";       // name of our window class
static char szHookName[ ] = "StatusBarHook";    // name of our hook

#define     MAXCELLS            10

typedef struct StatusRec
{
        HFONT       statusFont;             // handle to our special font
        int         border;                 // width of border
        int         height;                 // height of status bar
        int         numParts;               // number of defined cells
        HLOCAL      hText [MAXCELLS];        // handle to text data
        int         frames [MAXCELLS];      // right edge of each cell
        int         flags [MAXCELLS];       // flag information

} StatusRec, NEAR * PStatusRec;

static LONG hookKey;

//————————————————————————————————————————————————————————————————
// Name:     DrawSunkenRect
// Purpose:  Draw a sunken rectangle at specified location.
//————————————————————————————————————————————————————————————————

static void PASCAL DrawSunkenRect (HDC dc, LPRECT lpr)
{
        HBRUSH hbr;
        int width, height;

        width = lpr–>right – lpr–>left;
        height = lpr–>bottom – lpr–>top;

        hbr = SelectObject (dc, CreateSolidBrush (GetSysColor
                        (COLOR_BTNHIGHLIGHT)));
        PatBlt (dc, lpr–>right, lpr–>top, 1, height, PATCOPY);
        PatBlt (dc, lpr–>left, lpr–>bottom, width, 1, PATCOPY);
        DeleteObject (SelectObject (dc,CreateSolidBrush (GetSysColor
                        (COLOR_BTNSHADOW))));
        PatBlt (dc, lpr–>left, lpr–>top, 1, height, PATCOPY);
        PatBlt (dc, lpr–>left, lpr–>top, width, 1, PATCOPY);
        DeleteObject (SelectObject (dc, hbr));
}

//————————————————————————————————————————————————————————————————
// Name:     GetStatusFont
// Purpose:  Return a handle to our special font.
//————————————————————————————————————————————————————————————————

static HFONT PASCAL GetStatusFont (int * height)
{
        HDC dc;
        HFONT font;
```

Figure 4.12   STATBAR5.C: the status bar module with the new API routines included.

```
        TEXTMETRIC tm;
        char faceName [50];
        int nHeight, pointSize;

        // Pickup point size and face name from WIN.INI

        pointSize = GetProfileInt ("Desktop", "StatusBarFaceHeight", 8);
        GetProfileString ("Desktop", "StatusBarFaceName",
                          "MS Sans Serif", faceName, 50);

        // Now create the font

        dc = GetDC (NULL);
        nHeight = (GetDeviceCaps (dc, LOGPIXELSY) * pointSize) / −72;

        font = CreateFont (nHeight, 0, 0, 0, FW_NORMAL, 0, 0, 0,
                          ANSI_CHARSET,
                          OUT_DEFAULT_PRECIS,
                          CLIP_DEFAULT_PRECIS,
                          DEFAULT_QUALITY,
                          FF_SWISS | VARIABLE_PITCH,
                          faceName);

        font = SelectObject (dc, font);
        GetTextMetrics (dc, &tm);
        font = SelectObject (dc, font);
        ReleaseDC (NULL, dc);
        if (height != NULL) *height = tm.tmHeight;
        return (font);
}

//——————————————————————————————————————————————————————————
// Name:     GetStatusRec
// Purpose:  Given a window handle, return a pointer to the corresponding
//           status record.
//——————————————————————————————————————————————————————————

static PStatusRec PASCAL GetStatusRec (HWND Wnd)
{
        return (PStatusRec) GetWindowWord (Wnd, 0);
}

//——————————————————————————————————————————————————————————
// Name:     AllocText
// Purpose:  Allocate a chunk of text, and return a handle to it.
//——————————————————————————————————————————————————————————

static HLOCAL PASCAL AllocText (LPCSTR text)
{
        HLOCAL hText;

        if (text == NULL || *text == '\0') return (NULL);
        hText = LocalAlloc (LHND, lstrlen (text) + 1);
        lstrcpy (LocalLock (hText), text);
        LocalUnlock (hText);
        return (hText);
}

//——————————————————————————————————————————————————————————
// Name:     ResizeWindow
// Purpose:  Routine to force status bar to proper size and position.
//——————————————————————————————————————————————————————————

static void PASCAL ResizeWindow (HWND Wnd)
{
        RECT r;
        PStatusRec p;

        p = GetStatusRec (Wnd);
        GetClientRect (GetParent (Wnd), &r);
```

```
        SetWindowPos (Wnd, 0, 0, r.bottom − p−>height, r.right,
                      p−>height, SWP_NOZORDER);
}

//———————————————————————————————————————————————————————————————————
// Name:    SubclassParentWndProc
// Purpose: Subclassing routine for the main application window.
//———————————————————————————————————————————————————————————————————

#pragma argsused

LONG FAR PASCAL _export SubclassParentWndProc (HWND Wnd, WORD Msg,
                                    WPARAM wParam, LPARAM lParam)
{
        if (Msg == WM_SIZE) ResizeWindow (GetStatusBarWindow (Wnd));
        return CallOldProc (Wnd, Msg, wParam, lParam, hookKey);
}

//———————————————————————————————————————————————————————————————————
// Name:    InitStatusWindow
// Purpose: Initialization code for setting up the status window.
//———————————————————————————————————————————————————————————————————

static LONG PASCAL InitStatusWindow (HWND Wnd, LONG lParam)
{
        LPCSTR text;
        PStatusRec p;
        LONG res = −1L;

        p = (PStatusRec) LocalAlloc (LPTR, sizeof (StatusRec));
        if (p != NULL)
        {
            // Initialize the StatusRec data structure

            p−>numParts = 0;
            p−>statusFont = GetStatusFont (&p−>height);
            p−>border = (GetSystemMetrics (SM_CXFRAME) + 1) / 2;
            p−>height += (p−>border * 4) + 1;
            SetWindowWord (Wnd, 0, (WORD) p);
            ResizeWindow (Wnd);
            SetProp (GetParent (Wnd), szClassName, Wnd);
            hookKey = HookWindow (GetParent (Wnd), (FARPROC)
                                  SubclassParentWndProc, szHookName);

            // Now check for any initial text

            text = ((LPCREATESTRUCT) lParam)−>lpCreateParams;
            if (text != NULL && *text != '\0')
                InsertCell (GetParent (Wnd), text, −1, −1);

            res = 0;
        }
        return (res);
}

//———————————————————————————————————————————————————————————————————
// Name:    GetCellRect
// Purpose: Return the frame rectangle for a given cell.
//———————————————————————————————————————————————————————————————————

static VOID PASCAL GetCellRect (PStatusRec p, int cellNum, LPRECT r)
{
        r−>left = (cellNum) ? p−>frames [cellNum − 1]
                 + (p−>border * 2) : p−>border;
        r−>top = p−>border + 1;
        r−>right = p−>frames [cellNum];
        r−>bottom = p−>height − p−>border;
}
```

```
//—————————————————————————————————————————————
// Name:    PaintCell
// Purpose: Paint a specified cell in the status bar.
//—————————————————————————————————————————————

static VOID PASCAL PaintCell (HDC dc, PStatusRec p, int cellNum)
{
        RECT r;
        int mode;
        LPSTR theText;

        GetCellRect (p, cellNum, &r);
        DrawSunkenRect (dc, &r);

        if (p−>hText [cellNum] != NULL)
        {
          mode = SetBkMode (dc, TRANSPARENT);
          p−>statusFont = SelectObject (dc, p−>statusFont);
          InflateRect (&r, −p−>border, −p−>border);
          theText = LocalLock (p−>hText [cellNum]);
          DrawText (dc, theText, −1, &r, p−>flags [cellNum] | DT_VCENTER);
          LocalUnlock (p−>hText [cellNum]);
          p−>statusFont = SelectObject (dc, p−>statusFont);
          SetBkMode (dc, mode);
        }
}

//—————————————————————————————————————————————
// Name:    StatusBarPaint
// Purpose: This routine is responsible for painting the status bar.
//—————————————————————————————————————————————

static int PASCAL StatusBarPaint (HWND Wnd)
{
        int i;
        RECT r;
        PStatusRec p;
        PAINTSTRUCT ps;

        BeginPaint (Wnd, &ps);
        p = GetStatusRec (Wnd);

        // First, draw the top edge of the status bar

        GetClientRect (Wnd, &r);
        MoveTo (ps.hdc, 0, 0);
        LineTo (ps.hdc, r.right, 0);
        PatBlt (ps.hdc, 0, 1, r.right − r.left, 1, WHITENESS);

        // Now draw each cell in turn

        for (i = 0; i < p−>numParts; i++)
           PaintCell (ps.hdc, p, i);

        EndPaint (Wnd, &ps);
        return (0);
}

//—————————————————————————————————————————————
// Name:    DestroyStatusWindow
// Purpose: Clean-up code for the status window.
//—————————————————————————————————————————————

static int PASCAL DestroyStatusWindow (HWND Wnd)
{
        int i;
        PStatusRec p;

        p = GetStatusRec (Wnd);
        DeleteObject (p−>statusFont);
```

```
            RemoveProp (GetParent (Wnd), szClassName);
            UnHookWindow (GetParent (Wnd), hookKey);

            // Deallocate text buffers

            for (i = 0; i < p−>numParts; i++)
               if (p−>hText [i] != NULL)
                  LocalFree (p−>hText [i]);
            LocalFree ((HLOCAL) p);
            return (0);
    }

    //─────────────────────────────────────────────────────────
    // Name:    StatusBarWndProc
    // Purpose: Window procedure for status bar windows.
    //─────────────────────────────────────────────────────────

    LONG FAR PASCAL _export StatusBarWndProc (HWND Wnd, WORD Msg,
                                    WPARAM wParam, LPARAM lParam)
    {
        switch (Msg)
        {
          case WM_PAINT:

            return StatusBarPaint (Wnd);

          case WM_CREATE:

            return InitStatusWindow (Wnd, lParam);

          case WM_DESTROY:

            return DestroyStatusWindow (Wnd);
        }

        return DefWindowProc (Wnd, Msg, wParam, lParam);
    }

    //─────────────────────────────────────────────────────────
    // Name:    RegisterStatusBar
    // Purpose: Register the status bar window procedure.
    //─────────────────────────────────────────────────────────

    static BOOL PASCAL RegisterStatusBar (HANDLE hInstance)
    {
        WNDCLASS cls;

        if (GetClassInfo (hInstance, szClassName, &cls) == 0)
        {
            cls.style            = 0;
            cls.lpfnWndProc      = (WNDPROC) StatusBarWndProc;
            cls.cbClsExtra       = 0;
            cls.cbWndExtra       = sizeof (void NEAR *);
            cls.hInstance        = hInstance;
            cls.hIcon            = 0;
            cls.hCursor          = LoadCursor (NULL, IDC_ARROW);
            cls.hbrBackground    = COLOR_BTNFACE + 1;
            cls.lpszMenuName     = NULL;
            cls.lpszClassName    = szClassName;

            return RegisterClass (&cls);
        }
        return TRUE;
    }

    //─────────────────────────────────────────────────────────
    // Name:    GetStatusBarWindow
    // Purpose: Return the handle of this window's status bar.
    //─────────────────────────────────────────────────────────
```

```
HWND PASCAL GetStatusBarWindow (HWND hWndParent)
{
    if (hWndParent != NULL && IsWindow (hWndParent))
      return GetProp (hWndParent, szClassName);
    else
      return NULL;
}

//————————————————————————————————————————————————————
// Name:    CreateStatusWindow
// Purpose: Create a status window and attach it to the designated parent.
//————————————————————————————————————————————————————

HWND PASCAL CreateStatusWindow (HANDLE hInstance,
                                HWND hWndParent, LPCSTR lpText)
{
    HWND Wnd = NULL;
    PStatusRec p;
    int fontHeight;

    // Check that we've got a valid parent window

    if (hWndParent != NULL && IsWindow (hWndParent))
    {
      // Ok so far, but has window already got a status bar ?

      Wnd = GetStatusBarWindow (hWndParent);
      if (Wnd == NULL)
        if (RegisterStatusBar (hInstance))
          Wnd = CreateWindow (szClassName, "", WS_CHILD | WS_VISIBLE,
                              0, 0, 100, 100, hWndParent, NULL,
                              hInstance, lpText);
    }

    return (Wnd);
}

//————————————————————————————————————————————————————
// Name:    GetNumCells
// Purpose: Return number of cells in status bar.
// Returns: −1 on failure.
//————————————————————————————————————————————————————

int PASCAL GetNumCells (HWND hWndParent)
{
    PStatusRec p;
    HWND hWndStatus;
    hWndStatus = GetStatusBarWindow (hWndParent);
    p = GetStatusRec (hWndStatus);
    return (hWndStatus != NULL && p != NULL) ? p->numParts : −1;
}

//————————————————————————————————————————————————————
// Name:    GetCellFlags
// Purpose: Return the flag word for a specified cell.
// Returns: −1 on failure.
//————————————————————————————————————————————————————

int PASCAL GetCellFlags (HWND hWndParent, int cellNum)
{
    PStatusRec p;
    HWND hWndStatus;

    hWndStatus = GetStatusBarWindow (hWndParent);
    p = GetStatusRec (hWndStatus);
    if (hWndStatus != NULL && p != NULL && cellNum >= 0 &&
        cellNum < p->numParts)
      return p->flags [cellNum];
```

```
        else
            return −1;
}

//─────────────────────────────────────────────────────────
// Name:     SetCellFlags
// Purpose:  Set the flag word for a specified cell.
// Returns:  Previous flag value or −1 on failure.
//─────────────────────────────────────────────────────────

int PASCAL SetCellFlags (HWND hWndParent, int cellNum, int flags)
{
        RECT r;
        int old;
        PStatusRec p;
        HWND hWndStatus;

        hWndStatus = GetStatusBarWindow (hWndParent);
        p = GetStatusRec (hWndStatus);
        if (hWndStatus != NULL && p != NULL && cellNum >= 0 &&
            cellNum < p−>numParts)
        {
            old = p−>flags [cellNum];
            p−>flags [cellNum] = flags & (DT_CENTER | DT_RIGHT);
            GetCellRect (p, cellNum, &r);
            InvalidateRect (hWndStatus, &r, TRUE);
            return (old);
        }

        return −1;
}

//─────────────────────────────────────────────────────────
// Name:     GetCellText
// Purpose:  Retrieve the text of a specified cell.
// Returns:  Number of bytes copied to destination (not including null byte).
//─────────────────────────────────────────────────────────

int PASCAL GetCellText (HWND hWndParent, int cellNum, LPSTR buffer, int
                        buffSize)
{
        int bytes;
        LPSTR text;
        HLOCAL th;
        PStatusRec p;
        char ch = '\0';
        HWND hWndStatus;

        hWndStatus = GetStatusBarWindow (hWndParent);
        p = GetStatusRec (hWndStatus);
        if (hWndStatus != NULL && p != NULL && cellNum >= 0 &&
            cellNum < p−>numParts)
          if (buffer != NULL)
          {
            *buffer = '\0';
            if ((th = p−>hText [cellNum]) != NULL)
            {
               text = LocalLock (th);
               if ((bytes = lstrlen (text)) > buffSize)
               {
                  ch = text [buffSize];
                  text [buffSize] = '\0';
                  bytes = buffSize;
               }
               lstrcpy (buffer, text);
               if (ch != '\0') text [buffSize] = ch;
               LocalUnlock (th);
               return (bytes);
```

```
                }
            }

        return (0);
    }

//————————————————————————————————————————————————
// Name:     SetCellText
// Purpose:  Set the text of a specified cell to 'lpText'.
// Returns:  TRUE on success, FALSE on failure.
//————————————————————————————————————————————————

BOOL PASCAL SetCellText (HWND hWndParent, LPCSTR lpText, int cellNum)
{
    RECT r;
    PStatusRec p;
    HWND hWndStatus;

    hWndStatus = GetStatusBarWindow (hWndParent);
    p = GetStatusRec (hWndStatus);
    if (hWndStatus != NULL && p != NULL && cellNum >= 0 &&
        cellNum < p->numParts)
    {
        if (p->hText [cellNum] != NULL) LocalFree (p->hText [cellNum]);
        p->hText [cellNum] = AllocText (lpText);
        GetCellRect (p, cellNum, &r);
        InvalidateRect (hWndStatus, &r, TRUE);
        return (TRUE);
    }

    return (FALSE);
}

//————————————————————————————————————————————————
// Name:     InsertCell
// Purpose:  Insert a cell into the status bar.
// Returns:  TRUE on success, FALSE on failure.
//————————————————————————————————————————————————

BOOL PASCAL InsertCell (HWND hWndParent, LPCSTR text, int nWidth, int pos)
{
    HDC dc;
    int i, left;
    HFONT hFont;
    PStatusRec p;
    HWND hWndStatus;

    hWndStatus = GetStatusBarWindow (hWndParent);
    p = GetStatusRec (hWndStatus);
    if (hWndStatus != NULL && p != NULL && p->numParts < MAXCELLS)
    {
        // Get pos parameter in range

        if (pos == -1 || pos > p->numParts) pos = p->numParts;

        // Do we need to shuffle ?

        if (pos < p->numParts)
        {
            // Yes, we do !

            memmove (&p->hText [pos + 1], &p->hText [pos],
                        (p->numParts - pos) * sizeof (p->hText [0]));
                        memmove (&p->frames [pos + 1], &p->frames [pos],
                        (p->numParts - pos) * sizeof (p->frames [0]));
                        memmove (&p->flags [pos + 1], &p->flags [pos],
                        (p->numParts - pos) * sizeof (p->flags [0]));
        }
```

```
        p->hText [pos] = AllocText (text);
        p->flags [pos] = DT_LEFT;

        // Calculate left edge of cell

        if (pos) left = p->frames [pos - 1] + (p->border * 2);
        else left = p->border;

        // Calculate width of string if necessary

        if (nWidth == -1 && p->hText [pos] != NULL)
        {
            dc = GetDC (NULL);
            hFont = SelectObject (dc, p->statusFont);
            nWidth = LOWORD (GetTextExtent (dc, text, lstrlen (text))) +
                               p->border * 3;
            SelectObject (dc, hFont);
            ReleaseDC (NULL, dc);
        }

        // And calculate position of right edge

        if (nWidth != -1)
        {
            p->frames [pos] = left + nWidth;

            // Do we need to shuffle position of following cells ?

            if (pos < p->numParts)
              for (i = pos + 1; i <= p->numParts; i++)
                p->frames [i] += nWidth + (p->border * 2);

            ++p->numParts;
            InvalidateRect (hWndStatus, NULL, TRUE);
            return (TRUE);
        }
    }

    return (FALSE);
}

//----------------------------------------------------------------
// Name:     DeleteCell
// Purpose:  Delete a cell from the status bar.
// Returns:  TRUE on success, FALSE on failure.
//----------------------------------------------------------------

BOOL PASCAL DeleteCell (HWND hWndParent, int pos)
{
    int i;
    RECT r;
    PStatusRec p;
    HWND hWndStatus;

    hWndStatus = GetStatusBarWindow (hWndParent);
    p = GetStatusRec (hWndStatus);
    if (hWndStatus != NULL && p != NULL && pos >= 0 && pos < p->numParts)
    {
        if (p->hText [pos] != NULL) LocalFree (p->hText [pos]);

        // Do we need to shuffle ?

        if (pos < p->numParts - 1)
        {
            GetCellRect (p, pos, &r);

            // Adjust any following right borders

            for (i = pos + 1; i < p->numParts; i++)
            p->frames [i] -= (r.right - r.left) + (p->border * 2);
```

```
                // And shuffle everything up one slot

                memmove (&p->hText [pos], &p->hText [pos + 1],
                        (p->numParts – pos – 1) * sizeof (p->hText [0]));
                memmove (&p->frames [pos], &p->frames [pos + 1],
                        (p->numParts – pos – 1) * sizeof (p->frames [0]));
                memmove (&p->flags [pos], &p->flags [pos + 1],
                        (p->numParts – pos – 1) * sizeof (p->flags [0]));
            }

            —p->numParts;
            InvalidateRect (hWndStatus, NULL, TRUE);
            return (TRUE);
        }

        return (FALSE);
    }
```

Figure 4.13 STATBAR3.H: the revised header file.

```
/* STATBAR3.H */

// © 1994 Dave Jewell and Addison-Wesley, ALL RIGHTS RESERVED

#ifndef _INC_STATBAR
#define _INC_STATBAR          /* #defined if statlib.h has been included */

#ifdef         __cplusplus
extern         "C" {
#endif

int PASCAL GetNumCells (HWND hWndParent);
int PASCAL GetCellFlags (HWND hWndParent, int cellNum);
int PASCAL SetCellFlags (HWND hWndParent, int cellNum, int flags);
HWND PASCAL GetStatusBarWindow (HANDLE hWndParent);
BOOL PASCAL SetCellText (HWND hWndParent, LPCSTR lpText, int cellNum);
int PASCAL GetCellText (HWND hWndParent, int cellNum, LPSTR buffer,
                        int buffSize);
BOOL PASCAL InsertCell (HWND hWndParent, LPCSTR text, int nWidth, int pos);
BOOL PASCAL DeleteCell (HWND hWndParent, int pos);
HWND PASCAL CreateStatusWindow (HANDLE hInstance, HWND hWndParent,
                        LPCSTR lpText);

#ifdef         __cplusplus
}
#endif

#endif
```

Keeping track of your keyboard

Now that we have a fully working status bar, let's try it out by writing an application that displays the state of the various keyboard 'modifiers' in three cells of the status bar. Many programs, such as Word for Windows, display the Caps Lock, Num Lock and Insert mode in the status bar so that the user always knows what to expect when he or she presses a key on the keyboard. These three cells should use the DT_CENTER flag so that the text appears centered within each cell.

```
if (CreateStatusWindow (hInstance, Wnd, NULL) != NULL)
{
    InsertCell (Wnd, NULL, 70, −1);
    InsertCell (Wnd, NULL, 70, −1);
    InsertCell (Wnd, NULL, 70, −1);

    for (i = 0; i < 3; i++)
        SetCellFlags (Wnd, i, DT_CENTER);
}
```

This fragment of code creates a status bar and then inserts three cells into it, each of which is initially empty. Here, each of the three cells is 70 client coordinates wide for the sake of simplicity, but in practice, you would naturally base the cell widths on the intended cell contents. After creating the cells, the SetCellFlags routine is called to set the DT_CENTER attribute for each of the cells.

The NumLock and CapsLock are system-wide keyboard toggles. This means that the state of the CapsLock and NumLock flags affect every application. Once you've pressed the CapsLock key on your keyboard, every character you type will be upper case. This is true even if you switch over to another Windows application. The same is true of the NumLock toggle. They're called toggles because you press them once to turn them on and you press them again to turn them off. In other words, they 'remember' their current state. This should be obvious from watching the CapsLock and NumLock lights on your keyboard.

The Insert key is quite different. For a start, it isn't system-wide, but is specific to each application. You might, for example, have two different instances of a word processing application running. Pressing the Insert key would toggle the active application between overwrite and insert mode, but it would do nothing for the other, inactive application. To toggle the other application, you would need first to make it the active window. This is an important point, as you'll see when we examine the code. The IBM PC has built-in hardware which 'latches' the state of the CapsLock and NumLock keys, but no such hardware exists for the Insert key. In fact, from a hardware point of view, the Insert key has no special significance at all; it's just another keystroke. It just happens to be convention that many Windows programs use it for toggling between insert and overwrite modes.

Because the Insert key is an ordinary key, we can handle it in our Windows program just as we handle any other keystroke. In other words, we need to intercept the WM_KEYDOWN message within the main application's window procedure. Here's how we would do it:

```
case WM_KEYDOWN:
if (wParam == VK_INSERT) SetCellText (Wnd, (insert ^= 1) ? "Insert" : NULL, 0);
break;
```

For the sake of simplicity, this code fragment doesn't show any other application-specific key processing that you might wish to perform. Here, we're only interested in the Insert key, which corresponds to the value VK_INSERT in the wParam field.

When an Insert keypress is detected, a global variable called insert is toggled. By exclusive-OR'ing this variable with 1, we can force it to flip from one state to another. In other words, if the insert flag is currently set to 0, then exclusive-

OR'ing with 1 will set it to 1. If it's already set to 1, then it will be set to 0. This is a little trick that will save you some code, but perhaps at the expense of a little readability! Depending on the final setting of the insert flag, the SetCellText routine is called to set the cell text either to Insert or to NULL, in which case no text is shown.

If you press either the CapsLock or NumLock key while your application is active, you will get a WM_KEYDOWN message with the wParam field set to either VK_CAPITAL or VK_NUMLOCK, respectively. This sounds ideal; it sounds like we can use the same mechanism as for the Insert key. Sadly, such is not the case.

The key (pun strictly intentional!) phrase above is 'while your application is active'. If the CapsLock or NumLock key is pressed while your application does not have the focus, then no WM_KEYDOWN message will be sent to your program's message queue. Consequently, your application won't see the keypress and will not be able to update the display in the status bar.

As was pointed out earlier, the CapsLock and NumLock keys are latched and have a persistent state. This means that we can actually interrogate their state at any time, irrespective of normal message processing. Windows has an API routine called GetKeyboardState that can be used to determine the state of every key on your keyboard. When called, GetKeyboardState fills a 256-byte buffer with information on the state of the keys. For most normal keys, this is effectively a snapshot of which keys are up and which are down. However, for toggles, like the CapsLock and NumLock keys, the GetKeyboardState routine can be used to determine whether or not they are turned on. If the least significant bit (bit 0) of a particular toggle key is set, then it indicates that this particular key is 'on'. The idea is illustrated below:

```
BYTE keys [256];

GetKeyboardState (keys);
if (numlock != (keys [VK_NUMLOCK] & 1))
{
      numlock = keys [VK_NUMLOCK] & 1;
      SetCellText (Wnd, (numlock) ? "NumLock" : NULL, 1);
}

if (caps != (keys [VK_CAPITAL] & 1))
{
      caps = keys [VK_CAPITAL] & 1;
      SetCellText (Wnd, (caps) ? "CapsLock" : NULL, 2);
}
```

In this sample code, the GetKeyboardState routine is first called to fill the keys array with information on the various characters. The numlock and caps variables are assumed to be global variables that reflect the current NumLock and CapsLock state of the keyboard. For each of these two variables, the keys array is interrogated to see if the state of that particular toggle has changed. If so, the appropriate global variable is updated and the SetCellText routine called to reflect the change in the status bar display.

```
/* STATUS4.C */

// © 1994 Dave Jewell and Addison-Wesley, ALL RIGHTS RESERVED

#include    <windows.h>
#include    "statbar.h"

char szAppName[] = "StatusTest";

int insert = 0, numlock = −1, caps = −1;

//──────────────────────────────────────────────────────
// Name:    CheckKeyboard
// Purpose: Routine to check the keyboard modifiers and set status bar.
//──────────────────────────────────────────────────────

void PASCAL CheckKeyboard (HWND Wnd, WORD Msg, WPARAM wParam)
{
     BYTE keys [256];

     GetKeyboardState (keys);
     if (numlock != (keys [VK_NUMLOCK] & 1))
     {
        numlock = keys [VK_NUMLOCK] & 1;
        SetCellText (Wnd, (numlock) ? "NumLock" : NULL, 1);
     }

     if (caps != (keys [VK_CAPITAL] & 1))
     {
        caps = keys [VK_CAPITAL] & 1;
        SetCellText (Wnd, (caps) ? "CapsLock" : NULL, 2);
     }

     if (Msg == WM_KEYDOWN && wParam == VK_INSERT)
        SetCellText (Wnd, (insert ^= 1) ? "Insert" : NULL, 0);
}

//──────────────────────────────────────────────────────
// Name:    WindowProc
// Purpose: Window procedure for main application window.
//──────────────────────────────────────────────────────

LONG FAR PASCAL _export WindowProc (HWND Wnd, WORD Msg,
                                    WPARAM wParam, LPARAM lParam)
{
     CheckKeyboard (Wnd, Msg, wParam);

     switch (Msg)
     {
       case WM_DESTROY:

       PostQuitMessage (0);
       return (0);
     }

     return DefWindowProc (Wnd, Msg, wPararn, lParam);
}

//──────────────────────────────────────────────────────
// Name:    InitAppClass
// Purpose: Register the main application window class.
//──────────────────────────────────────────────────────

BOOL PASCAL InitAppClass (HANDLE hInstance)
{
     WNDCLASS cls;

     if (GetClassInfo (hInstance, szAppName, &cls) == 0)
     {
       cls.style          = CS_VREDRAW | CS_HREDRAW;
```

```
                cls.lpfnWndProc        = (WNDPROC) WindowProc;
                cls.cbClsExtra         = 0;
                cls.cbWndExtra         = 0;
                cls.hInstance          = hInstance;
                cls.hIcon              = LoadIcon (NULL, IDI_APPLICATION);
                cls.hCursor            = LoadCursor (NULL, IDC_ARROW);
                cls.hbrBackground      = GetStockObject (WHITE_BRUSH);
                cls.lpszMenuName       = NULL;
                cls.lpszClassName      = szAppName;
                return RegisterClass (&cls);
            }

            return (TRUE);
        }

//─────────────────────────────────────────────────────────────────
// Name:    WinMain
// Purpose: Main application entry point.
//─────────────────────────────────────────────────────────────────

#pragma argsused

int PASCAL WinMain (HANDLE hInstance, HANDLE hPrevInstance,
                    LPSTR lpCmdLine, int nCmdShow)
{
        int i;
        HWND Wnd;
        MSG Msg;

        // Register application class if needed

        if (InitAppClass (hInstance) == FALSE)
            return (0);

        // Create the main application window

        Wnd = CreateWindow (szAppName, szAppName, WS_OVERLAPPEDWINDOW,
                            CW_USEDEFAULT, CW_USEDEFAULT,
                            CW_USEDEFAULT, CW_USEDEFAULT,
                            0, 0, hInstance, NULL);

        if (Wnd != NULL)
        {
            ShowWindow (Wnd, nCmdShow);
            UpdateWindow (Wnd);
            if (CreateStatusWindow (hInstance, Wnd, NULL) != NULL)
            {
                InsertCell (Wnd, NULL, 70, −1);
                InsertCell (Wnd, NULL, 70, −1);
                InsertCell (Wnd, NULL, 70, −1);

                for (i = 0; i < 3; i++)
                    SetCellFlags (Wnd, i, DT_CENTER);
            }
        }

        while (GetMessage (&Msg, 0, 0, 0))
        {
            TranslateMessage (&Msg);
            DispatchMessage (&Msg);
        }

        return (Msg.wParam);
}
```

Figure 4.14 shows the complete application source. In this example, the code that checks for keypresses and updates the status bar has been wrapped up into one routine called CheckKeyboard. Using this approach, we ensure that the status bar is updated as soon as possible when the relevant keys are pressed. You will find that this happens instantaneously when your application has the input focus. If the CapsLock or NumLock key is pressed while another program has the focus, the status bar will not be updated until your application receives a message. (Just moving the mouse over the application window without activating it will cause the status bar to change, as the application receives a series of WM_MOUSEMOVE messages.)

You will see the same behavior if you shrink down Word for Windows so that it occupies only part of the screen. Make another application such as the Program Manager active and press the CapsLock key. You won't see Word for Windows update its status bar until it receives a message, causing Word for Windows to perform the equivalent of the CheckKeyboard code shown above.

The code in Figure 4.14 is perfectly adequate for most purposes, and behaves pretty much like Word for Windows, as I've shown. Wouldn't it be nice, though, if the application's status bar immediately reflected changes to CapsLock and NumLock, even when the application didn't actually have the input focus? As it turns out, it's quite simple to achieve this: it's just a matter of ensuring that the application regularly gets a message even when it isn't active. This can be done simply by setting up a timer and checking the state of the CapsLock and NumLock keys in response to a WM_TIMER message. In a sense, this is taking things a little too far. The user shouldn't really expect the status bar of an inactive application to be updated, and you shouldn't consider worrying about cosmetic niceties such as this unless you have strong feelings one way or the other! However, if you want to do this, the code in Figure 4.15 shows how you would go about it.

```
/* STATUS5.C */

// © 1994 Dave Jewell and Addison-Wesley, ALL RIGHTS RESERVED

#include    <windows.h>
#include    "statbar.h"

char szAppName[] = "StatusTest";

int insert = 0, numlock = −1, caps = −1;

//—————————————————————————————————————
// Name:     CheckKeyboard
// Purpose:  Routine to check the keyboard modifiers and set status bar.
//—————————————————————————————————————

void PASCAL CheckKeyboard (HWND Wnd)
{
      BYTE keys [256];

      GetKeyboardState (keys);
      if (numlock != (keys [VK_NUMLOCK] & 1))
      {
         numlock = keys [VK_NUMLOCK] & 1;
         SetCellText (Wnd, (numlock) ? "NumLock" : NULL, 1);
      }
```

Figure 4.15   STATUS5.C: automatic updating of the status bar display.

```
        if (caps != (keys [VK_CAPITAL] & 1))
        {
            caps = keys [VK_CAPITAL] & 1;
            SetCellText (Wnd, (caps) ? "CapsLock" : NULL, 2);
        }
}

//--------------------------------------------------------------
// Name:    WindowProc
// Purpose: Window procedure for main application window.
//--------------------------------------------------------------
LONG FAR PASCAL _export WindowProc (HWND Wnd, WORD Msg,
                                    WPARAM wParam, LPARAM lParam)
{
    switch (Msg)
    {
      case WM_TIMER:

        CheckKeyboard (Wnd);
        break;

      case WM_CREATE:

        SetTimer (Wnd, 0x1000, 250, NULL);
        break;

      case WM_KEYDOWN:

        if (wParam == VK_INSERT)
            SetCellText (Wnd, (insert ^= 1) ? "Insert" : NULL, 0);
        break;

      case WM_DESTROY:

        KillTimer (Wnd, 0x1000);
        PostQuitMessage (0);
        break;

      default:

        return DefWindowProc (Wnd, Msg, wParam, lParam);
    }

    return (0);
}

//--------------------------------------------------------------
// Name:    InitAppClass
// Purpose: Register the main application window class.
//--------------------------------------------------------------
BOOL PASCAL InitAppClass (HANDLE hInstance)
{
    WNDCLASS cls;

    if (GetClassInfo (hInstance, szAppName, &cls) == 0)
    {
        cls.style           = CS_VREDRAW | CS_HREDRAW;
        cls.lpfnWndProc     = (WNDPROC) WindowProc;
        cls.cbClsExtra      = 0;
        cls.cbWndExtra      = 0;
        cls.hInstance       = hInstance;
        cls.hIcon           = LoadIcon (NULL, IDI_APPLICATION);
        cls.hCursor         = LoadCursor (NULL, IDC_ARROW);
        cls.hbrBackground   = GetStockObject (WHITE_BRUSH);
        cls.lpszMenuName    = NULL;
        cls.lpszClassName   = szAppName;
        return RegisterClass (&cls);
    }
```

```
        return (TRUE);
}

//———————————————————————————————————————————————————————————
// Name:    WinMain
// Purpose: Main application entry point.
//———————————————————————————————————————————————————————————

#pragma argsused

int PASCAL WinMain (HANDLE hInstance, HANDLE hPrevInstance,
                    LPSTR lpCmdLine, int nCmdShow)
{
    int i;
    HWND Wnd;
    MSG Msg;

    // Register application class if needed

    if (InitAppClass (hInstance) == FALSE)
        return (0);

    // Create the main application window

    Wnd = CreateWindow (szAppName, szAppName, WS_OVERLAPPEDWINDOW,
                    CW_USEDEFAULT, CW_USEDEFAULT,
                    CW_USEDEFAULT, CW_USEDEFAULT,
                    0, 0, hInstance, NULL);

    if (Wnd != NULL)
    {
        ShowWindow (Wnd, nCmdShow);
        UpdateWindow (Wnd);
        if (CreateStatusWindow (hInstance, Wnd, NULL) != NULL)
        {
            InsertCell (Wnd, NULL, 70, −1);
            InsertCell (Wnd, NULL, 70, −1);
            InsertCell (Wnd, NULL, 70, −1);

            for (i = 0; i < 3; i++)
                SetCellFlags (Wnd, i, DT_CENTER);
        }
    }

    while (GetMessage (&Msg, 0, 0, 0))
    {
        TranslateMessage (&Msg);
        DispatchMessage (&Msg);
    }

    return (Msg.wParam);
}
```

Incidentally, the initial state of the insert, numlock and caps global variables is quite important. The insert flag is initially turned off, which means that the application 'wakes up', in overwrite mode. You can obviously change this by altering the initialization statement for the global variable. Some text editors, such as Borland's development tools, allow you to specify whether the editor will start in insert or over-write mode. The other two flags must be initialized to an invalid value (−1). This ensures that the first time the CheckKeyboard routine is called, it will decide that the values of the CapsLock and NumLock toggles have changed, forcing the status bar

Figure 4.16 The status bar display produced by the STATUS5.C program.

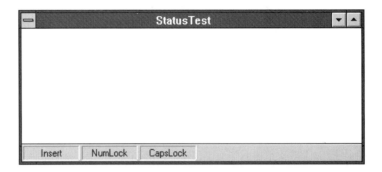

to be updated to reflect the true state of affairs. In situations like this, initializing a variable to some invalid value is always a good way of forcing an immediate update. The source code to the STATUS5.C file is on the companion disk, and the corresponding executable file is called STATUS6.EXE. The status bar display produced by the STATUS5.C program is shown in Figure 4.16.

The STATUS5.C code is probably somewhat more efficient than the previous version of the program. Although the overhead in calling the GetKeyboardState routine is relatively minor, as a general rule you should avoid calling some particular routine *every* time a message is received. By only checking when a WM_TIMER message is received, regular message processing will be more efficient, but against that you need to balance the loss of one of the available timers.

More subclassing skullduggery

In this chapter, we've used the generic subclasser from Chapter 3 in such a way as to hide the changes we've made to the main application window procedure. In this particular case, the change was pretty trivial; we only had to intercept the WM_SIZE message to keep the status bar window correctly sized. In the code developed in the previous section, we've made some further alterations to the application's window procedure in order to support keyboard status cells in the status bar.

This naturally begs the question: would it be possible to incorporate these changes behind the scenes, inside the subclassing mechanism, so as to make the operation of the keyboard status cells completely transparent to the main application?

The answer to this question is yes. It would be perfectly possible to extend the status bar API we've got to enable you to do something like this:

```
// Add a cell to the end of the status bar
InsertCell (Wnd, NULL, 70, −1);
// Mark the cell as a CapsLock status cell
SetCellFlags (Wnd, GetNumCells (Wnd) − 1, DT_CENTER | STATBAR_NUMLOCK);
```

In this fictitious example, the InsertCell routine is used to add an empty cell to the end of the status bar. The SetCellFlags call is then used in conjunction with the

GetNumCells function to set the flags for this cell. The DT_CENTER flag is used along with a new flag, called STATBAR_NUMLOCK. This flag would be recognized by the internal SetCellFlags code as an instruction to turn this cell into a NumLock 'reporter' cell. The necessary code could then be enabled in the subclassing routine to check for WM_KEYDOWN events and call the GetKeyboardState API routine as explained earlier.

If all this sounds very object-oriented, you'd be right. Although I have a certain healthy skepticism that the C++ programming language is going to cure all the world's programming problems, I am a great fan of the OOP philosophy in general. Fundamental to this is the concept of information hiding: burying detail away so that the application program doesn't need to be concerned with it. By modifying the status bar code to make it work as described here, we would be effectively turning the CapsLock, NumLock and Insert cells into independent little objects that almost seem to have a life of their own. The bad news is that I'm not going to implement this code for you. In time-honored tradition, this is being left as an exercise for the reader! However, if you do want to do this, you shouldn't find it difficult. All the code is already written; it's mainly a matter of moving things into the subclassing procedure and giving the SetCellFlags routine the ability to recognize and act upon the STATBAR_NUMLOCK flag and the other flags needed to implement the Insert and NumLock cells. Instead, we'll be looking at something of perhaps greater importance to most application developers: menu hinting.

Taking the hint

Menu hinting and status bars go hand in hand like bread and butter. It seems natural, therefore, to round out this chapter by adding a little more code to the status bar module to implement menu hinting.

So what exactly is menu hinting? Menu hinting is a useful technique that helps users find their way around the menu structure of a Windows application. As far as I know, the idea was pioneered by Microsoft. Every time that the user pulls down a drop-down menu, the contents of the status bar change to provide some help information on the menu item that is directly beneath the mouse. As the user moves the mouse up and down within the menu, the status bar keeps track, always displaying help information for the currently highlighted menu item. Things work just as well if you're not using a mouse; navigating around an application's menu using the keyboard will show you just the same information. When you close the menu (either by selecting a menu item, pressing the ESC key or clicking the mouse somewhere outside the menu area), the status bar immediately returns to normal.

Word for Windows is an example of a Microsoft application that implements menu hinting. Of the programs that come with Windows 3.1 itself, only the PIF Editor has menu hinting. As you move the mouse around inside the menu structure, you'll see useful 'hint' information appear for each menu item. An example is shown in Figure 4.17.

As it turns out, it's possible to put menu hinting capabilities into the status bar code module by adding a single routine to the interface. This routine, called SetHintText, allows the application program to pass a text string to the status bar code.

Figure 4.17 Menu hinting in Microsoft's PIF Editor program.

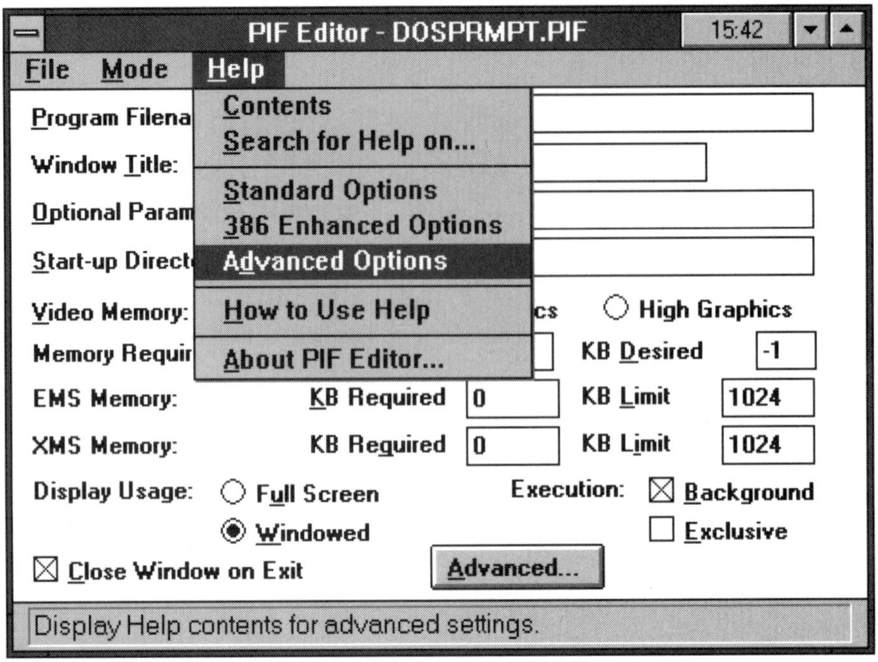

Here's how it works: firstly, we add a new handle to the StatusRec data structure called hintText. This field represents the handle of the current menu hint string passed in via the SetHintText routine. When the status bar drawing code comes to draw the status bar, it checks to see whether or not the hintText field is NULL. If it's NULL, it works in the usual way, drawing each cell in the status bar. On the other hand, if the handle is not NULL, then the hint text string is drawn instead.

```
//—————————————————————————————————————————————————————————————
// Name:    PaintHintText
// Purpose: Paint the special menu hint text.
//—————————————————————————————————————————————————————————————
static VOID PASCAL PaintHintText (HWND Wnd, PStatusRec p, HDC dc)
{
    RECT r;
    LPSTR theText;
    int width, mode;

    // Calculate the bounding box

    GetClientRect (GetParent (Wnd), &r);
    width = r.right − r.left − (p−>border * 2);
    GetCellRect (p, 0, &r);
    r.right = r.left + width;
    InflateRect (&r, −p−>border, −p−>border);

    // Now draw the text...

    mode = SetBkMode (dc, TRANSPARENT);
    p−>statusFont = SelectObject (dc, p−>statusFont);
    theText = LocalLock (p−>hintText);
    DrawText (dc, theText, −1, &r, DT_LEFT | DT_VCENTER | DT_EXPANDTABS);
    LocalUnlock (p−>hintText);
```

```
        p−>statusFont = SelectObject (dc, p−>statusFont);
        SetBkMode (dc, mode);
}

//————————————————————————————————————————————————————
// Name:     StatusBarPaint
// Purpose:  This routine is responsible for painting the status bar.
//————————————————————————————————————————————————————

static int PASCAL StatusBarPaint (HWND Wnd)
{
        int i;
        RECT r;
        PStatusRec p;
        PAINTSTRUCT ps;

        BeginPaint (Wnd, &ps);
        p = GetStatusRec (Wnd);

        // First, draw the top edge of the status bar

        GetClientRect (Wnd, &r);
        MoveTo (ps.hdc, 0, 0);
        LineTo (ps.hdc, r.right, 0);
        PatBlt (ps.hdc, 0, 1, r.right − r.left, 1, WHITENESS);

        // Are we in hint mode ?

        if (p−>hintText != NULL) PaintHintText (Wnd, p, ps.hdc);
        else
        {

          // Now draw each cell in turn

          for (i = 0; i < p−>numParts; i++)
             PaintCell (ps.hdc, p, i);
        }

        EndPaint (Wnd, &ps);
        return (0);
}
```

As you can see, the StatusBarPaint routine now checks to see if the handle to the hint text is NULL. If not, it calls a new routine, PaintHintText, to draw the current hint text rather than drawing the various cells of the status bar.

The PaintHintText routine determines the total width of the status bar and uses this as a basis for calling the DrawText routine. Hint text is always left-aligned, and the DT_EXPANDTABS flag has also been set in the call to DrawText so that you can embed tab characters into the menu hint information if desired.

With this mechanism in place, it's important to remember to do the right thing when the status bar window is created and destroyed. Thus the InitStatusWindow routine needs to be modified to initialize the hintText field to NULL, and the DestroyStatusWindow needs to call LocalFree for the hintText handle if it isn't NULL at the time that the window is destroyed. This shouldn't be necessary in practice since, as we shall see, the application code should clear the menu hint text when the menu is closed.

The SetHintText routine can be called from the application in one of three ways, as shown below:

```
SetHintText (Wnd, "Hello World");
SetHintText (Wnd, "");
SetHintText (Wnd, NULL);
```

In the first example, the menu hint text string is set to "Hello World". This text immediately appears in the menu bar and remains until the SetHintText routine is called again or the status bar window is destroyed. In the second case, an empty (zero length) string is passed. This causes the status bar code to display an empty status bar with no cells or menu hint text visible. You might wonder why this is necessary. The reason is that as the user navigates around in the application program's menu structure, there may well be places where it is not appropriate to draw any menu text. This will most typically happen when a menu separator is highlighted – the horizontal line between groups of similar menu items within the same drop-down menu.

It doesn't make sense to display any menu hint text when a separator is highlighted. Equally, we shouldn't revert to the 'normal' status bar view at this time. The normal status bar should not be restored until the menu has been dismissed. This is an important visual cue for the user, which shows that menu hinting is still in operation. It's therefore best to show an empty status bar at this point.

In the third case, a NULL pointer is passed to the SetHintText routine. This indicates to the status bar code that the menu hinting operation is over and normal operation should be resumed. With this in mind, the code below shows the operation of the SetHintText routine. Perhaps the only part of the code that requires some explanation is the comment relating to 'tweaking' the text. Recall that if the AllocText routine sees an empty string, it will return a NULL handle. In this particular case, we don't want a NULL handle to result, since setting the hintText handle to NULL indicates the end of the hinting operation. Therefore, if an empty string is passed to the SetHintText routine, it's replaced by a string containing a single space character. It's this single-space character string that actually gets drawn when a menu separator is highlighted and the status bar appears to be empty.

```
//---------------------------------------------------------------
// Name:     SetHintText
// Purpose:  Set up a text string for menu hinting.
// Returns:  TRUE on success, FALSE on failure.
// Notes:    Passing an empty string clears the status bar.
//           Passing NULL turns off menu hinting.
//           Anything else is interpreted as text and drawn as a hint.
//---------------------------------------------------------------

BOOL PASCAL SetHintText (HWND hWndParent, LPCSTR lpText)
{
    PStatusRec p;
    HWND hWndStatus;

    hWndStatus = GetStatusBarWindow (hWndParent);
    p = GetStatusRec (hWndStatus);
    if (hWndStatus != NULL && p != NULL)
    {
        // Delete any existing hint text

        if (p->hintText != NULL) LocalFree (p->hintText);

        // Tweak the text to get around AllocText "auto-NULL"

        if (lpText != NULL && *lpText == '\0') lpText = " ";

        p->hintText = AllocText (lpText);

        // Force redraw of status bar
```

```
        InvalidateRect (hWndStatus, NULL, TRUE);
        return (TRUE);
    }

    return (FALSE);

}
```

Now let's turn our attention to the changes needed in the application code. Figure 4.18 shows the full source code for STATUS6.C, the final version of our testbed code. This application has been modified to support menu hinting although, as I shall explain, the hints you'll get here will not be terribly informative!

The major change to the code is the inclusion of a new routine called MenuHint. This routine is called in response to a WM_MENUSELECT message. These messages are the key to menu hinting. While a menu is active (in other words, you have a drop-down menu on the screen) the Windows system will send a WM_MENUSELECT message to your application's main window whenever the currently highlighted menu item changes. By examining the various fields that comprise a WM_MENUSELECT message, the application can determine which menu item is currently highlighted and use the SetHintText routine to set up an appropriate hint text string in the status bar.

When a menu is closed (either by choosing an actual menu item or else by canceling the menu), a WM_MENUSELECT message is also sent to the application window. In this particular case, the lParam field is set to the value 0xFFFF. If you look at the code for the MenuHint routine, you'll see that when this condition is recognized, the code calls the SetHintText function with a NULL pointer. This causes the status bar to return to normal operation.

There's also an explicit check to see if the menu item now highlighted happens to be a menu separator line. In this case, there's obviously no hint text to be displayed and so the SetHintText routine is called with an empty string, causing the status bar to appear empty.

```
/* STATUS6.C */

// © 1994 Dave Jewell and Addison-Wesley, ALL RIGHTS RESERVED

#include    <windows.h>
#include    "statbar.h"

char szAppName[] = "StatusTest";

int insert = 0, numlock = −1, caps = −1;

//------------------------------------------------------------
// Name:     MenuHint
// Purpose:  Routine to set menu hint strings in status bar.
//------------------------------------------------------------

void PASCAL MenuHint (HWND Wnd, WPARAM wParam, LPARAM lParam)
{
        WORD flags;
        char buff [100];
        flags = LOWORD (lParam);

        // If menu closed, then return status bar to normal

        if (lParam == 0xFFFF) SetHintText (Wnd, NULL);
```

Figure 4.18 STATUS6.C: the application program with menu hinting support.

```
        else if (flags & MF_SEPARATOR) SetHintText (Wnd, "");
        else
        {
            GetMenuString (HIWORD (lParam), wParam, buff, sizeof (buff),
                    MF_BYCOMMAND);
            SetHintText (Wnd, buff);
        }
}

//----------------------------------------------------------------------
// Name:    CheckKeyboard
// Purpose: Routine to check the keyboard modifiers and set status bar.
//----------------------------------------------------------------------

void PASCAL CheckKeyboard (HWND Wnd)
{
        BYTE keys [256];

        GetKeyboardState (keys);

        if (numlock != (keys [VK_NUMLOCK] & 1))
        {
            numlock = keys [VK_NUMLOCK] & 1;
            SetCellText (Wnd, (numlock) ? "NumLock" : NULL, 1);
        }

        if (caps != (keys [VK_CAPITAL] & 1))
        {
            caps = keys [VK_CAPITAL] & 1;
            SetCellText (Wnd, (caps) ? "CapsLock" : NULL, 2);
        }
}

//----------------------------------------------------------------------
// Name:    WindowProc
// Purpose: Window procedure for main application window.
//----------------------------------------------------------------------

LONG FAR PASCAL _export WindowProc (HWND Wnd, WORD Msg,
                                    WPARAM wParam, LPARAM lParam)
{
        switch (Msg)
        {
        case WM_MENUSELECT:

            MenuHint (Wnd, wParam, lParam);
            break;

        case WM_TIMER:

            CheckKeyboard (Wnd);
            break;

        case WM_CREATE:

            SetTimer (Wnd, 0x1000, 250, NULL);
            break;

        case WM_KEYDOWN:

            if (wParam == VK_INSERT) SetCellText (Wnd, (insert ^= 1) ?
                                                "Insert" : NULL, 0);
            break;

        case WM_DESTROY:

            KillTimer (Wnd, 0x1000);
            PostQuitMessage (0);
            break;
```

```
        default:

        return DefWindowProc (Wnd, Msg, wParam, lParam);
    }

    return (0);
}

//────────────────────────────────────────────────────────────────
// Name:    InitAppClass
// Purpose: Register the main application window class.
//────────────────────────────────────────────────────────────────

BOOL PASCAL InitAppClass (HANDLE hInstance)
{
    WNDCLASS cls;

    if (GetClassInfo (hInstance, szAppName, &cls) == 0)
    {
        cls.style           = CS_VREDRAW | CS_HREDRAW;
        cls.lpfnWndProc     = (WNDPROC) WindowProc;
        cls.cbClsExtra      = 0;
        cls.cbWndExtra      = 0;
        cls.hInstance       = hInstance;
        cls.hIcon           = LoadIcon (NULL, IDI_APPLICATION);
        cls.hCursor         = LoadCursor (NULL, IDC_ARROW);
        cls.hbrBackground   = GetStockObject (WHITE_BRUSH);
        cls.lpszMenuName    = MAKEINTRESOURCE (1);
        cls.lpszClassName   = szAppName;
        return RegisterClass (&cls);
    }

    return (TRUE);
}

//────────────────────────────────────────────────────────────────
// Name:    WinMain
// Purpose: Main application entry point.
//────────────────────────────────────────────────────────────────

#pragma argsused

int PASCAL WinMain (HANDLE hInstance, HANDLE hPrevInstance,
                    LPSTR lpCmdLine, int nCmdShow)
{
    int i;
    HWND Wnd;
    MSG Msg;

    // Register application class if needed

    if (InitAppClass (hInstance) == FALSE)
      return (0);

    // Create the main application window

    Wnd = CreateWindow (szAppName, szAppName, WS_OVERLAPPEDWINDOW,
                        CW_USEDEFAULT, CW_USEDEFAULT,
                        CW_USEDEFAULT, CW_USEDEFAULT,
                        0, 0, hInstance, NULL);

    if (Wnd != NULL)
    {
      ShowWindow (Wnd, nCmdShow);
      UpdateWindow (Wnd);
      if (CreateStatusWindow (hInstance, Wnd, NULL) != NULL)
      {
        InsertCell (Wnd, NULL, 70, −1);
        InsertCell (Wnd, NULL, 70, −1);
```

```
                    InsertCell (Wnd, NULL, 70, −1);

                    for (i = 0; i < 3; i++)
                        SetCellFlags (Wnd, i, DT_CENTER);
                    }

                }

                while (GetMessage (&Msg, 0, 0, 0))
                {
                    TranslateMessage (&Msg);
                    DispatchMessage (&Msg);
                }

                return (Msg.wParam);
            }
```

More typically, an ordinary menu item will be highlighted. This is where I've cheated in the sample code: all I've done for demonstration purposes is copy the text of the menu item into a buffer, and then use the contents of this buffer as the text passed to the SetHintText routine! This is not going to be terribly informative for the user!

What's really needed, of course, is a means of mapping the highlighted menu ID onto a text string that you've defined yourself. In practice, this can be done quite easily using resource strings. My personal suggestion would be to set up a resource string for each of the menu identifiers in your program. Give each hint string a resource ID that corresponds to a particular menu item in your program. When the WM_MENUSELECT message is received, the wParam field corresponds to the menu ID of the highlighted menu item.

The STATUS6.C source code can be found on the companion disk, and the corresponding executable file is called STATUS7.EXE. In order to test out the program, I needed a menu structure to work with, so I just used Borland's Resource Workshop to copy over the menu from Microsoft's Program Manager. The resource script for this menu is shown in Appendix 4, along with the Pascal equivalent of the code that we've developed in this chapter.

An interesting aspect of the status bar code which may not be immediately obvious is the fact that you can make changes to the status bar even while menu hinting is in operation. Indeed, this is just what happens if you press the Insert, NumLock or CapsLock key while a menu is active. Because the hintText handle is not NULL, the normal status bar display is hidden until the SetHintText routine is called with a non-NULL handle. In fact, if your program makes a lot of changes to cells in the status bar, then it might be a good idea to call SetHintText (Wnd, "") as a means of effectively hiding the regular status display while these changes are taking place. Once done, the whole status bar can be updated in one operation to give a smoother effect.

The earlier discussion about hiding keyboard status cells 'behind' the subclassing mechanism applies equally well to the issue of menu hinting. It would be quite straightforward to intercept the WM_MENUSELECT message inside the status bar code and take the appropriate action. In this way, a menu hinting capability could be provided without any special action being taken by the main application code. This still leaves us with the issue of where do we get the hint messages from, but if we adopt the convention of loading resource strings with the same ID as the highlighted menu item, this is not a problem as it can easily done internally to the status bar code. There is, as you can see, plenty of opportunity for experimentation.

Figure 4.19 shows STATBAR6.C, the final state of the status bar code. I haven't shown the header file again since only one line has been added to it, this being the definition for the SetHintText routine as shown below. The final version of this file can be found on the disk as STATBAR4.H.

```
BOOL PASCAL SetHintText (HWND hWndParent, LPCSTR lpText);
```

Figure 4.19 STATBAR6.C: the finished status bar and menu hinting code.

```
/* STATBAR6.C */

// © 1993 Dave Jewell and Addison-Wesley, ALL RIGHTS RESERVED

#include    <mem.h>
#include    <windows.h>
#include    "statbar.h"
#include    "sclaslib.h"

static char szClassName[] = "StatusBar";      // name of our window class
static char szHookName[] = "StatusBarHook";// name of our hook

#define     MAXCELLS              10

typedef struct StatusRec
{
      HLOCAL  hintText;               // handle of menu hint text
      HFONT   statusFont;             // handle to our special font
      int       border;                 // width of border
      int       height;                 // height of status bar
      int       numParts;              // number of defined cells
      HLOCAL  hText [MAXCELLS];   // handle to text data
      int       frames [MAXCELLS]; // right edge of each cell
      int       flags [MAXCELLS];   // flag information

} StatusRec, NEAR * PStatusRec;

static LONG hookKey;

//————————————————————————————————————————————————
// Name:    DrawSunkenRect
// Purpose: Draw a sunken rectangle at specified location.
//————————————————————————————————————————————————

static void PASCAL DrawSunkenRect (HDC dc, LPRECT lpr)
{
      HBRUSH hbr;
      int width, height;

      width = lpr−>right − lpr−>left;
      height = lpr−>bottom − lpr−>top;

      hbr = SelectObject (dc, CreateSolidBrush (GetSysColor
                  (COLOR_BTNHIGHLIGHT)));

      PatBlt (dc, lpr−>right, lpr−>top, 1, height, PATCOPY);
      PatBlt (dc, lpr−>left, lpr−>bottom, width, 1, PATCOPY);
      DeleteObject (SelectObject (dc,CreateSolidBrush
                  (GetSysColor(COLOR_BTNSHADOW))));
```

```
        PatBlt (dc, lpr−>left, lpr−>top, 1, height, PATCOPY);
        PatBlt (dc, lpr−>left, lpr−>top, width, 1, PATCOPY);
        DeleteObject (SelectObject (dc, hbr));
}

//————————————————————————————————————————————————————————
// Name:    GetStatusFont
// Purpose: Return a handle to our special font.
//————————————————————————————————————————————————————————

static HFONT PASCAL GetStatusFont (int * height)
{
        HDC dc;
        HFONT font;
        TEXTMETRIC tm;
        char faceName [50];
        int nHeight, pointSize;

        // Pickup point size and face name from WIN.INI

        pointSize = GetProfileInt ("Desktop", "StatusBarFaceHeight", 8);
        GetProfileString ("Desktop", "StatusBarFaceName", "MS Sans Serif",
                        faceName, 50);

        // Now create the font

        dc = GetDC (NULL);
        nHeight = (GetDeviceCaps (dc, LOGPIXELSY) * pointSize) / −72;

        font = CreateFont (nHeight, 0, 0, 0, FW_NORMAL, 0, 0, 0,
                        ANSI_CHARSET,
                        OUT_DEFAULT_PRECIS,
                        CLIP_DEFAULT_PRECIS,
                        DEFAULT_QUALITY,
                        FF_SWISS | VARIABLE_PITCH,
                        faceName);

        font = SelectObject (dc, font);
        GetTextMetrics (dc, &tm);
        font = SelectObject (dc, font);
        ReleaseDC (NULL, dc);
        if (height != NULL) *height = tm.tmHeight;
        return (font);
}

//————————————————————————————————————————————————————————
// Name:    GetStatusRec
// Purpose: Given a window handle, return a pointer to the corresponding
//          status record.
//————————————————————————————————————————————————————————

static PStatusRec PASCAL GetStatusRec (HWND Wnd)
{
        return (PStatusRec) GetWindowWord (Wnd, 0);
}

//————————————————————————————————————————————————————————
// Name:    AllocText
// Purpose: Allocate a chunk of text, and return a handle to it.
//————————————————————————————————————————————————————————

static HLOCAL PASCAL AllocText (LPCSTR text)
{
        HLOCAL hText;

        if (text == NULL || *text == '\0') return (NULL);
        hText = LocalAlloc (LHND, lstrlen (text) + 1);
        lstrcpy (LocalLock (hText), text);
```

```
        LocalUnlock (hText);
        return (hText);
}

//————————————————————————————————————————————————————
// Name:    ResizeWindow
// Purpose: Routine to force status bar to proper size and position.
//————————————————————————————————————————————————————

static void PASCAL ResizeWindow (HWND Wnd)
{
        RECT r;
        PStatusRec p;

        p = GetStatusRec (Wnd);
        GetClientRect (GetParent (Wnd), &r);
        SetWindowPos (Wnd, 0, 0, r.bottom − p−>height, r.right, p−>height,
                        SWP_NOZORDER);
}

//————————————————————————————————————————————————————
// Name:    SubclassParentWndProc
// Purpose: Subclassing routine for the main application window.
//————————————————————————————————————————————————————

#pragma argsused

LONG FAR PASCAL _export SubclassParentWndProc (HWND Wnd, WORD Msg,
                                            WPARAM wParam, LPARAM
                                            lParam)
{
        if (Msg == WM_SIZE) ResizeWindow (GetStatusBarWindow (Wnd));
        return CallOldProc (Wnd, Msg, wParam, lParam, hookKey);
}

//————————————————————————————————————————————————————
// Name:    InitStatusWindow
// Purpose: Initialization code for setting up the status window.
//————————————————————————————————————————————————————

static LONG PASCAL InitStatusWindow (HWND Wnd, LONG lParam)
{
        LPCSTR text;
        PStatusRec p;
        LONG res = −1L;

        p = (PStatusRec) LocalAlloc (LPTR, sizeof (StatusRec));
        if (p != NULL)
        {
          // Initialize the StatusRec data structure

          p−>numParts = 0;
          p−>hintText = NULL;
          p−>statusFont = GetStatusFont (&p−>height);
          p−>border = (GetSystemMetrics (SM_CXFRAME) + 1) / 2;
          p−>height += (p->border * 4) + 1;
          SetWindowWord (Wnd, 0, (WORD) p);
          ResizeWindow (Wnd);
          SetProp (GetParent (Wnd), szClassName, Wnd);
          hookKey = HookWindow (GetParent (Wnd), (FARPROC)
                                SubclassParentWndProc, szHookName);

          // Now check for any initial text

          text = ((LPCREATESTRUCT) lParam)−>lpCreateParams;
          if (text != NULL && *text != '\0')
                InsertCell (GetParent (Wnd), text, −1, −1);
```

```
            res = 0;
        }

    return (res);
}

//————————————————————————————————————————————————
// Name:    GetCellRect
// Purpose: Return the frame rectangle for a given cell.
//————————————————————————————————————————————————

static VOID PASCAL GetCellRect (PStatusRec p, int cellNum, LPRECT r)
{
        r->left = (cellNum) ? p->frames [cellNum − 1] + (p->border * 2) :
                p->border;
        r->top = p->border + 1;
        r->right = p->frames [cellNum];
        r->bottom = p->height − p->border;
}

//————————————————————————————————————————————————
// Name:    PaintCell
// Purpose: Paint a specified cell in the status bar.
//————————————————————————————————————————————————

static VOID PASCAL PaintCell (HDC dc, PStatusRec p, int cellNum)
{
        RECT r;
        int mode;
        LPSTR theText;

        GetCellRect (p, cellNum, &r);
        DrawSunkenRect (dc, &r);

        if (p->hText [cellNum] != NULL)
        {
            mode = SetBkMode (dc, TRANSPARENT);
            p->statusFont = SelectObject (dc, p->statusFont);
            InflateRect (&r, −p->border, −p->border);
            theText = LocalLock (p->hText [cellNum]);
            DrawText (dc, theText, −1, &r, p->flags [cellNum] | DT_VCENTER);
            LocalUnlock (p->hText [cellNum]);
            p->statusFont = SelectObject (dc, p->statusFont);
            SetBkMode (dc, mode);
        }
}

//————————————————————————————————————————————————
// Name:    PaintHintText
// Purpose: Paint the special menu hint text.
//————————————————————————————————————————————————

static VOID PASCAL PaintHintText (HWND Wnd, PStatusRec p, HDC dc)
{
        RECT r;
        LPSTR theText;
        int width, mode;

        // Calculate the bounding box

        GetClientRect (GetParent (Wnd), &r);
        width = r.right − r.left − (p->border * 2);
        GetCellRect (p, 0, &r);
        r.right = r.left + width;
        InflateRect (&r, −p->border, −p->border);

        // Now draw the text...

        mode = SetBkMode (dc, TRANSPARENT);
```

```
        p->statusFont = SelectObject (dc, p->statusFont);
        theText = LocalLock (p->hintText);
        DrawText (dc, theText, -1, &r, DT_LEFT | DT_VCENTER | DT_EXPANDTABS);
        LocalUnlock (p->hintText);
        p->statusFont = SelectObject (dc, p->statusFont);
        SetBkMode (dc, mode);
}

//------------------------------------------------------------------------
// Name:     StatusBarPaint
// Purpose:  This routine is responsible for painting the status bar.
//------------------------------------------------------------------------

static int PASCAL StatusBarPaint (HWND Wnd)
{
        int i;
        RECT r;
        PStatusRec p;
        PAINTSTRUCT ps;

        BeginPaint (Wnd, &ps);
        p = GetStatusRec (Wnd);

        // First, draw the top edge of the status bar

        GetClientRect (Wnd, &r);
        MoveTo (ps.hdc, 0, 0);
        LineTo (ps.hdc, r.right, 0);
        PatBlt (ps.hdc, 0, 1, r.right - r.left, 1, WHITENESS);

        // Are we in hint mode?

        if (p->hintText != NULL) PaintHintText (Wnd, p, ps.hdc);
        else
        {
            // Now draw each cell in turn

            for (i = 0; i < p->numParts; i++)
                PaintCell (ps.hdc, p, i);
        }
        EndPaint (Wnd, &ps);
        return (0);
}

//------------------------------------------------------------------------
// Name:     DestroyStatusWindow
// Purpose:  Clean-up code for the status window.
//------------------------------------------------------------------------

static int PASCAL DestroyStatusWindow (HWND Wnd)
{
        int i;
        PStatusRec p;

        p = GetStatusRec (Wnd);
        DeleteObject (p->statusFont);
        if (p->hintText != NULL) LocalFree (p->hintText);
        RemoveProp (GetParent (Wnd), szClassName);
        UnHookWindow (GetParent (Wnd), hookKey);

        // Deallocate text buffers

        for (i = 0; i < p->numParts; i++)
            if (p->hText [i] != NULL)
                LocalFree (p->hText [i]);

        LocalFree ((HLOCAL) p);
        return (0);
}
```

```
//-------------------------------------------------------------------
// Name:     StatusBarWndProc
// Purpose:  Window procedure for status bar windows.
//-------------------------------------------------------------------

LONG FAR PASCAL _export StatusBarWndProc (HWND Wnd, WORD Msg,
                                          WPARAM wParam, LPARAM lParam)
{
    switch (Msg)
    {
      case WM_PAINT:

      return StatusBarPaint (Wnd);

      case WM_CREATE:

      return InitStatusWindow (Wnd, lParam);

      case WM_DESTROY:

      return DestroyStatusWindow (Wnd);
    }

    return DefWindowProc (Wnd, Msg, wParam, lParam);
}

//-------------------------------------------------------------------
// Name:     RegisterStatusBar
// Purpose:  Register the status bar window procedure.
//-------------------------------------------------------------------

static BOOL PASCAL RegisterStatusBar (HANDLE hInstance)
{
    WNDCLASS cls;

    if (GetClassInfo (hInstance, szClassName, &cls) == 0)
    {
        cls.style              = 0;
        cls.lpfnWndProc        = (WNDPROC) StatusBarWndProc;
        cls.cbClsExtra         = 0;
        cls.cbWndExtra         = sizeof (void NEAR *);
        cls.hInstance          = hInstance;
        cls.hIcon              = 0;
        cls.hCursor            = LoadCursor (NULL, IDC_ARROW);
        cls.hbrBackground      = COLOR_BTNFACE + 1;
        cls.lpszMenuName       = NULL;
        cls.lpszClassName      = szClassName;

        return RegisterClass (&cls);
    }

    return TRUE;
}

//-------------------------------------------------------------------
// Name:     GetStatusBarWindow
// Purpose:  Return the handle of this window's status bar.
//-------------------------------------------------------------------

HWND PASCAL GetStatusBarWindow (HWND hWndParent)
{
    if (hWndParent != NULL && IsWindow (hWndParent))
        return GetProp (hWndParent, szClassName);
    else
        return NULL;
}

//-------------------------------------------------------------------
// Name:     CreateStatusWindow
// Purpose: Create a status window and attach it to the designated parent.
//-------------------------------------------------------------------
```

```
HWND PASCAL CreateStatusWindow (HANDLE hInstance, HWND hWndParent,
                                LPCSTR lpText)
{
    HWND Wnd = NULL;

    // Check that we've got a valid parent window

    if (hWndParent != NULL && IsWindow (hWndParent))
    {
        // Ok so far, but has window already got a status bar ?

        Wnd = GetStatusBarWindow (hWndParent);
        if (Wnd == NULL)
          if (RegisterStatusBar (hInstance))
            Wnd = CreateWindow (szClassName, "", WS_CHILD | WS_VISIBLE,
                                0, 0, 0, 0, hWndParent, NULL, hInstance, lpText);
    }

    return (Wnd);
}

//————————————————————————————————————————————————————————————
// Name:    GetNumCells
// Purpose: Return number of cells in status bar.
// Returns: −1 on failure.
//————————————————————————————————————————————————————————————

int PASCAL GetNumCells (HWND hWndParent)
{
    PStatusRec p;
    HWND hWndStatus;

    hWndStatus = GetStatusBarWindow (hWndParent);
    p = GetStatusRec (hWndStatus);
    return (hWndStatus != NULL && p != NULL) ? p−>numParts : −1;
}

//————————————————————————————————————————————————————————————
// Name:    GetCellFlags
// Purpose: Return the flag word for a specified cell.
// Returns: −1 on failure.
//————————————————————————————————————————————————————————————

int PASCAL GetCellFlags (HWND hWndParent, int cellNum)
{
    PStatusRec p;
    HWND hWndStatus;

    hWndStatus = GetStatusBarWindow (hWndParent);
    p = GetStatusRec (hWndStatus);
    if (hWndStatus != NULL && p != NULL && cellNum >= 0 &&
          cellNum < p−>numParts)
      return p−>flags [cellNum];
    else
      return −1;
}

//————————————————————————————————————————————————————————————
// Name:    SetCellFlags
// Purpose: Set the flag word for a specified cell.
// Returns: Previous flag value or −1 on failure.
//————————————————————————————————————————————————————————————

int PASCAL SetCellFlags (HWND hWndParent, int cellNum, int flags)
{
    RECT r;
    int old;
    PStatusRec p;
    HWND hWndStatus;
```

```
        hWndStatus = GetStatusBarWindow (hWndParent);
        p = GetStatusRec (hWndStatus);
        if (hWndStatus != NULL && p != NULL && cellNum >= 0 && cellNum
            < p->numParts)
        {
            old = p->flags [cellNum];
            p->flags [cellNum] = flags & (DT_CENTER | DT_RIGHT);
            GetCellRect (p, cellNum, &r);
            InvalidateRect (hWndStatus, &r, TRUE);
            return (old);
        }

        return -1;
}

//------------------------------------------------------------------
// Name:    GetCellText
// Purpose: Retrieve the text of a specified cell.
// Returns: Number of bytes copied to destination (not including null byte).
//------------------------------------------------------------------

int PASCAL GetCellText (HWND hWndParent, int cellNum, LPSTR buffer,
                    int buffSize)
{
        int bytes;
        LPSTR text;
        HLOCAL th;
        PStatusRec p;
        char ch = '\0';
        HWND hWndStatus;

        hWndStatus = GetStatusBarWindow (hWndParent);
        p = GetStatusRec (hWndStatus);
        if (hWndStatus != NULL && p != NULL && cellNum >= 0 && cellNum
            < p->numParts)
          if (buffer != NULL)
          {
            *buffer = '\0';
            if ((th = p->hText [cellNum]) != NULL)
            {
                text = LocalLock (th);
                if ((bytes = lstrlen (text)) > buffSize)
                {
                    ch = text [buffSize];
                    text [buffSize] = '\0';
                    bytes = buffSize;
                }

                lstrcpy (buffer, text);
                if (ch != '\0') text [buffSize] = ch;
                LocalUnlock (th);
                return (bytes);
            }
          }

        return (0);
}

//------------------------------------------------------------------
// Name:    SetCellText
// Purpose: Set the text of a specified cell to 'lpText'.
// Returns: TRUE on success, FALSE on failure.
//------------------------------------------------------------------

BOOL PASCAL SetCellText (HWND hWndParent, LPCSTR lpText, int cellNum)
{
        RECT r;
        PStatusRec p;
        HWND hWndStatus;
```

```
        hWndStatus = GetStatusBarWindow (hWndParent);
        p = GetStatusRec (hWndStatus);
        if (hWndStatus != NULL && p != NULL && cellNum >= 0 && cellNum
                < p->numParts)
        {
            if (p->hText [cellNum] != NULL) LocalFree (p->hText [cellNum]);
            p->hText [cellNum] = AllocText (lpText);
            GetCellRect (p, cellNum, &r);
            InvalidateRect (hWndStatus, &r, TRUE);
            return (TRUE);
        }

        return (FALSE);
}

//—————————————————————————————————————————————————
// Name:     InsertCell
// Purpose:  Insert a cell into the status bar.
// Returns:  TRUE on success, FALSE on failure.
//—————————————————————————————————————————————————

BOOL PASCAL InsertCell (HWND hWndParent, LPCSTR text, int nWidth, int pos)
{
        HDC dc;
        int i, left;
        HFONT hFont;
        PStatusRec p;
        HWND hWndStatus;

        hWndStatus = GetStatusBarWindow (hWndParent);
        p = GetStatusRec (hWndStatus);
        if (hWndStatus != NULL && p != NULL && p->numParts < MAXCELLS)
        {
            // Get pos parameter in range

            if (pos == -1 || pos > p->numParts) pos = p->numParts;

            // Do we need to shuffle ?

            if (pos < p->numParts)
            {
                // Yes, we do !

                memmove (&p->hText [pos + 1], &p->hText [pos],
                            (p->numParts - pos) * sizeof (p->hText [0]));
                memmove (&p->frames [pos + 1], &p->frames [pos],
                            (p->numParts - pos) * sizeof (p->frames [0]));
                memmove (&p->flags [pos + 1], &p->flags [pos],
                            (p->numParts - pos) * sizeof (p->flags [0]));
            }

            p->hText [pos] = AllocText (text);
            p->flags [pos] = DT_LEFT;

            // Calculate left edge of cell

            if (pos) left = p->frames [pos - 1] + (p->border * 2);
            else left = p->border;

            // Calculate width of string if necessary

            if (nWidth == -1 && p->hText [pos] != NULL)
            {
                dc = GetDC (NULL);
                hFont = SelectObject (dc, p->statusFont);
                nWidth = LOWORD (GetTextExtent (dc, text,
                                                lstrlen (text))) + p->border * 3;
                SelectObject (dc, hFont);
                ReleaseDC (NULL, dc),
            }
```

```
                    // And calculate position of right edge

                    if (nWidth != -1)
                    {
                        p->frames [pos] = left + nWidth;

                        // Do we need to shuffle position of following cells?

                        if (pos < p->numParts)
                            for (i = pos + 1; i <= p->numParts; i++)
                                p->frames [i] += nWidth + (p->border * 2);

                        ++p->numParts;
                        InvalidateRect (hWndStatus, NULL, TRUE);
                        return (TRUE);
                    }
                }
            }

            return (FALSE);
}

//─────────────────────────────────────────────────────────────
// Name:     DeleteCell
// Purpose:  Delete a cell from the status bar.
// Returns:  TRUE on success, FALSE on failure.
//─────────────────────────────────────────────────────────────
BOOL PASCAL DeleteCell (HWND hWndParent, int pos)
{
        int i;
        RECT r;
        PStatusRec p;
        HWND hWndStatus;

        hWndStatus = GetStatusBarWindow (hWndParent);
        p = GetStatusRec (hWndStatus);
        if (hWndStatus != NULL && p != NULL && pos >= 0 && pos < p->numParts)
        {
            if (p->hText [pos] != NULL) LocalFree (p->hText [pos]);

            // Do we need to shuffle?

            if (pos < p->numParts - 1)
            {
                GetCellRect (p, pos, &r);

                // Adjust any following right borders

                for (i = pos + 1; i < p->numParts; i++)
                    p->frames [i] -= (r.right - r.left) + (p->border * 2);

                // And shuffle everything up one slot

                memmove (&p->hText [pos], &p->hText [pos + 1],
                        (p->numParts - pos - 1) * sizeof (p->hText [0]));
                memmove (&p->frames [pos], &p->frames [pos + 1],
                        (p->numParts - pos - 1) * sizeof (p->frames [0]));
                memmove (&p->flags [pos], &p->flags [pos + 1],
                        (p->numParts - pos - 1) * sizeof (p->flags [0]));
            }

            --p->numParts;
            InvalidateRect (hWndStatus, NULL, TRUE);
            return (TRUE);
        }

        return (FALSE);
}
```

```
//————————————————————————————————————————————————
// Name:     SetHintText
// Purpose:  Set up a text string for menu hinting.
// Returns:  TRUE on success, FALSE on failure.
// Notes:    Passing an empty string clears the status bar.
//           Passing NULL turns off menu hinting.
//           Anything else is interpreted as text and drawn as a hint.
//————————————————————————————————————————————————

BOOL PASCAL SetHintText (HWND hWndParent, LPCSTR lpText)
{
    PStatusRec p;
    HWND hWndStatus;

    hWndStatus = GetStatusBarWindow (hWndParent);
    p = GetStatusRec (hWndStatus);
    if (hWndStatus != NULL && p != NULL)
    {
        // Delete any existing hint text

        if (p->hintText != NULL) LocalFree (p->hintText);

        // Tweak the text to get around AllocText "auto-NULL"

        if (lpText != NULL && *lpText == '\0') lpText = " ";

        p->hintText = AllocText (lpText);

        // Force redraw of status bar

        InvalidateRect (hWndStatus, NULL, TRUE);
        return (TRUE);
    }

    return (FALSE);
}
```

Note

Pascal equivalents of the C code developed in this chapter can be found in Appendix 4. The file STATBAR.PAS contains a Pascal unit that you can use in your own programs, while STATUS.PAS is a small Pascal application that demonstrates the operation of the unit.

Better-looking dialog boxes

5

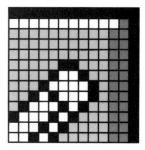

When I put together the generic window subclassing routines in Chapter 3, I began developing some code which showed you how to give a more professional, Excel-style look to your dialog boxes. Chapter 3 was a convenient place to do this, since the basic dialog box code was a useful way of showing how the generic subclassing routines operated.

In this chapter, we're going to build on the foundation laid in Chapter 3. In particular, I'm going to show you how to transparently subclass the other controls in your dialog box to get an even better effect. As with the earlier code, we will do this very simply by making just one function call to a single routine that will set up the dialog box subclassing. There's no sense in building a complex programming interface where a simple one will do.

Figure 5.1 shows how each of the different control types in a dialog box gets subclassed. In this example, the radio buttons, check boxes, group box, and push buttons have all been subclassed. The push buttons shown here might look quite ordinary, but recall the heavy bold text that Windows normally uses to display text in a dialog box. This has been replaced in the push buttons, in the static text item, and in fact, everywhere else in the dialog box. As with the code in Chapter 3, all this can be achieved just through a single call that you make in your dialog box procedure in response to a WM_INITDIALOG message. Although not shown in Figure 5.1, edit boxes also get modified and end up with an enhanced appearance.

Doing it the hard way...

You may wonder why I'm making such a big deal about being able to do all this from a single function call. To understand why, it's useful to review the 'official' way of getting the sort of effects that I'm talking about here. Microsoft first pioneered the concept of custom controls in early versions of Windows. The code for a custom

Figure 5.1 Subclassing the controls in a dialog box.

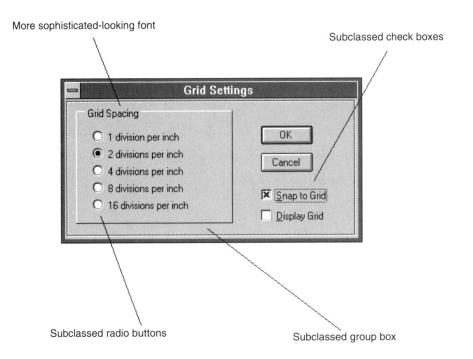

More sophisticated-looking font

Subclassed check boxes

Subclassed radio buttons

Subclassed group box

control was packaged up as a DLL, with a nice tight interface to the outside world. Using this approach, it was possible to create an installable custom control that could be utilized by one or more programs at the same time. Unfortunately, the Microsoft approach was somewhat limited – for one thing, a particular DLL file could only contain one type of custom control.

Borland improved considerably upon the custom control API and made it possible to place the code for a number of custom controls into a single DLL. They did this by adding new calls such as ListClasses, which enables an application program to get a list of all custom control names supported by the DLL. Almost all of Borland's Windows-based utilities and applications now use a standard custom control DLL called BWCC.DLL. (BWCC is an abbreviation for Borland Windows Custom Controls.) BWCC is designed to provide a chiseled-steel appearance to DLLs. An example of the typical Borland 'look' is shown in Figure 5.2.

In order to use the BWCC library, a programmer has to do two things, one of which is very simple and the other a little more work. The easy bit involves making sure that the BWCC library is loaded when the application is running. When the BWCC library is loaded, it calls the RegisterClass API routine for each of the custom control classes that it contains. Because it's a DLL, it uses the CS_GLOBALCLASS class style so that any application can then come along and create a window of that class.

As a concrete example, consider the BorDlg window class. This class is used by the dialog window itself, and it provides the chiseled-steel dialog background that you can see in Figure 5.2. In order to get those nice-looking bit-mapped push-

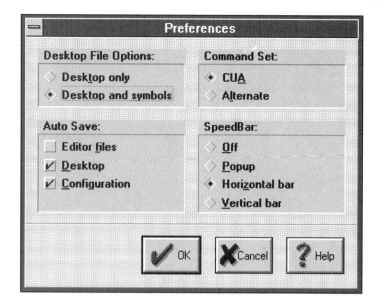

Figure 5.2   The characteristic
Borland look and feel for dialog
boxes.

buttons, you need to create push-button controls that use the window class BorBtn.
For those neat, diamond-shaped radio buttons, you need to use the BorRadio class,
and so forth. All these classes are available when the BWCC DLL has been loaded.
Therefore, if you use the Borland custom control library, you must call the
LoadLibrary routine near the beginning of your program to ensure that these global
window classes are available. That's the easy bit, but what else is there to do?

The not-quite-so-simple part involves using all these different window names
when you create your dialog resource template. To do this, you need to use a
Windows-based dialog editor. Microsoft include a dialog editor as part of the SDK,
and Borland include the Borland Resource Workshop with their application development systems. Both these programs allow you to install a DLL-based custom control
library, which effectively makes your library of custom controls available to the
dialog editor. With the Resource Workshop, a floating toolbox palette displays all
the available custom controls once the BWCC DLL has been installed. Creating
dialog box templates for use in your program is then just a matter of selecting the
appropriate control and placing it where you want it on the dialog.

What you end up with is a dialog box template that makes extensive use of the
Borland class names. This is not a problem in itself, but it means that your application is now entirely dependent on the BWCC library. If a user inadvertently deletes
that DLL, then your application won't work at all. Another consideration involves
disk space: the version of BWCC.DLL I have on my machine is over 150 kbytes in
size. That's quite a large file. The size of BWCC.DLL has varied somewhat with each
release and in fairness, there may be significantly smaller versions available. The fact
remains, however, that if your actual application program is only 30 or 40 kbytes in
size (you can pack a lot into an EXE file this size using Borland Pascal's smart

linker!), then the user might not be too keen on having to find a home for a DLL file that dwarfs the application itself! There's no problem if your users are already using some other Borland Windows product because they will already have the BWCC.DLL file installed on their machines, but you obviously can't count on this. Similarly, when writing something like an installation program, space is particularly at a premium. For reasons of cost, it's important to minimize the number of disks in a distribution set. Equally, having launched the setup program on the first disk of the distribution set, the user may not like the long wait while BWCC.DLL is loaded from floppy.

Note
Let me stress that I am, and always have been, a great fan of Borland's language products. I'm simply seeking to show, in this section, that there's often more than one way to crack a nut and that some ways require considerably less effort and are a lot less hassle than others.

Well, that's the story as regards the application programmer, but what if you're in the business of creating custom control DLLs yourself? In a recent book devoted to the development of custom controls for Windows (*Windows Custom Controls* by William Smith and Robert Ward, published by R&D Technical Books, 1993), the authors admit that the implementation of the necessary code to interface a custom control library to a dialog editor represents the most unpleasant and tedious aspect of implementing custom controls in this way. They explain that it involves large amounts of uninteresting, repetitive code. In order to provide compatibility with Microsoft's Dialog Editor, the authors wisely restrict themselves to implementing each of their six basic custom controls as a separate DLL. This is because in the world of custom controls, the Microsoft Dialog Editor represents a sort of lowest common denominator from a compatibility point of view. The upshot of this approach, of course, is that they end up with no fewer than six separate DLLs.

To be fair, only four of these DLLs are likely to be used by the average application (custom control classes for check boxes, push buttons, radio buttons and static items), but let me ask you: do you really want to distribute your application with four DLLs just to get a nice-looking dialog? No? Neither do I.

The actual implementation of the dialog editor interface involves writing a number of routines that pass information to the dialog editor. In addition, you will typically need to implement a setup dialog, called from the dialog editor, that lets the user set up any special styles for the current custom control. The Borland Resource Workshop is more complex because it allows the custom control library to provide a bitmap to the Resource Workshop for displaying the custom control in the toolbox window.

Some commercial packages, such as the Blaise Control Palette, provide two different versions of each custom control DLL. There's a development version that includes the interface code needed to interact with a dialog editor, and there's a smaller release version that contains just the code required to implement the custom control itself. This is a better approach, but it means that you now have to modify your build files to support the two different versions of the DLL. Also, at the end of the day, your application is still going to be reliant upon a number of external DLLs.

None of the code involved in interfacing an installable custom control DLL to a dialog editor is especially difficult, but there's quite a bit of it, and it's true to say that most of the code is entirely incidental to the real operation of the custom control itself. For this reason, and the other issues discussed earlier, we will not be pursuing this approach in *Polishing Windows*.

...And the easy way

When Borland first introduced their BWCC library, it enjoyed a measure of popularity amongst developers and end users alike. Many commercial applications and shareware programs were released, all of which came with the obligatory, redistributable copy of BWCC.DLL. More recently, enthusiasm for this particular look and feel waned, and it came to be perceived as outdated and 'clunky'. Microsoft's Excel program featured an entirely new look and at the time of writing (June 1993) programmers and end users alike both now seem to favor the Microsoft Excel way of doing things (see Figure 5.1).

As an aside, isn't it interesting how tastes change? Just as fashion in clothes seems to come and go with no apparent rhyme or reason, the same phenomenon now seems to be coming to the graphical user interface. As far as clothes are concerned, one of the legendary characteristics of 'real' programmers is that they are totally immune to the whims of the fashion world (well, I am anyway!) but we do need to create programs that are visually appealing to prospective customers!

Having looked at the traditional DLL-based approach to custom controls, let's briefly review the advantages of doing things via window subclassing. I've already mentioned that the dialog box effects shown in Figure 5.1 were achieved by inserting a single procedure call into your existing dialog box procedure. In addition, we don't use any external DLLs so there's no possibility of the user inadvertently throwing away our custom control code. Having no additional DLLs improves reliability and simplifies installation of your software. The dialog box shown was created using a standard dialog editor without the need for any installable custom control library. Finally, for what it's worth, the amount of code increased by just under 5 kbytes when the program was linked with the fancy dialog code.

That sounds like a pretty convincing argument but, of course, there's no such thing as a free lunch. I'm not going to pretend to you that the subclassing scheme I use is a universal panacea. Custom controls such as gauges and speedometers (often used in installation programs) can't easily be implemented merely through subclassing an existing control class. The deservedly popular Visual Basic development system has spawned an incredible diversity of custom controls – you can have everything from a high-speed serial comms link to an OLE client/server linkup! You can't really get this breadth of functionality without developing your own custom window classes from scratch. The scheme presented here is primarily targeted at Windows developers who wish to build great-looking, Excel-style dialogs into their applications with minimum programming effort. Minimum programming effort is what it's all about!

Keeping track of your children

As our starting point in developing the code, let's quickly review the final state of play in Chapter 3. If you look back at Figure 3.14, you'll see the dialog subclassing code as we left it. By calling the SubClassDialog routine in response to the WM_INIT-DIALOG message, we arranged for the existing dialog box procedure to be supplemented in a number of ways. Specifically, the WM_ERASEBKGND message was intercepted and used to draw a gray background to the dialog with a fancy border. The WM_CTLCOLOR message was likewise intercepted and used to set the background color of each control to match the background color of the dialog. The only exception to this was for edit text controls – we decided that we'd leave these with a white background to make them stand out. Figure 3.17 shows the final effect we achieved.

The big limitation with this code is the fact that it only subclasses the overall dialog box window. Because the dialog box controls themselves aren't subclassed, it's impossible to modify the appearance of individual controls. We can change the background color of check boxes and radio buttons, but we can't make them look any different. This is why it's important to subclass the individual controls if we're going to get effects like those shown in Figure 5.1.

On the face of it, this sounds pretty tedious – are we going to have to laboriously subclass each control in the dialog? Well, yes we are, but it doesn't have to be too laborious. The most important thing to bear in mind is that the controls of a dialog box are all child windows of the dialog box. At the time the WM_INITDIALOG message is sent to the dialog procedure, all these child windows have already been created. This is true even though neither the controls nor the dialog box itself have appeared on the screen. This means that we can use one of the Windows API routines to step through the various controls and automatically subclass each one.

An obvious routine to use here is EnumChildWindows. This routine sounds as if it will do exactly what we want. Certainly, we could use the EnumChildWindows routine, but the most obvious choices aren't always the best choices! Because EnumChildWindows belongs to the family of 'Enum' routines, if we want to use it, we're going to have to set up an exported callback routine for the EnumChildWindows routine to use each time it passes back the handle of a new child window. This is hassle that we can do without.

A far more convenient routine is the GetWindow API call. If we pass this routine the handle of our dialog and set the second parameter to GW_CHILD, we'll get back the handle of the first child window belonging to the dialog box, for example:

```
Wnd = GetWindow (hDlg, GW_CHILD);
```

For each parent window, Windows maintains the various child windows as a linked list. This linked list is Z-ordered. In other words, the topmost child window comes first in the list, with the bottom-most child window as the last window in the list. (Every Windows programmer is familiar with the idea of the screen being addressed as a two-dimensional array of pixels along the X and Y axes. The Z axis is simply the third dimension, pointing straight out of the screen.)

To access the next window in the linked list, you only need to call the GetWindow routine again, using the GW_HWNDNEXT flag value. When a value of NULL is returned, this indicates that you've got to the end of the list of child windows. In this way, all the dialog controls belonging to the dialog box can be examined. The code looks something like this:

```
Wnd = GetWindow (hDlg, GW_CHILD);
while (Wnd != NULL)
{
        ... Do something with this child window ...
        Wnd = GetWindow (Wnd, GW_HWNDNEXT);
}
```

For each dialog control that we encounter, we need to decide whether or not to subclass it. Also, of course, some dialog controls will be subclassed in different ways than others. For example, edit boxes might be subclassed with one routine, whereas we might use a different subclassing routine to handle static text items. We therefore need to figure out the class of each child window. This is easily done by using the GetClassName routine. Given a window handle and a buffer location, this routine will return the class name of the specified window.

```
//------------------------------------------------------------
// Name:    ControlType
// Purpose: Given a window handle, return the control type.
//          −1 is returned for an unrecognized type.
//------------------------------------------------------------

static int PASCAL ControlType (HWND Wnd)
{
        int i;
        char ClassName [64];
        static char * controlNames [6] = {    "Button",
                                               "Edit",
                                               "Static",
                                               "ListBox",
                                               "ComboBox",
                                               "ComboLBox" };
        GetClassName (Wnd, ClassName, sizeof (ClassName) −1);

        for (i = 0; i < 6; i++)
           if (lstrcmpi (controlNames [i], ClassName) == 0)
              return (i);

        return (−1);
}
```

The ControlType routine shown above is used to obtain the control type of a specified dialog control. It simply calls the GetClassName routine and then checks an array of built-in control class names looking for a match. If a match is found, the control type is returned, otherwise −1 is returned, indicating an unrecognized control. Note that the lstrcmpi routine is used here so that there are no problems caused by a string match failing owing to case sensitivity.

We can define six constants based on the values returned from the ControlType routine, as shown below:

```
// Control types returned by ControlType()

#define     BUTTON       0
#define     EDITBOX      1
```

```
#define    STATIC       2
#define    LISTBOX      3
#define    COMBOBOX     4
#define    COMBOLBOX    5
```

With this done, we can rewrite the SubClassDialog routine to look like this:

```
//————————————————————————————————————————————
// Name:    SubClassDialog
// Purpose: This routine does the actual job of subclassing a
//          dialog. It should be called from WM_INITDIALOG.
//————————————————————————————————————————————
void PASCAL SubClassDialog (HWND hDlg)
{
    HWND Wnd;

    // Do nothing if we're running Windows 4 or later

    if (LOBYTE (LOWORD (GetVersion())) < 4)
    {
        hookKey = HookWindow (hDlg, (FARPROC) DlgSubClass, szHookName);

        // Now subclass the various dialog controls

        Wnd = GetWindow (hDlg, GW_CHILD);
        while (Wnd != NULL)
        {
            SubClassControl (Wnd, ControlType (Wnd));
            Wnd = GetWindow (Wnd, GW_HWNDNEXT);
        }
    }
}
```

For each dialog control, the routine calls SubClassControl, passing it the window handle of the dialog control and the type of control. It's inside this routine that we do the real work of subclassing the control. We'll look at the code to do this shortly.

Before leaving the SubClassDialog routine behind us, there is one useful addition that can be made to it. It's always nice to arrange for dialog boxes to be displayed in the center of the screen and we can move the dialog box to the screen center from within the SubClassDialog routine. This gives us a bit of 'added value' for very little work. Here's the code to do it:

```
//————————————————————————————————————————————
// Name:    CenterDialog
// Purpose: Center a given dialog window on the screen.
//————————————————————————————————————————————
static void PASCAL CenterDialog (HWND Wnd)
{
    RECT r;

    GetWindowRect (Wnd, &r);
    r.left = (GetSystemMetrics (SM_CXSCREEN) − r.right + r.left) / 2;
    r.top = (GetSystemMetrics (SM_CYSCREEN) − r.bottom + r.top) / 2;
    SetWindowPos (Wnd, 0, r.left, r.top, 0, 0, SWP_NOSIZE | SWP_NOZORDER);
}
```

By calling the CenterDialog routine from inside the SubClassDialog procedure, we can ensure that any dialog we subclass will automatically be positioned at the center of the screen. If, for some reason, you want to make this feature optional, you could just pass a Boolean flag as a parameter to the SubClassDialog, specifying whether or not you want the dialog to be centered.

When we finished with the code at the end of Chapter 3, the dialog handling stuff was buried in the same file as the generic subclassing code. This is obviously not a very clean approach. Accordingly, I've separated out the various source files and renamed them as shown below:

DIALOGS.C   The dialog subclassing routines
SCLASLIB.C   The generic window subclassing code
DIATEST.C   The main application test program

I won't show the SCLASLIB.C or SCLASLIB.H files here – suffice it to say that they haven't changed from Chapter 3 except that the GetControlBrush, DlgSubClass and SubClassDialog routines have been removed and transferred to the DIALOGS.C file. The DIATEST.C file is the same application test program that we were using in Chapter 3 except that it now #includes DIALOGS.H rather than SCLASLIB.H. I won't bother to list it here until we make more substantial changes to it. The resource script is also (for the time being) the same as it was before. It's now renamed to DIATEST.RC to fit in with the other name changes. Figure 5.3 shows the new, very simple DIALOGS.H file.

Note

As we proceed through this chapter, we will develop new routines that you may feel are useful in their own right. Most of these routines will be hidden away as static routines inside the DIALOGS.C source file. If you want to make them more generally available, then remove the static attribute and include them in the DIALOGS.H header file. I haven't done this here as it's a matter of personal choice. If you look at the Pascal implementation of these routines in the Appendices at the back of the book, you'll see that there's an additional unit, Tools, that contains most of these utility routines.

```
/* DIALOGS1.H */

// © 1994 Dave Jewell and Addison-Wesley, ALL RIGHTS RESERVED

#ifndef _INC_DIALOGS
#define _INC_DIALOGS /* #defined if dialogs.h has been included */

#ifdef __cplusplus
extern "C" {
#endif

void PASCAL SubClassDialog (HWND hDlg);

#ifdef __cplusplus
}
#endif

#endif
```

Figure 5.3 DIALOGS1.H: the new header file for the dialog handling code.

Similarly, the code in Figure 5.4 shows the DIALOGS.C file with the changes discussed so far. At this point, the SubClassControl routine does nothing. This file can be found on the disk as DIALOGS1.C, and the executable version of the complete program as DIATEST1.EXE.

Figure 5.4 DIALOGS1.C:
the restructured dialog code
ready for control subclassing.

```
/* DIALOGS1.C */

// © 1994 Dave Jewell and Addison-Wesley, ALL RIGHTS RESERVED

#include    <windows.h>
#include    "sclaslib.h"
#include    "dialogs.h"

// Control types returned by ControlType()

#define    BUTTON      0
#define    EDITBOX     1
#define    STATIC      2
#define    LISTBOX     3
#define    COMBOBOX    4
#define    COMBOLBOX   5

static char szHookName[] = "DialogsHook";
static LONG hookKey;

//————————————————————————————————————————————————————————
// Name:    CenterDialog
// Purpose: Center a given dialog window on the screen.
//————————————————————————————————————————————————————————

static void PASCAL CenterDialog (HWND Wnd)
{
    RECT r;

    GetWindowRect (Wnd, &r);

    r.left = (GetSystemMetrics (SM_CXSCREEN) − r.right + r.left) / 2;
    r.top = (GetSystemMetrics (SM_CYSCREEN) − r.bottom + r.top) / 2;
    SetWindowPos (Wnd, 0, r.left, r.top, 0, 0, SWP_NOSIZE | SWP_NOZORDER);
}

//————————————————————————————————————————————————————————
// Name:    GetControlBrush
// Purpose: Create a control brush for a given system color.
//————————————————————————————————————————————————————————

HBRUSH PASCAL GetControlBrush (int sysColor)
{
    COLORREF color;

    color = GetSysColor (sysColor);
    return (CreateSolidBrush (color));
}

//————————————————————————————————————————————————————————
// Name:    DlgSubClass
// Purpose: This is the subclasser for the dialog box itself.
//          Main embellishments are "gray" background for dialog and
//          any controls. Also draws a fancy border around the box.
//————————————————————————————————————————————————————————

LONG FAR PASCAL _export DlgSubClass (HWND hDlg, UINT Msg,
                                WPARAM wParam, LPARAM lParam)
{
    HDC dc;
    RECT r;
    HBRUSH hbr;
    static HBRUSH hbrBack = NULL;

    switch (Msg)
    {
      case WM_CTLCOLOR:
```

```
            if (HIWORD (lParam) == CTLCOLOR_EDIT)
            {
               SetBkColor ((HDC) wParam, 0xFFFFFF);
               return GetStockObject (WHITE_BRUSH);
            }
            else
            {
               SetBkColor ((HDC) wParam, GetSysColor (COLOR_BTNFACE));
               if (hbrBack == NULL) hbrBack = GetControlBrush (COLOR_BTNFACE);
               return (hbrBack);
            }

         case WM_ERASEBKGND:

            dc = (HDC) wParam;
            GetClientRect (hDlg, &r);
            hbr = SelectObject (dc, GetControlBrush (COLOR_BTNFACE));
            PatBlt (dc, r.left, r.top, r.right − r.left, r.bottom − r.top, PATCOPY);
            DeleteObject (SelectObject (dc, hbr));

            // Now draw the fancy border

            InflateRect (&r, −3, −3);
            FrameRect (dc, &r, GetStockObject (WHITE_BRUSH));
            −−r.left;
            −−r.right;
            −−r.top;
            −−r.bottom;
            FrameRect (dc, &r, hbr = GetControlBrush (COLOR_BTNSHADOW));
            DeleteObject (hbr);
            return (TRUE);

         case WM_DESTROY:

            if (hbrBack != NULL)
            {
               DeleteObject (hbrBack);
               hbrBack = NULL;
            }
      }

      return CallOldProc (hDlg, Msg, wParam, lParam, hookKey);
}

//−−−−−−−−−−−−−−−−−−−−−−−−−−−−−−−−−−−−−−−−−−−−−−−−−−−−−−−−−−−−−−−−−−−−−−−
// Name:    ControlType
// Purpose: Given a window handle, return the control type.
//          −1 is returned for an unrecognized type.
//−−−−−−−−−−−−−−−−−−−−−−−−−−−−−−−−−−−−−−−−−−−−−−−−−−−−−−−−−−−−−−−−−−−−−−−

static int PASCAL ControlType (HWND Wnd)
{
      int i;
      char ClassName [64];
      static char * controlNames [6] = { "Button",
                                         "Edit",
                                         "Static",
                                         "ListBox",
                                         "ComboBox",
                                         "ComboLBox" };

      GetClassName (Wnd, ClassName, sizeof (ClassName) − 1);

      for (i = 0; i < 6; i++)
         if (lstrcmpi (controlNames [i], ClassName) == 0)
            return (i);

      return (−1);
}
```

```
//---------------------------------------------------------------
// Name:    SubClassControl
// Purpose: Subclass an individual dialog box control, according to
//          type. Controls that we don't recognize or aren't interested
//          in are left alone.
//---------------------------------------------------------------

static void PASCAL SubClassControl (HWND Wnd, int type)
{
}

//---------------------------------------------------------------
// Name:    SubClassDialog
// Purpose: This routine does the actual job of subclassing a
//          dialog. It should be called from WM_INITDIALOG.
//---------------------------------------------------------------

void PASCAL SubClassDialog (HWND hDlg)
{
      HWND Wnd;

      CenterDialog (hDlg);

      // Do nothing if we're running Windows 4 or later

      if (LOBYTE (LOWORD (GetVersion()))) < 4)
      {
         hookKey = HookWindow (hDlg, (FARPROC) DlgSubClass,
                               szHookName);

         // Now subclass the various dialog controls

         Wnd = GetWindow (hDlg, GW_CHILD);
         while (Wnd != NULL)
         {
            SubClassControl (Wnd, ControlType (Wnd));
            Wnd = GetWindow (Wnd, GW_HWNDNEXT);
         }
      }
}
```

One of the easiest ways to improve the appearance of a dialog box is to use a finely defined, non-bold font such as that which Windows itself uses to display the names of minimized icon titles. This font looks good on today's high-resolution color displays whereas the rather chunky-looking, bold font that dialog boxes normally use is actually a hangover from earlier days. The routine shown below, CreateDialogFont, should be very familiar to you if you've read Chapter 4 on status bars – this routine works in almost the same way and sets up a font handle in the global variable called DialogFont. You could use the routine from Chapter 4 'as is', but I've separated it out here to simplify the development of the program code. In the Pascal units, this font creation routine is located in the common Tools unit.

```
//---------------------------------------------------------------
// Name:    CreateDialogFont
// Purpose: Create the dialog font.
//---------------------------------------------------------------
void PASCAL CreateDialogFont (void)
{
      HDC dc;
```

```
        char faceName [50];
        int nHeight, pointSize;

        // Pickup point size and face name from WIN.INI

        pointSize = GetProfileInt ("Desktop", "StatusBarFaceHeight", 8);
        GetProfileString ("Desktop", "StatusBarFaceName", "MS Sans Serif", faceName, 50);

        dc = GetDC (NULL);
        nHeight = (GetDeviceCaps (dc, LOGPIXELSY) * pointSize) / −72;
        ReleaseDC (NULL, dc);

        // Now create the font

        DialogFont = CreateFont (nHeight, 0, 0, 0, FW_NORMAL, 0, 0, 0,
                                 ANSI_CHARSET,
                                 OUT_DEFAULT_PRECIS,
                                 CLIP_DEFAULT_PRECIS,
                                 DEFAULT_QUALITY,
                                 FF_SWISS | VARIABLE_PITCH,
                                 faceName);
}
```

With the code as it is in Figure 5.4, whenever a WM_DESTROY message is received by the dialog procedure the hbrBack background brush will be destroyed. This is fine so long as only one dialog has been subclassed, but in a real-world application, you might typically have one dialog box leading to another, and so on. This means that the hbrBack brush will be needlessly created and destroyed each time WM_CTLCOLOR and WM_DESTROY messages are received. In any event, it's messy to create our brushes and fonts in different places: a better approach is to do all the initialization in one place and put all the 'clean-up' code in another place, so that there are no tools we forget to destroy. This leads to the approach shown below:

```
static HFONT       DialogFont = NULL;   // special dialog font
static HBRUSH      hbrBack = NULL;      // background brush
static int         DialogCount = 0;     // number of subclassed dialogs
```

Three global variables are declared. DialogFont contains the handle to our special dialog font and hbrBack contains the handle to the background brush which, you will remember, is set up according to the value of the COLOR_BTNFACE constant for compatibility with the user's chosen color scheme. The DialogCount variable is used to keep track of the number of dialog boxes that have been subclassed. It is incremented each time the SubClassDialog routine is called and decremented each time a subclassed dialog procedure receives the WM_DESTROY window message. Only when the count falls back to zero are the brush and font handles destroyed. In this way, all the initialization and clean-up code can be nicely compartmentalized. All three variables are declared as static so that they are not accessible from outside the Dialogs source code module.

Note

It has to be admitted that the Windows-based Borland implementation of Pascal has certain advantages over C. Each Pascal unit has the ability to run some initialization code 'behind the scenes' before the main body of the application starts executing. In this case, we could use this to initialize the font and brush handles. Similarly, Borland Pascal and Turbo Pascal have an ExitProc facility which permits clean-up code to be automatically executed when the program terminates. Again, this would be a natural place to delete any needed fonts and brushes. Because we're not using Pascal, we have to resort to other trickery if we want these things to happen behind the scenes. To some extent, you can achieve the same effects if you use the #pragma startup and #pragma exit facilities, but things then become a little compiler-specific.

```
//————————————————————————————————————————————————————
// Name:    InitTools
// Purpose: Set up needed tools.
//————————————————————————————————————————————————————

static void PASCAL InitTools (void)
{
    if (DialogCount++ == 0)
    {
        CreateDialogFont ();
        hbrBack = GetControlBrush (COLOR_BTNFACE);
    }
}
```

The InitTools routine is called from the SubClassDialog routine. As you can see, it will only actually initialize the tools if the DialogCount variable is zero at the time that it's first called; in other words, if there are not currently any other subclassed dialogs in existence.

```
//————————————————————————————————————————————————————
// Name:    FreeTools
// Purpose: Called to clean up tools when a dialog is closed.
//————————————————————————————————————————————————————

static void PASCAL FreeTools (void)
{
    if (--DialogCount == 0)
    {
        DeleteObject (hbrBack);
        DeleteObject (DialogFont);
    }
}
```

Similarly, the FreeTools routine will only delete the two tool handles if the number of subclassed dialogs drops to zero. It is called from the WM_DESTROY handling code inside the DlgSubClass code. With these changes in place, we need to modify the SubClassControl routine like this:

```
//————————————————————————————————————————————————————
// Name:    SubClassControl
// Purpose: Subclass an individual dialog box control, according to
//          type. Controls that we don't recognize or aren't interested
//          in are left alone.
//————————————————————————————————————————————————————

static void PASCAL SubClassControl (HWND Wnd, int type)
{
    // Use our special font

    if (type != -1) SendMessage (Wnd, WM_SETFONT, DialogFont, 0);
}
```

Now, provided that the dialog control is one of the recognized types, it will automatically be set up to use our own font by passing it a WM_SETFONT message. Compiling the program with these changes leads to the result shown in Figure 5.5.

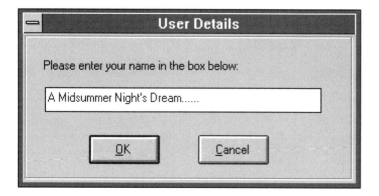

Figure 5.5   The effect of setting the font for each dialog control.

This is looking pretty good. Unfortunately, it's not looking quite as good as it ought to. If you look closely, you can see that the text inside the edit box doesn't appear to be properly aligned vertically: it's just a little too close to the top of the edit box. What's happening should be pretty obvious: the new font we're using isn't quite as tall as the default dialog font was, and therefore it doesn't look quite right. Well, I didn't say it was going to be *that* easy, did I?

Putting the squeeze on edit boxes

Clearly, we need to reduce the size of the edit text box on the fly. This would be difficult and inconvenient to do within a subclassing routine – for one thing, the edit box will already be in existence, so we have no chance of being able to trap the WM_CREATE message and resize the window at that time. A better approach is simply to resize the edit box when the SubClassControl routine is called, like this:

```
//------------------------------------------------------------------
// Name:     SubClassControl
// Purpose:  Subclass an individual dialog box control, according to
//           type. Controls that we don't recognize or aren't interested
//           in are left alone.
//------------------------------------------------------------------
static void PASCAL SubClassControl (HWND Wnd, int type)
{
    // Use our special font
    if (type != −1) SendMessage (Wnd, WM_SETFONT, DialogFont, 0);
    // Case out on control type
    switch (type)
    {
        case EDITBOX:    ShrinkEditBox (Wnd);
                         break;
    }
}
```

The SubClassControl routine now explicitly checks for an edit box control and, if found, it calls a new procedure called ShrinkEditBox to reduce the height of the control. Here's the code:

```
//------------------------------------------------------------
// Name:     ShrinkEditBox
// Purpose:  Reduce the size of an edit box to compensate for the
//           smaller font used.
//------------------------------------------------------------

static void PASCAL ShrinkEditBox (HWND Wnd)
{
        HDC dc;
        RECT r;
        TEXTMETRIC tm;
        int oldHeight, newHeight;

        // Get old font height

        dc = GetDC (NULL);
        GetTextMetrics (dc, &tm);
        oldHeight = tm.tmHeight + tm.tmInternalLeading;

        // Get new font height

        DialogFont = SelectObject (dc, DialogFont);
        GetTextMetrics (dc, &tm);
        DialogFont = SelectObject (dc, DialogFont);
        ReleaseDC (NULL, dc);
        newHeight = tm.tmHeight + tm.tmInternalLeading;

        // Now resize the window

        GetWindowRect (Wnd, &r);
        ScreenToClient (GetParent (Wnd), (LPPOINT) &r.left);
        ScreenToClient (GetParent (Wnd), (LPPOINT) &r.right);

        r.top += (oldHeight − newHeight) / 2;
        r.bottom −= (oldHeight − newHeight) / 2;

        SetWindowPos (Wnd, NULL, r.left, r.top,
                        r.right − r.left, r.bottom − r.top, SWP_NOZORDER);
}
```

The ShrinkEditBox routine works by comparing the height of the system font (the font that's normally used by dialog box controls) with the height of the new dialog font. The difference between the two represents the amount by which the edit box should be shrunk vertically. An important consideration here is maintaining the overall vertical position of the edit box – you might, for example, have aligned the edit box vertically with respect to some static text. In order to keep the same position, the top of the edit box is lowered, and the bottom is raised by the same amount.

The ShrinkEditBox routine assumes that when a device context is first created (using the GetDC (NULL) call) it will already have the system font selected into it. This is a valid assumption, and saves us from having to mess about explicitly selecting the system font into the device context. The SetWindowPos routine is then used to resize the edit box to the wanted height. Bringing this all together, Figure 5.6 shows the result of our efforts so far, DIALOGS2.C. This file and the compiled program, DIATEST2.EXE, can be found on the companion disk.

Figure 5.6   DIALOGS2.C:
with edit boxes now behaving
themselves.

```
/* DIALOGS2.C */

// © 1994 Dave Jewell and Addison-Wesley, ALL RIGHTS RESERVED

#include    <windows.h>
#include    "sclaslib.h"
#include    "dialogs.h"

// Control types returned by ControlType()

#define    BUTTON       0
#define    EDITBOX      1
#define    STATIC       2
#define    LISTBOX      3
#define    COMBOBOX     4
#define    COMBOLBOX    5

static char      szHookName[ ] = "DialogsHook";
static LONG      hookKey;
static HFONT     DialogFont = NULL;  // special dialog font
static HBRUSH    hbrBack = NULL;     // background brush
static int       DialogCount = 0;    // number of subclassed dialogs

//---------------------------------------------------------------
// Name:    GetControlBrush
// Purpose: Create a control brush for a given system color.
//---------------------------------------------------------------

HBRUSH PASCAL GetControlBrush (int sysColor)
{
    COLORREF color;

    color = GetSysColor (sysColor);
    return (CreateSolidBrush (color));
}

//---------------------------------------------------------------
// Name:    CenterDialog
// Purpose: Center a given dialog window on the screen.
//---------------------------------------------------------------

static void PASCAL CenterDialog (HWND Wnd)
{
    RECT r;

    GetWindowRect (Wnd, &r);
    r.left = (GetSystemMetrics (SM_CXSCREEN) − r.right + r.left) / 2;
    r.top = (GetSystemMetrics (SM_CYSCREEN) − r.bottom + r.top) / 2;
    SetWindowPos (Wnd, 0, r.left, r.top, 0, 0, SWP_NOSIZE | SWP_NOZORDER);
}

//---------------------------------------------------------------
// Name:    CreateDialogFont
// Purpose: Create the dialog font.
//---------------------------------------------------------------

void PASCAL CreateDialogFont (void)
{
    HDC dc;
    char faceName [50];
    int nHeight, pointSize;

    // Pickup point size and face name from WIN.INI

    pointSize = GetProfileInt ("Desktop", "StatusBarFaceHeight", 8);
    GetProfileString ("Desktop", "StatusBarFaceName", "MS Sans Serif",
                faceName, 50);

    dc = GetDC (NULL);
    nHeight = (GetDeviceCaps (dc, LOGPIXELSY) * pointSize) / −72;
```

```
                    ReleaseDC (NULL, dc);

                    // Now create the font

                    DialogFont = CreateFont (nHeight, 0, 0, 0, FW_NORMAL, 0, 0, 0,
                                             ANSI_CHARSET,
                                             OUT_DEFAULT_PRECIS,
                                             CLIP_DEFAULT_PRECIS,
                                             DEFAULT_QUALITY,
                                             FF_SWISS | VARIABLE_PITCH,
                                             faceName);
             }

//————————————————————————————————————————————————————
// Name:    InitTools
// Purpose:  Set up needed tools.
//————————————————————————————————————————————————————

static void PASCAL InitTools (void)
{
        if (DialogCount++ == 0)
        {
            CreateDialogFont ();
            hbrBack = GetControlBrush (COLOR_BTNFACE);
        }
}

//————————————————————————————————————————————————————
// Name:    FreeTools
// Purpose:  Called to clean up tools when a dialog is closed.
//————————————————————————————————————————————————————

static void PASCAL FreeTools (void)
{
        if (—DialogCount == 0)
        {
            DeleteObject (hbrBack);
            DeleteObject (DialogFont);
        }
}

//————————————————————————————————————————————————————
// Name:    DlgSubClass
// Purpose:  This is the subclasser for the dialog box itself.
//           Main embellishments are "gray" background for dialog and
//           any controls. Also draws a fancy border around the box.
//————————————————————————————————————————————————————

LONG FAR PASCAL _export DlgSubClass (HWND hDlg, UINT Msg,
                                     WPARAM wParam, LPARAM lParam)
{
        HDC dc;
        RECT r;
        HBRUSH hbr;

        switch (Msg)
        {
          case WM_CTLCOLOR:

            if (HIWORD (lParam) == CTLCOLOR_EDIT)
            {
                SetBkColor ((HDC) wParam, 0xFFFFFF);
                return GetStockObject (WHITE_BRUSH);
            }
            else
            {
                SetBkColor ((HDC) wParam, GetSysColor (COLOR_BTNFACE));
                return (hbrBack);
            }
```

```
        case WM_ERASEBKGND:

            dc = (HDC) wParam;
            GetClientRect (hDlg, &r);
            hbr = SelectObject (dc, GetControlBrush (COLOR_BTNFACE));
            PatBlt (dc, r.left, r.top, r.right − r.left, r.bottom − r.top, PATCOPY);
            DeleteObject (SelectObject (dc, hbr));

            // Now draw the fancy border

            InflateRect (&r, −3, −3);
            FrameRect (dc, &r, GetStockObject (WHITE_BRUSH));
            −−r.left;
            −−r.right;
            −−r.top;
            −−r.bottom;
            FrameRect (dc, &r, hbr = GetControlBrush (COLOR_BTNSHADOW));
            DeleteObject (hbr);
            return (TRUE);

        case WM_DESTROY:

            FreeTools ();
        }

    return CallOldProc (hDlg, Msg, wParam, lParam, hookKey);
}

//−−−−−−−−−−−−−−−−−−−−−−−−−−−−−−−−−−−−−−−−−−−−−−−−−−−−−−−−−−−−−
// Name:    ControlType
// Purpose: Given a window handle, return the control type.
//          −1 is returned for an unrecognized type.
//−−−−−−−−−−−−−−−−−−−−−−−−−−−−−−−−−−−−−−−−−−−−−−−−−−−−−−−−−−−−−

static int PASCAL ControlType (HWND Wnd)
{
    int i;
    char ClassName [64];
    static char * controlNames [6] = { "Button",
                                       "Edit",
                                       "Static",
                                       "ListBox",
                                       "ComboBox",
                                       "ComboLBox" };

    GetClassName (Wnd, ClassName, sizeof (ClassName) − 1);

    for (i = 0; i < 6; i++)
        if (lstrcmpi (controlNames [i], ClassName) == 0)
            return (i);

    return (−1);
}

//−−−−−−−−−−−−−−−−−−−−−−−−−−−−−−−−−−−−−−−−−−−−−−−−−−−−−−−−−−−−−
// Name:    ShrinkEditBox
// Purpose: Reduce the size of an edit box to compensate for the
//          smaller font used.
//−−−−−−−−−−−−−−−−−−−−−−−−−−−−−−−−−−−−−−−−−−−−−−−−−−−−−−−−−−−−−

static void PASCAL ShrinkEditBox (HWND Wnd)
{
    HDC dc;
    RECT r;
    TEXTMETRIC tm;
    int oldHeight, newHeight;


    // Get old font height
```

```
        dc = GetDC (NULL);
        GetTextMetrics (dc, &tm);
        oldHeight = tm.tmHeight + tm.tmInternalLeading;

        // Get new font height

        DialogFont = SelectObject (dc, DialogFont);
        GetTextMetrics (dc, &tm);
        DialogFont = SelectObject (dc, DialogFont);
        ReleaseDC (NULL, dc);
        newHeight = tm.tmHeight + tm.tmInternalLeading;

        // Now resize the window

        GetWindowRect (Wnd, &r);
        ScreenToClient (GetParent (Wnd), (LPPOINT) &r.left);
        ScreenToClient (GetParent (Wnd), (LPPOINT) &r.right);

        r.top += (oldHeight − newHeight) / 2;
        r.bottom −= (oldHeight − newHeight) / 2;

        SetWindowPos (Wnd, NULL, r.left,
                        r.top, r.right − r.left, r.bottom − r.top, SWP_NOZORDER);
}

//─────────────────────────────────────────────────────────────
// Name:    SubClassControl
// Purpose: Subclass an individual dialog box control, according to
//          type. Controls that we don't recognize or aren't interested
//          in are left alone.
//─────────────────────────────────────────────────────────────

static void PASCAL SubClassControl (HWND Wnd, int type)
{
        // Use our special font

        if (type != −1) SendMessage (Wnd, WM_SETFONT, DialogFont, 0);

        // Case out on control type

        switch (type)
        {
          case EDITBOX:    ShrinkEditBox (Wnd);
                           break;
        }
}

//─────────────────────────────────────────────────────────────
// Name:    SubClassDialog
// Purpose: This routine does the actual job of subclassing a
//          dialog. It should be called from WM_INITDIALOG.
//─────────────────────────────────────────────────────────────

void PASCAL SubClassDialog (HWND hDlg)
{
        HWND Wnd;

        // Center the dialog

        CenterDialog (hDlg);

        // Do nothing if we're running Windows 4 or later

        if (LOBYTE (LOWORD (GetVersion()))) < 4)
        {
          // Create needed tools

          InitTools ();

          // Hook the dialog box procedure
```

```
        hookKey = HookWindow (hDlg, (FARPROC) DlgSubClass,
                             szHookName);

        // Now subclass the various dialog controls

        Wnd = GetWindow (hDlg, GW_CHILD);
        while (Wnd != NULL)
        {
            SubClassControl (Wnd, ControlType (Wnd));
            Wnd = GetWindow (Wnd, GW_HWNDNEXT);
        }
    }
}
```

The result of running the DIATEST2.EXE program is shown in Figure 5.7. As you can see, the text is now correctly aligned within the edit box.

Better buttons

Let's get started now on subclassing some of the controls within the dialog box. If you look back at Figure 5.1, you'll see that the group boxes, check boxes and radio buttons have all had their appearance changed. It turns out that we can achieve all this by subclassing just one class, the BUTTON class. If you're familiar with Windows dialog box controls, you'll know that all these different dialog controls are implemented through variations on the one BUTTON window class. Windows does this by using the last few bits of the 32-bit window style to differentiate between different types of control. The various BUTTON styles are shown below.

```
/* Button Control Styles */

#define BS_PUSHBUTTON        0x00000000L
#define BS_DEFPUSHBUTTON     0x00000001L
#define BS_CHECKBOX          0x00000002L
#define BS_AUTOCHECKBOX      0x00000003L
#define BS_RADIOBUTTON       0x00000004L
```

Figure 5.7 Running the DIATEST2 program.

```
#define BS_3STATE              0x00000005L
#define BS_AUTO3STATE          0x00000006L
#define BS_GROUPBOX            0x00000007L
#define BS_USERBUTTON          0x00000008L
#define BS_AUTORADIOBUTTON     0x00000009L
#define BS_OWNERDRAW           0x0000000BL
#define BS_LEFTTEXT            0x00000020L
```

In actual fact, the BUTTON class is the only control class that we will be subclassing. If you want to add more sophisticated effects, such as changing the non-client area around an edit box or combo box, you can do this by subclassing the appropriate controls. However, in this chapter, we will be able to get all the effects we want merely by subclassing the BUTTON class.

As you can see from the list above, the BUTTON class implements push buttons, check boxes, radio buttons and group boxes. We can tell which type of control we're looking at by examining the low-order bytes in the window style. In order to be able to fool around with these different control types, we obviously need to be able to include some in our dialog box. Figure 5.8 shows the new DIATEST.RC file that we'll be using from now on. You can find this on the sample disk as DIATEST2.RC. Recall that the resource script file we've been using up to now came from Chapter 3.

Figure 5.8   DIATEST2.RC: the new resource script file we'll be using from now on.

```
USERNAME DIALOG 37, 30, 280, 102
STYLE DS_MODALFRAME | WS_POPUP | WS_CAPTION | WS_SYSMENU
CAPTION "User Details"
BEGIN
EDITTEXT 100, 10, 23, 137, 12,
    ES_LEFT | WS_CHILD | WS_VISIBLE | WS_BORDER | WS_GROUP | WS_TABSTOP
CONTROL "Married", 101,"BUTTON", BS_AUTOCHECKBOX | WS_CHILD |
    WS_VISIBLE | WS_GROUP | WS_TABSTOP, 18, 56, 86, 12
CONTROL "Likes Programming Windows", 102, "BUTTON", BS_AUTOCHECKBOX |
    WS_CHILD | WS_VISIBLE | WS_GROUP | WS_TABSTOP, 18, 68, 122, 12
CONTROL "&Female", 103, "BUTTON", BS_AUTORADIOBUTTON | WS_CHILD |
    WS_VISIBLE | WS_GROUP | WS_TABSTOP, 148, 56, 39, 12
CONTROL "&Male", 104, "BUTTON", BS_AUTORADIOBUTTON | WS_CHILD |
    WS_VISIBLE | WS_GROUP | WS_TABSTOP, 148, 68, 37, 12
CONTROL "Programmer", 105, "COMBOBOX", CBS_DROPDOWNLIST | WS_CHILD |
    WS_VISIBLE | WS_GROUP | WS_TABSTOP, 222, 23, 49, 31
CONTROL "&Cancel", 2, "BUTTON", BS_PUSHBUTTON | WS_CHILD | WS_VISIBLE |
    WS_GROUP | WS_TABSTOP, 231, 55, 35, 14
CONTROL "&OK", 1, "BUTTON", BS_DEFPUSHBUTTON | WS_CHILD | WS_VISIBLE |
    WS_GROUP | WS_TABSTOP, 231, 75, 35, 14
LTEXT "Please enter your name in the box below:", −1, 10, 12, 143, 11,
    WS_CHILD | WS_VISIBLE | WS_GROUP
LTEXT "Occupation:", −1, 225, 12, 43, 8, WS_CHILD |
    WS_VISIBLE | WS_GROUP
GROUPBOX "Personal Details", −1, 12, 44, 185, 47, WS_CHILD |
    WS_VISIBLE | WS_TABSTOP
END
```

Because I've arranged that edit boxes should have a white background, I felt that it would be good to make combo boxes look the same. Accordingly, the WM_CTLCOLOR handling code inside the DlgSubClass routine has been modified to look like this:

```
case WM_CTLCOLOR:

if (HIWORD (lParam) == CTLCOLOR_EDIT || HIWORD (lParam) == CTLCOLOR_LISTBOX)
{
    SetBkColor ((HDC) wParam, 0xFFFFFF);
    return GetStockObject (WHITE_BRUSH);
    ...
```

The combo box doesn't have a CTLCOLOR identifier of its own, but it shares the CTLCOLOR_LISTBOX identifier with listboxes. With the above change to the code, and the new resource script file, the program now displays a dialog box as shown in Figure 5.9.

As you can see, the check boxes, radio buttons and group boxes still look flat and uninteresting, despite being drawn on a gray background. Let's start building the BUTTON subclassing code which will give them a more sophisticated look.

In principle, we could write just one enormous subclassing procedure that dealt with all the different control types implemented by the BUTTON window class. However, this would be needlessly complicated and error-prone. Most of the code would be spending its time deciding what sort of control was being drawn! A better, neater approach is to assign a different subclassing procedure to each of the different control types supported by the BUTTON window class, just as if they were different window classes to start with – arguably, they should have been. It's rather confusing that Microsoft chose to implement radio buttons, check boxes and group boxes as variants on the same window class. After all, if you create a window of class BUTTON, you would expect to get a button, not a group box.

We'll begin with the group box implementation as it's easiest – it performs no interaction with the user. Based on the above comments, our SubClassControl procedure should now look as shown below. As you can see, there are two nested switch statements. Once a BUTTON window class is detected, the code gets the specific control type by calling the GetWindowLong routine to fetch the 32-bit style information for the window. Masking the style with 0xF can be used to determine the specific control type we're dealing with. If this turns out to be a group box, the window is subclassed by setting its window procedure to point to the SCGroupBox routine. We will add the code for dealing with check boxes and radio buttons later in the chapter.

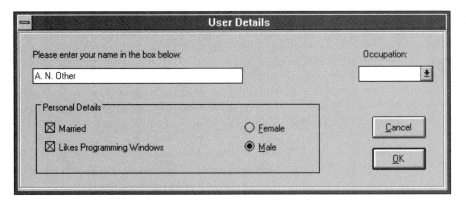

Figure 5.9 The new dialog box in operation.

```
//————————————————————————————————
// Name:    SubClassControl
// Purpose: Subclass an individual dialog box control, according to
//          type. Controls that we don't recognize or aren't interested
//          in are left alone.
//————————————————————————————————

static void PASCAL SubClassControl (HWND Wnd, int type)
{
     // Use our special font

     if (type != −1) SendMessage (Wnd, WM_SETFONT, DialogFont, 0);

     // Case out on control type

     switch (type)
     {
       case EDITBOX:

       ShrinkEditBox (Wnd);
       break;

       case BUTTON:

       type = GetWindowLong (Wnd, GWL_STYLE) & 0xF;
       switch (type)
       {
         case GROUPBOX:

         HookWindow (Wnd, (FARPROC) SCGroupBox, szHookName);
         break;
       }
     }
}
```

The code for the SCGroupBox function is shown below. Because SCGroupBox
is a subclassing routine, it must be exported using the _export directive. Note that we
don't need to store the hook key which is returned from subclassing the group box
window because it will already have been set up when the dialog box itself was
subclassed. Because the same service name is used, the hook key returned will be
identical.

```
//————————————————————————————————
// Name:    SCGroupBox
// Purpose: Subclassing routine for GROUPBOX controls.
//————————————————————————————————

LONG FAR PASCAL _export SCGroupBox (HWND Wnd, UINT Msg,
                                    WPARAM wParam, LPARAM lParam)
{
     RECT r;
     DWORD dwExtent;
     HFONT hFont;
     COLORREF bkColor;
     PAINTSTRUCT ps;
     char szText [128];
     switch (Msg)
     {
       case WM_PAINT:

       BeginPaint (Wnd, &ps);
       if (SendMessage (Wnd, WM_GETTEXT, 120, (LONG)(LPSTR) &szText [1]) <= 0)
          szText[0] = '\0';
       else
       {
          szText [0] = ' ';
          lstrcat (szText, " ");
```

```
        }

        GetClientRect (Wnd, &r);
        DrawRaisedRect (ps.hdc, &r);

        if (szText [0] != '\0')
        {
            hFont = SelectObject (ps.hdc, DialogFont);
            dwExtent = GetTextExtent (ps.hdc, "Yy", 2);
            r.top -= HIWORD (dwExtent) / 2;
            r.left += LOWORD (dwExtent) / 2;
            bkColor = SetBkColor (ps.hdc, GetSysColor (COLOR_BTNFACE));
            DrawText (ps.hdc, szText, -1, &r, DT_SINGLELINE);
            SetBkColor (ps.hdc, bkColor);
            SelectObject (ps.hdc, hFont);
        }

        EndPaint (Wnd, &ps);
        return (0);
    }

    return CallOldProc (Wnd, Msg, wParam, lParam, hookKey);
}
```

The above code requires some explanation. Firstly, it's important to bear in mind that a group box doesn't necessarily have to have any text associated with it. For this reason, the code specifically checks to see if there's any text. If not, the routine skips the code that's responsible for positioning and drawing the text. You can get a copy of the text associated with a BUTTON control by sending a WM_GETTEXT message, and that's what the code does here. If the group box does have a title, then two extra space characters are inserted at the beginning and end of the title string. This gives a more pleasing appearance, as we end up with a small gap between the title text and the outline of the group box itself.

```
//----------------------------------------------------------------
// Name:    DrawRaisedRect
// Purpose: Draw a raised rectangle at specified location.
//----------------------------------------------------------------
static void PASCAL DrawRaisedRect (HDC dc, LPRECT lpr)
{
    HBRUSH hbr;
    int width, height;

    width = lpr->right - lpr->left;
    height = lpr->bottom - lpr->top;

    PatBlt (dc, lpr->left, lpr->top, 1, height -1, WHITENESS);
    PatBlt (dc, lpr->left, lpr->top, width -1, 1, WHITENESS);
    hbr = SelectObject (dc, CreateSolidBrush (GetSysColor (COLOR_BTNSHADOW)));
    PatBlt (dc, lpr->right -1, lpr->top, 1, height, PATCOPY);
    PatBlt (dc, lpr->left, lpr->bottom -1, width, 1, PATCOPY);
    DeleteObject (SelectObject (dc, hbr));
}
```

The DrawRaisedRect routine is used to draw the outline of the group box. This routine is a close cousin (a very close cousin!) of the DrawSunkenRect routine which, you will remember, was used in Chapter 4 to draw the various cells within a status bar. Once the DrawRaisedRect routine has been called, the code checks to see whether there's any text to draw.

It isn't possible to draw the text directly using the client rectangle that was used for the call to the DrawRaisedRect routine. This is because the title string of a group

Figure 5.10 The new group box subclassing routine in operation.

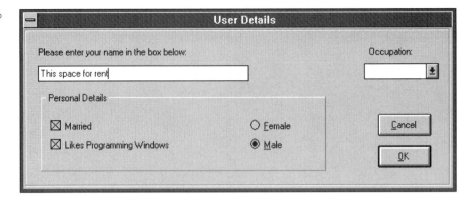

box is supposed to sit actually on the group box outline, rather than below it or above it. Accordingly, the GetTextExtent routine is called to obtain the dimensions of a small string consisting of the letters "Yy". This string is chosen to include descenders but also to come fairly high off the baseline. As an alternative, you could call the GetTextMetrics routine, but in this case you would have to allocate a TEXTMETRIC data structure. Using the returned character height, the top coordinate of the rectangle is moved up by half this distance so that the text sits squarely on the group box outline. Similarly, the left edge of the rectangle is moved over by half the width of the string. This prevents the displayed text from obscuring the upper left corner of the group box outline, which would not look good. Finally, the background color is set up and the group box title is drawn.

The only window message that we're concerned with in this subclassing routine is the WM_PAINT message. Things get much more interesting (not to say complicated!) when we develop the code for check boxes and radio buttons. With the changes made so far, the dialog box now looks as shown in Figure 5.10.

The complete source code for the Dialogs module, DIALOGS3.C, is now as shown in Figure 5.11, and it can be found on disk together with the corresponding executable file, DIATEST3.EXE.

Figure 5.11 The DIALOGS3.C source incorporating the group box subclassing code.

```
/* DIALOGS3.C */

// © 1994 Dave Jewell and Addison-Wesley, ALL RIGHTS RESERVED

#include    <windows.h>
#include    "sclaslib.h"
#include    "dialogs.h"

// Control types returned by ControlType()

#define     BUTTON          0
#define     EDITBOX         1
#define     STATIC          2
#define     LISTBOX         3
#define     COMBOBOX        4
#define     COMBOLBOX       5
```

```
// BUTTON types

#define    PUSHBUTTON           0x0
#define    DEFPUSHBUTTON        0x1
#define    CHECKBOX             0x2
#define    AUTOCHECKBOX         0x3
#define    RADIOBUTTON          0x4
#define    THREESTATE           0x5
#define    AUTO3STATE           0x6
#define    GROUPBOX             0x7
#define    USERBUTTON           0x8
#define    AUTORADIOBUTTON      0x9
#define    OWNERDRAW            0xB

static char      szHookName[ ] = "DialogsHook";
static LONG      hookKey;
static HFONT     DialogFont = NULL;      // special dialog font
static HBRUSH    hbrBack = NULL;         // background brush
static int       DialogCount = 0;        // number of subclassed dialogs

//————————————————————————————————————————————————————————
// Name:    GetControlBrush
// Purpose: Create a control brush for a given system color.
//————————————————————————————————————————————————————————

static HBRUSH PASCAL GetControlBrush (int sysColor)
{
    COLORREF color;

    color = GetSysColor (sysColor);
    return (CreateSolidBrush (color));
}

//————————————————————————————————————————————————————————
// Name:    DrawRaisedRect
// Purpose: Draw a raised rectangle at specified location.
//————————————————————————————————————————————————————————

static void PASCAL DrawRaisedRect (HDC dc, LPRECT lpr)
{
    HBRUSH hbr;
    int width, height;

    width = lpr−>right − lpr−>left;
    height = lpr−>bottom − lpr−>top;
    PatBlt (dc, lpr−>left, lpr−>top, 1, height − 1, WHITENESS);
    PatBlt (dc, lpr−>left, lpr−>top, width − 1, 1, WHITENESS);
    hbr = SelectObject (dc, CreateSolidBrush (GetSysColor (COLOR_BTNSHADOW)));
    PatBlt (dc, lpr−>right − 1, lpr−>top, 1, height, PATCOPY);
    PatBlt (dc, lpr−>left, lpr−>bottom − 1, width, 1, PATCOPY);
    DeleteObject (SelectObject (dc, hbr));
}

//————————————————————————————————————————————————————————
// Name:    CenterDialog
// Purpose: Center a given dialog window on the screen.
//————————————————————————————————————————————————————————

static void PASCAL CenterDialog (HWND Wnd)
{
    RECT r;

    GetWindowRect (Wnd, &r);
    r.left = (GetSystemMetrics (SM_CXSCREEN) − r.right + r.left) / 2;
    r.top = (GetSystemMetrics (SM_CYSCREEN) − r.bottom + r.top) / 2;
    SetWindowPos (Wnd, 0, r.left, r.top, 0, 0, SWP_NOSIZE | SWP_NOZORDER);
}
```

```
//————————————————————————————————————————————————————
// Name:    CreateDialogFont
// Purpose: Create the dialog font.
//————————————————————————————————————————————————————

void PASCAL CreateDialogFont (void)
{
    HDC dc;
    char faceName [50];
    int nHeight, pointSize;

    // Pickup point size and face name from WIN.INI

    pointSize = GetProfileInt ("Desktop", "StatusBarFaceHeight", 8);
    GetProfileString ("Desktop", "StatusBarFaceName", "MS Sans Serif",
            faceName, 50);

    dc = GetDC (NULL);
    nHeight = (GetDeviceCaps (dc, LOGPIXELSY) * pointSize) / −72;
    ReleaseDC (NULL, dc);

    // Now create the font

    DialogFont = CreateFont (nHeight, 0, 0, 0, FW_NORMAL, 0, 0, 0,
            ANSI_CHARSET,
            OUT_DEFAULT_PRECIS,
            CLIP_DEFAULT_PRECIS,
            DEFAULT_QUALITY,
            FF_SWISS | VARIABLE_PITCH,
            faceName);
}

//————————————————————————————————————————————————————
// Name:    InitTools
// Purpose: Set up needed tools.
//————————————————————————————————————————————————————

static void PASCAL InitTools (void)
{
    if (DialogCount++ == 0)
    {
        CreateDialogFont ();
        hbrBack = GetControlBrush (COLOR_BTNFACE);
    }
}

//————————————————————————————————————————————————————
// Name:    FreeTools
// Purpose: Called to clean up tools when a dialog is closed.
//————————————————————————————————————————————————————

static void PASCAL FreeTools (void)
{
    if (—DialogCount == 0)
    {
        DeleteObject (hbrBack);
        DeleteObject (DialogFont);
    }
}

//————————————————————————————————————————————————————
// Name:    SCGroupBox
// Purpose: Subclassing routine for GROUPBOX controls.
//————————————————————————————————————————————————————

LONG FAR PASCAL _export SCGroupBox (HWND Wnd, UINT Msg,
                                    WPARAM wParam, LPARAM lParam)
{
    RECT r;
```

```
          DWORD dwExtent;
          HFONT hFont;
          COLORREF bkColor;
          PAINTSTRUCT ps;
          char szText [128];

          switch (Msg)
          {
            case WM_PAINT:

              BeginPaint (Wnd, &ps);
              if (SendMessage (Wnd, WM_GETTEXT, 120,
                (LONG)(LPSTR) &szText [1]) <= 0) szText[0] = '\0';
              else
              {
                szText [0] = ' ';
                lstrcat (szText, " ");
              }

              GetClientRect (Wnd, &r);
              DrawRaisedRect (ps.hdc, &r);

              if (szText [0] != '\0')
              {
                hFont = SelectObject (ps.hdc, DialogFont);
                dwExtent = GetTextExtent (ps.hdc, "Yy", 2);
                r.top -= HIWORD (dwExtent) / 2;
                r.left += LOWORD (dwExtent) / 2;
                bkColor = SetBkColor (ps.hdc, GetSysColor (COLOR_BTNFACE));
                DrawText (ps.hdc, szText, -1, &r, DT_SINGLELINE);
                SetBkColor (ps.hdc, bkColor);
                SelectObject (ps.hdc, hFont);
              }

              EndPaint (Wnd, &ps);
              return (0);
          }

        return CallOldProc (Wnd, Msg, wParam, lParam, hookKey);
      }

//----------------------------------------------------------------
// Name:    DlgSubClass
// Purpose: This is the subclasser for the dialog box itself.
//          Main embellishments are "gray" background for dialog and
//          any controls. Also draws a fancy border around the box.
//----------------------------------------------------------------

LONG FAR PASCAL _export DlgSubClass (HWND hDlg, UINT Msg,
                                     WPARAM wParam, LPARAM lParam)
{
        HDC dc;
        RECT r;
        HBRUSH hbr;

        switch (Msg)
        {
          case WM_CTLCOLOR:

            if (HIWORD (lParam) == CTLCOLOR_EDIT ||
                HIWORD (lParam) == CTLCOLOR_LISTBOX)
            {
              SetBkColor ((HDC) wParam, 0xFFFFFF);
              return GetStockObject (WHITE_BRUSH);
            }
            else
            {
              SetBkColor ((HDC) wParam, GetSysColor (COLOR_BTNFACE));
```

```
                return (hbrBack);
            }

            case WM_ERASEBKGND:

            dc = (HDC) wParam;
            GetClientRect (hDlg, &r);
            hbr = SelectObject (dc, GetControlBrush (COLOR_BTNFACE));
            PatBlt (dc, r.left, r.top, r.right - r.left, r.bottom - r.top, PATCOPY);
            DeleteObject (SelectObject (dc, hbr));

            // Now draw the fancy border

            InflateRect (&r, -3, -3);
            FrameRect (dc, &r, GetStockObject (WHITE_BRUSH));
            --r.left;
            --r.right;
            --r.top;
            --r.bottom;
            FrameRect (dc, &r, hbr = GetControlBrush (COLOR_BTNSHADOW));
            DeleteObject (hbr);
            return (TRUE);

            case WM_DESTROY:

            FreeTools ();
        }

        return CallOldProc (hDlg, Msg, wParam, lParam, hookKey);
}

//-----------------------------------------------------------------------------
// Name:    ControlType
// Purpose: Given a window handle, return the control type.
//          -1 is returned for an unrecognized type.
//-----------------------------------------------------------------------------

static int PASCAL ControlType (HWND Wnd)
{
        int i;
        char ClassName [64];
        static char * controlNames [6] = { "Button",
                                           "Edit",
                                           "Static",
                                           "ListBox",
                                           "ComboBox",
                                           "ComboLBox" };

        GetClassName (Wnd, ClassName, sizeof (ClassName) - 1);

        for (i = 0; i < 6; i++)
           if (lstrcmpi (controlNames [i], ClassName) == 0)
               return (i);

        return (-1);
}

//-----------------------------------------------------------------------------
// Name:    ShrinkEditBox
// Purpose: Reduce the size of an edit box to compensate for the smaller
//          font used.
//-----------------------------------------------------------------------------

static void PASCAL ShrinkEditBox (HWND Wnd)
{
        HDC dc;
        RECT r;
        TEXTMETRIC tm;
        int oldHeight, newHeight;
```

```
        // Get old font height

        dc = GetDC (NULL);
        GetTextMetrics (dc, &tm);
        oldHeight = tm.tmHeight + tm.tmInternalLeading;

        // Get new font height

        DialogFont = SelectObject (dc, DialogFont);
        GetTextMetrics (dc, &tm);
        DialogFont = SelectObject (dc, DialogFont);
        ReleaseDC (NULL, dc);
        newHeight = tm.tmHeight + tm.tmInternalLeading;

        // Now resize the window

        GetWindowRect (Wnd, &r);
        ScreenToClient (GetParent (Wnd), (LPPOINT) &r.left);
        ScreenToClient (GetParent (Wnd), (LPPOINT) &r.right);

        r.top += (oldHeight − newHeight) / 2;
        r.bottom −= (oldHeight − newHeight) / 2;

        SetWindowPos (Wnd, NULL, r.left, r.top,
                        r.right − r.left, r.bottom − r.top, SWP_NOZORDER);
}

//───────────────────────────────────────────────────────────
// Name:     SubClassControl
// Purpose:  Subclass an individual dialog box control, according to
//           type. Controls that we don't recognize or aren't interested
//           in are left alone.
//───────────────────────────────────────────────────────────

static void PASCAL SubClassControl (HWND Wnd, int type)
{
        // Use our special font

        if (type != −1) SendMessage (Wnd, WM_SETFONT, DialogFont, 0);

        // Case out on control type

        switch (type)
        {
          case EDITBOX:

            ShrinkEditBox (Wnd);
            break;

          case BUTTON:

            type = GetWindowLong (Wnd, GWL_STYLE) & 0xF;
            switch (type)
            {
              case GROUPBOX:

              HookWindow (Wnd, (FARPROC) SCGroupBox, szHookName);
              break;
            }
        }
}

//───────────────────────────────────────────────────────────
// Name:     SubClassDialog
// Purpose:  This routine does the actual job of subclassing a
//           dialog. It should be called from WM_INITDIALOG.
//───────────────────────────────────────────────────────────

void PASCAL SubClassDialog (HWND hDlg)
{
```

```
    HWND Wnd;

    // Center the dialog

    CenterDialog (hDlg);

    // Do nothing if we're running Windows 4 or later

    if (LOBYTE (LOWORD (GetVersion()))) < 4)
    {
      // Create needed tools

      InitTools ();

      // Hook the dialog box procedure

      hookKey = HookWindow (hDlg, (FARPROC) DlgSubClass,
                            szHookName);

      // Now subclass the various dialog controls

      Wnd = GetWindow (hDlg, GW_CHILD);
      while (Wnd != NULL)
      {
        SubClassControl (Wnd, ControlType (Wnd));
        Wnd = GetWindow (Wnd, GW_HWNDNEXT);
      }
    }
  }
```

Of bitmaps and buttons

So far, the only variant of the BUTTON window class that we've modified is the group box. Now let's turn our attention to push buttons and check boxes. In principle, it would be possible to produce the effect shown in Figure 5.1 by directly drawing the shapes of the new check boxes and radio buttons onto the screen. However, doing so would involve a lot of intricate drawing code, and if you ever wanted to modify the appearance of your custom check boxes and radio buttons, you would find it very difficult and tedious to do so.

A much better approach is to use a bitmap containing the image of each different control type. This bitmap image can then be blitted directly onto the screen when a control needs to be drawn. If you want to modify the appearance of controls, you can visually edit the bitmap using something like Borland's Resource Workshop. This is obviously a lot easier and less error-prone than modifying a large chunk of drawing code. The bitmap we'll be using is shown in Figure 5.12. The actual appearance of the buttons is intended to duplicate those used by Microsoft in applications such as Excel, Microsoft Golf, and so forth.

It's very obvious that the row of images in the top half of the bitmap are related to check boxes, while those in the bottom half are concerned with radio buttons. Since a control can appear in various 'states', we need to have an image of each control type in each of its possible states. That's the reason why there are so many similar-looking images in the bitmap. Don't worry about the cool dude; he's only along for the ride. The leftmost column of the bitmap shows what the two different

Figure 5.12 The bitmap used to draw radio buttons and check boxes.

control types look like in their normal, unchecked state. The second column shows the appearance of the controls when the mouse is clicked on them from the unchecked state. This state will only be shown while the mouse is actually held down over one of the controls. As soon as the mouse button is released, the image displayed will be taken from the third column, which shows the controls in their checked state. The fourth column shows the image that is displayed when the mouse is clicked on a control while in its checked state. As soon as the mouse button is released, the image displayed will move back to the unchecked state, as shown in column one.

In a sense, the two images shown in columns two and four are transient: they're only displayed while the mouse button is held down on a control. You might wonder why we bother to show these transient states at all. The code could be simplified, and the bitmap image would certainly be smaller without them. This is really a question of good user interface design. For any action that the user might take, it's important to give some sort of visual feedback. By highlighting a pressed control in this way, we're indicating that its state is going to change when the mouse button is released. Also, the highlighting is removed if the user drags the mouse button away from the clicked-on control. This is a way of telling the user that OK, he or she's made a choice, but it isn't irrevocable and can be canceled. Good interface design always provides a 'way out' for inexperienced users who are unfamiliar with an interface's design.

You could implement each control image as a separate bitmap, but doing so would be wasteful: a bunch of small bitmaps takes up more room than a single, larger bitmap. It would also make editing the bitmap more tedious if you wanted to change the appearance of any of the controls. Each of the images in the bitmap is a square, 13 pixels high and 13 pixels wide. If you want to change the size of the bitmap, you will need to change a couple of #defines in the code that specifies these values. Not doing so will produce some very strange effects! The bitmap in Figure 5.12 is obviously shown much larger than actual size. If you don't have the companion disk, you can manually enter it using this figure. The bitmap is incorporated into the next revision of the resource script file, DIATEST3.RC, which is on the disk.

It would be nice if Windows-hosted C/C++ development systems supported the inclusion of multiple .RC files into a single project. This would allow us to neatly compartmentalize the dialog handling code along with its resource data.

Unfortunately, we can't do that. Borland C/C++, for example, will complain if you try to add a second resource script to an existing project. This being the case, the DIATEST3.RC incorporates both the bitmap shown above and the existing dialog box template.

Keeping color-coordinated

How do we load this bitmap so that we can make use of it within the dialog handling code? You might be forgiven for thinking that we need do nothing more complex than this:

```
hbmTools = LoadBitmap (hInstance, MAKEINTRESOURCE (1));
```

This code assumes that we've given a resource ID of 1 to the bitmap resource, and it stores the bitmap handle into a global variable called hbmTools. Unfortunately, we've got a real problem here. The code will work – most of the time, but what happens if the user decides to change his or her color scheme? Recall that we want to make our code as flexible as possible; we want to be able to adopt the appearance of our Excel-style dialog boxes to suit the currently selected settings for COLOR_BTN-FACE, COLOR_BTNSHADOW, and so on. How are we going to do this if we just blast parts of a predefined bitmap onto the screen? This looks pretty bad. Have we got to load up the bitmap and then modify the colors in it pixel by pixel? Yeugh.

Fortunately, the answer is no. Like most things in Windows, there is a simple solution if you look hard enough. The answer lies inside a Windows data structure called BITMAPINFO. The C definition of this data structure is given below. There's a header followed by an array of RGBQUADs. Although only one RGBQUAD is shown in the array, there will be 16 entries for a 16-bit color bitmap.

```
typedef struct tagBITMAPINFO
{
    BITMAPINFOHEADER bmiHeader;
    RGBQUAD          bmiColors[1];
} BITMAPINFO;

typedef struct tagRGBQUAD
{
    BYTE rgbBlue;
    BYTE rgbGreen;
    BYTE rgbRed;
    BYTE rgbReserved;
} RGBQUAD;
```

Tweaking the bitmap to be consistent with the currently selected color scheme involves little more than altering the relevant RGBQUAD entries in this data structure. Each RGBQUAD describes a color in the bitmap and by modifying these entries, the bitmap colors effectively change, too. The code to perform this magic is shown below:

```
//-----------------------------------------------------------
// Name:    ColorFix
// Purpose: Fix up a color value for the LoadButtonBitmap routine.
//-----------------------------------------------------------
```

```
static COLORREF PASCAL ColorFix (COLORREF color)
{
      return RGB (GetBValue (color), GetGValue (color), GetRValue (color));
}

//————————————————————————————————————————————————————
// Name:    LoadButtonBitmap
// Purpose: Load a bitmap and tweak it for current system colors.
//————————————————————————————————————————————————————

HBITMAP PASCAL LoadButtonBitmap (HANDLE hInstance, int bmID)
{
      HDC dc;
      HBITMAP hbm;
      HANDLE hRes;
      LPDWORD lprgb;
      LPVOID lpb;
      LPBITMAPINFOHEADER lpbi;

      hRes = LoadResource (hInstance, FindResource (hInstance,
                        MAKEINTRESOURCE(bmID), RT_BITMAP));

      lpbi = (LPBITMAPINFOHEADER) LockResource (hRes);
      if (lpbi == NULL) return (NULL);

      lprgb = (LPDWORD) ((LPSTR) lpbi + (int) lpbi->biSize);
      lpb = (LPVOID) (lprgb + 16);

      lprgb [0] = ColorFix (GetSysColor (COLOR_WINDOWTEXT));        // Black
      lprgb [8] = ColorFix (GetSysColor (COLOR_BTNFACE));           // Light gray
      lprgb [7] = ColorFix (GetSysColor (COLOR_BTNSHADOW));         // Gray
      lprgb [15] = ColorFix (GetSysColor (COLOR_BTNHIGHLIGHT));     // White

      dc = GetDC (NULL);
      hbm = CreateDIBitmap (dc, lpbi, CBM_INIT, lpb,
                        (LPBITMAPINFO) lpbi, DIB_RGB_COLORS);

      ReleaseDC (NULL, dc);
      GlobalUnlock (hRes);
      FreeResource (hRes);
      return (hbm);
}
```

As you can see, an extra routine called ColorFix is required. This routine takes a color specification in RGB format and returns the corresponding color in the form of an RBGQUAD data structure. Once the necessary changes have been made to the bmiColors array, the CreateDIBitmap routine is called to create an entirely new bitmap that reflects the changes made to the color information. The old bitmap is then deallocated. Using this routine we can ensure that the appearance of the radio buttons and check boxes in our dialog will reflect any changes that the user makes to the color scheme. It is important, though, that the bitmap resource should be a 16-color bitmap, as this is assumed by the above code.

With this change, the InitTools and FreeTools routines now look as shown below. The SubClassDialog routine now takes an instance handle as an additional parameter. This is needed in order to load the bitmap resource via the LoadButtonBitmap routine. The instance handle passed in via SubClassDialog is kept as a static global inside the dialog handling code. This change is reflected in the new header file, DIALOGS2.H, which takes an instance handle as a parameter to the SubClassDialog routine and uses it to set up hInst.

```
//—————————————————————————————————————————————————————
// Name:    InitTools
// Purpose: Set up needed tools.
//—————————————————————————————————————————————————————

static void PASCAL InitTools (void)
{
      if (DialogCount++ == 0)
      {
        CreateDialogFont ();
        hbrBack = GetControlBrush (COLOR_BTNFACE);
        hbmTools = LoadButtonBitmap (hInst, 1);
      }
}

//—————————————————————————————————————————————————————
// Name:    FreeTools
// Purpose: Called to clean up tools when a dialog is closed.
//—————————————————————————————————————————————————————

static void PASCAL FreeTools (void)
{
      if (—DialogCount == 0)
      {
        DeleteObject (hbrBack);
        DeleteObject (DialogFont);
        DeleteObject (hbmTools);
      }
}
```

It became obvious while testing this code that the DrawRaisedRect routine also needed to be modified slightly in order to fit in with the user's choice of color scheme. Previously, I overlooked the fact that the button highlight color wasn't always going to be white. A revised version of the DrawRaisedRect code is shown below. The DrawRaisedRect routine, DrawSunkenRect routine and LoadButtonBitmap routine are included in the Pascal Tools unit, because of their usefulness. As mentioned at the end of Chapter 2, the LoadButtonBitmap routine should be likewise used to load the toolbox bitmap so that the application program's toolbox remains consistent with the current color scheme.

```
//—————————————————————————————————————————————————————
// Name:    DrawRaisedRect
// Purpose: Draw a raised rectangle at specified location.
//—————————————————————————————————————————————————————

static void PASCAL DrawRaisedRect (HDC dc, LPRECT lpr)
{
      HBRUSH hbr;
      int width, height;

      width = lpr—>right — lpr—>left;
      height = lpr—>bottom — lpr—>top;

      hbr = SelectObject (dc, CreateSolidBrush (GetSysColor (COLOR_BTNHIGHLIGHT)));
      PatBlt (dc, lpr—>left, lpr—>top, 1, height — 1, PATCOPY);
      PatBlt (dc, lpr—>left, lpr—>top, width — 1, 1, PATCOPY);
      DeleteObject (SelectObject (dc, CreateSolidBrush (GetSysColor (COLOR_BTNSHADOW))));
      PatBlt (dc, lpr—>right — 1, lpr—>top, 1, height, PATCOPY);
      PatBlt (dc, lpr—>left, lpr—>bottom — 1, width, 1, PATCOPY);
      DeleteObject (SelectObject (dc, hbr));
}
```

Note

It's surprising how few programs bother to implement color scheme compatibility properly. Borland C/C++, for example, totally ignores the current color scheme and will stubbornly continue to display light gray button bars and status bars no matter what changes you make via the Control Panel application. Even Microsoft aren't blameless here; if you change the colors of a button, you'll see the Word for Windows toolbar and status bar change to reflect the new button face color, but the button highlight color is ignored by Word for Windows – it always use white for button highlighting. It may be that Microsoft are aware of these shortcomings since, strangely enough, all of the color schemes offered by the Control Panel use a standard light-gray button.

Admittedly, keeping in step with the current color scheme is a pain. What do we do if the color scheme changes while there's a button displayed? Fortunately, this isn't a problem because Windows sends a special notification message to all top-level windows. This message, called WM_SYSCOLORCHANGE, is Windows' way of telling you that the system colors have changed. We can add the following code to our dialog subclassing routine to handle this message:

```
case WM_SYSCOLORCHANGE:

DeleteObject (hbmTools);
DeleteObject (hbrBack);
hbmTools = LoadButtonBitmap (hInst, 1);
hbrBack = GetControlBrush (COLOR_BTNFACE);
return (0);
```

We can't call the FreeTools and InitTools routines here since we may already have more than one dialog box in operation. If this is the case, the DialogCount variable wouldn't be decremented to zero and no reloading of the bitmap and background brush would take place. Unfortunately, Windows only sends the WM_SYSCOLOR-CHANGE message to top-level windows. If your application is structured in the normal way, with a main application window, then your dialog boxes will not get this message. The solution is to intercept the WM_SYSCOLORCHANGE message in your main application window procedure and use the SendMessage routine to just 'pass it on' to any active dialog box. If several dialog boxes are active, it's only necessary to send the message to one of them.

If your program is implemented as a single dialog window (like Petzold's ubiquitous HEXCALC program), the dialog box will effectively be a top-level window and it will automatically receive WM_SYSCOLORCHANGE messages. If this isn't the case, you may wish to consider subclassing the main application window within the dialog handling code to make the dialog code more self-contained. Although I haven't pursued this approach here, it wouldn't be difficult to do.

OK, so we've got our bitmap handle; now let's look at how we're going to display this bitmap on the screen. The routine below, PaintTool, is used to draw a tool bitmap on to the screen. When I say 'tool bitmap', I'm referring to one small part of the overall bitmap that corresponds to a single control in a particular state. The routine takes three parameters: a handle to the dialog item itself, a state word that specifies the current state of the item, and a flags word that can contain a combination of these two bit flags:

```
// Control flags for PaintTool routine

#define          PTDOWN   1
#define          PTPAINT  2

//————————————————————————————————————————————————————————————————
// Name:    PaintTool
// Purpose: Draw a subsection of the tool bitmap as required.
//————————————————————————————————————————————————————————————————

static void PASCAL PaintTool (HWND Wnd, WORD bsState, WORD flags)
{
      RECT r;
      HDC SrcDC;
      WORD dtFlags;
      PAINTSTRUCT ps;
      BOOL bLeftAlign;
      char szText [128];
      int bskind, x, y, blitHeight;

      bLeftAlign = LOWORD (GetWindowLong (Wnd, GWL_STYLE)) & BS_LEFTTEXT;
      bskind = LOWORD (GetWindowLong (Wnd, GWL_STYLE)) & 0xF;

      x = bsState * 2;
      if (flags & PTDOWN) ++x;
      y = 0;
      if (bskind == BS_RADIOBUTTON || bskind == BS_AUTORADIOBUTTON) ++y;
      x *= TOOLWIDTH;
      y *= TOOLHEIGHT;

      if (flags & PTPAINT) BeginPaint (Wnd, &ps);
      else ps.hdc = GetDC (Wnd);
      DialogFont = SelectObject (ps.hdc, DialogFont);
      SetBkMode (ps.hdc, TRANSPARENT);

      GetClientRect (Wnd, &r);
      blitHeight = r.top + ((r.bottom − r.top) − TOOLHEIGHT) / 2;
      SrcDC = CreateCompatibleDC (ps.hdc);
      hbmTools = SelectObject (SrcDC, hbmTools);

      if (bLeftAlign)
      {
         BitBlt (ps.hdc, r.right − TOOLWIDTH, blitHeight,
               TOOLWIDTH, TOOLHEIGHT, SrcDC, x, y, SRCCOPY);
         r.right −= (TOOLWIDTH * 3) / 2;
         dtFlags = DT_SINGLELINE | DT_RIGHT | DT_VCENTER;
      }
      else
      {
         BitBlt (ps.hdc, r.left, blitHeight, TOOLWIDTH,
               TOOLHEIGHT, SrcDC, x, y, SRCCOPY);
         r.left += (TOOLWIDTH * 3) / 2;
         −−r.left;
         dtFlags = DT_SINGLELINE | DT_VCENTER;
      }

      ++r.top;
      CallOldProc (Wnd, WM_GETTEXT, sizeof (szText), (LPARAM) szText, hookKey);
      DrawText (ps.hdc, szText, −1, &r, dtFlags);

      hbmTools = SelectObject (SrcDC, hbmTools);

      DeleteDC (SrcDC);

      DialogFont = SelectObject (ps.hdc, DialogFont);
      if (flags & PTPAINT) EndPaint (Wnd, &ps);
      else ReleaseDC (Wnd, ps.hdc);
}
```

The PTDOWN flag indicates whether the control should be drawn in the 'up' or
'pushed down' position, while the PTPAINT flag indicates whether or not PaintTool is
being called as the result of a WM_PAINT message. If so, a destination device context

is obtained in the usual way via a call to the BeginPaint routine. If PaintTool is not being called in response to a WM_PAINT message, a device context is obtained through a call to the GetDC routine.

This might seem odd, but you need to bear in mind that a dialog control needs to be redrawn at various times, and not just in response to a WM_PAINT message. For example, as soon as a WM_LBUTTONDOWN message is received, a check box or radio button needs to be redrawn to indicate that it is responding to the mouse click.

```
//---------------------------------------------------------------------
// Name:    SCCheckBox
// Purpose: Subclassing routine for CHECKBOX controls.
//---------------------------------------------------------------------

LONG FAR PASCAL _export SCCheckBox (HWND Wnd, UINT Msg,
                                    WPARAM wParam, LPARAM lParam)
{
    RECT r;
    POINT pt;
    WORD buttonState;
    WORD buttonKind;

    buttonKind = LOWORD (GetWindowLong (Wnd, GWL_STYLE)) & 0xF;
    buttonState = GetWindowWord (Wnd, 0);

    switch (Msg)
    {
      case WM_PAINT:

        PaintTool (Wnd, buttonState & 3, PTPAINT);
        return (0);

      case WM_LBUTTONDOWN:

        if (GetFocus() != Wnd) SetFocus (Wnd);

        fPressed = TRUE;
        fCapture = TRUE;
        SetCapture (Wnd);
        PaintTool (Wnd, buttonState & 3, PTDOWN);
        return (0);

      case WM_LBUTTONUP:

        fCapture = FALSE;
        ReleaseCapture();
        if (fPressed == FALSE) return (0);
        fPressed = FALSE;

        if (buttonKind == BS_AUTOCHECKBOX)
        {
            buttonState ^= (buttonState ^ ((buttonState & 3) == 0)) & 3;
            SetWindowWord (Wnd, 0, buttonState);
            PaintTool (Wnd, buttonState & 3, 0);
        }

        SendMessage (GetParent (Wnd), WM_COMMAND,
                     GetWindowWord (Wnd, GWW_ID), MAKELONG (Wnd, 0));
        return (0);

      case WM_MOUSEMOVE:

        if (fCapture)
        {
            GetClientRect (Wnd, &r);
            pt.x = LOWORD (lParam);
            pt.y = HIWORD (lParam);
```

```
                                    if (PtInRect (&r, pt))

                                    {
                                        if (fPressed == FALSE) PaintTool (Wnd, buttonState & 3, PTDOWN);
                                        fPressed = TRUE;
                                    }
                                    else
                                    {
                                        if (fPressed) PaintTool (Wnd, buttonState & 3, 0);
                                        fPressed = FALSE;
                                    }
                                    return (0);
                                }
                                return DefWindowProc (Wnd, Msg, wParam, lParam);

                            case WM_SETFOCUS:
                            case WM_GETFONT:
                            case WM_KILLFOCUS:
                            case WM_GETDLGCODE:

                                return CallOldProc (Wnd, Msg, wParam, lParam, hookKey);

                            case WM_ENABLE:

                                InvalidateRect (Wnd, NULL, FALSE);
                                return (0);

                            case BM_SETCHECK:

                                SetWindowWord (Wnd, 0, (buttonState & ~3) | (wParam & 3));
                                PaintTool (Wnd, wParam, 0);
                                return (0);

                            case BM_GETCHECK:

                                return buttonState & 3;

                            default:

                                return DefWindowProc (Wnd, Msg, wParam, lParam);
                        }
                    }
```

The code above, SCCheckBox, is the actual subclassing routine for checkboxes. It may look rather intimidating, but it's fairly straightforward if you look at it on a message-by-message basis. The state of a button control can be retrieved by calling GetWindowWord with an index of zero. The state can likewise be obtained by sending a BM_GETSTATE message to the control.

The SDK documentation provides some insight into how to interpret the word value which is obtained. Bit 0 and bit 1 together specify the check state of the control. This has a value of 0 for an unchecked control, 1 for a checked control, and 2 for the indeterminate state of a tri-state check box. Bit 2 specifies the highlight state of a control. A button is highlighted when the user presses and holds the left mouse button. A highlight state corresponds to the transient states discussed earlier when we were looking at the layout of the bitmap. Finally, bit 3 indicates whether or not the button has the focus.

The revised SubClassControl code needed to subclass any checkbox controls is shown below. As you can see, this is pretty straightforward. We simply look for control types of CHECKBOX and AUTOCHECKBOX and, if found, the HookWindow routine is used to subclass them with the SCCheckBox code. At this stage, the dialog box now looks as shown in Figure 5.13.

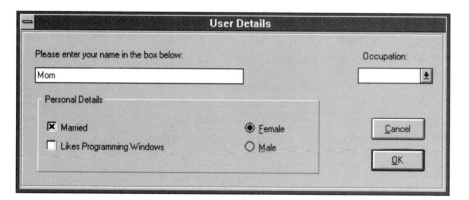

Figure 5.13 The dialog test
program with the check box
subclassing code in place.

```
//————————————————————————————————————————————————————
// Name:     SubClassControl
// Purpose:  Subclass an individual dialog box control, according to
//           type. Controls that we don't recognize or aren't interested
//           in are left alone.
//————————————————————————————————————————————————————

static void PASCAL SubClassControl (HWND Wnd, int type)
{
      // Use our special font

      if (type != -1) SendMessage (Wnd, WM_SETFONT, DialogFont, 0);

      // Case out on control type

      switch (type)
      {
        case EDITBOX:

        ShrinkEditBox (Wnd);
        break;

        case BUTTON:

        type = GetWindowLong (Wnd, GWL_STYLE) & 0xF;
        switch (type)
        {
          case GROUPBOX:

          HookWindow (Wnd, (FARPROC) SCGroupBox, szHookName);
          break;

          case CHECKBOX:
          case AUTOCHECKBOX:

          HookWindow (Wnd, (FARPROC) SCCheckBox, szHookName);
        }
      }
}
```

Flushed from our success with check boxes, let's tackle the radio button code
next. One wrinkle concerning the implementation of the radio button code is relevant
to the operation of so-called auto radio buttons. An auto radio button, when pressed,
will automatically uncheck any other radio buttons in the same group. Looking at the
sample dialog template that we're using, we have two auto radio buttons in this dialog, one for each possible sex. Despite the miracles of modern science, most people
tend to be either male or female, so when one radio button is clicked we obviously

want the other one to be automatically unchecked! This behavior usually happens for free – you don't have to take any special action in your dialog procedure. However, that's from the viewpoint of the application programmer. From our viewpoint, as custom control implementors, the business of unchecking other buttons in the same group is our responsibility.

The routine below, SetRadioGroup, and the associated routine IsRadioButton are used to scan forwards and backwards from the current control, looking for more auto radio buttons in the group. When the group limits have been determined, the CheckRadioButton routine is called to set the wanted radio button and to clear all the others. The working of the IsAutoRadioButton routine should be pretty obvious: it calls the ButtonType routine to get a match on the window class name and then checks that it's the button variant that is being dealt with. As an alternative, you could check for a match on the window procedure address, but you would still have to differentiate between radio buttons and auto radio buttons, since both variants of the control class are subclassed to the same window procedure.

```
//------------------------------------------------------------------
// Name:    IsAutoRadioButton
// Purpose: Determine if specified control is an auto radio button.
//------------------------------------------------------------------
static BOOL PASCAL IsAutoRadioButton (HWND Dlg, int ID)
{
        HWND Wnd;

        if ((Wnd = GetDlgItem (Dlg, ID)) != NULL)
          if (ControlType (Wnd) == BUTTON)
            if ((GetWindowLong (Wnd, GWL_STYLE) & 0xF) == BS_AUTORADIOBUTTON)
              return (TRUE);

        return (FALSE);
}

//------------------------------------------------------------------
// Name:    SetRadioGroup
// Purpose: Check the specified button and uncheck all other auto
//          radio buttons in the current group.
//------------------------------------------------------------------
static void PASCAL SetRadioGroup (HWND Dlg, HWND Wnd)
{
        int first, last, current;

        first = last = current = GetWindowWord (Wnd, GWW_ID);
        while (IsAutoRadioButton (Dlg, first - 1)) —first;
        while (IsAutoRadioButton (Dlg, last + 1)) ++last;
        CheckRadioButton (Dlg, first, last, current);
}
```

The actual subclassing routine for the radio button controls is shown below. There are some obvious similarities to the check box subclassing code and you may feel that you'd rather implement all the BUTTON variants within the same subclassing routine. As mentioned earlier, this could certainly be done, although I feel that the code would get rather messy. Personally, I would prefer to implement duplicate chunks of code as procedures – the code for handling WM_LBUTTON-DOWN and WM_MOUSEMOVE are obvious candidates for this approach.

```
//------------------------------------------------------------------
// Name:    SCRadioButton
// Purpose: Subclassing routine for RADIOBUTTON controls.
//------------------------------------------------------------------
```

```
LONG FAR PASCAL _export SCRadioButton (HWND Wnd, UINT Msg,
                                WPARAM wParam, LPARAM lParam)
{
    RECT r;
    POINT pt;
    WORD buttonState;
    WORD buttonKind;

    buttonKind = LOWORD (GetWindowLong (Wnd, GWL_STYLE)) & 0xF;
    buttonState = GetWindowWord (Wnd, 0);

    switch (Msg)
    {
      case WM_PAINT:

        PaintTool (Wnd, buttonState & 3, PTPAINT);
        return (0);

      case WM_LBUTTONDOWN:

        if (GetFocus() != Wnd) SetFocus (Wnd);
        fPressed = TRUE;
        fCapture = TRUE;
        SetCapture (Wnd);
        PaintTool (Wnd, buttonState & 3, PTDOWN);
        return (0);

      case WM_LBUTTONUP:

        fCapture = FALSE;
        ReleaseCapture();
        if (fPressed == FALSE) return (0);
        fPressed = FALSE;

        if (buttonKind == BS_AUTORADIOBUTTON)
        {
          buttonState = (buttonState & ~2) | 1;
          SetWindowWord (Wnd, 0, buttonState);
          PaintTool (Wnd, buttonState & 3, 0);
          SetRadioGroup (GetParent (Wnd), Wnd);
        }
        SendMessage (GetParent (Wnd), WM_COMMAND,
                    GetWindowWord (Wnd, GWW_ID), MAKELONG (Wnd, 0));
        return (0);

      case WM_MOUSEMOVE:

        if (fCapture)
        {
          GetClientRect (Wnd, &r);
          pt.x = LOWORD (lParam);
          pt.y = HIWORD (lParam);

          if (PtInRect (&r, pt))
          {
            if (fPressed == FALSE) PaintTool (Wnd, buttonState & 3, PTDOWN);
            fPressed = TRUE;
          }
          else
          {
            if (fPressed) PaintTool (Wnd, buttonState & 3, 0);
            fPressed = FALSE;
          }
          return (0);
        }
        return DefWindowProc (Wnd, Msg, wParam, lParam);

      case WM_GETFONT:
      case WM_KILLFOCUS:
      case WM_GETDLGCODE:

        return CallOldProc (Wnd, Msg, wParam, lParam, hookKey);

      case WM_SETFOCUS:

        buttonState = (buttonState & ~2) | 1;
```

```
                SetWindowWord (Wnd, 0, buttonState);
                PaintTool (Wnd, buttonState & 3, 0);
                SetRadioGroup (GetParent (Wnd), Wnd);
                SendMessage (GetParent (Wnd), WM_COMMAND,
                          GetWindowWord (Wnd, GWW_ID), MAKELONG (Wnd, 0));
                return CallOldProc (Wnd, Msg, wParam, lParam, hookKey);

              case WM_ENABLE:
                InvalidateRect (Wnd, NULL, FALSE);
                return (0);

              case BM_SETCHECK:
                SetWindowWord (Wnd, 0, buttonState ^ ((wParam ^ buttonState) & 3));
                PaintTool (Wnd, buttonState & 3, 0);
                return (0);

              case BM_GETCHECK:
                return buttonState & 3;

              default:
                return DefWindowProc (Wnd, Msg, wParam, lParam);
          }
      }
```

In order to 'activate' the radio button subclassing code, it's only necessary to add the needed cases to the SubClassControl code as shown below. At this point, the dialog box appears as shown in Figure 5.14.

```
//───────────────────────────────────────────────────────────
// Name:     SubClassControl
// Purpose:  Subclass an individual dialog box control, according to
//           type. Controls that we don't recognize or aren't interested
//           in are left alone.
//───────────────────────────────────────────────────────────
static void PASCAL SubClassControl (HWND Wnd, int type)
{
        // Use our special font
        if (type != −1) SendMessage (Wnd, WM_SETFONT, DialogFont, 0);

        // Case out on control type
        switch (type)
        {
          case EDITBOX:
            ShrinkEditBox (Wnd);
            break;

          case BUTTON:
            type = GetWindowLong (Wnd, GWL_STYLE) & 0xF;
            switch (type)
            {
              case GROUPBOX:
                HookWindow (Wnd, (FARPROC) SCGroupBox, szHookName);
                break;

              case CHECKBOX:
              case AUTOCHECKBOX:
                HookWindow (Wnd, (FARPROC) SCCheckBox, szHookName);
                break;

              case RADIOBUTTON:
              case AUTORADIOBUTTON:
                HookWindow (Wnd, (FARPROC) SCRadioButton, szHookName);
                break;
            }
        }
}
```

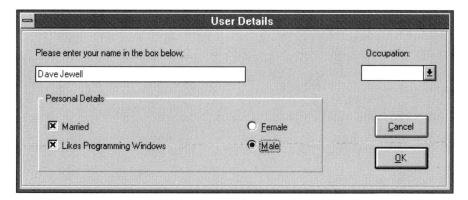

Figure 5.14 The dialog test program with radio button sub-classing added.

As it stands, the dialog subclassing code is now almost complete. The source code listing in Figure 5.15 shows all the changes made so far, and also includes a few minor changes required to implement tri-state and auto tri-state radio buttons. The source code can be found on the disk as DIALOGS4.C, and the corresponding compiled executable file as DIATEST4.EXE.

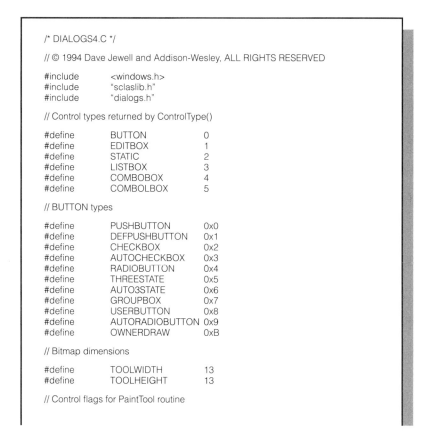

Figure 5.15 DIALOGS4.C: the working dialog subclassing code, with all control subclassing in place.

```
/* DIALOGS4.C */

// © 1994 Dave Jewell and Addison-Wesley, ALL RIGHTS RESERVED

#include     <windows.h>
#include     "sclaslib.h"
#include     "dialogs.h"

// Control types returned by ControlType()

#define     BUTTON         0
#define     EDITBOX        1
#define     STATIC         2
#define     LISTBOX        3
#define     COMBOBOX       4
#define     COMBOLBOX      5

// BUTTON types

#define     PUSHBUTTON          0x0
#define     DEFPUSHBUTTON       0x1
#define     CHECKBOX            0x2
#define     AUTOCHECKBOX        0x3
#define     RADIOBUTTON         0x4
#define     THREESTATE          0x5
#define     AUTO3STATE          0x6
#define     GROUPBOX            0x7
#define     USERBUTTON          0x8
#define     AUTORADIOBUTTON 0x9
#define     OWNERDRAW           0xB

// Bitmap dimensions

#define     TOOLWIDTH      13
#define     TOOLHEIGHT     13

// Control flags for PaintTool routine
```

```
#define          PTDOWN           1
#define          PTPAINT          2

static char      szHookName[ ]= "DialogsHook";
static LONG      hookKey;
static HFONT     DialogFont = NULL;   // special dialog font
static HBRUSH    hbrBack = NULL;      // background brush
static int       DialogCount = 0;     // number of subclassed dialogs
static HBITMAP   hbmTools = NULL;     // handle to tool bitmap
static HANDLE    hInst;               // application instance handle
static BOOL      fPressed = FALSE;    // TRUE if a control is pressed
static BOOL      fCapture = FALSE;    // TRUE if mouse captured

//————————————————————————————————————————————————
// Name:    GetControlBrush
// Purpose: Create a control brush for a given system color.
//————————————————————————————————————————————————

static HBRUSH PASCAL GetControlBrush (int sysColor)
{
     COLORREF color;

     color = GetSysColor (sysColor);
     return (CreateSolidBrush (color));
}

//————————————————————————————————————————————————
// Name:    DrawRaisedRect
// Purpose: Draw a raised rectangle at specified location.
//————————————————————————————————————————————————

static void PASCAL DrawRaisedRect (HDC dc, LPRECT lpr)
{
     HBRUSH hbr;
     int width, height;

     width = lpr−>right − lpr−>left;
     height = lpr−>bottom − lpr−>top;

     hbr = SelectObject (dc, CreateSolidBrush (GetSysColor
                         (COLOR_BTNHIGHLIGHT)));
     PatBlt (dc, lpr−>left, lpr−>top, 1, height − 1, PATCOPY);
     PatBlt (dc, lpr−>left, lpr−>top, width − 1, 1, PATCOPY);
     DeleteObject (SelectObject (dc, CreateSolidBrush (GetSysColor
                         (COLOR_BTNSHADOW))));
     PatBlt (dc, lpr−>right − 1, lpr−>top, 1, height, PATCOPY);
     PatBlt (dc, lpr−>left, lpr−>bottom − 1, width, 1, PATCOPY);
     DeleteObject (SelectObject (dc, hbr));
}

//————————————————————————————————————————————————
// Name:    CenterDialog
// Purpose: Center a given dialog window on the screen.
//————————————————————————————————————————————————

static void PASCAL CenterDialog (HWND Wnd)
{
     RECT r;

     GetWindowRect (Wnd, &r);
     r.left = (GetSystemMetrics (SM_CXSCREEN) − r.right + r.left) / 2;
     r.top = (GetSystemMetrics (SM_CYSCREEN) − r.bottom + r.top) / 2;
     SetWindowPos (Wnd, 0, r.left, r.top, 0, 0, SWP_NOSIZE | SWP_NOZORDER);
}

//————————————————————————————————————————————————
// Name:    CreateDialogFont
// Purpose: Create the dialog font.
//————————————————————————————————————————————————
```

```
void PASCAL CreateDialogFont (void)
{
    HDC dc;
    char faceName [50];
    int nHeight, pointSize;

    // Pickup point size and face name from WIN.INI

    pointSize = GetProfileInt ("Desktop", "StatusBarFaceHeight", 8);
    GetProfileString ("Desktop", "StatusBarFaceName",
                    "MS Sans Serif", faceName, 50);

    dc = GetDC (NULL);
    nHeight = (GetDeviceCaps (dc, LOGPIXELSY) * pointSize) / −72;
    ReleaseDC (NULL, dc);

    // Now create the font

    DialogFont = CreateFont (nHeight, 0, 0, 0, FW_NORMAL, 0, 0, 0,
                            ANSI_CHARSET,
                            OUT_DEFAULT_PRECIS,
                            CLIP_DEFAULT_PRECIS,
                            DEFAULT_QUALITY,
                            FF_SWISS | VARIABLE_PITCH,
                            faceName);

}

//──────────────────────────────────────────────────────────
// Name:    ColorFix
// Purpose: Fix up a color value for the LoadButtonBitmap routine.
//──────────────────────────────────────────────────────────

static COLORREF PASCAL ColorFix (COLORREF color)
{
    return RGB (GetBValue (color), GetGValue (color), GetRValue (color));
}

//──────────────────────────────────────────────────────────
// Name:    LoadButtonBitmap
// Purpose: Load a bitmap and tweak it for current system colors.
//──────────────────────────────────────────────────────────

HBITMAP PASCAL LoadButtonBitmap (HANDLE hInstance, int bmID)
{
    HDC dc;
    HBITMAP hbm;
    HANDLE hRes;
    LPDWORD lprgb;
    LPVOID lpb;
    LPBITMAPINFOHEADER lpbi;

    hRes = LoadResource (hInstance, FindResource (hInstance,
                        MAKEINTRESOURCE(bmID), RT_BITMAP));

    lpbi = (LPBITMAPINFOHEADER) LockResource (hRes);
    if (lpbi == NULL) return (NULL);
    lprgb = (LPDWORD) ((LPSTR) lpbi + (int) lpbi−>biSize);
    lpb = (LPVOID) (lprgb + 16);

    lprgb [0] = ColorFix (GetSysColor (COLOR_WINDOWTEXT));    // Black
    lprgb [8] = ColorFix (GetSysColor (COLOR_BTNFACE));       // Light gray
    lprgb [7] = ColorFix (GetSysColor (COLOR_BTNSHADOW));     // Gray
    lprgb [15] = ColorFix (GetSysColor (COLOR_BTNHIGHLIGHT)); // White

    dc = GetDC (NULL);
    hbm = CreateDIBitmap (dc, lpbi, CBM_INIT, lpb,
                        (LPBITMAPINFO) lpbi, DIB_RGB_COLORS);
```

```
            ReleaseDC (NULL, dc);
            GlobalUnlock (hRes);
            FreeResource (hRes);
            return (hbm);
}

//————————————————————————————————————————————————————————————
// Name:    InitTools
// Purpose: Set up needed tools.
//————————————————————————————————————————————————————————————

static void PASCAL InitTools (void)
{
        if (DialogCount++ == 0)
        {
            CreateDialogFont ();
            hbrBack = GetControlBrush (COLOR_BTNFACE);
            hbmTools = LoadButtonBitmap (hInst, 1);
        }
}

//————————————————————————————————————————————————————————————
// Name:    FreeTools
// Purpose: Called to clean up tools when a dialog is closed.
//————————————————————————————————————————————————————————————

static void PASCAL FreeTools (void)
{
        if (—DialogCount == 0)
        {
            DeleteObject (hbrBack);
            DeleteObject (DialogFont);
            DeleteObject (hbmTools);
        }
}

//————————————————————————————————————————————————————————————
// Name:    SCGroupBox
// Purpose: Subclassing routine for GROUPBOX controls.
//————————————————————————————————————————————————————————————

LONG FAR PASCAL _export SCGroupBox (HWND Wnd, UINT Msg,
                                    WPARAM wParam, LPARAM lParam)
{
        RECT r;
        DWORD dwExtent;
        HFONT hFont;
        COLORREF bkColor;
        PAINTSTRUCT ps;
        char szText [128];

        switch (Msg)
        {
          case WM_PAINT:

            BeginPaint (Wnd, &ps);
            if (SendMessage (Wnd, WM_GETTEXT, 120,
              (LONG)(LPSTR) &szText [1]) <= 0) szText[0] = '\0';
            else
            {
              szText [0] = ' ';
              lstrcat (szText, " ");
            }

            GetClientRect (Wnd, &r);
            DrawRaisedRect (ps.hdc, &r);

            if (szText [0] != '\0')
            {
```

```
            hFont = SelectObject (ps.hdc, DialogFont);
            dwExtent = GetTextExtent (ps.hdc, "Yy", 2);
            r.top -= HIWORD (dwExtent) / 2;
            r.left += LOWORD (dwExtent) / 2;
            bkColor = SetBkColor (ps.hdc, GetSysColor (COLOR_BTNFACE));
            DrawText (ps.hdc, szText, -1, &r, DT_SINGLELINE);
            SetBkColor (ps.hdc, bkColor);
            SelectObject (ps.hdc, hFont);
        }

        EndPaint (Wnd, &ps);
        return (0);
    }

    return CallOldProc (Wnd, Msg, wParam, lParam, hookKey);
}

//————————————————————————————————————————————————————————————
// Name:    PaintTool
// Purpose: Draw a subsection of the tool bitmap as required.
//————————————————————————————————————————————————————————————

static void PASCAL PaintTool (HWND Wnd, WORD bsState, WORD flags)
{
    RECT r;
    HDC SrcDC;
    WORD dtFlags;
    PAINTSTRUCT ps;
    BOOL bLeftAlign;
    char szText [128];
    int bskind, x, y, blitHeight;

    bLeftAlign = LOWORD (GetWindowLong (Wnd, GWL_STYLE)) & BS_LEFTTEXT;
    bskind = LOWORD (GetWindowLong (Wnd, GWL_STYLE)) & 0xF;

    x = bsState * 2;
    if (flags & PTDOWN) ++x;
    y = 0;
    if (bskind == BS_RADIOBUTTON || bskind == BS_AUTORADIOBUTTON) ++y;
    x *= TOOLWIDTH;
    y *= TOOLHEIGHT;

    if (flags & PTPAINT) BeginPaint (Wnd, &ps);
    else ps.hdc = GetDC (Wnd);
    DialogFont = SelectObject (ps.hdc, DialogFont);
    SetBkMode (ps.hdc, TRANSPARENT);

    GetClientRect (Wnd, &r);
    blitHeight = r.top + ((r.bottom - r.top) - TOOLHEIGHT) / 2;
    SrcDC = CreateCompatibleDC (ps.hdc);
    hbmTools = SelectObject (SrcDC, hbmTools);

    if (bLeftAlign)
    {
        BitBlt (ps.hdc, r.right - TOOLWIDTH, blitHeight,
                TOOLWIDTH, TOOLHEIGHT, SrcDC, x, y, SRCCOPY);
        r.right -= (TOOLWIDTH * 3) / 2;
        dtFlags = DT_SINGLELINE | DT_RIGHT | DT_VCENTER;
    }
    else
    {
        BitBlt (ps.hdc, r.left, blitHeight, TOOLWIDTH,
                TOOLHEIGHT, SrcDC, x, y, SRCCOPY);
        r.left += (TOOLWIDTH * 3) / 2;
        —r.left;
        dtFlags = DT_SINGLELINE | DT_VCENTER;
    }
```

```
        ++r.top;
        CallOldProc (Wnd, WM_GETTEXT, sizeof (szText), (LPARAM) szText, hookKey);
        DrawText (ps.hdc, szText, −1, &r, dtFlags);

        hbmTools = SelectObject (SrcDC, hbmTools);

        DeleteDC (SrcDC);

        DialogFont = SelectObject (ps.hdc, DialogFont);
        if (flags & PTPAINT) EndPaint (Wnd, &ps);
        else ReleaseDC (Wnd, ps.hdc);
}

//────────────────────────────────────────────────────────────
// Name:     ControlType
// Purpose:  Given a window handle, return the control type.
//           −1 is returned for an unrecognized type.
//────────────────────────────────────────────────────────────

static int PASCAL ControlType (HWND Wnd)
{
        int i;
        char ClassName [64];
        static char * controlNames [6] = { "Button",
                                           "Edit",
                                           "Static",
                                           "ListBox",
                                           "ComboBox",
                                           "ComboLBox" };

        GetClassName (Wnd, ClassName, sizeof (ClassName) − 1);

        for (i = 0; i < 6; i++)
        if (lstrcmpi (controlNames [i], ClassName) == 0)
             return (i);

        return (−1);
}

//────────────────────────────────────────────────────────────
// Name:     IsAutoRadioButton
// Purpose:  Determine if specified control is an auto radio button.
//────────────────────────────────────────────────────────────

static BOOL PASCAL IsAutoRadioButton (HWND Dlg, int ID)
{
        HWND Wnd;

        if ((Wnd = GetDlgItem (Dlg, ID)) != NULL)
          if (ControlType (Wnd) == BUTTON)
            if ((GetWindowLong (Wnd, GWL_STYLE) & 0xF) == BS_AUTORADIOBUTTON)
                return (TRUE);

        return (FALSE);
}

//────────────────────────────────────────────────────────────
// Name:     SetRadioGroup
// Purpose:  Check the specified button and uncheck all other auto
//           radio buttons in the current group.
//────────────────────────────────────────────────────────────

static void PASCAL SetRadioGroup (HWND Dlg, HWND Wnd)
{
        int first, last, current;

        first = last = current = GetWindowWord (Wnd, GWW_ID);
        while (IsAutoRadioButton (Dlg, first − 1)) −−first;
        while (IsAutoRadioButton (Dlg, last + 1)) ++last;
        CheckRadioButton (Dlg, first, last, current);
}
```

```
//--------------------------------------------------------------------------------
// Name:    SCRadioButton
// Purpose: Subclassing routine for RADIOBUTTON controls.
//--------------------------------------------------------------------------------
LONG FAR PASCAL _export SCRadioButton (HWND Wnd, UINT Msg,
                                       WPARAM wParam, LPARAM lParam)
{
    RECT r;
    POINT pt;
    WORD buttonState;
    WORD buttonKind;

    buttonKind = LOWORD (GetWindowLong (Wnd, GWL_STYLE)) & 0xF;
    buttonState = GetWindowWord (Wnd, 0);

    switch (Msg)
    {
      case WM_PAINT:

        PaintTool (Wnd, buttonState & 3, PTPAINT);
        return (0);

      case WM_LBUTTONDOWN:

        if (GetFocus() != Wnd) SetFocus (Wnd);
        fPressed = TRUE;
        fCapture = TRUE;
        SetCapture (Wnd);
        PaintTool (Wnd, buttonState & 3, PTDOWN);
        return (0);

      case WM_LBUTTONUP:

        fCapture = FALSE;
        ReleaseCapture();
        if (fPressed == FALSE) return (0);
        fPressed = FALSE;

        if (buttonKind == BS_AUTORADIOBUTTON)
        {
           buttonState = (buttonState & ~2) | 1;
           SetWindowWord (Wnd, 0, buttonState);
           PaintTool (Wnd, buttonState & 3, 0);
           SetRadioGroup (GetParent (Wnd), Wnd);
        }
        else if (buttonKind == BS_AUTO3STATE)
        {
           buttonState ^= (((((buttonState & 3) + 1) % 3) ^ buttonState) & 3);
           SetWindowWord (Wnd, 0, buttonState);
           PaintTool (Wnd, buttonState & 3, 0);
        }

        SendMessage (GetParent (Wnd), WM_COMMAND,
                     GetWindowWord (Wnd, GWW_ID), MAKELONG (Wnd, 0));
        return (0);

      case WM_MOUSEMOVE:

        if (fCapture)
        {
           GetClientRect (Wnd, &r);
           pt.x = LOWORD (lParam);
           pt.y = HIWORD (lParam);

           if (PtInRect (&r, pt))
           {
              if (fPressed == FALSE) PaintTool (Wnd, buttonState & 3, PTDOWN);
              fPressed = TRUE;
```

```
            }
            else
            {
               if (fPressed) PaintTool (Wnd, buttonState & 3, 0);
               fPressed = FALSE;
            }
            return (0);
         }
         return DefWindowProc (Wnd, Msg, wParam, lParam);

      case WM_GETFONT:
      case WM_KILLFOCUS:
      case WM_GETDLGCODE:

         return CallOldProc (Wnd, Msg, wParam, lParam, hookKey);

      case WM_SETFOCUS:

         if (buttonKind == BS_RADIOBUTTON || buttonKind == BS_AUTORADIOBUTTON)
         {
            buttonState = (buttonState & ~2) | 1;
            SetWindowWord (Wnd, 0, buttonState);
            PaintTool (Wnd, buttonState & 3, 0);
            SetRadioGroup (GetParent (Wnd), Wnd);
            SendMessage (GetParent (Wnd), WM_COMMAND,
                        GetWindowWord (Wnd, GWW_ID), MAKELONG (Wnd, 0));
         }
         return CallOldProc (Wnd, Msg, wParam, lParam, hookKey);

      case WM_ENABLE:

         InvalidateRect (Wnd, NULL, FALSE);
         return (0);

      case BM_SETCHECK:

         SetWindowWord (Wnd, 0, buttonState ^ ((wParam ^ buttonState) & 3));
         PaintTool (Wnd, buttonState & 3, 0);
         return (0);

      case BM_GETCHECK:

         return buttonState & 3;

      default:

         return DefWindowProc (Wnd, Msg, wParam, lParam);
   }
}

//─────────────────────────────────────────────────────────────────
// Name:    SCCheckBox
// Purpose: Subclassing routine for CHECKBOX controls.
//─────────────────────────────────────────────────────────────────

LONG FAR PASCAL _export SCCheckBox (HWND Wnd, UINT Msg,
                                    WPARAM wParam, LPARAM lParam)
{
   RECT r;
   POINT pt;
   WORD buttonState;
   WORD buttonKind;

   buttonKind = LOWORD (GetWindowLong (Wnd, GWL_STYLE)) & 0xF;
   buttonState = GetWindowWord (Wnd, 0);

   switch (Msg)
   {
      case WM_PAINT:
```

```
PaintTool (Wnd, buttonState & 3, PTPAINT);
return (0);

case WM_LBUTTONDOWN:

if (GetFocus() != Wnd) SetFocus (Wnd);
fPressed = TRUE;
fCapture = TRUE;
SetCapture (Wnd);
PaintTool (Wnd, buttonState & 3, PTDOWN);
return (0);

case WM_LBUTTONUP:

fCapture = FALSE;
ReleaseCapture();
if (fPressed == FALSE) return (0);
fPressed = FALSE;

if (buttonKind == BS_AUTOCHECKBOX)
{
   buttonState ^= (buttonState ^ ((buttonState & 3) == 0)) & 3;
   SetWindowWord (Wnd, 0, buttonState);
   PaintTool (Wnd, buttonState & 3, 0);
}

SendMessage (GetParent (Wnd), WM_COMMAND,
               GetWindowWord (Wnd, GWW_ID), MAKELONG (Wnd, 0));
return (0);

case WM_MOUSEMOVE:

if (fCapture)
{
   GetClientRect (Wnd, &r);
   pt.x = LOWORD (lParam);
   pt.y = HIWORD (lParam);

   if (PtInRect (&r, pt))
   {
      if (fPressed == FALSE) PaintTool (Wnd, buttonState & 3, PTDOWN);
      fPressed = TRUE;
   }
   else
   {
      if (fPressed) PaintTool (Wnd, buttonState & 3, 0);
      fPressed = FALSE;
   }
   return (0);
}
return DefWindowProc (Wnd, Msg, wParam, lParam);

case WM_SETFOCUS:
case WM_GETFONT:
case WM_KILLFOCUS:
case WM_GETDLGCODE:

return CallOldProc (Wnd, Msg, wParam, lParam, hookKey);

case WM_ENABLE:

InvalidateRect (Wnd, NULL, FALSE);
return (0);

case BM_SETCHECK:

SetWindowWord (Wnd, 0, (buttonState & ~3) | (wParam & 3));
PaintTool (Wnd, wParam, 0);
return (0);
```

```
            case BM_GETCHECK:

            return buttonState & 3;

            default:

            return DefWindowProc (Wnd, Msg, wParam, lParam);
        }
}

//————————————————————————————————————————————————————————————
// Name:     DlgSubClass
// Purpose:  This is the subclasser for the dialog box itself.
//           Main embellishments are "gray" background for dialog and
//           any controls. Also draws a fancy border around the box.
//————————————————————————————————————————————————————————————

LONG FAR PASCAL _export DlgSubClass (HWND hDlg, UINT Msg,
                                        WPARAM wParam, LPARAM lParam)
{
    HDC dc;
    RECT r;
    HBRUSH hbr;

    switch (Msg)
    {
      case WM_SYSCOLORCHANGE:

        DeleteObject (hbmTools);
        DeleteObject (hbrBack);
        hbmTools = LoadButtonBitmap (hInst, 1);
        hbrBack = GetControlBrush (COLOR_BTNFACE);
        return (0);

      case WM_CTLCOLOR:

        if (HIWORD (lParam) == CTLCOLOR_EDIT || HIWORD (lParam) ==
          CTLCOLOR_LISTBOX)
        {
          SetBkColor ((HDC) wParam, 0xFFFFFF);
          return GetStockObject (WHITE_BRUSH);
        }
        else
        {
          SetBkColor ((HDC) wParam, GetSysColor (COLOR_BTNFACE));
          return (hbrBack);
        }

      case WM_ERASEBKGND:

        dc = (HDC) wParam;
        GetClientRect (hDlg, &r);
        hbr = SelectObject (dc, GetControlBrush (COLOR_BTNFACE));
        PatBlt (dc, r.left, r.top, r.right — r.left, r.bottom — r.top, PATCOPY);
        DeleteObject (SelectObject (dc, hbr));

        // Now draw the fancy border

        InflateRect (&r, −3, −3);
        FrameRect (dc, &r, GetStockObject (WHITE_BRUSH));
        —r.left;
        —r.right;
        —r.top;
        —r.bottom;
        FrameRect (dc, &r, hbr = GetControlBrush (COLOR_BTNSHADOW));
        DeleteObject (hbr);
        return (TRUE);

      case WM_DESTROY:
```

```
        FreeTools ();
    }

    return CallOldProc (hDlg, Msg, wParam, lParam, hookKey);
}

//------------------------------------------------------------------
// Name:    ShrinkEditBox
// Purpose: Reduce the size of an edit box to compensate for the
//              smaller font used.
//------------------------------------------------------------------

static void PASCAL ShrinkEditBox (HWND Wnd)
{
    HDC dc;
    RECT r;
    TEXTMETRIC tm;
    int oldHeight, newHeight;

    // Get old font height

    dc = GetDC (NULL);
    GetTextMetrics (dc, &tm);
    oldHeight = tm.tmHeight + tm.tmInternalLeading;

    // Get new font height

    DialogFont = SelectObject (dc, DialogFont);
    GetTextMetrics (dc, &tm);
    DialogFont = SelectObject (dc, DialogFont);
    ReleaseDC (NULL, dc);
    newHeight = tm.tmHeight + tm.tmInternalLeading;

    // Now resize the window

    GetWindowRect (Wnd, &r);
    ScreenToClient (GetParent (Wnd), (LPPOINT) &r.left);
    ScreenToClient (GetParent (Wnd), (LPPOINT) &r.right);

    r.top += (oldHeight − newHeight) / 2;
    r.bottom −= (oldHeight − newHeight) / 2;

    SetWindowPos (Wnd, NULL, r.left, r.top,
                    r.right − r.left, r.bottom − r.top, SWP_NOZORDER);
}

//------------------------------------------------------------------
// Name:    SubClassControl
// Purpose: Subclass an individual dialog box control, according to
//              type. Controls that we don't recognize or aren't interested
//              in are left alone.
//------------------------------------------------------------------

static void PASCAL SubClassControl (HWND Wnd, int type)
{
    // Use our special font

    if (type != −1) SendMessage (Wnd, WM_SETFONT, DialogFont, 0);

    // Case out on control type

    switch (type)
    {
      case EDITBOX:

        ShrinkEditBox (Wnd);
        break;

      case BUTTON:
```

```
                      type = GetWindowLong (Wnd, GWL_STYLE) & 0xF;
                      switch (type)
                      {
                         case GROUPBOX:

                         HookWindow (Wnd, (FARPROC) SCGroupBox, szHookName);
                         break;

                         case CHECKBOX:
                         case AUTOCHECKBOX:

                         HookWindow (Wnd, (FARPROC) SCCheckBox, szHookName);
                         break;

                         case THREESTATE:
                         case AUTO3STATE:
                         case RADIOBUTTON:
                         case AUTORADIOBUTTON:

                         HookWindow (Wnd, (FARPROC) SCRadioButton, szHookName);
                         break;
                      }
                   }
             }

//————————————————————————————————————————————————————————————
// Name:    SubClassDialog
// Purpose: This routine does the actual job of subclassing a
//          dialog. It should be called from WM_INITDIALOG.
//————————————————————————————————————————————————————————————

void PASCAL SubClassDialog (HANDLE hInstance, HWND hDlg)
{
      HWND Wnd;

      // Stash the dreaded instance handle

      hInst = hInstance;

      // Center the dialog

      CenterDialog (hDlg);

      // Do nothing if we're running Windows 4 or later

      if (LOBYTE (LOWORD (GetVersion()))) < 4)
      {
         // Create needed tools

         InitTools ();

         // Hook the dialog box procedure

         hookKey = HookWindow (hDlg, (FARPROC) DlgSubClass,
                                     szHookName);

         // Now subclass the various dialog controls

         Wnd = GetWindow (hDlg, GW_CHILD);
         while (Wnd != NULL)
         {
            SubClassControl (Wnd, ControlType (Wnd));
            Wnd = GetWindow (Wnd, GW_HWNDNEXT);
         }
      }
}
```

Doing it with mirrors: the magic of Windows hooks

If you feel that, as it stands, the dialog subclassing code is suitable for your purposes, then that's fine. However, there is one more thing we can do to make it more convenient to use. As you know, for every dialog you want to subclass, you have to insert a call to the SubClassDialog routine in the WM_INITDIALOG message handling code of that dialog procedure. Putting in all these calls to SubClassDialog can be a little tedious if you have a very large, sophisticated program with many dialogs. Wouldn't it be nice if the dialog subclassing code worked automatically, with absolutely no need to call any special routines in the dialog procedure?

As a matter of fact, this is perfectly feasible using the built-in Windows hook mechanism. Using Windows hooks, we can arrange for the dialog subclassing code to lurk in the background, waiting for your application to create a dialog window. As soon as a dialog window is created, the dialog can be transparently subclassed, all without any changes whatsoever to the dialog procedure.

Maybe you're thinking that this is all very well, but you're perfectly happy with things as they are. After all, the once-only addition of the SubClassDialog call to each and every dialog procedure is no big deal, and you're not sure you like the idea of something 'lurking in the background', ready to subclass your dialogs for you. Well, there is one other good reason for doing things this way. Read on....

In the normal course of events, your program will create two sorts of dialog boxes; firstly, it will create dialog boxes specific to your application, where the dialog procedure is contained within your program code. The second type of dialog box is created on behalf of your application, and the dialog procedure is not contained in your program, and possibly not accessible at all. An example of the second type of dialog box is the standard 'Open File...' dialog, one of the standard dialog boxes implemented inside the Microsoft COMMDLG.DLL library. A Windows program that wishes to present a standard interface should use the COMMDLG routines whenever it wants to open files, save files, select fonts, and so forth. Wouldn't it be great if you could add our new Excel-style 'look' to these dialogs, too? Using the window hook procedure discussed here, we can do exactly that. If you're at all familiar with the COMMDLG DLL, you'll know that it's possible to install a subclassing hook into the common dialog procedures. However, we won't make use of this facility since, with the technique discussed here, the subclassing happens for free, and no special subclassing hook needs to be installed.

Another example of this is the Windows MessageBox API routine. Message boxes are frequently used in Windows programming to indicate some error, report on the successful completion of an operation, and so on. Although they're very well camouflaged from the application programmer, message boxes are really just ordinary dialogs, too. The only difference is that the dialog box procedure is hidden deep inside the USER DLL. Using the Windows hook routine, any time that your program makes use of the MessageBox routine, the dialog displayed will have the same style as that of all the other subclassed dialogs displayed by the program.

OK, hopefully you're convinced. Now let's see how it works. The technique makes use of the SetWindowsHookEx routine. This API call allows an application or DLL to install different types of hook that allow you to gain control when specific events occur. The hook that we'll be using is called the CBT (Computer Based Training) Hook. It has this name because, used in the right way, it allows you almost to run a Windows session 'on autopilot' for training purposes. For example, the CBT hook allows you to get control when a window is created, destroyed, activated, moved, resized, and so forth. For our purposes, we're really only interested in a window being created. If it turns out to be a dialog window, then we want to subclass it at this time.

```
//—————————————————————————————————————————————————————
// Name:     InstallAutoHook
// Purpose:  Install the auto-subclassing hook.
//—————————————————————————————————————————————————————
void PASCAL InstallAutoHook (HANDLE hInstance)
{
    if (AutoHook == NULL)
    {
        // Stash the dreaded instance handle
        hInst = hInstance;
        // Install the autohook for automatic dialog subclassing
        AutoHook = SetWindowsHookEx (WH_CBT, (HOOKPROC) CBTHook,
                                     hInstance, GetCurrentTask());
    }
}
```

The InstallAutoHook routine, shown above, must be called from the main application program. Unlike the SubClassDialog routine, it only needs to be called once at the beginning of the program. Similarly, the small routine RemoveAutoHook, shown below, MUST be called when the application terminates. There's no harm in calling RemoveAutoHook when there are still subclassed dialogs in existence. It just means that any subsequently created dialogs will not be subclassed. It is crucially important, however, to ensure that RemoveAutoHook is called before the program terminates. If this isn't done, Windows will die a horrible death the next time a window is created.

```
//—————————————————————————————————————————————————————
// Name:       RemoveAutoHook
// Purpose:    Remove the auto-subclassing hook.
//—————————————————————————————————————————————————————
void PASCAL RemoveAutoHook (void)
{
    if (AutoHook != NULL)
    {
        UnhookWindowsHookEx (AutoHook);
        AutoHook = NULL;
    }
}
```

The InstallAutoHook routine installs a hook procedure, called CBTHook, which is called at certain specific points from the internals of Windows. Because CBTHook is a callback routine (that is, Windows calling your code, rather than you calling Windows code), it's essential that this routine is exported so that the DS register is properly set up to point to your application's data segment. If you're using Borland C/C++, you can just use the _export qualifier when you declare the routine. With other development systems, you may have to add the CBTHook procedure name to the .DEF file for your program.

```
//----------------------------------------------------------------
// Name:    CBTHook
// Purpose: This routine hooks the dialog window and subclasses it
//          with the HookWindow routine.
//----------------------------------------------------------------
LONG FAR PASCAL _export CBTHook (int code, WPARAM wParam, LPARAM lParam)
{
    CREATESTRUCT FAR * cs;
    static HWND theDlg = NULL;

    if (code == HCBT_CREATEWND)
    {
      cs = ((LPCBT_CREATEWND) lParam)->lpcs;
      if (cs->lpszClass == WC_DIALOG) theDlg = wParam;
      else if (theDlg != NULL)
      {
         hookKey = HookWindow (theDlg, (FARPROC) DlgSubClass,
                                  szHookName);
         theDlg = NULL;
      }
    }

    return CallNextHookEx (AutoHook, code, wParam, lParam);
}
```

The CBTHook routine is only interested in window creation events, so it checks the code parameter for the value HCBT_CREATEWND, which indicates that a window is indeed being created. Obviously, we need to ensure that only dialog boxes get subclassed, so the class name of the window is checked to see if it's equal to WC_DIALOG. WC_DIALOG is a special internal class name (defined in the WINDOWS.H header file) which is always used to implement dialog boxes.

If these tests check out OK, the wParam parameter is saved in a static variable. This corresponds to the handle of the window being created. The routine then exits and the subclassing doesn't actually occur until the next time the CBTHook is called. This might seem like very odd behavior, and requires a little explanation.

When the CBTHook routine is called, the dialog box window is in a very early stage of creation. In fact, it hasn't yet received a WM_CREATE or WM_NCCREATE message and the dialog box controls (the child windows) don't yet exist. The Dialog box may not even be set up with a valid parent window handle at this point. Because the state of the dialog box is so embryonic, it's rather dangerous to start subclassing it and manipulating it in any other way at this point. Contrast this state of affairs with the situation when WM_INITDIALOG is called – at this time, the window has been completely created, all its child windows exist and all that remains to do is display it on the screen.

Because of this problem, it's not entirely safe to call the HookWindow routine when the CBTHook procedure is called. Instead, the window handle is saved in a static variable and the subclassing takes place when the next subsequent window is created. How do we know that another window is going to be created so soon? The answer, of course, is that the dialog box controls will be created quite soon after the dialog box itself is in existence and it's when the first dialog box control is created that the actual subclassing takes place. If you think about it, this is an entirely logical sequence of events – it's unrealistic, for example, to create the dialog box controls before the parent dialog box exists, because they must each be given the window handle of their parent when they are created via the CreateWindow routine.

Using this approach, things are quite safe at the time the HookWindow routine gets called. There is, however, one other change that needs to be made. With the SubClassDialog routine, the subclassing took place at the time the WM_INITDIALOG message was received. Now, using the CBTHook approach, the subclassing takes place way before the WM_INITDIALOG message is generated. It's therefore important to ensure that the equivalent actions take place behind the scenes when the subclassed dialog receives its WM_INITDIALOG message. This can easily be done by adding a WM_INITDIALOG message handler to the DlgSubClass code as shown below.

```
case WM_INITDIALOG:

CenterDialog (hDlg);
if (LOBYTE (LOWORD (GetVersion()))) < 4)
{
    // Create needed tools

    InitTools ();

    // Now subclass the various dialog controls

    Wnd = GetWindow (hDlg, GW_CHILD);
    while (Wnd != NULL)
    {
        SubClassControl (Wnd, ControlType (Wnd));
        Wnd = GetWindow (Wnd, GW_HWNDNEXT);
    }
}
break;
```

It's very important that this handler should terminate with a break instruction and thereby end up calling the CallOldProc routine at the end of the procedure. In other words, a dialog that has been subclassed in this way must 'pass on' the WM_INITDIALOG message to the original dialog procedure so that any custom dialog initialization code in the application will be executed properly.

With these changes in place, we can add the InstallAutoHook and RemoveAutoHook routines to the DIALOGS.H header file. The revised header file is shown in Figure 5.16.

Figure 5.16 The revised DIALOGS3.H file with the auto hook function prototypes.

```
/* DIALOGS3.H */

// © 1994 Dave Jewell and Addison-Wesley, ALL RIGHTS RESERVED

#ifndef _INC_DIALOGS
#define _INC_DIALOGS /* #defined if dialogs.h has been included */

#ifdef __cplusplus
extern "C" {
#endif

void PASCAL InstallAutoHook (HANDLE hInstance);
void PASCAL RemoveAutoHook (void);
void PASCAL SubClassDialog (HANDLE hInstance, HWND hDlg);

#ifdef __cplusplus
}
#endif

#endif
```

The revised source code for the Dialogs module is shown in Figure 5.17 and the new application code is shown in Figure 5.18. These files are on the disk as DIALOGS5.C and DIATEST.C respectively, and the new executable file is named DIATEST5.EXE.

```
/* DIALOGS5.C */

// © 1994 Dave Jewell and Addison-Wesley, ALL RIGHTS RESERVED

#include    <windows.h>
#include    "sclaslib.h"
#include    "dialogs.h"

// Control types returned by ControlType()

#define    BUTTON          0
#define    EDITBOX         1
#define    STATIC          2
#define    LISTBOX         3
#define    COMBOBOX        4
#define    COMBOLBOX       5

// BUTTON types

#define    PUSHBUTTON         0x0
#define    DEFPUSHBUTTON      0x1
#define    CHECKBOX           0x2
#define    AUTOCHECKBOX       0x3
#define    RADIOBUTTON        0x4
#define    THREESTATE         0x5
#define    AUTO3STATE         0x6
#define    GROUPBOX           0x7
#define    USERBUTTON         0x8
#define    AUTORADIOBUTTON    0x9
#define    OWNERDRAW          0xB

// Bitmap dimensions

#define    TOOLWIDTH       13
#define    TOOLHEIGHT      13

// Control flags for PaintTool routine

#define    PTDOWN          1
#define    PTPAINT         2

static char     szHookName[ ] = "DialogsHook";
static LONG     hookKey;
static HFONT    DialogFont = NULL;   // special dialog font
static HBRUSH   hbrBack = NULL;      // background brush
static int      DialogCount = 0;     // number of subclassed dialogs
static HBITMAP  hbmTools = NULL;     // handle to tool bitmap
static HANDLE   hInst;               // application instance handle
static BOOL     fPressed = FALSE;    // TRUE if a control is pressed
static BOOL     fCapture = FALSE;    // TRUE if mouse captured
static HHOOK    AutoHook = NULL;     // for WH_CBT trickery...

//──────────────────────────────────────────────────────
// Name:    GetControlBrush
// Purpose: Create a control brush for a given system color.
//──────────────────────────────────────────────────────

static HBRUSH PASCAL GetControlBrush (int sysColor)
{
    COLORREF color;
```

Figure 5.17   The dialog subclassing code with the auto-hook facility incorporated.

```
          color = GetSysColor (sysColor);
          return (CreateSolidBrush (color));
}

//----------------------------------------------------------------
// Name:    DrawRaisedRect
// Purpose: Draw a raised rectangle at specified location.
//----------------------------------------------------------------

static void PASCAL DrawRaisedRect (HDC dc, LPRECT lpr)
{
          HBRUSH hbr;
          int width, height;

          width = lpr->right - lpr->left;
          height = lpr->bottom - lpr->top;

          hbr = SelectObject (dc, CreateSolidBrush (GetSysColor
                          (COLOR_BTNHIGHLIGHT)));
          PatBlt (dc, lpr->left, lpr->top, 1, height - 1, PATCOPY);
          PatBlt (dc, lpr->left, lpr->top, width - 1, 1, PATCOPY);
          DeleteObject (SelectObject (dc, CreateSolidBrush (GetSysColor
                          (COLOR_BTNSHADOW))));
          PatBlt (dc, lpr->right - 1, lpr->top, 1, height, PATCOPY);
          PatBlt (dc, lpr->left, lpr->bottom - 1, width, 1, PATCOPY);
          DeleteObject (SelectObject (dc, hbr));
}

//----------------------------------------------------------------
// Name:    CenterDialog
// Purpose: Center a given dialog window on the screen.
//----------------------------------------------------------------

static void PASCAL CenterDialog (HWND Wnd)
{
          RECT r;

          GetWindowRect (Wnd, &r);
          r.left = (GetSystemMetrics (SM_CXSCREEN) - r.right + r.left) / 2;
          r.top = (GetSystemMetrics (SM_CYSCREEN) - r.bottom + r.top) / 2;
          SetWindowPos (Wnd, 0, r.left, r.top, 0, 0, SWP_NOSIZE | SWP_NOZORDER);
}

//----------------------------------------------------------------
// Name:    CreateDialogFont
// Purpose: Create the dialog font.
//----------------------------------------------------------------

void PASCAL CreateDialogFont (void)
{
          HDC dc;
          char faceName [50];
          int nHeight, pointSize;

          // Pickup point size and face name from WIN.INI

          pointSize = GetProfileInt ("Desktop", "StatusBarFaceHeight", 8);
          GetProfileString ("Desktop", "StatusBarFaceName", "MS Sans Serif",
                          faceName, 50);

          dc = GetDC (NULL);
          nHeight = (GetDeviceCaps (dc, LOGPIXELSY) * pointSize) / -72;
          ReleaseDC (NULL, dc);

          // Now create the font

          DialogFont = CreateFont (nHeight, 0, 0, 0, FW_NORMAL, 0, 0, 0,
                          ANSI_CHARSET,
                          OUT_DEFAULT_PRECIS,
```

```
                              CLIP_DEFAULT_PRECIS,
                              DEFAULT_QUALITY,
                              FF_SWISS I VARIABLE_PITCH,
                              faceName);
}

//————————————————————————————————————————————————————————
// Name:    ColorFix
// Purpose: Fix up a color value for the LoadButtonBitmap routine.
//————————————————————————————————————————————————————————

static COLORREF PASCAL ColorFix (COLORREF color)
{
     return RGB (GetBValue (color), GetGValue (color), GetRValue (color));
}

//————————————————————————————————————————————————————————
// Name:    LoadButtonBitmap
// Purpose: Load a bitmap and tweak it for current system colors.
//————————————————————————————————————————————————————————

HBITMAP PASCAL LoadButtonBitmap (HANDLE hInstance, int bmID)
{
     HDC dc;
     HBITMAP hbm;
     HANDLE hRes;
     LPDWORD lprgb;
     LPVOID lpb;
     LPBITMAPINFOHEADER lpbi;

     hRes = LoadResource (hInstance, FindResource (hInstance,
                          MAKEINTRESOURCE(bmID), RT_BITMAP));

     lpbi = (LPBITMAPINFOHEADER) LockResource (hRes);
     if (lpbi == NULL) return (NULL);

     lprgb = (LPDWORD) ((LPSTR) lpbi + (int) lpbi->biSize);
     lpb = (LPVOID) (lprgb + 16);

     lprgb [0] = ColorFix (GetSysColor (COLOR_WINDOWTEXT));      // Black
     lprgb [8] = ColorFix (GetSysColor (COLOR_BTNFACE));        // Light gray
     lprgb [7] = ColorFix (GetSysColor (COLOR_BTNSHADOW));      // Gray
     lprgb [15] = ColorFix (GetSysColor (COLOR_BTNHIGHLIGHT));  // White

     dc = GetDC (NULL);
     hbm = CreateDIBitmap (dc, lpbi, CBM_INIT, lpb,
                           (LPBITMAPINFO) lpbi, DIB_RGB_COLORS);

     ReleaseDC (NULL, dc);
     GlobalUnlock (hRes);
     FreeResource (hRes);
     return (hbm);
}

//————————————————————————————————————————————————————————
// Name:    InitTools
// Purpose: Set up needed tools.
//————————————————————————————————————————————————————————

static void PASCAL InitTools (void)
{
     if (DialogCount++ == 0)
     {
       CreateDialogFont ();
       hbrBack = GetControlBrush (COLOR_BTNFACE);
       hbmTools = LoadButtonBitmap (hInst, 1);
     }
}
```

```
//─────────────────────────────────────────────────────
// Name:    FreeTools
// Purpose: Called to clean up tools when a dialog is closed.
//─────────────────────────────────────────────────────

static void PASCAL FreeTools (void)
{
    if (—DialogCount == 0)
    {
      DeleteObject (hbrBack);
      DeleteObject (DialogFont);
      DeleteObject (hbmTools);
    }
}

//─────────────────────────────────────────────────────
// Name:    SCGroupBox
// Purpose: Subclassing routine for GROUPBOX controls.
//─────────────────────────────────────────────────────

LONG FAR PASCAL _export SCGroupBox (HWND Wnd, UINT Msg,
                                    WPARAM wParam, LPARAM lParam)
{
    RECT r;
    DWORD dwExtent;
    HFONT hFont;
    COLORREF bkColor;
    PAINTSTRUCT ps;
    char szText [128];

    switch (Msg)
    {
      case WM_PAINT:

      BeginPaint (Wnd, &ps);
      if (SendMessage (Wnd, WM_GETTEXT, 120,
        (LONG)(LPSTR) &szText [1]) <= 0) szText[0] = '\0';
      else
      {
        szText [0] = ' ';
        lstrcat (szText, "" );
      }

      GetClientRect (Wnd, &r);
      DrawRaisedRect (ps.hdc, &r);

      if (szText [0] != '\0')
      {
        hFont = SelectObject (ps.hdc, DialogFont);
        dwExtent = GetTextExtent (ps.hdc, "Yy", 2);
        r.top -= HIWORD (dwExtent) / 2;
        r.left += LOWORD (dwExtent) / 2;
        bkColor = SetBkColor (ps.hdc, GetSysColor (COLOR_BTNFACE));
        DrawText (ps.hdc, szText, −1, &r, DT_SINGLELINE);
        SetBkColor (ps.hdc, bkColor);
        SelectObject (ps.hdc, hFont);
      }

      EndPaint (Wnd, &ps);
      return (0);
    }

    return CallOldProc (Wnd, Msg, wParam, lParam, hookKey);
}

//─────────────────────────────────────────────────────
// Name:    PaintTool
// Purpose: Draw a subsection of the tool bitmap as required.
//─────────────────────────────────────────────────────
```

```
static void PASCAL PaintTool (HWND Wnd, WORD bsState, WORD flags)
{
    RECT r;
    HDC SrcDC;
    WORD dtFlags;
    PAINTSTRUCT ps;
    BOOL bLeftAlign;
    char szText [128];
    int bskind, x, y, blitHeight;

    bLeftAlign = LOWORD (GetWindowLong (Wnd, GWL_STYLE)) & BS_LEFTTEXT;
    bskind = LOWORD (GctWindowLong (Wnd, GWL_STYLE)) & 0xF;

    x = bsState * 2;
    if (flags & PTDOWN) ++x;
    y = 0;
    if (bskind == BS_RADIOBUTTON || bskind == BS_AUTORADIOBUTTON) ++y;
    x *= TOOLWIDTH;
    y *= TOOLHEIGHT;

    if (flags & PTPAINT) BeginPaint (Wnd, &ps);
    else ps.hdc = GetDC (Wnd);
    DialogFont = SelectObject (ps.hdc, DialogFont);
    SetBkMode (ps.hdc, TRANSPARENT);

    GetClientRect (Wnd, &r);
    blitHeight = r.top + ((r.bottom − r.top) − TOOLHEIGHT) / 2;
    SrcDC = CreateCompatibleDC (ps.hdc);
    hbmTools = SelectObject (SrcDC, hbmTools);

    if (bLeftAlign)
    {
        BitBlt (ps.hdc, r.right − TOOLWIDTH, blitl leight,
            TOOLWIDTH, TOOLHEIGHT, SrcDC, x, y, SRCCOPY);
        r.right −= (TOOLWIDTH * 3) / 2;
        dtFlags = DT_SINGLELINE | DT_RIGHT | DT_VCENTER;
    }
    else
    {
        BitBlt (ps.hdc, r.left, blitHeight, TOOLWIDTH,
            TOOLHEIGHT, SrcDC, x, y, SRCCOPY);
        r.left += (TOOLWIDTH * 3) / 2;
        −−r.left;
        dtFlags = DT_SINGLELINE | DT_VCENTER;
    }

    ++r.top;
    CallOldProc (Wnd, WM_GETTEXT, sizeof (szText), (LPARAM) szText, hookKey);
    DrawText (ps.hdc, szText, −1, &r, dtFlags);

    hbmTools = SelectObject (SrcDC, hbmTools);

    DeleteDC (SrcDC);

    DialogFont = SelectObject (ps.hdc, DialogFont);
    if (flags & PTPAINT) EndPaint (Wnd, &ps);
    else ReleaseDC (Wnd, ps.hdc);
}

//─────────────────────────────────────────────
// Name:     ControlType
// Purpose:  Given a window handle, return the control type.
//           −1 is returned for an unrecognized type.
//─────────────────────────────────────────────

static int PASCAL ControlType (HWND Wnd)
{
    int i;
```

```
            char ClassName [64];
            static char * controlNames [6] = { "Button",
                                               "Edit",
                                               "Static",
                                               "ListBox",
                                               "ComboBox",
                                               "ComboLBox" };

            GetClassName (Wnd, ClassName, sizeof (ClassName) − 1);

            for (i = 0; i < 6; i++)
               if (lstrcmpi (controlNames [i], ClassName) == 0)
                  return (i);

            return (−1);
}

//─────────────────────────────────────────────────────────────────
// Name:    IsAutoRadioButton
// Purpose: Determine if specified control is an auto radio button.
//─────────────────────────────────────────────────────────────────
static BOOL PASCAL IsAutoRadioButton (HWND Dlg, int ID)
{
            HWND Wnd;

            if ((Wnd = GetDlgItem (Dlg, ID)) != NULL)
               if (ControlType (Wnd) == BUTTON)
                  if ((GetWindowLong (Wnd, GWL_STYLE) & 0xF) ==
                        BS_AUTORADIOBUTTON)
                     return (TRUE);

            return (FALSE);
}

//─────────────────────────────────────────────────────────────────
// Name:    SetRadioGroup
// Purpose: Check the specified button and uncheck all other auto
//          radio buttons in the current group.
//─────────────────────────────────────────────────────────────────
static void PASCAL SetRadioGroup (HWND Dlg, HWND Wnd)
{
            int first, last, current;

            first = last = current = GetWindowWord (Wnd, GWW_ID);
            while (IsAutoRadioButton (Dlg, first − 1)) —first;
            while (IsAutoRadioButton (Dlg, last + 1)) ++last;
            CheckRadioButton (Dlg, first, last, current);
}

//─────────────────────────────────────────────────────────────────
// Name:    SCRadioButton
// Purpose: Subclassing routine for RADIOBUTTON controls.
//─────────────────────────────────────────────────────────────────
LONG FAR PASCAL _export SCRadioButton (HWND Wnd, UINT Msg,
                                    WPARAM wParam, LPARAM lParam)
{
            RECT r;
            POINT pt;
            WORD buttonState;
            WORD buttonKind;

            buttonKind = LOWORD (GetWindowLong (Wnd, GWL_STYLE)) & 0xF;
            buttonState = GetWindowWord (Wnd, 0);

            switch (Msg)
            {
               case WM_PAINT:
```

```
        PaintTool (Wnd, buttonState & 3, PTPAINT);
        return (0);

    case WM_LBUTTONDOWN:

        if (GetFocus() != Wnd) SetFocus (Wnd);
        fPressed = TRUE;
        fCapture = TRUE;
        SetCapture (Wnd);
        PaintTool (Wnd, buttonState & 3, PTDOWN);
        return (0);

    case WM_LBUTTONUP:

        fCapture = FALSE;
        ReleaseCapture();
        if (fPressed == FALSE) return (0);
        fPressed = FALSE;

        if (buttonKind == BS_AUTORADIOBUTTON)
        {
            buttonState = (buttonState & ~2) | 1;
            SetWindowWord (Wnd, 0, buttonState);
            PaintTool (Wnd, buttonState & 3, 0);
            SetRadioGroup (GetParent (Wnd), Wnd);
        }
        else if (buttonKind == BS_AUTO3STATE)
        {
            buttonState ^= (((((buttonState & 3) + 1) % 3) ^ buttonState) & 3);
            SetWindowWord (Wnd, 0, buttonState);
            PaintTool (Wnd, buttonState & 3, 0);
        }

        SendMessage (GetParent (Wnd), WM_COMMAND,
                    GetWindowWord (Wnd, GWW_ID), MAKELONG (Wnd, 0));
        return (0);

    case WM_MOUSEMOVE:

        if (fCapture)
        {
            GetClientRect (Wnd, &r);
            pt.x = LOWORD (lParam);
            pt.y = HIWORD (lParam);

            if (PtInRect (&r, pt))
            {
                if (fPressed == FALSE) PaintTool (Wnd, buttonState & 3, PTDOWN);
                fPressed = TRUE;
            }
            else
            {
                if (fPressed) PaintTool (Wnd, buttonState & 3, 0);
                fPressed = FALSE;
            }
            return (0);
        }
        return DefWindowProc (Wnd, Msg, wParam, lParam);

    case WM_GETFONT:
    case WM_KILLFOCUS:
    case WM_GETDLGCODE:

        return CallOldProc (Wnd, Msg, wParam, lParam, hookKey);

    case WM_SETFOCUS:

        if (buttonKind == BS_RADIOBUTTON ||
            buttonKind == BS_AUTORADIOBUTTON)
        {
```

```
                buttonState = (buttonState & ~2) | 1;
                SetWindowWord (Wnd, 0, buttonState);
                PaintTool (Wnd, buttonState & 3, 0);
                SetRadioGroup (GetParent (Wnd), Wnd);
                SendMessage (GetParent (Wnd), WM_COMMAND,
                              GetWindowWord (Wnd, GWW_ID), MAKELONG (Wnd, 0));
            }
            return CallOldProc (Wnd, Msg, wParam, lParam, hookKey);

        case WM_ENABLE:

            InvalidateRect (Wnd, NULL, FALSE);
            return (0);

        case BM_SETCHECK:

            SetWindowWord (Wnd, 0, buttonState ^ ((wParam ^ buttonState) & 3));
            PaintTool (Wnd, buttonState & 3, 0);
            return (0);

        case BM_GETCHECK:

            return buttonState & 3;

        default:

            return DefWindowProc (Wnd, Msg, wParam, lParam);
        }
    }

//--------------------------------------------------------------------------------
// Name:    SCCheckBox
// Purpose: Subclassing routine for CHECKBOX controls.
//--------------------------------------------------------------------------------

LONG FAR PASCAL _export SCCheckBox (HWND Wnd, UINT Msg,
                                    WPARAM wParam, LPARAM lParam)
{
    RECT r;
    POINT pt;
    WORD buttonState;
    WORD buttonKind;

    buttonKind = LOWORD (GetWindowLong (Wnd, GWL_STYLE)) & 0xF;
    buttonState = GetWindowWord (Wnd, 0);

    switch (Msg)
    {
        case WM_PAINT:

            PaintTool (Wnd, buttonState & 3, PTPAINT);
            return (0);

        case WM_LBUTTONDOWN:

            if (GetFocus() != Wnd) SetFocus (Wnd);
            fPressed = TRUE;
            fCapture = TRUE;
            SetCapture (Wnd);
            PaintTool (Wnd, buttonState & 3, PTDOWN);
            return (0);

        case WM_LBUTTONUP:

            fCapture = FALSE;
            ReleaseCapture();
            if (fPressed == FALSE) return (0);
            fPressed = FALSE;
```

```
            if (buttonKind == BS_AUTOCHECKBOX)
            {
                buttonState ^= (buttonState ^ ((buttonState & 3) == 0)) & 3;
                SetWindowWord (Wnd, 0, buttonState);
                PaintTool (Wnd, buttonState & 3, 0);
            }

            SendMessage (GetParent (Wnd), WM_COMMAND,
                        GetWindowWord (Wnd, GWW_ID), MAKELONG (Wnd, 0));
            return (0);

        case WM_MOUSEMOVE:

            if (fCapture)
            {
                GetClientRect (Wnd, &r);
                pt.x = LOWORD (lParam);
                pt.y = HIWORD (lParam);

                if (PtInRect (&r, pt))
                {
                    if (fPressed == FALSE) PaintTool (Wnd, buttonState & 3, PTDOWN);
                    fPressed = TRUE;
                }
                else
                {
                    if (fPressed) PaintTool (Wnd, buttonState & 3, 0);
                    fPressed = FALSE;
                }
                return (0);
            }
            return DefWindowProc (Wnd, Msg, wParam, lParam);

        case WM_SETFOCUS:
        case WM_GETFONT:
        case WM_KILLFOCUS:
        case WM_GETDLGCODE:

            return CallOldProc (Wnd, Msg, wParam, lParam, hookKey);

        case WM_ENABLE:

            InvalidateRect (Wnd, NULL, FALSE);
            return (0);

        case BM_SETCHECK:

            SetWindowWord (Wnd, 0, (buttonState & ~3) | (wParam & 3));
            PaintTool (Wnd, wParam, 0);
            return (0);

        case BM_GETCHECK:

            return buttonState & 3;

        default:

            return DefWindowProc (Wnd, Msg, wParam, lParam);
    }
}

//---------------------------------------------------------------
// Name:    DlgSubClass
// Purpose: This is the subclasser for the dialog box itself.
//          Main embellishments are "gray" background for dialog and
//          any controls. Also draws a fancy border around the box.
//---------------------------------------------------------------
```

```
LONG FAR PASCAL _export DlgSubClass (HWND hDlg, UINT Msg,
                                     WPARAM wParam, LPARAM lParam)
{
    HDC dc;
    RECT r;
    HWND Wnd;
    HBRUSH hbr;
    void PASCAL SubClassControl (HWND Wnd, int type);

    switch (Msg)
    {
      case WM_INITDIALOG:

        CenterDialog (hDlg);
        if (LOBYTE (LOWORD (GetVersion()))) < 4)
        {
            // Create needed tools

            InitTools ();

            // Now subclass the various dialog controls

            Wnd = GetWindow (hDlg, GW_CHILD);
            while (Wnd != NULL)
            {
                SubClassControl (Wnd, ControlType (Wnd));
                Wnd = GetWindow (Wnd, GW_HWNDNEXT);
            }
        }
        break;

      case WM_SYSCOLORCHANGE:

        DeleteObject (hbmTools);
        DeleteObject (hbrBack);
        hbmTools = LoadButtonBitmap (hInst, 1);
        hbrBack = GetControlBrush (COLOR_BTNFACE);
        return (0);

      case WM_CTLCOLOR:

        if (HIWORD (lParam) == CTLCOLOR_EDIT || HIWORD (lParam) ==
            CTLCOLOR_LISTBOX)
        {
            SetBkColor ((HDC) wParam, 0xFFFFFF);
            return GetStockObject (WHITE_BRUSH);
        }
        else
        {
            SetBkColor ((HDC) wParam, GetSysColor (COLOR_BTNFACE));
            return (hbrBack);
        }

      case WM_ERASEBKGND:

        dc = (HDC) wParam;
        GetClientRect (hDlg, &r);
        hbr = SelectObject (dc, GetControlBrush (COLOR_BTNFACE));
        PatBlt (dc, r.left, r.top, r.right − r.left, r.bottom − r.top, PATCOPY);
        DeleteObject (SelectObject (dc, hbr));

        // Now draw the fancy border

        InflateRect (&r, −3, −3);
        FrameRect (dc, &r, GetStockObject (WHITE_BRUSH));
        −−r.left;
        −−r.right;
        −−r.top;
        −−r.bottom;
```

```
            FrameRect (dc, &r, hbr = GetControlBrush (COLOR_BTNSHADOW));
            DeleteObject (hbr);
            return (TRUE);

        case WM_DESTROY:

            FreeTools ();
        }

        return CallOldProc (hDlg, Msg, wParam, lParam, hookKey);
}

//----------------------------------------------------------------------------
// Name:    ShrinkEditBox
// Purpose: Reduce the size of an edit box to compensate for the
//          smaller font used.
//----------------------------------------------------------------------------

static void PASCAL ShrinkEditBox (HWND Wnd)
{
        HDC dc;
        RECT r;
        TEXTMETRIC tm;
        int oldHeight, newHeight;

        // Get old font height

        dc = GetDC (NULL);
        GetTextMetrics (dc, &tm);
        oldHeight = tm.tmHeight + tm.tmInternalLeading;

        // Get new font height

        DialogFont = SelectObject (dc, DialogFont);
        GetTextMetrics (dc, &tm);
        DialogFont = SelectObject (dc, DialogFont);
        ReleaseDC (NULL, dc);
        newHeight = tm.tmHeight + tm.tmInternalLeading;

        // Now resize the window

        GetWindowRect (Wnd, &r);
        ScreenToClient (GetParent (Wnd), (LPPOINT) &r.left);
        ScreenToClient (GetParent (Wnd), (LPPOINT) &r.right);

        r.top += (oldHeight − newHeight) / 2;
        r.bottom −= (oldHeight − newHeight) / 2;

        SetWindowPos (Wnd, NULL, r.left, r.top,
                        r.right − r.left, r.bottom − r.top, SWP_NOZORDER);
}

//----------------------------------------------------------------------------
// Name:    SubClassControl
// Purpose: Subclass an individual dialog box control, according to
//          type. Controls that we don't recognize or aren't interested
//          in are left alone.
//----------------------------------------------------------------------------

static void PASCAL SubClassControl (HWND Wnd, int type)
{
        // Use our special font

        if (type != −1) SendMessage (Wnd, WM_SETFONT, DialogFont, 0);

        // Case out on control type

        switch (type)
        {
          case EDITBOX:
```

```
                    ShrinkEditBox (Wnd);
                    break;

                 case BUTTON:

                    type = GetWindowLong (Wnd, GWL_STYLE) & 0xF;
                    switch (type)
                    {
                       case GROUPBOX:

                          HookWindow (Wnd, (FARPROC) SCGroupBox, szHookName);
                          break;

                       case CHECKBOX:
                       case AUTOCHECKBOX:

                          HookWindow (Wnd, (FARPROC) SCCheckBox, szHookName);
                          break;

                       case THREESTATE:
                       case AUTO3STATE:
                       case RADIOBUTTON:
                       case AUTORADIOBUTTON:

                          HookWindow (Wnd, (FARPROC) SCRadioButton, szHookName);
                          break;
                    }
              }
       }

//─────────────────────────────────────────────────────────────
// Name:     SubClassDialog
// Purpose:  This routine does the actual job of subclassing a
//           dialog. It should be called from WM_INITDIALOG.
//─────────────────────────────────────────────────────────────

void PASCAL SubClassDialog (HANDLE hInstance, HWND hDlg)
{
       HWND Wnd;

       // Stash the dreaded instance handle

       hInst = hInstance;

       // Center the dialog

       CenterDialog (hDlg);

       // Do nothing if we're running Windows 4 or later

       if (LOBYTE (LOWORD (GetVersion())) < 4)
       {
          // Create needed tools

          InitTools ();

          // Hook the dialog box procedure

          hookKey = HookWindow (hDlg, (FARPROC) DlgSubClass, szHookName);

          // Now subclass the various dialog controls

          Wnd = GetWindow (hDlg, GW_CHILD);
          while (Wnd != NULL)
          {
             SubClassControl (Wnd, ControlType (Wnd));
             Wnd = GetWindow (Wnd, GW_HWNDNEXT);
          }
       }
}
```

```
//—————————————————————————————————————————————
// Name:     CBTHook
// Purpose:  This routine hooks the dialog window and subclasses it
//           with the HookWindow routine.
//—————————————————————————————————————————————

LONG FAR PASCAL _export CBTHook (int code, WPARAM wParam, LPARAM lParam)
{
    CREATESTRUCT FAR * cs;
    static HWND theDlg = NULL;

    if (code == HCBT_CREATEWND)
    {
      cs = ((LPCBT_CREATEWND) lParam)->lpcs;
      if (cs->lpszClass == WC_DIALOG) theDlg = wParam;
      else if (theDlg != NULL)
      {
        hookKey = HookWindow (theDlg, (FARPROC) DlgSubClass, szHookName);
        theDlg = NULL;
      }
    }

    return CallNextHookEx (AutoHook, code, wParam, lParam);
}

//—————————————————————————————————————————————
// Name:     InstallAutoHook
// Purpose:  Install the auto-subclassing hook.
//—————————————————————————————————————————————

void PASCAL InstallAutoHook (HANDLE hInstance)
{
    if (AutoHook == NULL)
    {
      // Stash the dreaded instance handle

      hInst = hInstance;

      // Install the autohook for automatic dialog subclassing

      AutoHook = SetWindowsHookEx (WH_CBT, (HOOKPROC) CBTHook,
                                   hInstance, GetCurrentTask());
    }
}

//—————————————————————————————————————————————
// Name:     RemoveAutoHook
// Purpose:  Remove the auto-subclassing hook.
//—————————————————————————————————————————————

void PASCAL RemoveAutoHook (void)
{
    if (AutoHook != NULL)
    {
      UnhookWindowsHookEx (AutoHook);
      AutoHook = NULL;
    }
}
```

Figure 5.18 The revised application program code, using the auto-hook facility.

```
/* DIATEST.C */

// © 1994 Dave Jewell and Addison-Wesley, ALL RIGHTS RESERVED

#include    <windows.h>
#include    "dialogs.h"

#define     UNAMEBOX            100

//————————————————————————————————————————————
// Name:      UserNameWndProc
// Purpose:  Dialog procedure for user name dialog.
//————————————————————————————————————————————

#pragma argsused
BOOL FAR PASCAL _export UserNameWndProc (HWND hDlg, UINT Msg,
                                            WPARAM wParam, LPARAM lParam)
{
    switch (Msg)
    {
      case WM_INITDIALOG:

      SetFocus (GetDlgItem (hDlg, UNAMEBOX));
      return (FALSE);

      case WM_COMMAND:

      if (wParam == IDOK || wParam == IDCANCEL)
         EndDialog (hDlg, wParam);
      break;

      default:

      return (FALSE);
    }

    return (TRUE);
}

//————————————————————————————————————————————
// Name:      WinMain
// Purpose:  Program entry point.
//————————————————————————————————————————————

#pragma argsused

int PASCAL WinMain (HANDLE hInstance, HANDLE hPrevInstance,
                    LPSTR lpCmdLine, int nCmdShow)
{
    InstallAutoHook (hInstance);
    MessageBox (0, "Hello :- I'm a subclassed Message box !",
                    "Hello", MB_OK | MB_ICONEXCLAMATION);
    DialogBox (hInstance, "USERNAME", NULL, UserNameWndProc);
    RemoveAutoHook ();
    return (0);
}
```

If your application uses the auto-hook facility, you should avoid calling the SubClassDialog routine altogether: the subclassing routines are written such that they will ignore an attempt to subclass an already-subclassed window, but it's probably not a good idea. To summarize, therefore, use the DialogSubClass routine if you want to manually subclass individual dialogs within your application OR use the InstallAutoHook and RemoveAutoHook routines if you want to subclass all the dialogs in your application.

As you can see from an examination of Figure 5.18, I've added a call to the MessageBox routine just to show you what a subclassed message box looks like. The result of running the program (before the main dialog box appears) is shown in Figure 5.19.

Note
Pascal equivalents of the code developed in this chapter can be found in Appendix 5. There's a listing of a Pascal unit that provides dialog box subclassing, and a sample Pascal application to demonstrate its operation.

Tempting toolbars

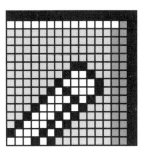

6

In this chapter, we concentrate on the last of the major user interface elements that users have come to expect from professional-looking applications, namely, the toolbar. We'll work through the development of the toolbar code, ending up with a full-featured code module that you can easily slot into your existing applications. As always, if you want to skip the theory and the development process, you can just go to the end of the chapter and pick up the finished code from there.

Toolbars versus toolboxes

In Chapter 2, we developed a floating toolbox which could be moved around anywhere within the client area of the application. Toolbars, on the other hand, are generally not moveable: they take up residence directly beneath the menu bar of the main application window, and that's where they remain. A toolbar runs right across the width of the application window and has one or more clickable button controls along its length. A good example of a toolbar is the one used by Borland's Pascal development system, shown in Figure 6.1. The C/C++ development system also has a very similar toolbar.

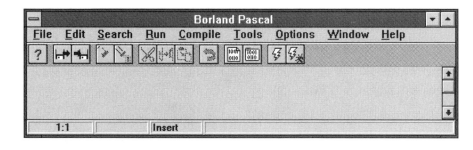

Figure 6.1 An example of a toolbar, courtesy of Borland Pascal for Windows.

Some programs (including Borland's development systems) give the user the option of having either a toolbar or a floating toolbox. This gives maximum flexibility and allows the user to decide how he or she wants to utilize the client area of the application. With a floating toolbox, a larger client area is available, but this needs to be offset against the occasional need to move the toolbox out of the way as you work. A toolbar, on the other hand, never gets in the way of your work, but it does reduce the usable client area, which may be a factor if you're using a smaller, low-resolution display. By giving users the choice, they can use whichever scheme works best for them.

An important factor here is the bitmaps displayed by the toolbar or toolbox. If you are going to allow the user to choose between a toolbar and a toolbox, then you don't really want to have two sets of bitmaps, one for the toolbox code and one for the toolbar. That's why the toolbar code developed here uses exactly the same format bitmaps as were utilized in Chapter 2 when we developed the floating toolbox code. Again, the toolbar code makes no assumptions about the size of the bitmaps: you can use whatever size bitmaps you choose (within reason!) and the toolbar will automatically adjust to accommodate them. The only restriction – a not unreasonable one – is that the bitmaps should all be the same size.

Variations on a theme

A number of applications implement a toolbar simply as an array of menu shortcuts. In other words, clicking on a toolbar button is just a fast way of accessing an often-used menu item. Both Word for Windows and the Borland development systems contain a set of toolbar buttons that correspond to the frequently-used cut, copy and paste operations. These operations can also be found on the program's Edit menu too, of course, but clicking on a button is generally a lot faster than pulling down a menu and selecting the item you want.

This sort of toolbar is easy to implement and is very straightforward from the user's point of view. However, often a toolbar is more complex than a simple array of clickable bitmaps. Sometimes, you encounter Windows programs that contain 'sticky' toolbar buttons. By sticky, I mean that once a button is pushed in, it stays that way until it's clicked again. To use the proper terminology, we're really talking about the difference between modal and non-modal operations. A menu shortcut button is non-modal: it doesn't change the mode of operation of the program. Once pressed and released, it looks just like it did before, and the program is in the same state after the corresponding operation has finished. A modal button, on the other hand, influences the mode of the program until it's pushed a second time. It's rather like the difference between a push button and a check box in a dialog.

If you look at the Word for Windows toolbar illustrated in Figure 6.2, you'll see that it's actually comprised of two toolbars stacked one on top of another. The top toolbar is non-modal: almost all of the buttons'in this toolbar correspond directly to menu operations such as Cut, Copy, Paste, Open, Save, Spell Check, Print, and so forth. The bottom toolbar is modal: it contains buttons such as left-align, justify, right-align, bold, italic, underline, and so on. The buttons may be either pressed or not depending on the style of the text that is currently being edited. If you press the

With the exception of user-installed buttons and the page view buttons, all the buttons in the top toolbar are non-modal shortcuts.

Figure 6.2 The Word for Windows toolbar.

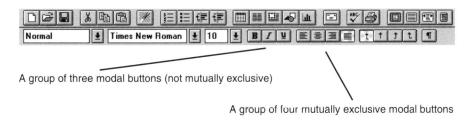

A group of three modal buttons (not mutually exclusive)

A group of four mutually exclusive modal buttons

italic button, any text from then on will use the italic style. The state of the button will change to reflect this. Similarly, pressing the right-align button changes the current paragraph to use this style. All these changes are modal in nature.

The Word for Windows example illustrates another point. Buttons should be arranged together into functional groups. The bold, italic and underline buttons are all grouped together and it's clear that they are related in some way. These particular buttons are not mutually exclusive – in other words, it's possible to have a chunk of text that includes any combination of the bold, italic and underline attributes. Pressing any button in this group of three does not automatically turn off all the other buttons in the same group.

The text alignment group, however, is a mutually exclusive group. Obviously, a chunk of text can only be left-aligned or right-aligned or centered or justified. It's impossible for it to take on more than one of these four attributes at the same time. For this reason, pushing any button in this group of four will automatically turn off all the other buttons in the same group. It's rather like a set of auto radio buttons in a dialog box. The toolbar code developed here allows buttons to be positionally grouped on the toolbar and also supports the concept of a mutually exclusive group.

Building the code

If you think about it, the toolbar has something in common with the status bar code we developed in Chapter 4, and it also has things in common with the toolbox palette code from Chapter 2. It seems reasonable to start with the status bar code and change it so that it sits at the top of the window rather than at the bottom.

Let's begin then, by taking the bare bones of the status bar code as the foundation for our toolbar window. One pretty obvious change is the fact that toolbars live at the top of the application window, whereas status bars live at the bottom! We can make the toolbar window upwardly mobile simply by changing a line or two in the ResizeWindow routine, so that it looks like this:

```
//———————————————————————————————————————
// Name:     ResizeWindow
// Purpose:  Routine to force toolbar to proper size and position.
//———————————————————————————————————————

static void PASCAL ResizeWindow (HWND Wnd)
{
```

```
        RECT r;
        PToolBarRec p;

        p = GetToolBarRec (Wnd);
        GetClientRect (GetParent (Wnd), &r);
        SetWindowPos (Wnd, 0, 0, 0, r.right, p−>height, SWP_NOZORDER);
}
```

We'll use the same technique for subclassing the main application window that we developed in Chapter 4. In other words, any time that a WM_SIZE message is received by the main window, we'll ensure that we get to see it first and call the ResizeWindow routine. With the code above, the toolbar window will stay at the top of the application window, immediately beneath the menu bar, if any.

A small change is also required to the painting code: because the status bar was located at the bottom of the screen, we needed to add a nice-looking 3D top edge to separate it from the main window client area. With a toolbar, on the other hand, it's obviously the bottom edge that needs to get the decorative treatment. This is shown in the code below:

```
//─────────────────────────────────────────────────────────
// Name:     ToolBarPaint
// Purpose:  This routine is responsible for painting the tool bar.
//─────────────────────────────────────────────────────────
static int PASCAL ToolBarPaint (HWND Wnd)
{
        int i;
        RECT r;
        PAINTSTRUCT ps;

        BeginPaint (Wnd, &ps);

        // First, draw the bottom edge of the toolbar

        GetClientRect (Wnd, &r);
        PatBlt (ps.hdc, 0, r.bottom − 1, r.right − r.left, 1, BLACKNESS);
        PatBlt (ps.hdc, 0, 0, r.right − r.left, 1, WHITENESS);

        EndPaint (Wnd, &ps);
        return (0);
}
```

As for the status bar code, there should be no real problem in using the hard-wired color values shown above. However, if you want to be absolutely accurate, you can use the COLOR_BTNHIGHLIGHT color to draw the highlight line along the top of the button bar. Figure 6.3 shows the source code for the initial toolbar code module, TOOLBAR1.C, and Figure 6.4 shows the initial test application source, BARTEST1.C. Both these files can be found on the companion disk, and the executable file is named BARTEST1.EXE. The initial header file is shown in Figure 6.5.

Figure 6.3 TOOLBAR1.C: the initial skeletal toolbar implementation.

```
/* TOOLBAR1.C */

// © 1994 Dave Jewell and Addison-Wesley, ALL RIGHTS RESERVED

#include    <mem.h>
#include    <windows.h>
#include    "toolbar.h"
#include    "sclaslib.h
```

```
"static char szClassName[ ]  = "ToolBar";        // name of our window class
static char szHookName[ ]   = "ToolBarHook";    // name of our hook

typedef struct ToolBarRec
{
    int height;                                 // height of the toolbar
} ToolBarRec, NEAR * PToolBarRec;

static LONG hookKey;

//─────────────────────────────────────────────────────────────────
// Name:    GetToolBarRcc
// Purpose: Given a window handle, return a pointer to the corresponding
//          toolbar record.
//─────────────────────────────────────────────────────────────────

static PToolBarRec PASCAL GetToolBarRec (HWND Wnd)
{
    return (PToolBarRec) GetWindowWord (Wnd, 0);
}

// ─────────────────────────────────────────────────────────────────
// Name:    ResizeWindow
// Purpose: Routine to force toolbar to proper size and position.
//─────────────────────────────────────────────────────────────────

static void PASCAL ResizeWindow (HWND Wnd)
{
    RECT r;
    PToolBarRec p;

    p = GetToolBarRec (Wnd);
    GetClientRect (GetParent (Wnd), &r);
    SetWindowPos (Wnd, 0, 0, 0, r.right, p−>height, SWP_NOZORDER);
}

//─────────────────────────────────────────────────────────────────
// Name:    SubclassParentWndProc
// Purpose: Subclassing routine for the main application window.
//─────────────────────────────────────────────────────────────────

#pragma argsused
LONG FAR PASCAL _export SubclassParentWndProc (HWND Wnd, WORD Msg,
                                               WPARAM wParam,
                                               LPARAM lParam)

{
    if (Msg == WM_SIZE) ResizeWindow (GetToolBarWindow (Wnd));
    return CallOldProc (Wnd, Msg, wParam, lParam, hookKey);
}

//─────────────────────────────────────────────────────────────────
// Name:    InitToolBarWindow
// Purpose: Initialization code for setting up the toolbar window.
//─────────────────────────────────────────────────────────────────

static LONG PASCAL InitToolBarWindow (HWND Wnd, LONG lParam)
{
    LPCSTR text;
    PToolBarRec p;
    LONG res = −1L;

    p = (PToolBarRec) LocalAlloc (LPTR, sizeof (ToolBarRec));
    if (p != NULL)
    {
        // Initialize the ToolBarRec data structure

        p−>height = 25; // !!! Temporary !!!
        SetWindowWord (Wnd, 0, (WORD) p);
        ResizeWindow (Wnd);
        SetProp (GetParent (Wnd), szClassName, Wnd);
```

```
                hookKey = HookWindow (GetParent (Wnd), (FARPROC)
                                      SubclassParentWndProc, szHookName);

        res = 0;
    }

    return (res);
}

//——————————————————————————————————————————————————————
// Name:    ToolBarPaint
// Purpose: This routine is responsible for painting the tool bar.
//——————————————————————————————————————————————————————

static int PASCAL ToolBarPaint (HWND Wnd)
{
    int i;
    RECT r;
    PAINTSTRUCT ps;

    BeginPaint (Wnd, &ps);

    // First, draw the bottom edge of the toolbar

    GetClientRect (Wnd, &r);
    PatBlt (ps.hdc, 0, r.bottom — 1, r.right — r.left, 1, BLACKNESS);
    PatBlt (ps.hdc, 0, 0, r.right — r.left, 1, WHITENESS);
    EndPaint (Wnd, &ps);
    return (0);
}

//——————————————————————————————————————————————————————
// Name:    DestroyToolBarWindow
// Purpose: Clean-up code for the toolbar window.
//——————————————————————————————————————————————————————

static int PASCAL DestroyToolBarWindow (HWND Wnd)
{
    PToolBarRec p;

    p = GetToolBarRec (Wnd);
    RemoveProp (GetParent (Wnd), szClassName);
    UnHookWindow (GetParent (Wnd), hookKey);

    LocalFree ((HLOCAL) p);
    return (0);
}

//——————————————————————————————————————————————————————
// Name:    ToolBarWndProc
// Purpose: Window procedure for toolbar windows.
//——————————————————————————————————————————————————————

LONG FAR PASCAL _export ToolBarWndProc (HWND Wnd, WORD Msg,
                                        WPARAM wParam, LPARAM lParam)
{
    switch (Msg)
    {
      case WM_PAINT:

        return ToolBarPaint (Wnd);

      case WM_CREATE:

        return InitToolBarWindow (Wnd, lParam);

      case WM_DESTROY:

        return DestroyToolBarWindow (Wnd);
    }
```

```
      return DefWindowProc (Wnd, Msg, wParam, lParam);
}

//————————————————————————————————————————————————————
// Name:    RegisterToolBar
// Purpose: Register the toolbar window procedure.
//————————————————————————————————————————————————————

static BOOL PASCAL RegisterToolBar (HANDLE hInstance)
{
      WNDCLASS cls;

      if (GetClassInfo (hInstance, szClassName, &cls) == 0)
      {
          cls.style            = 0;
          cls.lpfnWndProc      = (WNDPROC) ToolBarWndProc;
          cls.cbClsExtra       = 0;
          cls.cbWndExtra       = sizeof (void NEAR *);
          cls.hInstance        = hInstance;
          cls.hIcon            = 0;
          cls.hCursor          = LoadCursor (NULL, IDC_ARROW);
          cls.hbrBackground    = COLOR_BTNFACE + 1;
          cls.lpszMenuName     = NULL;
          cls.lpszClassName    = szClassName;

          return RegisterClass (&cls);
      }

      return TRUE;
}

//————————————————————————————————————————————————————
// Name:    GetToolBarWindow
// Purpose: Return the handle of this window's tool bar.
//————————————————————————————————————————————————————

HWND PASCAL GetToolBarWindow (HWND hWndParent)
{
      if (hWndParent != NULL && IsWindow (hWndParent))
        return GetProp (hWndParent, szClassName);
      else
        return NULL;
}

//————————————————————————————————————————————————————
// Name:    CreateToolBarWindow
// Purpose: Create a toolbar window and attach it to the designated parent.
//————————————————————————————————————————————————————

HWND PASCAL CreateToolBarWindow (HANDLE hInstance, HWND hWndParent)
{
      HWND Wnd = NULL;

      // Check that we've got a valid parent window

      if (hWndParent != NULL && IsWindow (hWndParent))
      {
        // Ok so far, but has window already got a toolbar?

        Wnd = GetToolBarWindow (hWndParent);
        if (Wnd == NULL)
          if (RegisterToolBar (hInstance))
            Wnd = CreateWindow (szClassName, "", WS_CHILD | WS_VISIBLE,
                                0, 0, 0, 0, hWndParent, NULL, hInstance, NULL);
      }

      return (Wnd);
}
```

Figure 6.4 BARTEST1.C: the initial test application for the toolbar code.

```
/* BARTEST1.C */

// © 1994 Dave Jewell and Addison-Wesley, ALL RIGHTS RESERVED

#include   <windows.h>
#include   "toolbar.h"

char szAppName[ ] = "ToolBarTest";

//————————————————————————————————————————————————
// Name:    WindowProc
// Purpose: Window procedure for main application window.
//————————————————————————————————————————————————

LONG FAR PASCAL _export WindowProc (HWND Wnd, WORD Msg,
                                    WPARAM wParam, LPARAM lParam)
{
    switch (Msg)
    {
      case WM_DESTROY:

        PostQuitMessage (0);
        break;
        default:

        return DefWindowProc (Wnd, Msg, wParam, lParam);
    }

    return (0);
}

//————————————————————————————————————————————————
// Name:    InitAppClass
// Purpose: Register the main application window class.
//————————————————————————————————————————————————

BOOL PASCAL InitAppClass (HANDLE hInstance)
{
    WNDCLASS cls;

    if (GetClassInfo (hInstance, szAppName, &cls) == 0)
    {
        cls.style            = CS_VREDRAW | CS_HREDRAW;
        cls.lpfnWndProc      = (WNDPROC) WindowProc;
        cls.cbClsExtra       = 0;
        cls.cbWndExtra       = 0;
        cls.hInstance        = hInstance;
        cls.hIcon            = LoadIcon (NULL, IDI_APPLICATION);
        cls.hCursor          = LoadCursor (NULL, IDC_ARROW);
        cls.hbrBackground    = GetStockObject (WHITE_BRUSH);
        cls.lpszMenuName     = MAKEINTRESOURCE (1);
        cls.lpszClassName    = szAppName;
        return RegisterClass (&cls);
    }

    return (TRUE);
}

//————————————————————————————————————————————————
// Name:    WinMain
// Purpose: Main application entry point.
//————————————————————————————————————————————————

#pragma argsused

int PASCAL WinMain (HANDLE hInstance, HANDLE hPrevInstance,
                    LPSTR lpCmdLine, int nCmdShow)
{
    HWND Wnd;
    MSG Msg;
```

```
              // Register application class if needed

              if (InitAppClass (hInstance) == FALSE)
                 return (0);

              // Create the main application window

              Wnd = CreateWindow (szAppName, szAppName, WS_OVERLAPPEDWINDOW,
                           CW_USEDEFAULT, CW_USEDEFAULT,
                           CW_USEDEFAULT, CW_USEDEFAULT,
                           0, 0, hInstance, NULL);

              if (Wnd != NULL)
              {
                 ShowWindow (Wnd, nCmdShow);
                 UpdateWindow (Wnd);
                 if (CreateToolBarWindow (hInstance, Wnd) != NULL)
                 {
                    // Watch this space...
                 }
              }

              while (GetMessage (&Msg, 0, 0, 0))
              {
                 TranslateMessage (&Msg);
                 DispatchMessage (&Msg);
              }

              return (Msg.wParam);
        }
```

Figure 6.5   TOOLBAR1.H: the header file for the toolbar code.

```
        /* TOOLBAR1.H */

        // © 1994 Dave Jewell and Addison-Wesley, ALL RIGHTS RESERVED

        #ifndef _INC_TOOLBAR
        #define _INC_TOOLBAR          /* #defined if toolbar.h has been included */

        #ifdef      __cplusplus
        extern      "C" {
        #endif

        HWND PASCAL GetToolBarWindow (HWND hWndParent);
        HWND PASCAL CreateToolBarWindow (HANDLE hInstance, HWND hWndParent);

        #ifdef      __cplusplus
        }
        #endif

        #endif
```

As you can see, there are only two routines exported by the toolbar module. These are CreateToolBarWindow, which does the work of creating the actual toolbar, and GetToolBarWindow, which, given the handle of the parent application window, returns a handle to the toolbar window.

Figure 6.6 The initial, empty toolbar window.

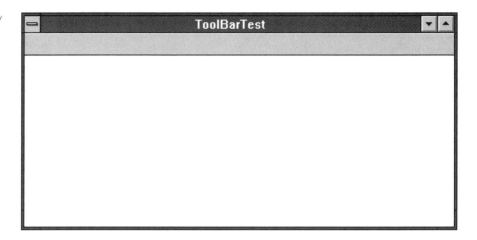

As for the status bar code, we will design the various routines so that they take the window handle of the parent application window, rather than the window handle of the toolbar itself. In this way, the application code does not have to keep accessing the toolbar window handle and, indeed, does not even have to know that the toolbar is implemented as a window. In other words, the toolbar becomes a natural extension to the main application window and is accessed using the same window handle.

You can see from Figure 6.3 that I have tried to structure the toolbar code in much the same way as the status bar module. In particular, when the toolbar window is created, a small data structure is allocated and attached to the toolbar window using the SetWindowWord API call. This same data structure is deallocated automatically when the toolbar window is destroyed.

In this first pass through the code, the data structure contains a single field, height, which is used to contain the height of the toolbar window. This field is accessed in the ResizeWindow code when the size and position of the toolbar window are being established. In the initial code, the toolbar height is set to an arbitrary value so as to provide a reasonable looking toolbar as shown in Figure 6.6.

Specifying the wanted bitmaps

In practice, of course, we want the height of the toolbar to be automatically adjusted according to the size of the toolbar bitmaps used. This is analogous to the operation of the floating palette toolbox. The question is, how do we pass the toolbar bitmaps to the toolbar code? We don't want to make a separate call each time we want to add a bitmap to the toolbar. The easiest approach is to pass a pointer to an array of bitmap resource IDs. In this way, the client code (that is, the main application) only needs to generate an array of integers and pass this to the toolbar module at the time the toolbar window is created. It's then the responsibility of the toolbar code to load up the wanted bitmaps and adjust the vertical size of the toolbar.

With this in mind, let's add a third parameter to the CreateToolBarWindow routine. This parameter will be a far pointer to the array of bitmap resource IDs and we'll assume that these bitmaps are accessible using the instance handle passed to the CreateToolBarWindow call. (You always need an instance handle in order to load a resource – effectively, the instance handle tells Windows what file to search for the wanted resource.)

We'll specify that a bitmap resource ID of −1 terminates the list. So, for example, to specify a toolbar with just two bitmaps, we might set up an array of IDs like this:

```
static int bitMaps [3] = { 1000, 1001, −1 };
```

This tells the toolbar code to load bitmap 1000 as the first bitmap in the toolbar and bitmap 1001 as the second. The −1 terminates the list. The declaration for the CreateToolBarWindow routine now looks as below, and the new header file is called TOOLBAR2.H, although I won't show it again until we make some more substantial changes to the file.

```
HWND PASCAL CreateToolBarWindow (HANDLE hInstance, HWND hWndParent,
                                 LPINT lpButtons);
```

I've added the array of bitmap IDs to the main application file and modified the CreateToolBarWindow call to pass the address of the array like this:

```
if (CreateToolBarWindow (hInstance, Wnd, bitMaps) != NULL)
{
        // Watch this space...
}
```

The result is the BARTEST2.C file. Again, I won't show this file again until we make some more substantial changes to it.

Of course, now that we're referencing some bitmaps, we need to ensure that we've got the needed bitmap resources in our executable file. I just copied the ten bitmap resources from Chapter 2 into a .RES file and renamed it BARTEST.RES. Be sure to include it into your project so that the bitmaps get bound into the .EXE file.

OK, that's the view from the application side. Now let's look at the changes we need to make to the CreateToolBarWindow routine itself:

```
//——————————————————————————————————————————
// Name:    CreateToolBarWindow
// Purpose: Create a toolbar window and attach it to the designated parent.
//——————————————————————————————————————————

HWND PASCAL CreateToolBarWindow (HANDLE hInstance, HWND hWndParent,
                                 LPINT lpButtons)
{
        HWND Wnd = NULL;

        // Check that we've got a valid parent window

        if (hWndParent != NULL && IsWindow (hWndParent))
        {
            // Ok so far, but has window already got a toolbar ?

            Wnd = GetToolBarWindow (hWndParent);
            if (Wnd == NULL)
```

```
        if (RegisterToolBar (hInstance))
            Wnd = CreateWindow (szClassName, "", WS_CHILD | WS_VISIBLE,
                                0, 0, 0, 0, hWndParent, NULL, hInstance, lpButtons);
    }

    return (Wnd);
}
```

In the revised code, we've simply added the lpButtons parameter to the function definition and passed the integer pointer through as the last parameter to the CreateWindow routine. At this point, we could check that the lpButtons parameter is not equal to NULL and fail immediately if it is. However, it's equally easy just to pass the address through to the CreateWindow call and do this checking further along the line.

By passing the bitmap ID array address as the final parameter to CreateWindow, we get a chance to examine the array when a WM_CREATE message is generated for the window. This is a technique that we used before when developing the status bar code and the floating toolbox. It saves us from having to mess about with separate initialization routines and makes the whole thing a lot neater from the application's viewpoint. We've already got a rudimentary InitToolBarWindow which is called in response to a WM_CREATE message, so let's flesh it out a little more now that we've got the bitmap array available.

```
//------------------------------------------------------------------
// Name:     InitToolBarWindow
// Purpose:  Initialization code for setting up the toolbar window.
//------------------------------------------------------------------

static LONG PASCAL InitToolBarWindow (HWND Wnd, LONG lParam)
{
    LPCSTR text;
    LPINT pBitmaps;
    PToolBarRec p;
    LONG res = -1L;
    HANDLE hInstance;

    p = (PToolBarRec) LocalAlloc (LPTR, sizeof (ToolBarRec));
    if (p != NULL)
    {
        // Initialize the ToolBarRec data structure

        p->border = (GetSystemMetrics (SM_CXFRAME) + 3) / 2;
        p->height = -1;
        SetWindowWord (Wnd, 0, (WORD) p);

        // Load the various bitmaps

        pBitmaps = (LPINT) ((LPCREATESTRUCT) lParam)->lpCreateParams;
        hInstance = GetWindowWord (Wnd, GWW_HINSTANCE);

        if (LoadToolBitmaps (p, pBitmaps, hInstance) == 0)
        {
            ResizeWindow (Wnd);
            SetProp (GetParent (Wnd), szClassName, Wnd);
            hookKey = HookWindow (GetParent (Wnd),
                            (FARPROC) SubclassParentWndProc,
                            szHookName);

            res = 0;
        }
    }

    return (res);
}
```

Here's the revised code for InitToolBarWindow. I've added a new field called border to the ToolBarRec data structure. As for the status bar implementation, this field is used to specify the size of the border between the bitmaps and the sides of the toolbar. In the code above, the height field is initially set to −1. This indicates that we haven't yet seen a bitmap. The pBitmaps pointer is obtained by typecasting lParam to an LPCREATESTRUCT and then dereferencing from it. Finally, a new routine, LoadToolBitmaps, is called which, as the name suggests, is responsible for the actual business of loading the various bitmaps into memory. Because this routine needs to load resources, it also needs an instance handle. As a sneaky way of getting the instance handle without resorting to a global variable (remember: we hate those darned global variables!), the GetWindowWord routine is used to retrieve the instance handle from the window handle.

```
//———————————————————————————————————————————————————
// Name:    LoadToolBitmaps
// Purpose: Load all specified bitmaps into the ToolBarRec structure.
//———————————————————————————————————————————————————
static int LONG LoadToolBitmaps (PToolBarRec p, LPINT pBitmaps,
                                 HANDLE hInstance)
{
    BITMAP bm;
    int ret = −1;

    if (pBitmaps != NULL)
    {
        while (*pBitmaps != −1 && p−>NumButtons < MAXBUTTONS − 1)
        {
            p−>bmHandles [p−>NumButtons] = LoadButtonBitmap (hInstance,
                                                             *pBitmaps);

            if (p−>bmHandles [p−>NumButtons] == NULL) return (ret);

            // If this is first bitmap, determine dimensions

            if (p−>height == −1)
            {
                GetObject (p−>bmHandles [p−>NumButtons],
                    sizeof (BITMAP), &bm);

                p−>bmWidth = bm.bmWidth / 2;
                p−>bmHeight = bm.bmHeight;
                p−>height = bm.bmHeight + (p−>border * 2);
            }

            p−>NumButtons++;
            pBitmaps++;
        }
        if (p−>NumButtons != 0) ret = 0;
    }

    return (ret);
}
```

The code for the LoadToolBitmaps routine is shown above. It simply scans through the array of bitmap resource IDs until a value of −1 is detected. Note that our old friend the LoadButtonBitmap routine is used here, making a special guest appearance in the toolbar code. Although the code for LoadButtonBitmap is included in the toolbar code, it should really be in a separate module of reusable routines, as for the Pascal code. (See the source code for the Tools unit in Chapter 8.) By using the LoadButtonBitmap routine, we ensure that the displayed toolbar bitmaps remain consistent with the current Windows color scheme.

The toolbar is designed to allow a maximum of 40 bitmap buttons, and this is determined by the value of a #defined constant called MAXBUTTONS. As each bitmap is loaded into memory, the NumButtons field is incremented by one. (This field was implicitly set to zero when the ToolBarRec data structure was allocated using LocalAlloc with the LPTR specifier, since this automatically clears the newly allocated memory block to all zeros.) If the height field is set to −1 then the bitmap dimensions are obtained and the height of the toolbar is calculated. Bear in mind that this all happens at WM_CREATE time, so the toolbar is not yet visible on the screen. The current definition of the ToolBarRec structure is shown below:

```
#define          MAXBUTTONS   40           // maximum buttons per window

typedef struct ToolBarRec
{
      int        border;                   // width of border
      int        height;                   // height of the toolbar
      int        bmWidth;                  // width of bitmaps
      int        bmHeight;                 // height of bitmaps
      int        NumButtons;               // number of buttons
      HANDLE     bmHandles [MAXBUTTONS];   // bitmap handles

} ToolBarRec, NEAR * PToolBarRec;
```

With all the above code in place, the ToolBarRec data structure will be correctly initialized when the CreateToolBarWindow is called. However, we're obviously not going to see any bitmaps in the toolbar until we've implemented the WM_PAINT code! Let's do that now.

```
// Now draw each cell in turn

for (i = 0; i < p−>NumButtons; i++)
      PaintCell (ps.hdc, p, i);
```

Firstly, we need to add the above code to the ToolBarPaint routine. This loops through each of the loaded bitmaps calling PaintCell for each bitmap in turn.

```
//────────────────────────────────────────────────────────────────
// Name:    PaintCell
// Purpose: Paint a specified cell in the toolbar.
//────────────────────────────────────────────────────────────────

static void PASCAL PaintCell (HDC dc, PToolBarRec p, int cellNum)
{
      HDC hMemDC;
      HBITMAP hbm;
      hMemDC = CreateCompatibleDC (dc);
      hbm = SelectObject (hMemDC, p−>bmHandles [cellNum]);
      BitBlt (dc, p−>border + cellNum * (p−>bmWidth + 2),
            p−>border, p−>bmWidth, p−>bmHeight, hMemDC, 0, 0, SRCCOPY);
      SelectObject (hMemDC, hbm);
      DeleteDC (hMemDC);
}
```

The PaintCell routine is quite straightforward. It uses the standard Windows technique of creating a memory device context, selecting the wanted bitmap handle into the DC and using BitBlt to copy the bitmap onto the destination DC. The horizontal position of the displayed bitmap is calculated in a very straightforward way using the passed cellNum parameter.

At this stage, the current state of play for the toolbar code is shown in Figure 6.7. This file can be found on the disk as TOOLBAR2.C, the corresponding header file as TOOLBAR2.H, and the test application as BARTEST2.C. The header file and application source haven't been shown here because of the relatively minor changes involved. The corresponding executable file is called BARTEST2.EXE and it is shown running in Figure 6.8.

Figure 6.7 TOOLBAR2.C: the toolbar implementation with bitmap loading and painting in place.

```
/* TOOLBAR2.C */

// © 1994 Dave Jewell and Addison-Wesley, ALL RIGHTS RESERVED

#include    <mem.h>
#include    <windows.h>
#include    "toolbar.h"
#include    "sclaslib.h"

static char szClassName[ ] = "ToolBar";         // name of our window class
static char szHookName[ ] = "ToolBarHook";      // name of our hook

#define     MAXBUTTONS         40               // maximum buttons per window

typedef struct ToolBarRec
{
    int         border;                         // width of border
    int         height;                         // height of the toolbar
    int         bmWidth;                        // width of bitmaps
    int         bmHeight;                       // height of bitmaps
    int         NumButtons;                     // number of buttons
    HANDLE      bmHandles [MAXBUTTONS];         // bitmap handles
} ToolBarRec, NEAR * PToolBarRec;

static LONG hookKey;

//––––––––––––––––––––––––––––––––––––––––––––––––––––––––––––––––––
// Name:      GetToolBarRec
// Purpose:   Given a window handle, return a pointer to the corresponding
//            toolbar record.
//––––––––––––––––––––––––––––––––––––––––––––––––––––––––––––––––––
static PToolBarRec PASCAL GetToolBarRec (HWND Wnd)
{
    return (PToolBarRec) GetWindowWord (Wnd, 0);
}

//––––––––––––––––––––––––––––––––––––––––––––––––––––––––––––––––––
// Name:      ResizeWindow
// Purpose:   Routine to force toolbar to proper size and position.
//––––––––––––––––––––––––––––––––––––––––––––––––––––––––––––––––––
static void PASCAL ResizeWindow (HWND Wnd)
{
    RECT r;
    PToolBarRec p;

    p = GetToolBarRec (Wnd);
    GetClientRect (GetParent (Wnd), &r);
    SetWindowPos (Wnd, 0, 0, 0, r.right, p–>height, SWP_NOZORDER);
}

//––––––––––––––––––––––––––––––––––––––––––––––––––––––––––––––––––
// Name:      SubclassParentWndProc
// Purpose:   Subclassing routine for the main application window.
//––––––––––––––––––––––––––––––––––––––––––––––––––––––––––––––––––
#pragma argsused

LONG FAR PASCAL _export SubclassParentWndProc (HWND Wnd, WORD Msg,
                                               WPARAM wParam, LPARAM
                                               lParam)
```

```
        {
                if (Msg == WM_SIZE) ResizeWindow (GetToolBarWindow (Wnd));
                return CallOldProc (Wnd, Msg, wParam, lParam, hookKey);
        }

        //————————————————————————————————————————————————
        // Name:     ColorFix
        // Purpose:  Fix up a color value for the LoadButtonBitmap routine.
        //————————————————————————————————————————————————

        static COLORREF PASCAL ColorFix (COLORREF color)
        {
                return RGB (GetBValue (color), GetGValue (color), GetRValue (color));
        }

        //————————————————————————————————————————————————
        // Name:     LoadButtonBitmap
        // Purpose:  Load a bitmap and tweak it for current system colors.
        //————————————————————————————————————————————————

        static HBITMAP PASCAL LoadButtonBitmap (HANDLE hInstance, int bmID)
        {
                HDC dc;
                HBITMAP hbm;
                HANDLE hRes;
                LPDWORD lprgb;
                LPVOID lpb;
                LPBITMAPINFOHEADER lpbi;

                hRes = LoadResource (hInstance, FindResource (hInstance,
                                        MAKEINTRESOURCE(bmID), RT_BITMAP));

                lpbi = (LPBITMAPINFOHEADER) LockResource (hRes);
                if (lpbi == NULL) return (NULL);

                lprgb = (LPDWORD) ((LPSTR) lpbi + (int) lpbi–>biSize);
                lpb = (LPVOID) (lprgb + 16);

                lprgb [0] = ColorFix (GetSysColor (COLOR_WINDOWTEXT));      // Black
                lprgb [8] = ColorFix (GetSysColor (COLOR_BTNFACE));         // Light gray
                lprgb [7] = ColorFix (GetSysColor (COLOR_BTNSHADOW));       // Gray
                lprgb [15] = ColorFix (GetSysColor (COLOR_BTNHIGHLIGHT));   // White

                dc = GetDC (NULL);
                hbm = CreateDIBitmap (dc, lpbi, CBM_INIT, lpb,
                                        (LPBITMAPINFO) lpbi, DIB_RGB_COLORS);

                ReleaseDC (NULL, dc);
                GlobalUnlock (hRes);
                FreeResource (hRes);
                return (hbm);
        }

        //————————————————————————————————————————————————
        // Name:     LoadToolBitmaps
        // Purpose:  Load all specified bitmaps into the ToolBarRec structure.
        //————————————————————————————————————————————————

        static int LONG LoadToolBitmaps (PToolBarRec p, LPINT pBitmaps,
                                        HANDLE hInstance)
        {
                BITMAP bm;
                int ret = –1;

                if (pBitmaps != NULL)
                {
                  while (*pBitmaps != –1 && p–>NumButtons < MAXBUTTONS – 1)
                  {
                    p–>bmHandles [p–>NumButtons] = LoadButtonBitmap (hInstance,
                                                        *pBitmaps);
                    if (p–>bmHandles [p–>NumButtons] == NULL) return (ret);
```

```
                // If this is first bitmap, determine dimensions

                if (p->height == -1)
                {
                    GetObject (p->bmHandles [p->NumButtons],
                            sizeof (BITMAP), &bm);

                    p->bmWidth = bm.bmWidth / 2;
                    p->bmHeight = bm.bmHeight;
                    p->height = bm.bmHeight + (p->border * 2);
                }

                p->NumButtons++;
                pBitmaps++;
            }

            if (p->NumButtons != 0) ret = 0;
        }

        return (ret);
}

//------------------------------------------------------------
// Name:    InitToolBarWindow
// Purpose: Initialization code for setting up the toolbar window.
//------------------------------------------------------------

static LONG PASCAL InitToolBarWindow (HWND Wnd, LONG lParam)
{
        LPCSTR text;
        LPINT pBitmaps;
        PToolBarRec p;
        LONG res = -1L;
        HANDLE hInstance;

        p = (PToolBarRec) LocalAlloc (LPTR, sizeof (ToolBarRec));
        if (p != NULL)
        {
            // Initialize the ToolBarRec data structure

            p->border = (GetSystemMetrics (SM_CXFRAME) + 3) / 2;
            p->height = -1;
            SetWindowWord (Wnd, 0, (WORD) p);

            // Load the various bitmaps

            pBitmaps = (LPINT) ((LPCREATESTRUCT) lParam)->lpCreateParams;
            hInstance = GetWindowWord (Wnd, GWW_HINSTANCE);

            if (LoadToolBitmaps (p, pBitmaps, hInstance) == 0)
            {
                ResizeWindow (Wnd);
                SetProp (GetParent (Wnd), szClassName, Wnd);
                hookKey = HookWindow (GetParent (Wnd),
                                (FARPROC) SubclassParentWndProc,
                                szHookName);

                res = 0;
            }
        }

        return (res);
}

//------------------------------------------------------------
// Name:    PaintCell
// Purpose: Paint a specified cell in the toolbar.
//------------------------------------------------------------

static void PASCAL PaintCell (HDC dc, PToolBarRec p, int cellNum)
{
        HDC hMemDC;
        HBITMAP hbm;

        hMemDC = CreateCompatibleDC (dc);
```

```
        hbm = SelectObject (hMemDC, p->bmHandles [cellNum]);
        BitBlt (dc, p->border + cellNum * (p->bmWidth + 2),
                p->border, p->bmWidth, p->bmHeight, hMemDC, 0, 0, SRCCOPY);
        SelectObject (hMemDC, hbm);
        DeleteDC (hMemDC);
}

//─────────────────────────────────────────────────────────────
// Name:    ToolBarPaint
// Purpose: This routine is responsible for painting the tool bar.
//─────────────────────────────────────────────────────────────

static int PASCAL ToolBarPaint (HWND Wnd)
{
        int i;
        RECT r;
        PToolBarRec p;
        PAINTSTRUCT ps;

        BeginPaint (Wnd, &ps);
        p = GetToolBarRec (Wnd);

        // First, draw the bottom edge of the toolbar

        GetClientRect (Wnd, &r);
        PatBlt (ps.hdc, 0, r.bottom - 1, r.right - r.left, 1, BLACKNESS);
        PatBlt (ps.hdc, 0, 0, r.right - r.left, 1, WHITENESS);

        // Now draw each cell in turn

        for (i = 0; i < p->NumButtons; i++)
            PaintCell (ps.hdc, p, i);

        EndPaint (Wnd, &ps);
        return (0);
}

//─────────────────────────────────────────────────────────────
// Name:    DestroyToolBarWindow
// Purpose: Clean-up code for the toolbar window.
//─────────────────────────────────────────────────────────────

static int PASCAL DestroyToolBarWindow (HWND Wnd)
{
        PToolBarRec p;

        p = GetToolBarRec (Wnd);
        RemoveProp (GetParent (Wnd), szClassName);
        UnHookWindow (GetParent (Wnd), hookKey);
        LocalFree ((HLOCAL) p);
        return (0);
}

//─────────────────────────────────────────────────────────────
// Name:    ToolBarWndProc
// Purpose: Window procedure for toolbar windows.
//─────────────────────────────────────────────────────────────

LONG FAR PASCAL _export ToolBarWndProc (HWND Wnd, WORD Msg,
                                        WPARAM wParam, LPARAM lParam)
{
        switch (Msg)
        {
          case WM_PAINT:

          return ToolBarPaint (Wnd);

          case WM_CREATE:

          return InitToolBarWindow (Wnd, lParam);

          case WM_DESTROY:

          return DestroyToolBarWindow (Wnd);
        }
```

```
            return DefWindowProc (Wnd, Msg, wParam, lParam);
    }
    //─────────────────────────────────────────────────────────────
    // Name:     RegisterToolBar
    // Purpose:  Register the toolbar window procedure.
    //─────────────────────────────────────────────────────────────
    static BOOL PASCAL RegisterToolBar (HANDLE hInstance)
    {
        WNDCLASS cls;

        if (GetClassInfo (hInstance, szClassName, &cls) == 0)
        {
          cls.style              = 0;
          cls.lpfnWndProc        = (WNDPROC) ToolBarWndProc;
          cls.cbClsExtra         = 0;
          cls.cbWndExtra         = sizeof (void NEAR *);
          cls.hInstance          = hInstance;
          cls.hIcon              = 0;
          cls.hCursor            = LoadCursor (NULL, IDC_ARROW);
          cls.hbrBackground      = COLOR_BTNFACE + 1;
          cls.lpszMenuName       = NULL;
          cls.lpszClassName      = szClassName;

          return RegisterClass (&cls);
        }

        return TRUE;
    }

    //─────────────────────────────────────────────────────────────
    // Name:     GetToolBarWindow
    // Purpose:  Return the handle of this window's tool bar.
    //─────────────────────────────────────────────────────────────
    HWND PASCAL GetToolBarWindow (HWND hWndParent)
    {
        if (hWndParent != NULL && IsWindow (hWndParent))
          return GetProp (hWndParent, szClassName);
        else
          return NULL;
    }
    //─────────────────────────────────────────────────────────────
    // Name:     CreateToolBarWindow
    // Purpose:  Create a toolbar window and attach it to the designated parent.
    //─────────────────────────────────────────────────────────────
    HWND PASCAL CreateToolBarWindow (HANDLE hInstance, HWND hWndParent,
                            LPINT lpButtons)

    {
        HWND Wnd = NULL;

        // Check that we've got a valid parent window

        if (hWndParent != NULL && IsWindow (hWndParent))
        {
          // Ok so far, but has window already got a toolbar?

          Wnd = GetToolBarWindow (hWndParent);
          if (Wnd == NULL)
            if (RegisterToolBar (hInstance))
                Wnd = CreateWindow (szClassName, "", WS_CHILD | WS_VISIBLE,
                                    0, 0, 0, 0, hWndParent, NULL, hInstance, lpButtons);
        }

        return (Wnd);
    }
```

Figure 6.8 Running the
TOOLBAR2.EXE program

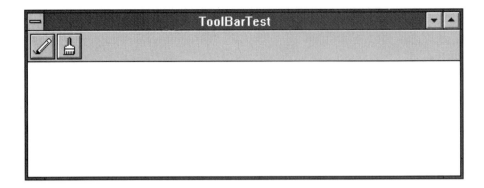

Button groups

At the moment, the existing code is a little too simplistic. A major limitation is the fact that the bitmaps can only be placed at equal intervals along the toolbar. This leads to a boring, visually uninteresting appearance, and makes it harder for the user to immediately locate the bitmap that he or she wants. If you look back to the sample toolbars in Figures 6.1 and 6.2, you'll see that it's good practice to group together functionally related buttons along the toolbar. The question is, how are we going to implement this?

The solution that I adopted was to give a special meaning to a bitmap resource ID of zero. Effectively, we've already given a special meaning to the value −1, by using it to signify the end of the list of bitmap resource IDs. In a similar way, I've used the value zero to indicate that a gap should be left after the preceding bitmap. In essence, the code says to itself, 'OK, this zero means I should just move along a bit, and not load a bitmap.' Because the values zero and −1 have been used in this way, we obviously can't use any bitmaps with those particular resource IDs in our toolbar code. This is a very minor restriction, however.

Let's create a more comprehensive-looking toolbar by using all ten of the available bitmaps from our .RES file. The code fragment below shows the new bitMaps ID array in the BARTEST application program. You can see that I've divided the bitmaps into three groups, inserting two zeros between each group to separate them clearly.

```
static int bitMaps [15] = { 1000, 1001, 0, 0, 1002, 1003, 1004,
                            1005, 1006, 1007, 0, 0, 1008, 1009, −1 };
```

To get this scheme to work, we need to add another array to the ToolBarRec data structure. This array, which I've given the rather nondescript name of edges, is used to store the horizontal starting position for every bitmap in the toolbar.

```
int    edges [MAXBUTTONS];        // bitmap positions
```

Using the edges array, we can rewrite the PaintCell routine to look like this:

```
//————————————————————————————————————————————————
// Name:    PaintCell
// Purpose: Paint a specified cell in the toolbar.
//————————————————————————————————————————————————

static void PASCAL PaintCell (HDC dc, PToolBarRec p, int cellNum)
{
     HDC hMemDC;
     HBITMAP hbm;

     hMemDC = CreateCompatibleDC (dc);
     hbm = SelectObject (hMemDC, p->bmHandles [cellNum]);
     BitBlt (dc, p->edges [cellNum], p->border, p->bmWidth,
          p->bmHeight, hMemDC, 0, 0, SRCCOPY);
     SelectObject (hMemDC, hbm);
     DeleteDC (hMemDC);
}
```

The PaintCell routine now uses the edges array to define the horizontal position of each bitmap. Before we can use this array, we need to initialize it and this is best done inside the LoadToolBitmaps routine as shown below:

```
//————————————————————————————————————————————————
// Name:    LoadToolBitmaps
// Purpose: Load all specified bitmaps into the ToolBarRec structure.
//————————————————————————————————————————————————

static int LONG LoadToolBitmaps (PToolBarRec p, LPINT pBitmaps,
                                 HANDLE hInstance)
{
     int x;
     BITMAP bm;
     int ret = -1;

     if (pBitmaps != NULL)
     {
       x = p->border;
       while (*pBitmaps != -1 && p->NumButtons < MAXBUTTONS - 1)
       {
         if (*pBitmaps == 0) x += p->border * 3;
         else
           {
             p->bmHandles [p->NumButtons] = LoadButtonBitmap (hInstance,
                                                     *pBitmaps);

             if (p->bmHandles [p->NumButtons] == NULL) return (ret);

             // If this is first bitmap, determine dimensions

             if (p->height == -1)
             {
                GetObject (p->bmHandles [p->NumButtons],
                        sizeof (BITMAP), &bm);

                p->bmWidth = bm.bmWidth / 2;
                p->bmHeight = bm.bmHeight;
                p->height = bm.bmHeight + (p->border * 2);
             }

             p->edges [p->NumButtons++] = x;
             x += p->bmWidth + p->border;
           }
         pBitmaps++;
       }
       if (p->NumButtons != 0) ret = 0;
     }

     return (ret);
}
```

Figure 6.9 Splitting the buttons into functional groups.

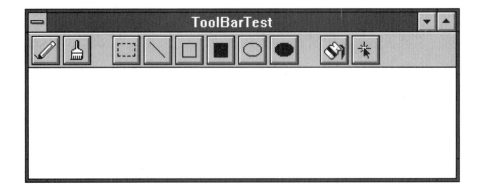

This routine works by maintaining a variable, x, which specifies the horizontal position of the next found bitmap. Each time round the loop, whenever a bitmap is loaded the value of the x variable is increased by the width of the bitmap and the border field. This gives a small gap between each bitmap. You may wish to adjust this to suit your own preferences. Whenever a bitmap resource ID of zero is encountered, the code simply adds three times the border variable to x and continues round the loop. Again, you can adjust this to suit your own taste. Be careful, however, not to base this 'shift factor' on the width of a bitmap, otherwise you won't be able to use an ID of zero until at least one bitmap has been loaded and the bmWidth field initialized. With these changes, the toolbar now looks as shown in Figure 6.9.

Responding to mouse clicks

Because the location of the bitmaps in the toolbar is no longer linear, we need a routine that will return a bounding rectangle for each of the bitmaps present. We'll need this routine in order to implement the hit-testing code when we respond to mouse clicks in the toolbar. This code is shown below.

```
//—————————————————————————————————————————————
// Name:     GetCellRect
// Purpose:  Return the frame rectangle for a given cell.
//—————————————————————————————————————————————

static void PASCAL GetCellRect (PToolBarRec p, int cellNum, LPRECT r)
{
    r−>left = p−>edges [cellNum];
    r−>right = r−>left + p−>bmWidth;
    r−>top = p−>border;
    r−>bottom = r−>top + p−>bmHeight;
}
```

With the GetCellRect routine as a basis, we can now write a hit-testing routine, ButtonHitTest, which tests for a mouse click on any button in the toolbar. If the mouse was clicked on a button, the routine returns the number of the button. If the mouse didn't land on any button, a value of −1 is returned.

```
//—————————————————————————————————————————————————————————
// Name:    ButtonHitTest
// Purpose: Test for a hit on any button in the toolbar.
//—————————————————————————————————————————————————————————
static int PASCAL ButtonHitTest (PToolBarRec p, LPARAM lParam)
{
    RECT r;
    POINT pt;
    int buttonNum;

    pt.x = LOWORD (lParam);
    pt.y = HIWORD (lParam);

    for (buttonNum = 0; buttonNum < p−>NumButtons; buttonNum++)
    {
      GetCellRect (p, buttonNum, &r);
      if (PtInRect (&r, pt)) return (buttonNum);
    }

    return (−1);
}
```

Some programs make use of mouse clicks that aren't in the button parts of a toolbar. For example, Word for Windows will bring up an Options dialog if you double-click on the topmost (non-modal) toolbar. Double-clicking on the lower, modal toolbar will bring up a dialog that allows you to quickly change type characteristics such as superscript, strike through, font size and so forth. This is a useful shortcut, and you can get similar behavior in your own applications by watching for a result of −1 when you call the ButtonHitTest routine. You'll have to make a few minor modifications to the code here and, of course, if you want to use double clicks rather than just single clicks, you'll need to specify the CS_DBLCLKS style when the toolbar window class is registered.

Let's continue developing the hit-testing code by looking at the routine that's needed to handle WM_LBUTTONDOWN messages in the toolbar. Here's the code:

```
//—————————————————————————————————————————————————————————
// Name:       HandleButtonDown
// Purpose:    Handle mouse clicks in the toolbar.
//—————————————————————————————————————————————————————————
static LONG PASCAL HandleButtonDown (HWND Wnd, LPARAM lParam)
{
    RECT r;
    int buttonNum;
    PToolBarRec p;

    p = GetToolBarRec (Wnd);
    buttonNum = ButtonHitTest (p, lParam);
    if (buttonNum != −1)
    {
      SetCapture (Wnd);
      p−>CaptureButton = buttonNum;
      p−>CapturePressed = TRUE;
      GetCellRect (p, buttonNum, &r);
      InvalidateRect (Wnd, &r, FALSE);
    }
    return (0);
}
```

This routine is called directly from the ToolBarWndProc procedure whenever a WM_LBUTTONDOWN message is received. It tests for a hit on a particular mouse button and, if found, sets a couple of new variables in the ToolBarRec data structure. The first of these is called CaptureButton. This is an integer variable that contains the number of the toolbar button that's got the capture.

Because buttons are numbered from zero, we need some way of discriminating between button zero having the capture and no button having the capture. We do this by setting the CaptureButton variable to −1 if no button has the capture. This must be done in the InitToolBarWindow code when the toolbar window is first created.

The second of our two new variables is called CapturePressed. It's only relevant if the CaptureButton variable is not equal to −1, that is, if a button currently has the mouse cursor. In this case, it indicates whether the capturing button is currently pushed in or released. If the mouse is held down and moved around, we'll use this variable to indicate whether the button should be drawn in a pushed-in or released state.

Note

If you make these changes to the above code and then try clicking the mouse on one of the toolbar controls, you won't find the result very satisfying – in fact, you'll cause Windows to hang up! This is because we've used the SetCapture routine without a corresponding call to ReleaseCapture. SetCapture is an innocent-looking little routine, but it needs to be used with a great deal of care. Don't EVER call SetCapture without making a corresponding call to ReleaseCapture! Because we've called SetCapture in response to a mouse-down event, we need to call ReleaseCapture when a mouse-up event (WM_LBUTTONUP) is received. Here's the code to do it:

```
//----------------------------------------------------------------
// Name:     HandleButtonUp
// Purpose:  Handle mouse ups in the toolbar.
//----------------------------------------------------------------
static LONG PASCAL HandleButtonUp (HWND Wnd, LPARAM lParam)
{
    RECT r;
    PToolBarRec p;

    p = GetToolBarRec (Wnd);
    if (p->CaptureButton != −1)
    {
      ReleaseCapture();
      if (p->CapturePressed)
      {
        GetCellRect (p, p->CaptureButton, &r);
        InvalidateRect (Wnd, &r, FALSE);
      }

      p->CapturePressed = FALSE;
      p->CaptureButton = −1;
    }

    return (0);
}
```

Like the HandleButtonDown routine, this code is called directly from the ToolBarWndProc routine. It releases the mouse capture and restores the state of the CapturePressed and CaptureButton variables. These two routines together maintain the variables that we need in order to determine whether or not the captured button is pressed.

Despite these new routines, clicking on a button won't make the button appear to 'push in' until we make the appropriate changes to the drawing code. As you'll remember from Chapter 2, we need to display the leftmost half of the button bitmap to make it appear raised, and the rightmost half of the button to make it appear to be pushed in.

```
//——————————————————————————————————————————————————
// Name:     PaintCell
// Purpose:  Paint a specified cell in the toolbar.
//——————————————————————————————————————————————————

static void PASCAL PaintCell (HDC dc, PToolBarRec p, int cellNum)
{
    int XSrc;
    HDC hMemDC;
    HBITMAP hbm;

    hMemDC = CreateCompatibleDC (dc);
    hbm = SelectObject (hMemDC, p->bmHandles [cellNum]);
    XSrc = (cellNum == p->CaptureButton && p->CapturePressed) ? p->bmWidth : 0;
    BitBlt (dc, p->edges [cellNum], p->border, p->bmWidth,
        p->bmHeight, hMemDC, XSrc, 0, SRCCOPY);
    SelectObject (hMemDC, hbm);
    DeleteDC (hMemDC);
}
```

This is taken care of by the PaintCell routine shown above. In this code, the XSrc variable is set up to select between the two different halves of the bitmap. If the button being displayed is the CaptureButton and the button is in the pressed-down state, the PaintCell routine draws the rightmost half of the bitmap. With this code in place, you'll be able to push buttons to your heart's content.

Figure 6.10 shows TOOLBAR3.C. The corresponding executable is BARTEST3.EXE and the source file for the application is BARTEST3.C. As ever, all these files can be found on the accompanying disk.

```
/* TOOLBAR3.C */

// © 1994 Dave Jewell and Addison-Wesley, ALL RIGHTS RESERVED

#include    <mem.h>
#include    <windows.h>
#include    "toolbar.h"
#include    "sclaslib.h"

static char szClassName[ ] = "ToolBar";        // name of our window class
static char szHookName[ ] = "ToolBarHook";  // name of our hook

#define    MAXBUTTONS    40              // maximum buttons per window

typedef struct ToolBarRec
{
    int        border;                    // width of border
    int        height;                    // height of the toolbar
    int        bmWidth;                   // width of bitmaps
    int        bmHeight;                  // height of bitmaps
    int        NumButtons;                // number of buttons
    int        CaptureButton;             // capturing button
    BOOL       CapturePressed;            // if 'CaptureButton' down
    int        edges [MAXBUTTONS];        // bitmap positions
```

Figure 6.10 The TOOLBAR3.C code with the mouse handling code in place.

```
        HANDLE   bmHandles [MAXBUTTONS];  // bitmap handles
}       ToolBarRec, NEAR * PToolBarRec;

static LONG hookKey;

//————————————————————————————————————————————————————————————————
// Name:     GetToolBarRec
// Purpose:  Given a window handle, return a pointer to the corresponding
//           toolbar record.
//————————————————————————————————————————————————————————————————

static PToolBarRec PASCAL GetToolBarRec (HWND Wnd)
{
        return (PToolBarRec) GetWindowWord (Wnd, 0);
}

//————————————————————————————————————————————————————————————————
// Name:     ResizeWindow
// Purpose:  Routine to force toolbar to proper size and position.
//————————————————————————————————————————————————————————————————

static void PASCAL ResizeWindow (HWND Wnd)
{
        RECT r;
        PToolBarRec p;

        p = GetToolBarRec (Wnd);
        GetClientRect (GetParent (Wnd), &r);
        SetWindowPos (Wnd, 0, 0, 0, r.right, p->height, SWP_NOZORDER);
}

//————————————————————————————————————————————————————————————————
// Name:     SubclassParentWndProc
// Purpose:  Subclassing routine for the main application window.
//————————————————————————————————————————————————————————————————

#pragma argsused

LONG FAR PASCAL _export SubclassParentWndProc (HWND Wnd, WORD Msg,
                                               WPARAM wParam,
                                               LPARAM lParam)
{
        if (Msg == WM_SIZE) ResizeWindow (GetToolBarWindow (Wnd));
        return CallOldProc (Wnd, Msg, wParam, lParam, hookKey);
}

//————————————————————————————————————————————————————————————————
// Name:     ColorFix
// Purpose:  Fix up a color value for the LoadButtonBitmap routine.
//————————————————————————————————————————————————————————————————

static COLORREF PASCAL ColorFix (COLORREF color)
{
        return RGB (GetBValue (color), GetGValue (color), GetRValue (color));
}

//————————————————————————————————————————————————————————————————
// Name:     LoadButtonBitmap
// Purpose:  Load a bitmap and tweak it for current system colors.
//————————————————————————————————————————————————————————————————

static HBITMAP PASCAL LoadButtonBitmap (HANDLE hInstance, int bmID)
{
        HDC dc;
        HBITMAP hbm;
        HANDLE hRes;
        LPDWORD lprgb;
        LPVOID lpb;
        LPBITMAPINFOHEADER lpbi;

hRes = LoadResource (hInstance, FindResource (hInstance,
                        MAKEINTRESOURCE(bmID), RT_BITMAP));
```

```
            lpbi = (LPBITMAPINFOHEADER) LockResource (hRes);
            if (lpbi == NULL) return (NULL);

            lprgb = (LPDWORD) ((LPSTR) lpbi + (int) lpbi->biSize);
            lpb = (LPVOID) (lprgb + 16);

            lprgb [0] = ColorFix (GetSysColor (COLOR_WINDOWTEXT));      // Black
            lprgb [8] = ColorFix (GetSysColor (COLOR_BTNFACE));        // Light gray
            lprgb [7] = ColorFix (GetSysColor (COLOR_BTNSHADOW));      // Gray
            lprgb [15] = ColorFix (GetSysColor (COLOR_BTNHIGHLIGHT)); // White

            dc = GetDC (NULL);
            hbm = CreateDIBitmap (dc, lpbi, CBM_INIT, lpb,
                                  (LPBITMAPINFO) lpbi, DIB_RGB_COLORS);

            ReleaseDC (NULL, dc);
            GlobalUnlock (hRes);
            FreeResource (hRes);
            return (hbm);
}

//---------------------------------------------------------------
// Name:    LoadToolBitmaps
// Purpose: Load all specified bitmaps into the ToolBarRec structure.
//---------------------------------------------------------------

static int LONG LoadToolBitmaps (PToolBarRec p, LPINT pBitmaps,
                                 HANDLE hInstance)
{
        int x;
        BITMAP bm;
        int ret = -1;

        if (pBitmaps != NULL)
        {
           x = p->border;
           while (*pBitmaps != -1 && p->NumButtons < MAXBUTTONS - 1)
           {
              if (*pBitmaps == 0) x += p->border * 3;
              else
              {
                 p->bmHandles [p->NumButtons] = LoadButtonBitmap (hInstance,
                                                                  *pBitmaps);

                 if (p->bmHandles [p->NumButtons] == NULL) return (ret);

                 // If this is first bitmap, determine dimensions

                 if (p->height == -1)
                 {
                    GetObject (p->bmHandles [p->NumButtons],
                               sizeof (BITMAP), &bm);

                    p->bmWidth = bm.bmWidth / 2;
                    p->bmHeight = bm.bmHeight;
                    p->height = bm.bmHeight + (p->border * 2);

                 }

                 p->edges [p->NumButtons++] = x;
                 x += p->bmWidth + p->border;
              }

              pBitmaps++;
           }

           if (p->NumButtons != 0) ret = 0;

        }

        return (ret);

}
```

```
//----------------------------------------------------------------
// Name:     InitToolBarWindow
// Purpose:  Initialization code for setting up the toolbar window.
//----------------------------------------------------------------

static LONG PASCAL InitToolBarWindow (HWND Wnd, LONG lParam)
{
    LPCSTR text;
    LPINT pBitmaps;
    PToolBarRec p;
    LONG res = -1L;
    HANDLE hInstance;

    p = (PToolBarRec) LocalAlloc (LPTR, sizeof (ToolBarRec));
    if (p != NULL)
    {
        // Initialize the ToolBarRec data structure

        p->CaptureButton = -1;
        p->border = (GetSystemMetrics (SM_CXFRAME) + 3) / 2;
        p->height = -1;
        SetWindowWord (Wnd, 0, (WORD) p);

        // Load the various bitmaps

        pBitmaps = (LPINT) ((LPCREATESTRUCT) lParam)->lpCreateParams;
        hInstance = GetWindowWord (Wnd, GWW_HINSTANCE);

        if (LoadToolBitmaps (p, pBitmaps, hInstance) == 0)
        {
            ResizeWindow (Wnd);
            SetProp (GetParent (Wnd), szClassName, Wnd);
            hookKey = HookWindow (GetParent (Wnd),
                            (FARPROC) SubclassParentWndProc,
                            szHookName);

            res = 0;
        }
    }

    return (res);
}

//----------------------------------------------------------------
// Name:     GetCellRect
// Purpose:  Return the frame rectangle for a given cell.
//----------------------------------------------------------------

static void PASCAL GetCellRect (PToolBarRec p, int cellNum, LPRECT r)
{
    r->left = p->edges [cellNum];
    r->right = r->left + p->bmWidth;
    r->top = p->border;
    r->bottom = r->top + p->bmHeight;
}

//----------------------------------------------------------------
// Name:     PaintCell
// Purpose:  Paint a specified cell in the toolbar.
//----------------------------------------------------------------

static void PASCAL PaintCell (HDC dc, PToolBarRec p, int cellNum)
{
    int XSrc;
    HDC hMemDC;
    HBITMAP hbm;

    hMemDC = CreateCompatibleDC (dc);
    hbm = SelectObject (hMemDC, p->bmHandles [cellNum]);
    XSrc = (cellNum == p->CaptureButton && p->CapturePressed) ? p->bmWidth : 0;
```

```
        BitBlt (dc, p−>edges [cellNum], p−>border, p−>bmWidth,
            p−>bmHeight, hMemDC, XSrc, 0, SRCCOPY);
        SelectObject (hMemDC, hbm);
        DeleteDC (hMemDC);
}

//────────────────────────────────────────────────────────────
// Name:    ToolBarPaint
// Purpose: This routine is responsible for painting the tool bar.
//────────────────────────────────────────────────────────────

static int PASCAL ToolBarPaint (HWND Wnd)
{
        int i;
        RECT r;
        PToolBarRec p;
        PAINTSTRUCT ps;

        BeginPaint (Wnd, &ps);
        p = GetToolBarRec (Wnd);

        // First, draw the bottom edge of the toolbar

        GetClientRect (Wnd, &r);
        PatBlt (ps.hdc, 0, r.bottom − 1, r.right − r.left, 1, BLACKNESS);
        PatBlt (ps.hdc, 0, 0, r.right − r.left, 1, WHITENESS);

        // Now draw each cell in turn

        for (i = 0; i < p−>NumButtons; i++)
            PaintCell (ps.hdc, p, i);

        EndPaint (Wnd, &ps);
        return (0);
}

//────────────────────────────────────────────────────────────
// Name:    DestroyToolBarWindow
// Purpose: Clean-up code for the toolbar window.
//────────────────────────────────────────────────────────────

static int PASCAL DestroyToolBarWindow (HWND Wnd)
{
        int i;
        PToolBarRec p;

        p = GetToolBarRec (Wnd);
        RemoveProp (GetParent (Wnd), szClassName);
        UnHookWindow (GetParent (Wnd), hookKey);

        // Deallocate bitmap handles

        for (i = 0; i < p−>NumButtons; i++)
            DeleteObject (p−>bmHandles [i]);

        LocalFree ((HLOCAL) p);
        return (0);
}

//────────────────────────────────────────────────────────────
// Name:    ButtonHitTest
// Purpose: Test for a hit on any button in the toolbar.
//────────────────────────────────────────────────────────────

static int PASCAL ButtonHitTest (PToolBarRec p, LPARAM lParam)
{
        RECT r;
        POINT pt;
        int buttonNum;
```

```
          pt.x = LOWORD (lParam);
          pt.y = HIWORD (lParam);

          for (buttonNum = 0; buttonNum < p−>NumButtons; buttonNum++)
          {
            GetCellRect (p, buttonNum, &r);
            if (PtInRect (&r, pt)) return (buttonNum);
          }

          return (−1);
}
```

```
//───────────────────────────────────────────────────────────────────
// Name:     HandleButtonDown
// Purpose:  Handle mouse clicks in the toolbar.
//───────────────────────────────────────────────────────────────────

static LONG PASCAL HandleButtonDown (HWND Wnd, LPARAM lParam)
{
          RECT r;
          int buttonNum;
          PToolBarRec p;

          p = GetToolBarRec (Wnd);
          buttonNum = ButtonHitTest (p, lParam);
          if (buttonNum != −1)
          {
            SetCapture (Wnd);
            p−>CaptureButton = buttonNum;
            p−>CapturePressed = TRUE;
            GetCellRect (p, buttonNum, &r);
            InvalidateRect (Wnd, &r, FALSE);
          }

          return (0);
}
```

```
//───────────────────────────────────────────────────────────────────
// Name:     HandleButtonUp
// Purpose:  Handle mouse ups in the toolbar.
//───────────────────────────────────────────────────────────────────

static LONG PASCAL HandleButtonUp (HWND Wnd, LPARAM lParam)
{
          RECT r;
          PToolBarRec p;

          p = GetToolBarRec (Wnd);
          if (p−>CaptureButton != −1)
          {
            ReleaseCapture();
            if (p−>CapturePressed)
            {
              GetCellRect (p, p−>CaptureButton, &r);
              InvalidateRect (Wnd, &r, FALSE);
            }

            p−>CapturePressed = FALSE;
            p−>CaptureButton = −1;
          }

          return (0);
}
```

```
//───────────────────────────────────────────────────────────────────
// Name:     ToolBarWndProc
// Purpose:  Window procedure for toolbar windows.
//───────────────────────────────────────────────────────────────────
```

```
LONG FAR PASCAL _export ToolBarWndProc (HWND Wnd, WORD Msg,
                                        WPARAM wParam, LPARAM lParam)
{
    switch (Msg)
    {
      case WM_LBUTTONDOWN:

      return HandleButtonDown (Wnd, lParam);

      case WM_LBUTTONUP:

      return HandleButtonUp (Wnd, lParam);

      case WM_PAINT:

      return ToolBarPaint (Wnd);

      case WM_CREATE:

      return InitToolBarWindow (Wnd, lParam);

      case WM_DESTROY:

      return DestroyToolBarWindow (Wnd);
    }

    return DefWindowProc (Wnd, Msg, wParam, lParam);
}

//--------------------------------------------------------------------
// Name:    RegisterToolBar
// Purpose: Register the toolbar window procedure.
//--------------------------------------------------------------------
static BOOL PASCAL RegisterToolBar (HANDLE hInstance)
{
    WNDCLASS cls;

    if (GetClassInfo (hInstance, szClassName, &cls) == 0)
    {
        cls.style           = 0;
        cls.lpfnWndProc     = (WNDPROC) ToolBarWndProc;
        cls.cbClsExtra      = 0;
        cls.cbWndExtra      = sizeof (void NEAR *);
        cls.hInstance       = hInstance;
        cls.hIcon           = 0;
        cls.hCursor         = LoadCursor (NULL, IDC_ARROW);
        cls.hbrBackground   = COLOR_BTNFACE + 1;
        cls.lpszMenuName    = NULL;
        cls.lpszClassName   = szClassName;

        return RegisterClass (&cls);
    }

    return TRUE;
}

//--------------------------------------------------------------------
// Name:    GetToolBarWindow
// Purpose: Return the handle of this window's tool bar.
//--------------------------------------------------------------------

HWND PASCAL GetToolBarWindow (HWND hWndParent)
{
    if (hWndParent != NULL && IsWindow (hWndParent))
        return GetProp (hWndParent, szClassName);
    else
        return NULL;
}
```

```
//--------------------------------------------------------------------------
// Name:    CreateToolBarWindow
// Purpose: Create a toolbar window and attach it to the designated parent.
//--------------------------------------------------------------------------

HWND PASCAL CreateToolBarWindow (HANDLE hInstance, HWND hWndParent,
                                 LPINT lpButtons)
{
      HWND Wnd = NULL;

      // Check that we've got a valid parent window

      if (hWndParent != NULL && IsWindow (hWndParent))
      {
         // Ok so far, but has window already got a toolbar?

        Wnd = GetToolBarWindow (hWndParent);
        if (Wnd == NULL)
          if (RegisterToolBar (hInstance))
            Wnd = CreateWindow (szClassName, "", WS_CHILD | WS_VISIBLE,
                                0, 0, 0, 0, hWndParent, NULL, hInstance,
                                lpButtons);
      }

      return (Wnd);
}
```

If you try out the BARTEST3.EXE program, you'll see that it's possible to push down a toolbar button and then, with the mouse still held down, drag the mouse right away from the button. The button will stay pressed down, just as if the mouse were on top of it, and won't 'pop up' again until the mouse is released, even if the mouse happens to be over the other side of the screen! This is unprofessional and confusing to the user. The proper thing to do is to make the button pop back up as soon as the mouse moves away from it. This is a visual cue to the user – it's a way of indicating that the action just taken is not irreversible. It shows the user that the button click can be canceled by simply dragging the mouse away from the button and releasing it.

We can modify the code to behave in this way by intercepting the WM_MOUSE-MOVE message within the toolbar. In fact, we implemented similar code to handle the check box and radio button subclassers in Chapter 5. Here's the new code below. It needs to be called directly from the ToolBarWndProc in response to a WM_MOUSEMOVE message.

```
//--------------------------------------------------------------------------
// Name:    HandleMouseMoves
// Purpose: Handle mouse movement in the toolbar.
//--------------------------------------------------------------------------

static LONG PASCAL HandleMouseMoves (HWND Wnd, LPARAM lParam)
{
      RECT r;
      int buttonNum;
      PToolBarRec p;

      p = GetToolBarRec (Wnd);
      if (p->CaptureButton != -1)
      {
         buttonNum = ButtonHitTest (p, lParam);
```

```
                  if (buttonNum == p->CaptureButton)
                  {
                     if (p->CapturePressed == FALSE)
                     {
                        p->CapturePressed = TRUE;
                        GetCellRect (p, p->CaptureButton, &r);
                        InvalidateRect (Wnd, &r, FALSE);
                     }
                  }
                  else
                  {
                     if (p->CapturePressed == TRUE)
                     {
                        p->CapturePressed = FALSE;
                        GetCellRect (p, p->CaptureButton, &r);
                        InvalidateRect (Wnd, &r, FALSE);
                     }
                  }

               }

         return (0);
      }
```

With this code in place, the toolbar buttons will behave properly, popping back up as soon as the mouse is moved away from them. Not all Windows programmers bother to put this code in – for example, try the same test on the drive buttons in the Windows File Manager. You'll see that you can keep a drive button held down while moving the mouse right outside of the File Manager window. To be fair, though, the drive selection is ignored if the mouse wasn't inside the drive button at the time that it was released.

Making your buttons sticky

So far so good. At this stage, we've got a neat little toolbar that could easily be used to implement one-for-one menu selection shortcuts. In other words, it would be simple to arrange for a WM_COMMAND message to be sent to the parent window each time a button was released. For real flexibility, however, we want our toolbar to be able to support modal or 'sticky' buttons, as discussed at the beginning of the chapter. A sticky button stays down when it's pressed and must be pushed again to release it. A sticky button indicates to the user that some persistent change has taken place in the operation of the program.

Ideally, we want to be able to make any of the toolbar buttons modal. In order to do this, we really need an array of flag values, one for each of the buttons in the toolbar. We also need to define a couple of constants which relate to the contents of the flags field. The end result looks like this:

```
// Constants for the flags field

#define      FPUSHED      0x80      // If set, button is pushed
#define      FSTICKY      0x40      // If set, button is modal

typedef struct ToolBarRec
{
     int          border;                // width of border
     int          height;                // height of the toolbar
```

```
        int       bmWidth;                 // width of bitmaps
        int       bmHeight;                // height of bitmaps
        int       NumButtons;              // number of buttons
        int       CaptureButton;           // capturing button
        BOOL      CapturePressed;          // if 'CaptureButton' down
        int       edges [MAXBUTTONS];      // bitmap positions
        HANDLE    bmHandles [MAXBUTTONS];  // bitmap handles
        BYTE      flags [MAXBUTTONS];      // flags for each button
    } ToolBarRec, NEAR * PToolBarRec;
```

The FPUSHED constant is used to indicate whether a button is currently in a pushed-in state. This is not to be confused with the CapturePressed field, which only applies to the currently captured button. Similarly, the FSTICKY flag indicates whether a particular button is modal or non-modal. By default, a newly created toolbar contains only non-pushed, non-modal buttons.

To exploit these flags, we need to make a few changes to the existing code. Obviously, the PaintCell routine needs to be modified so that it will examine the FPUSHED flag to see how a button should be drawn. There's a slight wrinkle here – what do we do if the button being painted happens to be the currently captured button? The code below shows how to handle this problem.

```
//--------------------------------------------------------------------
// Name:    PaintCell
// Purpose: Paint a specified cell in the toolbar.
//--------------------------------------------------------------------
static void PASCAL PaintCell (HDC dc, PToolBarRec p, int cellNum)
{
        int XSrc;
        HDC hMemDC;
        HBITMAP hbm;
        BOOL fDown;

        fDown = (p−>flags [cellNum] & FPUSHED) ? TRUE : FALSE;
        if (cellNum == p−>CaptureButton && p−>CapturePressed) fDown = !fDown;
        XSrc = fDown ? p−>bmWidth : 0;

        hMemDC = CreateCompatibleDC (dc);
        hbm = SelectObject (hMemDC, p−>bmHandles [cellNum]);
        BitBlt (dc, p−>edges [cellNum], p−>border, p−>bmWidth,
                  p−>bmHeight, hMemDC, XSrc, 0, SRCCOPY);
        SelectObject (hMemDC, hbm);
        DeleteDC (hMemDC);
}
```

Initially, the fDown flag is set up according to the state of the FPUSHED flag. If the button being drawn is the captured button and it happens to be pushed in, then the current 'pushed-in' state is inverted. This might not make much sense at first glance, but think about it for a moment. If we happen to have clicked the mouse down on a button that wasn't previously pushed-in, then we need to draw the button in a pushed-in state while the mouse is over it and a popped-out state otherwise. On the other hand, if we've just clicked the mouse on a button that was previously pushed in, then it needs to be drawn in a popped-out state while the mouse is over it, and pushed in otherwise! That's why we need the Boolean NOT operation in the above code.

We also need to make some changes to the code that handles mouse button up events. This is so that the FPUSHED flag can be set in a sticky, modal button. Obviously, for non-modal buttons, we don't set this flag and the appearance of the button returns to normal as soon as the mouse is released.

```
//--------------------------------------------------------------------------------
// Name:    HandleButtonUp
// Purpose:  Handle mouse ups in the toolbar.
//--------------------------------------------------------------------------------

#pragma argsused

static LONG PASCAL HandleButtonUp (HWND Wnd, LPARAM lParam)
{
     PToolBarRec p;

     p = GetToolBarRec (Wnd);
     if (p->CaptureButton != −1)
     {
       ReleaseCapture();
       if (p->CapturePressed) ClickButton (Wnd, p, p->CaptureButton);
       p->CapturePressed = FALSE;
       p->CaptureButton = −1;
     }

     return (0);
}
```

The revised code for the HandleButtonUp routine is shown above. It now calls a new routine, ClickButton, which is responsible for actually changing the FPUSHED state of a specific toolbar button. The reason why we've put this code into a separate routine is one of reusability; we're also going to need a new API routine that will enable the application program to press toolbar buttons under program control. In order to do this, it will make use of the ClickButton routine.

```
//--------------------------------------------------------------------------------
// Name:    ClickButton
// Purpose:  Adjust state of a button and send message to parent.
//--------------------------------------------------------------------------------

static void PASCAL ClickButton (HWND Wnd, PToolBarRec p, int ClickedButton)
{
     RECT r;

     if (p->flags [ClickedButton] & FSTICKY)
        p->flags [ClickedButton] ^= FPUSHED;

     // Redraw the button in its new state

     GetCellRect (p, ClickedButton, &r);
     InvalidateRect (Wnd, &r, FALSE);

     // Send message to parent window

     SendMessage (GetParent (Wnd), WM_COMMAND, p->bmIDS [ClickedButton],
                  p->flags [ClickedButton] & FPUSHED);
}
```

The ClickButton routine toggles the FPUSHED state of sticky buttons, but leaves non-sticky buttons alone. For all types of button, it sends a WM_COMMAND message to the parent window that owns the toolbar. This, of course, will be the main application window. For non-modal buttons, the lParam field of the WM_COMMAND message will always be zero. For modal buttons, on the other hand, the lParam field is zero if the button has just been released, and non-zero if the button has been pushed. In all cases, the wParam field will contain the command ID of the button in question, which just happens to be the same number as the resource ID of that particular button's bitmap. As you can see, this number is obtained from a new field, pbmIDS, in the ToolBarRec data structure. This field is defined as below:

```
WORD          bmIDS [MAXBUTTONS];        // ID of each button
```

Of course, having defined a new array, we need to ensure that it's properly initialized. (Have you ever noticed that computer programming is a bit like home decorating – one job always seems to lead to another?!) The final code for the LoadToolBitmaps routine is shown below. This code now initializes the bmIDS array as each bitmap is loaded into memory.

```
//------------------------------------------------------------
// Name:    LoadToolBitmaps
// Purpose: Load all specified bitmaps into the ToolBarRec structure.
//------------------------------------------------------------

static int LONG LoadToolBitmaps (PToolBarRec p, LPINT pBitmaps,
                                 HANDLE hInstance)
{
    int x;
    BITMAP bm;
    int ret = -1;

    if (pBitmaps != NULL)
    {
        x = p->border;
        while (*pBitmaps != -1 && p->NumButtons < MAXBUTTONS - 1)
        {
            if (*pBitmaps == 0) x += p->border * 3;
            else
            {
                p->bmIDS [p->NumButtons] = *pBitmaps;
                p->bmHandles [p->NumButtons] = LoadButtonBitmap (hInstance,
                                                            *pBitmaps);

                if (p->bmHandles [p->NumButtons] == NULL) return (ret);

                // If this is first bitmap, determine dimensions

                if (p->height == -1)
                {
                    GetObject (p->bmHandles [p->NumButtons],
                            sizeof (BITMAP), &bm);
                    p->bmWidth = bm.bmWidth / 2;
                    p->bmHeight = bm.bmHeight;
                    p->height = bm.bmHeight + (p->border * 2);

                }

                p->edges [p->NumButtons++] = x;
                x += p->bmWidth + p->border;
            }

            pBitmaps++;
        }

        if (p->NumButtons != 0) ret = 0;
    }

    return (ret);
}
```

That completes the implementation of the sticky button code apart from the one small detail – we have no way of making a button modal. A new API routine is called for!

```
//------------------------------------------------------------
// Name:    SetButtonModal
// Purpose: Make a button modal or non-modal.
//------------------------------------------------------------

int PASCAL SetButtonModal (HWND hWndParent, int buttonNum, BOOL fModal)
```

```
{
    int ret;
    HWND Wnd;
    PToolBarRec p;

    ret = 0;
    Wnd = GetToolBarWindow (hWndParent);
    p = GetToolBarRec (Wnd);
    if (Wnd != NULL && p != NULL && buttonNum < p->NumButtons)
    {
        ret = (p->flags [buttonNum] & FSTICKY) ? TRUE : FALSE;
        p->flags [buttonNum] &= ~FSTICKY;
        if (fModal) p->flags [buttonNum] |= FSTICKY;
    }

    return (ret);
}
```

The above routine, SetButtonModal, has been added to the programming interface, and therefore appears in the revised header file, TOOLBAR3.H. As parameters,
it takes the handle of the application window, the number of the wanted button, and
a flag that indicates whether the button should be made modal or non-modal. As the
function return result, SetButtonModal returns TRUE if the button was previously
modal, and FALSE if it was previously non-modal.

In the above code, I don't discriminate between an error condition (for example,
button number out of range, invalid window handle and so forth) and a zero function
result. If you want to do this, then you can just set the initial value of the ret local
variable to −1 so as to return this number if an error occurs.

In order to test the new routine, I've added a couple of calls to SetButtonModal
that make the first and second buttons in the toolbar sticky. This code needs
to be added to the BARTEST source code immediately after the call to
CreateToolBarWindow, like this:

```
if (CreateToolBarWindow (hInstance, Wnd, bitMaps) != NULL)
{
    // Make button 0 and 1 modal

    SetButtonModal (Wnd, 0, TRUE);
    SetButtonModal (Wnd, 1, TRUE);
}
```

With these changes, the toolbar source code now looks as shown in Figure 6.11,
the application source code is shown in Figure 6.12 and the revised header file in
Figure 6.13.

```
/* TOOLBAR4.C */

// © 1994 Dave Jewell and Addison-Wesley, ALL RIGHTS RESERVED

#include    <mem.h>
#include    <windows.h>
#include    "toolbar.h"
#include    "sclaslib.h"

static char szClassName[ ] = "ToolBar";        // name of our window class
static char szHookName[ ] = "ToolBarHook";     // name of our hook

#define    MAXBUTTONS    40                     // maximum buttons per window
```

Figure 6.11   TOOLBAR4.C:
the toolbar code with support
for modal and non-modal
buttons

```
// Constants for the flags field

#define    FPUSHED         0x80            // If set, button is pushed
#define    FSTICKY         0x40            // If set, button is modal

typedef struct ToolBarRec
{
        int      border;                           // width of border
        int      height;                           // height of the toolbar
        int      bmWidth;                          // width of bitmaps
        int      bmHeight;                         // height of bitmaps
        int      NumButtons;                       // number of buttons
        int      CaptureButton;                    // capturing button
        BOOL     CapturePressed;                   // if 'CaptureButton' down
        int      edges [MAXBUTTONS];               // bitmap positions
        HANDLE   bmHandles [MAXBUTTONS];           // bitmap handles
        WORD     bmIDS [MAXBUTTONS];               // ID of each button
        BYTE     flags [MAXBUTTONS];               // flags for each button

}  ToolBarRec, NEAR * PToolBarRec;

static LONG hookKey;

//————————————————————————————————————————————————————————————————————
// Name:    GetToolBarRec
// Purpose: Given a window handle, return a pointer to the corresponding
//          toolbar record.
//————————————————————————————————————————————————————————————————————

static PToolBarRec PASCAL GetToolBarRec (HWND Wnd)
{
        return (PToolBarRec) GetWindowWord (Wnd, 0);
}

//————————————————————————————————————————————————————————————————————
// Name:    ResizeWindow
// Purpose: Routine to force toolbar to proper size and position.
//————————————————————————————————————————————————————————————————————

static void PASCAL ResizeWindow (HWND Wnd)
{
        RECT r;
        PToolBarRec p;

        p = GetToolBarRec (Wnd);
        GetClientRect (GetParent (Wnd), &r);
        SetWindowPos (Wnd, 0, 0, 0, r.right, p—>height, SWP_NOZORDER);
}

//————————————————————————————————————————————————————————————————————
// Name:    SubclassParentWndProc
// Purpose: Subclassing routine for the main application window.
//————————————————————————————————————————————————————————————————————

#pragma argsused

LONG FAR PASCAL _export SubclassParentWndProc (HWND  Wnd,  WORD  Msg,
                                               WPARAM wParam, LPARAM
                                               lParam)

{
        if (Msg == WM_SIZE) ResizeWindow (GetToolBarWindow (Wnd));
        return CallOldProc (Wnd, Msg, wParam, lParam, hookKey);
}

//————————————————————————————————————————————————————————————————————
// Name:    ColorFix
// Purpose: Fix up a color value for the LoadButtonBitmap routine.
//————————————————————————————————————————————————————————————————————
```

```
static COLORREF PASCAL ColorFix (COLORREF color)
{
     return RGB (GetBValue (color), GetGValue (color), GetRValue (color));
}


//——————————————————————————————————————————————
// Name:    LoadButtonBitmap
// Purpose:  Load a bitmap and tweak it for current system colors.
//——————————————————————————————————————————————
static HBITMAP PASCAL LoadButtonBitmap (HANDLE hInstance, int bmID)
{
     HDC dc;
     HBITMAP hbm;
     HANDLE hRes;
     LPDWORD lprgb;
     LPVOID lpb;
     LPBITMAPINFOHEADER lpbi;

     hRes = LoadResource (hInstance, FindResource (hInstance,
                           MAKEINTRESOURCE(bmID), RT_BITMAP));
     lpbi = (LPBITMAPINFOHEADER) LockResource (hRes);
     if (lpbi == NULL) return (NULL);

     lprgb = (LPDWORD) ((LPSTR) lpbi + (int) lpbi->biSize);
     lpb = (LPVOID) (lprgb + 16);

     lprgb [0] = ColorFix (GetSysColor (COLOR_WINDOWTEXT));    // Black
     lprgb [8] = ColorFix (GetSysColor (COLOR_BTNFACE));       // Light gray
     lprgb [7] = ColorFix (GetSysColor (COLOR_BTNSHADOW));     // Gray
     lprgb [15] = ColorFix (GetSysColor (COLOR_BTNHIGHLIGHT));// White

     dc = GetDC (NULL);
     hbm = CreateDIBitmap (dc, lpbi, CBM_INIT, lpb,
                           (LPBITMAPINFO) lpbi, DIB_RGB_COLORS);

     ReleaseDC (NULL, dc);
     GlobalUnlock (hRes);
     FreeResource (hRes);
     return (hbm);
}


//——————————————————————————————————————————————
// Name:    LoadToolBitmaps
// Purpose:  Load all specified bitmaps into the ToolBarRec structure.
//——————————————————————————————————————————————
static int LONG LoadToolBitmaps (PToolBarRec p, LPINT pBitmaps,
                           HANDLE hInstance)
{
     int x;
     BITMAP bm;
     int ret = -1;

     if (pBitmaps != NULL)
     {
       x = p->border;
       while (*pBitmaps != -1 && p->NumButtons < MAXBUTTONS - 1)
       {
         if (*pBitmaps == 0) x += p->border * 3;
         else
         {
           p->bmIDS [p->NumButtons] = *pBitmaps;
           p->bmHandles [p->NumButtons] = LoadButtonBitmap (hInstance,
                                                *pBitmaps);

           if (p->bmHandles [p->NumButtons] == NULL) return (ret);

           // If this is first bitmap, determine dimensions
```

```
                        if (p->height == -1)
                        {
                            GetObject (p->bmHandles [p->NumButtons],
                                        sizeof (BITMAP), &bm);

                            p->bmWidth = bm.bmWidth / 2;
                            p->bmHeight = bm.bmHeight;
                            p->height = bm.bmHeight + (p->border * 2);

                        }

                        p->edges [p->NumButtons++] = x;
                        x += p->bmWidth + p->border;
                    }

                    pBitmaps++;
                }

            if (p->NumButtons != 0) ret = 0;
        }

        return (ret);
}

//------------------------------------------------------------------
// Name:      InitToolBarWindow
// Purpose:   Initialization code for setting up the toolbar window.
//------------------------------------------------------------------

static LONG PASCAL InitToolBarWindow (HWND Wnd, LONG lParam)
{
        LPCSTR text;
        LPINT pBitmaps;
        PToolBarRec p;
        LONG res = -1L;
        HANDLE hInstance;

        p = (PToolBarRec) LocalAlloc (LPTR, sizeof (ToolBarRec));
        if (p != NULL)
        {
            // Initialize the ToolBarRec data structure

            p->CaptureButton = -1;
            p->border = (GetSystemMetrics (SM_CXFRAME) + 3) / 2;
            p->height = -1;
            SetWindowWord (Wnd, 0, (WORD) p);

            // Load the various bitmaps

            pBitmaps = (LPINT) ((LPCREATESTRUCT) lParam)->lpCreateParams;
            hInstance = GetWindowWord (Wnd, GWW_HINSTANCE);

            if (LoadToolBitmaps (p, pBitmaps, hInstance) == 0)
            {
                ResizeWindow (Wnd);
                SetProp (GetParent (Wnd), szClassName, Wnd);
                hookKey = HookWindow (GetParent (Wnd),
                                        (FARPROC) SubclassParentWndProc,
                                        szHookName);
                res = 0;
            }
        }

        return (res);
}

//------------------------------------------------------------------
// Name:      GetCellRect
// Purpose:   Return the frame rectangle for a given cell.
//------------------------------------------------------------------
```

```
static void PASCAL GetCellRect (PToolBarRec p, int cellNum, LPRECT r)
{
    r->left = p->edges [cellNum];
    r->right = r->left + p->bmWidth;
    r->top = p->border;
    r->bottom = r->top + p->bmHeight;
}

//———————————————————————————————————————————————
// Name:    PaintCell
// Purpose: Paint a specified cell in the toolbar.
//———————————————————————————————————————————————

static void PASCAL PaintCell (HDC dc, PToolBarRec p, int cellNum)
{
    int XSrc;
    HDC hMemDC;
    HBITMAP hbm;
    BOOL fDown;

    fDown = (p->flags [cellNum] & FPUSHED) ? TRUE : FALSE;
    if (cellNum == p->CaptureButton && p->CapturePressed) fDown = !fDown;
    XSrc = fDown ? p->bmWidth : 0;

    hMemDC = CreateCompatibleDC (dc);
    hbm = SelectObject (hMemDC, p->bmHandles [cellNum]);
    BitBlt (dc, p->edges [cellNum], p->border, p->bmWidth,
            p->bmHeight, hMemDC, XSrc, 0, SRCCOPY);
    SelectObject (hMemDC, hbm);
    DeleteDC (hMemDC);
}

//———————————————————————————————————————————————
// Name:    ToolBarPaint
// Purpose: This routine is responsible for painting the tool bar.
//———————————————————————————————————————————————

static int PASCAL ToolBarPaint (HWND Wnd)
{
    int i;
    RECT r;
    PToolBarRec p;
    PAINTSTRUCT ps;

    BeginPaint (Wnd, &ps);
    p = GetToolBarRec (Wnd);

    // First, draw the bottom edge of the toolbar

    GetClientRect (Wnd, &r);
    PatBlt (ps.hdc, 0, r.bottom - 1, r.right - r.left, 1, BLACKNESS);
    PatBlt (ps.hdc, 0, 0, r.right - r.left, 1, WHITENESS);

    // Now draw each cell in turn

    for (i = 0; i < p->NumButtons; i++)
        PaintCell (ps.hdc, p, i);

    EndPaint (Wnd, &ps);
    return (0);
}

//———————————————————————————————————————————————
// Name:    DestroyToolBarWindow
// Purpose: Clean-up code for the toolbar window.
//———————————————————————————————————————————————

static int PASCAL DestroyToolBarWindow (HWND Wnd)
{
```

```
        int i;
        PToolBarRec p;

        p = GetToolBarRec (Wnd);
        RemoveProp (GetParent (Wnd), szClassName);
        UnHookWindow (GetParent (Wnd), hookKey);

        // Deallocate bitmap handles

        for (i = 0; i < p->NumButtons; i++)
            DeleteObject (p->bmHandles [i]);

        LocalFree ((HLOCAL) p);
        return (0);
}

//----------------------------------------------------------------
// Name:     ClickButton
// Purpose:  Adjust state of a button and send message to parent.
//----------------------------------------------------------------

static void PASCAL ClickButton (HWND Wnd, PToolBarRec p, int ClickedButton)
{
        RECT r;

        if (p->flags [ClickedButton] & FSTICKY)
        p->flags [ClickedButton] ^= FPUSHED;

        // Redraw the button in its new state

        GetCellRect (p, ClickedButton, &r);
        InvalidateRect (Wnd, &r, FALSE);

        // Send message to parent window

        SendMessage (GetParent (Wnd), WM_COMMAND, p->bmIDS [ClickedButton],
                        p->flags [ClickedButton] & FPUSHED);

}

//----------------------------------------------------------------
// Name:     ButtonHitTest
// Purpose:  Test for a hit on any button in the toolbar.
//----------------------------------------------------------------

static int PASCAL ButtonHitTest (PToolBarRec p, LPARAM lParam)
{
        RECT r;
        POINT pt;
        int buttonNum;

        pt.x = LOWORD (lParam);
        pt.y = HIWORD (lParam);

        for (buttonNum = 0; buttonNum < p->NumButtons; buttonNum++)
        {
          GetCellRect (p, buttonNum, &r);
          if (PtInRect (&r, pt)) return (buttonNum);
        }

        return (-1);
}

//----------------------------------------------------------------
// Name:     HandleButtonDown
// Purpose:  Handle mouse clicks in the toolbar.
//----------------------------------------------------------------

static LONG PASCAL HandleButtonDown (HWND Wnd, LPARAM lParam)
{
```

```
        RECT r;
        int buttonNum;
        PToolBarRec p;

        p = GetToolBarRec (Wnd);
        buttonNum = ButtonHitTest (p, IParam);
        if (buttonNum != −1)
        {
          SetCapture (Wnd);
          p−>CaptureButton = buttonNum;
          p−>CapturePressed = TRUE;
          GetCellRect (p, buttonNum, &r);
          InvalidateRect (Wnd, &r, FALSE);
        }

        return (0);
}

//─────────────────────────────────────────────────────────
// Name:    HandleButtonUp
// Purpose: Handle mouse ups in the toolbar.
//─────────────────────────────────────────────────────────

#pragma argsused

static LONG PASCAL HandleButtonUp (HWND Wnd, LPARAM IParam)
{
        PToolBarRec p;

        p = GetToolBarRec (Wnd);
        if (p−>CaptureButton != −1)
        {
          ReleaseCapture();
          if (p−>CapturePressed) ClickButton (Wnd, p, p−>CaptureButton);
          p−>CapturePressed = FALSE;
          p−>CaptureButton = −1;
        }

        return (0);
}

//─────────────────────────────────────────────────────────
// Name:    HandleMouseMoves
// Purpose: Handle mouse movement in the toolbar.
//─────────────────────────────────────────────────────────

static LONG PASCAL HandleMouseMoves (HWND Wnd, LPARAM IParam)
{
        RECT r;
        int buttonNum;
        PToolBarRec p;

        p = GetToolBarRec (Wnd);
        if (p−>CaptureButton != −1)
        {
          buttonNum = ButtonHitTest (p, IParam);
          if (buttonNum == p−>CaptureButton)
          {
            if (p−>CapturePressed == FALSE)
            {
              p−>CapturePressed = TRUE;
              GetCellRect (p, p−>CaptureButton, &r);
              InvalidateRect (Wnd, &r, FALSE);
            }
          }
          else
          {
            if (p−>CapturePressed == TRUE)
```

```
                    {
                        p->CapturePressed = FALSE;
                        GetCellRect (p, p->CaptureButton, &r);
                        InvalidateRect (Wnd, &r, FALSE);
                    }
                }
            }

        return (0);
}
```

```
//------------------------------------------------------------------
// Name:    ToolBarWndProc
// Purpose: Window procedure for toolbar windows.
//------------------------------------------------------------------

LONG FAR PASCAL _export ToolBarWndProc (HWND Wnd, WORD Msg,
                                        WPARAM wParam, LPARAM lParam)
{
    switch (Msg)
    {
        case WM_LBUTTONDOWN:

        return HandleButtonDown (Wnd, lParam);

        case WM_LBUTTONUP:

        return HandleButtonUp (Wnd, lParam);

        case WM_MOUSEMOVE:

        return HandleMouseMoves (Wnd, lParam);

        case WM_PAINT:

        return ToolBarPaint (Wnd);

        case WM_CREATE:

        return InitToolBarWindow (Wnd, lParam);

        case WM_DESTROY:

        return DestroyToolBarWindow (Wnd);
    }

        return DefWindowProc (Wnd, Msg, wParam, lParam);
}
```

```
//------------------------------------------------------------------
// Name:    RegisterToolBar
// Purpose: Register the toolbar window procedure.
//------------------------------------------------------------------

static BOOL PASCAL RegisterToolBar (HANDLE hInstance)
{
    WNDCLASS cls;

    if (GetClassInfo (hInstance, szClassName, &cls) == 0)
    {
        cls.style           = 0;
        cls.lpfnWndProc     = (WNDPROC) ToolBarWndProc;
        cls.cbClsExtra      = 0;
        cls.cbWndExtra      = sizeof (void NEAR *);
        cls.hInstance       = hInstance;
        cls.hIcon           = 0;
        cls.hCursor         = LoadCursor (NULL, IDC_ARROW);
        cls.hbrBackground   = COLOR_BTNFACE + 1;
        cls.lpszMenuName    = NULL;
        cls.lpszClassName   = szClassName;
```

```
            return RegisterClass (&cls);
        }

        return TRUE;
    }

//————————————————————————————————————————————————————————
// Name:    GetToolBarWindow
// Purpose:  Return the handle of this window's tool bar.
//————————————————————————————————————————————————————————

HWND PASCAL GetToolBarWindow (HWND hWndParent)
{
        if (hWndParent != NULL && IsWindow (hWndParent))
            return GetProp (hWndParent, szClassName);
        else
            return NULL;
    }

//————————————————————————————————————————————————————————
// Name:    CreateToolBarWindow
// Purpose:  Create a toolbar window and attach it to the designated parent.
//————————————————————————————————————————————————————————

HWND PASCAL CreateToolBarWindow (HANDLE hInstance, HWND hWndParent,
                                        LPINT lpButtons)
{
        HWND Wnd = NULL;

        // Check that we've got a valid parent window

        if (hWndParent != NULL && IsWindow (hWndParent))
        {
            // Ok so far, but has window already got a toolbar?

            Wnd = GetToolBarWindow (hWndParent);
            if (Wnd == NULL)
              if (RegisterToolBar (hInstance))
                Wnd = CreateWindow (szClassName, "", WS_CHILD | WS_VISIBLE,
                                        0, 0, 0, 0, hWndParent, NULL, hInstance, lpButtons);
        }

        return (Wnd);
    }

//————————————————————————————————————————————————————————
// Name:    SetButtonModal
// Purpose:  Make a button modal or non-modal.
//————————————————————————————————————————————————————————

int PASCAL SetButtonModal (HWND hWndParent, int buttonNum, BOOL fModal)
{
        int ret;
        HWND Wnd;
        PToolBarRec p;

        ret = 0;
        Wnd = GetToolBarWindow (hWndParent);
        p = GetToolBarRec (Wnd);
        if (Wnd != NULL && p != NULL && buttonNum < p->NumButtons)
        {
            ret = (p->flags [buttonNum] & FSTICKY) ? TRUE : FALSE;
            p->flags [buttonNum] &= ~FSTICKY;
            if (fModal) p->flags [buttonNum] |= FSTICKY;
        }

        return (ret);
    }
```

Figure 6.12 BARTEST4.C:
the sample toolbar application.

```
/* BARTEST4.C */

// © 1994 Dave Jewell and Addison-Wesley, ALL RIGHTS RESERVED

#include    <windows.h>
#include    "toolbar.h"

char szAppName[ ] = "ToolBarTest";

//————————————————————————————————————————————————————
// Name:    WindowProc
// Purpose: Window procedure for main application window.
//————————————————————————————————————————————————————

LONG FAR PASCAL _export WindowProc (HWND Wnd, WORD Msg,
                                    WPARAM wParam, LPARAM lParam)
{
    switch (Msg)
    {
      case WM_DESTROY:

        PostQuitMessage (0);
        break;

        default:

        return DefWindowProc (Wnd, Msg, wParam, lParam);
    }

    return (0);
}

//————————————————————————————————————————————————————
// Name:    InitAppClass
// Purpose: Register the main application window class.
//————————————————————————————————————————————————————

BOOL PASCAL InitAppClass (HANDLE hInstance)
{
    WNDCLASS cls;

    if (GetClassInfo (hInstance, szAppName, &cls) == 0)
    {
        cls.style           = CS_VREDRAW | CS_HREDRAW;
        cls.lpfnWndProc     = (WNDPROC) WindowProc;
        cls.cbClsExtra      = 0;
        cls.cbWndExtra      = 0;
        cls.hInstance       = hInstance;
        cls.hIcon           = LoadIcon (NULL, IDI_APPLICATION);
        cls.hCursor         = LoadCursor (NULL, IDC_ARROW);
        cls.hbrBackground   = GetStockObject (WHITE_BRUSH);
        cls.lpszMenuName    = MAKEINTRESOURCE (1);
        cls.lpszClassName   = szAppName;
        return RegisterClass (&cls);
    }

    return (TRUE);
}

//————————————————————————————————————————————————————
// Name:    WinMain
// Purpose: Main application entry point.
//————————————————————————————————————————————————————

#pragma argsused

int PASCAL WinMain (HANDLE hInstance, HANDLE hPrevInstance,
                    LPSTR lpCmdLine, int nCmdShow)
{
    HWND Wnd;
```

```
      MSG Msg;
      static int bitMaps [15] = { 1000, 1001, 0, 0, 1002, 1003, 1004,
                                   1005, 1006, 1007, 0, 0, 1008, 1009, −1 };

      // Register application class if needed

      if (InitAppClass (hInstance) == FALSE)
          return (0);

      // Create the main application window

      Wnd = CreateWindow (szAppName, szAppName,
                           WS_OVERLAPPEDWINDOW,
                           CW_USEDEFAULT, CW_USEDEFAULT,
                           CW_USEDEFAULT, CW_USEDEFAULT,
                           0, 0, hInstance, NULL);

      if (Wnd != NULL)
      {
         ShowWindow (Wnd, nCmdShow);
         UpdateWindow (Wnd);
         if (CreateToolBarWindow (hInstance, Wnd, bitMaps) != NULL)
         {
            // Make button 0 and 1 modal
            SetButtonModal (Wnd, 0, TRUE);
            SetButtonModal (Wnd, 1, TRUE);
         }
      }

      while (GetMessage (&Msg, 0, 0, 0))
      {
         TranslateMessage (&Msg);
         DispatchMessage (&Msg);
      }

      return (Msg.wParam);
   }
```

Figure 6.13   TOOLBAR3.H.

```
   /* TOOLBAR3.H */

   // © 1994 Dave Jewell and Addison-Wesley, ALL RIGHTS RESERVED

   #ifndef _INC_TOOLBAR
   #define _INC_TOOLBAR        /* #defined if toolbar.h has been included */

   #ifdef __cplusplus
   extern "C" {
   #endif

   HWND PASCAL GetToolBarWindow (HWND hWndParent);
   int PASCAL SetButtonModal (HWND hWndParent, int buttonNum, BOOL fModal);
   HWND PASCAL CreateToolBarWindow (HANDLE hInstance, HWND hWndParent,
                                    LPINT lpButtons);

   #ifdef __cplusplus
   }
   #endif

   #endif
```

Figure 6.14 Two 'sticky'
buttons doing their stuff.

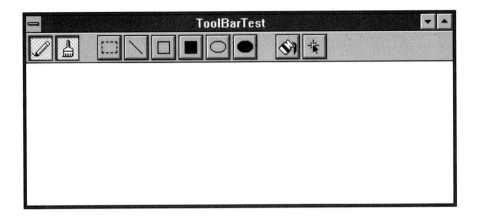

Figure 6.14 shows the result of running the BARTEST4.EXE executable. In this screen shot, both of the sticky buttons on the left-hand side of the toolbar have been selected.

Enabling and disabling toolbar buttons

There are a few more features that need adding to our toolbar code in order to make it sufficiently flexible for use in a general-purpose, commercial-quality application. The first of these is the ability to make different toolbar buttons either enabled or disabled under program control. An enabled button can be clicked on, and will respond to mouse actions, sending a WM_COMMAND message to the parent window as already described. Disabled buttons, on the other hand, have a 'grayed-out' appearance, just like a disabled menu option. They don't respond to user activity and do nothing when clicked on. Typically, your application will disable toolbar buttons when it doesn't make sense for those particular buttons to be available. You can either hide them (more on that later) or disable them so as to indicate to the user that the option is not currently available.

This sounds quite straightforward to implement, with the exception of the grayed-out appearance. How are we going to implement this in a straightforward, simple fashion? One possible way to do this would be to have a third, disabled image attached to each of our toolbar bitmaps. The problem here is that we've got to go back and modify all of our existing bitmaps, and we lose compatibility with the floating toolbox palette code.

As a matter of fact, it is possible to create a grayed-out bitmap from a normal one, but to do so requires a lot of complexity, involving the creation of a custom brush. In the end, I decided to stick to the KISS (Keep It Simple, Stupid!) principle, and came up with an alternative way of doing things.

If you remember, the LoadButtonBitmap routine is designed to load a bitmap into memory and return a bitmap handle. The routine automatically takes care of mapping the bitmap colors into the currently selected Windows color scheme. The technique described here is a simple extension of this approach: it simply involves replacing any black parts of the bitmap with the currently selected COLOR_BTNSHADOW color. This will have the effect of graying out the bitmap, or making it less distinct. Of course, there is one disadvantage with this technique: if your bitmap doesn't happen to contain any black pixels, then the disabled version won't look any different! Just make sure that the bitmaps you use do contain some black elements.

This leads to the code shown below. We now have two different routines, LoadButtonBitmap which functions as it always did, and LoadDisabledButtonBitmap, which creates a bitmap with a disabled look to it. In the interests of code space, both of these routines call a common routine to do the real work.

```
//-----------------------------------------------------------------
// Name:     InternalLoadButtonBitmap
// Purpose:  Called by LoadButtonBitmap and LoadDisabledButtonBitmap.
//-----------------------------------------------------------------

static HBITMAP PASCAL InternalLoadButtonBitmap (HANDLE hInstance, int bmID,
                                                BOOL fEnable)
{
    HDC dc;
    HBITMAP hbm;
    HANDLE hRes;
    LPDWORD lprgb;
    LPVOID lpb;
    LPBITMAPINFOHEADER lpbi;

    hRes = LoadResource (hInstance, FindResource (hInstance,
                     MAKEINTRESOURCE(bmID), RT_BITMAP));

    lpbi = (LPBITMAPINFOHEADER) LockResource (hRes);
    if (lpbi == NULL) return (NULL);

    lprgb = (LPDWORD) ((LPSTR) lpbi + (int) lpbi->biSize);
    lpb = (LPVOID) (lprgb + 16);

    // Black

    if (fEnable)
        lprgb [0] = ColorFix (GetSysColor (COLOR_WINDOWTEXT));
    else
        lprgb [0] = ColorFix (GetSysColor (COLOR_BTNSHADOW));

    lprgb [8] = ColorFix (GetSysColor (COLOR_BTNFACE));        // Light gray
    lprgb [7] = ColorFix (GetSysColor (COLOR_BTNSHADOW));      // Gray
    lprgb [15] = ColorFix (GetSysColor (COLOR_BTNHIGHLIGHT));  // White

    dc = GetDC (NULL);
    hbm = CreateDIBitmap (dc, lpbi, CBM_INIT, lpb,
                          (LPBITMAPINFO) lpbi, DIB_RGB_COLORS);

    ReleaseDC (NULL, dc);
    GlobalUnlock (hRes);
    FreeResource (hRes);
    return (hbm);
}

//-----------------------------------------------------------------
// Name      LoadButtonBitmap
// Purpose:  Load a button bitmap and tweak for system colors.
//-----------------------------------------------------------------

static HBITMAP PASCAL LoadButtonBitmap (HANDLE hInstance, int bmID)
{
    return InternalLoadButtonBitmap (hInstance, bmID, TRUE);
}
```

```
//————————————————————————————————————————
// Name:    LoadDisabledButtonBitmap
// Purpose: Load a button bitmap and make it look disabled.
//————————————————————————————————————————
static HBITMAP PASCAL LoadDisabledButtonBitmap (HANDLE hInstance, int bmID)
{
    return InternalLoadButtonBitmap (hInstance, bmID, FALSE);
}
```

Let's define a new flag value, FDISABLED, like this:

```
#define        FDISABLED          0x20        // if set, button is disabled
```

Using this flag, we can mark a particular toolbar button as either enabled or
disabled. In principle, we could hold two bitmaps in memory for each button, one
showing the button in an enabled state, and the other showing it in a disabled state.
In practice though, a button isn't likely to change state often, and such an approach
would therefore be wasteful of memory. A better technique is to reload the wanted
bitmap only when a button changes state. With this in mind, the code below shows
another new API routine, EnableToolBarButton, which can be used to enable or
disable a button in the toolbar.

```
//————————————————————————————————————————
// Name:    EnableToolBarButton
// Purpose: Enable or disable a button in the toolbar.
//————————————————————————————————————————
int PASCAL EnableToolBarButton (HWND hWndParent, int buttonNum, BOOL fDisable)
{
    int ret;
    RECT r;
    HWND Wnd;
    HANDLE hInstance;
    PToolBarRec p;

    ret = 0;
    Wnd = GetToolBarWindow (hWndParent);
    p = GetToolBarRec (Wnd);
    if (Wnd != NULL && p != NULL && buttonNum < p−>NumButtons)
    {
        ret = (p−>flags [buttonNum] & FDISABLED) ? TRUE : FALSE;
        p−>flags [buttonNum] &= ~FDISABLED;
        if (fDisable) p−>flags [buttonNum] |= FDISABLED;

        if (ret != fDisable)
        {
            // Reload the button bitmap

            hInstance = GetWindowWord (Wnd, GWW_HINSTANCE);
            DeleteObject (p−>bmHandles [buttonNum]);
            p−>bmHandles [buttonNum] = (fDisable) ?
                LoadDisabledButtonBitmap (hInstance, p−>bmIDS [buttonNum]) :
                LoadButtonBitmap (hInstance, p−>bmIDS [buttonNum]);

            // Redisplay the button

            GetCellRect (p, buttonNum, &r);
            InvalidateRect (Wnd, &r, TRUE);
        }
    }

    return (ret);
}
```

Like the SetButtonModal routine, the EnableToolBarButton call returns the previous state of the associated flag. Unlike the SetButtonModal routine, this new call directly affects the visual appearance of the toolbar, so the InvalidateRect routine is called to redraw the toolbar button in its new state.

Of course, with the code as it is at the moment, a disabled button will still respond to mouse clicks. We need to modify the hit-testing code so that mouse clicks on a disabled button are ignored. This is simply done by modifying the HandleButtonDown routine as shown below:

```
//————————————————————————————————
// Name:    HandleButtonDown
// Purpose: Handle mouse clicks in the toolbar.
//————————————————————————————————

static LONG PASCAL HandleButtonDown (HWND Wnd, LPARAM lParam)
{
    RECT r;
    int buttonNum;
    PToolBarRec p;

    p = GetToolBarRec (Wnd);
    buttonNum = ButtonHitTest (p, lParam);
    if (buttonNum != −1 && (p−>flags [buttonNum] & FDISABLED) == 0)
    {
        SetCapture (Wnd);
        p−>CaptureButton = buttonNum;
        p−>CapturePressed = TRUE;
        GetCellRect (p, buttonNum, &r);
        InvalidateRect (Wnd, &r, FALSE);
    }

    return (0);
}
```

We also need to be able to test out the button disabling code, so I added the following message handling code to the window procedure of the BARTEST application:

```
static BOOL fDisable = FALSE;

switch (Msg)
{
    case WM_RBUTTONDOWN:

    EnableToolBarButton (Wnd, 9, fDisable ^= 1);
    break;
```

With this code in place, each time the right-hand mouse button is clicked in the main application window, the last button in the toolbar (button 9) will be toggled between its disabled and its enabled state.

Hiding toolbar buttons

An alternative to disabling a toolbar button is to hide it altogether. This is, if anything, even easier to accomplish than creating the disabled effect. Whether you hide buttons or disable them is a matter of personal choice, and also has some bearing on the application under development. In situations where screen space is tight and there are a large number of buttons in the toolbar, it might make more sense to hide those that aren't needed.

Once again, we'll define another flag, FHIDDEN, which specifies whether or not a button is hidden.

```
#define          FHIDDEN  0x10        // If set, button is hidden
```

The necessary changes to the drawing code are very simple: if the button is hidden, we just don't draw it! Here's the revised code:

```
//——————————————————————————————————————————————————————
// Name:    PaintCell
// Purpose: Paint a specified cell in the toolbar.
//——————————————————————————————————————————————————————
static void PASCAL PaintCell (HDC dc, PToolBarRec p, int cellNum)
{
      int XSrc;
      HDC hMemDC;
      HBITMAP hbm;
      BOOL fDown;
      if ((p->flags [cellNum] & FHIDDEN) == 0)
      {
          fDown = (p->flags [cellNum] & FPUSHED) ? TRUE : FALSE;
          if (cellNum == p->CaptureButton && p->CapturePressed) fDown = !fDown;
          XSrc = fDown ? p->bmWidth : 0;

          hMemDC = CreateCompatibleDC (dc);
          hbm = SelectObject (hMemDC, p->bmHandles [cellNum]);
          BitBlt (dc, p->edges [cellNum], p->border, p->bmWidth,
                   p->bmHeight, hMemDC, XSrc, 0, SRCCOPY);
          SelectObject (hMemDC, hbm);
          DeleteDC (hMemDC);
      }
}
```

Since we don't want hit-testing to apply to hidden buttons, we have to change one line of code in the HandleButtonDown routine. The code must now test for disabled and hidden buttons. If either flag is set, the routine exits and the mouse click is ignored.

```
if (buttonNum != -1 && (p->flags [buttonNum] & (FDISABLED | FHIDDEN)) == 0)
```

Naturally, we also need a new API routine that will enable us to hide and unhide buttons under program control. It's becoming clear, however, that all of these API routines work in pretty much the same way. They get a handle to the toolbar window, get a pointer to the toolbar record, perform any needed validation and then do the actual business of setting up the needed bits within the flags field belonging to the specified button. What's really needed is an internal, common routine that can handle all of these functions for each API routine. In this way, we can simplify the code and produce a more compact implementation.

```
//——————————————————————————————————————————————————————
// Name:    InternalSetButtonFlags
// Purpose: Set a button flag either true or false.
//——————————————————————————————————————————————————————
static int PASCAL InternalSetButtonFlags (HWND hWndParent, int buttonNum,
                              WORD Mask, BOOL val)
```

```
{
    RECT r;
    int ret;
    HWND Wnd;
    HANDLE hInstance;
    PToolBarRec p;

    ret = 0;
    Wnd = GetToolBarWindow (hWndParent);
    p = GetToolBarRec (Wnd);
    if (Wnd != NULL && p != NULL && buttonNum < p->NumButtons)
    {
        ret = (p->flags [buttonNum] & Mask) ? TRUE : FALSE;
        p->flags [buttonNum] &= ~Mask;
        if (val) p->flags [buttonNum] |= Mask;

        // If this is a button enable/disable, reload the bitmap

        if (Mask == FDISABLED)
        {
            hInstance = GetWindowWord (Wnd, GWW_HINSTANCE);
            DeleteObject (p->bmHandles [buttonNum]);
            p->bmHandles [buttonNum] = (val) ?
                LoadDisabledButtonBitmap (hInstance, p->bmIDS [buttonNum]) :
                LoadButtonBitmap (hInstance, p->bmIDS [buttonNum]);
        }

        // If change to hide or disable state, then update display

        if (Mask & (FHIDDEN | FDISABLED))
        {
            GetCellRect (p, buttonNum, &r);
            InvalidateRect (Wnd, &r, TRUE);
        }

    }

    return (ret);
}
```

The new routine is shown above. InternalSetButtonFlags takes care of setting
and clearing the various parts of a button's flags. If the bit being set or cleared is the
FDISABLED bit, the routine automatically reloads the needed bitmap. If the visual
state of the button is being changed (either hidden or disabled), the code calls
GetCellRect to determine a bounding rectangle for the button and invalidates the
rectangle, forcing a redraw of the button in its new state. Note that because we're
potentially hiding buttons with this code, it's important here to call the InvalidateRect
routine with the final parameter set to TRUE, so as to force a redraw of the window
background in the invalidated area. This will cause the button to disappear in
conjunction with the drawing code which ignores buttons that have the FHIDDEN bit
set high.

Using the new InternalSetButtonFlags code, our two previous API routines
become trivially simple. Here they are in all their glory:

```
//————————————————————————————————————————
// Name:     SetButtonModal
// Purpose:  Make a button modal or non-modal.
//————————————————————————————————————————

int PASCAL SetButtonModal (HWND hWndParent, int buttonNum, BOOL fModal)
{
    return InternalSetButtonFlags (hWndParent, buttonNum, FSTICKY, fModal);
}
```

```
//————————————————————————————————————————————————
// Name:     EnableToolBarButton
// Purpose:  Enable or disable a button in the toolbar.
//————————————————————————————————————————————————

int PASCAL EnableToolBarButton (HWND hWndParent, int buttonNum, BOOL fDisable)
{
       return InternalSetButtonFlags (hWndParent, buttonNum, FDISABLED, fDisable);
}
```

Quite a worthwhile reduction in code size. This is a good example of how you can reduce the amount of code you write by looking for routines that perform a similar job. The new routine for button hiding, HideToolBarButton, is equally simple:

```
//————————————————————————————————————————————————
// Name:     HideToolBarButton
// Purpose:  Hide or unhide a toolbar button.
//————————————————————————————————————————————————

int PASCAL HideToolBarButton (HWND hWndParent, int buttonNum, BOOL fHide)
{
       return InternalSetButtonFlags (hWndParent, buttonNum, FHIDDEN, fHide);
}
```

After incorporating the HideToolBarButton prototype into the header file, we can add the following message handling code to the BARTEST program:

```
case WM_LBUTTONDOWN:

HideToolBarButton (Wnd, 8, fHide ^= 1);
break;
```

With this code, any left mouse button clicks in the application window client area will toggle button number eight (the ninth button in the toolbar) between a hidden and a non-hidden state.

Implementing modal button groups

As I mentioned at the beginning of this chapter, you sometimes have a situation where a number of toolbar buttons form a mutually exclusive group. In other words, for that particular group, it only makes sense for one button to be pushed at any one time. A good example of this is the text justification group shown in Figure 6.2. Any arbitrary chunk of text can be left-aligned, right-aligned, justified or centered, but it cannot be more than one of these at any one time.

In this section, we concentrate on building the concept of a mutually exclusive group of buttons into the toolbar code. The toolbar code will then take the responsibility of deselecting all other buttons in a group once one particular button is pressed. This is much like the operation of auto radio buttons in a dialog box. Whenever one of the radio buttons is pushed, the Windows dialog manager automatically turns off all other auto radio buttons within the same group.

In order to implement this feature, I chose to use the remaining bits in the flags array, as shown below:

```
// Constants for the flags field#

 define       FPUSHED      0x80         // If set, button is pushed
#define       FSTICKY      0x40         // If set, button is modal
#define       FDISABLED    0x20         // if set, button is disabled
#define       FHIDDEN      0x10         // If set, button is hidden
#define       FGROUPBITS   0x0F         // Space for four groups
```

As you can see, the top four bits of the flags field are used for the bit constants we've already discussed. This leaves four bits to use as group bits. I defined a new constant, FGROUPBITS, which can be used to select these four group bits. This allows us to define up to four mutually exclusive groups within our toolbar, which should be adequate for most purposes. If you need more, you can increase the size of the flags field to an integer array rather than a byte array. This will give you up to 12 groups $(16 - 4 = 12)$.

Here's how it works. If a button belongs to a group, it will have the appropriate bit set in its flags field. So, for example, if a button belongs to group 2, it will have bit 2 of the flags field set. If it belongs to group 0, then bit 0 will be set, and so forth. This gives us four groups, numbered 0–3. A button cannot belong to more than one mutually exclusive group at the same time. If a button does not belong to any group, then the lower four bits of its flags field are all set to zero. A simple API routine will be defined that will allow us to add and remove buttons from a group. Adding a button to a group will automatically make it a modal (sticky) button. For obvious reasons, buttons belonging to a group must also be modal.

When a button is clicked, we'll need a routine that will check to see if the button belongs to a group. If so, the routine will search for any other buttons in the same group and make sure that they're all turned off. This routine, AdjustButtonGroup, is shown below:

```
//--------------------------------------------------------------------
// Name:     AdjustButtonGroup
// Purpose:  Release any pressed buttons in the same group.
//--------------------------------------------------------------------

static void PASCAL AdjustButtonGroup (HWND Wnd, PToolBarRec p, int ClickedButton)
{
     RECT r;
     int groupMask;
     int num;

     groupMask = p->flags [ClickedButton] & FGROUPBITS;
     if (groupMask != 0)
     {
       for (num = 0; num < p->NumButtons; num++)
       {
         if (num != ClickedButton &&
            (p->flags [num] & FGROUPBITS) == groupMask &&
            (p->flags [num] & FPUSHED))
         {
           p->flags [num] &= ~FPUSHED;
           GetCellRect (p, num, &r);
           InvalidateRect (Wnd, &r, FALSE);
         }
       }
     }
}
```

The AdjustButtonGroup routine needs to be called from the ClickButton code so that the buttons in a group are adjusted whenever a button is pressed and released.

```
//————————————————————————————————————————————————
// Name:    ClickButton
// Purpose: Adjust state of a button and send message to parent.
//————————————————————————————————————————————————

static void PASCAL ClickButton (HWND Wnd, PToolBarRec p, int ClickedButton)
{
    RECT r;

    if (p−>flags [ClickedButton] & FSTICKY)
        p−>flags [ClickedButton] ^= FPUSHED;

    // Redraw the button in its new state

    GetCellRect (p, ClickedButton, &r);
    InvalidateRect (Wnd, &r, FALSE);

    // If this is a group button, adjust the group

    AdjustButtonGroup (Wnd, p, ClickedButton);

    // Send message to parent window

    SendMessage (GetParent (Wnd), WM_COMMAND, p−>bmIDS [ClickedButton],
                    p−>flags [ClickedButton] & FPUSHED);
}
```

There's one other important change we need to make. When dealing with ordinary modal buttons, recall that we press them once to select them and press them again to deselect them. This is obviously no good for a group button. If a group button is selected, we want to ignore a subsequent press of the same button. This involves adding a bit more logic to the HandleButtonDown routine.

```
//————————————————————————————————————————————————
// Name:    HandleButtonDown
// Purpose: Handle mouse clicks in the toolbar.
//————————————————————————————————————————————————

static LONG PASCAL HandleButtonDown (HWND Wnd, LPARAM lParam)
{
    RECT r;
    BYTE flgs;
    int buttonNum;
    PToolBarRec p;

    p = GetToolBarRec (Wnd);
    buttonNum = ButtonHitTest (p, lParam);
    if (buttonNum != −1 && (p−>flags [buttonNum] & (FDISABLED | FHIDDEN)) == 0)
    {
        flgs = p−>flags [buttonNum];

        // If button is in a modal group and already pushed, do nothing.

        if ((flgs & FGROUPBITS) == 0 || (flgs & FPUSHED) == 0)
        {
            SetCapture (Wnd);
            p−>CaptureButton = buttonNum;
            p−>CapturePressed = TRUE;
            GetCellRect (p, buttonNum, &r);
            InvalidateRect (Wnd, &r, FALSE);
        }
    }
    return (0);
}
```

With this code in place, we can now define a new API routine, SetButtonGroup, which adds a button to a specified group number in the range 0–3. If the group number is set to −1, the code removes the button from any group in which it may be.

```
//————————————————————————————————————————————————
// Name:    SetButtonGroup
// Purpose: Assign a button to a group.
//          If groupNum is −1, resigns from a group
//————————————————————————————————————————————————

void PASCAL SetButtonGroup (HWND hWndParent, int buttonNum, int groupNum)
{
    InternalSetButtonFlags (hWndParent, buttonNum, FGROUPBITS, FALSE);
    if (groupNum >= 0 && groupNum <= 3)
        InternalSetButtonFlags (hWndParent, buttonNum, 1 << groupNum, TRUE);
}
```

The new routine uses our old friend InternalSetButtonFlags. Firstly, it's called to clear any group bits in the flags field, and then (provided that the group number is in range) it's called once more to set the needed group flag. This necessitates a couple of further modifications to the InternalSetButtonFlags code. Firstly, we need to ensure that the FSTICKY bit gets turned on whenever a button is added to a group. Secondly, as a convenience, if the button that's being added to a group is already pushed down, we call the AdjustButtonGroup routine to clear any other buttons in the group. These changes are illustrated in the new InternalSetButtonFlags routine below.

```
//————————————————————————————————————————————————
// Name:    InternalSetButtonFlags
// Purpose: Set a button flag either true or false.
//————————————————————————————————————————————————

static int PASCAL InternalSetButtonFlags (HWND hWndParent, int buttonNum,
                                          WORD Mask, BOOL val)
{
    RECT r;
    int ret;
    HWND Wnd;
    HANDLE hInstance;
    PToolBarRec p;

    ret = 0;
    Wnd = GetToolBarWindow (hWndParent);
    p = GetToolBarRec (Wnd);
    if (Wnd != NULL && p != NULL && buttonNum < p->NumButtons)
    {
        ret = (p->flags [buttonNum] & Mask) ? TRUE : FALSE;
        p->flags [buttonNum] &= ~Mask;
        if (val)
        {
            p->flags [buttonNum] |= Mask;

            if (Mask < FHIDDEN)
            {
                // We're adding to a group : better set sticky bit

                p->flags [buttonNum] |= FSTICKY;

                // If button is down, adjust group

                if (p->flags [buttonNum] & FPUSHED)
                    AdjustButtonGroup (Wnd, p, buttonNum);
            }
        }
    }
```

```
                // If this is a button enable/disable, reload the bitmap

                if (Mask == FDISABLED)
                {
                    hInstance = GetWindowWord (Wnd, GWW_HINSTANCE);
                    DeleteObject (p->bmHandles [buttonNum]);
                    p->bmHandles [buttonNum] = (val) ?
                        LoadDisabledButtonBitmap (hInstance, p->bmIDS [buttonNum]) :
                        LoadButtonBitmap (hInstance, p->bmIDS [buttonNum]);
                }
                // If change to hide or disable state, then update display

                if (Mask & (FHIDDEN | FDISABLED))
                {
                    GetCellRect (p, buttonNum, &r);
                    InvalidateRect (Wnd, &r, TRUE);
                }
            }
        }
        return (ret);
    }
```

This new code completes the implementation of mutually exclusive toolbar groups. In order to test out the implementation, we can just add the following statements to the BARTEST.C application. These statements replace the existing SetButtonModal calls that were in there.

```
if (CreateToolBarWindow (hInstance, Wnd, bitMaps) != NULL)
{
    // Make button 0 and 1 into a group

    SetButtonGroup (Wnd, 0, 0);
    SetButtonGroup (Wnd, 1, 0);
}
```

You should now find that the first two buttons of the toolbar interact with one another. When one of them is pressed, the other automatically pops up, and vice versa.

The icing on the cake

This leaves us with just a couple of holes in our API. Firstly, we've no way of setting a specific button under program control, and secondly, there's no way of interrogating a particular button to determine whether or not it's in a pushed-in state. Let's plug those two holes now with the code shown below:

```
//———————————————————————————————————————————————
// Name:     SetButtonPushed
// Purpose:  Set a modal button to be pushed or unpushed.
//———————————————————————————————————————————————

int PASCAL SetButtonPushed (HWND hWndParent, int buttonNum, BOOL fPush)
{
    int ret;
    HWND Wnd;
    RECT r;
    PToolBarRec p;

    ret = 0;
    Wnd = GetToolBarWindow (hWndParent);

    p = GetToolBarRec (Wnd);
    if (Wnd != NULL && p != NULL && buttonNum < p->NumButtons)
    {
```

```
            // Only makes sense for modal buttons
            if (p->flags [buttonNum] & FSTICKY)
            {
                ret = (p->flags [buttonNum] & FPUSHED) ? TRUE : FALSE;
                p->flags [buttonNum] &= ~FPUSHED;
                if (fPush)
                {
                    p->flags [buttonNum] |= FPUSHED;
                    AdjustButtonGroup (Wnd, p, buttonNum);
                }
                GetCellRect (p, buttonNum, &r);
                InvalidateRect (Wnd, &r, FALSE);
            }
        }
    }
    return (ret);
}
//─────────────────────────────────────────────────────────────
// Name:    IsButtonPushed
// Purpose: Determine if a modal button is pushed or unpushed.
//─────────────────────────────────────────────────────────────
int PASCAL IsButtonPushed (HWND hWndParent, int buttonNum)
{
    int ret;
    HWND Wnd;
    PToolBarRec p;

    ret = 0;
    Wnd = GetToolBarWindow (hWndParent);
    p = GetToolBarRec (Wnd);
    if (Wnd != NULL && p != NULL && buttonNum < p->NumButtons)
        if (p->flags [buttonNum] & FSTICKY)
            ret = (p->flags [buttonNum] & FPUSHED) ? TRUE : FALSE;
    return (ret);
}
```

This completes the development of the toolbar routines. The following code
fragment was added to the BARTEST program to demonstrate the operation of the
SetButtonPushed routine. Pressing any key while the program is active will push the
first button on the toolbar and deselect the other button in the group.

```
case WM_CHAR:
SetButtonPushed (Wnd, 0, TRUE);
break;
```

Figure 6.15 shows the completed toolbar source code, TOOLBAR5.C. The
revised header file, TOOLBAR4.H, is shown in Figure 6.16, and the new source for
the test application, BARTEST5.C, is given in Figure 6.17. All these files are present
on the companion disk, along with the executable file, BARTEST5.EXE.

Figure 6.15 TOOLBAR5.C:
the finished toolbar code.

```
/* TOOLBAR5.C */

// © 1994 Dave Jewell and Addison-Wesley, ALL RIGHTS RESERVED

#include    <mem.h>
#include    <windows.h>
#include    "toolbar.h"
#include    "sclaslib.h"
```

```
static char szClassName[ ] = "ToolBar";        // name of our window class
static char szHookName[ ] = "ToolBarHook";     // name of our hook

#define    MAXBUTTONS         40               // maximum buttons per window

// Constants for the flags field

#define    FPUSHED            0x80             // If set, button is pushed
#define    FSTICKY            0x40             // If set, button is modal
#define    FDISABLED          0x20             // if set, button is disabled
#define    FHIDDEN            0x10             // If set, button is hidden
#define    FGROUPBITS         0x0F             // Space for four groups

typedef struct ToolBarRec
{
        int        border;                     // width of border
        int        height;                     // height of the toolbar
        int        bmWidth;                    // width of bitmaps
        int        bmHeight;                   // height of bitmaps
        int        NumButtons;                 // number of buttons
        int        CaptureButton;              // capturing button
        BOOL       CapturePressed;             // if 'CaptureButton' down
        int        edges [MAXBUTTONS];         // bitmap positions
        HANDLE     bmHandles [MAXBUTTONS];     // bitmap handles
        WORD       bmIDS [MAXBUTTONS];         // ID of each button
        BYTE       flags [MAXBUTTONS];         // flags for each button

}       ToolBarRec, NEAR * PToolBarRec;

static LONG hookKey;

//─────────────────────────────────────────────────────────────────
// Name:     GetToolBarRec
// Purpose:  Given a window handle, return a pointer to the corresponding
//           toolbar record.
//─────────────────────────────────────────────────────────────────

static PToolBarRec PASCAL GetToolBarRec (HWND Wnd)
{
        return (PToolBarRec) GetWindowWord (Wnd, 0);
}

//─────────────────────────────────────────────────────────────────
// Name:     ResizeWindow
// Purpose:  Routine to force toolbar to proper size and position.
//─────────────────────────────────────────────────────────────────

static void PASCAL ResizeWindow (HWND Wnd)
{
        RECT r;
        PToolBarRec p;

        p = GetToolBarRec (Wnd);
        GetClientRect (GetParent (Wnd), &r);
        SetWindowPos (Wnd, 0, 0, 0, r.right, p−>height, SWP_NOZORDER);
}

//─────────────────────────────────────────────────────────────────
// Name:     SubclassParentWndProc
// Purpose:  Subclassing routine for the main application window.
//─────────────────────────────────────────────────────────────────

#pragma argsused

LONG FAR PASCAL _export SubclassParentWndProc (HWND  Wnd,  WORD  Msg,
                                               WPARAM wParam, LPARAM
                                               lParam)

{
        if (Msg == WM_SIZE) ResizeWindow (GetToolBarWindow (Wnd));
        return CallOldProc (Wnd, Msg, wParam, lParam, hookKey);
}
```

```
//---------------------------------------------------------------
// Name:    ColorFix
// Purpose: Fix up a color value for the LoadButtonBitmap routine.
//---------------------------------------------------------------

static COLORREF PASCAL ColorFix (COLORREF color)
{
    return RGB (GetBValue (color), GetGValue (color), GetRValue (color));
}

//---------------------------------------------------------------
// Name:    InternalLoadButtonBitmap
// Purpose: Called by LoadButtonBitmap and LoadDisabledButtonBitmap.
//---------------------------------------------------------------

static HBITMAP PASCAL InternalLoadButtonBitmap (HANDLE hInstance,
                                      int bmID, BOOL fEnable)
{
    HDC dc;
    HBITMAP hbm;
    HANDLE hRes;
    LPDWORD lprgb;
    LPVOID lpb;
    LPBITMAPINFOHEADER lpbi;

    hRes = LoadResource (hInstance, FindResource (hInstance,
                    MAKEINTRESOURCE(bmID), RT_BITMAP));

    lpbi = (LPBITMAPINFOHEADER) LockResource (hRes);
    if (lpbi == NULL) return (NULL);

    lprgb = (LPDWORD) ((LPSTR) lpbi + (int) lpbi->biSize);
    lpb = (LPVOID) (lprgb + 16);

    // Black

    if (fEnable)
        lprgb [0] = ColorFix (GetSysColor (COLOR_WINDOWTEXT));
    else
        lprgb [0] = ColorFix (GetSysColor (COLOR_BTNSHADOW));

    lprgb [8] = ColorFix (GetSysColor (COLOR_BTNFACE));      // Light gray
    lprgb [7] = ColorFix (GetSysColor (COLOR_BTNSHADOW));    // Gray
    lprgb [15] = ColorFix (GetSysColor (COLOR_BTNHIGHLIGHT)); // White

    dc = GetDC (NULL);
    hbm = CreateDIBitmap (dc, lpbi, CBM_INIT, lpb,
                        (LPBITMAPINFO) lpbi, DIB_RGB_COLORS);

    ReleaseDC (NULL, dc);
    GlobalUnlock (hRes);
    FreeResource (hRes);
    return (hbm);
}

//---------------------------------------------------------------
// Name:    LoadButtonBitmap
// Purpose: Load a button bitmap and tweak for system colors.
//---------------------------------------------------------------

static HBITMAP PASCAL LoadButtonBitmap (HANDLE hInstance, int bmID)
{
    return InternalLoadButtonBitmap (hInstance, bmID, TRUE);
}

//---------------------------------------------------------------
// Name:    LoadDisabledButtonBitmap
// Purpose: Load a button bitmap and make it look disabled.
//---------------------------------------------------------------

static HBITMAP PASCAL LoadDisabledButtonBitmap (HANDLE hInstance, int bmID)
```

```
{
        return InternalLoadButtonBitmap (hInstance, bmID, FALSE);
}

//─────────────────────────────────────────────────────────────
// Name:     LoadToolBitmaps
// Purpose: Load all specified bitmaps into the ToolBarRec structure.
//─────────────────────────────────────────────────────────────

static int LONG LoadToolBitmaps (PToolBarRec p, LPINT pBitmaps,
                                 HANDLE hInstance)
{
        int x;
        BITMAP bm;
        int ret = −1;

        if (pBitmaps != NULL)
        {
          x = p−>border;
          while (*pBitmaps != −1 && p−>NumButtons < MAXBUTTONS − 1)
          {
            if (*pBitmaps == 0) x += p−>border * 3;
            else
            {
              p−>bmIDS [p−>NumButtons] = *pBitmaps;
              p−>bmHandles [p−>NumButtons] = LoadButtonBitmap (hInstance,
                                                               *pBitmaps);

              if (p−>bmHandles [p−>NumButtons] == NULL) return (ret);

              // If this is first bitmap, determine dimensions

              if (p−>height == −1)
              {
                  GetObject (p−>bmHandles [p−>NumButtons],
                             sizeof (BITMAP), &bm);

                  p−>bmWidth = bm.bmWidth / 2;
                  p−>bmHeight = bm.bmHeight;
                  p−>height = bm.bmHeight + (p−>border * 2);
              }

              p−>edges [p−>NumButtons++] = x;
              x += p−>bmWidth + p−>border;
            }

            pBitmaps++;
          }

          if (p−>NumButtons != 0) ret = 0;
        }

        return (ret);
}

//─────────────────────────────────────────────────────────────
// Name:     InitToolBarWindow
// Purpose: Initialization code for setting up the toolbar window.
//─────────────────────────────────────────────────────────────

static LONG PASCAL InitToolBarWindow (HWND Wnd, LONG lParam)
{
        LPCSTR text;
        LPINT pBitmaps;
        PToolBarRec p;
        LONG res = −1L;
        HANDLE hInstance;
```

```
        p = (PToolBarRec) LocalAlloc (LPTR, sizeof (ToolBarRec));
        if (p != NULL)
        {
            // Initialize the ToolBarRec data structure

            p->CaptureButton = -1;
            p->border = (GetSystemMetrics (SM_CXFRAME) + 3) / 2;
            p->height = -1;
            SetWindowWord (Wnd, 0, (WORD) p);

            // Load the various bitmaps

            pBitmaps = (I PINT) ((LPCREATESTRUCT) lParam)->lpCreateParams;
            hInstance = GetWindowWord (Wnd, GWW_HINSTANCE);

            if (LoadToolBitmaps (p, pBitmaps, hInstance) == 0)
            {
                ResizeWindow (Wnd);
                SetProp (GetParent (Wnd), szClassName, Wnd);
                hookKey = HookWindow (GetParent (Wnd),
                                    (FARPROC) SubclassParentWndProc,
                                        szHookName);

                res = 0;
            }
        }

        return (res);
}

//-----------------------------------------------------------------
// Name:    GetCellRect
// Purpose: Return the frame rectangle for a given cell.
//-----------------------------------------------------------------

static void PASCAL GetCellRect (PToolBarRec p, int cellNum, LPRECT r)
{
        r->left = p->edges [cellNum];
        r->right = r->left + p->bmWidth;
        r->top = p->border;
        r->bottom = r->top + p->bmHeight;
}

//-----------------------------------------------------------------
// Name:    PaintCell
// Purpose: Paint a specified cell in the toolbar.
//-----------------------------------------------------------------

static void PASCAL PaintCell (HDC dc, PToolBarRec p, int cellNum)
{
        int XSrc;
        HDC hMemDC;
        HBITMAP hbm;
        BOOL fDown;

        if ((p->flags [cellNum] & FHIDDEN) == 0)
        {
            fDown = (p->flags [cellNum] & FPUSHED) ? TRUE : FALSE;
            if (cellNum == p->CaptureButton && p->CapturePressed) fDown = !fDown;
            XSrc = fDown ? p->bmWidth : 0;

            hMemDC = CreateCompatibleDC (dc);
            hbm = SelectObject (hMemDC, p->bmHandles [cellNum]);
            BitBlt (dc, p->edges [cellNum], p->border, p->bmWidth,
                    p->bmHeight, hMemDC, XSrc, 0, SRCCOPY);
            SelectObject (hMemDC, hbm);
            DeleteDC (hMemDC);
        }
}
```

```
//————————————————————————————————————————————————
// Name:     ToolBarPaint
// Purpose:  This routine is responsible for painting the tool bar.
//————————————————————————————————————————————————

static int PASCAL ToolBarPaint (HWND Wnd)
{
    int i;
    RECT r;
    PToolBarRec p;
    PAINTSTRUCT ps;

    BeginPaint (Wnd, &ps);
    p = GetToolBarRec (Wnd);

    // First, draw the bottom edge of the toolbar

    GetClientRect (Wnd, &r);
    PatBlt (ps.hdc, 0, r.bottom −1, r.right − r.left, 1, BLACKNESS);
    PatBlt (ps.hdc, 0, 0, r.right − r.left, 1, WHITENESS);

    // Now draw each cell in turn

    for (i = 0; i < p−>NumButtons; i++)
        PaintCell (ps.hdc, p, i);

    EndPaint (Wnd, &ps);
    return (0);
}

//————————————————————————————————————————————————
// Name:     DestroyToolBarWindow
// Purpose:  Clean-up code for the toolbar window.
//————————————————————————————————————————————————

static int PASCAL DestroyToolBarWindow (HWND Wnd)
{
    int i;
    PToolBarRec p;

    p = GetToolBarRec (Wnd);
    RemoveProp (GetParent (Wnd), szClassName);
    UnHookWindow (GetParent (Wnd), hookKey);

    // Deallocate bitmap handles

    for (i = 0; i < p−>NumButtons; i++)
        DeleteObject (p−>bmHandles [i]);

    LocalFree ((HLOCAL) p);
    return (0);
}

//————————————————————————————————————————————————
// Name:     AdjustButtonGroup
// Purpose:  Release any pressed buttons in the same group.
//————————————————————————————————————————————————

static void PASCAL AdjustButtonGroup (HWND Wnd, PToolBarRec p, int ClickedButton)
{
    RECT r;
    int groupMask;
    int num;

    groupMask = p−>flags [ClickedButton] & FGROUPBITS;
    if (groupMask != 0)
    {
        for (num = 0; num < p−>NumButtons; num++)
        {
            if (num != ClickedButton &&
```

```
                    (p−>flags [num] & FGROUPBITS) == groupMask &&
                    (p−>flags [num] & FPUSHED))
                {
                    p−>flags [num] &= ~FPUSHED;
                    GetCellRect (p, num, &r);
                    InvalidateRect (Wnd, &r, FALSE);
                }
            }
        }
}

//─────────────────────────────────────────────────────────────
// Name:    ClickButton
// Purpose: Adjust state of a button and send message to parent.
//─────────────────────────────────────────────────────────────

static void PASCAL ClickButton (HWND Wnd, PToolBarRec p, int ClickedButton)
{
    RECT r;

    if (p−>flags [ClickedButton] & FSTICKY)
        p−>flags [ClickedButton] ^= FPUSHED;

    // Redraw the button in its new state

    GetCellRect (p, ClickedButton, &r);
    InvalidateRect (Wnd, &r, FALSE);

    // If this is a group button, adjust the group

    AdjustButtonGroup (Wnd, p, ClickedButton);

    // Send message to parent window

    SendMessage (GetParent (Wnd), WM_COMMAND, p−>bmIDS
                    [ClickedButton], p−>flags [ClickedButton] & FPUSHED);
}

//─────────────────────────────────────────────────────────────
// Name:    ButtonHitTest
// Purpose: Test for a hit on any button in the toolbar.
//─────────────────────────────────────────────────────────────

static int PASCAL ButtonHitTest (PToolBarRec p, LPARAM lParam)
{
    RECT r;
    POINT pt;
    int buttonNum;

    pt.x = LOWORD (lParam);
    pt.y = HIWORD (lParam);

    for (buttonNum = 0; buttonNum < p−>NumButtons; buttonNum++)
    {
        GetCellRect (p, buttonNum, &r);
        if (PtInRect (&r, pt)) return (buttonNum);
    }

    return (−1);
}

//─────────────────────────────────────────────────────────────
// Name:    HandleButtonDown
// Purpose: Handle mouse clicks in the toolbar.
//─────────────────────────────────────────────────────────────

static LONG PASCAL HandleButtonDown (HWND Wnd, LPARAM lParam)
{
    RECT r;
    BYTE flgs;
```

```
        int buttonNum;
        PToolBarRec p;

        p = GetToolBarRec (Wnd);
        buttonNum = ButtonHitTest (p, lParam);
        if (buttonNum != −1 && (p−>flags [buttonNum] & (FDISABLED | FHIDDEN)) == 0)
        {
            flgs = p−>flags [buttonNum];

            // If button is in a modal group and already pushed, do nothing.

            if ((flgs & FGROUPBITS) == 0 || (flgs & FPUSHED) == 0)
            {
                SetCapture (Wnd);
                p−>CaptureButton = buttonNum;
                p−>CapturePressed = TRUE;
                GetCellRect (p, buttonNum, &r);
                InvalidateRect (Wnd, &r, FALSE);
            }
        }

        return (0);
}

//————————————————————————————————————————————————————————————————
// Name:    HandleButtonUp
// Purpose: Handle mouse ups in the toolbar.
//————————————————————————————————————————————————————————————————

#pragma argsused
static LONG PASCAL HandleButtonUp (HWND Wnd, LPARAM lParam)
{
        PToolBarRec p;

        p = GetToolBarRec (Wnd);
        if (p−>CaptureButton != −1)
        {
            ReleaseCapture();
            if (p−>CapturePressed) ClickButton (Wnd, p, p−>CaptureButton);
            p−>CapturePressed = FALSE;
            p−>CaptureButton = −1;
        }

        return (0);
}

//————————————————————————————————————————————————————————————————
// Name:    HandleMouseMoves
// Purpose: Handle mouse movement in the toolbar.
//————————————————————————————————————————————————————————————————

static LONG PASCAL HandleMouseMoves (HWND Wnd, LPARAM lParam)
{
        RECT r;
        int buttonNum;
        PToolBarRec p;

        p = GetToolBarRec (Wnd);
        if (p−>CaptureButton != −1)
        {
            buttonNum = ButtonHitTest (p, lParam);
            if (buttonNum == p−>CaptureButton)
            {
                if (p−>CapturePressed == FALSE)
                {
                    p−>CapturePressed = TRUE;
                    GetCellRect (p, p−>CaptureButton, &r);
```

```
                    InvalidateRect (Wnd, &r, FALSE);
                }
            }
            else
            {
                if (p->CapturePressed == TRUE)
                {
                    p->CapturePressed = FALSE;
                    GetCellRect (p, p->CaptureButton, &r);
                    InvalidateRect (Wnd, &r, FALSE);
                }
            }
        }

        return (0);
}

//----------------------------------------------------------------------
// Name:     ToolBarWndProc
// Purpose:  Window procedure for toolbar windows.
//----------------------------------------------------------------------

LONG FAR PASCAL _export ToolBarWndProc (HWND Wnd, WORD Msg,
                                        WPARAM wParam, LPARAM
                                        lParam)
{
        switch (Msg)
        {
        case WM_LBUTTONDOWN:

            return HandleButtonDown (Wnd, lParam);

        case WM_LBUTTONUP:

            return HandleButtonUp (Wnd, lParam);

        case WM_MOUSEMOVE:

            return HandleMouseMoves (Wnd, lParam);

        case WM_PAINT:

            return ToolBarPaint (Wnd);

        case WM_CREATE:

            return InitToolBarWindow (Wnd, lParam);

        case WM_DESTROY:

            return DestroyToolBarWindow (Wnd);
        }

        return DefWindowProc (Wnd, Msg, wParam, lParam);
}

//----------------------------------------------------------------------
// Name:     RegisterToolBar
// Purpose:  Register the toolbar window procedure.
//----------------------------------------------------------------------

static BOOL PASCAL RegisterToolBar (HANDLE hInstance)
{
        WNDCLASS cls;

        if (GetClassInfo (hInstance, szClassName, &cls) == 0)
        {
            cls.style           = 0;
            cls.lpfnWndProc     = (WNDPROC) ToolBarWndProc;
            cls.cbClsExtra      = 0;
```

```
            cls.cbWndExtra        = sizeof (void NEAR *);
            cls.hInstance         = hInstance;
            cls.hIcon             = 0;
            cls.hCursor           = LoadCursor (NULL, IDC_ARROW);
            cls.hbrBackground     = COLOR_BTNFACE + 1;
            cls.lpszMenuName      = NULL;
            cls.lpszClassName     = szClassName;

        return RegisterClass (&cls);
    }

    return TRUE;
}

//─────────────────────────────────────────────────────────
// Name:     GetToolBarWindow
// Purpose:  Return the handle of this window's tool bar.
//─────────────────────────────────────────────────────────

HWND PASCAL GetToolBarWindow (HWND hWndParent)
{
    if (hWndParent != NULL && IsWindow (hWndParent))
        return GetProp (hWndParent, szClassName);
    else
        return NULL;
}

//─────────────────────────────────────────────────────────
// Name:     CreateToolBarWindow
// Purpose:  Create a toolbar window and attach it to the designated parent.
//─────────────────────────────────────────────────────────

HWND PASCAL CreateToolBarWindow (HANDLE hInstance,
                          HWND hWndParent, LPINT lpButtons)
{
    HWND Wnd = NULL;

    // Check that we've got a valid parent window

    if (hWndParent != NULL && IsWindow (hWndParent))
    {
        // Ok so far, but has window already got a toolbar?

        Wnd = GetToolBarWindow (hWndParent);
        if (Wnd == NULL)
            if (RegisterToolBar (hInstance))
                Wnd = CreateWindow (szClassName, "", WS_CHILD | WS_VISIBLE,
                          0, 0, 0, 0, hWndParent, NULL, hInstance,
                          lpButtons);
    }

    return (Wnd);
}

//─────────────────────────────────────────────────────────
// Name:     InternalSetButtonFlags
// Purpose:  Set a button flag either true or false.
//─────────────────────────────────────────────────────────

static int PASCAL InternalSetButtonFlags (HWND hWndParent, int buttonNum,
                          WORD Mask, BOOL val)
{
    RECT r;
    int ret;
    HWND Wnd;
    HANDLE hInstance;

    PToolBarRec p;
```

```
        ret = 0;
        Wnd = GetToolBarWindow (hWndParent);
        p = GetToolBarRec (Wnd);
        if (Wnd != NULL && p != NULL && buttonNum < p−>NumButtons)
        {
            ret = (p−>flags [buttonNum] & Mask) ? TRUE : FALSE;
            p−>flags [buttonNum] &= ~Mask;
            if (val)
            {
                p−>flags [buttonNum] |= Mask;

                if (Mask < FHIDDEN)
                {
                    // We're adding to a group :- better set sticky bit

                    p−>flags [buttonNum] |= FSTICKY;

                    // If button is down, adjust group

                    if (p−>flags [buttonNum] & FPUSHED)
                        AdjustButtonGroup (Wnd, p, buttonNum);
                }
            }

            // If this is a button enable/disable, reload the bitmap

            if (Mask == FDISABLED)
            {
                hInstance = GetWindowWord (Wnd, GWW_HINSTANCE);
                DeleteObject (p−>bmHandles [buttonNum]);
                p−>bmHandles [buttonNum] = (val) ?
                    LoadDisabledButtonBitmap (hInstance, p−>bmIDS [buttonNum]) :
                    LoadButtonBitmap (hInstance, p−>bmIDS [buttonNum]);
            }

            // If change to hide or disable state, then update display

            if (Mask & (FHIDDEN | FDISABLED))
            {
                GetCellRect (p, buttonNum, &r);
                InvalidateRect (Wnd, &r, TRUE);
            }
        }

        return (ret);
}

//─────────────────────────────────────────────────────────────────
// Name:    SetButtonModal
// Purpose: Make a button modal or non-modal.
//─────────────────────────────────────────────────────────────────

int PASCAL SetButtonModal (HWND hWndParent, int buttonNum, BOOL fModal)
{
        return InternalSetButtonFlags (hWndParent, buttonNum, FSTICKY, fModal);
}

//─────────────────────────────────────────────────────────────────
// Name:    EnableToolBarButton
// Purpose: Enable or disable a button in the toolbar.
//─────────────────────────────────────────────────────────────────

int PASCAL EnableToolBarButton (HWND hWndParent, int buttonNum, BOOL fDisable)
{
        return InternalSetButtonFlags (hWndParent, buttonNum, FDISABLED, fDisable);
}
```

```
//————————————————————————————————————————————————
// Name:    HideToolBarButton
// Purpose: Hide or unhide a toolbar button.
//————————————————————————————————————————————————

int PASCAL HideToolBarButton (HWND hWndParent, int buttonNum, BOOL fHide)
{
    return InternalSetButtonFlags (hWndParent, buttonNum, FHIDDEN, fHide);
}


//————————————————————————————————————————————————
// Name:    SetButtonGroup
// Purpose: Assign a button to a group.
//          If groupNum is −1, resigns from a group
//————————————————————————————————————————————————

void PASCAL SetButtonGroup (HWND hWndParent, int buttonNum, int groupNum)
{
    InternalSetButtonFlags (hWndParent, buttonNum, FGROUPBITS, FALSE);
    if (groupNum >= 0 && groupNum <= 3)
        InternalSetButtonFlags (hWndParent, buttonNum, 1 << groupNum, TRUE);
}


//————————————————————————————————————————————————
// Name:    SetButtonPushed
// Purpose: Set a modal button to be pushed or unpushed.
//————————————————————————————————————————————————

int PASCAL SetButtonPushed (HWND hWndParent, int buttonNum, BOOL fPush)
{
    int ret;
    HWND Wnd;
    RECT r;
    PToolBarRec p;

    ret = 0;
    Wnd = GetToolBarWindow (hWndParent);
    p = GetToolBarRec (Wnd);
    if (Wnd != NULL && p != NULL && buttonNum < p->NumButtons)
    {
        // Only makes sense for modal buttons
        if (p->flags [buttonNum] & FSTICKY)
        {
            ret = (p->flags [buttonNum] & FPUSHED) ? TRUE : FALSE;
            p->flags [buttonNum] &= ~FPUSHED;
            if (fPush)
            {
                p->flags [buttonNum] |= FPUSHED;
                AdjustButtonGroup (Wnd, p, buttonNum);
            }

            GetCellRect (p, buttonNum, &r);
            InvalidateRect (Wnd, &r, FALSE);
        }
    }

    return (ret);
}


//————————————————————————————————————————————————
// Name:    IsButtonPushed
// Purpose: Determine if a modal button is pushed or unpushed.
//————————————————————————————————————————————————

int PASCAL IsButtonPushed (HWND hWndParent, int buttonNum)
{
    int ret;
    HWND Wnd;
    PToolBarRec p;
```

```
        ret = 0;
        Wnd = GetToolBarWindow (hWndParent);
        p = GetToolBarRec (Wnd);
        if (Wnd != NULL && p != NULL && buttonNum < p−>NumButtons)
          if (p−>flags [buttonNum] & FSTICKY)
            ret = (p−>flags [buttonNum] & FPUSHED) ? TRUE : FALSE;
        return (ret);
}
```

```
/* TOOLBAR4.H */

// © 1994 Dave Jewell and Addison-Wesley, ALL RIGHTS RESERVED

#ifndef _INC_TOOLBAR
#define _INC_TOOLBAR          /* #defined if toolbar.h has been included */

#ifdef __cplusplus
extern "C" {
#endif

HWND PASCAL GetToolBarWindow (HWND hWndParent);
int PASCAL SetButtonModal (HWND hWndParent, int buttonNum, BOOL fModal);
int PASCAL HideToolBarButton (HWND hWndParent, int buttonNum, BOOL fHide);
int PASCAL IsButtonPushed (HWND hWndParent, int buttonNum);
void PASCAL SetButtonGroup (HWND hWndParent, int buttonNum, int groupNum);
int PASCAL SetButtonPushed (HWND hWndParent, int buttonNum, BOOL fPush);
int PASCAL EnableToolBarButton (HWND hWndParent, int buttonNum, BOOL fDisable);
HWND PASCAL CreateToolBarWindow (HANDLE hInstance, HWND hWndParent,
                                 LPINT lpButtons);

#ifdef __cplusplus
}
#endif

#endif
```

Figure 6.16 TOOLBAR4.H: the finished header file for the toolbar code.

```
/* BARTEST5.C

// © 1994 Dave Jewell and Addison-Wesley, ALL RIGHTS RESERVED

*/#include  <windows.h>
#include   "toolbar.h"

char szAppName[] = "ToolBarTest";

//————————————————————————————————————
// Name:    WindowProc
// Purpose: Window procedure for main application window.
//————————————————————————————————————
LONG FAR PASCAL _export WindowProc (HWND Wnd, WORD Msg,
                                    WPARAM wParam, LPARAM lParam)
{
    static BOOL fDisable = FALSE;
    static BOOL fHide = FALSE;

    switch (Msg)
    {
      case WM_CHAR:
```

Figure 6.17 BARTEST5.C: the test program for the toolbar code.

```
                    SetButtonPushed (Wnd, 0, TRUE);
                    break;

                case WM_LBUTTONDOWN:

                    HideToolBarButton (Wnd, 8, fHide ^= 1);
                    break;

                case WM_RBUTTONDOWN:

                    EnableToolBarButton (Wnd, 9, fDisable ^= 1);
                    break;

                case WM_DESTROY:

                    PostQuitMessage (0);
                    break;

                default:

                    return DefWindowProc (Wnd, Msg, wParam, lParam);
            }

            return (0);
}

//─────────────────────────────────────────────────────────────
// Name:    InitAppClass
// Purpose: Register the main application window class.
//─────────────────────────────────────────────────────────────

BOOL PASCAL InitAppClass (HANDLE hInstance)
{
        WNDCLASS cls;

        if (GetClassInfo (hInstance, szAppName, &cls) == 0)
        {
            cls.style            = CS_VREDRAW | CS_HREDRAW;
            cls.lpfnWndProc      = (WNDPROC) WindowProc;
            cls.cbClsExtra       = 0;
            cls.cbWndExtra       = 0;
            cls.hInstance        = hInstance;
            cls.hIcon            = LoadIcon (NULL, IDI_APPLICATION);
            cls.hCursor          = LoadCursor (NULL, IDC_ARROW);
            cls.hbrBackground    = GetStockObject (WHITE_BRUSH);
            cls.lpszMenuName     = MAKEINTRESOURCE (1);
            cls.lpszClassName    = szAppName;
            return RegisterClass (&cls);
        }

        return (TRUE);
}

//─────────────────────────────────────────────────────────────
// Name:    WinMain
// Purpose: Main application entry point.
//─────────────────────────────────────────────────────────────

#pragma argsused

int PASCAL WinMain (HANDLE hInstance, HANDLE hPrevInstance,
                    LPSTR lpCmdLine, int nCmdShow)
{
        HWND Wnd;
        MSG Msg;
        static int bitMaps [15] = { 1000, 1001, 0, 0, 1002, 1003, 1004,
                                    1005, 1006, 1007, 0, 0, 1008, 1009, −1 };

        // Register application class if needed
```

```
    if (InitAppClass (hInstance) == FALSE)
        return (0);

    // Create the main application window

    Wnd = CreateWindow (szAppName, szAppName, WS_OVERLAPPEDWINDOW,
                        CW_USEDEFAULT, CW_USEDEFAULT,
                        CW_USEDEFAULT, CW_USEDEFAULT,
                        0, 0, hInstance, NULL);

    if (Wnd != NULL)
    {
        ShowWindow (Wnd, nCmdShow);
        UpdateWindow (Wnd);
        if (CreateToolBarWindow (hInstance, Wnd, bitMaps) != NULL)
        {
            // Make button 0 and 1 into a group

            SetButtonGroup (Wnd, 0, 0);
            SetButtonGroup (Wnd, 1, 0);
        }
    }

    while (GetMessage (&Msg, 0, 0, 0))
    {
        TranslateMessage (&Msg);
        DispatchMessage (&Msg);
    }

    return (Msg.wParam);
}
```

Note

Appendix 6 contains the toolbar source code in the form of a Pascal unit, TOOLBAR.PAS. The Pascal equivalent of the test program, BARTEST.PAS, is also included in the appendix and both files can be found on the disk.

Super spin buttons 7

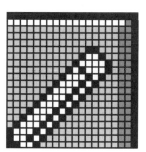

In a sense, spin buttons started it all. They appeared in Windows applications (in particular, Microsoft's own Windows applications!) long before toolbars, status bars, floating tool palettes and the like were first seen. This led to a lot of curiosity on the part of other developers: how do you go about implementing a spin button in your own application, and how can you make your spin button code reusable? Jeffrey Richter's excellent book, *Windows 3: A Developer's Guide* (M&T Books, 1991), acknowledged this interest by including a chapter on spin buttons.

So what exactly is a spin button, and why are they so called? Anyone who has used a one-armed bandit gambling machine will be familiar with the way in which numbers (and other symbols) spin round on several drums inside the machine. This is really the essence of a spin button, which actually has very little to do with spinning at all. A spin button is a dialog box control that looks, if anything, like a tiny scroll-bar with just the arrows at either end visible. Pressing the uppermost arrow will increase the value of some numeric variable, while pressing the lower arrow will decrease its value. A good example of spin button usage can be found in the Control Panel, where they're used to set up the system date and time. This is illustrated in Figure 7.1.

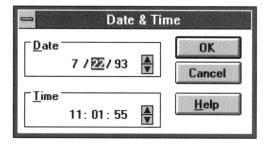

Figure 7.1 Spin button usage in the Microsoft Control Panel.

Generally speaking, a spin button is always associated with an edit box control which contains the value being changed. For example, in a CAD application, you might have a spin button that controls grid spacing. An edit box would allow you to type a grid spacing value directly into the dialog, or you could use the spin button to adjust the value already there. From one point of view, spin buttons are simply a convenience for those people who don't like taking their fingers off the mouse! With a spin button, you can avoid moving your hand continually between the mouse and the keyboard. For some people, this is a significant productivity benefit, depending on the type of work they're doing.

Spin buttons come in two flavors: vertical and horizontal. The vertical type (as shown in Figure 7.1) is the most common, because there is an obvious relationship between pressing the up and down parts of the spin button and increasing or decreasing the value in the associated edit box. Horizontal spin buttons are not so widely used, but the code developed here supports both types. In addition, the code is written in such a way that it can be used with or without an edit box. If you use a spin button in isolation, notification messages will be sent directly to the parent window. This is usually the dialog box window, although, of course, there's nothing to stop you using the spin button in a normal application window.

In Microsoft's literature, they refer to the spin button's associated edit box as a 'buddy', and we'll adopt the same convention here. Buddies are so called because the two controls cooperate together in a seamless way. If a spin button has a buddy, then no notification message is sent to the parent window. Instead, the highlighted selection in the buddy control is incremented or decremented according to which part of the spin button control was pressed.

If you look back at Figure 7.1, you'll see that only part of the date field is highlighted. The day of the month (22 in this case) is highlighted, but the rest of the control isn't. In these circumstances, the spin button control will try to interpret the highlighted part of the buddy text as a number, and increment or decrement it as appropriate. If there is no text selection, the entire text of the buddy control is assumed to be a number. In either case, code inside the spin button control checks that a valid number is present, and calls the MessageBeep routine if this isn't the case. All this functionality is built into the code that we'll put together.

One size fits all

Because of the popularity of the spin button, a number of different specimens can be found. Aside from Richter's code, which I've already mentioned, you can also get a spin button control packaged as a VBX (Visual Basic Extension) so that it can be used from Visual Basic and from Visual C++. A number of other suppliers of programmers' utilities also implement a spin button control and, of course, there are the proprietary implementations buried deep inside the Windows Control Panel, Word for Windows, and the like.

You often find that these different implementations allow you to create a spin button of any size. Personally, this isn't something I like. You sometimes see spin buttons of truly gargantuan proportions which just look terrible. Other times, you see spin buttons so small that it's difficult to realize exactly what you're looking at. These variable-sized spin buttons work by explicitly drawing the shape of the spin button in the device context. In other words, rather than using a bitmap (as we've done for the toolbox palette, Excel-style dialog box effects and toolbar) these spin buttons use GDI drawing routines to paint the control.

There are a couple of disadvantages with this approach. Firstly, it's difficult (as I've already implied) to make the control look good when drawn very large or small. Secondly, unless you're prepared to expend a lot of effort in refining the drawing code, it's hard to provide a nice-looking pushed-in appearance while the mouse is held down over one or other of the control's arrows. It's been said that a picture is worth a thousand words. In this modern age of WYSIWYG, fancy GUIs and so forth, we might coin another adage: 'A bitmap is worth a thousand GDI drawing instructions!' Certainly, it's far easier blitting a bitmap onto the screen than trying to fine-tune a complex piece of drawing code so as to get a polished appearance at all possible sizes.

Of course, this does mean that we're restricted to one size for our spin buttons, but the advantages outweigh the disadvantages. You get simplified drawing code, and you know that your spin button is going to look neat no matter what. Figure 7.2 shows the bitmap used to implement the spin button control. You can ignore the thick border around the image – this is just to show the limits of the bitmap on the printed page. When loading the bitmap, we need to remember to use our old friend the LoadButtonBitmap routine, so that the bitmap remains consistent with the currently defined Windows color scheme.

As you can see, the bitmap contains all the images needed for the horizontal and vertical variants of the spin button, shown in both the normal and the pushed-in state, making a total of eight small images in all. The drawing code will obviously need to be able to select the appropriate image to use when drawing the bitmap. This is analogous to the bitmap used in Chapter 5, which was used to contain the various states of the check boxes and radio buttons. The bitmap shown here can be found on the companion disk as SPIN.RC and SPIN.RES.

Let's begin developing the spin button code along the same lines that we've used for other code modules in this book. In order to make things simple, we'll create the

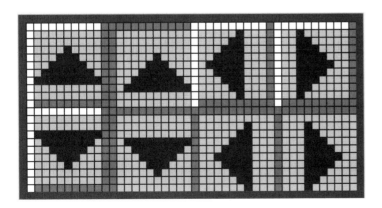

Figure 7.2 The bitmap used to create the spin button controls.

spin button window as a child of a normal application window. Once the code is finished, we'll consider the best way of implementing spin buttons inside an actual dialog box. The aim with this approach is to minimize the amount of interaction needed with a dialog editor. As I implied in Chapter 5, it's perfectly possible to create custom control dialogs without the need to build specialized custom control libraries, and without the necessity of providing all the interface routines that allow those custom controls to interact with a dialog editor such as Borland's Resource Workshop. Towards the end of this chapter, we'll explore a very simple technique that can be used to create custom dialog controls 'on the fly' within a dialog box.

One problem is that we don't have any direct control over the way dialog box controls are created. When we created floating toolbox palettes and tool bars in previous chapters, we were able to make use of the final parameter of the CreateWindow call. In the case of the tool bar, if you remember, we used it to pass a far pointer to an array of bitmap IDs. We can't resort to any such trickery here because the individual controls of a dialog box are created internally by the dialog manager when the dialog is initialized. This raises a question: how do we tell a spin button whether to have a horizontal or vertical orientation? The correct way to approach this problem is to use the available bits in the low-order word of the window's style. This is the same approach taken by Microsoft when they designed the internal control classes such as BUTTON, STATIC, and so forth. In all cases, the low-order style bits are used to define properties of the control such as whether a BUTTON window will be a check box control, whether an edit box will left- or right-align the text and so forth. The low-order style bits of each built-in control class are known and understood by dialog editors such as Borland's Resource Workshop, and you can use such resource editors to set up each control's style as required.

OK, then. We'll specify that bit 7 of the style word is going to differentiate between vertical and horizontal spin buttons. With the addition of a few more definitions, our header file looks as shown in Figure 7.3.

Figure 7.3 SPIN.H: the header file for implementing spin buttons.

```
/* SPIN.H */

// © 1994 Dave Jewell and Addison-Wesley, ALL RIGHTS RESERVED

#ifndef    _SPINBTN
#define    _SPINBTN         /* #defined if SPIN.H has been included */

#ifdef     __cplusplus
extern     "C" {
#endif

#define    SP_VERT          0x00        // Style for vertical spin buttons
#define    SP_HORIZ         0x80        // Style for horizontal spin buttons
#define    SPINCLASSNAME    "SpinButton" // Class name for spin buttons
#define    SPINMESSAGE      WM_USER     // Spin notification message

BOOL PASCAL InitSpinButton (HANDLE hInstance);

#ifdef     __cplusplus
extern     "C" {
#endif

#endif     /* _SPINBTN */
```

As usual, the header file is written in such a way that it can be used for C++ programming as well as for regular C work. The SP_VERT and SP_HORIZ constants are used to specify the horizontal or vertical orientation of a spin button, as just explained. The SPINCLASSNAME constant gives the name of the window class used to implement spin buttons and the SPINMESSAGE constant is used to indicate the message number used by the spin button control when notifying its parent window that it has been clicked. You might need to modify its value so as not to conflict with other custom messages used in your application. We'll talk more about the spin notification message later.

The only routine defined in the header file is InitSpinButton. This routine is responsible for registering the spin button class. The application must call this routine before attempting to create any spin button windows, or before invoking a dialog box which contains spin button controls.

The skeletal spin button code, SPIN1.C, is shown in Figure 7.4 and the test application is shown in Figure 7.5. As you can see, the test code creates two spin buttons, children of the main application window, one of which has the SP_VERT style, and the other the SP_HORIZ style.

Figure 7.4   SPIN1.C: the beginnings of the spin button code module.

```
/* SPIN1.C */

// © 1994 Dave Jewell and Addison-Wesley, ALL RIGHTS RESERVED

#include    <windows.h>
#include    "spin.h"

typedef struct SpinButtonRec
{
      BOOL            horiz;        // spinbutton orientation
} SpinButtonRec, NEAR * PSpinButtonRec;

//------------------------------------------------------------------
// Name:    SpinButtonWndProc
// Purpose: Window procedure for the spin button window class.
//------------------------------------------------------------------

LONG FAR PASCAL _export SpinButtonWndProc (HWND Wnd, WORD Msg,
                               WPARAM wParam,
                               LPARAM lParam)
{
      return DefWindowProc (Wnd, Msg, wParam, lParam);
}


//------------------------------------------------------------------
// Name:    InitSpinButton
// Purpose: Register the spin button window class.
//------------------------------------------------------------------

BOOL PASCAL InitSpinButton (HANDLE hInstance)
{
      WNDCLASS cls;

      if (GetClassInfo (hInstance, SPINCLASSNAME, &cls) == FALSE)
      {
        cls.style             = CS_DBLCLKS;
        cls.lpfnWndProc       = (WNDPROC) SpinButtonWndProc;
        cls.cbClsExtra        = 0;
        cls.cbWndExtra        = sizeof (PSpinButtonRec);
```

```
            cls.hInstance            = hInstance;
            cls.hIcon                = 0;
            cls.hCursor              = LoadCursor (NULL, IDC_ARROW);
            cls.hbrBackground        = 0;
            cls.lpszMenuName         = NULL;
            cls.lpszClassName        = SPINCLASSNAME;

            return RegisterClass (&cls);
        }

        return (TRUE);
    }
```

Figure 7.5 SPINTST1.C: the
spin button test application.

```
/* SPINTST1.C */

// © 1994 Dave Jewell and Addison-Wesley, ALL RIGHTS RESERVED

#include   <windows.h>
#include   "spin.h"

char szAppName [] = "SpinTest";

//----------------------------------------------------------------------
// Name:    WindowProc
// Purpose: Window procedure for the main application window.
//----------------------------------------------------------------------

LONG FAR PASCAL _export WindowProc (HWND Wnd, WORD Msg,
                                    WPARAM wParam, LPARAM lParam)
{
    switch (Msg)
    {
      case WM_DESTROY:

        PostQuitMessage (0);
        return (0);
    }

        return DefWindowProc (Wnd, Msg, wParam, lParam);
}

//----------------------------------------------------------------------
// Name:    InitApplication
// Purpose: Register the application window class.
//----------------------------------------------------------------------

BOOL PASCAL InitApplication (HANDLE hInstance)
{
    WNDCLASS cls;

    if (GetClassInfo (hInstance, SPINCLASSNAME, &cls) == FALSE)
    {
        cls.style                = 0;
        cls.lpfnWndProc          = (WNDPROC) WindowProc;
        cls.cbClsExtra           = 0;
        cls.cbWndExtra           = 0;
        cls.hInstance            = hInstance;
        cls.hIcon                = LoadIcon (NULL, IDI_APPLICATION);
        cls.hCursor              = LoadCursor (NULL, IDC_ARROW);
        cls.hbrBackground        = COLOR_BTNFACE + 1;
        cls.lpszMenuName         = NULL;
        cls.lpszClassName        = szAppName;
```

```
              return RegisterClass (&cls);
         }

         return (TRUE);
}

//────────────────────────────────────────────────────
// Name:    WinMain
// Purpose: Program entry point.
//────────────────────────────────────────────────────

#pragma argsused

int PASCAL WinMain (HANDLE hInstance, HANDLE hPrevInstance,
                    LPSTR lpCmdLine, int nCmdShow)
{
         HWND Wnd;
         MSG Msg;

         InitApplication (hInstance);
         InitSpinButton (hInstance);

         Wnd = CreateWindow (szAppName, "Spin Button Test",
                    WS_OVERLAPPEDWINDOW,
                    CW_USEDEFAULT, CW_USEDEFAULT,
                    CW_USEDEFAULT, CW_USEDEFAULT,
                    NULL, NULL, hInstance, NULL);

         if (Wnd != NULL)
         {
            ShowWindow (Wnd, nCmdShow);
            UpdateWindow (Wnd);

            CreateWindow (SPINCLASSNAME, "", WS_CHILD | WS_VISIBLE | SP_VERT,
                    100, 100, 10, 10, Wnd, NULL, hInstance, NULL);
            CreateWindow (SPINCLASSNAME, "", WS_CHILD | WS_VISIBLE | SP_HORIZ,
                    200, 100, 10, 10, Wnd, NULL, hInstance, NULL);
         }

         while (GetMessage (&Msg, 0, 0, 0))
         {
            TranslateMessage (&Msg);
            DispatchMessage (&Msg);
         }

         return Msg.wParam;
}
```

The compiled version of this file (including the bitmap resource from SPIN.RES) can be found on the disk as SPINTST1.EXE. If you execute the program, you'll probably be unsurprised to see that the spin buttons are conspicuous by their absence – all you'll see is a uniformly gray window. Before we can make the spin buttons visible, we need to flesh out the spin button code module.

Spin button initialization

The first job is to add some code to take care of spin button initialization. We need to deal with the WM_CREATE message and set up some fields in the SpinButtonRec data structure.

Let's begin by adding some more fields to the PSpinButtonRec data structure –
we weren't using this structure at all in the skeletal code shown in Figure 7.4.

```
typedef struct SpinButtonRec
{
        BOOL      horiz;        // spin button orientation
        int       bmWidth;      // width of bitmap image
        int       bmHeight;     // height of bitmap image
        HBITMAP   bmBitmap;     // handle to spin button bitmap

}       SpinButtonRec, NEAR * PSpinButtonRec;
```

The bmWidth and bmHeight fields are used to store the width and height of the
bitmap. Note that this is not the width and height of the entire bitmap, but just the
size of one of the eight bitmap images shown in Figure 7.2. Similarly, the bmBitmap
field is the handle of the bitmap, obtained via a call to the LoadButtonBitmap routine.

```
//————————————————————————————————————————————————
// Name:          InitSpinButtonWindow
// Purpose:       Initialize the spin button data structure.
//————————————————————————————————————————————————
static LONG PASCAL InitSpinButtonWindow (HWND Wnd, LPCREATESTRUCT lpcs)
{
        RECT rc;
        BITMAP bm;
        PSpinButtonRec p;

        p = (PSpinButtonRec) LocalAlloc (LPTR, sizeof (SpinButtonRec));
        if (p == NULL) return (−1);
        p−>bmBitmap = LoadButtonBitmap (GetWindowWord (Wnd, GWW_HINSTANCE),
                                SPINCLASSNAME);
        if (p−>bmBitmap == NULL) return (−1);

        // Figure out the size of the bitmap

        GetObject (p−>bmBitmap, sizeof (BITMAP), &bm);
        p−>bmWidth = bm.bmWidth / 4;
        p−>bmHeight = bm.bmHeight / 2;

        // Resize window according to the dimensions of the current bitmap

        GetWindowRect (Wnd, &rc);
        ScreenToClient (GetParent (Wnd), (LPPOINT) &rc);
        p−>horiz = (GetWindowLong (Wnd, GWL_STYLE) & SP_HORIZ) ? TRUE : FALSE;
        if (p−>horiz)
          MoveWindow (Wnd, rc.left, rc.top, p−>bmWidth * 2, p−>bmHeight, FALSE);
        else MoveWindow (Wnd, rc.left, rc.top, p−>bmWidth, p−>bmHeight * 2, FALSE);

        SetWindowWord (Wnd, 0, (WORD) p);
        return (0);
}
```

The code above, InitSpinButtonWindow, is called from the spin button window
procedure in response to a WM_CREATE message. As you can see, we're passing it
the LPCREATESTRUCT pointer which accompanies a WM_CREATE message, and
you might be surprised by this. After all, we said we wouldn't do anything special
with the final Param parameter to CreateWindow. You'll understand later why I've
passed this pointer through to the initialization code. Suffice to say that the spin
button window is eventually going to need to look at its own window name. At the
moment, an empty window name is used, and the lpcs parameter is ignored.

The InitSpinButtonWindow routine has several tasks to perform. Firstly, it
allocates memory for the SpinButtonRec data structure, and then it loads our special
bitmap using the LoadButtonBitmap routine. This is a slightly different version of the

LoadButtonBitmap code that takes a pointer to a bitmap name, rather than a bitmap ID. On reflection, I guess I should have used this version of the code all along: you can pass resource IDs to a routine that expects a string (using the MAKEINTRESOURCE macro), but you can't pass a string to a routine that's designed only to expect an integer ID. Thus, designing a routine to expect a string provides maximum flexibility. Oh well, it's easy to be wise after the event.

Having loaded the bitmap, the GetObject routine is then called to determine the width and height of the total bitmap, and the bmHeight and bmWidth fields are then set up accordingly. The horiz field is set up by looking at bit 7 of the window style, and this information is then used to resize the window so that it's an exact fit with the bitmap. Although I said earlier that our spin button was going to be a fixed size, I really meant that it was fixed relative to the bitmap used. If you create a larger version of the bitmap shown in Figure 7.2, then you'll automatically get a larger spin button control. If you do create an alternative bitmap, though, do remember that it must be subdivided into eight cells in the same arrangement as the bitmap we're using here.

Finally, the SetWindowWord routine is called to associate the data structure with the spin button window handle. We reserved the appropriate number of bytes when the window class was registered.

With this code in place, the two spin buttons created by the test program will now resize themselves automatically when they're created. However, you still won't be able to see them. This is because we haven't yet implemented the drawing code and also, the window class was registered with a null background brush which means that the spin button window doesn't even have any background drawn. At the moment, our spin buttons are totally invisible. Without further ado, let's rectify this situation.

Drawing the spin buttons

If you think about it, a spin button control can be drawn in one of three states. Either the up arrow is pressed, or the down arrow is pressed, or else neither part of the control is pressed. When I use the terms up and down here, I'm not referring specifically to the vertically aligned spin button – the same argument applies to both. The spin button code obviously needs to know which of these three states it's in, and in order to do this, I've added another field, called State, to the SpinButtonRec data structure. If this integer variable is set to zero, the spin button is drawn in its normal, unpressed state. With the state set to 1, the spin button will be drawn with the up arrow pressed, and with the state set to −1, the control is drawn with the down arrow pressed. The code that's responsible for doing this drawing, PaintSpinButton, is shown below.

You should be able to figure out how it works by referring back to the bitmap shown in Figure 7.2. Firstly, the code works out whether it's painting a horizontal or vertical spin button, and it then examines the State field in order to decide how to draw the two halves of the control. This routine uses the BeginPaint and EndPaint functions, and must therefore be called from the SpinButtonWndProc code in response to a WM_PAINT message.

```
//————————————————————————————————————————————————————————————————
// Name:     PaintSpinButton
// Purpose:  Paint the spin button bitmap.
//————————————————————————————————————————————————————————————————
static LONG PASCAL PaintSpinButton (HWND Wnd)
{
    HDC hdcMem;
    HBITMAP hbm;
    PAINTSTRUCT ps;
    PSpinButtonRec p;
    int xSrc, ySrc;

    BeginPaint (Wnd, &ps);
    hdcMem = CreateCompatibleDC (ps.hdc);
    p = GetSpinButtonRec (Wnd);
    hbm = SelectObject (hdcMem, p–>bmBitmap);

    if (p–>horiz)
    {
        ySrc = (p–>State == 1) ? p–>bmHeight : 0;
        BitBlt (ps.hdc, p–>bmWidth, 0, p–>bmWidth, p–>bmHeight,
                hdcMem, 3 * p–>bmWidth, ySrc, SRCCOPY);
        ySrc = (p–>State == –1) ? p–>bmHeight : 0;
        BitBlt (ps.hdc, 0, 0, p–>bmWidth, p–>bmHeight, hdcMem,
                2 * p–>bmWidth, ySrc, SRCCOPY);
    }
    else
    {
        xSrc = (p–>State == 1) ? p–>bmWidth : 0;
        BitBlt (ps.hdc, 0, 0, p–>bmWidth, p–>bmHeight, hdcMem, xSrc, 0, SRCCOPY);
        xSrc = (p–>State == –1) ? p–>bmWidth : 0;
        BitBlt (ps.hdc, 0, p–>bmHeight, p–>bmWidth, p–>bmHeight,
                hdcMem, xSrc, p–>bmHeight, SRCCOPY);
    }
    if (hbm) SelectObject (hdcMem, hbm);
    DeleteDC (hdcMem);
    EndPaint (Wnd, &ps);
    return (0);
}
```

If you compile and execute the code with the changes discussed so far, the main application window should now look as shown in Figure 7.6. The spin buttons have now appeared, and are looking pretty good. You can find the executable file, SPINTST2.EXE, on the disk and at this stage, the spin button source code looks as shown in Figure 7.7. The application test program remains unchanged at this time.

Figure 7.6   The spin buttons put in their first appearance.

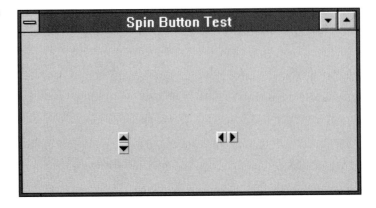

```c
/* SPIN2.C */

// © 1994 Dave Jewell and Addison-Wesley, ALL RIGHTS RESERVED

#include    <windows.h>
#include    "spin.h"

typedef struct SpinButtonRec
{
    int             State;          // state of play flag
    BOOL            horiz;          // spinbutton orientation
    int             bmWidth;        // width of bitmap image
    int             bmHeight;       // height of bitmap image
    HBITMAP         bmBitmap;       // handle to spin button bitmap
}   SpinButtonRec, NEAR * PSpinButtonRec;

//────────────────────────────────────────────────────────────
// Name:     GetSpinButtonRec
// Purpose:  Given a spin button window handle, return a pointer to
//           the SpinButtonRec data structure.
//────────────────────────────────────────────────────────────

static PSpinButtonRec PASCAL GetSpinButtonRec (HWND Wnd)
{
    return (PSpinButtonRec) GetWindowWord (Wnd, 0);
}

//────────────────────────────────────────────────────────────
// Name:     ColorFix
// Purpose:  Fix up a color value for the LoadButtonBitmap routine.
//────────────────────────────────────────────────────────────

static COLORREF PASCAL ColorFix (COLORREF color)
{
    return RGB (GetBValue (color), GetGValue (color), GetRValue (color));
}

//────────────────────────────────────────────────────────────
// Name:     LoadButtonBitmap
// Purpose:  Load a bitmap and tweak it for current system colors.
//────────────────────────────────────────────────────────────

static HBITMAP PASCAL LoadButtonBitmap (HANDLE hInstance,
                                        LPCSTR bitmapName)
{
    HDC dc;
    HBITMAP hbm;
    HANDLE hRes;
    LPDWORD lprgb;
    LPVOID lpb;
    LPBITMAPINFOHEADER lpbi;

    hRes = LoadResource (hInstance, FindResource (hInstance,
                        bitmapName, RT_BITMAP));
    lpbi = (LPBITMAPINFOHEADER) LockResource (hRes);
    if (lpbi == NULL) return (NULL);

    lprgb = (LPDWORD) ((LPSTR) lpbi + (int) lpbi->biSize);
    lpb = (LPVOID) (lprgb + 16);

    lprgb [0] = ColorFix (GetSysColor (COLOR_WINDOWTEXT));     // Black
    lprgb [8] = ColorFix (GetSysColor (COLOR_BTNFACE));        // Light gray
    lprgb [7] = ColorFix (GetSysColor (COLOR_BTNSHADOW));      // Gray
    lprgb [15] = ColorFix (GetSysColor (COLOR_BTNHIGHLIGHT));  // White

    dc = GetDC (NULL);
    hbm = CreateDIBitmap (dc, lpbi, CBM_INIT, lpb,
                        (LPBITMAPINFO) lpbi, DIB_RGB_COLORS);
```

```
            ReleaseDC (NULL, dc);
            GlobalUnlock (hRes);
            FreeResource (hRes);
            return (hbm);
    }

    //--------------------------------------------------------------
    // Name:    InitSpinButtonWindow
    // Purpose: Initialize the spin button data structure.
    //--------------------------------------------------------------

    static LONG PASCAL InitSpinButtonWindow (HWND Wnd,
                                       LPCREATESTRUCT lpcs)

    {
            RECT rc;
            BITMAP bm;
            PSpinButtonRec p;

            p = (PSpinButtonRec) LocalAlloc (LPTR, sizeof (SpinButtonRec));
            if (p == NULL) return (-1);
            p->bmBitmap = LoadButtonBitmap (GetWindowWord (Wnd,
                                GWW_HINSTANCE), SPINCLASSNAME);
            if (p->bmBitmap == NULL) return (-1);

            // Figure out the size of the bitmap

            GetObject (p->bmBitmap, sizeof (BITMAP), &bm);
            p->bmWidth = bm.bmWidth / 4;
            p->bmHeight = bm.bmHeight / 2;

            // Resize window according to the dimensions of the current bitmap

            GetWindowRect (Wnd, &rc);
            ScreenToClient (GetParent (Wnd), (LPPOINT) &rc);
            p->horiz = (GetWindowLong (Wnd, GWL_STYLE) & SP_HORIZ) ? TRUE : FALSE;
            if (p->horiz)
                MoveWindow (Wnd, rc.left, rc.top, p->bmWidth * 2, p->bmHeight, FALSE);
            else MoveWindow (Wnd, rc.left, rc.top, p->bmWidth, p->bmHeight * 2, FALSE);

            SetWindowWord (Wnd, 0, (WORD) p);
            return (0);
    }

    //--------------------------------------------------------------
    // Name:    PaintSpinButton
    // Purpose: Paint the spinbutton bitmap.
    //--------------------------------------------------------------

    static LONG PASCAL PaintSpinButton (HWND Wnd)
    {
            HDC hdcMem;
            HBITMAP hbm;
            PAINTSTRUCT ps;
            PSpinButtonRec p;
            int xSrc, ySrc;

            BeginPaint (Wnd, &ps);
            hdcMem = CreateCompatibleDC (ps.hdc);
            p = GetSpinButtonRec (Wnd);
            hbm = SelectObject (hdcMem, p->bmBitmap);

            if (p->horiz)
            {
                ySrc = (p->State == 1) ? p->bmHeight : 0;
                BitBlt (ps.hdc, p->bmWidth, 0, p->bmWidth, p->bmHeight,
                        hdcMem, 3 * p->bmWidth, ySrc, SRCCOPY);
                ySrc = (p->State == -1) ? p->bmHeight : 0;
                BitBlt (ps.hdc, 0, 0, p->bmWidth, p->bmHeight, hdcMem,
                        2 * p->bmWidth, ySrc, SRCCOPY);
```

```
        }
        else
        {
          xSrc = (p->State == 1) ? p->bmWidth : 0;
          BitBlt (ps.hdc, 0, 0, p->bmWidth, p->bmHeight, hdcMem, xSrc, 0, SRCCOPY);
          xSrc = (p->State == -1) ? p->bmWidth : 0;
          BitBlt (ps.hdc, 0, p->bmHeight, p->bmWidth, p->bmHeight,
                  hdcMem, xSrc, p->bmHeight, SRCCOPY);
        }

        if (hbm) SelectObject (hdcMem, hbm);
        DeleteDC (hdcMem);
        EndPaint (Wnd, &ps);
        return (0);
}

//------------------------------------------------------------------
// Name:    SpinButtonWndProc
// Purpose: Window procedure for the spin button window class.
//------------------------------------------------------------------

LONG FAR PASCAL _export SpinButtonWndProc (HWND Wnd, WORD Msg,
                                           WPARAM wParam, LPARAM lParam)
{
        switch (Msg)
        {
          case WM_CREATE:

          return InitSpinButtonWindow (Wnd, (LPCREATESTRUCT) lParam);

          case WM_PAINT:

          return PaintSpinButton (Wnd);
        }

        return DefWindowProc (Wnd, Msg, wParam, lParam);
}

//------------------------------------------------------------------
// Name:    InitSpinButton
// Purpose: Register the spin button window class.
//------------------------------------------------------------------

BOOL PASCAL InitSpinButton (HANDLE hInstance)
{
        WNDCLASS cls;

        if (GetClassInfo (hInstance, SPINCLASSNAME, &cls) == FALSE)
        {
          cls.style           = CS_DBLCLKS;
          cls.lpfnWndProc     = (WNDPROC) SpinButtonWndProc;
          cls.cbClsExtra      = 0;
          cls.cbWndExtra      = sizeof (PSpinButtonRec);
          cls.hInstance       = hInstance;
          cls.hIcon           = 0;
          cls.hCursor         = LoadCursor (NULL, IDC_ARROW);
          cls.hbrBackground   = 0;
          cls.lpszMenuName    = NULL;
          cls.lpszClassName   = SPINCLASSNAME;

          return RegisterClass (&cls);
        }

        return (TRUE);

}
```

At this stage, pressing on the spin buttons will not, of course, have any effect because we haven't got any hit-testing logic or code to handle the WM_LBUTTONDOWN message. Let's build that code now. This stuff should be pretty familiar to you if you've followed through the rest of the book. We need to determine the part of the spin button where the mouse has been clicked, call the SetCapture routine so as to be able to track WM_MOUSEMOVE messages as the mouse is moved around and then call the ReleaseCapture routine and establish the new state of the spin button.

The hit test routine is shown below:

```
//----------------------------------------------------------------
// Name:    HitTest
// Returns: 0 – Mouse wasn't in spin button.
//          1 – Mouse was in increment part of button.
//          −1 – Mouse was in decrement part of button.
//----------------------------------------------------------------
static int PASCAL HitTest (HWND Wnd, LONG lParam)
{
        int hit;
        POINT pt;
        RECT rc;
        PSpinButtonRec p;

        pt.x = LOWORD (lParam);
        pt.y = HIWORD (lParam);
        GetClientRect (Wnd, &rc);
        p = GetSpinButtonRec (Wnd);

        if (PtInRect (&rc, pt) == FALSE) hit = 0;
        else if (p−>horiz) hit = (pt.x >= rc.right / 2) ? 1 : −1;
        else hit = (pt.y >= rc.bottom / 2) ? −1 : 1;
        return hit;

}
```

This should be pretty straightforward. The HitTest routine is intended to return an integer code that can be plugged straight into the State field of the data structure. Therefore, as discussed earlier, it returns either 0, 1 or −1. The HitTest code is called in response to mouse-down events, and it's repeatedly called as WM_MOUSEMOVE messages are received so that the appearance of the spin button changes according to whether or not the mouse is pressed down over the control.

```
case WM_LBUTTONDOWN:
case WM_LBUTTONDBLCLK:

SetCapture (Wnd);
p−>State = HitTest (Wnd, lParam);
InvalidateRect (Wnd, NULL, FALSE);
SpinNotify (Wnd);
return (0);
```

As you can see, the InvalidateRect routine is called as soon as the State field has been set up. This will cause the spin button to be redrawn in its new state. When the mouse button is released, the State field is reset to zero, and the InvalidateRect routine called again as shown below.

```
case WM_LBUTTONUP:

if (Wnd == GetCapture())
{
```

```
        ReleaseCapture();
        p->State = 0;
        InvalidateRect (Wnd, NULL, FALSE);
    }
    return (0);
```

The final piece of mouse handling code is the WM_MOUSEMOVE message handler. This continually polls the HitTest routine for as long as the spin button window has the capture. If the HitTest routine returns a hit code different from the currently selected state, the State field is updated and the InvalidateRect routine called to show the new spin button state.

```
case WM_MOUSEMOVE:
if (Wnd == GetCapture())
{
        hitCode = HitTest (Wnd, lParam);
        if (hitCode != p->State)
        {
            p->State = hitCode;
            InvalidateRect (Wnd, NULL, FALSE);
        }
}
return (0);
```

With this code in place, the mouse will now interact properly with the spin button controls. What's missing is the code for the SpinNotify routine, which is called whenever a spin button is clicked. Here's the code for SpinNotify. It simply sends a SPINMESSAGE message to the parent window. The wParam field of the message is set to the window handle of the spin button (this is important in case there are multiple spin buttons and the parent needs to discriminate between them) and the State variable is passed in the lParam field of the message. This lets the parent window know whether the up or down part of the control was pressed.

```
//─────────────────────────────────────────────────
// Name:     SpinNotify
// Returns:  Send spin button notification message.
//─────────────────────────────────────────────────
static void PASCAL SpinNotify (HWND Wnd)
{
        PSpinButtonRec p;

        p = GetSpinButtonRec (Wnd);
        SendMessage (GetParent (Wnd), SPINMESSAGE, Wnd, p->State);
}
```

If you add the following three lines of code to the test program's window procedure, you'll find that, sure enough, you get a beep each time one of the spin buttons is clicked.

```
case SPINMESSAGE:

MessageBeep (0);
return (0);
```

Adding auto-repeat

Open up the Control Panel application and bring up the date/time dialog shown in Figure 7.1. If you try holding down the mouse over one of the spin buttons, you'll see that the corresponding numeric value in the buddy edit box is continually incremented or decremented – you don't have to keep clicking on the spin button. This feature is quite standard in spin buttons and we ought to add it to our spin button code, too.

The easiest way of doing this is to create a timer that will send WM_TIMER messages to the spin button window. Each time a WM_TIMER message is received, the spin button can then call the SpinNotify routine to send a message to the parent window. Because timers are a scarce system resource, it's important to use a timer resource only when it's actually needed. In other words, we'll create the timer when the spin button is clicked, and destroy the timer when the mouse button is released.

It's important to ensure that the SpinNotify routine is only called if the mouse is actually held down over the spin button. We don't want auto-repeat notification messages to be sent while the mouse is held down outside of the control.

The changes needed to make this work are very simple. Here's the revised code that creates a system timer when a spin button is clicked:

```
case WM_LBUTTONDOWN:
case WM_LBUTTONDBLCLK:

SetCapture (Wnd);
p−>State = HitTest (Wnd, lParam);
InvalidateRect (Wnd, NULL, FALSE);
SetTimer (Wnd, 100, p−>SpinRate, NULL);
SpinNotify (Wnd);
return (0);
```

I've used a timer ID of 100 here, and you will see that there's a new field in the SpinButtonRec data structure called SpinRate. This specifies the number of auto-repeats per millisecond while the mouse button is held down. We'll discuss the initialization of this field shortly.

```
case WM_LBUTTONUP:

if (Wnd == GetCapture())
{
    ReleaseCapture();
    KillTimer (Wnd, 100);
    p−>State = 0;
    InvalidateRect (Wnd, NULL, FALSE);
}
return (0);
```

The WM_LBUTTONUP code now includes a call to KillTimer so that the timer is automatically destroyed as soon as the mouse button is released. The actual WM_TIMER handing code is equally straightforward:

```
case WM_TIMER:

if (p−>State) SpinNotify (Wnd);
return (0);
```

If you compile and run this code, you'll find that you'll get auto-repeat action, but it will be very fast! The reason is that the SpinRate field hasn't been initialized. Actually, it did get initialized – but to zero. Because we're using the LPTR memory option to create the SpinButtonRec data structure, all members of that data structure are pre-initialized to zero when the data structure is allocated. Passing a zero value to the SetTimer routine is another way of saying, 'I want WM_TIMER messages just as fast as you can send 'em', so that's what we get. Obviously, we need some way of initializing the SpinRate field to some sensible value.

Unfortunately, there's no 'best' value to use here. Some applications might need to set a variable anywhere between 0 and 10, so a low auto-repeat rate would be appropriate. Another application might have a variable with a much higher dynamic range, such as 0–1000. Obviously, a much higher repeat rate would be required in the latter case.

OK, so how are we going to set up the spin button's auto-repeat rate? One solution would be to define some sort of special custom message, and send such a message to a spin button in order to tell it what value of repeat rate we want. This approach requires extra application code because it involves you using the SendMessage API routine at WM_INITDIALOG time to initialize each of the spin button controls in your dialog. A better approach, in my view, is to encode the auto-repeat rate for a particular spin button into that spin button's window style bits. If you remember, this is exactly what we did with the horizontal/vertical flag: we used bit 7 to indicate the orientation that the spin button should use.

Since we've already used bit 7, it seems reasonable to use the remaining low-order seven bits to specify the auto-repeat rate. This gives us a range of 0–127, or from very fast to approximately eight updates per second. Some programmers might want a wider range than this, with the ability to select an even lower repeat rate. I therefore decided to take the low-order seven bits of the style word as the repeat rate, and multiply this by four to give an effective range of 0–512. This amounts to a slowest possible auto-repeat rate of twice per second which ought to be slow enough for anyone. The code to set up the SpinRate field needs to be added to the InitSpinButtonWindow routine, and is shown below.

```
// Set up auto-repeat rate

p->SpinRate = GetWindowLong (Wnd, GWL_STYLE) & 0x7F;

if (p->SpinRate == 0) p->SpinRate = 125;
else p->SpinRate *= 4;
```

Notice that if no repeat rate was specified (low-order seven bits all zero), a default value of 125 is assumed – in other words, a default rate of eight updates per second.

While we're at it, we ought to add the following code to the SpinButtonWndProc routine. This takes care of cleaning things up when a spin button is destroyed.

```
case WM_DESTROY:

DeleteObject (p->bmBitmap);
LocalFree ((HANDLE) p);
return (0);
```

Buddy, can you spare a paradigm?

With the changes outlined above, the spin button code is essentially complete with the exception of the buddy code discussed earlier. Before we can write the code that communicates with a buddy control, we obviously need to create the buddy window. Add the following CreateWindow call to the SPINTEST program immediately before the spin buttons are created:

```
CreateWindow ("Edit", "Hello World", WS_CHILD | WS_VISIBLE | WS_BORDER,
              100, 300, 100, 25, Wnd, 999, hInstance, NULL);
```

This will create a new edit box control which, like the spin buttons, is a child of the main application window. Note that we've assigned an ID of 999 to this window. For non-child windows, this parameter specifies a menu handle, but for child windows, it specifies the ID of the window.

We now need some way of telling a spin button control about the existence of a buddy control. There might be several different edit boxes in a given dialog, so we can't blindly search for the first edit box we come across. Although we could use some more window style bits to store the ID of the associated buddy control, a better technique in this case is to use the window name. By storing the ID of the associated edit text control as the window name of the spin button, we're easily and conveniently telling the spin button that it has a buddy control and giving it the control's ID.

Because the various controls of a dialog are created deep inside the Windows dialog manager, we have no control over the order in which those controls are created. Accordingly, we can't be certain that the buddy exists at the time the spin button window is created and initialized. This is an important point since it means that the spin button control must defer checking for the existence of the buddy control and performing other validation until the show is under way. An appropriate point at which to do this would be when it's time to send the first notification to the buddy – in other words, when the spin button control is first clicked on. If, for any reason, the buddy control turns out to be invalid, then the spin button reverts to sending notifications to its parent window as already discussed.

```
//────────────────────────────────────────────────────────────
// Name:     InitSpinButtonWindow
// Purpose:  Initialize the spin button data structure.
//────────────────────────────────────────────────────────────

static LONG PASCAL InitSpinButtonWindow (HWND Wnd, LPCREATESTRUCT lpcs)
{
    RECT rc;
    BITMAP bm;
    PSpinButtonRec p;
    char szWindowName [128];

    p = (PSpinButtonRec) LocalAlloc (LPTR, sizeof (SpinButtonRec));
    if (p == NULL) return (-1);
    p->bmBitmap = LoadButtonBitmap (GetWindowWord (Wnd,
                        GWW_HINSTANCE), SPINCLASSNAME);

    if (p->bmBitmap == NULL) return (-1);

    // Set up auto-repeat rate
```

```
    p−>SpinRate = GetWindowLong (Wnd, GWL_STYLE) & 0x7F;
    if (p−>SpinRate == 0) p−>SpinRate = 125;
    else p−>SpinRate *= 4;

    // Figure out the size of the bitmap

    GetObject (p−>bmBitmap, sizeof (BITMAP), &bm);
    p−>bmWidth = bm.bmWidth / 4;
    p−>bmHeight = bm.bmHeight / 2;

    // Resize window according to the dimensions of the current bitmap

    GetWindowRect (Wnd, &rc);
    ScreenToClient (GetParent (Wnd), (LPPOINT) &rc);
    p−>horiz = (GetWindowLong (Wnd, GWL_STYLE) & SP_HORIZ) ? TRUE : FALSE;
    if (p−>horiz)
        MoveWindow (Wnd, rc.left, rc.top, p−>bmWidth * 2, p−>bmHeight, FALSE);
    else MoveWindow (Wnd, rc.left, rc.top, p−>bmWidth, p−>bmHeight * 2, FALSE);

    // Set up buddy ID

    if (lpcs−>lpszName != NULL && *lpcs−>lpszName != '\0')
    {
        lstrcpy (szWindowName, lpcs−>lpszName);
        p−>BuddyID = atoi (szWindowName);
    }

    SetWindowWord (Wnd, 0, (WORD) p);
    return (0);
}
```

Amalgamating all the changes so far, the InitSpinButtonWindow code now
looks as shown above. Towards the end of the routine, a check is made for a non-
NULL, non-empty window name. If found, the atoi routine is called to convert the
(supposedly) numeric string in the window name into an integer value. This integer
is stored in a new field, BuddyID, which is used to store the ID of the buddy window.
Like everything else in the SpinButtonRec structure, the BuddyID field is initialized
to zero, and a zero value is taken to indicate that the spin button has no associated
buddy window. As it turns out, the atoi run-time library routine will return zero if it's
unable to convert the text string (in other words, if the text string isn't a valid
number), so this fits in with how we want things to work – an invalid text string will
have the effect of leaving the BuddyID field set to zero.

```
//─────────────────────────────────────────────────────────────
// Name:     SpinNotify
// Returns:  Send spin button notification message.
//─────────────────────────────────────────────────────────────
static void PASCAL SpinNotify (HWND Wnd)
{
    PSpinButtonRec p;
    char szClassName [64];

    if ((p = GetSpinButtonRec (Wnd))−>BuddyID != 0)
    {
        if (p−>BuddyHWnd == NULL)
        {
            // Try and find our buddy window

            p−>BuddyHWnd = GetDlgItem (GetParent (Wnd), p−>BuddyID);
            if (p−>BuddyHWnd == NULL) p−>BuddyID = 0;
            else
            {
```

```
                    GetClassName (p->BuddyHWnd, szClassName, sizeof (szClassName));
                    if (lstrcmpi (szClassName, "Edit") != 0)
                        {
                        p->BuddyHWnd = NULL;
                        p->BuddyID = 0;
                        }
                    }
                }
            if (p->BuddyHWnd != NULL)
                {
                BuddyTalk (p);
                return;
                }
            }
        SendMessage (GetParent (Wnd), SPINMESSAGE, Wnd, p->State);
    }
```

The revised SpinNotify code is shown above. If the BuddyID field is non-zero, the routine examines a new field, BuddyHWnd, which contains the window handle of the buddy edit box. If this window handle is NULL, which it will be the first time the SpinNotify code is called, an attempt is made to obtain the window handle of the buddy control. Recall the earlier comments about timing considerations: we can't go searching for our buddy at the time the spin button itself is created. The GetDlgItem routine is used to retrieve the window handle of the buddy. This routine works perfectly well whether or not it's being used in the context of the dialog manager – it will operate correctly in any child-parent window relationship. If a non-NULL window handle is retrieved, the class name of the window is obtained and a check is made to ensure that we're talking to an edit box. Clearly, we don't want to start sending edit-control-specific messages to a push button or list box! If any of these checks fail, the BuddyHWnd and BuddyID fields are set to zero, indicating that only parent notifications should be used.

If a buddy window has been correctly set up, the BuddyTalk routine is eventually called. It's this code that is responsible for actually updating the contents of the buddy edit box control.

```
//──────────────────────────────────────────────────────
// Name:           BuddyTalk
// Returns:        Increment or decrement the value in the buddy control.
//──────────────────────────────────────────────────────
static void PASCAL BuddyTalk (PSpinButtonRec p)
    {
    int i;
    HWND Wnd;
    BOOL fValid;
    char szText [64];
    LONG sel, oldsel;
    BOOL gotSel = FALSE;

    Wnd = p->BuddyHWnd;
    if (IsWindow (Wnd) && SendMessage (Wnd, WM_GETTEXTLENGTH, 0, 0) < sizeof (szText))
        {
        SendMessage (Wnd, WM_GETTEXT, sizeof (szText) - 1, (LONG) (LPSTR) szText);
        oldsel = sel = SendMessage (Wnd, EM_GETSEL, 0, 0);

        // Have we got a selection?

        if (LOWORD (sel) == HIWORD (sel)) sel = MAKELONG (0, lstrlen (szText));
        else gotSel = TRUE;
        szText [HIWORD (sel)] = '\0';
```

```
// Convert to numeric value

i = MyAtoi (&szText [LOWORD (sel)], &fValid) + p−>State;
if (fValid == FALSE)
{
    MessageBeep (0);
    return;
}

wvsprintf (szText, "%d", (LPVOID) &i);

// If got a selection, replace it

if (gotSel)
{
    SendMessage (Wnd, EM_REPLACESEL, 0, (LONG) (LPSTR) szText);
    SendMessage (Wnd, EM_SETSEL, 0, MAKELONG (LOWORD (oldsel),
                    LOWORD (oldsel) + lstrlen (szText)));
}
else
{
    SendMessage (Wnd, WM_SETTEXT, 0, (LONG) (LPSTR) szText);
    SendMessage (Wnd, EM_SETSEL, 0, MAKELONG (0, 0x7fff));
}
}
}
}
```

The BuddyTalk routine first checks to ensure that the BuddyHWnd window is still in existence by calling the IsWindow function. Perhaps this is rather over-cautious programming, but it allows for cases where a reconfigurable dialog box might end up deleting some of the controls that are not needed. The BuddyTalk routine also checks to see that the buddy control text can safely be accommodated within the szText buffer.

If things check out so far, the text is copied into the szText buffer and an EM_GETSEL message is sent to the buddy control to get the current text selection limits. As mentioned earlier, the spin button will attempt to increment or decrement only the selected part of the text. If there is no selection, then the entire text is assumed to be a numeric value. This is the purpose of the next chunk of code which sets up the sel, gotsel, and oldsel parameters according to whether or not there is a text selection. In all cases, the low word of the sel variable is the index of the first character to check, and the high word is one past the index of the last character to be examined.

```
//——————————————————————————————————————————————————
// Name:    MyAtoi
// Returns: Convert a string to its numeric representation.
//——————————————————————————————————————————————————

static int PASCAL MyAtoi (LPCSTR p, BOOL * fValid)
{
    int result = 0;
    BOOL neg = FALSE;

    while (*p == ' ' || *p == '\t' || *p == '\r' || *p == '\n') p++;
    if (*p == '+') p++;
    if (*p == '−')
    {
        neg = TRUE;
        p++;
    }

    while (*p >= '0' && *p <= '9')
        result = (result * 10) + *p++ − '0';
```

```
*fValid = (*p == '\0');
if (neg) result = −result;
return result;
}
```

Another new routine, MyAtoi, is then called to convert the text into its corresponding numeric value. You might be wondering why I haven't used the standard run-time library atoi routine here – after all, I've used it elsewhere in the spin button code. The reason is this: atoi will return zero if it's faced with an invalid, non-numeric string. Using atoi, therefore, we can't determine that the passed string was invalid because we can't tell whether a zero result means that the string was invalid, or was a valid representation of zero. This wasn't a problem when we used atoi earlier to determine the ID of the buddy window because you wouldn't use an ID of zero anyway. Here, however, it is a problem. The MyAtoi routine sets up a Boolean variable, fValid, according to whether or not the passed string could be converted into a number. If not, the system speaker is beeped via the MessageBeep routine and the function terminates.

The State field (which should be 1 or −1) is added to the number retrieved from the buddy window at this time. Now you can see why I chose 1 and −1 as the numbers to use! Finally, the wvsprintf routine is called to convert back to a string representation, and the new string is put back into the buddy window using either EM_REPLACESEL or WM_SETTEXT, depending on whether or not there was a selection in the buddy window.

Figure 7.8 Showing the buddy facility in operation.

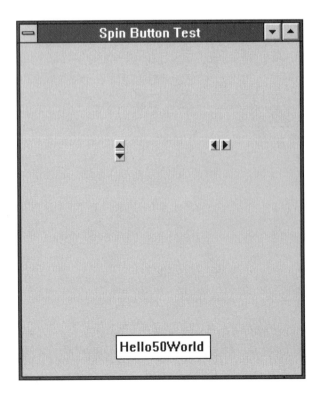

To make use of this facility, there are a couple of small changes we need to make to the CreateWindow calls in the SPINTEXT application. We just need to change the window name to 999 so that the spin buttons will go looking for a buddy window with that ID. In a real application, you wouldn't normally have two spin buttons jealously fighting over the same buddy window, but I've set things up that way here for illustrative purposes.

```
CreateWindow (SPINCLASSNAME, "999", WS_CHILD | WS_VISIBLE | SP_VERT,
        100, 100, 10, 10, Wnd, NULL, hInstance, NULL);
CreateWindow (SPINCLASSNAME, "999", WS_CHILD | WS_VISIBLE | SP_HORIZ,
        200, 100, 10, 10, Wnd, NULL, hInstance, NULL);
```

With all these changes in place, we get the effect shown in Figure 7.8. With a numeric value highlighted in the buddy window, either spin button can be used to increment or decrement the value. With no highlighting, the entire contents of the edit box are assumed to be a numeric string.

Figure 7.9 shows the completed spin button code while Figure 7.10 contains the code for the test application. The corresponding filenames on disk are SPIN3.C and SPINTST2.C. The executable filename is named SPINTST3.EXE.

Figure 7.9   SPIN3.C: the completed spin button code.

```c
/* SPIN3.C */

// © 1994 Dave Jewell and Addison-Wesley, ALL RIGHTS RESERVED

#include    <stdlib.h>
#include    <windows.h>
#include    "spin.h"

typedef struct SpinButtonRec
{
        int         State;          // state of play flag
        BOOL        horiz;          // spinbutton orientation
        int         bmWidth;        // width of bitmap image
        int         bmHeight;       // height of bitmap image
        int         SpinRate;       // auto-repeat rate
        int         BuddyID;        // ID of buddy control
        HWND        BuddyHWnd;      // handle to buddy control
        HBITMAP     bmBitmap;       // handle to spin button bitmap
}       SpinButtonRec, NEAR * PSpinButtonRec;

//-------------------------------------------------------------------
// Name:     GetSpinButtonRec
// Purpose:  Given a spin button window handle, return a pointer to
//           the SpinButtonRec data structure.
//-------------------------------------------------------------------

static PSpinButtonRec PASCAL GetSpinButtonRec (HWND Wnd)
{
        return (PSpinButtonRec) GetWindowWord (Wnd, 0);
}

//-------------------------------------------------------------------
// Name:     ColorFix
// Purpose:  Fix up a color value for the LoadButtonBitmap routine.
//-------------------------------------------------------------------

static COLORREF PASCAL ColorFix (COLORREF color)
{
        return RGB (GetBValue (color), GetGValue (color), GetRValue (color));
}
```

```
//————————————————————————————————————————————————————————————————
// Name:   LoadButtonBitmap
// Purpose: Load a bitmap and tweak it for current system colors.
//————————————————————————————————————————————————————————————————

static HBITMAP PASCAL LoadButtonBitmap (HANDLE hInstance,
                                        LPCSTR bitmapName)
{
    HDC dc;
    HBITMAP hbm;
    HANDLE hRes;
    LPDWORD lprgb;
    LPVOID lpb;
    LPBITMAPINFOHEADER lpbi;

    hRes = LoadResource (hInstance, FindResource (hInstance,
                             bitmapName, RT_BITMAP));

    lpbi = (LPBITMAPINFOHEADER) LockResource (hRes);
    if (lpbi == NULL) return (NULL);

    lprgb = (LPDWORD) ((LPSTR) lpbi + (int) lpbi->biSize);
    lpb = (LPVOID) (lprgb + 16);

    lprgb [0] = ColorFix (GetSysColor (COLOR_WINDOWTEXT));      // Black
    lprgb [8] = ColorFix (GetSysColor (COLOR_BTNFACE));         // Light gray
    lprgb [7] = ColorFix (GetSysColor (COLOR_BTNSHADOW));       // Gray
    lprgb [15] = ColorFix (GetSysColor (COLOR_BTNHIGHLIGHT));   // White

    dc = GetDC (NULL);
    hbm = CreateDIBitmap (dc, lpbi, CBM_INIT, lpb,
                          (LPBITMAPINFO) lpbi, DIB_RGB_COLORS);

    ReleaseDC (NULL, dc);
    GlobalUnlock (hRes);
    FreeResource (hRes);
    return (hbm);
}

//————————————————————————————————————————————————————————————————
// Name:    InitSpinButtonWindow
// Purpose: Initialize the spin button data structure.
//————————————————————————————————————————————————————————————————

static LONG PASCAL InitSpinButtonWindow (HWND Wnd, LPCREATESTRUCT lpcs)
{
    RECT rc;
    BITMAP bm;
    PSpinButtonRec p;
    char szWindowName [128];

    p = (PSpinButtonRec) LocalAlloc (LPTR, sizeof (SpinButtonRec));
    if (p == NULL) return (-1);
    p->bmBitmap = LoadButtonBitmap (GetWindowWord (Wnd,
                          GWW_HINSTANCE), SPINCLASSNAME);
    if (p->bmBitmap == NULL) return (-1);

    // Set up auto-repeat rate

    p->SpinRate = GetWindowLong (Wnd, GWL_STYLE) & 0x7F;
    if (p->SpinRate == 0) p->SpinRate = 125;
    else p->SpinRate *= 4;

    // Figure out the size of the bitmap

    GetObject (p->bmBitmap, sizeof (BITMAP), &bm);
    p->bmWidth = bm.bmWidth / 4;
    p->bmHeight = bm.bmHeight / 2;

    // Resize window according to the dimensions of the current bitmap
```

```
        GetWindowRect (Wnd, &rc);
        ScreenToClient (GetParent (Wnd), (LPPOINT) &rc);
        p->horiz = (GetWindowLong (Wnd, GWL_STYLE) & SP_HORIZ) ? TRUE :
            FALSE;
        if (p->horiz) MoveWindow (Wnd, rc.left, rc.top,
                                p->bmWidth * 2, p->bmHeight, FALSE);
        else MoveWindow (Wnd, rc.left, rc.top, p->bmWidth, p->bmHeight * 2,
                        FALSE);

        // Set up buddy ID

        if (lpcs->lpszName != NULL && *lpcs->lpszName != '\0')
        {
            lstrcpy (szWindowName, lpcs->lpszName);
            p->BuddyID = atoi (szWindowName);
        }

        SetWindowWord (Wnd, 0, (WORD) p);
        return (0);
}

//─────────────────────────────────────────────────────────────
// Name:    PaintSpinButton
// Purpose: Paint the spinbutton bitmap.
//─────────────────────────────────────────────────────────────

static LONG PASCAL PaintSpinButton (HWND Wnd)
{
        HDC hdcMem;
        HBITMAP hbm;
        PAINTSTRUCT ps;
        PSpinButtonRec p;
        int xSrc, ySrc;

        BeginPaint (Wnd, &ps);
        hdcMem = CreateCompatibleDC (ps.hdc);
        p = GetSpinButtonRec (Wnd);
        hbm = SelectObject (hdcMem, p->bmBitmap);

        if (p->horiz)
        {
            ySrc = (p->State == 1) ? p->bmHeight : 0;
            BitBlt (ps.hdc, p->bmWidth, 0, p->bmWidth,
                    p->bmHeight, hdcMem, 3 * p->bmWidth, ySrc, SRCCOPY);
            ySrc = (p->State == -1) ? p->bmHeight : 0;
            BitBlt (ps.hdc, 0, 0, p->bmWidth, p->bmHeight, hdcMem,
                    2 * p->bmWidth, ySrc, SRCCOPY);
        }
        else
        {
            xSrc = (p->State == 1) ? p->bmWidth : 0;
            BitBlt (ps.hdc, 0, 0, p->bmWidth, p->bmHeight, hdcMem,
                    xSrc, 0, SRCCOPY);
            xSrc = (p->State == -1) ? p->bmWidth : 0;
            BitBlt (ps.hdc, 0, p->bmHeight, p->bmWidth, p->bmHeight,
                    hdcMem, xSrc, p->bmHeight, SRCCOPY);
        }

        if (hbm) SelectObject (hdcMem, hbm);
        DeleteDC (hdcMem);
        EndPaint (Wnd, &ps);
        return (0);
}

//─────────────────────────────────────────────────────────────
// Name:    HitTest
// Returns: 0 – Mouse wasn't in spin button.
//          1 – Mouse was in increment part of button.
//          -1 – Mouse was in decrement part of button.
//─────────────────────────────────────────────────────────────
```

```
static int PASCAL HitTest (HWND Wnd, LONG lParam)
{
    int hit;
    POINT pt;
    RECT rc;
    PSpinButtonRec p;

    pt.x = LOWORD (lParam);
    pt.y = HIWORD (lParam);
    GetClientRect (Wnd, &rc);
    p = GetSpinButtonRec (Wnd);

    if (PtInRect (&rc, pt) == FALSE) hit = 0;
    else if (p->horiz) hit = (pt.x >= rc.right / 2) ? 1 : -1;
    else hit = (pt.y >= rc.bottom / 2) ? -1 : 1;
    return hit;
}

//------------------------------------------------------------------
// Name:    MyAtoi
// Returns: Convert a string to its numeric representation.
//------------------------------------------------------------------

static int PASCAL MyAtoi (LPCSTR p, BOOL * fValid)
{
    int result = 0;
    BOOL neg = FALSE;

    while (*p == ' ' || *p == '\t' || *p == '\r' || *p == '\n') p++;
    if (*p == '+') p++;
    if (*p == '-')
    {
        neg = TRUE;
        p++;
    }

    while (*p >= '0' && *p <= '9')
        result = (result * 10) + *p++ - '0';

    *fValid = (*p == '\0');
    if (neg) result = -result;
    return result;
}

//------------------------------------------------------------------
// Name:    BuddyTalk
// Returns: Increment or decrement the value in the buddy control.
//------------------------------------------------------------------

static void PASCAL BuddyTalk (PSpinButtonRec p)
{
    int i;
    HWND Wnd;
    BOOL fValid;
    char szText [64];
    LONG sel, oldsel;
    BOOL gotSel = FALSE;

    Wnd = p->BuddyHWnd;
    if (IsWindow (Wnd) && SendMessage (Wnd, WM_GETTEXTLENGTH, 0, 0)
        < sizeof (szText))
    {
        SendMessage (Wnd, WM_GETTEXT, sizeof (szText) - 1, (LONG)(LPSTR)
                szText);
        oldsel = sel = SendMessage (Wnd, EM_GETSEL, 0, 0);

        // Have we got a selection?

        if (LOWORD (sel) == HIWORD (sel)) sel = MAKELONG (0, lstrlen (szText));
        else gotSel = TRUE;
        szText [HIWORD (sel)] = '\0';
```

```
                // Convert to numeric value

                i = MyAtoi (&szText [LOWORD (sel)], &fValid) + p->State;
                if (fValid == FALSE)
                {
                    MessageBeep (0);
                    return;
                }

                wvsprintf (szText, "%d", (LPVOID) &i);

                // If got a selection, replace it

                If (gotSel)
                {
                    SendMessage (Wnd, EM_REPLACESEL, 0, (LONG) (LPSTR) szText);
                    SendMessage (Wnd, EM_SETSEL, 0, MAKELONG (LOWORD (oldsel),
                                    LOWORD (oldsel) + lstrlen (szText)));
                }
                else
                {
                    SendMessage (Wnd, WM_SETTEXT, 0, (LONG) (LPSTR) szText);
                    SendMessage (Wnd, EM_SETSEL, 0, MAKELONG (0, 0x7fff));
                }
            }
    }
//---------------------------------------------------------------------
// Name:    SpinNotify
// Returns: Send spin button notification message.
//---------------------------------------------------------------------
static void PASCAL SpinNotify (HWND Wnd)
{
        PSpinButtonRec p;
        char szClassName [64];

    if ((p = GetSpinButtonRec (Wnd))->BuddyID != 0)
    {
        if (p->BuddyHWnd == NULL)
        {
            // Try and find our buddy window

            p->BuddyHWnd = GetDlgItem (GetParent (Wnd), p->BuddyID);
            if (p->BuddyHWnd == NULL) p->BuddyID = 0;
            else
            {
                GetClassName (p->BuddyHWnd, szClassName, sizeof
                                (szClassName));
                if (lstrcmpi (szClassName, "Edit") != 0)
                {
                    p->BuddyHWnd = NULL;
                    p->BuddyID = 0;
                }
            }
        }
        if (p->BuddyHWnd != NULL)
        {
            BuddyTalk (p);
            return;
        }
    }

    SendMessage (GetParent (Wnd), SPINMESSAGE, Wnd, p->State);
}
//---------------------------------------------------------------------
// Name:    SpinButtonWndProc
// Purpose: Window procedure for the spin button window class.
//---------------------------------------------------------------------
```

```
LONG FAR PASCAL _export SpinButtonWndProc (HWND  Wnd,  WORD  Msg,
                                           WPARAM wParam, LPARAM
                                           lParam)
{
    int hitCode;
    PSpinButtonRec p;

    p = GetSpinButtonRec (Wnd);

    switch (Msg)
    {
    case WM_LBUTTONDOWN:
    case WM_LBUTTONDBLCLK:

        SetCapture (Wnd);
        p->State = HitTest (Wnd, lParam);
        InvalidateRect (Wnd, NULL, FALSE);
        SetTimer (Wnd, 100, p->SpinRate, NULL);
        SpinNotify (Wnd);
        return (0);

    case WM_LBUTTONUP:

        if (Wnd == GetCapture())
        {
            ReleaseCapture();
            KillTimer (Wnd, 100);
            p->State = 0;
            InvalidateRect (Wnd, NULL, FALSE);
        }
        return (0);

    case WM_MOUSEMOVE:

        if (Wnd == GetCapture())
        {
            hitCode = HitTest (Wnd, lParam);
            if (hitCode != p->State)
            {
                p->State = hitCode;
                InvalidateRect (Wnd, NULL, FALSE);
            }
        }
        return (0);

    case WM_CREATE:

        return InitSpinButtonWindow (Wnd, (LPCREATESTRUCT) lParam);

    case WM_PAINT:

        return PaintSpinButton (Wnd);

    case WM_TIMER:

        if (p->State) SpinNotify (Wnd);
        return (0);

    case WM_DESTROY:

        DeleteObject (p->bmBitmap);
        LocalFree ((HANDLE) p);
        return (0);
    }

    return DefWindowProc (Wnd, Msg, wParam, lParam);
}
//———————————————————————————————————————————
// Name:     InitSpinButton
// Purpose:  Register the spin button window class.
//———————————————————————————————————————————
```

```
BOOL PASCAL InitSpinButton (HANDLE hInstance)
{
    WNDCLASS cls;

    if (GetClassInfo (hInstance, SPINCLASSNAME, &cls) == FALSE)
    {
        cls.style           = CS_DBLCLKS;
        cls.lpfnWndProc     = (WNDPROC) SpinButtonWndProc;
        cls.cbClsExtra      = 0;
        cls.cbWndExtra      = sizeof (PSpinButtonRec);
        cls.hInstance       = hInstance;
        cls.hIcon           = 0;
        cls.hCursor         = LoadCursor (NULL, IDC_ARROW);
        cls.hbrBackground   = 0;
        cls.lpszMenuName    = NULL;
        cls.lpszClassName   = SPINCLASSNAME;

        return RegisterClass (&cls);
    }

    return (TRUE);
}
```

Figure 7.10 SPINTST2.C: the spin button test application.

```
/* SPINTST2.C */

// © 1994 Dave Jewell and Addison-Wesley, ALL RIGHTS RESERVED

#include    <windows.h>
#include    "spin.h"

char szAppName [ ] = "SpinTest";

//—————————————————————————————————————————————
// Name:     WindowProc
// Purpose:  Window procedure for the main application window.
//—————————————————————————————————————————————

LONG FAR PASCAL _export WindowProc (HWND Wnd, WORD Msg,
                                    WPARAM wParam, LPARAM lParam)
{
    switch (Msg)
    {
        case SPINMESSAGE:

        MessageBeep (0);
        return (0);

        case WM_DESTROY:

        PostQuitMessage (0);
        return (0);
    }

    return DefWindowProc (Wnd, Msg, wParam, lParam);
}

//—————————————————————————————————————————————
// Name:     InitApplication
// Purpose:  Register the application window class.
//—————————————————————————————————————————————

BOOL PASCAL InitApplication (HANDLE hInstance)
```

```
{
    WNDCLASS cls;

    if (GetClassInfo (hInstance, SPINCLASSNAME, &cls) == FALSE)
    {
        cls.style           = 0;
        cls.lpfnWndProc     = (WNDPROC) WindowProc;
        cls.cbClsExtra      = 0;
        cls.cbWndExtra      = 0;
        cls.hInstance       = hInstance;
        cls.hIcon           = LoadIcon (NULL, IDI_APPLICATION);
        cls.hCursor         = LoadCursor (NULL, IDC_ARROW);
        cls.hbrBackground   = COLOR_BTNFACE + 1;
        cls.lpszMenuName    = NULL;
        cls.lpszClassName   = szAppName;

        return RegisterClass (&cls);
    }

    return (TRUE);
}

//————————————————————————————————————————————————————————
// Name:    WinMain
// Purpose: Program entry point.
//————————————————————————————————————————————————————————

#pragma argsused

int PASCAL WinMain (HANDLE hInstance, HANDLE hPrevInstance,
                    LPSTR lpCmdLine, int nCmdShow)
{
    HWND Wnd;
    MSG Msg;

    InitApplication (hInstance);
    InitSpinButton (hInstance);

    Wnd = CreateWindow (szAppName, "Spin Button Test",
                        WS_OVERLAPPEDWINDOW, CW_USEDEFAULT,
                        CW_USEDEFAULT, CW_USEDEFAULT,
                        CW_USEDEFAULT, NULL, NULL, hInstance,
                        NULL);

    if (Wnd != NULL)
    {
        ShowWindow (Wnd, nCmdShow);
        UpdateWindow (Wnd);

    CreateWindow ("Edit", "Hello World", WS_CHILD | WS_VISIBLE | WS_BORDER,
                100, 300, 100, 25, Wnd, 999, hInstance, NULL);
    CreateWindow (SPINCLASSNAME, "999", WS_CHILD | WS_VISIBLE | SP_VERT,
                100, 100, 10, 10, Wnd, NULL, hInstance, NULL);
    CreateWindow (SPINCLASSNAME, "999", WS_CHILD | WS_VISIBLE | SP_HORIZ,
                200, 100, 10, 10, Wnd, NULL, hInstance, NULL);
    }

    while (GetMessage (&Msg, 0, 0, 0))
    {
        TranslateMessage (&Msg);
        DispatchMessage (&Msg);
    }

    return Msg.wParam;
}
```

Incidentally, if you try double-clicking on the time or date buddy edit boxes in the Windows Control Panel (see Figure 7.1), you'll probably notice that the edit boxes automatically set the highlighted portion of the text to a single numeric field such as the month, day, year or whatever. Similarly, if you click and drag the mouse inside these controls, you'll find that you can only highlight a single field at a time. This non-standard edit box selection behavior is great for the date/time setting dialog, but it may not be so great for your own application and so I'm not going to try to emulate it here. Such details are implementation-specific, and they really have nothing to do with the spin button control. They're the buddy window's business.

Dialog box integration

Of course, for some applications it might not be appropriate to have the number in the buddy window increment or decrement by one. As pointed out earlier, some programs might want to accept a very wide range of numbers, and you don't want your users to have to hold down their mouse buttons for half an hour while they wait for the wanted number to come round. The solution to this problem would be to allow a specific increment value to be applied each time the spin button is clicked. Rather than incrementing by one, we might increment by 5, 10, 100 or whatever. The best place to do this is in the BuddyTalk routine, like this:

```
// Convert to numeric value
i = MyAtoi (&szText [LOWORD (sel)], &fValid) + (p–>State * p–>Increment);
```

Here, a new field, called Increment, is used to store the increment value. Setting this field to ten will cause the buddy number to be incremented or decremented in steps of ten. I'm not going to outline the code needed to initialize this field because, in a sense, it's up to you. If you want, you can define a new message that you send to a spin button that sets up this field. Alternatively, you could make use of more of the window name to hold these additional parameters. For example, you could set the window name to something like this: "999 10". This might tell the spin button to look for a buddy with an ID of 999, and use an increment value of ten.

Really, these sorts of issue relate to how you want to handle your spin button control. Conventional wisdom dictates that we should spend a lot of time writing a set of routines that interface the spin button to a dialog editor. What does this buy us? Other than the ability to visually add and position spin buttons within dialog boxes, not a great deal. Being able to do this is certainly nice, but there's always more than one way to skin a cat. Look at it like this: a spin button is almost invariably linked to an edit box, so if we knew which edit box needed to have an associated spin button, we could create the spin button on the fly before the dialog is displayed on the screen.

The simplest way to do this is to set up some attribute of the edit box such as the style bits or the window text. Of the two, the window text seems like the better bet. Wouldn't it be great if you could just set up the text of an edit box to, say, "SPIN 25". This would automatically create a spin button to the right-hand side of the edit box with an increment value of 25. In other words, the number in the edit box increments or decrements by 25 each time the spin button is clicked.

By now, you've probably realized how we might go about this: our old friend, window subclassing! There's no reason why we couldn't extend the dialog sub-classing code of Chapter 5 to give us the effect we want. If you look back at the chapter, you'll see that the code iterates through every dialog box control and sub-classes those that are of interest. In the case of edit box controls, a routine is called which reduces the size of edit boxes so that they are a better 'fit' with the smaller font that we use.

It would be a simple matter to examine the window text of each edit control and, if it contains the string SPIN, create a new spin button immediately to the right of the edit box in question. When creating the spin button, it should be assigned a name that allows it to find the associated buddy edit box. Once the spin button has been created, the window text of the original edit box can be reset to an empty string.

Although I haven't provided code to do this, you should have little difficulty in implementing such a technique if you've absorbed the material in the rest of the book. Care needs to be taken when positioning the spin button alongside the edit control. As far as horizontal positioning is concerned, you can either butt the spin button right up again the edit box (see the 'Copies' box in the Print dialog of Word for Windows) or else allow a small space between the two controls. Vertical spacing is a little more tricky. You should first execute the existing code which reduces the vertical height of the edit box before attempting to align it with the spin button control. Once done, you can then explicitly load the spin button bitmap in order to determine the final height of the control. You then have all the information required to vertically align the centers of the two controls.

Note

For Pascal programmers, Appendix 7 contains a Pascal unit, SPIN.PAS, that is equivalent to the spin button code developed in this chapter. A Pascal equivalent of the test program, SPINTEST.PAS, is also included in the appendix.

The CTL3D library and WiDE

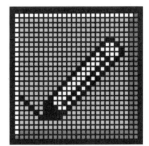

8

No book that's concerned with improving the appearance of your Windows applications would be complete without a chapter on Microsoft's CTL3D library. This DLL isn't part of the retail version of Windows 3.1, but it's been made available as part of Microsoft's support for Windows developers (MSDN – the Microsoft Developer Network) and is classified as one of the distributable files that can be supplied as part of a commercial package.

The CTL3D DLL is concerned with improving the appearance of your Windows dialogs. It was originally written by Wes Cherry of the Excel development group, which explains why it was Excel that first got the 'new look' dialog boxes. Subsequently, the code was repackaged as a DLL and became part of the MSDN package, supported by Kyle Marsh. The initially released version of CTL3D included full source code in C, but this was later withdrawn. A number of changes have been made to provide compatibility with the Microsoft Foundation Classes (MFC) and the code is now very stable.

The CTL3D code explicitly checks for the presence of Windows 4.0 or later, and bows out gracefully if found. The obvious implication, of course, is that Windows 4.0 (also known as the Chicago project) will implement the enhanced dialog box appearance as standard, without the need for any additional DLLs to be used. Once Windows 4.0 achieves critical mass and support for older versions of Windows is no longer an issue, you'll be able to remove the calls to CTL3D from your application, and you'll still get the improved dialog look. Taking its cue from CTL3D, the dialog enhancing code covered in Chapter 5 also becomes very shy if Windows 4.0 (or later) is detected!

If you like the CTL3D 'look', you might be tempted to use this Microsoft DLL rather than the code in Chapter 5. After all, the likelihood is that this will become the new, standard appearance of dialog boxes once Chicago hits the streets. There are a few points to make here, though. Firstly, if you have the source code in Chapter 5, you've got the freedom to customize the appearance of your application's dialog boxes the way it suits *you*. Looking back at what happened with Windows 3.0 and 3.1, history tends to suggest that people will initially love the appearance of Chicago dialog boxes, but only a few months down the road, some company will come out with an even cuter 'look', and soon everyone else will want it, too. We're talking about matters of fashion here, and as I've said elsewhere in this book, fashion is a very fickle thing!

Secondly, you may wish to ensure that your program is as self-contained as possible. DLLs are great, and you can always rely on the system ones (USER, GDI and KERNEL) being around. But what do you do if someone accidentally deletes the CTL3D.DLL from your Windows setup? If you've linked your application with CTL3D, your application won't even start running. A number of commercial programs get around this by using the LoadLibrary call to check for the CTL3D library, and they then use the GetProcAddress to access routines in the DLL. This is run-time DLL linking, rather than link-time DLL linking. This approach means that your applications will be able to run properly without CTL3D (although without fancy-looking dialog boxes), but it means more programming work for you.

I've seen the new Chicago system running and it looks great, but I couldn't help noticing that radio buttons have now taken on a diamond shape, rather like those used by Borland's BWCC library. Put another way, Microsoft's idea of the ideal dialog box is still evolving, just like everyone else's views on the same subject! If you want to retain maximum flexibility, the code in Chapter 5 enables you to choose the appearance you want for your applications.

Using CTL3D in your applications

For your experimentation, the CTL3D DLL is included on the disk that accompanies this book. If you're programming in C, you use the DLL just like any other – the CTL3D package includes programming documentation, a header file, a library file for linking to the DLL, and of course, the DLL itself. There is also some example source code and a Pascal unit for Pascal programmers who wish to use CTL3D. Figure 8.1 shows the CTL3D DLL being used to subclass the standard File Open dialog.

Using the DLL is quite straightforward. Other than the obvious steps of #including the header file and linking with CTL3D.LIB, you only need to make a couple of minor modifications to your application code.

Firstly, make a call to the Ctl3dRegister routine early on in your application. This is best done early in your WinMain code. Here's the function prototype for Ctl3DRegister:

```
BOOL Ctl3dRegister (HANDLE hinstApp);
```

Calling this routine effectively registers an application as a client of the DLL. Because the DLL is written in such a way as to handle multiple clients at the same time, this step is very important. You pass your program's instance handle as the only parameter. The function result will be TRUE if the client registration was successful, and FALSE otherwise. Realistically, there are only two reasons why the routine is likely to fail:

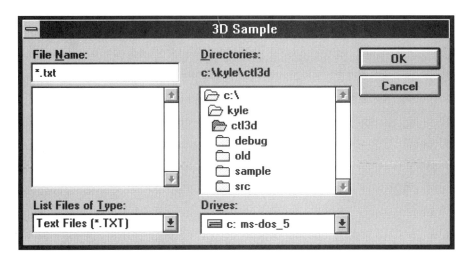

(1) If the DLL detects that it's being used with a display card of less than VGA resolution (less than 640×480 pixels) or with a monochrome display, it will return FALSE.

(2) As previously stated, if CTL3DDLL detects that it's being used with Windows 4.0 or greater, it will likewise return FALSE.

If you get a FALSE function result, the application should not attempt to make any further calls to the DLL.

The second change needed in your application is to add a call to the Ctl3DAutoSubClass routine. This installs a task-specific CBT hook in a manner similar to that described in Chapter 5. The effect is that any dialog box or message box created by the application will automatically benefit from the enhanced look and feel that CTL3D provides. If your program also uses a Windows CBT hook for any reason, you must take care to install the hook before calling the Ctl3DAutoSubClass routine. Also, in your own hook procedure, be sure to 'pass on' the hook by calling CallNextHookEx as dictated by the Microsoft SDK documentation. If you neglect to do this, then CTL3D's hook routine won't get called, and no automatic subclassing of dialog boxes and message boxes will take place.

```
PUBLIC BOOL FAR PASCAL Ctl3dAutoSubclass(HANDLE hinstApp);
```

The CBT hook requires Windows 3.1 or later. Consequently, this routine will return a FALSE function result if it detects an earlier version of Windows. Likewise, a FALSE function result will be returned if more than 32 client applications are trying to use the DLL at once. On success, a function result of TRUE will be returned.

The code in Figure 8.2 shows how easy it is to interface your application to the CTL3D DLL. This small program, which is adopted from the Microsoft MSDN material, displays a custom, application-specific dialog box. Clicking on buttons in this dialog box will bring up a message box that has been subclassed to have the Excel dialog style, and a File Open dialog box, courtesy of the COMMDLG library, that has received the same treatment. The code was compiled with Borland C/C++. The dialog box definition is shown in Figure 8.3.

Figure 8.2 CTL3DTST.C: a sample application which uses the CTL3D code.

```c
/* CTL3DTST.C */

// © 1994 Dave Jewell and Addison-Wesley, ALL RIGHTS RESERVED

#include <windows.h>
#include <commdlg.h>
#include <mem.h>
#include "ctl3d.h"

//--------------------------------------------------------------
// Name:    FileOpen
// Purpose: Select a file using the COMMDLG GetOpenFileName routine.
//--------------------------------------------------------------
void PASCAL FileOpen (HWND Wnd)
{
        OPENFILENAME ofn;
        char szFileName [120];

        szFileName [0] = '\0';
        memset (&ofn, 0, sizeof (ofn));

        ofn.lStructSize     = sizeof (ofn);
        ofn.hwndOwner       = Wnd;
        ofn.lpstrFilter     = "Text Files (*.TXT)\0*.TXT\0All Files (*.*)\0*.*\0";
        ofn.nFilterIndex    = 1;
        ofn.lpstrFile       = szFileName;
        ofn.nMaxFile        = sizeof (szFileName);
        ofn.nMaxFileTitle   = sizeof (szFileName);
        ofn.lpstrTitle      = "CTL3D Test";
        ofn.lpstrDefExt     = "TXT";

        GetOpenFileName ((LPOPENFILENAME) &ofn);
}

//--------------------------------------------------------------
// Name:    DialogProc
// Purpose: Dialog procedure for main dialog.
//--------------------------------------------------------------
#pragma argsused
BOOL FAR PASCAL _export DialogProc (HWND Wnd, UINT Msg,
                                    WPARAM wParam, LPARAM lParam)
{
    switch (Msg)
    {
      case WM_SYSCOLORCHANGE:
      Ctl3dColorChange();
      break;
      case WM_COMMAND:
      {
         if (wParam == IDOK) EndDialog (Wnd, TRUE);
         if (wParam == 130) MessageBox (Wnd, "A Message Box !",
                                    "CTL3D Test", MB_OK);
         if (wParam == 131) FileOpen (Wnd);
      }
      break;
      default:
      return FALSE;
    }
    return TRUE;
}
```

```
//----------------------------------------------------------------
// Name:    WinMain
// Purpose: Program entry point.
//----------------------------------------------------------------
#pragma argsused

int PASCAL WinMain (HANDLE hInstance, HANDLE hPrevInstance,
                    LPSTR lpszCmdLine, int nCmdShow)
{
    Ctl3dRegister (hInstance);
    Ctl3dAutoSubclass (hInstance);
    DialogBox (hInstance, MAKEINTRESOURCE (100), NULL, DialogProc);
    Ctl3dUnregister (hInstance);
    return 0;
}
```

```
/* CTL3DTST.RC */

// © 1994 Dave Jewell and Addison-Wesley, ALL RIGHTS RESERVED

100 DIALOG 83, −11, 327, 96

STYLE DS_MODALFRAME | WS_POPUP | WS_VISIBLE | WS_CAPTION | WS_SYSMENU
CAPTION "CTL3D Test Program"
FONT 8, "Helv"
BEGIN
    PUSHBUTTON "&OK", 1, 56, 70, 56, 16
    PUSHBUTTON "&Message Box", 130, 214, 70, 56, 16
    PUSHBUTTON "&File Open", 131, 135, 70, 56, 16
    CONTROL "", 101, "EDIT", ES_LEFT | ES_AUTOHSCROLL | WS_CHILD |
            WS_VISIBLE | WS_BORDER | WS_TABSTOP, 54, 23, 72, 12
    CONTROL "Auto Indent", 112, "BUTTON", BS_AUTOCHECKBOX | WS_CHILD I
            WS_VISIBLE | WS_TABSTOP, 186, 15, 57, 10
    CONTROL "Save on Exit", 113, "BUTTON", BS_AUTOCHECKBOX | WS_CHILD |
            WS_VISIBLE | WS_TABSTOP, 186, 25, 59, 10
    CONTROL "Snap to Grid", 114, "BUTTON", BS_AUTOCHECKBOX | WS_CHILD |
            WS_VISIBLE | WS_TABSTOP, 186, 35, 57, 10
    CONTROL "1"" Grid", 115, "BUTTON", BS_AUTORADIOBUTTON | WS_CHILD |
            WS_VISIBLE, 252, 15, 39, 10
    CONTROL "2"" Grid", 116, "BUTTON", BS_AUTORADIOBUTTON | WS_CHILD |
            WS_VISIBLE, 252, 25, 58, 10
    CONTROL "4"" Grid", 117, "BUTTON", BS_AUTORADIOBUTTON | WS_CHILD |
            WS_VISIBLE, 252, 35, 39, 10
    CONTROL "Preferences", 121, "BUTTON", BS_GROUPBOX | WS_CHILD |
            WS_VISIBLE, 175, 3, 140, 52
    CONTROL "Templates", 103, "BUTTON", BS_GROUPBOX | WS_CHILD |
            WS_VISIBLE, 4, 3, 165, 52
    LTEXT "Default:", −1, 17, 25, 31, 9, WS_CHILD | WS_VISIBLE | WS_GROUP
END
```

Figure 8.3 CTL3DTST.RC: the dialog box used by the sample application.

Naturally, there is more to the CTL3D library than this. You can, for example, choose to give the enhanced look only to certain specific dialog boxes. There are calls to determine the version number of the CTL3D library, and so forth. For a complete description of what's available, read the Help information that's included in the ZIP file. Figure 8.4 shows what you can expect to see when you execute the sample program.

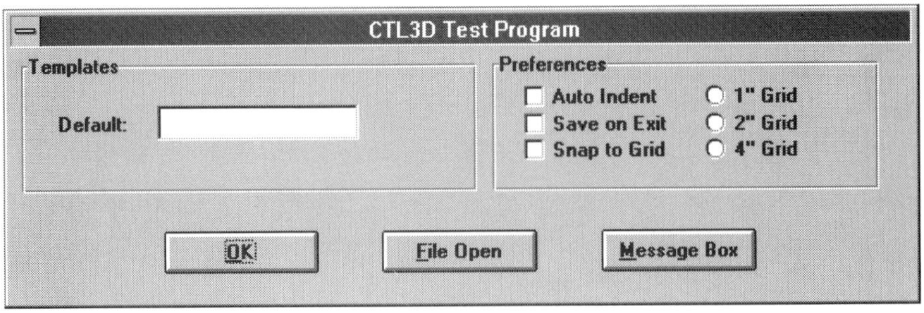

Figure 8.4 The result of running the CTL3DTST program.

Introducing WiDE: Windows Dialog Extensions

Of course, having got used to these cute, Excel-style dialog boxes in your own programs, ordinary Windows programs begin to look very plain. This includes the standard parts of Windows, such as the Program Manager and the File Manager. Wouldn't it be great if these applications could be made to have the same great-looking appearance?

Amazingly enough, it's perfectly possible to do this using the power of Windows hooks. The dialog subclassing code in Chapter 5 showed you something of what can be achieved by installing a Windows hook. In this particular case, the hook was

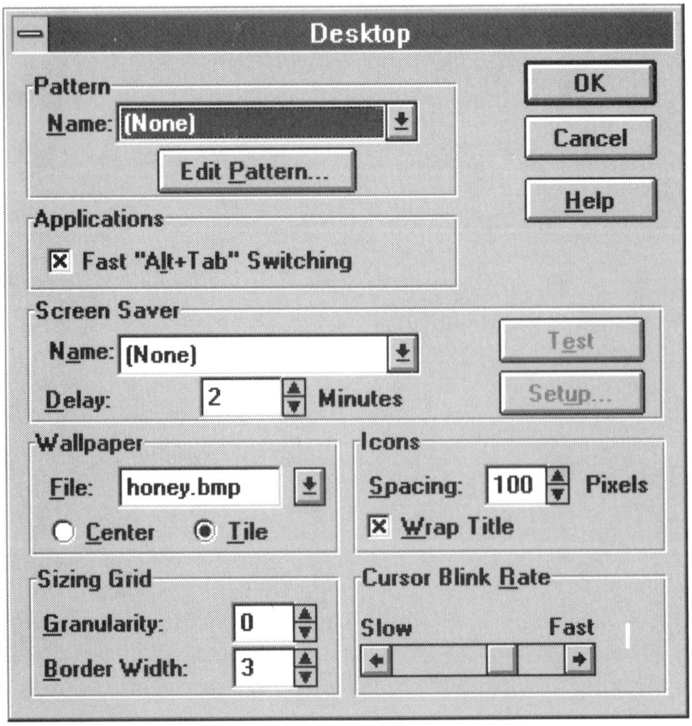

Figure 8.5 Using WiDE, the whole system takes on the CTL3D look.

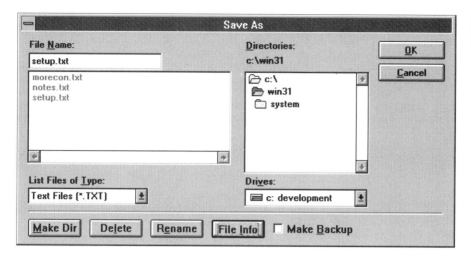

Figure 8.6   The WiDE extensions to the COMMDLG dialogs.

task-specific; in other words, it only affected the operation of the program that installed the hook. However, it's also possible to install system-wide hooks which influence every application running under Windows.

Mark Woollard, a British programmer, has developed a neat little shareware utility called WiDE. WiDE is an abbreviation for 'Windows Dialog Extensions'. Using WiDE, almost all of your Windows applications will automatically use the CTL3D library, and will display correspondingly nicer-looking dialogs. Figure 8.5 shows the Control Panel's preferences dialog on a system that has WiDE installed.

Why do I say, 'almost all of your Windows programs...'? The answer is that a very small number of applications, such as Microsoft Word for Windows, use a totally different means of displaying dialog boxes, and this can't be intercepted by the WiDE code.

Useful as this is, WiDE is also capable of modifying the common dialogs that are built into Windows 3.1. For example, with WiDE installed and the Common Dialog Extensions feature turned on, the File Save As dialog changes to look as shown in Figure 8.6.

As you can see, a new row of buttons has appeared underneath the existing dialog controls. Using these buttons, you effectively get a subset of the File Manager's functionality at any time that a file-oriented common dialog appears on the screen. Using the extra buttons, you can create new subdirectories, delete and rename files, and even bring up a 'File Info' dialog that allows you to view and change the attributes of any given file.

This additional functionality is so useful that the author of WiDE refers to it as 'The File Manager Inside'. You can try out the WiDE software by copying it from the companion disk and following the installation instructions. If you like the software and want to keep using it, then do please remember to register the software as explained in the accompanying documentation.

Appendix 1: The **STRLIB** unit

This appendix contains the equivalent Pascal code for the string access routines developed in Chapter 1. The code here differs in minor respects from the C implementation. For example, it makes use of Pascal's ability to have initialization code within a unit – the string buffer array is allocated when the program is first started in this case. The actual interface, however, remains the same as for the C code.

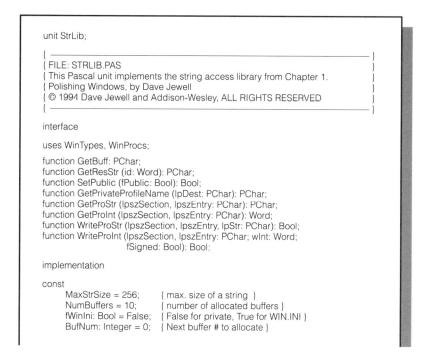

```
unit StrLib;

{ ———————————————————————————————————————— }
{ FILE: STRLIB.PAS                                          }
{ This Pascal unit implements the string access library from Chapter 1.  }
{ Polishing Windows, by Dave Jewell                         }
{ © 1994 Dave Jewell and Addison-Wesley, ALL RIGHTS RESERVED }
{ ———————————————————————————————————————— }

interface

uses WinTypes, WinProcs;

function GetBuff: PChar;
function GetResStr (id: Word): PChar;
function SetPublic (fPublic: Bool): Bool;
function GetPrivateProfileName (lpDest: PChar): PChar;
function GetProStr (lpszSection, lpszEntry: PChar): PChar;
function GetProInt (lpszSection, lpszEntry: PChar): Word;
function WriteProStr (lpszSection, lpszEntry, lpStr: PChar): Bool;
function WriteProInt (lpszSection, lpszEntry: PChar; wInt: Word;
                      fSigned: Bool): Bool;

implementation

const
        MaxStrSize = 256;       { max. size of a string  }
        NumBuffers = 10;        { number of allocated buffers }
        fWinIni: Bool = False;  { False for private, True for WIN.INI }
        BufNum: Integer = 0;    { Next buffer # to allocate }
```

Figure A1.1   STRLIB.PAS: string access routines.

```
type
      Buffer = array [0..MaxStrSize − 1] of Char;
      BufferArray = array [0..NumBuffers − 1] of Buffer;
var
      TheBuffer: ^BufferArray;

function GetTaskDS: THandle; far; external 'KERNEL' index 155;

{ ------------------------------------------------------------------- }
{ Name:    GetBuff                                                    }
{ Purpose: This is the buffer allocator. Each time it's called, it    }
{          returns a pointer to a 256-byte temporary buffer. As a     }
{          convenience to the caller, the first byte of the buffer is }
{          set to zero.                                               }
{ ------------------------------------------------------------------- }

function GetBuff: PChar;

var
      p: PChar;

begin
      p := TheBuffer^ [BufNum];
      Inc (BufNum);
      if BufNum >= NumBuffers then BufNum := 0;
      p^ := #0;
      GetBuff := p;
end;

{ ------------------------------------------------------------------- }
{ Name:    GetResStr                                                  }
{ Purpose: This version of GetResStr uses GetBuff to get a temporary  }
{          buffer for holding the returned string.                    }
{ ------------------------------------------------------------------- }

function GetResStr (id: Word): PChar;
var
      p: PChar;

begin
      p := GetBuff;
      LoadString (GetTaskDS, id, p, MAXSTRSIZE − 1);
      GetResStr := p;
end;

{ ------------------------------------------------------------------- }
{ Name:    GetPrivateProfileName                                      }
{ Purpose: This routine determines the name of the private initialization }
{          file, based on the executable file name.                   }
{ ------------------------------------------------------------------- }

function GetPrivateProfileName (lpDest: PChar): PChar;
var
      szBuffer: array [0..127] of Char;

begin
      { Allocate a buffer if user hasn't given us one }

      if lpDest = Nil then lpDest := GetBuff;

      if fWinIni then LStrCpy (lpDest, 'WIN.INI')
      else
      begin
        GetModuleFileName (GetTaskDS, szBuffer, sizeof (szBuffer));
        LStrCpy (@szBuffer [LStrlen (szBuffer) − 3], 'INI');
        LStrCpy (lpDest, szBuffer);
      end;

      GetPrivateProfileName := lpDest;
end;
```

```
{ ------------------------------------------------------------------- }
{ Name:    SetPublic                                                  }
{ Purpose: Specify whether to use the private initialization file or the }
{          public one (WIN.INI).                                      }
{ ------------------------------------------------------------------- }

function SetPublic (fPublic: Bool): Bool;
begin
      SetPublic := fWinIni;
      fWinIni := fPublic;
end;

{ ------------------------------------------------------------------- }
{ Name:    GetProStr                                                  }
{ Purpose: Return the value of a designated profile string.           }
{ ------------------------------------------------------------------- }

function GetProStr (lpszSection, lpszEntry: PChar): PChar;
var
      p: PChar;
      szfName: array [0..127] of Char;
begin
      p := GetBuff;
      GetPrivateProfileName (szfName);
      GetPrivateProfileString (lpszSection, lpszEntry, '',
                               p, MaxStrSize − 1, szfName);
      GetProStr := p;
end;

{ ------------------------------------------------------------------- }
{ Name:    GetProInt                                                  }
{ Purpose: Return the value of a designated profile integer.          }
{ ------------------------------------------------------------------- }

function GetProInt (lpszSection, lpszEntry: PChar): Word;
var
      p: PChar;
      Result, Code: Word;
      Buff: String [128];

begin
      GetProInt := $ffff;
      p := GetProStr (lpszSection, lpszEntry);
      if p^ <> #0 then
      begin
        { Convert to String for 'Val' call }
        LStrCpy (@Buff [1], p);
        Buff [0] := Chr (LStrLen (p));
        Val (Buff, Result, Code);
        if Code = 0 then GetProInt := Result;
      end;
end;

{ ------------------------------------------------------------------- }
{ Name:    WriteProStr                                                }
{ Purpose: Write a profile string to an initialization file.          }
{ ------------------------------------------------------------------- }

function WriteProStr (lpszSection, lpszEntry, lpStr: PChar): Bool;
var
      szfName: array [0..127] of Char;

begin
      GetPrivateProfileName (szfName);
      WriteProStr := WritePrivateProfileString (lpszSection,
                                     lpszEntry, lpStr, szfName);
end;
```

```
{ --------------------------------------------------------------- }
{ Name:     WriteProInt                                           }
{ Purpose: Write a profile integer to an initialization file.     }
{ --------------------------------------------------------------- }
function WriteProInt (lpszSection, lpszEntry: PChar; wInt: Word;
                        fSigned: Bool): Bool;
var
      szBuff: array [0..19] of Char;
begin
      { Special test to see if we want to remove entry }

      if (wInt = $ffff) and fSigned then
        WriteProInt := WriteProStr (lpszSection, lpszEntry, Nil)
      else

      begin
        if fSigned then wvsprintf (szBuff, '%d', wInt)
        else wvsprintf (szBuff, '%u', wInt);
        WriteProInt := WriteProStr (lpszSection, lpszEntry, szBuff);
      end;
end;
{ --------------------------------------------------------------- }
{ Name:     InitUnit                                              }
{ Purpose: Initialization code for the unit.                      }
{ Note:     We don't need a good-bye kiss because TheBuffer will be }
{           deallocated automatically when the program terminates. }
{ --------------------------------------------------------------- }

begin
      GetMem (TheBuffer, sizeof (BufferArray));
end.
```

Appendix 2:
The **PALETTE** unit

This appendix shows the source code for PALETTE.PAS, the Pascal source code that implements the floating toolbox palette described in Chapter 2. Unlike the C code, this Pascal unit does not require a separate initialization call. In fact, there is only one routine exported by the unit! The PALTEST.PAS program implements a small test application to show the toolbox palette in action. To build the PALTEST.EXE file, you will need the PALETTE.RES file, which contains the bitmaps used by the program. This file can be found on the companion disk.

```pascal
unit Palette;
{$R PALETTE.RES }

{ ———————————————————————————————————————————————— }
{ FILE: PALETTE.PAS                                                          }
{ This Pascal unit implements the floating toolbox palette from Chapter 2.   }
{ Polishing Windows, by Dave Jewell                                          }
{ © 1994 Dave Jewell and Addison-Wesley, ALL RIGHTS RESERVED                 }
{ ———————————————————————————————————————————————— }

interface

uses WinTypes, WinProcs;

const
        pm_GetTool   =   wm_User;
        pm_SetTool   =   wm_User + 1;

function CreatePaletteWindow (rows, cols, curTool: Integer; hWndCmd: hWnd;
                             bmBaseID: Word): hWnd;

implementation

const
        szClassName = 'Palette';   { name of our window class }

type
        pToolBoxInfo = ^ToolBoxInfo;
```

Figure A2.1 PALETTE.PAS: Pascal implementation of the floating tool palette code.

```
ToolBoxInfo = record
   rows: Integer;          { number of rows of bitmaps }
   cols: Integer;          { number of columns of bitmaps }
   curTool: Integer;       { currently selected tool bitmap }
   bmBaseID: Word;         { starting ID of bitmap resources }
   bmWidth: Integer;       { width of each bitmap resource }
   bmHeight: Integer;      { height of each bitmap resource }
   bmHandles: array [0..0] of THandle;
end;
```

```
{ --------------------------------------------------------------------- }
{ Name:     FakeCaptionHeight                                           }
{ Purpose:  Return height of fake caption bar                           }
{ --------------------------------------------------------------------- }
```

```
function FakeCaptionHeight: Integer;
begin
   FakeCaptionHeight := (GetSystemMetrics (sm_cyCaption) div 3) + 2;
end;
```

```
{ --------------------------------------------------------------------- }
{ Name:     DrawFakeCaption                                             }
{ Purpose:  This routine draws our fake caption bar, complete with      }
{           miniature system menu close box.                            }
{ --------------------------------------------------------------------- }
```

```
procedure DrawFakeCaption (dc: hDC; Wnd: hWnd);
var
   hbr: hBrush;
   rClient: TRect;
   width, height, brushKind: Integer;

begin
   GetClientRect (Wnd, rClient);
   rClient.bottom := rClient.top + FakeCaptionHeight;
   if GetParent (Wnd) = Getfocus then brushKind := Color_ActiveCaption
   else brushKind := Color_InActiveCaption;
   hbr := CreateSolidBrush (GetSysColor (brushKind));
   FillRect (dc, rClient, hbr);
   DeleteObject (hbr);

   MoveTo (dc, rClient.left, rClient.bottom);
   LineTo (dc, rClient.right, rClient.bottom);

   { Now draw the close box }

   rClient.right := (FakeCaptionHeight * 3) div 2;
   MoveTo (dc, rClient.right, rClient.top);
   LineTo (dc, rClient.right, rClient.bottom);
   FillRect (dc, rClient, GetStockObject (LtGray_Brush));

   { And the close box bar }

   width := rClient.right − rClient.left;
   Inc (rClient.left, (width div 4) + 1);
   rClient.right := rClient.left + (width div 2) + 1;

   height := rClient.bottom − rClient.top;
   Inc (rClient.top, height div 2);
   rClient.bottom := rClient.top + 3;

   FillRect (dc, rClient, GetStockObject (Gray_Brush));
   OffsetRect (rClient, −1, −1);
   FillRect (dc, rClient, GetStockObject (White_Brush));
   FrameRect (dc, rClient, GetStockObject (Black_Brush));
end;
```

```
{ --------------------------------------------------------------------- }
{ Name:     GetInfo                                                     }
{ Purpose:  Return a pointer to window's associated data.               }
{ --------------------------------------------------------------------- }
```

```
function GetInfo (Wnd: hWnd): PToolBoxInfo;
begin
      GetInfo := PToolBoxInfo (GetWindowLong (Wnd, 0));
end;
{ ———————————————————————————————————— }
{ Name:    GetBitmapRect                                         }
{ Purpose:  Return the bounding rectangle of a specific item.    }
{ ———————————————————————————————————— }
procedure GetBitmapRect (var r: TRect; num: Integer; info: PToolBoxInfo);
begin
      r.left     := (num mod info^.cols) * (info^.bmWidth − 1) + 3;
      r.top      := (num div info^.cols) * (info^.bmHeight − 1) +
                         FakeCaptionHeight + 3;
      r.right    := r.left + info^.bmWidth;
      r.bottom := r.top + info^.bmHeight;
end;
{ ———————————————————————————————————— }
{ Name:    DrawBitmap                                            }
{ Purpose:  Draw a specified bitmap in its own rectangle.        }
{ ———————————————————————————————————— }
procedure DrawBitmap (dc: hDC; info: PToolBoxInfo; num: Integer);
var
      hbm: HBitmap;
      hMemDC: hDC;
      r: TRect;
      XSrc: Integer;
begin
      with info^ do
      begin
        if bmHandles [num] <> 0 then
        begin
          GetBitmapRect (r, num, info);
          hMemDC := CreateCompatibleDC (dc);
          hbm := SelectObject (hMemDC, bmHandles [num]);
          if num <> curTool then XSrc := 0 else XSrc := bmWidth;
          BitBlt (dc, r.left, r.top, r.right − r.left, r.bottom − r.top,
               hMemDC, XSrc, 0, SrcCopy);
          SelectObject (hMemDC, hbm);
          DeleteDC (hMemDC);
        end;
      end;
end;
{ ———————————————————————————————————— }
{ Name:    CreateToolBoxWindow                                   }
{ Purpose:  Called in response to WM_CREATE message.            }
{ ———————————————————————————————————— }
function CreateToolBoxWindow (Wnd: hWnd; lParam: LongInt): LongInt;
var
      bm: TBitmap;
      i, numTools: Integer;
      NewInfo, Info: pToolBoxInfo;
begin
      CreateToolBoxWindow := −1;
      Info := PToolBoxInfo ((PCreateStruct (lParam))^.lpCreateParams);
      if Info = Nil then Exit;

      { Perform some sanity checks }

      numTools := Info^.rows * Info^.cols;
      if (numTools = 0) or (Info^.curTool >= numTools) then Exit;

      { Allocate the 'real' info structure }
```

```
            GetMem (NewInfo, sizeof (ToolBoxInfo) + (numTools − 1) * sizeof (HBitmap));
            NewInfo^ := Info^;

         with NewInfo^ do
         begin
           { Now load the tool bitmaps }

           bmWidth := −1;
           for i := 0 to numTools − 1 do
           begin
              bmHandles [i] := LoadBitmap (hInstance, PChar (bmBaseID + i));
              if (bmWidth = −1) and (bmHandles [i] <> 0) then
              begin
                GetObject (bmHandles [i], sizeof (bm), @bm);
                bmWidth := bm.bmWidth div 2;
                bmHeight := bm.bmHeight;
              end;
           end;

           { Check we've got at least one bitmap ! }

           if bmWidth = −1 then Exit;

           { Calculate the required size of the window }

           SetWindowPos (Wnd, 0, 0, 0,
                          (cols * bmWidth) − (cols − 1) + 6,
                          (rows * bmHeight) − (rows − 1) + FakeCaptionHeight + 6,
                          swp_NoMove or swp_NoActivate or swp_NoZOrder);

           { Associate the Info data structure with the window }

           SetWindowLong (Wnd, 0, LongInt (NewInfo));
           SendMessage (GetParent (Wnd), wm_Command, bmBaseID + curTool, 0);
           CreateToolBoxWindow := 0;
         end;
   end;

{ ---------------------------------------------------------------------- }
{ Name:    CaptionHitTest                                                }
{ Purpose:  Test for mouse hits in the caption bar.                      }
{ ---------------------------------------------------------------------- }

function CaptionHitTest (Wnd: hWnd; lParam: LongInt; CloseBoxOnly: Bool): Bool;
var
      rClient: TRect;
      pt: TPoint absolute lParam;

begin
      GetClientRect (Wnd, rClient);
      rClient.bottom := rClient.top + FakeCaptionHeight;
      if CloseBoxOnly then rClient.right := (FakeCaptionHeight * 3) div 2;
      ScreenToClient (Wnd, pt);
      CaptionHitTest := PtInRect (rClient, pt);
end;

{ ---------------------------------------------------------------------- }
{ Name:    ChangeTool                                                    }
{ Purpose:  Change to a new tool in the palette window.                  }
{ ---------------------------------------------------------------------- }

function ChangeTool (Wnd: hWnd; newTool: Integer): Bool;
var
      r: TRect;
      info: PToolBoxInfo;

begin
      info := GetInfo (Wnd);
      if (newTool <> info^.curTool) and (info^.bmHandles [newTool] <> 0) then
      begin
        GetBitmapRect (r, newTool, info);
```

```
            InvalidateRect (Wnd, @r, True);
            GetBitmapRect (r, info^.curTool, info);
            InvalidateRect (Wnd, @r, True);
            info^.curTool := newTool;
            UpdateWindow (Wnd);
            SendMessage (GetParent (Wnd), wm_Command, info^.bmBaseID +
                         newTool, 0);
          ChangeTool := True;
        end
        else ChangeTool := False;
end;

{ ——————————————————————————————————————————————————— }
{ Name:    ButtonHitTest                                                    }
{ Purpose: This routine tests for a mouse click in a tool slot.             }
{ ——————————————————————————————————————————————————— }

function ButtonHitTest (Wnd: hWnd; lParam: LongInt): Integer;
var
      r: TRect;
      num: Integer;
      info: PToolBoxInfo;
      pt: TPoint absolute lParam;

begin
      ButtonHitTest := −1;
      info := GetInfo (Wnd);

      for num := 0 to (info^.rows * info^.cols) − 1 do
      begin
        GetBitmapRect (r, num, info);
        if PtInRect (r, pt) then
        begin
          ButtonHitTest := num;
          Exit;
        end;
      end;
end;

{ ——————————————————————————————————————————————————— }
{ Name:    PaletteWndProc                                                   }
{ Purpose: Window procedure for our floating toolbox palette.              }
{ ——————————————————————————————————————————————————— }

function PaletteWndProc (Wnd: hWnd; Msg, wParam: Word; lParam: LongInt):
                         LongInt; export;

var
      i: Integer;
      r: TRect;
      ps: TPaintStruct;
      numTools: Integer;
      info: PToolBoxInfo;

begin
      PaletteWndProc := 0;
      info := GetInfo (Wnd);
      case Msg of
        wm_LButtonDown:

        begin
          i := ButtonHitTest (Wnd, lParam);
          if i <> −1 then ChangeTool (Wnd, i);
        end;

        wm_NCLButtonDown:

        begin
          if CaptionHitTest (Wnd, lParam, True) then
```

```
                        PostMessage (Wnd, wm_SysCommand, sc_Close, 0)
                    else PaletteWndProc := DefWindowProc (Wnd, Msg, wParam, lParam);
                end;

            wm_NCHitTest:

            begin
                if CaptionHitTest (Wnd, lParam, False) then
                    PaletteWndProc := HTCaption
                else
                    PaletteWndProc := DefWindowProc (Wnd, Msg, wParam, lParam);
            end;

            wm_Activate:

            begin
                GetClientRect (Wnd, r);
                r.bottom := r.top + FakeCaptionHeight;
                InvalidateRect (Wnd, @r, False);
            end;

            wm_Paint:

            begin
                BeginPaint (Wnd, ps);
                DrawFakeCaption (ps.hdc, Wnd);

                for i := 0 to (info^.rows * info^.cols) − 1 do
                    DrawBitmap (ps.hdc, info, i);

                GetClientRect (Wnd, r);
                FrameRect (ps.hdc, r, GetStockObject (Black_Brush));

                EndPaint (Wnd, ps);
            end;

            wm_Create:

            PaletteWndProc := CreateToolBoxWindow (Wnd, lParam);

            wm_Destroy:

            begin
                numTools := info^.rows * info^.cols;
                for i := 0 to numTools − 1 do
                    if info^.bmHandles [i] <> 0 then
                        DeleteObject (info^.bmHandles [i]);

                { Send good-bye kiss... }

                SendMessage (GetParent (Wnd), wm_Command, $ffff, 0);
                FreeMem (info, sizeof (ToolBoxInfo) + (numTools − 1)
                            * sizeof (HBitmap));

            end;

            pm_GetTool:

            PaletteWndProc := info^.curTool + info^.bmBaseID;

            pm_SetTool:

            begin
                Dec (wParam, info^.bmBaseID);
                numTools := info^.rows * info^.cols;
                if (Int (wParam) >= 0) and (wParam < numTools) then
                    PaletteWndProc := LongInt (ChangeTool (Wnd, wParam));
            end;
        else PaletteWndProc := DefWindowProc (Wnd, Msg, wParam, lParam);
    end;
end;
```

```
{ ------------------------------------------------------------------- }
{ Name:    InitToolPalette                                            }
{ Purpose: Routine to initialize palette code.                       }
{ ------------------------------------------------------------------- }
function InitToolPalette: Bool;
var
      cls: TWndClass;
begin
      if not GetClassInfo (hInstance, szClassName, cls) then
      begin
          cls.style              := cs_SaveBits;
          cls.lpfnWndProc        := @PaletteWndProc;
          cls.cbClsExtra         := 0;
          cls.cbWndExtra         := sizeof (pToolBoxInfo);
          cls.hInstance          := hInstance;
          cls.hIcon              := 0;
          cls.hCursor            := LoadCursor (0, idc_Arrow);
          cls.hbrBackground      := GetStockObject (LtGray_Brush);
          cls.lpszMenuName := Nil;
          cls.lpszClassName := szClassName;

          InitToolPalette := RegisterClass (cls);
      end
      else InitToolPalette := True;
end;
{ ------------------------------------------------------------------- }
{ Name:    CreatePaletteWindow                                       }
{ Purpose: Create a new toolbox palette and return handle.           }
{ ------------------------------------------------------------------- }
function CreatePaletteWindow (rows, cols, curTool: Integer; hWndCmd: hWnd;
                             bmBaseID: Word): hWnd;
var
      Wnd: hWnd;
      info: ToolBoxInfo;
begin
      CreatePaletteWindow := 0;
      if (hWndCmd <> 0) and InitToolPalette then
      begin
          { Initialize ToolBoxInfo data structure }

          info.rows       := rows;
          info.cols       := cols,
          info.curTool    := curTool;
          info.bmBaseID := bmBaseID;

          { Create the palette window }

          Wnd := CreateWindow (szClassName, Nil, ws_Child,
                              GetSystemMetrics (sm_cxFrame),
                              GetSystemMetrics (sm_cxFrame),
                              0, 0, hWndCmd, 0, hInstance,
                              @info);

          { If you've got it, flaunt it... }

          if Wnd <> 0 then
          begin
              ShowWindow (Wnd, sw_Show);
              UpdateWindow (Wnd);
              CreatePaletteWindow := Wnd;
          end;
      end;
end;
end.
```

Figure A2.2 PALTEST.PAS:
test application for the Palette
unit.

```pascal
program PalTest;

uses WinTypes, WinProcs, Palette;

const
      szClassName = 'PalTest';
      ToolBaseID = 1000;
var
      hPalWnd: hWnd; { Give me a break :- we need *some* global variables ! }

{ ------------------------------------------------------------------ }
{ Name:    AppWndProc                                                }
{ Purpose: Window procedure for application window.                  }
{ ------------------------------------------------------------------ }

function AppWndProc (Wnd: hWnd; Msg, wParam: Word; lParam: LongInt):
                        LongInt; export;

var
      curTool: Integer;
      ToolRect: TRect;
      pt: array [0..1] of TPoint absolute ToolRect;
      szBuffer: array [0..127] of Char;
      ps: TPaintStruct;
begin
      AppWndProc := 0;

      case Msg of
        wm_ActivateApp:

        if hPalWnd <> 0 then
        begin
          GetWindowRect (hPalWnd, ToolRect);
          ScreenToClient (Wnd, pt [0]);
          ScreenToClient (Wnd, pt [1]);
          InvalidateRect (Wnd, @ToolRect, True);
        end;

        wm_Char:

        begin
          Dec (wParam, Ord ('0'));
          if (Integer (wParam) >= 0) and (wParam <= 9) then
          begin
            if hPalWnd = 0 then MessageBeep (0)
            else SendMessage (hPalWnd, pm_SetTool, wParam + ToolBaseID, 0);
          end;
        end;

        wm_Command:

        begin
          if (wParam >= ToolBaseID) and (wParam <= ToolBaseID + 9) then
            InvalidateRect (Wnd, Nil, True);

          if wParam = $ffff then  { Good-bye kiss ? }
          begin
            InvalidateRect (Wnd, Nil, True);
            hPalWnd := 0;
          end;

          if hPalWnd <> 0 then
          begin
            GetWindowRect (hPalWnd, ToolRect);
            ScreenToClient (Wnd, pt [0]);
            ScreenToClient (Wnd, pt [1]);
            ValidateRect (Wnd, @ToolRect);
          end;
        end;

        wm_Paint:
```

```
      begin
        BeginPaint (Wnd, ps);
        if hPalWnd = 0 then
          LStrCpy (szBuffer, 'Palette window is out to lunch')
        else
        begin
          curTool := SendMessage (hPalWnd, pm_GetTool, 0, 0);
          wvsprintf (szBuffer, 'Currently selected tool is %d !', curTool);
        end;

        TextOut (ps.hdc, 10, 10, szBuffer, LStrLen (szBuffer));
        EndPaint (Wnd, ps);
      end;

      wm_Destroy:

      PostQuitMessage (0);

      else AppWndProc := DefWindowProc (Wnd, Msg, wParam, lParam);
    end;
end;

{ ---------------------------------------------------------------- }
{ Name:    InitApplication                                         }
{ Purpose: Register application window class.                      }
{ ---------------------------------------------------------------- }

function InitApplication: Bool;
var
    cls: TWndClass;

begin
    if not GetClassInfo (hInstance, szClassName, cls) then
    begin
        cls.style          := cs_HRedraw or cs_VRedraw;
        cls.lpfnWndProc    := @AppWndProc;
        cls.cbClsExtra     := 0;
        cls.cbWndExtra     := 0;
        cls.hInstance      := hInstance;
        cls.hIcon          := LoadIcon (0, idi_Application);
        cls.hCursor        := LoadCursor (0, idc_Arrow);
        cls.hbrBackground  := GetStockObject (White_Brush);
        cls.lpszMenuName   := Nil;
        cls.lpszClassName  := szClassName;
        InitApplication    := RegisterClass (cls);
    end
    else InitApplication :  = True;
end;

{ ---------------------------------------------------------------- }
{ Name:    WinMain                                                 }
{ Purpose: Main application entry point.                           }
{ ---------------------------------------------------------------- }

procedure WinMain;
var
    Wnd: hWnd;
    Msg: TMsg;

begin
    { Register our window class }

    if not InitApplication then Halt (0);

    { Create main application window }

    Wnd := CreateWindow (szClassName, 'Sample Application',
                         ws_OverlappedWindow,
                         cw_UseDefault, 0,
                         cw_UseDefault, 0, 0, 0,
                         hInstance, Nil);
```

```
        if Wnd = 0 then Halt (0);

        ShowWindow (Wnd, CmdShow);
        UpdateWindow (Wnd);

        { Create palette window }

        hPalWnd := CreatePaletteWindow (5, 2, 0, Wnd, ToolBaseID);
        if hPalWnd = 0 then Halt (0);

        while GetMessage (Msg, 0, 0, 0) do
        begin
          TranslateMessage (Msg);
          DispatchMessage (Msg);
        end;

        Halt (Msg.wParam);
    end;

    begin
        WinMain;
    end.
```

Appendix 3: The **SUBCLASS** unit

This appendix lists the generic windows subclassing code from Chapter 3. The dialog subclassing code is not shown here. Instead, it has been incorporated into the Dialogs unit shown in Appendix 5. Similarly, no test application code is shown here since the test application in Appendix 5 is used for this purpose.

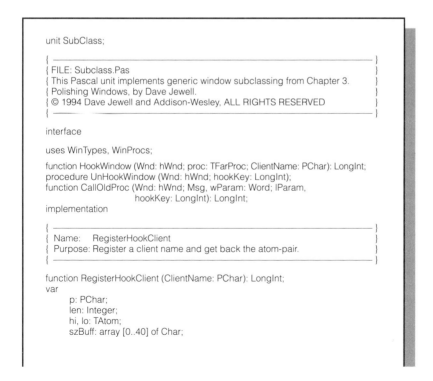

```
unit SubClass;

{ ——————————————————————————————————————————————— }
{ FILE: Subclass.Pas                                                        }
{ This Pascal unit implements generic window subclassing from Chapter 3.    }
{ Polishing Windows, by Dave Jewell.                                        }
{ © 1994 Dave Jewell and Addison-Wesley, ALL RIGHTS RESERVED                }
{ ——————————————————————————————————————————————— }

interface

uses WinTypes, WinProcs;

function HookWindow (Wnd: hWnd; proc: TFarProc; ClientName: PChar): LongInt;
procedure UnHookWindow (Wnd: hWnd; hookKey: LongInt);
function CallOldProc (Wnd: hWnd; Msg, wParam: Word; lParam,
                      hookKey: LongInt): LongInt;
implementation

{ ——————————————————————————————————————————————— }
{ Name:    RegisterHookClient                                               }
{ Purpose: Register a client name and get back the atom-pair.               }
{ ——————————————————————————————————————————————— }

function RegisterHookClient (ClientName: PChar): LongInt;
var
        p: PChar;
        len: Integer;
        hi, lo: TAtom;
        szBuff: array [0..40] of Char;
```

Figure A3.1 SUBCLASS.PAS: the generic window subclassing unit.

```
begin
      RegisterHookClient := 0;
      len := LStrLen (ClientName);
      if (len > 0) and (len < sizeof (szBuff)) then
      begin
        p := ClientName;
        szBuff [len] := #0;
        while len > 0 do
        begin
          Dec (len);
          szBuff [len] := p^;
          Inc (p);
        end;

        hi := GlobalAddAtom (ClientName);
        lo := GlobalAddAtom (szBuff);
        RegisterHookClient := MakeLong (lo, hi);
      end;
end;
{ ------------------------------------------------------------------- }
{ Name:    UnRegisterHookClient                                       }
{ Purpose: Unregister a client hook atom-pair.                        }
{ ------------------------------------------------------------------- }

procedure UnRegisterHookClient (hookKey: LongInt);
begin
      GlobalDeleteAtom (LoWord (hookKey));
      GlobalDeleteAtom (HiWord (hookKey));
end;
{ ------------------------------------------------------------------- }
{ Name:    HookWindow                                                 }
{ Purpose: Hook the window with our new window procedure.             }
{ ------------------------------------------------------------------- }

function HookWindow (Wnd: hWnd; proc: TFarProc; ClientName: PChar): LongInt;
var
      oldProc: LongInt;
      hookKey: LongInt;
begin
      hookKey := RegisterHookClient (ClientName);

      { Check if we're already hooked.... }

      if (GetProp (Wnd, PChar (LoWord (hookKey))) = 0) and
         (GetProp (Wnd, PChar (HiWord (hookKey))) = 0) then
      begin
        { Stash the old proc }

        oldProc := GetWindowLong (Wnd, gwl_WndProc);
        SetProp (Wnd, PChar (LoWord (hookKey)), LoWord (oldProc));
        SetProp (Wnd, PChar (HiWord (hookKey)), HiWord (oldProc));

        { And set the new one.... }

        SetWindowLong (Wnd, gwl_WndProc, LongInt (proc));
        HookWindow := hookKey;
      end
      else
      begin
        UnRegisterHookClient (hookKey);
        HookWindow := 0;
      end;
end;
{ ------------------------------------------------------------------- }
{ Name:    UnHookWindow                                               }
{ Purpose: Unhook a hooked window.                                    }
{ ------------------------------------------------------------------- }
```

```
procedure UnHookWindow (Wnd: hWnd; hookKey: LongInt);
var
     lo, hi: Word;
begin
     lo := GetProp (Wnd, PChar (LoWord (hookKey)));
     hi := GetProp (Wnd, PChar (HiWord (hookKey)));

     { Check that this is a hooked window }

     if (lo <> 0) or (hi <> 0) then
     begin
       RemoveProp (Wnd, PChar (LoWord (hookKey)));
       RemoveProp (Wnd, PChar (HiWord (hookKey)));
       UnRegisterHookClient (hookKey);
       SetWindowLong (Wnd, gwl_WndProc, MakeLong (lo, hi));
     end;
end;


{ --------------------------------------------------------------- }
{ Name:     CallOldProc                                           }
{ Purpose:  Call the old window procedure and return result.      }
{           For convenience, this routine takes care of unhooking }
{           a window in response to a WM_DESTROY message.         }
{ --------------------------------------------------------------- }

function CallOldProc (Wnd: hWnd; Msg, wParam: Word; lParam,
                     hookKey: LongInt): LongInt;
var
     lo, hi: Word;

begin
     lo := GetProp (Wnd, PChar (LoWord (hookKey)));
     hi := GetProp (Wnd, PChar (HiWord (hookKey)));

     { Check that this is a hooked window }

     if (lo <> 0) or (hi <> 0) then
     begin
       { If it's a WM_DESTROY message, then unhook now... }

       if Msg = wm_Destroy then UnHookWindow (Wnd, hookKey);

       CallOldProc := CallWindowProc (TFarProc (MakeLong (lo, hi)),
                                 Wnd, Msg, wParam, lParam);
     end
     else CallOldProc := DefWindowProc (Wnd, Msg, wParam, lParam);
end;
end.
```

Appendix 4:
The **STATBAR** unit

This appendix lists STATBAR.PAS, the Pascal equivalent of the status bar code developed in Chapter 4. In addition, you will find STATUS.PAS, the corresponding test application which is designed to demonstrate the operation of the StatBar unit. At the end of this appendix is the resource script file which contains the Program Manager's menu structure. This file, referred to in the text as STATUS.RC, was used as a sample menu structure to illustrate the menu hinting capabilities of the code.

The Tools unit, which is used by STATBAR.PAS, is shown in Appendix 8.

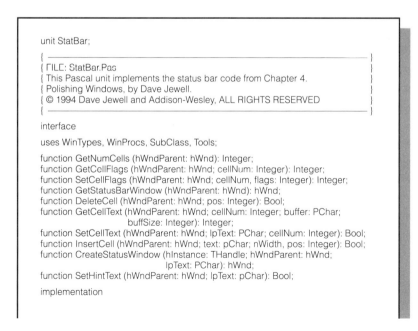

```
unit StatBar;

{ ———————————————————————————————————————————————————————— }
{ FILE: StatBar.Pas                                          }
{ This Pascal unit implements the status bar code from Chapter 4. }
{ Polishing Windows, by Dave Jewell.                         }
{ © 1994 Dave Jewell and Addison-Wesley, ALL RIGHTS RESERVED }
{ ———————————————————————————————————————————————————————— }

interface

uses WinTypes, WinProcs, SubClass, Tools;

function GetNumCells (hWndParent: hWnd): Integer;
function GetCellFlags (hWndParent: hWnd; cellNum: Integer): Integer;
function SetCellFlags (hWndParent: hWnd; cellNum, flags: Integer): Integer;
function GetStatusBarWindow (hWndParent: hWnd): hWnd;
function DeleteCell (hWndParent: hWnd; pos: Integer): Bool;
function GetCellText (hWndParent: hWnd; cellNum: Integer; buffer: PChar;
                     buffSize: Integer): Integer;
function SetCellText (hWndParent: hWnd; lpText: PChar; cellNum: Integer): Bool;
function InsertCell (hWndParent: hWnd; text: pChar; nWidth, pos: Integer): Bool;
function CreateStatusWindow (hInstance: THandle; hWndParent: hWnd;
                     lpText: PChar): hWnd;
function SetHintText (hWndParent: hWnd; lpText: pChar): Bool;

implementation
```

Figure A4.1 STATBAR.PAS: the Pascal Status Bar unit.

```
const
    szClassName = 'StatusBar';          { name of our window class    }
    szHookName  = 'StatusBarHook';      { name of our hook service    }
    MaxCells    = 10;                   { maximum cells per window    }

type
    pStatusRec = ^StatusRec;

    StatusRec = record
    hintText: PChar;                            { pointer to hint text, if any    }
    statusFont: HFont;                          { handle to our special font      }
    border: Integer;                            { width of border                 }
    height: Integer;                            { height of status bar            }
    numCells: Integer;                          { number of defined cells         }
    pText: array [0..MaxCells − 1] of PChar;    { pointer to cell text            }
    frames: array [0..MaxCells − 1] of Integer; { right edge of each cell         }
    flags: array [0..MaxCells − 1] of Word;     { flag info for each cell         }
    end;

var
    hookKey: LongInt;

{ -------------------------------------------------------------- }
{ Name:    GetStatusRec                                          }
{ Purpose: Given a window handle, return a pointer to the        }
{          corresponding status record.                          }
{ -------------------------------------------------------------- }

function GetStatusRec (Wnd: hWnd): pStatusRec;
begin
    GetStatusRec := pStatusRec (GetWindowLong (Wnd, 0));
end;

{ -------------------------------------------------------------- }
{ Name:    AllocText                                             }
{ Purpose: Allocate a chunk of text and return a pointer to it.. }
{ -------------------------------------------------------------- }

function AllocText (text: PChar): PChar;
var
    pText: PChar;

begin
    if (text = Nil) or (text^ = #0) then AllocText := Nil
    else
    begin
      GetMem (pText, LStrlen (text) + 1);
      LStrCpy (pText, text);
      AllocText := pText;
    end;
end;

{ -------------------------------------------------------------- }
{ Name:    ResizeWindow                                          }
{ Purpose: Routine to force status bar to proper size and position. }
{ -------------------------------------------------------------- }

procedure ResizeWindow (Wnd: hWnd);
var
    r: TRect;
    p: pStatusRec;

begin
    p := GetStatusRec (Wnd);
    GetClientRect (GetParent (Wnd), r);
    SetWindowPos (Wnd, 0, 0, r.bottom − p^.height, r.right,
                  p^.height, swp_NoZOrder);
end;
```

```
{ ------------------------------------------------------------------- }
{ Name:    GetStatusBarWindow                                         }
{ Purpose: Return the handle of this window's status bar.             }
{ ------------------------------------------------------------------- }

function GetStatusBarWindow (hWndParent: hWnd): hWnd;
begin
      GetStatusBarWindow := 0;
      if (hWndParent <> 0) and IsWindow (hWndParent) then
        GetStatusBarWindow := hWnd (GetProp (hWndParent, szClassName));
end;

{ ------------------------------------------------------------------- }
{ Name:    SubClassParentWbdProc                                      }
{ Purpose: Subclassing routine for the main application window.       }
{ ------------------------------------------------------------------- }

function SubClassParentWndProc (Wnd: hWnd; Msg, wParam: Word;
                                      lParam: LongInt): LongInt; export;
begin
      if Msg = wm_Size then ResizeWindow (GetStatusBarWindow (Wnd));
      SubClassParentWndProc := CallOldProc (Wnd, Msg, wParam, lParam,
                                      hookKey);
end;

{ ------------------------------------------------------------------- }
{ Name:    InitStatusWindow                                           }
{ Purpose: Initialization code for setting up the status window.      }
{ ------------------------------------------------------------------- }

function InitStatusWindow (Wnd: hWnd; lParam: LongInt): LongInt;
var
      text: PChar;
      p: PStatusRec;

begin
      GetMem (p, sizeof (StatusRec));
      if p = Nil then InitStatusWindow := -1
      else with p^ do
      begin
        { Initialize the StatusRec data structure }

        numCells := 0;
        hintText := Nil;
        statusFont := GetStatusFont (@height);
        border := (GetSystemMetrics (sm_cxFrame) + 1) div 2;
        Inc (height, (border * 4) + 1);
        SetWindowLong (Wnd, 0, LongInt (p));
        ResizeWindow (Wnd);
        SetProp (GetParent (Wnd), szClassName, Wnd);
        hookKey = HookWindow (GetParent (Wnd), @SubclassParentWndProc,
                            szHookName);

        { Now check for any initial text }

        text := (PCreateStruct (lParam))^.lpCreateParams;
        if (text <> Nil) and (text^ <> #0) then
          InsertCell (GetParent (Wnd), text, -1, -1);
        InitStatusWindow := 0;
      end;
end;

{ ------------------------------------------------------------------- }
{ Name:    GetCellRect                                                }
{ Purpose: Return the frame rectangle for a given cell.               }
{ ------------------------------------------------------------------- }

procedure GetCellRect (p: PStatusRec; cellNum: Integer; var r: TRect);
begin
      with p^ do
      begin
```

```
              if cellNum = 0 then r.left := border else
                  r.left := frames [cellNum − 1] + (border * 2);
              r.top := border + 1;
              r.right := frames [cellNum];
              r.bottom := height − border;
          end;
  end;

  { ———————————————————————————————————————————— }
  { Name:    PaintCell                                              }
  { Purpose:  Paint a specfied cell in the status bar.              }
  { ———————————————————————————————————————————— }
  procedure PaintCell (dc: hDC; p: PStatusRec; cellNum: Integer);
  var
        r: TRect;
        mode: Integer;

  begin
        with p^ do
        begin
          GetCellRect (p, cellNum, r);
          DrawSunkenRect (dc, r);

          if pText [cellNum] <> Nil then
          begin
            mode := SetBkMode (dc, Transparent);
            statusFont := SelectObject (dc, statusFont);
            InflateRect (r, −border, −border);
            DrawText (dc, pText [cellNum], −1, r, flags [cellNum] or dt_VCenter);
            statusFont := SelectObject (dc, statusFont);
            SetBkMode (dc, mode);
          end;
        end;
  end;

  { ———————————————————————————————————————————— }
  { Name:    PaintHintText                                          }
  { Purpose:  Paint the special menu hint text.                     }
  { ———————————————————————————————————————————— }
  procedure PaintHintText (Wnd: hWnd; p: PStatusRec; dc: hDC);
  var
        r: TRect;
        width, mode: Integer;

  begin
        with p^ do
        begin
          { Calculate the bounding box }

          GetClientRect (GetParent (Wnd), r);
          width := r.right − r.left − (border * 2);
          GetCellRect (p, 0, r);
          r.right := r.left + width;
          InflateRect (r, −border, −border);

          { Now draw the text... }

          mode := SetBkMode (dc, Transparent);
          statusFont := SelectObject (dc, statusFont);
          DrawText (dc, hintText, −1, r, dt_Left or dt_VCenter or dt_ExpandTabs);
          statusFont := SelectObject (dc, statusFont);
          SetBkMode (dc, mode);
        end;
  end;

  { ———————————————————————————————————————————— }
  { Name:    StatusBarPaint                                         }
  { Purpose:  This routine is responsible for painting the status bar. }
  { ———————————————————————————————————————————— }
```

```
function StatusBarPaint (Wnd: hWnd): Integer;
var
      i: Integer;
      r: TRect;
      p: pStatusRec;
      ps: TPaintStruct;

begin
      BeginPaint (Wnd, ps);
      p := GetStatusRec (Wnd);

      { First, draw the top edge of the status bar }

      GetClientRect (Wnd, r);
      MoveTo (ps.hdc, 0, 0);
      LineTo (ps.hdc, r.right, 0);
      PatBlt (ps.hdc, 0, 1, r.right − r.left, 1, Whiteness);

      { Are we in hint mode }

      if p^.hintText <> Nil then PaintHintText (Wnd, p, ps.hdc)
      else
        { Now draw each cell in turn }

        for i := 0 to p^.numCells − 1 do
        PaintCell (ps.hdc, p, i);

      EndPaint (Wnd, ps);
      StatusBarPaint := 0;
end;

{ ------------------------------------------------------------- }
{ Name:    DestroyStatusWindow                                  }
{ Purpose: Clean-up code for the status window.                 }
{ ------------------------------------------------------------- }

function DestroyStatusWindow (Wnd: hWnd): Integer;
var
      i: Integer;
      p: PStatusRec;

begin
      p := GetStatusRec (Wnd);
      with p^ do
      begin
        DeleteObject (statusFont);
        if hintText <> Nil then FreeMem (hintText, LStrLen (hintText) + 1);
        RemoveProp (GetParent (Wnd), szClassName);
        UnHookWindow (GetParent (Wnd), hookKey);

        { Deallocate text buffers }

        for i := 0 to numCells − 1 do
        if pText [i] <> Nil then
          FreeMem (pText [i], LStrLen (pText [i]) + 1);
      end;

      FreeMem (p, sizeof (StatusRec));
      DestroyStatusWindow := 0;
end;

{ ------------------------------------------------------------- }
{ Name:    StatusBarWndProc                                     }
{ Purpose: Window procedure for status bar windows.             }
{ ------------------------------------------------------------- }

function StatusBarWndProc (Wnd: hWnd; Msg, wParam: Word;
                              lParam: LongInt): LongInt; export;

begin
      case Msg of
```

```
           wm_Paint:     StatusBarWndProc  := StatusBarPaint (Wnd);
           wm_Create:    StatusBarWndProc  := InitStatusWindow (Wnd, lParam);
           wm_Destroy:   StatusBarWndProc  := DestroyStatusWindow (Wnd);
           else          StatusBarWndProc  := DefWindowProc (Wnd, Msg,
                                                        wParam, lParam);
      end;
end;

{ ----------------------------------------------------------------- }
{ Name:    RegisterStatusBar                                        }
{ Purpose: Register the status bar window class.                    }
{ ----------------------------------------------------------------- }

function RegisterStatusBar: Bool;
var
     cls: TWndClass;

begin
     if not GetClassInfo (hInstance, szClassName, cls) then
     begin
          cls.style            := 0;
          cls.lpfnWndProc      := @StatusBarWndProc;
          cls.cbClsExtra       := 0;
          cls.cbWndExtra       := sizeof (pStatusRec);
          cls.hInstance        := hInstance;
          cls.hIcon            := 0;
          cls.hCursor          := LoadCursor (0, idc_Arrow);
          cls.hbrBackground    := Color_BtnFace + 1;
          cls.lpszMenuName     := Nil;
          cls.lpszClassName    := szClassName;

          RegisterStatusBar    := RegisterClass (cls);
     end
     else RegisterStatusBar   := True;
end;

{ ----------------------------------------------------------------- }
{ Name:    CreateStatusWindow                                       }
{ Purpose: Create a status window and attach it to the parent.      }
{ ----------------------------------------------------------------- }

function CreateStatusWindow (hInstance: THandle; hWndParent:
                             hWnd; lpText: PChar): hWnd;
var
     Wnd: hWnd;

begin
     Wnd := 0;

     { Check that we've got a valid parent window }

     if (hWndParent <> 0) and IsWindow (hWndParent) then
     begin
          { Ok so far, but has window already got a status bar? }

          Wnd := GetStatusBarWindow (hWndParent);
          if Wnd = 0 then
            if RegisterStatusBar then
               Wnd := CreateWindow (szClassName, '', ws_Child or ws_Visible,
                            0, 0, 0, 0, hWndParent, 0, hInstance, lpText);
     end;
     CreateStatusWindow := Wnd;
end;

{ ----------------------------------------------------------------- }
{ Name:    GetNumCells                                              }
{ Purpose: Return number of cells in status bar.                    }
{ Returns:  −1 on failure.                                          }
{ ----------------------------------------------------------------- }

function GetNumCells (hWndParent: hWnd): Integer;
```

```
var
      p: PStatusRec;
      hWndStatus: hWnd;

begin
      hWndStatus := GetStatusBarWindow (hWndParent);
      p := GetStatusRec (hWndStatus);
      if (hWndStatus <> 0) and (p <> Nil) then GetNumCells := p^.numCells
      else GetNumCells := −1;
end;
```

```
{ ———————————————————————————————————————————— }
{ Name:    GetCellFlags                                    }
{ Purpose: Return the flag word for a specified cell.      }
{ Returns:  −1 on failure.                                 }
{ ———————————————————————————————————————————— }
```

```
function GetCellFlags (hWndParent: hWnd; cellNum: Integer): Integer;
var
      p: PStatusRec;
      hWndStatus: hWnd;

begin
      hWndStatus := GetStatusBarWindow (hWndParent);
      p := GetStatusRec (hWndStatus);
      if (hWndStatus <> 0) and (p <> Nil) and (cellNum >= 0) and
          (cellNum < p^.numCells) then
        GetCellFlags := p^.flags [cellNum]
      else
        GetCellFlags := −1;
end;
```

```
{ ———————————————————————————————————————————— }
{ Name:    SetCellFlags                                    }
{ Purpose: Set the flag word for a specified cell.         }
{ Returns:  Previous flag value or −1 on failure.          }
{ ———————————————————————————————————————————— }
```

```
function SetCellFlags (hWndParent: hWnd; cellNum, flags: Integer): Integer;
var
      r: TRect;
      p: PStatusRec;
      hWndStatus: hWnd;

begin
      hWndStatus := GetStatusBarWindow (hWndParent);
      p := GetStatusRec (hWndStatus);
      if (hWndStatus <> 0) and (p <> Nil) and (cellNum >= 0) and
          (cellNum < p^.numCells) then
      begin
        SetCellFlags := p^.flags [cellNum];
        p^.flags [cellNum] := flags and (dt_Center or dt_Right);
        GetCellRect (p, cellNum, r);
        InvalidateRect (hWndStatus, @r, True);
      end
      else SetCellFlags := −1;
end;
```

```
{ ———————————————————————————————————————————— }
{ Name:    GetCellText                                     }
{ Purpose: Retrieve the text of a specified cell.          }
{ Returns:  Number of bytes copied to dest (not including null byte). }
{ ———————————————————————————————————————————— }
```

```
function GetCellText (hWndParent: hWnd; cellNum: Integer; buffer: PChar;
                      buffSize: Integer): Integer;
var
      bytes: Integer;
```

```
        text: PChar;
        p: PStatusRec;
        ch: Char;
        hWndStatus: hWnd;
begin
        ch := #0;
        hWndStatus := GetStatusBarWindow (hWndParent);
        p := GetStatusRec (hWndStatus);
        if (hWndStatus <> 0) and (p <> Nil) and (cellNum >= 0) and
            (cellNum < p^.numCells) then
          if buffer <> Nil then with p^ do
          begin
            buffer^ := #0;
            if pText [cellNum] <> Nil then
            begin
              text := pText [cellNum];
              bytes := LStrLen (text);
              if bytes > buffSize then
              begin
                ch := text [buffSize];
                text [buffSize] := #0;
                bytes := buffSize;
              end;

              LStrCpy (buffer, text);
              if ch <> #0 then text [buffSize] := ch;
              GetCellText := bytes;
              Exit;
            end;
          end;
        end;
        GetCellText := 0;
end;

{ ------------------------------------------------------------------- }
{ Name:    SetCellText                                                }
{ Purpose: Set the text of a specified cell to 'lpText'.              }
{ Returns: TRUE on success, FALSE on failure.                         }
{ ------------------------------------------------------------------- }

function SetCellText (hWndParent: hWnd; lpText: PChar; cellNum: Integer): Bool;
var
        r: TRect;
        p: pStatusRec;
        hWndStatus: hWnd;

begin
        hWndStatus := GetStatusBarWindow (hWndParent);
        p := GetStatusRec (hWndStatus);
        if (hWndStatus <> 0) and (p <> Nil) and (cellNum >= 0) and
            (cellNum < p^.numCells) then
        with p^ do
        begin
          if pText [cellNum] <> Nil then FreeMem (pText [cellNum],
                                            LStrLen (pText [cellNum]) + 1);
          pText [cellNum] := AllocText (lpText);
          GetCellRect (p, cellNum, r);
          InvalidateRect (hWndStatus, @r, True);
          SetCellText := True;
        end
        else SetCellText := False;
end;

{ ------------------------------------------------------------------- }
{ Name:    InsertCell                                                 }
{ Purpose: Insert a cell into the status bar.                         }
{ Returns: TRUE on success, FALSE on failure.                         }
{ ------------------------------------------------------------------- }
```

```
function InsertCell (hWndParent: hWnd; text: pChar; nWidth, pos: Integer): Bool;
var
      dc: hDC;
      i, left: Integer;
      font: hFont;
      p: PStatusRec;
      hWndStatus: hWnd;
begin
      hWndStatus := GetStatusBarWindow (hWndParent);
      p := GetStatusRec (hWndStatus);
      if (hWndStatus <> 0) and (p <> Nil) and (p^.NumCells < MaxCells) then
      with p^ do
      begin
        { Get pos parameter in range }

        if (pos = −1) or (pos > numCells) then pos := numCells;

        { Do we need to shuffle? }

        if pos < numCells then
        begin
          { Yes, we do! }

          Move (pText [pos], pText [pos + 1], (numCells − pos) *
                  sizeof (pText [0]));
          Move (frames [pos], frames [pos + 1], (numCells − pos) *
                  sizeof (frames [0]));
          Move (flags [pos], flags [pos + 1], (numCells − pos) *
                  sizeof (flags [0]));
        end;

        pText [pos] := AllocText (text);
        flags [pos] := dt_Left;

        { Calculate left edge of cell }

        if pos <> 0 then left := frames [pos − 1] + (border * 2)
        else left := border;

        { Calculate width of string if necessary }

        if (nWidth = −1) and (pText [pos] <> Nil) then
        begin
          dc := GetDC (0);
          Font := SelectObject (dc, statusFont);
          nWidth := LoWord (GetTextExtent (dc, text, LStrLen (text))) + border * 3;
          SelectObject (dc, Font);
          ReleaseDC (0, dc);
        end;

        { And calculate position of right edge }

        if nWidth <> −1 then
        begin
          frames [pos] := left + nWidth;

          { Do we need to shuffle position of following cells? }

          if pos < numCells then
            for i := pos + 1 to numCells do
              Inc (frames [i], nWidth + (border * 2));

          Inc (numCells);
          InvalidateRect (hWndStatus, Nil, True);
          InsertCell := True;
          Exit;
        end;
      end;

      InsertCell := False;
end;
```

```
{ ------------------------------------------------------------------- }
{ Name:     DeleteCell                                                }
{ Purpose:  Delete a cell from the status bar                         }
{ Returns:  TRUE on success, FALSE on failure.                        }
{ ------------------------------------------------------------------- }

function DeleteCell (hWndParent: hWnd; pos: Integer): Bool;
var
      i: Integer;
      r: TRect;
      p: pStatusRec;
      hWndStatus: hWnd;

begin
      hWndStatus := GetStatusBarWindow (hWndParent);
      p := GetStatusRec (hWndStatus);
      if (hWndStatus <> 0) and (p <> Nil) and (pos >= 0) and
            (pos < p^.numCells) then
      with p^ do
      begin
         if pText [pos] <> Nil then
            FreeMem (pText [pos], LStrLen (pText [pos]) + 1);

         { Do we need to shuffle? }

         if pos < numCells − 1 then
         begin
            GetCellRect (p, pos, r);

            { Adjust any following right borders }

            for i := pos + 1 to numCells − 1 do
               Dec (frames [i], (r.right − r.left) + (border * 2));

            { And shuffle everything up one slot }

            Move (pText [pos + 1], pText [pos], (numCells − pos − 1) *
                  sizeof (pText [0]));
            Move (frames [pos + 1], frames [pos], (numCells − pos − 1) *
                  sizeof (frames [0]));
            Move (flags [pos + 1], flags [pos], (numCells − pos − 1) *
                  sizeof (flags [0]));
         end;

         Dec (numCells);
         InvalidateRect (hWndStatus, Nil, True);
         DeleteCell := True;
      end
      else DeleteCell := False;
end;

{ ------------------------------------------------------------------- }
{ Name:     SetHintText                                               }
{ Purpose:  Set up a text string for menu hinting.                    }
{ Returns:  TRUE on success, FALSE on failure.                        }
{ Notes:    Passing an empty string clears the status bar.            }
{           Passing NULL turns off menu hinting.                      }
{           Anything else is interpreted as text and drawn as a hint. }
{ ------------------------------------------------------------------- }

function SetHintText (hWndParent: hWnd; lpText: pChar): Bool;
var
      r: TRect;
      p: PStatusRec;
      hWndStatus: hWnd;

begin
      hWndStatus := GetStatusBarWindow (hWndParent);
      p := GetStatusRec (hWndStatus);
      if (hWndStatus <> 0) and (p <> Nil) then
      with p^ do
```

```
begin
    { Delete any existing hint text }
    if hintText <> Nil then FreeMem (hintText, LStrLen (hintText) + 1);

    { Tweak the text to get around AllocText "auto-NULL" }
    if (lpText <> Nil) and (lpText^ = #0) then lpText := ' ';

    hintText := AllocText (lpText);

    { Force redraw of status bar }
    InvalidateRect (hWndStatus, Nil, True);
    SetHintText := True;
  end
  else SetHintText := False;
end;
end.
```

```
program Status;

{$R Status.Res }

uses WinTypes, WinProcs, StatBar;

const
    szAppName = 'StatusTest';
    insert: Integer = 0;
    numLock: Integer = -1;
    caps: Integer = -1;

{ ------------------------------------------------------------------ }
{ Name:     MenuHint                                                  }
{ Purpose:  Routine to set menu hint strings in status bar.          }
{ ------------------------------------------------------------------ }

procedure MenuHint (Wnd: hWnd; wParam: Word; lParam: LongInt);
var
    flags: Word;
    buff: array [0..100] of char;

begin
    flags := LoWord (lParam);

    { If menu closed, then return status bar to normal }

    if lParam = $ffff then SetHintText (Wnd, Nil)
    else if (flags and mf_Separator) <> 0 then SetHintText (Wnd, '')
    else
    begin
      GetMenuString (HiWord (lParam), wParam, buff,
                       sizeof (buff), mf_ByCommand);
      SetHintText (Wnd, buff);
    end;
end;

{ ------------------------------------------------------------------ }
{ Name:     CheckKeyboard.                                            }
{ Purpose:  Routine to check keyboard modifiers and set status bar.  }
{ ------------------------------------------------------------------ }

procedure CheckKeyboard (Wnd: hWnd);
var
    keys: TKeyBoardState;

begin
    GetKeyboardState (keys);
```

Figure A4.2 STATUS.PAS: the test application for the Status Bar unit.

```
        if numlock <> (Ord (keys [vk_NumLock]) and 1) then
        begin
          numlock := Ord (keys [vk_NumLock]) and 1;
          if numlock <> 0 then SetCellText (Wnd, 'NumLock', 1)
          else SetCellText (Wnd, Nil, 1);
        end;

        if caps <> (Ord (keys [vk_Capital]) and 1) then
        begin
          caps := Ord (keys [vk_Capital]) and 1;
          if caps <> 0 then SetCellText (Wnd, 'CapsLock', 2)
          else SetCellText (Wnd, Nil, 2);
        end;
end;
{ ───────────────────────────────────────────────────────────────── }
{ Name:    WindowProc                                                 }
{ Purpose: Windows procedure for main application window.             }
{ ───────────────────────────────────────────────────────────────── }
function WindowProc (Wnd: hWnd; Msg, wParam: Word; lParam: LongInt):
                     LongInt; export;

begin
     WindowProc := 0;

     case Msg of
       wm_MenuSelect: MenuHint (Wnd, wParam, lParam);
       wm_Timer:      CheckKeyboard (Wnd);
       wm_Create:     SetTimer (Wnd, $1000, 250, Nil);
       wm_KeyDown:    if wParam = vk_Insert then
                        begin
                          insert := insert xor 1;
                          if insert <> 0 then SetCellText (Wnd, 'Insert', 0)
                          else SetCellText (Wnd, Nil, 0);
                        end;

       wm_Destroy:    begin
                        KillTimer (Wnd, $1000);
                        PostQuitMessage (0);
                      end;
       else WindowProc := DefWindowProc (Wnd, Msg, wParam, lParam);
     end;
end;

{ ───────────────────────────────────────────────────────────────── }
{ Name:    InitAppClass                                               }
{ Purpose: Register the main application window class.                }
{ ───────────────────────────────────────────────────────────────── }
function InitAppClass: Bool;
var
     cls: TWndClass;
begin
     if not GetClassInfo (hInstance, szAppName, cls) then
       begin
         cls.style          := cs_VRedraw or cs_HRedraw;
         cls.lpfnWndProc    := @WindowProc;
         cls.cbClsExtra     := 0;
         cls.cbWndExtra     := 0;
         cls.hInstance      := hInstance;
         cls.hIcon          := LoadIcon (0, idi_Application);
         cls.hCursor        := LoadCursor (0, idc_Arrow);
         cls.hbrBackground  := GetStockObject (White_Brush);
         cls.lpszMenuName   := PChar (1);
         cls.lpszClassName  := szAppName;
         InitAppClass       := RegisterClass (cls);
       end
     else InitAppClass      := True;
end;
```

```
{ ------------------------------------------------------------- }
{ Name:     WinMain                                             }
{ Purpose:  Main application entry point.                       }
{ ------------------------------------------------------------- }

procedure WinMain;
var
      i: Integer;
      Wnd: hWnd;
      Msg: TMsg;
begin
      { Register application class if needed }

      if not InitAppClass then Halt (0);

      { Create the main application window }

      Wnd := CreateWindow (szAppName, szAppName, ws_OverlappedWindow,
                           cw_UseDefault, cw_UseDefault,
                           cw_UseDefault, cw_UseDefault,
                           0, 0, hInstance, Nil);
      if Wnd <> 0 then
      begin
        ShowWindow (Wnd, cmdShow);
        UpdateWindow (Wnd);
        if CreateStatusWindow (hInstance, Wnd, Nil) <> 0 then
        begin
          InsertCell (Wnd, Nil, 70, -1);
          InsertCell (Wnd, Nil, 70, -1);
          InsertCell (Wnd, Nil, 70, -1);

          for i := 0 to 2 do
             SetCellFlags (Wnd, i, dt_Center);
        end;
      end;

      while GetMessage (Msg, 0, 0, 0) do
      begin
        TranslateMessage (Msg);
        DispatchMessage (Msg);
      end;

      Halt (Msg.wParam);
end;

begin
      WinMain;
end.
```

```
1 MENU PRELOAD MOVEABLE DISCARDABLE
BEGIN
      POPUP "&File"
      BEGIN
        MENUITEM "&New...", 101
        MENUITEM "&Open\tEnter", 102
        MENUITEM "&Move...\tF7", 103
        MENUITEM "&Copy...\tF8", 104
        MENUITEM "&Delete\tDel", 105
        MENUITEM "&Properties...\tAlt+Enter", 106
        MENUITEM SEPARATOR
        MENUITEM "&Run...", 107
```

Figure A4.3 STATUS.RC: the menu resource used by STATUS.PAS.

```
        MENUITEM SEPARATOR
        MENUITEM "E&xit Windows...", 108
    END

    POPUP "&Options"
    BEGIN
        MENUITEM "&Auto Arrange", 201
        MENUITEM "&Minimize on Use", 202
        MENUITEM "&Save Settings on Exit", 204
    END

    POPUP "&Window"
    BEGIN
        MENUITEM "&Cascade\tShift+F5", 301
        MENUITEM "&Tile\tShift+F4", 302
        MENUITEM "&Arrange Icons", 303
    END

    POPUP "&Help"
    BEGIN
        MENUITEM "&Contents", 401
        MENUITEM "&Search for Help on...", 404
        MENUITEM SEPARATOR
        MENUITEM "&How to Use Help", 402
        MENUITEM "&Windows Tutorial", 405
        MENUITEM SEPARATOR
        MENUITEM "&About Program Manager...", 403
    END

END
```

Appendix 5 :
The **DIALOGS** unit

Figure A5.1 gives the Pascal source code for the Dialogs unit, which implements the dialog box embellishments developed in Chapter 5. In this variation of the code, the auto-hook facility is permanently enabled and will be automatically installed if your program includes the Dialogs unit in its USES clause. The DialogSubClass routine has been removed, and this unit requires no interface part at all! The WH_CBT hook is removed automatically when the application terminates.

The code in Figure A5.2 contains the equivalent code for the DIATEST.C program shown in Chapter 5. Because of the behind-the-scenes initialization and cleanup code which can be built into Pascal units, no InstallAutoHook or RemoveAutoHook routines are required. Pascal units also have the ability to each include their own resource file and accordingly, the DIALOGS.RES file included by the Dialogs unit contains only the bitmap resource required for implementation of the custom check boxes and radio buttons, while the DIATEST.RES file included by the test program contains only the dialog template. In this way, the Pascal Dialogs unit becomes fully self-contained and is about as close to the ideal 'black box' approach as one could expect to find.

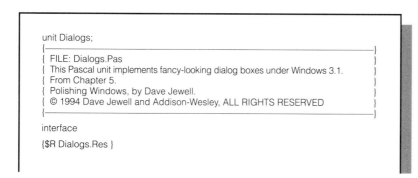

```
unit Dialogs;
{————————————————————————————————————————————————}
{ FILE: Dialogs.Pas                                                            }
{ This Pascal unit implements fancy-looking dialog boxes under Windows 3.1.     }
{ From Chapter 5.                                                               }
{ Polishing Windows, by Dave Jewell.                                            }
{ © 1994 Dave Jewell and Addison-Wesley, ALL RIGHTS RESERVED                    }
{————————————————————————————————————————————————}

interface

{$R Dialogs.Res }
```

Figure A5.1 The Dialogs unit for implementing Excel-style dialog boxes.

```
uses WinTypes, WinProcs, Win31, Tools, SubClass;

{ Look :− no interface! }

implementation

const
     { Service name for HookWindow }

     szHookName = 'DialogsHook';

     { Control types returned by ControlType }

     Button      = 0;
     EditBox     = 1;
     Static      = 2;
     Listbox     = 3;
     ComboBox    = 4;
     ComboLBox   = 5;

     { Bitmap dimensions }

     ToolWidth = 13;
     ToolHeight = 13;

     { Control flags for PaintTool routine }

     PtDown = 1;
     PtPaint = 2;

     DialogFont: hBrush = 0;      { special dialog font          }
     hbrBack: hBrush = 0;         { background brush             }
     DialogCount: Integer = 0;    { number of subclassed dialogs }
     hbmTools: HBitmap = 0;       { handle to tool bitmap        }
     fPressed: Bool = False;      { True if a control is pressed }
     fCapture: Bool = False;      { True if mouse captured       }
     AutoHook: HHook = 0;         { for WH_CBT trickery...       }
     OldExitProc: Pointer = Nil;  { for good-bye kiss            }
     hookKey: LongInt = 0;        { for subclasser              }

{────────────────────────────────────────────────────────────────────────}
{ Name:    InitTools                                                       }
{ Purpose: Initialize needed tools.                                        }
{────────────────────────────────────────────────────────────────────────}

procedure InitTools;
begin
     if DialogCount = 0 then
     begin
        DialogFont := GetStatusFont (nil);
        hbrBack  := GetControlBrush (Color_BtnFace);
        hbmTools := LoadButtonBitmap (hInstance, 1);
     end;

     Inc (DialogCount);
end;

{────────────────────────────────────────────────────────────────────────}
{ Name:    FreeTools                                                       }
{ Purpose: Called to clean up tools when a dialog is closed.               }
{────────────────────────────────────────────────────────────────────────}

procedure FreeTools;
begin
     Dec (DialogCount);
     if DialogCount = 0 then
     begin
        DeleteObject (hbrBack);
        DeleteObject (DialogFont);
        DeleteObject (hbmTools);
     end;
end;
```

```
{--------------------------------------------------------------------}
{ Name:     SCGroupBox                                               }
{ Purpose:  Subclassing routine for GROUPBOX controls.              }
{--------------------------------------------------------------------}

function SCGroupBox (Wnd: hWnd; Msg, wParam: Word;
                         lParam: LongInt): LongInt; export;
var
     r: TRect;
     dwExtent: LongInt;
     Font: HFont;
     bkColor: TColorRef;
     ps: TPaintStruct;
     szText: array [0..127] of Char;
begin
     if Msg = wm_Paint then
     begin
       BeginPaint (Wnd, ps);
       if SendMessage (Wnd, wm_GetText, sizeof (szText) − 1,
                        LongInt (@szText [1])) <= 0 then
         szText [0] := #0
       else
       begin
         szText [0] := ' ';
         LStrCat (szText, ' ');
       end;

       GetClientRect (Wnd, r);
       DrawRaisedRect (ps.hdc, r);

       if szText [0] <> #0 then
       begin
         Font := SelectObject (ps.hdc, DialogFont);
         dwExtent := GetTextExtent (ps.hdc, 'Yy', 2);
         Dec (r.top, HiWord (dwExtent) div 2);
         Inc (r.left, LoWord (dwExtent) div 2);
         bkColor := SetBkColor (ps.hdc, GetSysColor (Color_BtnFace));
         DrawText (ps.hdc, szText, −1, r, dt_SingleLine);
         SetBkColor (ps.hdc, bkColor);
         SelectObject (ps.hdc, Font);
       end;

       EndPaint (Wnd, ps);
       SCGroupBox := 0;
     end
     else SCGroupBox := CallOldProc (Wnd, Msg, wParam, lParam, hookKey);
end;

{--------------------------------------------------------------------}
{ Name:     PaintTool                                                }
{ Purpose:  Draw a subsection of the tool bitmap as required.       }
{--------------------------------------------------------------------}

procedure PaintTool (Wnd: hWnd; bsState, flags: Word);
var
     r: TRect;
     SrcDC: hDC;
     dtFlags: Word;
     ps: TPaintStruct;
     bLeftAlign: Bool;
     szText: array [0..127] of Char;
     bskind, x, y, blitHeight: Integer;
begin
     bLeftAlign := (LoWord (GetWindowLong (Wnd, gwl_Style))
           and bs_LeftText) <> 0;
     bskind := LoWord (GetWindowLong (Wnd, gwl_Style)) and $F;
```

```
      x := bsState * 2;
      if (flags and PtDown) <> 0 then Inc (x);
      y := 0;
      if (bskind = bs_RadioButton) or (bskind = bs_AutoRadioButton) then Inc (y);
      x := x * ToolWidth;
      y := y * ToolHeight;

      if (flags and PtPaint) <> 0 then BeginPaint (Wnd, ps)
      else ps.hdc := GetDC (Wnd);
      DialogFont := SelectObject (ps.hdc, DialogFont);
      SetBkMode (ps.hdc, Transparent);

      GetClientRect (Wnd, r);
      blitHeight := r.top + ((r.bottom − r.top) − ToolHeight) div 2;
      SrcDC := CreateCompatibleDC (ps.hdc);
      hbmTools := SelectObject (SrcDC, hbmTools);

      if bLeftAlign then
      begin
          BitBlt (ps.hdc, r.right − ToolWidth, blitHeight,
                  ToolWidth, ToolHeight, SrcDC, x, y, SrcCopy);
          Dec (r.right, (ToolWidth * 3) div 2);
              dtFlags := dt_SingleLine or dt_Right or dt_VCenter;
      end
      else
      begin
          BitBlt (ps.hdc, r.left, blitHeight, ToolWidth,
                  ToolHeight, SrcDC, x, y, SrcCopy);
          Inc (r.left, (ToolWidth * 3) div 2);
          Dec (r.left);
              dtFlags := dt_SingleLine or dt_VCenter;
      end;

      Inc (r.top);
      CallOldProc (Wnd, wm_GetText, sizeof (szText), LongInt (@szText), hookKey);
      DrawText (ps.hdc, szText, −1, r, dtFlags);

      hbmTools := SelectObject (SrcDC, hbmTools);
      DeleteDC (SrcDC);

      DialogFont := SelectObject (ps.hdc, DialogFont);
      if (flags and PtPaint) <> 0 then EndPaint (Wnd, ps)
      else ReleaseDC (Wnd, ps.hdc);
end;
{───────────────────────────────────────────────────────────────────}
{ Name:      ControlType                                             }
{ Purpose:   Given a window handle, return the control type.         }
{            −1 is returned for an unrecognized type.                }
{───────────────────────────────────────────────────────────────────}
function ControlType (Wnd: hWnd): Integer;
const
      controlNames: array [0..5] of PChar = ( 'Button',
                                              'Edit',
                                              'Static',
                                              'ListBox',
                                              'ComboBox',
                                              'ComboLBox' );
var
      i: Integer;
      ClassName: array [0..63] of Char;
begin
      GetClassName (Wnd, ClassName, sizeof (ClassName) − 1);
      for i := 0 to 5 do
        if LStrCmpi (controlNames [i], ClassName) = 0 then
          begin
            ControlType := i;
            Exit;
```

```
            end;
        ControlType := −1;
end;
{─────────────────────────────────────────────────────────────}
{ Name:     IsAutoRadioButton                                  }
{ Purpose:  Determine if specified control is an auto radio button. }
{─────────────────────────────────────────────────────────────}

function IsAutoRadioButton (Dlg: hWnd; ID: Integer): Bool;
var
      Wnd: hWnd;

begin
      Wnd := GetDlgItem (Dlg, ID);
      if Wnd <> 0 then
        if ControlType (Wnd) = Button then
          if (GetWindowLong (Wnd, gwl_Style) and $f) = bs_AutoRadioButton then
          begin
            IsAutoRadioButton := True;
            Exit;
          end;
      IsAutoRadioButton := False;
end;
{─────────────────────────────────────────────────────────────}
{ Name:     SetRadioGroup                                      }
{ Purpose:  Check the specified button and uncheck all other auto }
{           radio buttons in the current group.                }
{─────────────────────────────────────────────────────────────}

procedure SetRadioGroup (Dlg, Wnd: hWnd);
var
      first, last, current: Integer;

begin
      current := GetWindowWord (Wnd, Gww_Id);
      first := current; last := current;
      while IsAutoRadioButton (Dlg, first − 1) do Dec (first);
      while IsAutoRadioButton (Dlg, last + 1) do Inc (last);
      CheckRadioButton (Dlg, first, last, current);
end;
{─────────────────────────────────────────────────────────────}
{ Name:     SCRadioButton                                      }
{ Purpose:  Subclassing routine for RADIOBUTTON controls.      }
{─────────────────────────────────────────────────────────────}

function SCRadioButton (Wnd: hWnd; Msg, wParam: Word;
                        lParam: LongInt): LongInt; export;
var
      r: TRect;
      pt: TPoint;
      buttonState, buttonKind: Word;

begin
      SCRadioButton := 0;
      buttonKind := LoWord (GetWindowLong (Wnd, gwl_Style)) and $f;
      buttonState := GetWindowWord (Wnd, 0);

      case Msg of
        wm_Paint:

        PaintTool (Wnd, buttonState and 3, PtPaint);

        wm_LButtonDown:

        begin
          if GetFocus <> Wnd then SetFocus (Wnd);
          fPressed := True;
          fCapture := True;
          SetCapture (Wnd);
```

```
        PaintTool (Wnd, buttonState and 3, PtDown);
    end;

  wm_LButtonUp:

  begin
    fCapture := False;
    ReleaseCapture;
    if not fPressed then Exit;
    fPressed := False;

    if buttonKind = bs_AutoRadioButton then
    begin
      buttonState := (buttonState and (not 2)) or 1;
      SetWindowWord (Wnd, 0, buttonState);
      PaintTool (Wnd, buttonState and 3, 0);
      SetRadioGroup (GetParent (Wnd), Wnd);
    end
    else if buttonKind = bs_Auto3State then
    begin
      buttonState := buttonState xor
         (((((buttonState and 3) + 1) mod 3) xor buttonState) and 3);
      SetWindowWord (Wnd, 0, buttonState);
      PaintTool (Wnd, buttonState and 3, 0);
    end;

    SendMessage (GetParent (Wnd), wm_Command,
                    GetWindowWord (Wnd, gww_id), MakeLong (Wnd, 0));

    Exit;
  end;

  wm_MouseMove:

  if fCapture then
  begin
    GetClientRect (Wnd, r);
    pt.x := LoWord (lParam);
    pt.y := HiWord (lParam);

    if PtInRect (r, pt) then
    begin
      if not fPressed then PaintTool (Wnd, buttonState and 3, PtDown);
      fPressed := True;
    end
    else
    begin
      if fPressed then PaintTool (Wnd, buttonState and 3, 0);
      fPressed := False;
    end;
    Exit;
  end else SCRadioButton := DefWindowProc (Wnd, Msg, wParam, lParam);

  wm_GetFont,
  wm_KillFocus,
  wm_GetDlgCode:

  SCRadioButton := CallOldProc (Wnd, Msg, wParam, lParam, hookKey);

  wm_SetFocus:

  begin
    if (buttonKind = bs_RadioButton) or (buttonKind = bs_AutoRadioButton) then
    begin
      buttonState := (buttonState and (not 2)) or 1;
      SetWindowWord (Wnd, 0, buttonState);
      PaintTool (Wnd, buttonState and 3, 0);
      SetRadioGroup (GetParent (Wnd), Wnd);
      SendMessage (GetParent (Wnd), wm_Command,
                    GetWindowWord (Wnd, gww_id),
                    MakeLong (Wnd, 0));
    end;
    SCRadioButton := CallOldProc (Wnd, Msg, wParam, lParam, hookKey);
  end;
```

```
        wm_Enable:

        InvalidateRect (Wnd, Nil, False);

        bm_SetCheck:

        begin
          SetWindowWord (Wnd, 0, buttonState xor ((wParam xor buttonState)
                            and 3));
          PaintTool (Wnd, buttonState and 3, 0);
          Exit;
        end;

        bm_GetCheck:

        SCRadioButton := buttonState and 3;

        else

        SCRadioButton := DefWindowProc (Wnd, Msg, wParam, lParam);
      end;
end;
{----------------------------------------------------------------------}
{ Name:     SCCheckBox                                                 }
{ Purpose:  Subclassing routine for CHECKBOX controls.                 }
{----------------------------------------------------------------------}

function SCCheckBox (Wnd: hWnd; Msg, wParam: Word;
                        lParam: LongInt): LongInt; export;
var
      r: TRect;
      pt: TPoint;
      buttonState, buttonKind: Word;
begin
      SCCheckBox   := 0;
      buttonKind   := LoWord (GetWindowLong (Wnd, gwl_Style)) and $f;
      buttonState  := GetWindowWord (Wnd, 0);

      case Msg of
        wm_Paint:

        PaintTool (Wnd, buttonState and 3, PtPaint);

        wm_LButtonDown:

        begin
          if GetFocus <> Wnd then SetFocus (Wnd);
          fPressed := True;
          fCapture := True;
          SetCapture (Wnd);
          PaintTool (Wnd, buttonState and 3, PtDown);
        end;

        wm_LButtonUp:

        begin
          fCapture := False;
          ReleaseCapture;
          if not fPressed then Exit;
          fPressed := False;
          if buttonKind = bs_AutoCheckBox then
          begin
            buttonState := buttonState xor
              ((buttonState xor Ord ((buttonState and 3) = 0)) and 3);
            SetWindowWord (Wnd, 0, buttonState);
            PaintTool (Wnd, buttonState and 3, 0);
          end;

          SendMessage (GetParent (Wnd), wm_Command,
                        GetWindowWord (Wnd, gww_Id),
                        MakeLong (Wnd, 0));
          Exit;
        end;
```

```
wm_MouseMove:
if fCapture then
begin
  GetClientRect (Wnd, r);
  pt.x := LoWord (lParam);
  pt.y := HiWord (lParam);

  if PtInRect (r, pt) then
  begin
    if not fPressed then PaintTool (Wnd, buttonState and 3, PtDown);
    fPressed := True;
  end
  else
  begin
    if fPressed then PaintTool (Wnd, buttonState and 3, 0);
    fPressed := False;
  end;
  Exit;
end else SCCheckBox := DefWindowProc (Wnd, Msg, wParam, lParam);

wm_SetFocus,
wm_GetFont,
wm_KillFocus,
wm_GetDlgCode:

SCCheckBox := CallOldProc (Wnd, Msg, wParam, lParam, hookKey);

wm_Enable:

InvalidateRect (Wnd, Nil, False);

bm_SetCheck:

begin
  SetWindowWord (Wnd, 0, (buttonState and (not 3)) or (wParam and 3));
  PaintTool (Wnd, wParam, 0);
  Exit;
end;

bm_GetCheck:

SCCheckBox := buttonState and 3;
else

SCCheckBox := DefWindowProc (Wnd, Msg, wParam, lParam);
  end;
end;

{-------------------------------------------------------------------}
{ Name:    ShrinkEditBox                                            }
{ Purpose: Reduce the size of an edit box to compensate for the     }
{          smaller font used.                                       }
{-------------------------------------------------------------------}
procedure ShrinkEditBox (Wnd: hWnd);
var
    dc: hDC;
    r: TRect;
    tm: TTextMetric;
    oldHeight, newHeight: Integer;
    pts: array [0..1] of TPoint absolute r;
begin
    { Get old font height }

    dc := GetDC (0);
    GetTextMetrics (dc, tm);
    oldHeight := tm.tmHeight + tm.tmInternalLeading;

    { Get new font height }

    DialogFont := SelectObject (dc, DialogFont);
    GetTextMetrics (dc, tm);
    DialogFont := SelectObject (dc, DialogFont);
```

```
            ReleaseDC (0, dc);
            newHeight := tm.tmHeight + tm.tmInternalLeading;

            { Now resize the window }

            GetWindowRect (Wnd, r);
            ScreenToClient (GetParent (Wnd), pts [0]);
            ScreenToClient (GetParent (Wnd), pts [1]);

            Inc (r.top, (oldHeight − newHeight) div 2);
            Dec (r.bottom, (oldHeight − newHeight) div 2);
            SetWindowPos (Wnd, 0, r.left, r.top, r.right − r.left,
                            r.bottom − r.top, swp_NoZOrder);
    end;

    {───────────────────────────────────────────────────────────────}
    { Name:    SubClassControl                                        }
    { Purpose: Subclass an individual dialog box control, according to}
    {          type. Controls that we don't recognize or aren't       }
    {          interested in are left alone.                          }
    {───────────────────────────────────────────────────────────────}

procedure SubClassControl (Wnd: hWnd; typ: Integer);
begin
        { Use our special font }

        if typ <> −1 then SendMessage (Wnd, wm_SetFont, DialogFont, 0);

        { Case out on control type }

        case typ of
          EditBox:

            ShrinkEditBox (Wnd);

            Button:

            begin
              typ := GetWindowLong (Wnd, gwl_Style) and $f;
              case typ of
                bs_GroupBox:

                HookWindow (Wnd, @SCGroupBox, szHookName);

                bs_CheckBox,
                bs_AutoCheckBox:

                HookWindow (Wnd, @SCCheckBox, szHookName);

                bs_3State,
                bs_Auto3State,
                bs_RadioButton,
                bs_AutoRadioButton:

                HookWindow (Wnd, @SCRadioButton, szHookName);
              end;
            end;
        end;
end;

    {───────────────────────────────────────────────────────────────}
    { Name:    DlgSubClass                                            }
    { Purpose: This is the subclasser for the dialog box itself.      }
    {          Main embellishments are 'gray' background for dialog and}
    {          any controls. Also draws a fancy border around the box.}
    {───────────────────────────────────────────────────────────────}

function DlgSubClass (hDlg: hWnd; Msg, wParam: Word; lParam: LongInt):
                        LongInt; export;
var
        dc: hDC;
        r: TRect;
        Wnd: hWnd;
        hbr: hBrush;
```

```
begin
    case Msg of
        wm_InitDialog:

        begin
            CenterDialog (hDlg);
            if LoByte (LoWord (GetVersion)) < 4 then
            begin
                { Create needed tools }

                InitTools;

                { Now subclass the various dialog controls }

                Wnd := GetWindow (hDlg, gw_Child);
                while Wnd <> 0 do
                begin
                    SubClassControl (Wnd, ControlType (Wnd));
                    Wnd := GetWindow (Wnd, gw_HWndNext);
                end;
            end;
        end;

        wm_SysColorChange:

        begin
            DeleteObject (hbmTools);
            DeleteObject (hbrBack);
            hbmTools := LoadButtonBitmap (hInstance, 1);
            hbrBack := GetControlBrush (Color_BtnFace);
            DlgSubClass := 0;
            Exit;
        end;

        wm_CtlColor:

        if (HiWord (lParam) = CtlColor_Edit) or
                    (HiWord (lParam) = CtlColor_ListBox) then

        begin
            SetBkColor (wParam, $ffffff);
            DlgSubClass := GetStockObject (White_Brush);
            Exit;
        end
        else
        begin
            SetBkColor (wParam, GetSysColor (Color_BtnFace));
            DlgSubClass := hbrBack;
            Exit;
        end;

        wm_EraseBkGnd:

        begin
            dc := wParam;
            GetClientRect (hDlg, r);
            hbr := SelectObject (dc, GetControlBrush (Color_BtnFace));
            PatBlt (dc, r.left, r.top, r.right − r.left, r.bottom − r.top, PatCopy);
            DeleteObject (SelectObject (dc, hbr));

            { Now draw the fancy border }

            InflateRect (r, −3, −3);
            FrameRect (dc, r, GetStockObject (White_Brush));
            Dec (r.left); Dec (r.right); Dec (r.top); Dec (r.bottom);
            hbr := GetControlBrush (Color_BtnShadow);
            FrameRect (dc, r, hbr);
            DeleteObject (hbr);
            DlgSubClass := Ord (True);
            Exit;
        end;
```

```
                wm_Destroy:
                    FreeTools;
                end;
                DlgSubClass := CallOldProc (hDlg, Msg, wParam, lParam, hookKey);
        end;
{————————————————————————————————————————————}
{ Name:     CBTHook                                                           }
{ Purpose:  This routine hooks the dialog window and subclasses it            }
{           with the HookWindow routine.                                      }
{————————————————————————————————————————————}
function CBTHook (code: Integer; wParam: Word; lParam: LongInt):
                    LongInt; export;
const
        theDlg: hWnd = 0;
var
        cs: PCreateStruct;
begin
        if code = hcbt_CreateWnd then
        begin
            cs := PCBT_CreateWnd (lParam)^.lpcs;
            if cs^.lpszClass = PChar (32770) then theDlg := wParam
            else if theDlg <> 0 then
            begin
                hookKey := HookWindow (theDlg, @DlgSubClass, szHookName);
                theDlg := 0;
            end;
        end;
        CBTHook := CallNextHookEx (AutoHook, code, wParam, lParam);
end;
{————————————————————————————————————————————}
{ Name:     MyExitProc                                                        }
{ Purpose:  Called on program termination to remove Windows hook.             }
{————————————————————————————————————————————}
procedure MyExitProc; far;
begin
        ExitProc := OldExitProc;
        UnhookWindowsHookEx (AutoHook);
end;
begin
        { Setup for good-bye kiss }
        OldExitProc := ExitProc;
        ExitProc := @MyExitProc;

        { Install the auto-hook }
        AutoHook := SetWindowsHookEx (wh_cbt, CBTHook, hInstance,
                            GetCurrentTask);
end.
```

```
program DiaTest;
{$R DiaTest.Res }
uses WinTypes, WinProcs, Dialogs;
const
        UNameBox = 100;   { the ID of the name box in the dialog }
```

Figure A5.2 The DIATEST.PAS program for testing the Dialogs unit.

```pascal
{-------------------------------------------------------------------}
{ Name:    UserNameWndProc                                          }
{ Purpose: Dialog procedure for user name dialog.                   }
{-------------------------------------------------------------------}

function UserNameWndProc (hDlg: hWnd; Msg, wParam: Word;
                          lParam: LongInt): Bool; export;
begin
     UserNameWndProc := False;

     case Msg of
       wm_InitDialog:

       SetFocus (GetDlgItem (hDlg, UNameBox));

       wm_Command:

       begin
         if (wParam = IdOk) or (wParam = IdCancel) then
           EndDialog (hDlg, wParam);
           UserNameWndProc := True;
       end;
     end;
end;

{-------------------------------------------------------------------}
{ Name:    WinMain                                                  }
{ Purpose: Program entry point.                                     }
{-------------------------------------------------------------------}

procedure WinMain;
begin
     MessageBox (0, 'Hello :- I''m a subclassed Message box!', 'Hello',
                 mb_Ok or mb_IconExclamation);
     DialogBox (hInstance, 'USERNAME', 0, @UserNameWndProc);
end;

begin
     WinMain;
end.
```

Appendix 6 : The TOOLBAR unit

This appendix contains the Pascal source code for TOOLBAR.PAS, a unit that implements the toolbar developed in Chapter 6. Another Pascal file, BARTEST.PAS, is also listed. This is the Pascal equivalent of the text program from the same chapter. Because the toolbar bitmaps required by an application are specific to that application, and not to the generic toolbar code, no RES file is invoked by the TOOLBAR.PAS code. However, the test program uses the same BARTEST.RES file as is used by the C test program in Chapter 6.

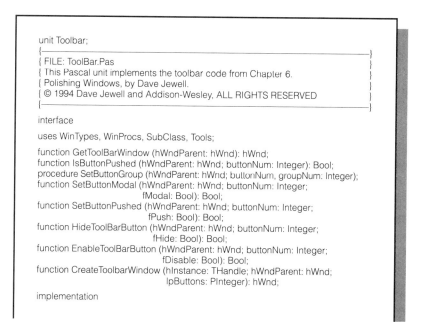

Figure A6.1 TOOLBAR.PAS: the Pascal implementation of the toolbar code.

```
unit Toolbar;
{----------------------------------------------------------------}
{ FILE: ToolBar.Pas                                              }
{ This Pascal unit implements the toolbar code from Chapter 6.   }
{ Polishing Windows, by Dave Jewell.                             }
{ © 1994 Dave Jewell and Addison-Wesley, ALL RIGHTS RESERVED     }
{----------------------------------------------------------------}

interface

uses WinTypes, WinProcs, SubClass, Tools;

function GetToolBarWindow (hWndParent: hWnd): hWnd;
function IsButtonPushed (hWndParent: hWnd; buttonNum: Integer): Bool;
procedure SetButtonGroup (hWndParent: hWnd; buttonNum, groupNum: Integer);
function SetButtonModal (hWndParent: hWnd; buttonNum: Integer;
                                fModal: Bool): Bool;
function SetButtonPushed (hWndParent: hWnd; buttonNum: Integer;
                                fPush: Bool): Bool;
function HideToolBarButton (hWndParent: hWnd; buttonNum: Integer;
                                fHide: Bool): Bool;
function EnableToolBarButton (hWndParent: hWnd; buttonNum: Integer;
                                fDisable: Bool): Bool;
function CreateToolbarWindow (hInstance: THandle; hWndParent: hWnd;
                                lpButtons: PInteger): hWnd;

implementation
```

```
const
    szClassName  = 'ToolBar';              { name of our window class   }
    szHookName   = 'ToolBarHook';          { name of our hook service   }
    MaxButtons   = 40;                     { maximum buttons per window}

    { Constants for flags field }

    fPushed      = $80;                    { if set, button was pushed  }
    fSticky      = $40;                    { if set, button is modal    }
    fDisabled    = $20;                    { if set, button is disabled }
    fHidden      = $10;                    { if set, button is hidden   }
    fGroupBits   = $0F;                    { space for four groups      }

type
    pToolBarRec = ^ToolBarRec;
    ToolBarRec = record
    border: Integer;                                          { width of border     }
    height: Integer;                                          { height of toolbar   }
    bmwidth: Integer;                                         { width of bitmaps    }
    bmheight: Integer;                                        { height of bitmaps   }
    NumButtons: Integer;                                      { number of buttons   }
    CaptureButton: Integer;                                   { capturing button    }
    CapturePressed: Bool;                                     { if CaptureButton down }
    edges: array [0..MaxButtons − 1] of Integer;              { bitmap positions    }
    bmHandles: array [0..MaxButtons − 1] of HBitmap;          { bitmap handles      }
    bmIDs: array [0..MaxButtons − 1] of Word;                 { ID of each bitmap   }
    flags: array [0..MaxButtons − 1] of Byte;                 { flags for each button }
    end;

var
    hookKey: LongInt;
```

```
{---------------------------------------------------------------}
{ Name:     GetToolBarRec                                       }
{ Purpose:  Given a window handle, return a pointer to the      }
{           corresponding toolbar record.                       }
{---------------------------------------------------------------}

function GetToolBarRec (Wnd: hWnd): pToolBarRec;
begin
    GetToolBarRec := pToolBarRec (GetWindowLong (Wnd, 0));
end;
```

```
{---------------------------------------------------------------}
{ Name:     ResizeWindow                                        }
{ Purpose:  Routine to force toolbar to proper size and position. }
{---------------------------------------------------------------}

procedure ResizeWindow (Wnd: hWnd);
var
    r: TRect;
    p: pToolBarRec;

begin
    p := GetToolBarRec (Wnd);
    GetClientRect (GetParent (Wnd), r);
    SetWindowPos (Wnd, 0, 0, 0, r.right, p^.height, swp_NoZOrder);
end;
```

```
{---------------------------------------------------------------}
{ Name:     GetToolBarWindow                                    }
{ Purpose:  Return the handle of this window's toolbar.         }
{---------------------------------------------------------------}

function GetToolBarWindow (hWndParent: hWnd): hWnd;
begin
    GetToolBarWindow := 0;
    if (hWndParent <> 0) and IsWindow (hWndParent) then
        GetToolBarWindow := hWnd (GetProp (hWndParent, szClassName));
end;
```

```
{———————————————————————————————————————————————————}
{ Name:    SubClassParentWbdProc                        }
{ Purpose:  Subclassing routine for the main application window.  }
{———————————————————————————————————————————————————}

function SubClassParentWndProc (Wnd: hWnd; Msg, wParam: Word;
                                 lParam: LongInt): LongInt; export;
begin
      if Msg = wm_Size then ResizeWindow (GetToolBarWindow (Wnd));
      SubClassParentWndProc := CallOldProc (Wnd, Msg, wParam, lParam,
                                 hookKey);
end;

{———————————————————————————————————————————————————}
{ Name:    LoadToolBitmaps                              }
{ Purpose:  Load all specified bitmaps into the ToolBarRec structure.  }
{———————————————————————————————————————————————————}

function LoadToolBitmaps (p: pToolBarRec; pBitmaps: pInteger): Integer;
var
      x: Integer;
      bm: TBitmap;

begin
      LoadToolBitmaps := −1;

      with p^ do

      begin
        x := border;
        while (pBitmaps^ <> −1) and (NumButtons < MaxButtons − 1) do
        begin
          if pBitmaps^ = 0 then Inc (x, border * 3)
          else
          begin
            bmIDs [NumButtons] := pBitmaps^;
            bmHandles [NumButtons] := LoadButtonBitmap (hInstance,
                                 pBitmaps^);
            if bmHandles [NumButtons] = 0 then Exit;

            { If this is first bitmap, determine dimensions }
            if height = −1 then
            begin
              GetObject (bmHandles [NumButtons], sizeof (TBitmap), @bm);
              bmWidth := bm.bmWidth div 2;
              bmHeight := bm.bmHeight;
              height := bmHeight + (border * 2);
            end;

            edges [NumButtons] := x;
            Inc (NumButtons);
            Inc (x, bmwidth + border);
          end;
          Inc (pBitmaps);
        end;

        if p^.NumButtons <> 0 then LoadToolBitmaps := 0;
      end;
end;

{———————————————————————————————————————————————————}
{ Name:    InitToolBarWindow                            }
{ Purpose:  Initialization code for setting up the toolbar window.  }
{———————————————————————————————————————————————————}

function InitToolBarWindow (Wnd: hWnd; lParam: LongInt): LongInt;
var
      text: PChar;
      pBitmaps: pInteger;
      p: PToolBarRec;
```

```
begin
      InitToolBarWindow := −1;
      GetMem (p, sizeof (ToolBarRec));
      if p <> Nil then with p^ do
      begin
         { Initialize the ToolBarRec data structure }

         FillChar (p^, sizeof (ToolBarRec), 0);
         CaptureButton := −1;
         border := (GetSystemMetrics (sm_cxFrame) + 3) div 2;
         height := −1;
         SetWindowLong (Wnd, 0, LongInt (p));

         { Load the various bitmaps }

         pBitmaps := PInteger ((PCreateStruct (lParam))^.lpCreateParams);
         if LoadToolBitmaps (p, pBitmaps) = 0 then
         begin
            ResizeWindow (Wnd);
            SetProp (GetParent (Wnd), szClassName, Wnd);
            hookKey := HookWindow (GetParent (Wnd),
                                 @SubclassParentWndProc, szHookName);
            InitToolBarWindow := 0;
         end;
      end;
end;

{------------------------------------------------------------------}
{ Name:    GetCellRect                                             }
{ Purpose: Return the frame rectangle for a given cell.            }
{------------------------------------------------------------------}

procedure GetCellRect (p: PToolBarRec; cellNum: Integer; var r: TRect);
begin
      with p^ do
      begin
         r.left := edges [cellNum];
         r.right := r.left + bmWidth;
         r.top := border;
         r.bottom := r.top + bmHeight;
      end;
end;

{------------------------------------------------------------------}
{ Name:    PaintCell                                              }
{ Purpose: Paint a specfied cell in the toolbar.                  }
{------------------------------------------------------------------}

procedure PaintCell (dc: hDC; p: PToolBarRec; cellNum: Integer);
var
      r: TRect;
      hMemDC: hDC;
      mode: Integer;
      hbm: hBitmap;
      fDown: Bool;
      XSrc: Integer;

begin
      with p^ do
      begin
         if (flags [cellNum] and fHidden) = 0 then
         begin
            fDown := (flags [cellNum] and fPushed) <> 0;
            if (cellNum = CaptureButton) and CapturePressed then
               fDown := not fDown;

            if fDown then XSrc := bmWidth else XSrc := 0;

            hMemDC := CreateCompatibleDC (dc);
            hbm := SelectObject (hMemDC, bmHandles [cellNum]);
            BitBlt (dc, edges [cellNum], border, bmWidth, bmHeight,
                    hMemDC, XSrc, 0, SrcCopy);
```

```
                SelectObject (hMemDC, hbm);
                DeleteDC (hMemDC);
            end;
        end;
end;

{————————————————————————————————————————————————————}
{ Name:    ToolBarPaint                                }
{ Purpose: This routine is responsible for painting the toolbar. }
{————————————————————————————————————————————————————}

function ToolBarPaint (Wnd: hWnd): Integer;
var
        i: Integer;
        r: TRect;
        p: pToolBarRec;
        ps: TPaintStruct;

begin
        BeginPaint (Wnd, ps);
        p := GetToolBarRec (Wnd);

        { First, draw the bottom edge of the toolbar }

        GetClientRect (Wnd, r);
        PatBlt (ps.hdc, 0, r.bottom − 1, r.right − r.left, 1, Blackness);
        PatBlt (ps.hdc, 0, 0, r.right − r.left, 1, Whiteness);

        { Now draw each cell in turn }

        for i := 0 to p^.NumButtons − 1 do
            PaintCell (ps.hdc, p, i);

        EndPaint (Wnd, ps);
        ToolBarPaint := 0;
end;

{————————————————————————————————————————————————————}
{ Name:    DestroyToolBarWindow                        }
{ Purpose: Clean up code for the toolbar window.       }
{————————————————————————————————————————————————————}

function DestroyToolBarWindow (Wnd: hWnd): Integer;
var
        i: Integer;
        p: PToolBarRec;

begin
        p := GetToolBarRec (Wnd);
        with p^ do
        begin
            RemoveProp (GetParent (Wnd), szClassName);
            UnHookWindow (GetParent (Wnd), hookKey);

            { Deallocate bitmap handles }

            for i := 0 to NumButtons − 1 do
                DeleteObject (bmHandles [i]);

        end;

        FreeMem (p, sizeof (ToolBarRec));
        DestroyToolBarWindow := 0;
end;

{————————————————————————————————————————————————————}
{ Name:    AdjustButtonGroup                           }
{ Purpose: Release any pressed buttons in the same group. }
{————————————————————————————————————————————————————}

procedure AdjustButtonGroup (Wnd: hWnd; p: pToolBarRec; ClickedButton:
                                    Integer);
var
        r: TRect;
```

```
              groupMask: Integer;
              num: Integer;
begin
        with p^ do
        begin
           GroupMask := flags [ClickedButton] and fGroupBits;
           if GroupMask <> 0 then
           begin
              for num := 0 to NumButtons − 1 do
              if (num <> ClickedButton) and
                 ((flags [num] and fGroupBits) = groupMask) and
                 ((flags [num] and fPushed) <> 0) then
                 begin
                    flags [num] := flags [num] and (not fPushed);
                    GetCellRect (p, num, r);
                    InvalidateRect (Wnd, @r, False);
                 end;
           end;
        end;
end;
```

```
{─────────────────────────────────────────────────────────────────}
{ Name:    ClickButton                                             }
{ Purpose: Adjust state of a button and send message to parent.    }
{─────────────────────────────────────────────────────────────────}

procedure ClickButton (Wnd: hWnd; p: pToolBarRec; ClickedButton:
                            Integer);
var
        r: TRect;
begin
        with p^ do
        begin
           if (flags [ClickedButton] and fSticky) <> 0 then
              flags [ClickedButton] := flags [ClickedButton] xor fPushed;

           { Redraw the button in its new state }

           GetCellRect (p, ClickedButton, r);
           InvalidateRect (Wnd, @r, False);

           { If this is a 'group' button, then adjust the group }

           AdjustButtonGroup (Wnd, p, ClickedButton);

           { Send message to parent window ... }

           SendMessage (GetParent (Wnd), wm_Command, bmIDS [ClickedButton],
                            flags [ClickedButton] and fPushed);
        end;
end;
```

```
{─────────────────────────────────────────────────────────────────}
{ Name:    ButtonHitTest                                           }
{ Purpose: Test for a hit on any button in the buttonbar.          }
{─────────────────────────────────────────────────────────────────}

function ButtonHitTest (p: PToolBarRec; lParam: LongInt): Integer;
var
        r: TRect;
        buttonNum: Integer;
        pt: TPoint absolute lParam;
begin
        ButtonHitTest := −1;
        with p^ do
           for buttonNum := 0 to NumButtons − 1 do
           begin
              GetCellRect (p, buttonNum, r);
              if PtInRect (r, pt) then
              begin
```

```
                ButtonHitTest := buttonNum;
                Exit;
            end;
        end;
end;

{————————————————————————————————————————————————}
{ Name:    HandleButtonDown                        }
{ Purpose:  Handle mouse clicks in the toolbar.     }
{————————————————————————————————————————————————}

function HandleButtonDown (Wnd: hWnd; lParam: LongInt): Integer;
var
    r: TRect;
    flgs: Byte;
    buttonNum: Integer;
    p: pToolBarRec;

begin
    p := GetToolBarRec (Wnd);
    with p^ do
    begin
        buttonNum := ButtonHitTest (p, lParam);
        if (buttonNum <> −1) and ((flags [buttonNum] and
            (fDisabled or fHidden)) = 0) then
        begin
            flgs := flags [buttonNum];

            { If button is in a modal group and it's pushed, do nothing }

            if ((flgs and fGroupBits) = 0) or ((flgs and fPushed) = 0) then
            begin
                SetCapture (Wnd);
                CaptureButton := buttonNum;
                CapturePressed := True;
                GetCellRect (p, ButtonNum, r);
                InvalidateRect (Wnd, @r, False);
            end;
        end;
    end;

    HandleButtonDown := 0;
end;

{————————————————————————————————————————————————}
{ Name:    HandleButtonUp                          }
{ Purpose:  Handle mouse ups in the toolbar.        }
{————————————————————————————————————————————————}

function HandleButtonUp (Wnd: hWnd; lParam: LongInt): Integer;
var
    p: pToolBarRec;

begin
    p := GetToolBarRec (Wnd);
    with p^ do
    begin
        if CaptureButton <> −1 then
        begin
            ReleaseCapture;
            if CapturePressed then ClickButton (Wnd, p, CaptureButton);
            CapturePressed := False;
            CaptureButton := −1;
        end;
    end;

    HandleButtonUp := 0;
end;
```

```
{----------------------------------------------------------------------}
{ Name:    HandleMouseMoves                                            }
{ Purpose: Handle mouse movement in the toolbar.                       }
{----------------------------------------------------------------------}

function HandleMouseMoves (Wnd: hWnd; lParam: LongInt): Integer;
var
      r: TRect;
      p: pToolBarRec;
      buttonNum: Integer;

begin
      p := GetToolBarRec (Wnd);
      with p^ do
        if CaptureButton <> −1 then
        begin
          buttonNum := ButtonHitTest (p, lParam);
          if buttonNum = CaptureButton then
          begin
            if not CapturePressed then
            begin
              CapturePressed := True;
              GetCellRect (p, CaptureButton, r);
              InvalidateRect (Wnd, @r, False);
            end;
          end
          else
          begin
            if CapturePressed then
            begin
              CapturePressed := False;
              GetCellRect (p, CaptureButton, r);
              InvalidateRect (Wnd, @r, False);
            end;
          end;
        end;
      HandleMouseMoves := 0;
end;

{----------------------------------------------------------------------}
{ Name:    ToolBarWndProc                                              }
{ Purpose: Window procedure for toolbar windows.                       }
{----------------------------------------------------------------------}

function ToolBarWndProc (Wnd: hWnd; Msg, wParam: Word; lParam:
                         LongInt): LongInt; export;
begin
      case Msg of
          wm_LButtonDown: ToolBarWndProc := HandleButtonDown (Wnd, lParam);
          wm_LButtonUp:   ToolBarWndProc := HandleButtonUp (Wnd, lParam);
          wm_MouseMove:   ToolBarWndProc := HandleMouseMoves (Wnd, lParam);
          wm_Paint:       ToolBarWndProc := ToolBarPaint (Wnd);
          wm_Create:      ToolBarWndProc := InitToolBarWindow (Wnd, lParam);
          wm_Destroy:     ToolBarWndProc := DestroyToolBarWindow (Wnd);
          else            ToolBarWndProc := DefWindowProc (Wnd, Msg,
                                                wParam, lParam);

      end;
end;

{----------------------------------------------------------------------}
{ Name:    RegisterToolBar                                             }
{ Purpose: Register the toolbar window class.                          }
{----------------------------------------------------------------------}

function RegisterToolBar: Bool;
var
      cls: TWndClass;
```

```
begin
    if not GetClassInfo (hInstance, szClassName, cls) then
    begin
        cls.style              := 0;
        cls.lpfnWndProc        := @ToolBarWndProc;
        cls.cbClsExtra         := 0;
        cls.cbWndExtra         := sizeof (pToolBarRec);
        cls.hInstance          := hInstance;
        cls.hIcon              := 0;
        cls.hCursor            := LoadCursor (0, idc_Arrow);
        cls.hbrBackground      := Color_BtnFace + 1;
        cls.lpszMenuName       := Nil;
        cls.lpszClassName      := szClassName;

        RegisterToolBar        := RegisterClass (cls);
    end
    else RegisterToolBar    := True;
end;
```

```
{————————————————————————————————————————————————————}
{ Name:    CreateToolbarWindow                                       }
{ Purpose: Create a toolbar window and attach it to the parent.      }
{————————————————————————————————————————————————————}

function CreateToolbarWindow (hInstance: THandle; hWndParent: hWnd;
                                lpButtons: PInteger): hWnd;
var
    Wnd: hWnd;
begin
    Wnd := 0;

    { Check that we've got a valid parent window }

    if (hWndParent <> 0) and IsWindow (hWndParent) and (lpButtons <> Nil) then
    begin
        { Ok so far, but has window already got a tool bar? }

        Wnd := GetToolBarWindow (hWndParent);
        if Wnd = 0 then
            if RegisterToolBar then
                Wnd := CreateWindow (szClassName, '', ws_Child or ws_Visible,
                                    0, 0, 0, 0, hWndParent, 0, hInstance,
                                    lpButtons);
    end;

    CreateToolbarWindow := Wnd;
end;
```

```
{————————————————————————————————————————————————————}
{ Name:    InternalSetButtonFlags                                    }
{ Purpose: Set a button flag either True or False.                   }
{————————————————————————————————————————————————————}

function InternalSetButtonFlags (hWndParent: hWnd; buttonNum: Integer;
                                Mask: Word; val: Bool): Bool;
var
    r: TRect;
    Wnd: hWnd;
    p: pToolBarRec;
    old: Word;
begin
    InternalSetButtonFlags := False;
    Wnd := GetToolBarWindow (hWndParent);
    p := GetToolBarRec (Wnd);
    if (Wnd <> 0) and (p <> Nil) and (buttonNum < p^.numButtons) then
    with p^ do
    begin
        InternalSetButtonFlags := (flags [buttonNum] and Mask) <> 0;
```

```
            flags [buttonNum] := flags [buttonNum] and (not Mask);
            if val then
            begin
              flags [buttonNum] := flags [ButtonNum] or Mask;

              if Mask < fHidden then
              begin
                { We're adding to a group :— better set sticky bit }

                flags [buttonNum] := flags [buttonNum] or fSticky;

                { If button is down, adjust group }

                if (flags [buttonNum] and fPushed) <> 0 then
                  AdjustButtonGroup (Wnd, p, buttonNum);
              end;
            end;

            { If this is a button enable/disable, reload the bitmap }

            if Mask = fDisabled then
            begin
              DeleteObject (bmHandles [buttonNum]);
              if val then bmHandles [buttonNum] :=
                LoadDisabledButtonBitmap (hInstance, bmIDs [buttonNum])
              else bmHandles [buttonNum] :=
                LoadButtonBitmap (hInstance, bmIDs [buttonNum]);
            end;

            { If change to Hide or Disable state, then update display }

            if (Mask and (fHidden or fDisabled)) <> 0 then
            begin
              GetCellRect (p, ButtonNum, r);
              InvalidateRect (Wnd, @r, True);
            end;
          end;
        end;
end;
```

```
{----------------------------------------------------------------------}
{ Name:     EnableToolBarButton                                        }
{ Purpose:  Enable or disable a toolbar button.                        }
{----------------------------------------------------------------------}

function EnableToolBarButton (hWndParent: hWnd; buttonNum: Integer;
                             fDisable: Bool): Bool;
begin
    EnableToolBarButton := InternalSetButtonFlags (hWndParent, buttonNum,
                                            fDisabled, fDisable);
end;
```

```
{----------------------------------------------------------------------}
{ Name:     HideToolBarButton                                          }
{ Purpose:  Hide or unhide a toolbar button.                           }
{----------------------------------------------------------------------}

function HideToolBarButton (hWndParent: hWnd; buttonNum: Integer;
                           fHide: Bool): Bool;
begin
    HideToolBarButton := InternalSetButtonFlags (hWndParent, buttonNum,
                                            fHidden, fHide);
end;
```

```
{----------------------------------------------------------------------}
{ Name:     SetButtonModal                                             }
{ Purpose:  Change a button from modal to non-modal.                   }
{----------------------------------------------------------------------}

function SetButtonModal (hWndParent: hWnd; buttonNum: Integer;
                        fModal: Bool): Bool;
begin
```

```
        SetButtonModal := InternalSetButtonFlags (hWndParent, buttonNum,
                                        fSticky, fModal);
end;

{------------------------------------------------------------------}
{ Name:    SetButtonGroup                                          }
{ Purpose: Assign a button to a group.                             }
{          If groupNum is −1, this resigns from a group.           }
{------------------------------------------------------------------}

procedure SetButtonGroup (hWndParent: hWnd; buttonNum, groupNum: Integer);
var
        mask: Integer;
begin
        InternalSetButtonFlags (hWndParent, buttonNum, fGroupBits, False);
        if groupNum in [0..3] then
            InternalSetButtonFlags (hWndParent, buttonNum, 1 shl groupNum, True);
end;

{------------------------------------------------------------------}
{ Name:    SetButtonPushed                                         }
{ Purpose: Set a modal button to be pushed or unpushed.            }
{------------------------------------------------------------------}

function SetButtonPushed (hWndParent: hWnd; buttonNum: Integer; fPush:
                        Bool): Bool;
var
        r: TRect;
        Wnd: hWnd;
        p: pToolBarRec;
begin
        SetButtonPushed := False;
        Wnd := GetToolBarWindow (hWndParent);
        p := GetToolBarRec (Wnd);
        if (Wnd <> 0) and (p <> Nil) and (buttonNum < p^.numButtons) then
        with p^ do
          { Only makes sense for modal buttons }

          if (Flags [ButtonNum and fSticky]) <> 0 then
          begin
            SetButtonPushed := (Flags [ButtonNum] and fPushed) <> 0;
            Flags [ButtonNum] := Flags [ButtonNum] and (not fPushed);
            if fPush then
            begin
              Flags [ButtonNum] := Flags [ButtonNum] or fPushed;
              AdjustButtonGroup (Wnd, p, ButtonNum);
            end;

            GetCellRect (p, ButtonNum, r);
            InvalidateRect (Wnd, @r, False);
          end;
end;

{------------------------------------------------------------------}
{ Name:    IsButtonPushed                                          }
{ Purpose: Determine if a modal button is pushed or unpushed.      }
{------------------------------------------------------------------}

function IsButtonPushed (hWndParent: hWnd; buttonNum: Integer): Bool;
var
        Wnd: hWnd;
        p: pToolBarRec;

begin
        IsButtonPushed := False;
        Wnd := GetToolBarWindow (hWndParent);
        p := GetToolBarRec (Wnd);
        if (Wnd <> 0) and (p <> Nil) and (buttonNum < p^.numButtons) then
        with p^ do
```

```
              if (Flags [ButtonNum and fSticky]) <> 0 then
                  IsButtonPushed := (Flags [ButtonNum] and fPushed) <> 0;
     end;
     end.
```

Figure A6.2 BARTEST.PAS:
the test program for trying out
the Toolbar unit.

```
program BarTest;

{$R BarTest.Res }

uses WinTypes, WinProcs, Toolbar;

const
     szAppName = 'Toolbar Test';

{————————————————————————————————————————————————————————————————————}
{ Name:    WindowProc                                                 }
{ Purpose:  Windows procedure for main application window.            }
{————————————————————————————————————————————————————————————————————}

function WindowProc (Wnd: hWnd; Msg, wParam: Word; lParam: LongInt):
                        LongInt; export;
const
     fHide: Bool = False;
     fDisable: Bool = False;

begin
     WindowProc := 0;

     case Msg of
        wm_Char:  SetButtonPushed (Wnd, 0, True);

        wm_LButtonDown: begin
                           fHide := not fHide;
                           HideToolBarButton (Wnd, 9, fHide);
                        end;

        wm_RButtonDown: begin
                           fDisable := not fDisable;
                           EnableToolBarButton (Wnd, 8, fDisable);
                        end;
        wm_Destroy:      PostQuitMessage (0);
        else WindowProc := DefWindowProc (Wnd, Msg, wParam, lParam);
     end;
end;

{————————————————————————————————————————————————————————————————————}
{ Name:    InitAppClass                                               }
{ Purpose:  Register the main application window class.               }
{————————————————————————————————————————————————————————————————————}

function InitAppClass: Bool;
var
     cls: TWndClass;

begin
     if not GetClassInfo (hInstance, szAppName, cls) then
     begin
        cls.style            := cs_VRedraw or cs_HRedraw;
        cls.lpfnWndProc      := @WindowProc;
        cls.cbClsExtra       := 0;
        cls.cbWndExtra       := 0;
        cls.hInstance        := hInstance;
        cls.hIcon            := LoadIcon (0, idi_Application);
        cls.hCursor          := LoadCursor (0, idc_Arrow);
        cls.hbrBackground    := GetStockObject (White_Brush);
        cls.lpszMenuName     := PChar (1);
```

```pascal
            cls.lpszClassName      := szAppName;
            InitAppClass           := RegisterClass (cls);
        end
        else InitAppClass          := True;
end;

{----------------------------------------------------------------}
{ Name:    WinMain                                               }
{ Purpose: Main application entry point.                         }
{----------------------------------------------------------------}

procedure WinMain;
const
        bitMaps: array [0..14] of Integer = ( 1000,1001,0,0,1002,1003,1004,
                                1005,1006,1007,0,0,1008,1009,−1);
var
        i: Integer;
        Wnd: hWnd;
        Msg: TMsg;
begin
        { Register application class if needed }

        if not InitAppClass then Halt (0);

        { Create the main application window }

        Wnd := CreateWindow (szAppName, szAppName, ws_OverlappedWindow,
                                cw_UseDefault, cw_UseDefault,
                                cw_UseDefault, cw_UseDefault,
                                0, 0, hInstance, Nil);

        if Wnd <> 0 then
        begin
           ShowWindow (Wnd, cmdShow);
           UpdateWindow (Wnd);
           if CreateToolbarWindow (hInstance, Wnd, @bitMaps) <> 0 then
           begin
             { Assign first two buttons to a modal group }

             SetButtonGroup (Wnd, 0, 0);
             SetButtonGroup (Wnd, 1, 0);
           end;
        end;

        while GetMessage (Msg, 0, 0, 0) do
        begin
           TranslateMessage (Msg);
           DispatchMessage (Msg);
        end;

        Halt (Msg.wParam);
end;

begin
        WinMain;
end.
```

Appendix 7 : The **SPIN** unit

This appendix contains two files, SPIN.PAS and SPINTEST.PAS. The first file replicates the spin button code from Chapter 7 while the second file is a small testbed application that can be used to test the code. The version of the spin button code presented here makes use of the initialization clause of Pascal units: the spin button window class is registered automatically on program startup and the main program code needs to make no explicit initialization call.

```
unit Spin;

{--------------------------------------------------------------------}
{ FILE: Spin.Pas                                                     }
{ This Pascal unit implements the toolbar code from Chapter 7.       }
{ Polishing Windows, by Dave Jewell.                                 }
{ © 1994 Dave Jewell and Addison-Wesley, ALL RIGHTS RESERVED        }
{--------------------------------------------------------------------}

{$R SPIN.RES }

interface

uses WinTypes, WinProcs, Tools;

const
     { Spin button window styles }

     sp_Vert        = $00;              { vertical spinbutton (default)   }
     sp_Horiz       = $80;              { horizontal spinbutton           }
     SpinClassName  = 'SpinButton';     { name of spin button class       }
     SpinMessage    = wm_User;          { notification message number     }

implementation

const
     BitmapID = $5350;                           { ID of spinbutton bitmap }

type pSpinButtonRec = ^SpinButtonRec;
     SpinButtonRec = record
        State: Integer;            { state of play flag              }
```

Figure A7.1 SPIN.PAS: the Pascal spin button unit.

```
            horiz: Bool;                    { spinbutton orientation       }
            bmWidth: Integer;               { width of bitmap image        }
            bmHeight: Integer;              { height of bitmap image       }
            SpinRate: Integer;              { auto-repeat rate             }
            BuddyID: Integer;               { ID of buddy control          }
            BuddyHWnd: hWnd;                { handle to buddy control      }
            bmBitmap: HBitmap;              { handle to spin button bitmap }
        end;
{---------------------------------------------------------------------------}
{ Name:    GetSpinButtonRec                                                  }
{ Purpose: Given a spin button window handle, return a pointer to           }
{          the SpinButtonRec data structure.                                }
{---------------------------------------------------------------------------}

function GetSpinButtonRec (Wnd: hWnd): pSpinButtonRec;
begin
        GetSpinButtonRec := PSpinButtonRec (GetWindowLong (Wnd, 0));
end;

{---------------------------------------------------------------------------}
{ Name:    InitSpinButtonWindow.                                            }
{ Purpose: Initialize the spin button data structure.                       }
{---------------------------------------------------------------------------}

function InitSpinButtonWindow (Wnd: hWnd; lpcs: PCreateStruct): LongInt;
var
        rc: TRect;
        bm: TBitmap;
        Code: Integer;
        p: PSpinButtonRec;
        pt: TPoint absolute rc;
        szWindowName: String;

begin
        InitSpinButtonWindow := -1;
        GetMem (p, sizeof (SpinButtonRec));
        FillChar (p^, sizeof (SpinButtonRec), 0);

        if p <> Nil then with p^ do
        begin
          bmBitmap := LoadButtonBitmap (GetWindowWord (Wnd,
                                      gww_hInstance), BitmapID);

          if bmBitmap <> 0 then
          begin
            { Set up auto-repeat rate }

            SpinRate := GetWindowLong (Wnd, gwl_Style) and $7F;
            if SpinRate = 0 then SpinRate := 125
            else SpinRate := SpinRate * 4;

            { Figure out the size of the bitmap }

            GetObject (bmBitmap, sizeof (TBitmap), @bm);
            bmWidth := bm.bmWidth div 4;
            bmHeight := bm.bmHeight div 2;

            { Resize window according to the dimensions of the bitmap }

            GetWindowRect (Wnd, rc);
            ScreenToClient (GetParent (Wnd), pt);
            horiz := (GetWindowLong (Wnd, gwl_Style) and sp_Horiz) <> 0;
            if horiz then
                MoveWindow (Wnd, rc.left, rc.top, bmWidth * 2, bmHeight, False)
            else
                MoveWindow (Wnd, rc.left, rc.top, bmWidth, bmHeight * 2, False);

            { Set up buddy ID }

            if (lpcs^.lpszName <> Nil) and (lpcs^.lpszName^ <> #0) then
            begin
```

```
                LStrCpy (@szWindowName[1], lpcs^.lpszName);
                szWindowName [0] := Chr (LStrLen (lpcs^.lpszName));
                Val (szWindowName, BuddyID, Code);
                if Code <> 0 then BuddyID := 0;
            end;

            SetWindowLong (Wnd, 0, LongInt (p));
            InitSpinButtonWindow := 0;
        end;
    end;
end;
{————————————————————————————————————————————————————————————————}
{ Name:    PaintSpinButton                                        }
{ Purpose: Paint the spin button bitmap.                          }
{————————————————————————————————————————————————————————————————}

function PaintSpinButton (Wnd: hWnd): LongInt;
var
    hdcMem: hDC;
    hbm: hBitmap;
    ps: TPaintStruct;
    p: PSpinButtonRec;
    xSrc, ySrc: Integer;

begin
    BeginPaint (Wnd, ps);
    hdcMem := CreateCompatibleDC (ps.hdc);
    p := GetSpinButtonRec (Wnd);
    with p^ do
    begin
        hbm := SelectObject (hdcMem, bmBitmap);

        if horiz then
        begin
            if State = 1 then ySrc := bmHeight else ySrc := 0;
            BitBlt (ps.hdc, bmWidth, 0, bmWidth, bmHeight, hdcMem,
                3 * bmWidth, ySrc, SrcCopy);
            if State = −1 then ySrc := bmHeight else ySrc := 0;
            BitBlt (ps.hdc, 0, 0, bmWidth, bmHeight, hdcMem,
                    2 * bmWidth, ySrc, SrcCopy);
        end
        else
        begin
            if State = 1 then xSrc := bmWidth else xSrc := 0;
            BitBlt (ps.hdc, 0, 0, bmWidth, bmHeight, hdcMem,
                    xSrc, 0, SrcCopy);
            if State = −1 then xSrc := bmWidth else xSrc := 0;
            BitBlt (ps.hdc, 0, bmHeight, bmWidth, bmHeight, hdcMem,
                    xSrc, bmHeight, SrcCopy);
        end;

        if hbm <> 0 then SelectObject (hdcMem, hbm);
        DeleteDC (hdcMem);
        EndPaint (Wnd, ps);
    end;

    PaintSpinButton := 0;
end;
{————————————————————————————————————————————————————————————————}
{ Name:    HitTest                                                }
{ Returns: 0 − Mouse wasn't in spin button.                       }
{          1 − Mouse was in increment part of button.             }
{         −1 − Mouse was in decrement part of button.             }
{————————————————————————————————————————————————————————————————}

function HitTest (Wnd: hWnd; lParam: LongInt): Integer;
var
    rc: TRect;
```

```
        hit: Integer;
        p: PSpinButtonRec;
        pt: TPoint absolute lParam;
begin
        GetClientRect (Wnd, rc);
        p := GetSpinButtonRec (Wnd);
        if not PtInRect (rc, pt) then hit := 0
        else if p^.horiz then
        begin
          if pt.x >= (rc.right div 2) then hit := 1 else hit := -1;
        end
        else
        begin
          if pt.y >= (rc.bottom div 2) then hit := -1 else hit := 1;
        end;

        HitTest := hit;
end;
{-----------------------------------------------------------------------}
{ Name:    BuddyTalk                                                    }
{ Returns: Increment or decrement the value in the buddy control.       }
{-----------------------------------------------------------------------}
procedure BuddyTalk (p: PSpinButtonRec);
var
        Wnd: hWnd;
        i, Code: Integer;
        gotSel: Bool;
        szText: array [0..63] of Char;
        szVal: String [128];
        sel, oldsel: LongInt;
begin
        gotSel := False;
        Wnd := p^.BuddyHWnd;
        if IsWindow (Wnd) and (SendMessage (Wnd, wm_GetTextLength, 0, 0)
             < sizeof (szText)) then
        begin
          SendMessage (Wnd, wm_GetText, sizeof (szText) - 1, LongInt (@szText));
          sel := SendMessage (Wnd, em_GetSel, 0, 0);
          oldsel := sel;

          { Have we got a selection? }

          if LoWord (sel) = HiWord (sel) then
             sel := MakeLong (0, lstrlen (szText))
          else
             gotSel := True;

          szText [HiWord (sel)] := #0;
          LStrCpy (@szVal [1], @szText [LoWord (sel)]);
          szVal [0] := Chr (LStrLen (@szText [LoWord (sel)]));

          { Convert to numeric value }

          Val (szVal, i, Code);
          if Code <> 0 then
          begin
             MessageBeep (0);
             Exit;
          end;

          Inc (i, p^.State);
          wvsprintf (szText, '%d', i);

          { If got a selection, replace it }

          if gotSel then
          begin
             SendMessage (Wnd, em_ReplaceSel, 0, LongInt (@szText));
```

```
                SendMessage (Wnd, em_SetSel, 0, MakeLong (LoWord (oldsel),
                             LoWord (oldsel) + LStrLen (szText)));
          end
          else
          begin
            SendMessage (Wnd, wm_SetText, 0, LongInt (@szText));
            SendMessage (Wnd, em_SetSel, 0, MakeLong (0, $7fff));
          end;
       end;
end;
{----------------------------------------------------------------------}
{ Name:    SpinNotify                                                   }
{ Returns: Send spin button notification message.                      }
{----------------------------------------------------------------------}

procedure SpinNotify (Wnd: hWnd);
var
    p: PSpinButtonRec;
    szClassName: array [0..63] of Char;

begin
    p := GetSpinButtonRec (Wnd);
    with p^ do
    begin
      if BuddyID <> 0 then
      begin
        if BuddyHWnd = 0 then
        begin
          { Try and find our buddy window }

          BuddyHWnd := GetDlgItem (GetParent (Wnd), BuddyID);
          if BuddyHWnd = 0 then BuddyID := 0
          else
          begin
            GetClassName (BuddyHWnd, szClassName, sizeof (szClassName));
            if lstrcmpi (szClassName, 'Edit') <> 0 then
            begin
              BuddyHWnd := 0;
              BuddyID := 0;
            end;
          end;
        end;

        if BuddyHWnd <> 0 then
        begin
          BuddyTalk (p);
          Exit;
        end;
      end;

      SendMessage (GetParent (Wnd), SpinMessage, Wnd, State);
    end;
end;
{----------------------------------------------------------------------}
{ Name:    SpinButtonWndProc                                           }
{ Purpose: Window procedure for the spin button window class.         }
{----------------------------------------------------------------------}

function SpinButtonWndProc (Wnd: hWnd; Msg, wParam: Word;
                            lParam: LongInt): LongInt; export;
var
    hitCode: Integer;
    p: PSpinButtonRec;

begin
    SpinButtonWndProc := 0;
    p := GetSpinButtonRec (Wnd);
```

```
      case Msg of
        wm_LButtonDown,
        wm_LButtonDblClk:

        begin
          SetCapture (Wnd);
          p^.State := HitTest (Wnd, lParam);
          InvalidateRect (Wnd, Nil, False);
          SetTimer (Wnd, 100, p^.SpinRate, Nil);
          SpinNotify (Wnd);
          Exit;
        end;

        wm_LButtonUp:

        begin
          if Wnd = GetCapture then
          begin
            ReleaseCapture;
            KillTimer (Wnd, 100);
            p^.State := 0;
            InvalidateRect (Wnd, Nil, False);
          end;
          Exit;
        end;

        wm_MouseMove:

        begin
          if Wnd = GetCapture then
          begin
            hitCode := HitTest (Wnd, lParam);
            if hitCode <> p^.State then
            begin
              p^.State := hitCode;
              InvalidateRect (Wnd, Nil, False);
            end;
          end;
          Exit;
        end;

        wm_Create:

        SpinButtonWndProc := InitSpinButtonWindow (Wnd, PCreateStruct (lParam));

        wm_Paint:

        SpinButtonWndProc := PaintSpinButton (Wnd);

        wm_Timer:

        begin
          if p^.State <> 0 then SpinNotify (Wnd);
          Exit;
        end;

        wm_Destroy:

        begin
          DeleteObject (p^.bmBitmap);
          FreeMem (p, sizeof (SpinButtonRec));
          Exit;
        end;

        else

        SpinButtonWndProc := DefWindowProc (Wnd, Msg, wParam, lParam);
      end;
end;

{----------------------------------------------------------------------}
{ Name:    InitSpinButton                                              }
{ Purpose: Register the spin button window class.                      }
{----------------------------------------------------------------------}
```

```
function InitSpinButton: Bool;
var
      cls: TWndClass;

begin
      if not GetClassInfo (hInstance, SPINCLASSNAME, cls) then
      begin
         cls.style              := cs_DblClks;
         cls.lpfnWndProc        := @SpinButtonWndProc;
         cls.cbClsExtra         := 0;
         cls.cbWndExtra         := sizeof (PSpinButtonRec);
         cls.hInstance          := hInstance;
         cls.hIcon              := 0;
         cls.hCursor            := LoadCursor (0, idc_Arrow);
         cls.hbrBackground      := 0;
         cls.lpszMenuName       := Nil;
         cls.lpszClassName      := SpinClassName;

         InitSpinButton         := RegisterClass (cls);
      end
      else InitSpinButton       := True;
end;

begin
      InitSpinButton;
end.
```

Figure A7.2 SPINTEST.PAS: the test application for the spin button unit.

```
program Generic;

uses WinTypes, WinProcs, Spin;

const
      AppName = 'Spin Test';

{—————————————————————————————————————————————————}
{ Name:    WindowProc                              }
{ Purpose: Window procedure for the main application window. }
{—————————————————————————————————————————————————}

function WindowProc (Wnd: hWnd; Msg, wParam: Word;
                     lParam: Longint): Longint; export;
begin
      WindowProc := 0;
      case Msg of
        wm_Destroy:

        PostQuitMessage(0);

        else
        WindowProc := DefWindowProc (Wnd, Msg, wParam, lParam);
      end;
end;

{—————————————————————————————————————————————————}
{ Name:    WinMain                                 }
{ Purpose: Program entry point.                    }
{—————————————————————————————————————————————————}

procedure WinMain;
var
      Wnd: hWnd;
      Msg: TMsg;
```

```
const
    cls: TWndClass = (
    style: 0;
    lpfnWndProc: @WindowProc;
    cbClsExtra: 0;
    cbWndExtra: 0;
    hInstance: 0;
    hIcon: 0;
    hCursor: 0;
    hbrBackground: Color_BtnFace + 1;
    lpszMenuName: Nil;
    lpszClassName: AppName);
begin
    if HPrevInst = 0 then
    begin
        cls.hInstance := HInstance;
        cls.hIcon := LoadIcon(0, idi_Application);
        cls.hCursor := LoadCursor(0, idc_Arrow);
        if not RegisterClass (cls) then Halt(255);
    end;

    Wnd := CreateWindow (AppName, 'Spin Test Program',
                        ws_OverlappedWindow,
                        cw_UseDefault, cw_UseDefault,
                        cw_UseDefault, cw_UseDefault,
                        0, 0, hInstance, nil);

    ShowWindow (Wnd, CmdShow);
    UpdateWindow (Wnd);

    CreateWindow ('Edit', 'Hello Mum', ws_Child or ws_Visible or ws_Border,
                100, 300, 100, 25, Wnd, 999, hInstance, Nil);
    CreateWindow (SpinClassName, '999', ws_Child or ws_Visible or sp_Vert,
                100, 100, 10, 10, Wnd, 0, hInstance, Nil);
    CreateWindow (SpinClassName, '999', ws_Child or ws_Visible or
                100 or sp_Horiz, 200, 100, 10, 10, Wnd, 0, hInstance, Nil);

    while GetMessage (Msg, 0, 0, 0) do
    begin
        TranslateMessage (Msg);
        DispatchMessage (Msg);
    end;
    Halt (Msg.wParam);
end;

begin
    WinMain;
end.
```

Appendix 8 : The TOOLS unit

This appendix contains the source code for the Pascal Tools unit, which implements a number of useful, general-purpose routines. These routines are used by a number of the other Pascal units in the earlier appendices.

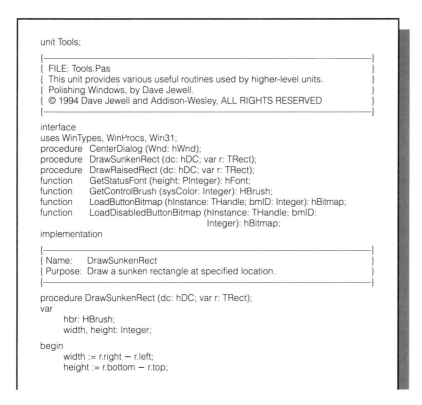

Figure A8.1 The Tools unit.

```
unit Tools;

{──────────────────────────────────────────────────────────────────────}
{ FILE: Tools.Pas                                                        }
{ This unit provides various useful routines used by higher-level units. }
{ Polishing Windows, by Dave Jewell.                                     }
{ © 1994 Dave Jewell and Addison-Wesley, ALL RIGHTS RESERVED             }
{──────────────────────────────────────────────────────────────────────}

interface
uses WinTypes, WinProcs, Win31;
procedure   CenterDialog (Wnd: hWnd);
procedure   DrawSunkenRect (dc: hDC; var r: TRect);
procedure   DrawRaisedRect (dc: hDC; var r: TRect);
function     GetStatusFont (height: PInteger): hFont;
function     GetControlBrush (sysColor: Integer): HBrush;
function     LoadButtonBitmap (hInstance: THandle; bmID: Integer): hBitmap;
function     LoadDisabledButtonBitmap (hInstance: THandle; bmID:
                                       Integer): hBitmap;
implementation

{──────────────────────────────────────────────────────────────────────}
{ Name:    DrawSunkenRect                                                }
{ Purpose: Draw a sunken rectangle at specified location.                }
{──────────────────────────────────────────────────────────────────────}

procedure DrawSunkenRect (dc: hDC; var r: TRect);
var
     hbr: HBrush;
     width, height: Integer;

begin
     width := r.right − r.left;
     height := r.bottom − r.top;
```

```
        hbr := SelectObject (dc, CreateSolidBrush (GetSysColor
                        (Color_BtnHighLight)));
    PatBlt (dc, r.right, r.top, 1, height, PatCopy);
    PatBlt (dc, r.left, r.bottom, width, 1, PatCopy);
    DeleteObject (SelectObject (dc, CreateSolidBrush (GetSysColor
                        (Color_BtnShadow))));
    PatBlt (dc, r.left, r.top, 1, height, PatCopy);
    PatBlt (dc, r.left, r.top, width, 1, PatCopy);
    DeleteObject (SelectObject (dc, hbr));
end;
{------------------------------------------------------------------}
{ Name:    DrawRaisedRect                                          }
{ Purpose: Draw a raised rectangle at specified location.          }
{------------------------------------------------------------------}

procedure DrawRaisedRect (dc: hDC; var r: TRect);
var
        hbr: HBrush;
        width, height: Integer;

begin
        width := r.right − r.left;
        height := r.bottom − r.top;
        hbr := SelectObject (dc, CreateSolidBrush (GetSysColor
                        (Color_BtnHighLight)));
        PatBlt (dc, r.left, r.top, 1, height − 1, PatCopy);
        PatBlt (dc, r.left, r.top, width − 1, 1, PatCopy);
        DeleteObject (SelectObject (dc, CreateSolidBrush (GetSysColor
                        (Color_BtnShadow))));
        PatBlt (dc, r.right − 1, r.top, 1, height, PatCopy);
        PatBlt (dc, r.left, r.bottom − 1, width, 1, PatCopy);
        DeleteObject (SelectObject (dc, hbr));
end;
{------------------------------------------------------------------}
{ Name:    GetStatusFont                                           }
{ Purpose: Return a handle to our special font.                    }
{------------------------------------------------------------------}

function GetStatusFont (height: PInteger): hFont;
var
        dc: hDC;
        font: hFont;
        tm: TTextMetric;
        faceName: array [0..50] of Char;
        nHeight, pointSize: Integer;

begin
        { Pickup point size and face name from WIN.INI }

        pointSize := GetProfileInt ('Desktop', 'StatusBarFaceHeight', 8);
        GetProfileString ('Desktop', 'StatusBarFaceName', 'MS Sans Serif',
                        faceName, 50);

        { Now create the font }

        dc := GetDC (0);
        nHeight := (GetDeviceCaps (dc, LogPixelsY) * pointSize) div −72;

        font := CreateFont (nHeight, 0, 0, 0, fw_Normal, 0, 0, 0,
                        Ansi_Charset,
                        Out_Default_Precis,
                        Clip_Default_Precis,
                        Default_Quality,
                        ff_Swiss or Variable_Pitch,
                        faceName);

        font := SelectObject (dc, font);
        GetTextMetrics (dc, tm);
        GetStatusFont := SelectObject (dc, font);
```

```
        ReleaseDC (0, dc);
        if height <> Nil then height^ := tm.tmHeight;
end;
{------------------------------------------------------------------}
{ Name:    InternalLoadButtonBitmap                                }
{ Purpose: Called by LoadButtonBitmap and LoadDisabledButtonBitmap.}
{------------------------------------------------------------------}

function InternalLoadButtonBitmap (hInstance: THandle; bmID: Integer;
                                   fEnable: Bool): hBitmap;
type
        lpColor = ^ColorArray;
        ColorArray = array [0..15] of TColorRef;

var
        dc: hDC;
        hRes: THandle;
        lpb: Pointer;
        lpbi: PBitmapInfoHeader;
        lpbiFudge: PBitmapInfo absolute lpbi;
        lprgb: lpColor;

        function ColorFix (color: TColorRef): TColorRef;
        begin
           ColorFix := RGB (GetBValue (color), GetGValue (color), GetRValue (color));
        end;
begin
        InternalLoadButtonBitmap := 0;
        hRes := LoadResource (hInstance, FindResource (hInstance,
                              PChar (bmID), rt_Bitmap));
        lpbi := PBitmapInfoHeader (LockResource (hRes));
        if lpbi = Nil then Exit;
        lprgb := lpColor (PChar (lpbi) + Integer (lpbi^.biSize));
        lpb := PChar (lprgb) + (16 * sizeof (TColorRef));

        { Black }

        if fEnable then lprgb^ [0] := ColorFix (GetSysColor (Color_WindowText))
        else lprgb^ [0] := ColorFix (GetSysColor (Color_BtnShadow));

        lprgb^ [8] := ColorFix (GetSysColor (Color_BtnFace));      { Light gray }
        lprgb^ [7] := ColorFix (GetSysColor (Color_BtnShadow));    { Gray }
        lprgb^ [15] := ColorFix (GetSysColor (Color_BtnHighlight)); { White }

        dc := GetDC (0);
        InternalLoadButtonBitmap := CreateDIBitmap (dc, lpbi^, cbm_Init, lpb,
                                                    lpbiFudge^, dib_rgb_Colors);

        ReleaseDC (0, dc);
        GlobalUnlock (hRes);
        FreeResource (hRes);
end;
{------------------------------------------------------------------}
{ Name:    LoadButtonBitmap                                        }
{ Purpose: Load a button bitmap and tweak for system colors.       }
{------------------------------------------------------------------}

function LoadButtonBitmap (hInstance: THandle; bmID: Integer): hBitmap;
begin
        LoadButtonBitmap := InternalLoadButtonBitmap (hInstance, bmID, True);
end;
{------------------------------------------------------------------}
{ Name:    LoadDisabledButtonBitmap                                }
{ Purpose: Load a button bitmap and make it look disabled.         }
{------------------------------------------------------------------}

function LoadDisabledButtonBitmap (hInstance: THandle; bmID: Integer): hBitmap;
begin
```

```
            LoadDisabledButtonBitmap := InternalLoadButtonBitmap (hInstance,
                                                                   bmID, False);
end;

{———————————————————————————————————————————————————}
{ Name:    GetControlBrush                                              }
{ Purpose: Create a control brush for a given system color.            }
{———————————————————————————————————————————————————}

function GetControlBrush (sysColor: Integer): HBrush;
var
      color: TColorRef;
begin
      color := GetSysColor (sysColor);
      GetControlBrush := CreateSolidBrush (color);
end;

{———————————————————————————————————————————————————}
{ Name:    CenterDialog                                                 }
{ Purpose: Center a given dialog window on the screen.                  }
{———————————————————————————————————————————————————}

procedure CenterDialog (Wnd: hWnd);
var
      r: TRect;

begin
      GetWindowRect (Wnd, r);
      r.left := (GetSystemMetrics (sm_CXScreen) − r.right + r.left) div 2;
      r.top := (GetSystemMetrics (sm_CYScreen) − r.bottom + r.top) div 2;
      SetWindowPos (Wnd, 0, r.left, r.top, 0, 0, swp_NoSize or
                    swp_NoZOrder);
end;

end.
```

Index